SHIMMERING DETAILS

VOLUME I

SHIMMERING DETAILS

A Memoir

VOLUME I

PÉTER NÁDAS

TRANSLATED FROM THE HUNGARIAN BY
JUDITH SOLLOSY

FARRAR, STRAUS AND GIROUX
NEW YORK

Farrar, Straus and Giroux
120 Broadway, New York 10271

Library of Congress Cataloging-in-Publication Data
Names: Nádas, Péter, 1942– author. | Sollosy, Judith, translator.
Title: Shimmering details : a memoir / Péter Nádas ; translated from the
    Hungarian by Judith Sollosy.
Other titles: Világló részletek. English
Description: First American edition. | New York : Farrar, Straus and
    Giroux, 2023.
Identifiers: LCCN 2023021275 | ISBN 9780374174590 (v. 1 ; hardcover) |
    ISBN 9780374611644 (v. 2 ; hardcover)
Subjects: LCSH: Nádas, Péter, 1942– | Authors, Hungarian—20th
    century—Biography. | LCGFT: Autobiographies.
Classification: LCC PH3291.N297 Z46 2023 | DDC 894/.511334
    [B]—dc23/eng/20230811
LC record available at https://lccn.loc.gov/2023021275

Our books may be purchased in bulk for promotional, educational,
or business use. Please contact your local bookseller or the Macmillan
Corporate and Premium Sales Department at 1-800-221-7945, extension
5442, or by email at MacmillanSpecialMarkets@macmillan.com.

www.fsgbooks.com
www.twitter.com/fsgbooks • www.facebook.com/fsgbooks

10 9 8 7 6 5 4 3 2 1

WHEN ON WEDNESDAY

THERE WERE NO IFS, ands, or buts about it, Sunday lunch had to be served punctually at noon. When the church bell rang out, the boiling hot soup had to be on the table. Not that Grandad wanted it like that. I'm referring to my maternal grandfather, Grandad Tauber. I knew him; he wouldn't have minded it at one and lukewarm, such things were of no concern to him. Besides, he hardly ate. He hardly spoke, and even then, he kept it brief. When he stood up from the table, he gave thanks for the lunch with a nod of the head, though there was no knowing who the thanks was meant for. It may have been meant for my grandmother, or Grandad may have been thinking of God, someone's god, I honestly don't know. I never saw him show the slightest interest in any of the worldly vanities. He was ethereal, all skin and bones. When he pulled me close, when he threw me up in the air, fly, Péter, fly, whoosh, there you go, and then as I came falling back down and he caught me after all, the little bird is falling down, I was very close to the bare skeleton that was my grandfather; even now I can feel his bony arms against my limbs. Except I can't understand how in his inordinate joy that falling little bird could have escaped his lips, even once. A little bird comes falling down when the hunter shoots it or its legs get frozen in the extreme cold of winter.

Grandad was sparing of his emotions and I never saw him lose his temper. At most he gave more than usual emphasis to things through his humor. Still, underneath that stoic facade there lurked something ominous and threatening, and his daughters were right to fear him, and I feared him too, quite a bit, even though I honestly couldn't imagine what would happen were he to lose control, just once. When he took offense his eyes shot off sparks, his cheeks turned crimson, but he never lost control; rather, he indulgently lowered his eyelids over his anger, like one who instantly thinks better of it and willingly turns a blind eye to what is taking place inside him.

My flight took longer than my fall, as if it would never end, that's what it felt like, and I even caught my breath; the wish to suffocate, possibly that's why I wanted him to make me fly; I came to only as I fell back down and he cradled me in his bony arms. Then again. Or else he rocked me on his knee, a game he must surely have enjoyed in his own way, though it must have bored him too, terribly. The rider had to sit securely in the saddle while the horse tossed him about, this was the rule of the game, the horse snorted, the horse bucked. Grandad simulated the chance occurrence, he mimicked randomness with his knee, and since I reacted to his efforts with good reflexes and good rhythm, because I knew what he was up to, I knew what he hoped to make me understand, he enjoyed the effect and roared with laughter.

He laughed silently, he roared with laughter silently, lips agape, in his delight raising his eyes up to the sky. Good. The boy's got good reflexes. I've never seen the likes of it, laughing without a sound.

He must have needed as much self-restraint for our game as I, except our self-restraint had different objects. Now when I think back on the details of the scene, replaying it each morning, tasting it, trying to make sense of it, as a result of which yet more details unfold one from the other and hook up to other, even more remote details, I can't help thinking that Grandad must have made a great point of keeping pleasure at bay. He didn't give in easily. I had to beg him, wiggle my way in between his knees, and when he succumbed, when

I found myself wrapped inside the live current of his body's warmth, his resistance melted and he picked me up onto his knee, though even then he held off, he continued aloof and surrendered to our proximity only under strict control. Surely the monotony, the mimetic nature of the game, the ritual must have bored him, I can see that now. For my part, I had to endure the sharp edges of his knees and the protruding bones. It hurt. Enduring the pain in the interest of the pleasure hurt. Imitation bores me, too; pretense latches on to it with all its amorphous parts. Still, the pleasure of the game outweighed the humiliation felt over the mimesis.

And also, there was the pleasure of persevering. The pleasure of the breath stuck inside, an advance on suffocation, and Grandad's silent laughter.

Grandad laughed into the air, but his laughter lacked air; his stubborn asthma may have been the cause. The slightest exertion made him gasp for air, his lungs wheezed; the doctors call it labored breathing. Doctors say that asthma is the disease of renunciation, of denial, of self-denial. Marcel Proust also suffered from asthma, though at the time his doctors did not yet recognize the psychological character of his illness. And if Proust and my grandfather suffered from the same disease, there's no knowing what an anti-mimetic person must be like, one who does not deny himself to himself and is free of all pretense. Surely, a man like that mimes only his most intrinsic traits, those most characteristic of him. On the other hand, what would be the use. This is what Grandad must have thought during the last ten years of his life. Besides, after a while you're bored with the thing that gives you pleasure, but you feel you've run out of options. The skin that stretched across the area just above his temples glistened, the thick veins curled and coiled on the backs of his hands. These veins fascinated me. Even when I was a child, their outlines and function thrilled me. To be perfectly frank, they repelled me. I dared hardly consider all the things that might be happening in the body under the epidermis, in the arteries, the heart, the groin, the lungs, the intestines, and the awe I felt at the regularity of their function made me shudder. I shuddered at the miracle of such consistency of function, and this shudder excited me. I had to be on guard lest this spiraling admiration of nature sweep me along. In my family, the path to romantic self-adulation came with a stop sign.

Grandad said I should press the veins with my finger and attend to the beating of his heart. Grandad and I attended to his pulse with equal amazement, and with this trick, the beating of his heart, or else by following his pulse with the help of his pocket watch, with the precision of the ticking in my ear and the rhythmic palpitation, he succeeded in diverting my attention. We followed the hand showing the seconds, we counted the beating of his heart until I had regained my composure. This is how I first learned to count to ten, I think; this is how I learned to relinquish the frenzy, to calm down, let the steam out of the valve. He didn't always let me, but from time to time I could coax the knotty veins on his temples from their place, after which they'd slide back only very, very slowly.

Grandad must have felt trapped, freed from one burdensome duty, the game, only to be followed by this other game.

He did not play cards, he did not play chess. When we stayed at the house in Göd, which the old man bought with the help of the members of the Workers' Physical Training Association on whose vacation grounds it was located and which everyone jokingly called the Tauber Villa; in short, even there, every afternoon, when the young people were off playing volleyball, Grandad would sit wearing his antiquated, formfitting swimming costume and his unruffled smile, and watch them from the timber terrace shaded by the leaves of the woodbine.

Also, he rarely joined us for a swim.

The small house stood on poles in order to keep the floodwaters at bay. On the other hand, this turned it into a sound box. You couldn't budge without it reverberating and booming, rumbling and thundering, and since many similar houses lined the riverbank, the riverbank rumbled and thundered too, from early morning till late at night.

They did not say that they were off for a swim; they said they were off for a dip.

We took a dip.

They hiked up a well-trodden footpath that ran along the riverbank and cut through the grassy thicket as it led up to Vác, then they swam at their leisure, entrusting themselves to the indolent current to bring them back down. Meanwhile they chatted leisurely on the surface of the sun-drenched water, as the water carried their voices afar, just as it carried the strains of the rumbling afar, too.

The riverbank on the other side brought their voices back.

We trickled back down, that's the expression they used.

Also, it was Grandad who taught me to play Mikado one wintry afternoon. It may have been the only game that interested him. Letting the sticks, their value determined by the different colored stripes painted on them, the Mandarin, the Bonzen, the Samurai, the Kuli, fall from your hand, then retrieving them from the pile one by one with the help of two other sticks, rolling them with great care, standing them up with your finger pressed down on the pointed end, or retrieving them with the two pointed ends pressed between your fingers, but so the other sticks shouldn't respond, they shouldn't stir, they shouldn't so much as quiver from the change. Not just see but, for all intents and purposes, intuit beforehand the position of the stick you've chosen to pull from the pack. Also, to control your breathing so the operation shouldn't fail because of some slight inadvertent movement.

Grandad was also the first to teach me that you should let out the air beforehand, only then can you hold your breath securely. If you hold it with your lungs full, the effort will make your hand shake. A decade and a half later, when I studied photography with a handheld camera and had to increase the exposure time without recourse to a tripod or support of any kind, I had to familiarize myself with this experience all over again.

When I was already familiar with it.

Grandad also taught me to play dominoes. Which made for two silent games.

Grandad's posture was straight, but he bowed his head meekly, almost bashfully; he bowed his head to the world when he was standing, and he bowed his head when he was sitting, as if to indicate that no, no, he doesn't want to carry the day, he doesn't even want to be right with respect to anything, though I wouldn't go so far as to say that he was a compliant man; if anything, under his thick, well-groomed mustache, behind his wire-rimmed spectacles, Grandad was smiling this compliantly for his own benefit. As I now see it, his steady smile was meant to bolster his patience, so it shouldn't end. He had an admirable way of lying on his back, enjoying his solitude in the grass, on a bed, on the damp gravel by the riverside, or on a hammock in Göd or Dömsöd among the locusts, the poplars, and the weeping willows as they spread their light, netlike shade along the water's edge. I envied him and tried to imitate him; he crossed one foot over the other and joined his hands over his chest, as if clasped in prayer. He invariably gave the impression of a man contemplating weighty matters with ease, in a state of suspension, as it were, and at such times we would not disturb him. Fifty years had passed, more or less, when I realized that for some time I'd been prone to lying like that myself under the open sky. Sometimes he dozed off as he meditated, sometimes I do, too, and when he lay like that for some time, with that self-effacing smile on his face, his asthmatic breathing let up as well. Possibly that's the explanation; he could best avoid the labored breathing in this position.

Grandad also smiled while he worked. At such times, he removed his wire-rimmed spectacles; without his glasses his face seemed naked, unfamiliar, exposed; he leaned over the piece he was working on with the loupe fitted in the socket of his eye, or else he used an even stronger lens. This Rodenstock that folds out from its safety frame and offers tenfold magnification is the only object I have inherited from him. He had a whole series of them. After all, he had to work on the details of details invisible to the naked eye. A single gas flame, a Bunsen burner adjusted as sharp as a needle, flickered and hissed close to his head. They let me sit by him for hours on a high stool; this was in his older sister's workshop in Holló Street, at least that's what it feels like now, though I can't vouch for those hours, it may have been just thirty or forty minutes before someone would come to pick me up. Once my grandmother Cecília Nusshaum, my mother's mother, came for me; she'd been to the farmers' market on Klauzál Square that lay in partial ruins, though I can't begin to imagine why, when she usually went to the Garay Square market. That's where her market woman was. And also her kosher butcher. But that particular early summer morning in the city I remember perfectly well, the sprinkled streets and the loaded basket she carried to Grandad's workshop from Klauzál Square, and her playing out for us, and surely for her own benefit too, the mighty drama of carrying that loaded basket. Another time my father came for me; he worked on the sunny sixth floor of a large building on a nearby street. But until they came for me I could watch my grandfather make things, and also how he went about it. I just had to make sure not to fall off the high stool and not move anything from its appointed place.

In his brief typed memoir of sorts in which my father attempted to record everything, and I do mean everything, about our dead mother for the benefit of his two sons before he leaves as well, he must have made up his mind months in advance, I'm leaving, this is the demure expression he'd used in the farewell letter he'd written before he sat down at his typewriter, but then he cut the memoir short in midsentence. This must have happened when he decided to take us along. This is the expression he used, to take us along. Please forgive me, but I must take them along; this is what he wrote in his farewell letter, but then he attached a note to it addressed to the two of us, the one whose lines were a lot more garbled. He stood over my younger brother with his gun and couldn't pull the trigger. This is what he wrote in the note. Had he started with me, he might have fared better.

Or else he cut the memoir short in midsentence because he realized the futility of his attempt, trying to draw a portrait of someone who, although she had valid, humble efforts to her credit even outside the immediate circle of her family, said efforts were doomed to fail, shrinking smaller than their worth not only because of the march of history, but because of his own awkward striving to record them for posterity. He'd have liked to draw the outlines of a heroic story about our mother. He must have done so hoping that sometime in the future someone would flesh out the heroic story, presenting it in its entirety. Except there was no heroine. The family commandments frowned upon bragging and swagger of all kinds, no heroic poses, no sacrificial martyrdom allowed. At most, you could be heroic in your self-restraint. You do what you do, but you don't do it to garner the gratitude of others. As he wrote in the main text of his farewell note, he wasn't about to saddle anyone else with the burden of caring for us, in which case, for whom should he write and why should he write the modest bits of information about his deceased wife, meant for the benefit of his two sons, Péter and Pál, whom he'd have to take with him so their existence should not be a burden to others. In his curtailed notes my father locates Grandad's workshop in Dob Street.

It may in fact have been there before, before the siege it may in fact have been in Dob Street, but in the years following the siege, I used to go see him in Holló Street. If my memory serves me right, there had been a silversmith's workshop in Dob Street where my grandmother worked as a polisher before she got married. It was in the course of one of these exceptional trips to the Klauzál Square market that she showed me where she and my grandfather had met. Both streets are in the heart of town. Afterward it gave me plenty of food for thought, trying to imagine, time and again, what would have happened had my grandmother not met my grandfather, in which case my mother wouldn't have been born, and then she wouldn't have met my father, and also, what would have been the consequence. I couldn't say. From then on my mind was more or less occupied with the same things all my life; the act of reflection did not abandon me; on the contrary, it grew more and more profound along with the furrows.

Holló Street was short, narrow, and dark, you could hardly see the sky. The other day I took a short detour so I could see that street again and also find the house. It's not all that narrow. It's not all that dark. I remember it differently from what it's like now, or what it has become, but the house was 1 Holló Street, I know that for a fact; at least, my memories identified this house more than any other with that former house. The workshop opened from the inner courtyard. As soon as you stepped inside, the automatic door closed behind you, and once it was closed, you couldn't get out again, because this door didn't have a doorknob on the inside, a circumstance that became a standard feature of my nightmares. On the other hand, it's a pity but I can't remember how many times my grandfather took me to Holló Street with him, possibly twice, possibly three times, certainly not more. At first the word came as a surprise, *holló*, raven; be that as it may, the street certainly surprised me. For at least a century Holló Street in Pest was the street of the goldsmiths. I didn't know that the *holló*, the raven, was a large bird; Grandad explained it to me in his workshop, he very softly did an imitation, cawing and kraaing, he imitated a raven with the back of his hand; the raven's feathers are black and shiny, maybe that's why the street continued dark in my mind for decades; this is how it hops about, holding in its beak a ring with the coat of arms of King Matthias the Just. We drew the raven. We drew the gold ring. We drew the coat of arms of King Matthias the Just. Quoth the raven. I had no idea what *just king* meant. There was hardly anything whose meaning I could understand.

It was quiet in Grandad's workshop, and I had to keep quiet as well. It wasn't even proper to talk in a whisper. If they couldn't avoid it, they spoke in subdued tones. This was their way of letting the others know that they didn't mean to keep anything from them, they were just being considerate. I assume that it must have been the value of the objects they were working on that prompted them to keep nothing from the others; they made sure that everything should take place before the eyes of their companions, and within hearing distance. A lack of trust must have been a nightmare to them. And also, unfounded trust. And that's not something they could make disappear by talking loudly. Besides, they had to pay close attention to the slightest move they made, lest the tools between their fingers slip. Four people worked in the shop, the master and his three assistants, each of them hunched over his own desk, and each of them a male, with only the burners, adjusted sharp as a needle, hissing in all that silence. The workshop looked out on the courtyard. At most, you could hear the sounds of the courtyard. Someone was beating rugs. The superintendent was washing the yard down with a hose, veritably flooding it; on the upstairs balcony and the back stairs children were playing catch; a door was being slammed shut, a window was being opened.

My grandfather made and repaired minuscule objects. He built jewelry. He resized rings, enlarging or downsizing them, and he changed or replaced the lost or loosened gemstones in colliers. These, too, were grand words from his workshop, *gemstone, collier, mounting, precious stone*, and *semi-precious stone*. Was a semi-precious stone anything like a semi-truth, I wondered, a half-truth. A half-truth, I often heard them say at home, and then they lost no time in chastising these half-truths with their contempt. Anyway, for years to come I wasn't really clear about which half of the truth they could possibly be referring to. And also, that diamonds are precious. Or brilliants. Yes, they say that, too. But we don't. Still, at times my grandfather said diamonds, at other times brilliants. He should know, he's the one working with them. And this here is a semi-precious stone. They lay hidden in the depths of long, velvet-lined boxes, and he removed one with his tweezers. They didn't look at all like they were only half real, one half real, the other half not. *Not true by half*, goes the saying. Which to me was not quite on par with a half-truth. They also said *the whole truth*, but I didn't understand that either. Besides, *semi-precious stone* was an expression long enough to confuse me. There was also *setting*. I saw it as a low-lying word, a flat word-plain. I also thought it peculiar, and so it filled me with a sense of uncertainty, seeing them work only one side of the stone, cutting and polishing it. Which is what turned them into semi-precious stones. They took the stone and laid it flat and then mounted it inside the word. From time to time, someone would get up and walk over to someone else with one of these very small objects or gems on a tray; he'd show it to someone, and that someone would look at it, or else lay it in his palm and examine it through the loupe he'd placed over his eye. Surely, at such times they must have seen what was precious in the stone, and where the borderline of the false was, or which half of the stone was false. They didn't talk about that either much, they just conferred in silence; they understood one another from slight gestures, nods, syllables. But strangely enough, these assistants,

I don't remember them, I remember only where they sat, but not their faces, not their figures, nor their ages. I remember their physical situation in the workshop, the place they occupied among the lights; I remember the condition of the lights. There was sufficient light in the spacious room, the windows were nice and tall, but you could see only through the top panes, the rest were so-called frosted glass, the recesses deep, and they reached all the way to the ceiling; but the huge panes could be opened wide despite the recesses, or if the sunlight was too direct, they could be closed, which today makes me conclude that it must have been a neoclassical building with thick walls.

Following in the wake of my memories, this is how I found the neoclassical building once designed in the uninviting, unassuming, no-nonsense barracks style characteristic of Pest's Inner City, and in this, too, Pest differs from Gothic and baroque Buda on the other side of the Danube. Pest, not Buda, is my native town.

Bright incandescent lamps were burning on turntables, and they were positioned under the magnifying glasses to shed light on the objects being worked on rather than the tables, which made sense, considering that the men worked with their backs to natural light. My grandfather worked with small tools, a small file, a small brass scale that he covered with a bell jar so the dust shouldn't settle on its plates, and there were several of these scales scattered over various parts of the workshop; my grandfather worked with small tweezers, a small vise, a small file, a small polisher, minuscule stone dishes, casting dies, jars and vessels with handles of various sizes, these are what he worked with; he brought the molten lead, the zinc, the precious metals, maybe gold and platinum, I don't really know, from the sizzling oven situated in the far recesses of the shop; he may have worked with pliers and a whole series of chisels; he applied nickel with wooden-handled pincers so he could soften silver threads or gold threads over the sharply sizzling flame. My grandfather was a goldsmith. There were also silversmiths back then; they made tableware, christening bowls with gold-plated insides, tobacco cases, sauce bowls, working the insides of the sauce bowls with gold, too, and also complete place settings along with all the accoutrements, as they said back then, of which a genteel household needed many kinds, candlesticks, napkin rings, trays and clever devices of all sorts for serving food, tongs, roasting forks, tiered fruit stands, jugs, saltcellars with cut crystal insides, separate ones for sal ammoniac, which they called smelling salts, separate ones for table salt, woven silver baskets of varying sizes for bread and rolls, ashtrays, candlesnuffers, dipping bowls for fruit and greasy fingers, and so on. Satisfaction over exacting work well done, the alleviation of concentrated effort, and the sense of permanence; this, I think, prompted Grandfather to smile to himself. Or perhaps it was some other consideration or sensation that prompted him to smile his way through his entire engrossed gold-smith's life. Who knows.

Throughout the city, throughout the country, throughout the whole of the Austro-Hungarian Empire, this was the established custom. The noonday ringing of the church bell marked the start of Sunday's meal. The soup had to be piping hot and steaming. In line with the dictates of established custom, a man could not tolerate his wife serving the soup lukewarm. In my maternal grandparents' home food was dished out, in my paternal grandparents' home it was served. Lunch or dinner is served. *Zum Tisch.* When they spoke in a foreign language, what they said gained a jocular or ironic character. *À table.* This was meant as the last warning, a summons to those who had been sitting on their ears, a common expression in our family. The soup was steaming, it was piping hot at my grandmother's house, whereas where was the Austro-Hungarian Empire by then, where were its bright hereditary dominions with their foreign words and distinctions in rank, where were the linguistic distinctions that sprang from them. Gone with the wind. The men had lost two world wars, they had fallen in two world wars. There was surely not a soul in the city who had not lost someone or something. Eviscerated, struggling with its losses and shortages and forced to its knees, at the time of our Sunday meals the city stood around us in ruins. Once a badly damaged house with its shell-shocked floors collapsed with a horrendous roar near City Park. I remember the scene and the characteristic protracted, seemingly endless rumbling sound as the house caved in, and yes, the smell as Grandad and I walked along; we may have been walking along István Street, it was peacetime, it was Sunday, and the tail end of the collapse was accompanied by a ringing sound as the people ran screaming from their homes, and there we stood in their midst, heading for City Park, except after a while we couldn't see the other side of the street anymore because of the dust cloud. At such times, the smell always came before the dust cloud. I knew that, everyone who had lived through the siege knew it. People were coughing, people were fleeing, and then the next day it got into the papers. One Saturday, Grandmother opened the paper, the *Népszava*, she showed it to us, here it is, I told you, it got into the paper. This is how the people of Pest said it. If it was a person, the individual in question got edited into the news, and for years to come I was under the impression that it would always be like this, that it could be like this at any time, buildings collapse, and then they get into the paper as a piece of news. Such is life. Just make sure you don't get edited into the news. God forbid. This is how the world around us works. Wouldn't you know, Elemér got edited into the news. The mutilated remains of blown-up bridges stick out of the Danube. This is my life.

I see them again now, these bridges, on contemporary photographs, they're like the broken wings of waterlogged birds, but back then I thought neither of birds nor broken wings; I gave no thought to the destruction, for destruction was life as we knew it. How could a bridge be any other way. This was their fate, it left no room for interpretation. Some people blow them up, others build them, this I had no trouble understanding; after all, following the siege, new bridges were being built in front of my very eyes. For years to come, one of the stone lions of the Chain Bridge lay on its side by the lower embankment, atop the debris of the tollhouse and its own pedestal. I admit that I preferred the lion lying on its side atop the debris to the newly carved one that replaced the old. The tollhouses were not rebuilt, though, neither the Chain Bridge's nor the Margaret Bridge's, because no one collected bridge tolls anymore.

The sappers of the Soviet army built a pile bridge so they could cross over to Buda with their troops, but the ice drifts swept this pile bridge along with them. The spring of the same year, amid constant ringing clatter, they then built a pontoon bridge over which you could reach Margaret Island, and through the slush and the mud, through the slime that those before us had trampled underfoot, past the decay that was the crumbled ornamental fountain, past the frozen shell casings, the maimed trees, you could reach the narrower branch of the Danube, across which another pontoon led to Buda. If there is such a thing as endless desolation, then for me this short path was and continues to be both endless and desolate.

The way I remember it today, my parents hardly ever picked me up in their arms, though that's not likely. It is much more likely that walking was the universal norm. Everyone walked, everyone was headed somewhere. The way I remember it, I walked and walked, I walked without end. Surely, my mother must have picked me up in her arms, surely, my father must have put me around his neck, if for no other reason than that I shouldn't impede their progress. I had two baby carriages, the deep carriage with a retractable hood and an open stroller, and I was proud of the fact that I had two; I don't know why I was proud of it, perhaps they told me that I should be proud of it, others, the poor proli children, don't even have one, whereas I have two to begin with; but basically, on the uneven postwar roads these baby carriages were best suited for hauling things, if that.

Just so I can give you a sense of the atmosphere of the times, I am quoting now, out of the blue as it were, from the surviving dated manuscript, a reminiscence my Aunt Magda wrote ten years later, in February 1955, on request from the editor of the *Literary Journal*, hoping that thanks to it it will emerge how a grown-up in the family saw what to me as a small child seemed the norm. We walked and walked. Where would they have left me and with whom. They took me with them during the very first post-siege days as well; besides, now that people could come up from the basements, they were all out on the street at long last, heading somewhere, hauling things.

The atmosphere of the times, I kept repeating to myself, but dear Sarolta, back then we had to look down in front of our feet and not up in the air when we headed from one nascent women's group to the next, my aunt wrote, though I never found out who Sarolta was, possibly the poet Sarolta Lányi, at whose request she had written the essay. For lack of public transportation of any kind, we had to walk, that goes without saying. We had to look strictly down in front of our feet, lest we come to grief on an unexploded mine or disappear in the depths of a shell crater, or trip over a corpse, an animal carcass, a piano, or a machine gun detached from its mounting, or a piece of fallen wall, foreign objects, things that had no business being there, my aunt writes, things that blanketed and blocked the once intact streets and roads of a city that now lay in ruins. But deadly danger did not lie in wait for us only in front of our feet. We had to help distraught mothers, undernourished babies, and abandoned children. This is what the times were like, this is what the atmosphere of the times was like when shells were still flying right and left. German units were still shelling Pest from Buda, and there was even shooting from some houses in Pest. The Soviet artillery retaliated. If we found ourselves too close to the Soviet positions, the soldiers were furious and started shouting, get these people out of here.

I had to walk, I had to overcome natural obstacles and keep pace with the grown-ups as best I could. Like them, I looked down at my feet; as we sidestepped the heaps of rubble, I couldn't very well look anywhere else. My aunt may have remembered it wrong, because our family papers bear witness that our first trip took us to Tisza Kálmán Square, hers as well as mine, and at the time they were really still shelling Pest from Buda. My parents had learned that the Hungarian Communist Party had seized the Volksbund headquarters on Tisza Kálmán Square; I don't know where the information came from, or from whom, that people were gathering there and that the Party, which had been illegal for twenty-five years, would legally reorganize itself at this address. The group we were marching with kept growing in size. My Aunt Magda came with us from Damjanich Street wearing her customary cashmere turban and silver fox stole wrapped around her shoulder, my Uncle Pali marching in his fur-trimmed coat and fur hat. On this particular march I sat on his shoulders, too. I also sat on Lombos's shoulders, they joined us on Rottenbiller Street, and I also sat on Kerekes's shoulders, he was the best-looking man in the crowd, a celebrated working-class athlete, and I was very impressed; he had a slight limp, and I bopped up and down around his neck to the uneven rhythm of his steps. The city that stood in ruins often re-appears in my dreams, though on the basis of these dreams I couldn't identify its patterns or places anymore. For instance, I seem to re-member a neighborhood in Újpest and I tried to find it repeatedly, whereas there is nothing of the sort there, not even anything remotely like it.

I didn't feel tired until it was over. We'd been in one place, then suddenly we were in another. We got there. We made it. It was always so sudden. In the heat I fell asleep without preamble; sometimes I fell asleep on my feet. I'd fall asleep even as we walked. To this day I can fall asleep at the drop of a hat. But back then, I reverted to the ethe-real calm of sleep in the midst of general amusement, as sleep, the reward for physical exertion, claimed my body, sweeping it along, tak-ing possession of it as with a single quick slip it tossed me, along with my sense of self, back into the protection of the womb. At times I'd return to self-consciousness on the sills of the boarded-up windows of half-ruined cafés, in the dark recesses of dingy cake shops, or else on a velvet settee reeking of cigarette smoke. These were pleasant awak-enings, I had no idea how we got there or what our role was amid the mighty hubbub of activity around us, amid so many laughing and ges-ticulating women who would soon depart to organize their women's groups; and from then on and for a long time to come, there are only women in my memories as the red-hot heat of a potbellied coke stove penetrates the convex panes of the frosted glass and illuminates my face in this banal rebirth that has survived the siege.

The pile bridge was the nicer bridge, but the ice floes soon swept it away. Meanwhile, I took pleasure in the words that came our way, the din of drifting floes, pontoon, ornamental fountain, the drifting ice floes really did make a great din, air raid, collier, semi-precious stone, shell casing, mounting, pile bridge. As we stood by the railing of the upper embankment in the cold and sparkling sunlight, amid the sharp splitting and thunder of the ice floes, my father explained how a pile bridge is made, what causes the ice to drift, what the currents in the water and the air are, what happens when the ice freezes over, or when they detonate a device to start the ice breaking up at long last, and where seagulls come from. We studied the concept of current by the way the seagulls moved, why it is that our breath is visible in the air, what *temperature* means, how the difference in temperature affects the amount of humidity in the air, what water vapor is, how it is created, how a pontoon is made and what makes it stay on the water's surface, and also why our own bodies sink in water, in short, the essence of relative density and how the differences in relative density affect the world subject to gravity, and also the meaning of body mass, the relationship between gravitational attraction and body mass, the secret of swimming bodies, the two physical conditions for staying afloat, and so on.

My father's explanations took on a characteristically soft, ingratiating melody, but were by no means attuned to the intellectual capacity of a three- or four-year-old child. At most he'd subdivide and slow the pace of what he had to say, he'd portion it out in what you might call easily digestible segments. The tone he assumed when explaining things, its higher than normal and thus rather offensive tessitura, still rings in my ears. Years later I heard an interesting expression from the drama critic Péter Molnár Gál, who said that someone's voice was not in place and that it would take a voice coach to put it there. The intonation of my father's various explanations has remained a concrete physical sensation, the rhythm of his sentences adjusted to the assumed grogginess of my intellectual faculties. When he explained something, his voice was not in place. But the modern conception of teaching in vogue at the time, which had originated with Imre Hermann and Emmi Pikler, held that everything should be explained to a child as often as is necessary. And for God's sake, never from above, never domineering, and as for the intellectual level, whatever you do, don't lower it. We're not explaining things to half-wits, but to children. It's all right if a child does not understand the phenomenon or the process in its entirety or in its full depth, if he doesn't quite grasp it, it's all right, he'll grasp it later or not at all, or he might misunderstand it, that doesn't matter either, we don't always grasp it ourselves, or just barely, what matters is that the child should retain his trust in us and, most important, his trust in knowledge. A child is entitled to a proper explanation. Even if intellectually he is not up to asking proper questions, the cause and effect of relationships should be made transparent. The structural frame of the explanation should rest on secure footing. Who, what, when, where, why. My parents even made a point of reciting the sequence of questions, who, what, when, where, why, and they laughed; it must have been a joke of some sort between them, and this wasn't the only thing they made me learn by heart; and I was confronted with this ironically incomplete sentence again and in the same strict order two decades later in journalism school, when Aladár Ritter, the venerable editor of the *Evening News*, who before the siege had been the editor of the *Evening Paper*, before the siege, after the siege, this constituted the borderline between the old regime and the new; in short, I was confronted with it once again as Aladár Ritter explained to us the essential and indispensable elements of a piece of news or a report. Anyone who doesn't answer these questions in a piece of news, who, what, when, where, why, anyone who leaves out a single element, can take his hat and go, for all I care, he's an amateur, a zero, a nobody, as far as I'm concerned, he shouldn't be writing about anything, a man like that should go find himself another profession, he's got no business writing for the papers.

My father also explained that we should admit in all honesty if we don't know something. And there are so many things we don't know. Even about the things that can be known we know hardly anything at all. This, too, was among my father's basic principles. Surely, he could have had no idea that, guided by basic modernist precepts, he had once again dislodged his voice from its place.

They tracked my brother Pali's progress in a large graph-paper notebook. They paid particular attention to his movements, they let him thrash about freely, without a baby bunting; I subsequently learned that in line with the modern principles for bringing up children, they had done the same with me. Today I know that they were adherents of Emmi Pikler's method of rearing infants. Besides, the names Pikler and Popper were a constant fixture of our family life, because there was plenty of mention of Piklers and Poppers in an entirely different context as well. For instance, there was Emmi, who first saw the light of day in Vienna as Emilie Madeleine Reich and who, when she was studying to be a pediatrician, met a Hungarian student at the university in Vienna, one György Pikler, who for his part was preparing to be a mathematician, and they were married. At the time there was also frequent mention of Gyula J. Pikler, the father of the statistician Pikler, in relationship to things I could not follow; they said that he was a Georgist sociologist who was a Galileist, that at the turn of the nineteenth and twentieth centuries, in the unimaginably distant past before the siege, he was one of the luminaries of the influential Galileo Circle of Budapest and one of the best planners of the land reform that had long been overdue, even if what he had planned with his impressive knowledge and reputation had come to naught.

If they did not know something, then in line with the agnostic mannerisms of modernist principles, both of them, my mother as well as my father, often said that they would look into it, look it up, find out, because they had to have an explanation for everything, just so they wouldn't have to bring the gods into the equation. All the same, my mother, who was prone to nihilism, preferred to say that she hasn't got the vaguest idea, or else that she hasn't got a clue. Both expressions were flippant, resorted to for the sake of their style. These linguistic gestures of hers, at variance, however slightly, with other people's, invariably caught my attention. I felt that there was a secret involved. Or else, in keeping with her custom, she launched a playful attack, shouting, how am I supposed to know, what am I, an oracle. Which was meant to convey that no one is blessed with omniscience, except maybe charlatans. I'll find an expert who knows, I'll look it up in the big all-knowing lexicon, which meant that only science matters, only expert knowledge matters, and we are not about to be taken in by hearsay, belief, and superstition. Or else she said, oh please, let's not go into that, don't pester me with your neverending questions, if you don't mind. We haven't got time for all your questions. We can't be expected to know everything. I'm not a wise qadi, you'll ask him in Constantinople someday. Constantinople became the city of miracles, where you could find out whatever you wanted to from the wise qadi. Except I had no idea what a qadi was and in what relationship a qadi stood to a caddy. Don't worry, your question won't run away, or if it does and tomorrow you can't remember it, then that's as much as it's worth. It's worth peanuts. The ironic, self-ironic, skeptical, and nihilistic edge to these statements, warnings, and promises made a lasting impression on me. I took them in stride because, after all, one will accept nearly anything from one's mother. But I did not approve. So many relativizations, flowery bits of rhetoric, exaggerations, playing with words, playing with where she put the emphasis, because she never looked up anyone or anything. As a result, I bore her a grudge. A question put to her hopped away like a bunny rabbit, but on her lips, even this bunny rabbit was no more than a joke. When it came to knowledge, my father would never allow himself this much cheeky playfulness, this sort of ironic linguistic distancing. On the contrary, he took a highly personal view of his own Socratic not-knowing. He seemed genuinely surprised, oh my, yet another thing I do not know. I never thought about it, whereas it's a thorny question, to be sure. He took the trouble to find out, he actually looked it up and came out with his supplementary explanations or corrections. It pleased him that, thanks to my curiosity, both of us would now know. He hoped to turn me into an agnostic, just as my mother hoped to turn me into a skeptic, but I resisted their efforts from very early on. Yesterday I forgot, but today I checked up on it. It was a mistake, I admit, I made a mistake. Unfortunately, the explanation I gave you yesterday was incorrect, but I've checked up on it since. Such formulas or similar courteous formulas pleased me inordinately, the fact that along with the newly gained knowledge, this too was coming to me, my father's obliging attitude, his thoroughness and acknowledgment of having erred. In this way he promoted my own lively curiosity to a higher class; without meaning to, he guided it toward gnosis. My mother, on the other hand, blocked its path, forcing it between practical limits. We can't be asking questions and looking for answers all the time, because sometimes we have other things to attend to, and instead of all the speculation we need to do things, eat lunch, eat dinner, go shopping.

Later on, my father caused no end of trouble with these obliging sentences. Because of his acknowledged ignorance and acknowledged errors, my confidence in his knowledge increased, rather than decreased. I did as he did. One might say that for a time my trust in him surpassed the requisite heights. To give you just one very simple example that influenced my whole life, when I was about ten years old, it dawned on me that he was a Communist, and if he's a Communist, then it goes without saying that I am a Communist, too, that's the conclusion I drew from what he'd been telling me, or else I would have to become one, I would have to become a Communist, like him, whereas I had more than one conclusive counterargument by then against my father and my mother being Communists. Consequently, I made sure to have examples other than theirs. Lest I turn into a monkey. Lest I be obliged to imitate everything all the time, just so they can say that I'm a good boy. But from then on, for three years or so, I practically bent under the burden of my filial obligations. A man who is a Communist is like this and he's like that; there I was, weighing my options, and if that's the case, what must I do to become a good Communist. The Communists rejected Grandad Tauber, while for his part, Grandad Nádas rejected the Communists. I didn't understand this either.

I first understood relative density, the essence of physical characteristics contingent on relative density, thanks to one of my father's early lectures, and when I was in school I just had to reach back to this early lecture so that I could understand it again, more or less, only to forget it again. Oh yes, I grasped this once before at such and such a time, in such and such a situation, because, needless to say, along with the thing to be grasped, I also remembered the situation in which I finally grasped or did not grasp it. I didn't understand how I could become a Communist, given that I couldn't be anything else, since I was a Communist to begin with. I've been studying the structure of the intellectual faculty ever since, its morphological constraints, that certain something that renders the intellect capable of understanding, and stores in their final place only those things whose meaning and system of relationships it has grasped. When with time I nevertheless began to grasp, however gradually, and along with all my previous knowledge and in spite of all my previous knowledge, what relative density was and what communism was, and many other things besides, I also noticed how many times I need to understand something yet again in greatly differing life situations, and even more time had to pass until, from various signs that I had formerly deemed of little consequence, I came to realize that others are the same way with respect to this and not just me, and that from the point of view of human consciousness, this bore special significance. The stages of comprehension, the various degrees of comprehension and incomprehension, the misunderstandings and fallacies are linked to highly concrete situation-images. Which means that the mind does not merely retain information as such. Not in the least. My personal dictionary is linked to an auxiliary gallery of images. The word *seagull* is also the snow-clad quay in Újpest sprawled in the glittering sunlight with the destroyed Margaret Bridge and its stumps frozen in the ice like so many wingless birds. Seagulls, these are seagulls. My first fundamental concepts of hydrodynamics are linked to the image of the reconstructed Margaret Bridge, specifically to the balustrade of the steps leading to the island, from where the acceleration of the current as it crashes against the pillars and from where the water's dramatic pulverization behind the pillars can best be seen. These scrapbook pages are bound up with my father's explanations of motion, velocity, and energy. And also, if we look up at the clouded sky, they are also bound up with the seagull hovering atop the current, or a seagull's feather, welcome contributions to my father's explanation of relative density.

My father leaned down slightly, he held my hand, he leaned in close, we walked, we were always walking, everyone was headed somewhere, and in the meantime he kept an eye on the object in need of an explanation, he tracked its process with words, the assembling of a pontoon bridge, for instance, or the reconstruction of the Margaret Bridge. As he leaned out of the curious odor of his body's warmth, he shared his knowledge with me. It is very difficult for me to say this, but I found his smell offensive. At the same time, I did my best to overcome my aversion, because it stood in the way of the affection I knew I should be feeling for him. And which I did feel. Though what I felt for him was more like sensual pleasure, attraction, and that can disarm the disgust or, at least, it doesn't make you turn your head away. Love, on the other hand, wants to be alone with its object. Love needs pleasant smells. I couldn't find my bearings in the love I felt for him. People mentioned so many of its forms and from such different, sometimes bizarre aspects, that for a long time, compared with the whole of human life for an excessively long time, for three decades at the very least, I couldn't understand or, to be precise, I couldn't make sense of the word as others used it, the word *love*. The word *caisson* and how and why bridge builders build caissons when they stabilize the piles in the riverbed and what the caisson builder does and the danger he faces, how they build a sluice, what pressure is, what the difference in pressure as such involves, how the outer and the inner pressure is equalized, the concept of equalization as such and the concept of pressure gauge, they're all stored in my mind, bound up with the visual memories of the rebuilding of the Margaret Bridge, with the musical echo and the boom of metal.

My father taught me to feed seagulls. He flung the small pieces of bread he'd rolled between his fingers in a wide arch. He said they were pellets. And from that moment on *pellet* ceased to be a piece of bread; thanks to this word, he basically separated form and substance while, taking advantage of the invisible current, the seagull glided and soared, then swooped down on the pellet to the accompaniment of the loud screeching of the other birds. We gauged the physical situation of the current from the bird's body and from the way the bird flapped its wings; he even pointed out the force of the current, more or less. We learned how to gauge and follow the strength and direction of the airflow by keeping our eye on natural objects. Sometimes several screeching seagulls dived at a single pellet. It's of no consequence, but I can trace with absolute certainty when these concepts of my mother tongue first found their way into my consciousness.

The southern roadway of the Margaret Bridge was officially opened to traffic on November 16, 1947. I know because my father gave his first lesson on hydrodynamics right after the official ceremony. I was five years old at the time. He had to attend in his official capacity, and since we had to be there on time, we hurried along and he jokingly hoisted me under his arm, and I liked that more than anything, him hoisting me under his arm. As I reconstruct it now, searching for the facts, since I'm curious to know why he had to attend the inauguration ceremony, I see that on October 16, 1947, exactly one month before the ceremony, György Szentpéteri, a gentleman of the old school, a retired colonel and vice president of the Reparations Bureau, had appointed him consultant to the bureau. In keeping with his profession, he was in charge of low-voltage current, meaning news and telecommunications in a country that had recently lost the war, and in accordance with the Soviet armistice deal and the Paris Peace Treaty, had been obliged to pay substantial reparations. The peace treaty was not new to me, because the previous year Uncle Pali had been sent to Paris to participate in the peace talks and was staying at the Hôtel Claridge on the Champs-Élysées with the government delegation so he could report back to his own newspaper and some other paper as well without delay.

At last he's working in his own field again, my father said repeatedly and with satisfaction, which surely caught my attention because he was generally averse to making statements of a personal nature. His previous job was with the Electrical Works, and that's high voltage. He never spoke about himself. He did not speak about himself for decades, as if he had no experiences relating to himself, and so had nothing personal to impart. Unfortunately, I inherited this trait of his, and have tried to get the better of it by being completely open, though my openness manifests itself mostly in the sphere of fiction and fantasy, genres that make it possible for me not to be the only I in my own sentences. The character trait we shared, and which in his case may have been partly professional and partly a Communist distortion, took a dramatic turn at the end of his life, when he spoke only about himself. He blamed and he accused. He used the accusations and self-accusations to conceal the fatal step that his most private hidden self was about to take. At the time, though, according to the evidence of his appointment papers and in the interest of the reparations consignments, he had the right and obligation to inspect all the factories, plants, and companies in Hungary, a right granted to him by Decree No. 1500/1946 M.E., Par. 3. Furthermore, his appointment obliged him to take action against those who stood in the way of him discharging his duties. He must surely have acted in accordance with his inspection rights, and in keeping with his radical temperament, he must just as surely have initiated proceedings against those who tried to prevent him from discharging his duties. Which in that historic moment was not Communist radicalism, but radical state interest. The armistice agreement concluded on January 20, 1945, followed by the peace treaty ratified in February 1947 specified the deadlines and default interest pertaining to the delivery of restitution. Although in the summer of 1946 the Soviet government had canceled a default interest charge that in the meantime had grown to $6 million, the moment it was canceled, the interest began to accrue again. Default and default interest were staples of their conversation, and so I had to learn these concepts at a very early age. For me, the concept of default interest is tied to the seventh-floor balcony of the house on Pozsonyi Street, and as I try to understand it, my eyes are fixed on the open door of our apartment and I see the long hallway, at the end of which I see my father's hands in the full-length mirror as, standing next to me, he explains it. Into the picture, out of the picture. Sometimes an official vehicle would come pick him up in front of our house, and it would bring him back only days later, the suit he wore saturated with unfamiliar smells. I liked to go down the stairs with him from the seventh floor and watch him slam the car door or watch the driver close the door for him once he was inside, and I liked watching the car drive off with him. Pozsonyi Street on an early spring morning, Pozsonyi Street on a summer's morning, my father's sundry departures lodged themselves firmly in my mind from this perspective. I was happy when he had to leave, because I could then watch him leave. After the siege, these were old-fashioned black cars with running boards, Bugattis, Adlers, Mercedeses, though somewhat later, colorful American cars appeared alongside the Soviet-made Zimek and Zis vehicles that were invariably black but with whitewall tires. Some of the American cars were mauve and turquoise, and people called them cruisers, because they were like warships; members of the diplomatic corps had brought them over, and they cruised the streets of Budapest with a variety of flags, only to disappear in the garages of various embassy buildings. Wherever they stopped, a noisy crowd of men and boys gathered around them.

The similarity in the men put me off. Though they looked different, they did everything alike, and so I felt a strong aversion to the behavioral models they suggested as well as their use of language. Not so the women. The women were mainly distinguished by their physique, which they emphasized by the way they dressed and, altogether, by the way they looked. This dazzled and excited me, all the things they did to themselves.

Back then, men wore overcoats, a lighter model in the spring and early fall until they switched to winter's weighty version. A strict protocol dictated when to shed the one and don the other. Come the first official day of spring or fall, that was that, the calendar ruled the day, and common meteorological sense be damned. I don't know why, but in such things there was no room for appeal. And while somehow the women managed to maintain their dignity despite the rule, I saw something unpleasantly servile in the men, and this impression of mine never let up. But once, back when I was about twenty-two or so and spring had arrived ahead of schedule, I grabbed my light topcoat, and not the winter one the date called for. My servile sex could sweat away, but spring had sprung, the day was warm, and so I decided to show my hand.

I recall the times our father came back home in such a rage he didn't even bother to remove his coat, whether light or otherwise. The irregularities he'd encountered must have infuriated him; someone cheating for his own or someone else's benefit or a consignment put at risk. He didn't, mind you, take it as a personal offense; it was rage as staged ritual. He must have been abroad, because he brought us presents, wonderful objects the likes of which I'd never seen before, and other surprises as well. Also, I assumed he'd been abroad because from time to time he borrowed one of Grandfather Tauber's better three-piece suits. The big stake in these compensation negotiations was the agenda, the object of the restitution consignment, and also the quantity and scheduling of the consignment, though what the great powers wanted or demanded, what they suffered a shortage of, was only part of the deal, the other part was what the Hungarian economy could afford. It was not in the interest of the victors to dismantle the industrial installations of a vanquished nation and ship them off *en masse*, because in that case they would have had to feed the population of the country they themselves had just brought to a standstill. The negotiations with the defeated nation were conducted with an eye to expediency. Besides, by the time my father received his appointment, the country was able to honor, at least on paper, the exorbitant reparations that the Allies had imposed. In the 1920s and '30s, two firms, Eliwest-Priteg and Standard, British and American respectively, organized the Hungarian telecommunications network according to the highest technological standards of the age, and my father had worked for them both. After the war, consignments had to be shipped abroad while ensuring that the telecommunications network would continue to function at full capacity and that plans for its eventual expansion would proceed apace, and they did. And so, in a way, I've had my eye on the state of Hungarian telecommunications for almost half a century; I read the news and the relevant statistics as if my father were still responsible for them.

Among the fruits his foreign travels yielded was a pair of ice skates with screw-on blades, a present perfectly timed, because the rink on the corner of Sziget and Pozsonyi streets had just opened near us, and we could all have skated there till ten at night with the music blaring, if only I had not been too small and didn't have to go back home ahead of the others. Yet I didn't feel at all small amid that whirl of dancing skaters and the crowd of dangerously zigzagging people, or those racing around the outer edge of the rink. The older girls even danced with me.

Signature. Seal. The illegible signature of the DASO, the deputy assistant of the subsidiary office, certified the official copy the same day. The subsidiary office was the administrative branch of the institution and the official copy was the delivered document or certificate. The day of the partial bridge inauguration was overcast and chill; it was November, but winter had not yet come, the air had retained something of the fall. Ten days later, at the headquarters of the Reparations Bureau at 12 Rombach Sebestyén Street, my father was sworn in before Vice-President Szentpéteri and Dr. Mrs. Géza Hazai. Though before the siege and after it the name of the street was written as Rombach, at the time the name fluctuated between Rombach and Rumbach. I visited that house several times. In the bright, sun-drenched sixth-floor rooms the mood was lively, at times even cheerful, and the tempo brusque. In the mid-nineteenth century, Rombach or Rumbach was Budapest's chief medical officer. He built thermal baths that had iron in the water, and thanks to these lucrative ventures, the city fathers of the future deemed him worthy of having a street named after him. I remember all the hustle and bustle, the smell of coffee, a chubby woman with heavy bones who, intent on taking one paper or another somewhere in a great hurry, kept kicking the chair from under her, while I, slightly taken aback, was allowed to make drawings at her typewriter desk. Grandad's workshop in Holló Street was not far from there. The woman gave me colored pencils to draw with, and she also gave me typing paper, but while I pretended to be absorbed in my drawing, I was actually intent on watching the woman and my father, who suddenly seemed like a stranger to me. As they leaned over a slip of paper, they ended up dangerously close, and as I looked at her, I tried to imagine what she'd be like as my mother. I couldn't tell if they were leaning over that slip of paper to discuss its contents, or if they were discussing its contents so they could lean close to each other. She must have been my father's secretary.

The official records have preserved the text of the oath my father had to take. I, László Nádas, swear on my conscience and honor that I will keep faith with the Hungarian Republic and its Constitution, will honor the laws of Hungary, its lawful customs and government decrees, will obey my superiors, will keep all official secrets, and will discharge my official duties conscientiously and to the letter, keeping the interests of the People before my eyes. Signatures. Seal. Surely, the long diacritical marks needed for Hungarian orthography must have been missing from the typewriter keys.

But I can't begin to imagine where my father got the self-confidence, the equanimity, and the faith in knowledge for these partial world exegeses. On the other hand, in our shared family psyche knowledge was perched on a higher shelf than God. The front had hardly retreated, and my father was already intent on his explanations, as if nothing out of the ordinary had happened, or to be exact, much had happened, to be sure, that we will not be able to forget, at most we will take it in stride, what he means is that we will have to remember even if we have managed to forget, but the world happens to have a more vital, a superior structural principle hidden in the depths of things that overrides past actions and events, which is to be found in the possible explanations, while for its part the key to these explanations lies in knowledge and research, which, as we recover from the universal chaos of world conflagration, we are once again embracing, one by one, we are flinging open the doors of the repositories and treasuries and we are leaving every one of them open, so the fresh air should penetrate them. Possibly, these explanations served him in celebrating his own return, the fact that he is here, in this one and only precious world of shadows, in the daylight, on the pockmarked surface of the earth marred by ruin and reeking of corpses. The five of them, my two uncles, István and Endre, as well as a couple, friends of the family, Ferenc Róna and Magda Róna whom, by the way, on the rowing tours and weekend outings everyone called Duci; they called her Duci so universally that I had to ask her daughter for her name; in seventy years it had never crossed my mind that she might have a different name; she was Duci, meaning Magda, Magduci; in brief, the five of them, bedecked with every imaginable symptom of scurvy, had just barely surfaced from the depths of the basement of the building at 7 Újpest Quay; the basement had been walled up illegally, and if my memory serves me right, my father launched into his explanations without delay, while I listened to him with a passion that nearly matched his own. I wasn't necessarily attending to his explanations as much as to his presence, the quality of his presence, the manner in which this strange man who they say is my father was explaining things to me.

Their written notes and recollections indicate that they were brought up from the basement into the daylight on January 16 or possibly January 17, 1945. Down there they had no reliable information about what was happening up above. From the second day of Christmas they were left alone with the sounds filtering in from the adjacent garage and bomb shelter. They had two guns. Uncle István had even prepared for the eventuality of one of them dying. He showed them the barrels, filled with paraffin almost to the brim, four of them, in which the bodies could be hidden. He removed just enough of the paraffin, he explained, so that it wouldn't overflow due to their presumptive weight. Of course, they had all lost a great deal of weight by then. These barrels had secure locks. In the pause between two air raids he showed the others how to make the locks airtight with wax. The garage next door was used to store army vehicles, and for a couple of days the vehicles drove off and came back at regular intervals. Then one fine day the vehicles did not come back. Then they heard some sort of irregular stamping coming from the garage, horrendous pounding against the walls that came at irregular intervals. Then they recognized the neighing of horses coming from the other side of the wall. The horses were kicking at the wall. By the first week of January, however, only the sound curtain of air raids and cannons remained. Four days later the two of us, my mother and I, moved back from Damjanich Street to our nearly intact original apartment on Pozsonyi Street, which at the time was still packed with strangers. I don't remember the move, but I remember perfectly well the sight of Újpest Quay strewn with corpses, the wide road ripped up by explosions and its filthy cover of snow smeared with blood and oil, the iron railing ripped up by bullets, and the maimed trees along the promenade. I also remember the position of the frozen corpses in the snow along the sidewalk and the road. I had to come to terms with the transfiguration of the world, which surely indicates that I remembered this quay, I'd remembered it from before, and I was stunned by the difference between the tranquil antecedents and their wartime aftermath. But when I try to recall that earlier picture of the quay as I had seen it in peacetime, its aspect from before the siege, I draw a blank; there is no such image, I can't find it, my conscious mind must have censored it.

Possibly the first visual memory of my life, one that keeps surfacing, is the dark stair landing of an apartment house in Budapest as it flares up in a sudden flash of cold light and my mother and I are hurled against a wall, crashing into it. I don't know what we are crashing into. Or possibly it's not us crashing into the wall, but the wall crashing into us. At this moment, the sense of inside and outside is not yet separate in the being that is I, the being that I was and will continue to be until the day I die, and who, with the utmost self-discipline, must place his intellect and memories at the service of providing a certain proscribed and preshaped coherence to things. Though my consciousness has retained traces of various sensations, because the mind has recorded the sensations tied to the images, in retrospect I cannot be sure whether these are in fact related to the visual sensations coming from the outside world or are perhaps impressions after the fact. On the other hand, at the moment of being hurled, traces of words already exist in my consciousness, even if I have not yet confirmed their meaning. For a long time, for a very long time to come, I won't know that without the linguistic settings mutually shaped by personal experience and impressions, there is in fact no lexicon of concepts in the mind, there is no comprehension. However, independent of this, there is visual memory. And it took me even longer to understand that my comprehension is not just my comprehension, but a thoroughly shared comprehension in which my comprehension, meaning the workings of my individual intellect, has a very small part to play. I see. But with my visual comprehension I am fortunately still residing with primordial creatures. The sounds are not yet consistently linked to the visual images and so, in retrospect and after the fantastic experience and painstaking effort of confirming given meanings and given chronologies in which a person initially engages with his parents, grandparents, or official guardians, and later with his teachers and peers, and later still, as the culmination of the process, with his own children, the origin of these early images is doubly difficult to determine.

The first image in my mind may not even be the first; I can't be a firm judge of this either anymore.

Having studied the various surviving documents, memoirs, and historical chronologies, I assume that the very first memory behind which I can discover nothing else dates from the summer of 1944, from the night of June 27, 1944, to be exact. Though who is to say that from among the images linked to the stored sensations an even earlier association might not surface at some point in time. Still, without detached observation, without the firm support of reflection, with reliance only on the visual content of consciousness, it is nevertheless very difficult, possibly even impossible to discover whether the memory is earlier, or possibly later.

When I think back on what I assume to be my very first staircase, a whole line of other staircases appear, all the staircases of my life appear along with this first one. Surely these staircases are stored in an identical place in my consciousness. Be that as it may, in this most probably the first staircase of mine I am flying, flying over the steps wrapped in someone's arm. We are flying through the air. I am probably turning my head every which way, a nervous little bird in mortal danger wanting to see everything, except I lack a sense of danger, my fundamental experience is that of safety, or to be exact, the surprising experience of the exceptional, of unpredictability comes into play against the sense of safety. Wanting to keep an eye on it. The rapid succession of images follows the basically neutral and by no means unsettling experience of danger; you might say that I am just about to lay down the foundations of the concept of danger in my conscious mind; I see the huge flat expanse of the stairwell wall, I see the wall as it closes in, an obstacle, and thanks to the brief, cold burst of light, through the railing I see the depth below as it suddenly appears out of the darkness and vanishes back into it. The images are linked in an unalterable sequence. And then there is no cold flare-up anymore, there is no plunging, there is no up and there is no down. There is only the collapsing wall. There is no sound, there is only the dark, the heat, the dark void. Just like my subsequent fainting spells. And possibly also the reverberating rumble of the debris after the collapse.

Later, armed with your validated concepts, you accept that you are about to lose your web of sensations, that you are about to lose consciousness. By now you are in possession of a conventionally agreed-upon word for the forthcoming loss of the conscious self, you already have a word for it, in fact, a number of formulas pertaining to fainting ready at hand, a cliché or two you've repeatedly heard from others. You may in fact have several words for it, and the sensation is prefigured in the word. The sensation is the semi-precious stone, the word the gold setting. The memory of the collapse of the wall must belong to the second year of my life. It is not the sensation of fainting that has survived. The sensation of fainting has various phases or stages. It was not the awareness of fainting with its phases that has survived. I will be aware of such a thing only when I will have a word for it. It is the moving image of the gradual disappearance of the visible world that has survived, the visible world giving way to the advent of darkness. The beauty of how we see the world before the acquisition of concepts dazzles me to this day; it is a sensation that goes hand in hand with the sensation of totality. At this early age, you are not supposed to have easily accessible memories, or just a very few, and the earliest section of the storehouse remains mostly inaccessible. But according to family lore, I was already potty-trained and I could speak clearly and fluently; as a reflective being ripe for mimesis, I was already able to exert diligent effort on differentiating the inner and the outer, the sensory and the conceptual, and could validate the concepts I was being taught.

I had never flown through the air on anyone's arms before, yet the sensation of flying was somehow not new to me. The essence of the sensation in no way differed from the sensation of subsequent flights and plunges. Péter is flying, he's flying. The little bird is falling down. Or when later I will fall from the top of a stone wall. Or as I see Tusi Szabó, properly Etelka Szabó, the little girl next door, shoving my little brother from the top of the same stone wall, who falls into a very deep hole filled with water that had been dug because of a burst pipe, but he bangs his head against the stones and the pipes stacked up on the rim and loses consciousness. Or when senseless of what I am doing, I fly through the air above the stairs, eager to rescue him. Or when I heave myself from the edge of the mound, flying above the snowy landscape and, keeping my skis balanced, touch the ground with a perfectly executed bounce. Or when, by lamplight at night, I fall out of the bunk bed in the Mátyás Rákosi summer camp for children at Balatonvilágos because, kneeling in bed, I want to throw a pillow, and as the pillow goes flying, intoxicated with the pleasure of throwing it, I let out a shout, and I feel someone, I don't know who, push me from behind, and my fall is inevitable, it is about to happen. Which is a heuristic novelty in my life. An addition to my father's earlier explanation. Gravity. I am flying in the wake of my pillow, but I see that my flight will be more precipitous. Which is an intoxicating experience. The observation ends with a cracking sound, and it's not until I regain consciousness in the hospital in Székesfehérvár that the first sounds emerge from inside this cracking sound, and also I can feel my weight again, and the big pillow and the bed, though I have no idea where I am or what I am actually feeling, and then the surprise propels me into consciousness and sends it on a voyage of discovery. It is a bright and sunny morning in the ward, where people are noisily going about their business, and it's fascinating, truly fascinating, because the place is new to me and I wonder how I got here, but even so, that cracking sound predominates, and then a nurse in a white cap comes in, she's shouting, she wants, she shouts as the tears come rolling down her cheeks, she wants to hear my name, which confuses me, because how can I give her my name when I don't know it myself; your name, give me your name, but how can I when I'm locked inside an echoing space; the effort hurts, I'm locked inside the echoing space with her screams and her laughter and my name and the settings of the words missing their gemstones, both the precious and the semi-precious, I'm locked inside the medley of sounds of the ward and the morning light; the light hurts, I'm going to tell her that the light hurts, but she won't understand, she won't take me seriously, after all, I don't understand myself why the light hurts, and besides, all she wants is my name. She's so happy she laughs, she showers me with kisses, and only now do I realize that the huge echoing space is actually my head, everything inside grown larger than life, and that on the periphery of its bulk, there's a bandage wrapped around and around it even bigger than my head. Which means that I'm far from my pillow now, I'm far from the night's fall. Which in turn makes me recall the last image from the previous night.

And then I hear someone call my name and Elza Baranyai comes striding in, my father trailing behind her with a fear-stricken smile trembling in the corners of his lips. And then I'm back again in this overbright ward. The light is too bright. The light hurts. But possibly, all this happened much later. Possibly days passed, possibly hours, I have never found out. Elza Baranyai is asking me a lot of questions, but I can't decipher my own reverberating answer. Instead, I feel that I must close my eyes, but I'm glad she's here. There must surely be something wrong with me, because she's been my doctor ever since I was born, and if there's something wrong with me, she's the one who always comes. They place a gauze pad on my eye or, to be exact, they replace the soothing bandage, the one that I had begged them for earlier. Then I begin to sink, then lose my earthly heft once again. It seems that behind the veil of recollection, there exists a less easily accessible yet highly stable domain of consciousness which in cases like this takes charge of coordination. If you have no interest in the esoteric, and I, for one, have always been interested in what other people think but was never interested in it myself, then given your rational mind, sensing this particular domain of consciousness terrifies you because theoretically, you'd have to admit that you have exact knowledge about phenomena from the times predating your own experience of them; what's more, that you'd be able to access it through the gates of memory, in short, that you are in possession of an inherited storehouse of memories. Of course, a sane person would hardly admit to any such thing out loud.

Once at night, when both of our parents were dead, I was sitting by my Aunt Magda's bed and I told her, at a loss, that I have images like this, wherever they may come from, and I don't know where to store them in my conscious mind or what to do about them.

Statements of a descriptive nature made my aunt recoil, though at such times the members of my family never let on. Their necks stiffened as if to say, come off it, and at most there appeared a belligerent flash in their eyes. I was baffled. Could these images of uncertain provenance originate with my storehouse of memories, or are they daydreams, the involuntary offshoots of fantasy, in short, notions or, as Hungarian literature from the time of the language reform would have it, imaginings. Or else, resisting such classification, could they originate from some inherited archetypal domain, transmitted into my conscious mind teeming with object and processes, all the while that I keep it under strict control, and function as the guideposts to the contents of consciousness.

I was studying photography by then, and after our parents' untimely death my aunt, Mrs. Aranyossi, née Magda Nádas, became our appointed guardian, and so I had a vested interest in light and image, the image-shaping attributes of light, the lightness of remembering, the gravity of the presence of things. As for the high, spacious room overlooking Teréz Boulevard where from time to time we could hear a late-night tram clatter past, only my aunt's reading lamp, a solitary sconce on the wall above her head, afforded us light. We'd been living together for about a year; they'd moved from a house across the way, while my brother and I moved from our apartment on Pozsonyi Street. It was a baroque sconce with wax paper shades, and though originally there had to be three, only two have survived and are now in my brother's living room. As it bounced off the ceiling, the reflected light from outside penetrated the darkness inside, but considering how well the reflected light brightened the room, the light sources from outside elongated the shadows of the baroque chandelier's arms along the ceiling more than one would have expected. Basically, ever since I took my first steps as a student of photography, I spent all my time watching the various light sources do their work. At that moment in that room on the boulevard, the direct lights and their reflections exercised their effect simultaneously with the indirect light. I observed the way the shadow of the arms of the baroque chandelier settled atop the shadow of the branches of the trees. An intriguing visual complexity on a flat wall, the lively patterns of complexity. Just like the sconces, the baroque chandelier found its way here from Aunt Erzsébet Mezei's pink salon, though originally it had served to illuminate our Viennese great-grandmother Eugenie Schlesinger's informal salon in her apartment on Nagykorona Street, from where it was transferred to Aunt Erzsébet's pink salon in the same house, and from there to our eldest aunt's apartment at 12 Dalszínház Street, and then to my Aunt Özsi's upstairs room at 12 Dobsinai Street, only to end up in our home; later still, my brother inherited it, only for it to be stolen when their apartment in Alvinczi Street was being painted, and they had to move everything into the garage. Nothing else, just that baroque chandelier, but that baroque chandelier they had to steal. Not the two sconces, though. As for the image, it lodged itself securely in my mind, though with it, the guest appearance of the Viennese baroque pretty much came to an end in my family. It was an interesting piece because it was originally made to hold candles and only later, after Eugénia Schlesinger had passed away, were the electric wires worked into it, as they said back then. In places the ancient electric cables jutted out from within.

My aunt laughed in the bright half-light in which, thanks to the reflective properties of the various surfaces, the lights and the shadows of the sundry objects were calligraphed into one; she laughed just like all the other members of the paternal side of my family, with a throaty sound, veritably gagging, barking, swallowing back the indecorous pleasure of her laughter. In my father's family, any public display of emotion was frowned upon. When they were children, they were not even allowed to laugh. If they did so, their governesses promptly put a stop to it; as for their father, who was by no means a man of refined manners, he punished them for the slightest infringement of decorum. My aunt was so surprised, she even cried out, oh, that's the house in Damjanich Street then, where one night, she was quick to add, when was it, in December, yes, sometime in December 1944, my mother, startled awake by the sound of sirens and an air raid in the fourth-floor blacked-out apartment where you couldn't see anything, and she meant anything, because the electricity was immediately cut off, and all you could hear was the shouting, Klári, get up this instant, and you could hear the frantic search for a candle and matches, Klári, Klári, and you could feel people bumping into one another, and I remember that from then on we always had to have candles and matches in the house, and I see to it to this day myself, there must be matches, no matter what, and there must be candles on hand, and also that somebody snatched me from bed and in the prolonged flare of the air defense tracers, ran with me down to the bomb shelter.

If in fact it was really the end of December, if my Aunt Magda was right and it didn't happen on June 22, on a summer's day, then my mother's younger sister Irén, Irén Tauber, must also have been there with her newborn baby, Mártuska, and Magda Bán and Ferenc Róna's two children, Péter and Erzsi, must have been there as well. And if that was the case, it is improbable that, forgetting about the other children, my mother should have run downstairs only with me, because in that case, it would have had to be another woman and another mother, and not my mother. She would never have done anything of the sort. She had unpleasant traits that others may have not known about or did not wish to know about, but she was not selfish, she was not an egotist. She always put other people first, regardless of who they were, only then did she concern herself with us, and only then with my father, and last of all with herself. I think that the date of this air raid, which forms the first sequence of images I remember, was not December, and it had to have occurred sometime in the summer.

On that memorable night, a bomb sliced clear through half of the house at 42 Damjanich Street, but it left the staircase and the other half of the building almost fully intact, along with us; the windows were shattered and the shards caused minor injuries, and this happened on June 27, 1944, when three hundred four-engine heavy bombers of the American air force originally headed for a Silesian target that had been obscured by clouds were redirected by their Anglo-Saxon allies to Budapest to grind the airport at Ferihegy, the railroad stations, and the Franz Joseph infantry barracks into dust. Which, by and large, they did. The following day, they counted 84 dead and 223 injured. If for no other reason, it had to happen then and in this manner, because issue number 30 of the *Municipal Gazette*, which published the decree ordering all Jews to relocate into houses marked with a yellow star, was put into effect on June 16, 1944, when the house at 12 Pozsonyi Street was also declared a yellow-star house. The decree further stipulated that each Jewish family could request one room, and with that our apartment ceased to be our apartment. This is when my mother decided to take advantage of the commotion caused by all the shifting about and exchanged our real papers for forged documents, thanks to which we could move ourselves. All I know is that on June 21, Ilona Ferber, a friend of ours whose nickname was Ferbi, moved into one of our rooms with several others, a circle of friends, no doubt, while on June 23 we moved into the house on Damjanich Street, just in time for me to acquire the first lasting memory of my life. If, however, what I experienced happened in the month of December after all, then surely, their wounded sister, Özsi, could not have been there yet, and then her daughter, Vera, couldn't have been there either. In her memoirs, my Aunt Magda writes that the two of them moved into Damjanich Street on December 26.

She makes two other assertions that also do not square with the first. She writes in her memoirs that in the summer she felt that because of the bombing my mother must leave Budapest with me posthaste, it's too dangerous for her and the child. And she was right. Except my mother would have none of it, which she later told me herself. She'd have had to curtail all communication with my father, who from May 1944 was building, not for the first time, an airport on the western frontier of the country, except this time in Szombathely, not Szentkirályszabadja. Even as a forced laborer he was engaged in professional work. I have it from him that he was in charge of a squad of engineering students responsible for building and developing telecommunications installations. The airport, which had originally been constructed with expert care and was being operated by soldiers, had to be enlarged at breakneck speed. The runway had to be overhauled and, as Tamás Révész writes in his monograph, *Airport at the Foot of the Alps*, they also put up new living quarters for the German training corps, who were arriving in increasingly large numbers. There was an urgent need for expansion because even before the German occupation of the country, the German High Command had transferred the IV./JG 27 fighter group with its Bf 109 fighters from Skopje to Szombathely. The planes arrived during the first days of March. The lion's share of the work was done by students serving as forced laborers, about two thousand young men all told. A teacher by the name of György Nagy was the commander of the unit. Under the circumstances, my mother would have had to suffer a great shock to leave Budapest with her impeccable forged papers and me in tow. Also, if she had left Budapest, they'd have had to abandon all hope not only of the monthly visits, but also communication by camp mail.

Half the house collapsed and the rubble from the staircase buried both of us underneath. Which suffices for a shock, after all. Otherwise the images I recall would not correspond to the dates. We must have left Budapest during the last days of June, when the cucumbers begin to grow and fill out in the vegetable gardens of the countryside, and when the forced laborers at the airport began dismantling the water tower that did double duty as the entrance gate, and which they had built the previous year, because the German High Command insisted that it would jeopardize the landings. According to data furnished by Révész, 141 adult forced laborers worked 1,058 hours and 268 students worked 2,005 hours on the dismantling. The demolition contractors were Ede Andráskay Müller & Son and the High Command paid them 36,343.42 pengős for the job. This time the dismantling was ordered not by Colonel Imre Torontály, commander of the airport, but the German High Command, namely *der Leiter des Bauwesens für den Bereich des Kommandierenden Generals der Deutschen Luftwaffe in Ungarn*. In one of my first memories, the ripe cucumber will be playing a vital role. According to the data published by Révész, they were also building domed shelter trenches and a battle position for the commander, they enlarged the hangar, and, needless to say, they had to upgrade the telephone lines for the new additions to the air base. The German command in Hungary also ordered the camouflage painting of the airport and published a tender for building new officers' and servicemen's barracks for a total of 782,000 pengős. The work had to be completed by June because by July, the Allied air force bombers taking off from the various Italian bases would have their choice of targets in Transdanubia. My aunt also writes that when in autumn, after the Arrow Cross putsch, they thought it best to return to their own apartment, which had remained intact even though a bomb had sliced off the other half of the house in the summer, and with help from higher quarters they had asked and received permission from the illegal Communist Party for the move, my mother was already in their apartment with me. It is only logical that when, in the first week of September, we came back to Pest from Bácska after all, we didn't go back to our apartment on Pozsonyi Street with our impeccably forged documents, but moved into the Aranyossis' empty apartment in Damjanich Street, where the superintendent dutifully asked for our papers but did not scrutinize them. He even accepted our obviously forged military travel documents without a word. No wonder that the house, which stood in ruins, was packed with deserters.

As far as Vera can remember, they spent Christmas with us in the Damjanich Street apartment, but they couldn't have moved in much before that, in which case my Aunt Magda is mistaken.

Vera's villa on Dobsinai Street in Orbánhegy was requisitioned by a certain General Görgényi. He took a liking to it, and they were given two days to pack up and leave, though I can't find a general by that name in any of the records. Neither a Honvéd general nor Gendarme general. I even looked for the name among the field officers, but came up empty-handed. Staff Captain Dániel Görgényi is the only one by this name, but at the time the villa was confiscated, he was a POW in Krasnogorsk, where he'd recently attended an anti-Fascist school, and so was among the few who issued a proclamation to the war-torn world to the effect that they had formed the Hungarian Legion and would fight alongside the Russian troops against the German and the Hungarian troops, in short, against their own compatriots, if need be.

From the house in Dobsinai Street they first moved in with friends at 15 Pozsonyi Street, which was a yellow-star house. Until their office was confiscated along with all its furnishings, Vera's father, Sándor Rendl, had a law practice with Elek Háy on Teréz Boulevard specializing in international business law. They were business partners as well as good friends. Elek Háy's numerous relatives were already occupying various rooms of the apartment on Pozsonyi Street. After approximately a year and a half of constant harassment, the government had put into effect the law ordering the confiscation of Jewish landed property, so the Háy relatives had to abandon their estates and country houses in Aszód and Jászberény. Soon after, when they decided to confiscate the yellow-star house, too, the Arrow Cross made them vacate these premises as well. They then moved into an apartment on the sixth floor of another yellow-star house, on nearby Návay Lajos Street, where eleven of them were crowded into that one-room apartment without a kitchen, just a single gas cooker in a corner of the hall that they called the kitchenette. As Vera remembers, they were able to keep the place clean and in order, there was never a loud word between them, no friction and no quarrels. Then on Christmas Eve, when they were sitting around the only table, the house suffered a direct hit. Those who were seriously injured, Vera's father, Sándor Rendl, Elek Háy and his wife, among others, were taken, along with the lightly injured Háy relatives, to Tátra Street where, relying only on their own resources, some Jewish doctors had set up an emergency hospital. My Aunt Özsi, Vera's mother, who had suffered light injuries, was also attended to there. Vera ended up alone in the one-room apartment, which now stood in ruins, and, until someone brought her freshly bandaged mother back later that night, she compulsively washed off the blood, she washed the blood off the damaged furnishings. She felt that she had to do it. She had to wipe the puddles of blood off the floor. While she worked she carried the bucket back and forth between the intact bathroom and the open depths below in the freezing, whistling wind; she traipsed atop the pile of ruins in a severe state of shock, surely realizing only quite belatedly that the walls were also bloody and that she herself had been wounded. The skin on the back of her hand was pierced by tiny splinters of shattered glass, she coaxed the splinters from her hand in the bathroom one by one, and by the time she was done, the back of her hand was bleeding from the open wounds. In a state of shock the horizon of human consciousness retreats, the universe, so to speak, is submerged. There is no looking out and no looking in. As if in an attempt to keep reflection at bay, consciousness is no longer concerned either with the past or the future, it is not even concerned with the present; it is concerned only with a single incidental, at times mind-boggling monomania. Vera could think of nothing else, just that she must wash up, she must soak the blood up to the last drop, get rid of the traces; she must even wash the blood off the walls so that her aunt Juliska should be pleased. Juliska, Elek Háy's wife, was herself badly injured. A large piece of shrapnel from the shell got lodged in Sándor Rendl's elbow; he managed to dislodge it with his uninjured hand, but the bone in his elbow was shattered; it was obvious that without medical assistance he wouldn't be able to bear the pain for too long without screaming and thrashing about. In Tátra Street he was immediately anesthetized and his elbow operated on. He and his mother spent the night in the hall of this badly damaged apartment that could not be cleared of blood. In the early hours of the next day, the architect György Koch showed up unexpectedly because, there's no knowing how, he got wind of what had happened and took the two of them to the house at 17 Pannónia Street. He had built it himself a couple of years before. He had built it slightly recessed from the street. The seven-story building has three main entrances for three separate parts of the house, two of these were designated yellow-star houses, but not so the third. Koch had his office in the latter. This is where he put them up with their fake Swiss safe-conduct passes. If there was an air raid, they had to go down to the basement of the yellow-star house. They could reach the basement without having to pass through the corridors of the part of the house inhabited by Christians, and for a couple of days managed to steer clear of the house's Arrow Cross superintendent as well. Koch supplied them with food. From 1941 to 1943, before he was called up for one of his ten stints of labor service, my father had been working as a technical supervisor to the prominent Bauhaus-trained architect.

I hasten to add that during the 102 days when Budapest was under siege, barely anyone would have thought to get undressed for the night and change into nightclothes. On this coldest winter of the war, the people of Budapest slept in their street clothes, in shoes or boots, wrapped up to the tip of their noses. There was hardly anything to start a fire with; as for the houses with central heating, where the coal or coke supplies had long since been depleted, they couldn't have taken advantage of the heating anyway, because the chimneys were gone. The people had to be ready to flee or join a column of marchers at a moment's notice.

From the basement up to the apartment, quickly, before the next air raid, from the apartment down to the bomb shelter, quickly, out for water when news came that there was water somewhere nearby, or out for a bit of kindling, quickly, provided you had a stove or had managed to stick the stovepipe out the window. Or with a knife or a pair of scissors, carve a piece out of the horses that had recently fallen. At the time Budapest was still crowded with horse-drawn carts and the horses that had broken loose from the damaged stables or the damaged carts wandered about the streets. When a horse fell, the news spread quickly. But at times they didn't just carve up the corpses; the starving people of Budapest also slaughtered freely roaming horses. They cut the flesh from the bodies of the poor animals with whatever was at hand. Best while the body was still warm. Once they were frozen, you needed an axe or a saw to carve out the meat, and not everyone had an axe or a saw.

Erzsi, who was six, and who became a radiologist, and who was given the nickname Worm because of her small stature, now says that my mother had to feed at least eleven people. She may have been small, but she told me that some funny little things were swimming atop the freshly made bean soup, and she cried out at the table, but these are worms, and that she wouldn't eat the soup, whereupon my mother grabbed her spoon, scooped out the worms, and ate them; wide-eyed, this made her reflect, and she also dipped into her soup.

In that terrible winter of 1944, my mother even managed to get hold of a Christmas tree. While the house in Návay Lajos Street was being hit by a shell and the Soviet army had finally succeeded in drawing a ring around Budapest, in the half of the Damjanich Street house that was still intact, upstairs in the fourth-floor apartment, we were lighting candles on the Christmas tree. Erzsi had a thick black braid that despite a veil of tears had to be cut off because of the lice that emerged when the two children came to us from an imperiled Jewish orphanage. At least, based on my mother's recollections, this is how I remember it, though Erzsi says that she had her braid cut off earlier, back at the Jewish orphanage. Anna Bán, who was their aunt and Milán Füst's physician, consigned them to my mother's care. As evidenced by their correspondence, she was one of Füst's trusted confidantes. But before that she had also promised Duci, when she, too, disappeared in the basement, that she'd look after them. We know from Füst's last diary entry, dated March 15, 1944, that he knew about the gas chambers in Budapest, of which nobody except a few insiders in Germany had any knowledge. Supposedly. And if Milán Füst knew, then Anna Bán must have known as well, and she had to get the children out of the orphanage with its precarious future.

As a consolation prize my mother gave Erzsi a wide red ribbon for Christmas, for when she'd have a long braid again. After the siege, Erzsi arranged her hair in a thick braid again, but instead of wearing the red ribbon, she wrapped it in tissue paper and put it away. Her brother Péter, who was thirteen at the time and who became a telecommunications engineer, was given a two-volume Lőrinc Kovai novel for Christmas. My mother also had to visit her parents, my maternal grandfather and grandmother, Arnold Tauber and Cecília Nussbaum, whom the Arrow Cross removed from their home in Péterfy Sándor Street, and who were now staying in her older sister Bözsi's home at 37 Dembinszky Street. Evading the Arrow Cross shakedowns or else managing to pass through them safely, she took them water or some of the newly acquired beans even if they were infested with weevils, or possibly a piece of horsemeat.

Until late December, my mother and my Aunt Magda also engaged in dangerous, illegal work. On the day after Christmas, my mother went down to the basement to bring up some forged documents. That was the last time she did so. They had a secret signaling device. If anyone touched the lock on the iron door of the basement, which, by the way, could also be removed from inside, or touched the live end of a loosely hanging electric cable to it, then in the lowest depths of the basement, which served as their illegal hideout, a buzzer gave off a very low signal. They had to touch the lock three times and then after the three buzzing sounds they could hand over what they had brought through a missing glass pane and also accept what they had to pass on. They hardly ever saw each other. They saw only each other's hand. With the exception of whispered messages brought from a comrade with the code name Pug Nose, they were not allowed to speak. On that certain day following Christmas night, my mother took Péter Róna's letter with her from Damjanich Street. My beloved parents, wrote the thirteen-year-old Péter, I can't tell you how I long to see you again. Erzsi is also crying after you all the time. I hope we can be together soon. Since we parted, I have seen only Anni from the family. We are both well. It is good that for the time being we are still together. Erzsi found out that they want to separate us and she won't hear of it. She's fighting tooth and nail against it. Erzsi is sick right now, but she is fine otherwise. She probably has the flu. Last night she had diarrhea. She may even have a bad stomach along with the flu. Thank God, I am well.

On the day after Christmas, my mother went back to the house on Újpest Quay, we know this from the letter Péter Róna wrote on December 26, 1944, which has survived. My beloved parents, he writes, I shouldn't have said that Erzsi has recovered. She is sick again. She ran a high fever yesterday, but I was very happy that I could at least see what you wrote. I had to read what you wrote three times to her. It looks like we can see each other soon. Erzsi misses you very much. No wonder. She has not seen you in over a month. Dear Mother, Péter writes in Worm's name, come as soon as you can, come and take me with you, please.

However, this letter never made it to the addressee, because my mother was forced to turn back with it. At the time, my mother and the others had no idea that there were two other resistance groups active in the neighborhood of Damjanich Street. In fact, one group was just a couple of houses away, at 41 Vilma királyné Street, while the other group had its secret headquarters in the building at 17 Dembinszky Street, but because of the incessant bombing, the cannon fire, and the frequent Arrow Cross raids, and somewhat later, the fighting in the streets, they, too, were soon forced into inactivity.

The front was drawing closer and closer. Then in the first days of January, when my mother and aunt tried to revive their former connections and resume their activities, the Arrow Cross, backed by the German security forces, raided the resistance group in the house on Vilma királyné Street. It must have been a major early morning operation that came about accidentally, after they heard from the tenants whose windows faced the gardens of Vilma királyné Street. This was on January 6. What they did not know was that Ferenc Dálnoki Nagy, one of Pál Aranyossi's nephews and the son of his younger sister, was among the young men who had been taken away. Just like his father, just like his mother, Irma Aranyossi, just like his grandfather and younger sister, Dálnoki Nagy was a gifted actor himself, except just then he was not only a member of the resistance, he was also a deserter along with nearly every member of the group, and as such, free prey; the first military patrol to bump into them could shoot them on sight on any street corner. They, Ferenc Rónai, Károly Nyeste, Vilmos Fuhrmann, Sándor Apsolon, László Füredi, and Füredi's wife, whose first name we don't know, were first taken to the German command post in Damjanich Street. The resistance group had used the Füredi Villa and the bomb shelter of a big neighboring house as their base of operations and ammunition depot. Down in the bomb shelter they must have aroused the suspicions of someone who then hastened to report them. Though they were not Communists, they called their action group the Red Brigade. They were taken in a tracked tank to Gestapo headquarters up in Buda Castle, and from there to the depths of the castle cave, the onetime ice pit now being used as a torture chamber. There were about 220 other apprehended resistance fighters down there at the time. But the family found out what had happened to them there only later, as part of the flotsam and jetsam of the war criminal trials, one might say, just when Ferenc Dálnoki Nagy's mother, Irma Aranyossi, had more or less succumbed to the comfort of thinking that her son must be on the list of those declared missing. In the years following the siege, to be missing remained a form of existence. You could not discount the possibility that the person might still be alive.

They never told Irma Aranyossi what had happened to her son.

The interrogation was conducted by the Gendarme Captain Endre Csergő, a commander of the National Accounting Bench, an organ of the Arrow Cross, and SS-Obersturmbannführer Reiner Gottstein. They availed themselves of the original, medieval instruments of torture, the Judas cradle, the thumbscrew, the thorn that they shoved up the anus, methods that far surpassed the usual repertoire. As a child and even as a young man, I could not look at Irma Aranyossi, whom the family called Irmus or Irmuska because she was such a sweet, cheerful person, energetic and a legendary beauty even in her old age, when she was no longer an actress but one of the best-known dance pedagogues in the country; in short, I could not look in her laughing eyes without compulsively repeating to myself, what did they do to her son, what did they do, and she knows nothing of what I know. But by now it's all right for me to know that she knew, even if not down to the smallest detail. She put up an act, pretending she didn't. It was for our sake. There was no language in which it could have been talked about anyway. We even knew that a certain Géza Sárándy was the Obersturmbannführer's interpreter. On January 26, 1945, they executed the remaining members of the group, but without extracting a confession from any of them, and so they did not denounce Kálmán Zsabka, their senior liaison and commander of the Auxiliary Honvéd Battalion Detachment, either. They had received their arms and the materials they needed to make explosives from him; they were on his list of those who needed supplies, and so their food probably came from him as well. Their bodies were hurled from the terrace of the winter garden of Buda Castle, where they were killed.

My mother and my aunt had the fake IDs and freshly printed flyers handed over to them through the basement opening of the building at 7 Újpest Quay, the one that looked out on Pozsonyi Street. It was safest just before dusk. From there they took them to the addresses they were given or handed them over to intermediaries, or else to their junior liaison whose name, in spite of regulations, they were familiar with. His name was György Markos, an exceptionally agile young man with a thorough knowledge of economic geography. Needless to say, all this was infinitely more complicated than I could ever describe here. If they set off before nightfall and were prevented from delivering the documents right away, they had to head back to Damjanich Street with their dangerous packages ahead of the curfew while long stretches of the city's streets were under bombardment or there was an air-raid alert, in which case they had to run down to an unfamiliar shelter with their packages in the dark. Or else they had to meet their senior liaison, Pug Nose, whose real name they did not learn till after the siege, at a given time and place, then head back with the blank forms and original documents he'd given them to Újpest Quay. They also had to take the blank forms and original documents they'd received from the resistance group at City Hall through the mediation of Pál Aranyossi and György Markos back to the Keeper of the Seal in the basement, meaning my Uncle István, for chemical cleaning. My mother also brought down to the basement blank religious birth and marriage certificates from Albert Bereczky, the Protestant minister at the Reformed Church on Pozsonyi Street. I still have some of these cleaned papers and empty forms in my possession. The cleaning meant that down in the illegal basement my uncle and my father stripped the papers of their unnecessary content by chemical means and, in line with Pug Nose's instructions, replaced the old data with the new by using the brown, blue, and black ink that they antiqued, meaning faded, as if by sunlight, according to old recipes.

They received the new data from Pug Nose on small slips. Some of these small slips have also survived among our papers. Down in the basement, Duci was in charge of entering the data. She was an expert at imitating old-style handwriting. All this by candlelight, need I add, or by oil lamp, or very weak lamplight. She could not afford to make a mistake, she could not damage the documents. Due to their most important printed elements, the secret numbers designating the names of towns and villages known only to the authorities and from time to time changed by them, as well as the original seals and signatures, these cleaned sheets could not be replaced. Luckily, they had an inside man at City Hall who informed them in time about changes to the place-name codes. They could change only certain specific data on the old documents; meanwhile my Uncle István made new round seals in imitation of the old seals. These tasks demanded great precision; the original writing style, the newly entered text, and the embossed round seal could in no way deviate from the original.

Still, there were modes of writing that Duci could not imitate. In such cases the chemically cleaned documents had to make their way to Gizi Várkonyi, the anointed priestess of graphology. I never found out where my mother and Aunt Magda had to take them.

There was no mode of writing, my aunt says in her memoirs, that Gizi could not imitate. In bed among her pillows, my Aunt Magda even showed me how Gizi went about it. She was greatly impressed by Gizi's know-how. She bent over the paper, studied the original writing for a while, then seemingly without a second thought, though we could just as well call it inspired, she picked up the suitable nib holder from her desk along with the nib whose thickness suited the written form, affixed the nib to the holder, never for a moment taking her eye from the written form, then, before she dipped the nib in one of the inks my Uncle Pista had concocted, she started to write in the air. She first duplicated the mode of writing in the air. Then, losing no more time looking down than was absolutely necessary for dipping the nib in the ink and making sure that she had picked up just the right quantity, without a trial run of any sort and in keeping with the original style, she wrote the proper word down in its proper place. Any further verbal instructions from Pug Nose were passed on to the Keeper of the Seal by my mother or Aunt Magda. They had a fail-safe method for this. Sometimes they saw Pista eye to eye in the obscure light of the passage to the basement or through the missing glass pane. On the other hand, my mother and my father could not see each other; they couldn't even hear each other, a safety measure set up by Pista that they accepted as a matter of course. If the others on the outside managed to get their hands on potatoes, vegetables, or in rarer instances fruit, they passed it down to the prisoners of the basement through the missing pane so that at least their scurvy would not get worse.

These illegal rounds were fraught with danger every step of the way. Also, they could not linger in any case, because delay could cost lives and could endanger the operation of the entire underground network. If anyone was caught and arrested, he was shot on the spot or, according to the language used at the time, slaughtered. Once in the basement passage my Aunt Magda found her younger brother Pista on the verge of a nervous collapse. She had first touched the loose electric wire to the lock of the closed basement door as she was supposed to, then right away heard the sound of the buzzer from the depths of the basement, and only then did she open the lock to go inside. A couple of minutes later Pista also appeared in the gloomy light, but the minute he opened his mouth, he began to whimper. All the Nádas brothers whimpered when they cried, they practically whined. Because of their father, they had to suppress their tears. At first, my Aunt Magda thought that someone had died. But as it turned out, Pista had been out earlier that day to bring something down, and on his way out, through a missing glass tile he saw that the kittens that had been born down in the basement and were passing in and out through the missing glass pane were playing in the sunlight up on the street. He sneaked closer to take pleasure in watching them, when he heard steps and a shadow obscured the sunlight. He saw only the hands, the hands of a man. He grabbed two kittens and slammed them to the ground. Down in the basement Pista was whimpering because he couldn't prevent it. But two of the kittens managed to sneak back in.

On Stefánia Street the Arrow Cross placed the bodies of those they'd killed on benches and hung signs around their necks. In City Park they hanged deserters from the trees and the bodies stayed there for weeks on end. Stray dogs, martens, and birds picked at the frozen corpses. Or else, if caught, they were beaten, taken away, interrogated, tortured, and then the four children would have ended up alone with Irén in Damjanich Street, where my Aunt Özsi must have arrived with her daughter, the fifteen-year-old Vera, only the last day of December, having come from their temporary hiding place injured and in a state of shock. My cousin Vera became an architect, a civil engineer; she now lives in Toronto. She was the one who decided that they must leave Pannónia Street. In the middle of an air raid, down in the basement of the yellow-star house in Pannónia Street, they had heard that the Arrow Cross units quartered nearby at 3 Lipót Boulevard had taken things into their own hands and, disregarding formalities, disregarding people's papers, safe-conduct passes or passports, to them it was all the same, marched the Jews down to Szent István Park or the Parliament access to the Danube and shot them into the frozen river.

I knew a man, his name was Miklós Békés, who was wounded, but he managed to swim ashore by maneuvering himself via the ice floes. He let the ice floes carry him along, he held on to their sides or else he held the ice floes in check with his arms and legs so they shouldn't decapitate him or cut off his limbs. He didn't know himself what his limbs were doing or what was happening to him. Injured and bleeding, he climbed out of the water, an adolescent boy gasping for air, he could just barely cross the road in the twilight, when on the corner of Balaton Street a solitary stranger had compassion for him. Wounded as he was, he had no physiologically acceptable explanation for how he managed to survive this interlude in his life, just as he had no explanation for why a stranger would take pity on him. He later became a cardiologist. And barely five hundred meters from the scene of this fortunate rescue and escape, Vera did not dare go upstairs to the office again, because she was possibly more terrified of yet another shelling than anything else.

The amplitude of the risk is a reliable indicator of the strength of the Communist commitment of the two women, my aunt, Magda Nádas, and my mother, Klára Tauber. The problems they faced in the course of their endeavors must have trumped their concern for their personal safety and this, in turn, and of necessity, must have in no small measure expanded the horizon of their sense of duty. Not only did their sight reach beyond the given moment, it also flung open the portal of their grudging instinct for survival. My mother was not timid by nature. What have you got in that basket, young woman, the Arrow Cross patrolman asked from a distance when she came up from the basement with her basket of forged papers and her flyers. Grinning all the while, without a second thought she said that she was carrying Jewish possessions. They screamed with laughter, slapped their knees, and she laughed heartily along with them, because as reward for the joke, she could walk on with her basket unhindered. Which also played a part in Vera's decision. They must go to Damjanich Street, she told her mother. This was the first grown-up decision of her life; at least, this was how she thought of it. Once in New York, on the street in the drizzling rain, I asked her, we had just come from a major Piranesi exhibition, to tell me why she loved my mother. What she loved about her. I wanted to know why people loved my mother. She said that she loved her spirit, her cheerful disposition. She talked to her as an equal, and not as a child. And anyway, in her opinion there was an understanding between her mother and the others that they shouldn't vex a young girl with their Communist views. Neither the men nor the women talked to her about such things, ever.

Your mother was always laughing, she made all of us laugh.

An idiot or a court jester can make anyone laugh, I said, because I wanted to see clearly.

I wasn't used to it, she reflected, and she even stopped short in the rain. It was a novelty to me, she went on, something out of the ordinary, because my own mother never laughed. At most she smiled. But your mother got up in a good mood and went to bed in a good mood. This was not the cheerfulness of an idiot. Also, it was surely intentional. She didn't want to spread sorrow and she never did, regardless of the circumstances.

In her memoirs, my Aunt Magda writes that she wasn't afraid either, and that's probably true as well. Her assessment of a situation, her fortitude, her ladylike manner brooking no argument or contradiction, must have made her formidable. She was like that even as a girl, authoritative, commanding, and the older she got, the more she was like this, a born lady, not a gentlewoman with acquired mannerisms, but a lady to the manor born who surely must have been a Communist only incidentally, even if she thought it was the other way around. She describes a number of astonishing scenes in her memoirs, hair-raising situations that she solved simply by force of character. She also admits that in the most critical days of the siege she broke down for five whole days, and not for the first time in her life either. This happened at the restaurant of the National Casino on Semmelweis Street, the favorite gathering place of the aristocracy, where she went for a clandestine meeting with Marquis György Pallavicini, while her husband was heading there to speak with a member of a resistance group from City Hall, but was arrested right in front of her eyes. Strangely enough, in one of the unpublished versions of her memoirs she mentions another place and not the casino, but at this point in time I have no way of knowing which of the two versions is correct. In all likelihood, the version that describes the scene at the National Casino. György Markos's own memoirs, which also give the casino as their meeting place, corroborate the likelihood. She probably wrote the other version because she didn't want György Markos on the scene. Markos was involved in the movements organized by free-thinkers that paved the way for the revolution of 1956, and in fact, he had taken an active part in the revolution itself. Possibly this is why she wanted to censor Markos out of their lives. Needless to say, Aunt Magda and her husband showed up separately for their appointments, except Pallavicini was nowhere in sight. She'd have waited in vain; the marquis had been arrested two days previously, and they found his diary on his desk. The fool kept a diary containing the names of those in the resistance along with their code names. The fool kept the diary in a drawer of his desk. Surely he thought it inconceivable that anyone would open his desk without his permission. Such things were simply not done in his circle; in fact, no person of breeding would touch another person's letters, diary, or desk. The desk was considered the sanctuary of one's private life. I opened my mother's desk maybe just once, and to this day I can see in my mind's eye the nature of its inner order. It was a black fold-down secrétaire, but it had blinding white rosewood inside, and the fold-down writing surface was covered in black leather. But I'd never have dared open my father's desk even once, not out of fear, but out of respect for the rules of conduct. My Aunt Magda was about to sit down at a table laid for lunch when she spotted György Markos, who had been taken there by detectives from the jail on Margit Boulevard as bait. Markos made faces. Get out of here. Don't recognize me. Don't come near me. I'm not alone. Which my Aunt Magda understood from a single flicker of the eye. And without acknowledging her junior liaison and their old friend from Paris, head held high, back straight, bearing upright, this tall, robust woman glided past to the room next door as if she were walking on air. You could never have caught this steadfast Communist woman when she was not wearing an immaculate suit, a hat, gloves, and fur. And if at all possible, on her hat a veil to cover her eyes. Which invariably lent an antiquated air to her appearance. Her husband, who entered the restaurant just as Markos was making faces, could feel that there was something off about Markos's mimicry, he even saw his wife depart in her veiled hat, her light muff, and the white fox stole enfolding her shoulder, but he concluded that Markos was fooling around as usual, and just as he was, in his coat and hat, he lost no time plopping down in a chair at Markos's table. Markos hissed between clenched teeth for him to go away. To get out of there. Right now. Right now. The two right nows he finally understood, but in his jovial, gentlemanly manner, he decided to counter Markos, saying, why on earth should he go right now, Markos should relax, he'd leave at his leisure. And does Markos know what the old bull said to the young bull. But he didn't proceed to tell the joke; he stood up, fixed his thick horn-rimmed spectacles on his nose, said farewell, replaced his hat on his handsome bald head, picked up his briefcase, conspicuously stuffed to the seams, neither of them knew with what. And as he headed for the door, at his leisure, with the angelic, unwavering trust that was so native to him, detectives in street clothes got up from a nearby table, flanking him, one on each side, like a good friend from old times, and immediately took from him the briefcase bursting at the seams with God only knows what, probably illegal papers or translations, and hissed in his ear to shut his trap, and he started walking faster on his small feet, and they took him to the dark Studebaker waiting outside in front of the casino. Another group flanked Markos, he too in a friendly manner, as old friends, and took him in another car back to the infamous prison on Margit Boulevard, where they would torture him, but could not get him to reveal anything he did not wish to reveal.

During those weeks, these people were not only courageous, they were reckless, and Markos was the most reckless of them all. Something that, as we know, Aristotle frowned upon in his *Nicomachean Ethics*. He lauds courage but rejects recklessness and cowardice as the two extremes of courage, neither of them being temperate.

I understand what he means and I applaud him with all my heart; my own experiences prove him right in every respect, but in this particular case, in the winter of 1944 in Budapest, I would rather not concur with him if I may. My aunt and my mother were right to act as they did, they were right to do so even if it meant jeopardizing the lives of the children in their care. Their recklessness was their strength. If they were unable to deliver the flyers and forged documents to their appointed place, they took them to the apartment in Damjanich Street where they were hiding at first four, then five minors with fake IDs. When my mother returned with me to Budapest in the middle of September, she gave the Aranyossis an account of the Yugoslav partisan movement. In order to join them, she'd only have had to go into the cornfield at night. She couldn't do it because of me; still, she could hardly restrain herself from doing so. There are situations when you run out of excuses for not being reckless.

To this day I am saddened that she did not head out to the cornfield at night out of concern for me, when she could have left me in care of the Biebers.

Magda and Klára loved and understood each other, and surely their sense of communality and unconditional mutuality must have bolstered their courage, and surely the family and comradely community they shared must have strengthened them in their resolve. We must also make allowances for the possibility that they loved each other with just a hint more warmth than was proper for a woman to love another woman in those days. If for no other reason, I can't discount this impression of mine, which dates from a later time, because my mother kept a photo of a woman in her snakeskin billfold. When I asked her once who that woman was, she blushed, whereas she never blushed; she wasn't given to blushing, but now she said the name of the young woman with a shock of curly hair with tender affection, of which I remember only Eta today, but I never heard the likes of it before, from her or anyone else's lips, the way she said it, and that she loved this Eta very much and had attended some sort of Communist seminar led by her, and the Arrow Cross slaughtered her openly on the street. There was another Eta among their friends, Eta Berényi, a breathtakingly beautiful gymnast who later married the hardline Communist Ferenc Münnich, who, unlike her, lived to a ripe old age. They killed her, she added, as if attempting to tame the fact of the brutal murder. Years after she died, my mother's snakeskin billfold fell apart at the scales, the lining held it together for another couple of years, then after some more decades the stitching, too, gave way in spots, so I removed its contents and threw it out.

The photograph of the shock-headed woman with the timid eyes has survived.

The outside observer first notices the intensity of comradely love, the intimate and enigmatic accord between those whose sight is set on the future. The weight of the accord. Its acerbic edge in the face of those who are in love with the present. That certain something that differs from all other familiar forms of love, and which surely contained within it a shared inclination for a bit of lesbian love. I have no way of knowing how pronounced this inclination may have been on my mother's part, it's only her blushing that makes me intuit it. On the other hand, my aunt's life was so jam-packed with girlfriends that, even at the time of the first flare-up of their youthful love, Aranyossi could barely get close to her because of her friends, and had his hands full trying to manage them. In the officers' hospital set up in the castle of Gödöllő, where after two years of service at the front his doctors tried to cure his chronic apical catarrh and helped him survive the war despite a variety of wounds, he launched into a short novel entitled *Magda's Girlfriends*, a feeble attempt to keep in check the wrath he felt for the women around his bride. Instead of love letters, he sent chapters of the novel from his sickbed addressed to Young Mistress Magda Nádas in Pannónia Street. Of the novel, only two short chapters and an outline have survived. But he had no need to finish the novel anyway, because as it turns out from a certain expression in the tenor of their correspondence, after months of love wrangling they did something that, according to the strict social etiquette of the time, was frowned upon.

The Communist utopia produced attractions at odds with other forms of attraction, and which may at times have seemed frightening to outside observers. As a child, I had to come to terms with them myself. After the siege, the two women called each other every day, staying on the line for hours. It was no use waiting for them to hang up. When they were talking, my father beat a courteous retreat. From time to time he appeared in the door with that strange little smile on his lips, waiting with utmost modesty for his wife and his sister to hang up. But they hadn't quite finished, they still had things to say to each other. Ten minutes later, they were still at it. Besides their activities in the illegal Communist movement, they helped about fourteen imperiled people survive the siege and the Arrow Cross bloodshed. Even the minimal feeding of this many people must have rivaled the labors of Sisyphus. Little wonder that for years after the siege, they were still soaring. Besides, my Aunt Magda lived the most illustrious period of her life during the four years after the siege. She was editor in chief of a newspaper she had founded, then in quick succession she wrote three books, two novels and an excellent piece of sociography in which she made good use of her experiences with the servants, field hands, and day laborers on her father's and grandfather's estate;

furthermore, she translated, and she launched into researching the history of the socialist women's and workers' movements, a circumstance that no doubt contributed to the euphoric character of their conversations. It wasn't their sentimentality that soared, because they were not sentimental, both of them recoiled at the least sign of sentiment, they turned sarcastic, and it wasn't their loquaciousness bubbling out of them either, neither of them had a penchant for heroic posturing; it was their intellect that frolicked in the shared joy of their free and loud exchange of ideas. Theirs was an exchange of rhetorical fireworks. Which is why it is surprising that soon afterward, when she wrote her first autobiography, my Aunt Magda nevertheless felt it incumbent upon herself to betray my mother, unobtrusively and consistently, all the while convinced that she was as steadfast in her morals as a rock, and you could build a church on her steadfastness. And it is to her credit that she did everything in her power to be like that. Nevertheless, as I read through the surviving documents, it seems to me that as we move further and further from the siege in time, her betrayal of my mother deepens. It's not that I don't understand her or that I blame her in retrospect.

She was bound to do as she did by the rules of the Communist movement pertaining to conspiracy, and without an understanding of these rules neither the movement nor its morals can be understood, nor for that matter our most recent history. In the interest of her integrity as a member of the movement, my Aunt Magda succumbed to pressure that subsequently violated not only her own integrity, but the integrity of the woman she adored, and she did a thorough job of it. Needless to say, in the Communist movement, this type of betrayal had its own appointed place and logic. I am almost willing to bet that they had discussed the betrayal between them. They had to agree on their priorities. A clumsy lie appears in my mother's autobiography as well. She writes that during the siege she was so busy looking after the children in her charge and caring for her family that she had to suspend her work for the movement. But even if they had not agreed, I hardly think they would have been at odds. Along with their senior and junior liaisons, they had infringed on the rules of the movement in the gravest possible way, but they did so in the toughest situation of their careers as Communists. They had no choice in the matter. My mother saw to some of the illegal duties of my Aunt Magda, and this was strictly against the rules. Or else they discharged their duties together, which was likewise strictly against the rules. Their senior liaison, Pug Nose, would sometimes charge my mother with a task directly, something he should not have done, unless my mother was officially part of his network. But she was not, and so they subsequently had to deny her having been engaged in actual activities, and in order to protect each other, they had to hide all relevant traces from the eyes of the overseeing apparatus. Not only my mother and not only Pál Aranyossi, but even Pug Nose was in direct contact with Markos, and surely, when they violated the rules, they did so out of necessity; as a matter of fact, each of them violated just about every square inch of the conspirative network. They managed jobs together that theoretically my mother shouldn't have even known about. And if they did so anyway, then my Aunt Magda should have reported it to Pug Nose, who was then supposed to report it to his superiors. But he couldn't very well have done so, since he himself repeatedly violated the rules. In order to obtain a fair picture of the situation, it suffices to place the memoirs of the same people written at various times side by side, or the various memoirs of various people, in which case it will be seen that these documents cannot be collated with regard to fact; what's more, even the verbal reports of certain individuals contradict their own written reports. In the late fifties, when my Aunt Magda told me about their late-night escapades, she spoke of their joint ventures with obvious relish, the same ventures that she had carefully omitted from the various autobiographies and memoirs she had written earlier. Also, she thought it best to acknowledge certain mutual actions as her own. My mother was long since dead when my aunt was still intensifying, revising, and perfecting the betrayal of the woman she loved. From a conspiratorial viewpoint, if nothing else, and at least in retrospect, she hoped to put her activities in the illegal Communist movement to rights.

She could not admit to it, she could not make a clean breast of it, because from the late forties onward, the Supervisory Commission of their party was intent upon bringing just such violations within the movement into the open. But at the time of their illegal activities, my Aunt Magda went even further and took upon herself the role of persecutor, whereby she managed to get György Markos punished for similar undisciplined actions within the movement. In the interest of restructuring the conspiratorial network, she even suggested his punishment, temporary expulsion from the movement. Which my Aunt Magda accomplished through her senior liaison, Pug Nose. A version detailing the arrest of Pál Aranyossi, in which there is no mention of Markos, must have been created with similar considerations in mind. For his part, even in the seventies, when he wrote his memoirs entitled *Itinerant Penitentiary*, Markos was still ignorant of the machinations that had taken place behind his back. Or else he pretended ignorance, even if he knew. From a comparison of the various published memoirs, handwritten memoirs, and autobiographies, it is clear that my Aunt Magda, who knows why, tried to blacken Markos in Pug Nose's eyes. They could exclude Markos from their midst, but they could not control him. Simply put, he could not be disciplined, he was not the kind of man you could turn on or off like a light switch. According to the rules governing conspiracy, Markos wasn't even supposed to know Pug Nose personally. But not only did they know each other, Markos was the only person who knew Pug Nose's real name, though as far as that goes, he went by the rules and never divulged it. They had met in Paris, where Pug Nose had gone to complete his college education. Pug Nose gave him orders directly, whereas in theory and according to the rules, he should have asked Magda to act as intermediary.

Because of such blatant violations of the rules, they should have expelled themselves from the resistance as well. As for Markos, even his official expulsion did not stop him; he continued his activities unrestrained, which made the others go into a raging frenzy. He played a lone hand, he engaged in the most reckless of adventures and, from the point of view of the Communist underground, he did so quite successfully, much like my aunt, who worked with my mother and who, in fact and in contravention of Pug Nose's strict interdictions, could be a passionate lone wolf herself, saving people in danger without waiting for orders from above, and in grave violation of the rules; actions that, in order to maintain appearances, she had to keep under wraps or else deny flat out for the rest of her life.

Thoroughly and repeatedly, my Aunt Magda had to edit appearance into her life. And not just one appearance, but an entire system of appearances. She didn't always succeed. Now, seventy years later, as I am engaged in collating data from various sources, the deceptions and half-truths of different magnitudes are becoming clear to me, even if I can't always discover the motive behind them. Still, none of this could have happened any other way. In their underground activities, they couldn't very well depend on chance, whether fortunate or otherwise. You can't build an underground movement based on chance, that's a given; this is why rules are called for, even if, let's face it, chance occurrences can't be discounted from human action altogether.

As my Aunt Magda recalls, on that certain night in December, she was about to step out of the apartment with the other two children when, in the intermittent glare of the tracer shell, she saw what happened with her own two eyes.

She couldn't budge, she couldn't scream. She stood ready for action, yet transfixed. The house on Damjanich Street has an enclosed staircase and no open balconies. She saw the blast propel my mother into the air along with me, and the same instant slam the two of us against the wall of the landing, which crumbled and collapsed at that instant. And if the two children, Erzsi and Péter, were really with her, as she later insisted, and she was really holding their hands, and in the midst of the various machinations of the effort of recall and cross-checking she wasn't mixing this scene up with an earlier scene, then I am the one who is mistaken, because in that case it really didn't happen in June but probably in December.

Today Erzsi Róna, or Worm, supports me in my supposition that this had to have happened in the summer, because had it happened in December, she'd remember it. However, she does not remember an air raid that sliced off one half of the house.

It is hardly likely that you could remember, my aunt said, laughing incredulously among her pillows the evening we were talking about this experience of mine and found ourselves at odds over when it happened.

If I'm right, if it was in fact Damjanich Street and not some recurring dream or fantasy, then I remember not just this, I said, laughing along with her, I remember a lot more, even if to this day I can't be sure which is the first of these intense memory fragments, or what belongs where or, in the interest of chronological order, what I should place where in retrospect for it to produce the proper sequence of events.

I was happy that she confirmed what happened in Damjanich Street, if only in part. It was happiness of a professional nature, I'm not mistaken about that, and it's not imagination but recall, because there is a clearly recognizable difference between original images and made-up images. With made-up images, the most you can do is determine which of their components are authentic. These can even be dreams, but dreams enhance the likelihood of delusion. Made-up images shift about, any one of their components is susceptible to change, while original images are static. Their appearance is fortuitous, they emerge from the system of associations belonging to the unconscious, or else they break free of it, and surely have their own repository in the conscious mind.

Your mother, Klári, must have told you about it, and since then you only think you remember, but in fact it's your imagination and not recall.

She loved to say my mother's name, Klári. She even loved her name.

But I wanted confirmation that it's in fact something I remember and not something I imagine, it's really Damjanich Street, really an air raid, and in that case I may even have earlier memories, except it seems that I can't verify them with anyone anymore.

A person animates, he adds to things, meaning he imagines, he fantasizes. It's all unintentional, involuntary, unconscious. Read Freud as soon as you can. Start with *Moses*, it's a must, then *The Interpretation of Dreams*, the *Introduction*. You must read these books. *Introduction to Psychoanalysis*, it's right there. Not there. The second shelf from the top. In Freud you'll see what the creation and the function of images is all about.

I got to read these books about seven years later, when the child psychologist Alaine Polcz, wife of my friend and mentor, the writer Miklós Mészöly, realized that I was struggling with thoughts of suicide. Of which, needless to say, I never spoke openly, neither with her nor with Miklós, nor anyone else, for that matter, not even with Magda Salamon, with whom I'd been for six years by then. As for Miklós and Alaine, our friendship was too new to discuss such a grave subject, but Alaine's suggestion was nearly identical, read *Moses* first, then read the *Interpretation*, but no, don't, you're better off reading the *Introduction* first and only then the others, and you must also read Jung, Carl Gustav Jung. After Freud, a person needs a fast-acting antidote. However, in line with my temperament, I again did things in reverse. I took the antidote, Jung, first, and only then did I attempt Freud. Still, the switch was in all probability contingent on happenstance. Miklós and Alaine gave me a copy of some of Jung's writings that a professional friend of theirs had translated into Hungarian, a typist friend of theirs had made five copies on thin sheets of carbon paper, and another friend, a bookbinder, bound them, and all this during the darkest years of Communist terror and in the greatest secrecy. Possibly in 1950, possibly 1951. These copies were passed around from hand to hand in the small group of adherents of the analytical school. In those years psychoanalysis was frowned upon and the Budapest School of Psychoanalysis was dissolved, and had barely just survived fifteen years of repression behind closed doors. After a while the now barely legible fifth copy was returned to Alaine for safekeeping, or else they had it all along, and she took out this historical relic for my sake. If memory serves me right, the first work in the collection was *Archetypes and the Collective Unconscious*, published in 1934, "On the Psychology of Eastern Meditation" was the second, which Jung initially published in 1943, and finally "The Phenomenology of the Spirit in Fairy Tales," a paper first delivered in 1945 in Ascona at the Eranos meeting honoring Jung's seventieth birthday.

I read the three essays in July and August 1968 and I finished reading them and taking notes just a couple of days before the Warsaw Pact troops marched into Prague and heavy military aircraft began flying overhead in the clear blue summer sky once again. They kept passing overhead in formation, and they made a lot of noise. What I had read turned my life topsy-turvy in every sense of the word; it made me turn my back on every intellectual and political view I had previously held. For days I couldn't leave the mansard I had rented in Kisoroszi for the summer months that afforded a spectacular view of the Danube Bend and the castle of Visegrád. What I read had brought on a fever and a malady, but it was a fever and a malady that needed at least another ten years of voluntary exile to subside. Only Kerényi's *Mythology* struck me with equal force or, when I was a child, Rabelais, Voltaire, Gogol, and the Holy Bible, and they struck me thoroughly. The defeat of the Prague Spring and the silencing of the Parisian student riots had affected me no less. After reading Jung, I could no longer separate the political, the emotional, and the impulsive animal being inside me; on the contrary, their interrelationship came to the fore. In the years that followed, Freud afforded the means of distinguishing between them, and luckily, as a brand-new Jungian, I was able to apply everything I'd learned to myself. There I stood on Szentendre Island, under the night sky by the shore of the Danube, poleaxed, trampled underfoot, depleted, knowing that once again, I'd have to start everything from scratch.

But on that particular night with my Aunt Magda we laughed in full accord as I held the works of Freud in my hand after taking them from the Biedermeier bookcase that had once belonged to Grandmother Mezei.

She laughed because she considered my assertion unlikely. How could I possibly remember something that happened when I was just two years of age. It's out of the question, she said. It's preposterous. Whereas in her memoirs she mentions her own recollections from an equally early age. She was just working on her memoirs at the time we were exchanging views on the nature of memory in general and concrete memories in particular. As for me, I was laughing with the same family-prescribed laugh, with whinnying, rasping pleasure, because her memories substantiated, and for the time being, at least, lent order to my own memory fragments.

The suddenly acquired new order, the brand-new knowledge resting on the foundations of the old, was the source of elemental joy. As Socrates said, you can only learn what you already know.

Visual reconstruction and the system of archiving are also among the most easily acquired photographic tasks. The customer handed us a fragment of a photograph, image tattered, torn, cracked, wrinkled, could you try to mend and enlarge it. Or else we were handed an enlargement that had been poorly developed and fixed and chemical decay had set in, with the emulsion peeling off the paper, or we were given a poorly developed, poorly fixed, and poorly stored negative swelling with moisture and stained with rainbowlike discoloration. We met with many such pieces in those years; they came from the depths of mildewed basements, they came from the musty cupboards of the best rooms of adobe houses, they came from the front, they came from POW camps or the billfolds of the dead, and our esteemed customers with no knowledge of photography were hoping for photographs on which the faces and figures of the persons dead or declared missing would be recognizable once again. We were fully aware of the nature of the photographs placed in our care, and this bolstered our professional aspirations. We worked on these restorations with an absorption that would never be properly acknowledged, and not just us, the photography students, but the older women retouchers, too, and the lab technicians in charge of adding sepia, of fading color out or, on the contrary, enhancing it. We were working on our shared past, the special respect of an unfamiliar nature had us in its grip. We had to salvage the figures and faces from the chaos of destruction, to reconstruct them from what little was left of them. In order to please the survivors, I always enhanced the facial features just a bit, while making sure that the person's character that could still be gleaned from the photograph should not be sacrificed to my effort.

In this faltering realm of probabilities, the chronological uncertainties were also at work.

I don't remember my mother telling me about it. She never told me about it.

Of course you don't remember, my Aunt Magda said. Of course she told you. You're compensating for the missing memory with fantasy. I'm not saying you're fantasizing, but you're adding to what she told you, you're enhancing it. It's the only way you can imagine it. That's why you think it's yours.

Okay, but she couldn't have told me what I saw on the other side of the collapsing wall.

What wall, what other side, my aunt exclaimed. My favorite aunt had a volatile temperament. She tried to rein it in so she wouldn't be like her own quick-tempered father, but she was; she resembled him even in her physique, and so her effort was mostly in vain. She'd have liked to resemble her wise and understanding grandfather, Mór Mezei, but she had nothing in common with him. She'd have had to be levelheaded, short and fragile, perceptive, with the mind of a mathematician. At times, she flew off the handle for no apparent reason; you could see her work herself up into a state, and you could tell that she even enjoyed it.

What other side, there was no other side, she yelled, raising herself off her pillows. There was an air raid, a blast. Nothing else.

But I see it clear as day. I can describe it to you, if you want.

Your mother managed to turn as she was falling so she could shield you with her body, to cover you, and the wall came tumbling down on top of you when she fell against it with her shoulder. There's nothing new you can possibly tell me. You couldn't have seen anything. We later thought she'd broken her shoulder, but there was no place we could take her, there were no X-rays in those days. She had to carry water and haul God only knows what with that fractured shoulder.

But I saw it. I know I did.

Under the light of the sconce, my aunt continued to wax indignant. You couldn't have seen anything, anything at all.

A brief second is made up of many parts.

Many parts indeed. Where did you read that. You're talking rubbish. It's made up of many parts, but not nearly enough to contain your fantasies. And that's the end of that. You couldn't have seen anything behind any wall whatsoever.

Probably no one could have understood the references contained in this furious aria except for me, but I enjoyed it tremendously. Such fussy, faultfinding discourse, even furious outbreaks of passion are accompanied by lighthearted laughter in our family because our family consciousness considers refutation, criticism, sarcasm, harshness, and skepticism as much a natural component of the acquisition of knowledge as hypothesis, assertion, proof, documentation, and reasoning.

I saw what was behind the wall that came tumbling down. I can tell you, and no problem. The yard of the house next door must have been on fire. Especially the trees were on fire. How in the dickens could I have seen anything of the sort, trees on fire, the trees along with their green leaves. They burn in Salvador Dalí's paintings, too.

He's phantasmagoric. He's mad. Where does he come into this.

They were burning in a soft and pleasant darkness in which I must have lost consciousness.

Fainting, the loss of consciousness as your own darkness absorbs the flames. They must have been locust trees, locusts burn easily. I realized this only decades later in the woods in Bak, when my friend Jakab Orsós taught me how to start a fire in rainy weather. So then, leafy locusts can burn, too. So I have not one but two authentic images of raw flames. They're like stills, independent images, they come one after the other, I explained to my aunt, except the sound is missing. Surely, they come in an order that corresponds to what I saw as I turned my head away in response to what was happening. In short, the sound is not situated where the images had been fixed in my mind. Still, the sound of burning is alive in my head. As a matter of fact, I even have an image that pre- or postdates this one. Or I should say that I have earlier and later images, except I have no idea where to place them along a continuum. But as soon as one visual fragment appears, another follows.

My favorite aunt came up with a number of reasons for why I'm exalted, phantasmagoric. I'm as mad as Dalí, Breton, and that Tristan Tzara. I'm not saying that her reasoning lacked basis in fact.

I'm standing on the shore of a large body of water, watching the ducks. This may be an image from a later time. I'm holding a raw cucumber in my hand. I'd never seen creatures like this that swim on top of the water and had no idea that they were ducks; only now can I say that they're ducks, because the concept came much later than the image. On the other hand, I know that what I'm holding is a cucumber; the name for the cucumber and the image of the cucumber may be linked in time. I shouldn't eat it because I have dysentery. I don't know what it means that I have dysentery, it's somehow related to the prohibition, except I don't understand that either. But along with the name of the cucumber, the feeling of not knowing and not understanding has remained intact. This is their first appearance. There is no cucumber and no dysentery before that. I stood by the table, I can tell you everything about this table down to the smallest detail, and the lady is scrubbing away at the cucumbers in a large washbowl, she's scrubbing them and stuffing them in a jar, and I'm standing there until she gives me one. I see the table from a low camera angle, from the angle of the half-filled jar, along with the washbowl, the dill, the cucumber, and the design on the lady's housedress. I must have asked her, I guess, though there's no sound to go with the image. The memory, the kernel of the memory, is of me wanting that cucumber. I've loved raw cucumbers ever since, the way they're full of moisture when they make a crunching sound.

In Gombosszeg, in our vegetable garden, from time to time I feel the urge to pick a fresh cucumber off the vine. In the morning, always in the morning, in the course of my first regular vegetable garden inspection when it's still cool and dewy from the night, I have to eat one unwashed; at most I rub it with the palm of my hand. Why one does something or why one feels compelled to repeat something throughout a lifetime of years remains a mystery.

It was the same sixty years before in Leányfalu, in my Aunt Magda's vegetable garden, when the early morning picking and eating of the cucumbers came into direct contact with the name for dysentery; if I eat cucumber unwashed, I'll get dysentery. I've enjoyed violating prohibitions ever since. Trying to find out what will happen if I violate them. Usually, nothing happens. To stand with those who are against, *pour ce qui est contre*, and against those who are for, *et contre ce qui est pour*. I cut this Tristan Tzara quote out of an issue of *Le Monde* because it reflects so well the logic of my own inclination to put up a staunch resistance. I enjoy rolling the name of the cucumber on my lips, puckering them up ever so slightly, rolling the amount of air needed to shape the word backward and forward. My mother flies into a rage, it's terrible when she flies into a rage; she's turning on me, she's turning on the lady, this, too, I remember, I remember the uproar. The disposition to resistance comes from my mother's side of the family, and not from my father's. I have tried to keep it in check all my life, because looking at it from the perspective of my father's family, it's not difficult to see that it makes no sense. Even so, you can't say no to everything, you can't do the opposite of everything. I can still hear the uproar, though I have no image to go with it, I remember no sentence either that makes sense; they may have been arguing someplace else and for some other reason, but all of a sudden, this sound experience and the fright that accompanies it bring to life the image of the room. Dysentery. Our room in Bácska. Where my mother is beside herself with rage, lamenting, what have I done, what have I done, and that woman, she knew I had dysentery, but she gave me a cucumber anyway, the old witch. Old witch, I heard this, too, for the first time. It's not the sound that has remained with me so much as the sense. It's a very rural-looking room, but not a peasant's; its armchairs are upholstered with tapestry fabric, the divan is upholstered in tapestry fabric, the pictures on the wall and the mirror, the so-called washbasin stand, the porcelain washbowl, and the porcelain pitcher with painted wreaths that lend it a gentrified air. I'm strolling along with the cucumber.

I don't know yet either, but I can see, my mind has faithfully retained it, that this reservoir with the ducks is the same regulationdesign wartime reservoir that I will soon encounter plenty of in

Budapest, where I'm already familiar with the concept of a reservoir and know their function in civil defense. They began dismantling them and filling them only in the late fifties. We can take great leaps in time inside me between concepts and images, we can determine the possible temporal order on the basis of the geographical provenance of the concepts. I also know that we're in Bácska. I know from my mother that this was where I learned to speak fluently. Bácska, Baja, air-raid warning, beware. The first full sentence of my life that I can say without botching it up and about which I have knowledge only because my mother kept saying with relish that this was the first meaningful sentence of my life. But as soon as she said it, the image of the original situation appeared alongside. Yes, to this day I know where the loudspeaker was on the roof of the house next door, and I have an intense acoustic experience to go with the image of the loudspeaker. When I hear the sentence and turn my face to the sky with sufficient steadfastness, the planes come in close formation. Basically, the names Bács and Baja occupy a more familiar place in my mind than the name of my native town. I first heard the name of my native town only after the siege. Until then I thought it was Pest, which is how the people living on this side of the city refer to all of Budapest. It seems that the associative systems described by Freud and the associative sequences employed by Proust superimpose the place where the concepts originate atop the concepts themselves.

The mechanics of remembering are wholly different, the topography of remembering is wholly different from what narrative literature would have us believe. I have never been back to Baja as a grown-up, but I'd gladly venture a pilgrimage there to experience this sensation. Besides, in my mind Baja functions as a descriptive name; when I hear it, the planes come flying overhead and there's plenty of *baj*, or trouble, and so I cannot sever the name from other catastrophic air raids, whether they pre- or postdate the raid in Baja. *Maga baja.* That's your problem.

During the course of my long life, not only did I not visit Baja, I haven't even bothered to check in any of my erudite dictionaries to find out what *dysentery* means. I don't know what home is, where my home is, if I have a home at all in this great big dysentery catastrophe, or why we are here in this strange place to begin with. But this not knowing suits me just fine, it gives me freedom to do what I want, though my mother takes center stage in this freedom of mine. I am absolutely sure that it was a small town and not a village, but despite the most assiduous research, I can no longer determine which small town of the Bácska region it may have been. Possibly it was the town of Baja itself, though why would Yugoslav partisans be sneaking about on its outskirts in the dead of night. My former consciousness is familiar neither with the concept of feeling at home nor with the concept of feeling like a stranger. Or Szabadka. Ancient associative links bind me to Szabadka as well. And so this earthly existence is good just as it is and it's good just where it is, bound as it is to the feeling to which it happens to be bound. In a person's conscious mind, not everything has a name; on the other hand, everything has a sensation associated with it. Or else something has a name, but the phonetic form of the name overrides the meaning. Montezuma's revenge. I've finally looked up what Montezuma's revenge is, and it's just as I thought. Dysentery. An infectious disease whose symptoms include inflammation of the bowels resulting in severe diarrhea, with the presence of blood and mucus in the excrement. It's a wartime contagion, the fatal illness of POW and concentration camps. At first the prisoners grow weak, then they become dehydrated, meaning that the body dries out, and then the blood circulation collapses. The cause may be an amoeba, in which case it is called *dysenteric amoebiasis*, or the cause may be a bacillus, in which case it is called *bacillary dysentery* or *shigellosis*.

Later, my mother said that I could repeat it at the drop of a hat, she had me memorize it, we're Transylvanian refugees in Pest, Transylvanian, don't forget, Transylvanian, and this Transylvanian got firmly fixed in my mind, though right away it was linked to something humorous; they bombed us out of our beautiful home, this bombed out was also the source of appreciable morphological pleasure, we even got bombed out of our lovely little Christian home in Pest, don't forget, Christian, and your daddy is fighting at the front for the homeland, you understand, the homeland. I must learn this, too, but even this knowledge is tinged with irony. I repeat it even when they don't ask, because the new knowledge, the new words make them happy. Their happiness is infectious, and this doubles my own happiness. It is reassuring. I remember this, too, perfectly, the exponential joy, the pleasant constraint of the linguistic performance. Szabadka. Daddy will come home from the front, he's sure to get a couple of days' leave and be free to visit us. At which I shout Szabadka, and they just love it. When it comes to Szabadka, I am self-propelled. For a long time, a very long time, in my mind Szabadka will remain a synonym for freedom. I'm sitting on the old man's lap, the old man's belly is big and firm. But I can't remember how I got on his lap with the cucumber. With the cucumber in one hand, I am feeling the uncle's big belly, I even lean my head against the uncle's big, firm belly. All newly acquired knowledge holds me in thrall, today I'd say that it makes me happy; the sensation of the uncle's big, firm belly is also newly acquired knowledge, but in place of the newly acquired knowledge that can't be put into words there hovers the vacuum of what I'm sensing, the ethereal order of things unknown. I stroke the uncle's big belly so I can feel it better. Which makes the uncle happy, the uncle gives a shrill laugh, he veritably chuckles, there's a rattle in his throat, which is yet another reason I repeat it. Given this experience, how could I not understand *exponential* later on, the exponential exponents. I learned early on that pleasure is always on the move; I give it, I take it, it bursts its banks, and consequently it can grow to dangerous proportions, it can transform itself into ecstasy, complication, shame.

An early morning image, me walking toward the uncle with the cucumber in my hand. I am crossing the barren yard under the scorching sun. I assume that the uncle's wife must have given me the cucumber in the kitchen, the one who is soon to be downgraded to old witch. Maybe she had told me to go to the uncle. Or maybe she told me not to. Not to cross the yard. All further details are missing. Possibly, my mother's raging at me in the room in Bácska has put all further details on hold. I am not allowed to leave the room. I am condemned to house arrest. They put me in the big bed with someone else, possibly another child, but this may be a much earlier image from the same small-town bedroom. Be that as it may, the uncle's ticklish laughter frightens me. His big belly trembles and it rumbles as it trembles, and we laugh, but after a while I'm so afraid of the rumbling, the laughter erupting from the depths of the uncle's belly, that I decide to pat it only if he asks.

I'm sitting on his lap and we're pretending to call Daddy at the front. He lets me crank up the phone, all the time that I'm readying myself for the eventuality of him asking me to pat his frightening, rumbling belly again.

On that certain night on the Grand Boulevard in the late fifties of the last century when the swaying, suspended streetlights had not yet been replaced by the lampposts with their bluish light, my aunt finally succumbed under the weight of my account. As I told her about these early images, as I listed them, though I could not put them in order, she finally succumbed. As she lay among her pillows, she attended to my recollection with some apprehension and confusion, but offered no more arguments to counter what she called my phantasmagoria. But she did not relinquish her right to doubt. Not that. In our family, it is never proper to give that up; at most you may retreat with it, so as not to burden others with it. You take cover. Though you may entertain justifiable doubts, you do not insist. You do not press your point. Instead, you muster your strength, collect arguments and information. Of our family obligations, this is the one the outside world least notices. They think nothing of the lack of platitudinous actions and the lack of resorting to platitudes, fools that they are. As I recalled each of the images, the corners of her lips trembled, no, that can't be true, it doesn't hold water, much like me, my own lips tremble, too, giving me away when someone posits something ridiculous, something that can't be followed rationally, something that can't be verified, confirmed, or documented.

She hid her doubt behind her lips' confusion, she questioned, she weighed the pros and cons. At such times you reach back to your memories, looking for facts and arguments, and you hope that with their help, you will be able to put all the drivel, all that is curious, peculiar, and contingent, in its proper place. From behind her confusion, which she laughingly enjoyed, she nevertheless allowed brief comments to pass her lips.

Yes, yes, I know. That nice uncle was the Arrow Cross district commander. You called your daddy at the front while sitting on his lap. And despite Klári's strict orders to the contrary, his wife gave you the cucumber. They didn't have children of their own, the wife was barren, they were Antal Bieber's next-door neighbors. If they didn't keep an eye on you, off you went to the Arrow Cross district commander next door so his wife could give you a cucumber or a peach, and so you could call your daddy at the front. Mrs. Bieber or your mother would run after you. They were afraid you'd say something you shouldn't, sitting on that man's lap. Bieber was with Pali in Vernet, and he escaped as well. He escaped soon after we helped Rajk and Pali escape.

When we moved from Damjanich Street back to Pozsonyi Street, there was still fighting in the Inner City, Pest was still being bombarded from Buda Castle. The next day, the retreating German troops blew up the Elizabeth Bridge. This was on January 18, 1945.

As for my father, he resumed where he'd left off, relentlessly explaining the world to me. He no doubt explained things even before he was called up for forced labor, except I have no such recollections, no traces have remained, just as nothing has remained of the times he was called up; he was called up ten times. Nor do I remember the times when he came back. On the other hand, the compound word they used to talk about my father's disappearances and reappearances I can't abide to this day. Forced laborer. It wasn't the meaning or its historical weight, but the phonetic shape burdened with those brutal consonants. And so I have no images of my pre-siege father. I have no images of my pre-siege mother either. The siege wiped out all traces of life before the siege. Or perhaps I should say that the siege showed me first what the only world I knew was like and where I was situated within it. Be that as it may, down in the basement, the teeth of the five of them came loose, or else fell out. My father spent four months in the basement, my Uncle István six months. Their body hair, their regular hair, and their pubic hair, fell out, and the surface of their skin was covered all over with scabrous spots. I think it must have been scabs or some fungal infection. Whenever they touched anything, however lightly, black and blue spots appeared under the skin, in which case I honestly can't begin to imagine where my father, marked as he was with these stigmata, could have drawn the temperate tone he used for his strictly descriptive explanations about earthy matter; I can't imagine it, I can only infer, but I can't explain it, though I can even remember his tone, whereas in theory I'm not supposed to remember that, either. To this day it's the tone, the characteristic intonation of his explanation, that conjures up his sentences.

In the bright January light suffused with intense cold, in the snow where people had just cleared away the corpses with their bare hands, my father was thirty-six years of age. His voice carried no trace of emotion or anger over what he had lived through; neither then nor later could I discover anything of the sort in his manner. We want to understand the phenomena of the world, and we want to understand them regardless of the situation. Our position does not shift in a catastrophe, and it does not shift in peace. Whether we truly understand is another matter. But in any case, beliefs and misunderstandings are also food for thought. He was the youngest son in the family, and surely, his older brothers, who were versed in the sciences, in the nature of the physical and mechanical world, gave him explanations of a similar nature, confident, cautious, objectively neutral, and strictly descriptive. The more phenomena we understand, the less margin there is for error in our actions. On the other hand, every generation passes on the knowledge, beliefs, and fallacies of a previous era to the next generation, and thus, for all intents and purposes, cognition is shaped by the patterns in this chain, and so we allow for a certain margin of error. The margin of error in our actions is a constant in the history of the human race. All the same, the chain-stitch pattern stands as a symbolic warning about dichotomous thinking. It means that civilizational knowledge is lodged in a different place and in a different manner in our consciousness than our daily joys and daily fears, the world of cognitive phenomena in a different place than cognitive knowledge. One bears with universal value and obeys the laws of physics and chemistry, the other bears with local and personal value and follows haphazard conventions and the laws of the individual's incidental customs or needs. Their function is coordinated neither in individual consciousness nor in social consciousness, nor is it coordinated with respect to the relationship between the two. Obviously, knowledge stands on the higher shelf of the hierarchy, but without emotion and passion, neither individual nor social action is possible. Perhaps this is why knowledge determines our actions to a far lesser extent than one would hope or expect, and this is why the margin of error is guaranteed. And this is why, in spite of our knowledge, and in spite of our most finely attuned and reasoned thinking, our emotions and passions control our decisions.

With his storehouse of knowledge, my father provided the fundamental tone to the norms of conduct legitimized by the family, and it functioned like the chorus in a Greek tragedy. With the heightened self-restraint of these fundamental tones, he also provided the model for the style of his didactics, and my aunts and uncles vouched for the model's universal validity. Or if any of them did not do so or acted otherwise, those present would eagerly jump in, they laughed, they waxed sarcastic, they protested vehemently or, in graver instances, they accompanied their protest with trembling lips and extremes of passion. Of the brothers, this latter was most characteristic of my Uncle István, the chemical engineer and polymath who was the avenging Nemesis of Knowledge in the family. If anyone talked nonsense or worse, his ascetic body bent into a spasm, his face a landscape of indignation; he stammered, he cried out, his eyes shot off sparks, just so the offender should desist and stop talking such colossal rubbish. Talking rubbish caused him physical anguish. Then, when the spasm of physical anguish had reached its climax, he would suddenly turn very calm, and softly, ever so softly, all he said was stuff and nonsense.

Furthermore, the model pertained not only to us, but to others as well. How we should conduct ourselves, given our knowledge and experience, how we should conduct ourselves with our teachers, and in general our fellow men who, with respect to knowledge and ignorance, share our own fate. How far we should stand our ground, in what way we should be on our guard, to what extent we should acknowledge the fate of other people as our own. When he was a soldier, my father said, I should be proud of him, because it was he who reannexed sweet Transylvania from the wicked Romanians, the Southlands from the villainous Serbs, and it was he who punished wicked Serbia, and he roared with laughter, it was offensive, awkward, he neighed, and in her own strident, brutal manner, my mother roared with laughter, too. They had plenty to laugh about. They laughed at the young irredentist *karpaszományos*, who was a Communist, and they laughed as they positioned themselves in the disastrous medium of Hungarian politics. After the two Vienna accords, from early May 1940, he served in Upper Hungary, from August through December of the same year he served in Transylvania, and from April through July 1941 in the Southlands. It fell to the lot of a repeatedly beaten and tortured illegal Communist to bask in the glory of the temporary reannexation of Upper Hungary, Transylvania, and the Southlands, in short, the revision of the Treaty of Trianon.

But here we reached an impasse; laugh as he might, I couldn't very well follow events before I was born. With his pedagogic ethos and exotic stories of the time before my birth, he barely penetrated the outer reaches of my consciousness, if that. Yet with his modern pedagogical views, he must have realized that yet again I didn't understand him. The only reason I haven't forgotten their joint laughter is because the very idea of a *karpaszományos*, a young irredentist army volunteer and a Communist to boot, made them laugh for years. This was their anti-nationalist amusement. No one ever explained its meaning to me, and yet I caught on to its tenor. No one should ever occupy another country, nor reoccupy it, the rule of the masses must eradicate all national boundaries. They showed me pictures in which, in spite of his knowledge and his convictions, my father marches in, a happy conqueror, or grinning, rests his elbows on the flower-bedecked windowsill of a house in Kolozsvár, Transylvania, or with his uniformed comrades in arms, their pants pulled down, sitting on a big, shared military latrine so they might pass in blissful unison what needed passing. It was the same tragicomical picture that, driven by the same motive, André

Kertész had taken in the previous world war. But regardless of how amusing or grave my father's words might have been, I couldn't get my head around the temporal structure and the storehouse of examples he assigned to them. For a long time, for a very long time, I couldn't understand my parents' past. Also, there was this *karpaszományos*, or young army volunteer. Its morphology was enchanting, but it made no sense. Today it seems to me that the majority of the historical store of examples was provided by my father's older brothers or possibly originated from before, from even more distant times, perhaps from their grandfather; there is plenty of information to suggest that they came from Mór Mezei's Sunday stories; these may have been the sources or *ur*-examples of their world exegesis.

They had some knowledge of psychology, but no psychological insight, neither my father nor his brothers and sisters, not even my mother, who at least had an affinity for it. I can't think of a single individual in my family who might have had some understanding of psychology. Even my Aunt Magda, who had actually read Freud and Adler and may have understood the simple mechanics, did not understand psychology; she may have even applied the knowledge she gleaned from their writings to others, but she made an exception for herself. Only the bare-bones information remained. They operated with rip-roaring conventions, killer prejudices, scandalous fallacies, and thus were no different from other people. Contemporary prejudices were engrained in their consciousness much more radically than their knowledge. They were familiar with mythology and the history of religion, and so should have known, in theory at least, that the gods also operate on the basis of affects and emotions, and why they prohibit one thing while recommending another; but just like their mostly high-quality literary experiences, this knowledge exercised little effect on their mental attitudes, neither on the attitudes of my highly cultivated and well-read paternal aunts nor on my paternal uncles versed in the mechanical and the social sciences, but otherwise spectacularly insensitive, not even on the attitudes of their husbands, wives, and children. Down to the last man, the members of my family were immune to everything related to the psyche. The soul is material. Lyrical word-trimming. Anyone with any self-respect keeps his emotions in check, he does not speak about his feelings, his thoughts, too, he keeps mostly to himself, because they can't be interesting enough to burden others with them. A sensible man does not concern himself with dreams, and so on. They acknowledged the world of the instincts, they even had knowledge relating to it insofar as they could apply it to their political consciousness or self-consciousness, but they considered it the product of material processes, and everything else balderdash. Put another way, they confined the horizons of their personal knowledge between the narrowest of limits. They acknowledged neither the duality of the body and the soul, nor the independence of the various elements of which they were constituted. They considered the social components and methodology of nurturing superior to natural endowment and character. One way or another, they linked character to duty. Not unlike the arching structure of a bridge, their concept of culture and civilization was supported by the pillars of the engineering sciences, historical heroes, and historical chronologies. They operated on the level of organized knowledge where the French mechanical materialists of the eighteenth century got stuck, because the deterministic attitude with which they created the causal links of materials, energies, and movements led them up against a wall and, acknowledging their fiasco, they abandoned, or were forced to abandon, their methodical thinking, all the while that, in their ecstatic state, they idolized Lully, dripping with sentimentality and drooping with charm, and Rameau, inebriated with the structure of emotional mechanisms, not to mention Handel, tripping along an infinitude of emotional modulations.

My father would launch into a profusion of explanations about all the things that did not happen in the world without us. He made an inventory of them, he heaped them on top of one another, and of these more than one continued to engage my imagination even after many decades had passed. He burdened my powers of apprehension with sadistic glee. He stuffed me full of facts. He kept returning to certain subjects as if at the same time and with the selfsame gesture he did not merely wish to pass on factual information, but hoped to call my attention to the quantity of knowledge needed for comprehension. Which I understood to mean that for the sake of endurance, meaning survival, the basic training course of which we had plenty during the siege, it is incumbent upon me to know about Zeus, the fatal eruption of Mount Vesuvius, Pliny, Dózsa, who led a rebellion against the grand squires and was tortured with red-hot irons, Walpurgis Night, the shepherd crying wolf on top of the mountain, the great German Peasants' War and the plague and Admiral Nelson, and the French revolution and Marianne, who, hoisting the French national banner in Delacroix's painting, called her gun-, revolver-, and blackjack-wielding countrymen the *sans culottes*, to what would clearly be a triumphant siege and final battle to be waged over the mound of rubble, even over the mound of corpses, if need be. And I also had to know about Napoleon, Robespierre, Engels, Darwin, and Lajos Kossuth, the Hungarian statesman and freedom fighter, whom my great-grandfather's younger brother Ernő Mezei knew personally, he looked him up several times in Turin while Kossuth was in exile there, wrote a book about him, and became a parliamentary representative thanks to Kossuth's recommendation; and there was the poet Endre Ady, too, who was also one of the luminaries of Hungarian journalism, and so on and so forth. If I do not understand all this, if I do not know it or do not develop a personal connection to history, I won't hack it, I won't survive; he didn't actually say so, but this is how I interpreted his admonition. After all, I was born in the midst of Europe's survival fever. Which laid the future bare to my understanding and made obvious all the things I would have to do in the interest of my survival. Except none of this eased my way toward an understanding of the past.

Only the merest hints of his explanations survived in my conscious mind. Thank the Lord. Some stray historical figures and concepts. Feudalism. I heard this, too, from him for the first time along with the etymology, feudal, feudalism, feudality, fief, fealty, fiefdom, as well as socage and vassal, the vassal swears allegiance to his lord, that goes without saying, then came mention of the first names in the family, Mór and Ernő, Mór Mezei's younger brother, who was a lawyer,

I heard this from him for the first time standing under some ceremoniously lit chandelier, in some ornate public building, no doubt, possibly Parliament, I really don't know. Lawyer. Law. Law-abiding. Good and true and upright. Proctor, procurator, prosecutor. So many conceptual hulks and shells that were filled with content only much later, if at all. In the best of cases, they were repeatedly filled with content. These hulks gorged themselves and grew fat with time, like a caterpillar; then one fine day they very nearly burst their bounds from the overabundance of knowledge garnished with an overabundance of footnotes; or else, only when they were abundantly fed did it come to light that they'd been nourished on misconception or, for that matter, superstition. My knowledge led me offtrack, or their knowledge led me offtrack because of their ignorance of psychology; I have been misinformed, I have been misled, they have stuffed me full of false knowledge, they are not what they seem. And then, leaving unsightly open wounds in their wake, these conceptual paunches, appendices, chrysalises, or shells burst their bounds, and all the putrid mistakes came pouring forth, all that fetid protein reeking to high heaven. But then, with its stray concepts, that's how the intellect advances in the deeper-than-deep layers of time, at times moving backward, at times forward. And also the other way around. For the time being, your conscious mind is aware of all the things it must do in the interest of a better understanding of the concept or phenomenon under consideration, all the things it must still find out, investigate, all the things it must still learn and comprehend, the experiments it must conduct for the sake of a hypothesis, but by the next day you have no time left for any of this, because you can't spare the time, and so you operate on the basis of imperfect knowledge, you rely on your scandalous gut instincts or the superstitions of your forebears, or else, because of the insecurities of your gut instinct, you eschew action altogether, clearing the way for minds more innocent than yours.

The bulks of the gradually expanding information clusters adhere to the oldest bits and pieces of cognizance, names and morphologies devoid of content. The stuff of experience that has been rightly or wrongly assigned to it settles down on top of it in layers; images, questions, footnotes, marginalia. He served in the army with the sappers, but he didn't build bridges, my father explained as we watched the bridge being built, he built communication lines. These communication lines left a deep impression on my mind. I can trace the first occurrence of the expression back to the days following the siege. The Germans were still shelling Pest from Buda. I can still see the ornate railing of the upper quay, recently shot to shreds, and the communication lines adhere to this image because I'm looking to see if I can find this something, this line on the ravaged asphalt and the frozen snow. But I can't. For the time being, the concept remains abstract, figurative. The concept of first appearance itself is of a much later date; possibly, it dates back to my study of chemistry in high school. The natural occurrences of the elements, the gaseous, solid, or fluid occurrence of the individual elements. They lay down the line, meaning that they advance with the cables as the front lines advance. Because of the front lines, this I more or less understood. I saw a real communications cable spool for the first time in the Endre Ságvári barracks, a bunch of chicken guts, as they called it in the military, and I had to pick it up and run with it, run, soldier, the buck sergeant yelled, run, if you don't run, soldier, if I catch up, I'm gonna fuck your ass. In the illegal Communist movement, my mother had attended Endre Ságvári's Communist seminars, and the barracks had been named in his honor. This much I knew. On the other hand, I had no idea that I was stationed in one of the barracks of military radio intelligence. By the time my training was completed, though, I knew for certain that I was no good at sending and receiving radio signals, for which I'd been singled out, I'm no good because I can't memorize Morse code, and even when I manage to memorize it, I can't make sense of it, I can't decode it. I mulled over these codes, which drove the intelligence officers to despair. They were at their wits' end. What are we gonna do with this muddleheaded photographer. Because of my incompetence, I was then transferred to the headquarters of Hungarian military and counterintelligence. It took me months before it dawned on me where I was.

As for the buck sergeant's yelling back in the Ságvári barracks, I never understood that either, it puzzled me from the start, and it took me another twenty years before I understood its logic and its function. No thanks to me, I was trained as a wireless officer, to the extent that I was up to it, of course, but at least my memory could reach back to my father's communication line without appreciable effort, and thanks to the admirable working of the mind, I was able, without the least effort, to identify the object with the concept of the object familiar to me from my childhood. It reached back, it knew where to reach, it knew what to look for. After two decades it identified the empty concept with the real object. Oh, I see. My father and his team had to unwind the communications lines from a cable spool just like the one here. Chicken-gut guys, this is what the other branches of the military called the communications men charged with laying the low-voltage lines. He'd been dead for five years when it finally dawned on me what he'd been explaining to me seventeen years before; this happened when, in the bars and men's locker rooms, swept along by the full extent of his fury, the buck sergeant would belt out his areas with respect to the prohibitions of his hardened instinctual life expressly for our edification, I might add. Except I couldn't understand why, with his fixation on anality and collectivity, he should be bent on committing something in words in the collective language of the bars and locker rooms that he must deny himself in fact.

Why they did something and how they did it in that even more distant past when I wasn't even born, and why did my father have to wear an incomprehensible name to mark his rank in the army. In Damjanich Street, the front line repeatedly swept over us. It meant fire, it meant infernal noise; it meant fear, cold, basements, darkness, screams, sirens, hysterical outbursts, fights, tea lights, wounded men, corpses flung out the gates, so they shouldn't be lying around inside. It meant the grating sound of the frozen windbreaker on the frozen corpse on the yellow clinker tiles. Being hit by a bomb. The sudden silence that makes you withhold your breath. Will it happen again, this is the question that the front line meant. Only years later, in November 1956, could I identify the experience and the atmospheric pressure, there it was again, propelling me, the breath caught

inside. It was back. Oh. So that's it. And then after the first quick in-
take of breath, veritably smelling the next one to come, then hearing
the roar of the collapse, and, as the last accord of the roar, the ringing
sound. The smell meant that the world around you was collapsing.
Your nose felt it before your eyes could see it. The rattle meant that for
now, at least, you have survived.

Still, for a long time, a very long time, the thought of the time
before I was born tortured me with its characteristic emptiness. For
instance, *karpaszományos*. I had no idea what it meant, but still, because in its quest for meaning the mind will latch on to knowledge
bound to physical sensations, *karpaszományos*, from the time before I
was born, had a meaning of sorts for me, unlike *forced laborer*, which
didn't. Needless to say, I didn't let on that I didn't understand. Also,
even if I had wanted to, I couldn't have put into words my problem
with compound words. Sometimes it was all too much, all the things
that got heaped up, all the things I didn't understand because I had
no place to store them, there was no place in my mind assigned to
them. It was an absence that, despite what people may say, is physical.
My temples and my frontal lobes ached. Which is why I understood
the physics of the heaped-up ice floes right away. When my father
explained the pile bridge being swept away, I could feel the situation
of the ice floes. I was the pile bridge. With its sharp edges, the ice
severed, it weighed down my pile legs. I was the ice being smashed to
bits by the pilings. It hurt. Given my empathic abilities, why couldn't
I be the ice and the piling as well. Anyway, I quickly realized how
to portion out my colossal lack of comprehension so my father's attention, caught up in his explanations, should keep turning to me
all the same and not disappear or dry up or be diverted; in short,
that I should bind him securely to me, along with the warmth of
his body and his repellent smell, his dark, male smell. Render him
helpless with my never-ending questions. Vulnerable, reined in. If he
wasn't explaining something, he wasn't present. I don't know where
he bided his time then. But he couldn't be made to speak except with
questions about the mechanical substance of the world. If I trespassed
beyond this charmed circle with my questions, he stared at me or

got annoyed, because I had disturbed him in his reflections on the workings of the physical world. The bad grace he felt almost always rendered his first sentence practically unintelligible. He was removed and absentminded by nature and couldn't get himself to say that it was high time I stopped asking him questions. The family code of conduct prescribed that he should be pleased with my questions, and so he was pleased, and by the second sentence he was his old self again as his explanations led to yet more questions. He let them lead to the outer limits of the physical universe, so that once there, he should use his relentless objectivity to block the way that might conceivably lead me to questions about the metaphysical, the spiritual, or the mystical. We mustn't make fools of ourselves by talking about nonexistent things. Much ado about nothing. This was one of his favorite expressions, and he thought it was amusing. On the other hand, he was intimately familiar with the positions and movements of the heavenly bodies and their names, but these he could never manage to teach me. There we stood under the starry sky, he pointed things out to me, he explained things, the mythological names, the course of the planets, the prorated distances, the seasonal changes, the wave propagation of light, and light-years, and I understood nothing whatsoever of these reciprocities. It suffices for us to concern ourselves with things that exist and can be measured. What doesn't exist doesn't exist. We are just laying the foundations of my knowledge with these explanations, this is how we are securing the foundations of the impartiality that knowledge calls for. Still, it took me decades to understand and not be aghast at the thought that in compounds the words on their own mean one thing, and together they mean something else, and how they mean this something else. Or to understand why, because of the way he explained it, I wasn't interested in the starry sky, and why, because of him, for a long time, for a very long time to come, I wasn't interested in the universe either, not even in the concept of the universe.

Based on the experience of incomprehension, I extrapolated a primitive system of rules so that at the cost of enormous difficulties I would be able to render the incomprehensible comprehensible. I realized that in order to understand compound words, I mustn't bind my comprehension to the partial meaning of either one or the other. Partial meaning was a goat bound to a post. This being bound to a post took up all my empathic capacities, it poleaxed me. Try as I might, I can't remember when I saw a goat for the first time; surely, it must have been in the summer of 1944 in Bácska. Once in Leány-falu I actually cut a goat's halter. I prepared for days so I could do it in secret. I wanted that goat to be free, and I wanted to tie that past the compound word that pulled my understanding in two directions at once. Later, too, I learned to count only by turning the numbers into mental images, notches, even though I knew that I was engaged in something that had nothing to do with counting, at most it had to do with my fingers, in short, with the primeval history of arithmetic. I counted on my fingers mentally, making sure no one caught on. That's why I needed the notches. I even know where I saw a notch for the first time. It was at the kosher grocer's in Dembinszky Street where my aunt Erzsébet Tauber sometimes sent me on an errand, and where, when they delivered the kindling and the coal, they drew notches by the entrance to the basement. Four notches and one across indicated five baskets of coal. As a result, I counted at a slower pace than the others, because I first had to turn the numbers into images. I envied the Russian children I saw in films and newsreels, who did their calculations by moving colorful balls around on an abacus. That, as least, was tangible. The western hemisphere preferred abstraction. When I started school, they deprived the children of these primitive aids, the colorful disks, the colorful balls, even their fingers. In first grade, Mrs. Koppány had started teaching with these, but then they deprived us of the tangible. They even called the highly respected parents' kind attention to the fact that these aids mustn't be used at home either. And so my parents got rid of them, over my protest. Later on, my teachers waited for me, at times patiently, at others impatiently; they knew I'd come up with the answer, except it would take me longer. We'll wait, Nádas, we'll wait, my arithmetic teacher who was called Gulyás kept repeating as he mesmerized me with his melancholy, shiftless gaze. He was robust and brown-skinned, and the great favorite of the female teachers. He'd come back from a POW camp, and traces of it were still visible on his face. As for me, I lived in fear that one fine day they'd catch me out and forbid me to use my trick. But luckily, they couldn't see inside my head. Which was a fantastic experience. Realizing that no one, but no one could see inside it. A triumph all my own, my secret joy. Whatever I think, whatever I may think, no one can see my thoughts. At the same time, I also realized how dangerous this was. It left me alone with God. The secret proof of His existence, of which my parents were wholly ignorant. And I must make sure that my face won't give me away. As if I were trying to convince myself that it was okay to lie.

The trousers were the trademark of the Guttmann department store on Rákóczi Street. Stylized figures, little sticklike men, tugged at the pants in two directions, three from the left, three from the right, but the Guttmann trousers were so marvelously hardy, you couldn't have torn them apart even with the strength of the six sticklike figures. Don't tug, don't pull, I kept reminding myself after the lesson I learned from the advertisement lest, driven by the separate meanings of the words, I end up tearing the meaning of the compound apart.

The pontoon bridge was erected near where we lived as soon as the ice was gone down the river.

Pontoon bridge was also a compound, yet it seemed easier to comprehend than the ornate, formal, prim *karpaszományos*, a young army volunteer who'd undergone reserve officer training and wore distinctive braids, or *paszomány*, on the *kar*, or sleeve, of his uniform, or the forced laborer creeping flat and awkward on his stomach, because all we had to do was go downstairs from the seventh floor, pass along the huge cross-shaped inner courtyard of the Palatinus houses that connected Újpest Quay with Pozsonyi Street, go past the entrance to my uncle's chemical works, where three steps led down to that certain basement and where during the spring following the siege his men sat outside, enjoying the sun, and my father and I were there in no time. It was, one might say, our bridge, it was being built for us. The plural didn't refer to the family but to the neighborhood, the city that stood in ruins and was in danger of collapse. Surely, my parents spoke about the city in this sense, in this special plural, which joined together person and object. I'd hardly sprouted out of the ground and there I was, smack in the middle of their utopia. This was how we plunged headlong into a lifetime of depersonalizations, which decades later I put an end to in my own way. In our home, *we* or *us* was a *we* or *us* that encompassed more than the members of our family. As for the personal, it was an attribute that one had to accept, even if its limits could not be defined. I couldn't make faces because of it, though. When this *we* or *us* referred not to the city or the collective majority of the country but to the family, with a certain distinctive, at times parodistic edge, they'd add our family name. It is an adopted name, and if someone says it, Nádas, they know right away that in common with other names it was fabricated from a botanical concept, *nádas* being the Hungarian word for a field of reeds, though to be sure, there's also a township near Debrecen called Nádas. Still, it did not catch on as a family name in the language, even though Hungarian-speakers use dozens of words every day that are neologisms and sound every bit as made-up as the name of my family. What's more, I can't even say for sure how our original family name should be written or pronounced. On some documents it appears as Neumayer, on other documents it appears as Neumeyer, and on still others the name is written as Naumayer or Niemayer.

Among the surviving documents, one of the first written occurrences of the name dates from 1847. In the document, my grandfather's grandfather, an Israelite and a resident of Pest, signs his name as Lázár Neumayer Freystadt, and so I insist on writing it the same way, though that's not how I pronounce it, because everyone always says Naumeyer. I don't know why. It's an amusing document, to say the least. Clearly, it wasn't my grandfather's grandfather who had written it, even his signature is not his own, but that of a lawyer by the name of Endre Szekránszky, who probably passed the task on to his clerk. In this manner, the three of them wrote a letter adorned with exquisite calligraphy, loops and curlicues, to His Majesty the Imperial and Royal Archduke, Heir Apparent and Royal Regent of Austria, though naturally not to the archduke personally; the letter was addressed to their Excellences, the Hungarian Royal Council of Regents.

Your Majesty, Your Excellences, this is how they were addressed. And in this case, too, I adhere strictly to the former mode of composition and the former spelling as I copy the work of the former clerk with clerical pleasure.

In order to earn my bred and butter and, furthermore, also, in the interest of the well fare of my seven offspring, I most humbly appeal to His Majesty and Their Excellences, the Hungarian Royal Council of Regents; this for the licence to brew coffee and to sell the beens by bulk over the counter. I was adopted by Lázár Freystadt in the 1820's as per no. 1 below,—in the year 1829 I was awarded in this same place residensy and merchant rights, as per no. 2 below,—since that time—I have paid the tax levied on me punctually every year, as the tax bills attest as appended most humbly by me as no. 3; but the manner in which I am thus earning my bred and butter and the veksation it has occasioned has so far weakened my constitution, that it is entirely and fundamentally impossible for me to continue my present manner of winning my bred without endangerment to my life, as the physician's statement affixed to no. 4 exhibits. With reference to the above, I most humbly entreat before the gracious presence of His Majesty the Archduke and their Excellences, the Hungarian Royal Council of Regents; that in view of the factors presented herein, they most kindly consider them and be kind enough to grant me, who otherwise am of the greatest respect toward Your Gracious Majesty the Archduke and Your Excellences, the Hungarian Royal Council of Regents, and also their most humble servant, a licence to brew coffee as well as sell the beens in bulk over the counter as per mentioned above.

Unfortunately, the supplements to this petition have not survived, but the official notations on the blank side of the huge sheet, which was first folded in two, then four, indicate that it is not really a petition at all, but an attempt to avoid having to pay a fine that can't be appealed through legal channels. My grandfather's grandfather was selling coffee in Pest without a license, his utensils were confiscated by the police, and that is why he mentions and documents in the supplements that he was an orphan, along with his virtues as a taxpayer, his old age and failing health, in the hope that his lamentable life would soften the heart of the Most Gracious Archduke, who should grant him a retail license to brew and sell coffee in bulk and see that the confiscated utensils are returned to him. Otherwise my children and I will starve to death on the spot. The administration was quite rapid. The document was entered in the records on April 8, 1847, and given the number 15914/847, and it was referred to His Majesty the Imperial and Royal Archduke, Heir Apparent and Royal Regent of Austria, Stephen and the Right Honorable Hungarian Royal Council of Governors, gracious lords and right honorable gentlemen, on April 13 with the accompanying comment that Lázár Neumayer Freysadt is a resident of Pest, and for the reasons above listed, he begs the right to brew coffee and sell coffee beans in bulk over the counter.

May passes, June passes, but at the end of July the Council of Governors finally meets and in another four days the writ signed by the functionary István Lukáts and addressed to the lawyer is in his hands, the gist of which is that their submitted application cannot be honored; on the other hand, with respect to the future return of the utensils confiscated from him, either in kind or in the amount decided on by the appraiser, the Pest City Council has taken the necessary steps, the decision copied from the Royal Council of Governors' yearly meeting on the 27th of the month in Szentjakab, 1847.

I know from family hearsay that my grandfather's grandfather, meaning my great-great-grandfather whom the Israelite Lázár Freystadt of Pest adopted and endowed with his name, arrived as an orphan; he came alone with his scant belongings, he came from someplace in Austria, he came on foot, according to family lore from Freistadt, in which case the Neumayers lived in the Austrian Freistadt. But if you scratch under the surface it will appear that he couldn't very well have come from there because until the last two decades of the nineteenth century Jews could not settle in Freistadt, and thus the town had no Jewish religious community. Possibly, he came from Freistett by the Rhine. Except, I couldn't find a gravestone with this name on it. Possibly Lázár Freystadt of Pest may have been a distant relative, but it is also possible that after my great-great-grandfather's father's death, a friend, business partner, acquaintance, or acquaintance's acquaintance, or more likely, the rabbi of the congregation of the town in Germany or possibly Austria, we shall never know, may have entrusted Lázár to his care. At least, so goes the family lore, and it may even be true. In those days, such things were not uncommon in Jewish communities. Still, whether it was in the vicinity of the Austrian Freistadt or Freistett by the Rhine, they couldn't have called him Lázár, that being a Hungarian name. I read about similar fates possibly from the great Galician writers, Olbracht, Franzon, Granach, Joseph Roth, Gregor von Rezzori, possibly Appelfeld. When a Jewish child was fully orphaned and they learned that in a distant Jewish community a couple was childless or would gladly take the orphan into their care, they sent him off, they let him go in God's name. In this case only the similarity in their first names is conspicuous. Theoretically, my great-grandfather's father should have arrived from Germany or Austria as Lazarus Neumayer. Because of their religious strictures, Jews cannot change their first names, just as a graveyard cannot be done away with and the bones thrown on a garbage heap to make room for a housing estate. Graveyards must remain forever and ever just as they are, and not be disturbed. The authorities can give Jews family surnames at their discretion, but first names are sacred and inviolate, like a covenant that stands for all time. Accordingly, had my great-great-grandfather, Lázár Neumayer, come to Pest with a first name bearing the Hungarian spelling and not Lazarus, it would be an entirely different story, and still a different story if, in spite of religious stricture, he changed it later, or if the authorities arbitrarily changed his first name from Lazarus to Lázár. The first version seems to indicate that he was born as the child of Lázár Freystadt, who had initially lived for a shorter or longer period in Freistett or possibly Rosenheim near the Austrian Freistadt, but in wedlock, and after his disgraced mother passed away at an early age in Rosenheim in the Upper Austrian Mühlviertel or Freistett by the Rhine, the local rabbi had no recourse but to send that unfortunate orphan, that accursed bantling, that bastard, that shame to the community, along with a letter to his natural father in Pest. However, as people conversant with the science of genealogy have pointed out to me, this adventurous version is itself not credible. In Ashkenazi communities they did not give a newborn the name of a person who was still alive, because they held that basically, by doing so, they would shorten the life of the older person. In Sephardic communities they thought otherwise, but I have no idea whether Lázár Neumayer, whom Lázár Freystadt adopted, came to Pest from a Sephardic or Ashkenazi community.

Let us concern ourselves with what can be documented. If in 1829 Lázár Neumayer Freystadt was awarded residential and commercial rights in Pest, then he had to be at least twenty-one years old at the time, meaning he had come of age. And if he had been adopted nine years before, he had to be twelve years of age when he came to Pest, before his bar mitzvah, which means that he had to be born in 1808 somewhere in Austria, possibly even in Rosenheim near Freistadt, or even Freistett near the Rhine. We also know from the authorized translation of an extant birth certificate that on April 8, 1847, Lázár Neumayer Freystadt, who for the abovementioned reasons petitioned the local Council of Governors for the right to brew coffee and sell it in bulk, was deceased by February 25, 1857. On this day the Israelite Congregation of Pest issued the authorized copy of circumcision certificate no. 6044 through one Dávid Schacherl, according to which József Neumayer, the lawful son of the deceased Lázár Neumayer Freystadt, local resident, was born locally on July 8, in the year 1832. The certificate was signed and supplied with a seal by the prefect Lipót A. Schulhof, and was further attested with the illegible signature of the head of the rabbinate, a chief rabbi, who also verified it with the seal of his office. But why the Hungarian translation was made or from which language the original certificate was translated, Hebrew or German, I am at a loss to discover.

The branches of the family tree disappear in the far reaches of time, and as I trace their path I cannot see more of the past.

My Neumayer grandfather, who was born in Szolnok, and who was Lázár's grandson and József's son, and who at birth was given the name Adolf Arnold, nevertheless appears on official documents and in one of my father's short autobiographies as Antal Arnold, I don't know why. Surely, a son knows his father's name. His original birth certificate does not verify this Antal, but curiously, the name Antal appears in several later documents. On the other hand, we know, because it can be documented, that along with the names of his children, and with the permission of the minister of the interior, on November 23, 1911, he magyarized his family name, the act being filed in the archives under number 49499/1911. We also know that from then on neither he nor his father, József Neumayer, used the Freystadt name. I also can't say when or where they lost their second name, the name of the adoptive father, and why they kept the name of their grandmother, who surely died early, perhaps in shame, perhaps in widowhood, or the name of their great-grandmother. On the other hand, I know that Klára Mezei, the mother of my Neumayer grandfather's seven children, in short, my paternal grandmother, was originally born with a Hungarian name. With Klára Mezei I can see a bit further back in time. On the occasion of his approaching ninetieth birthday, my great-grandfather Mór Mezei related the story of the magyarization of their surname to the reporter of *Pesti Napló*. This was on April 19, 1925, though the story is told and passed on differently in the family, and not as the journalist reported it on the basis of our great-grandfather's account. But that's the way it is; there are as many versions to something as there are documents, data, and legends.

Mezei leans back in his armchair, I read in the old paper, he forms a funnel with his hand so he can hear every word clearly, and meanwhile he relates that in the Piarist high school in Újhely, meaning Sátoraljaújhely, there was a principal by the name of Hutter, who gave all the students with German surnames a Hungarian name. The old gentleman, who is most content to talk about his student days, laughs when he says this. He was called Hutter, but he couldn't abide anyone else having a German name. He said to me, your father should adopt a Hungarian name. He should choose Zöldi or Mezei. And then, of the two names Hutter suggested, my father chose Mezei, because he didn't like Zöldi.

What the journalist neglects to mention, possibly my great-grandfather hadn't mentioned it to him either, but which is part of the truth or part of the family legend and so I wish to mention it, is that at one time this same principal called Hutter had looked up my great-great-grandfather in his tavern saying that Mr. Grünfeld must promise to send the boy to high school. Mr. Grünfeld's son will surely make something of himself. Mr. Grünfeld must keep in mind that a mathematical mind like his is very rare, it would be a sin to let such talent go to waste.

We will instruct him for free.

My innkeeper great-great-grandfather couldn't very well ignore such potent reasoning. This is why he later agreed to the name change, despite the fact that he himself was the great-grandson not only of a respected rabbi, but of the miracle-working Rabbi Izsák, or Isak, known throughout the empire. He read a great deal himself, especially philosophy. Though initially they wrote their family name as Grinfeld, Isak surely didn't write it any way at all, because the emperor was born just then and, following in the footsteps of his long-reigning mother, he would ordain the compulsory use of German surnames for all Jews, but by then he'd been a rabbi in Újhely under his own name for quite some time. And as was often the case with miracle rabbis, even the Christians turned to him for advice. I don't know when, and I don't know how Grinfeld became Grünfeld. Surely, some names are born of mishearing, even a string of mishearings and misspellings. Besides, it's impossible, or just barely possible to trace the spelling of names and the genealogy of Jewish individuals before the eighteenth century. There are no surnames in the surviving community records; next to their own name, Jews used their father's name. Were it not for Emperor Joseph II's sensible decree, I for instance would be Péter, son of László, which would be much to my liking. It would certainly sound better than Nádas. My younger brother would be Pál, son of László. However, let's face it, given such customs pertaining to names, it would have been impossible to keep a record of Jews living in the empire. Emperor Joseph II ordered the use of German names on July 23, 1787, and lost no time in forcing it through the Imperial public administration. *Die Judenschaft in allen Provinzen zu verhalten, dass ein jeder Hausvater für seine Familie, der Vormund für seine Waisen, und eine jede ledige, weder in der väterlischen gewalt, noch unter einer Vormundschaft, oder Kuratel stehende Mannsperson vom 1-en Jänner*

1788 einen bestimten Geschlechtsnamen führen, das wibliche Geschlecht im ledigen Stande, den Geschlechtsnamen ihres Vaters, verheiratet jenen ihres Mannes annehmen, jede einzelne Person aber ohne Ausnahme einen deutsche Vornamen sich beilegen und solchen Zeitlebens nicht abändern sol, in short, that the Jews of all the provinces must adopt a certain stipulated family name, which shall be the duty of every head of family, every guardian for the orphans under his care, as well as every individual, whether wedded or otherwise, who is not under the guardianship of a head of a family or a guardian, the unwedded women their mother's name, wedded women their husband's name; furthermore, every individual without exception must choose a German forename not to be abandoned as long as he lives.

Needless to say, this is language as transcribed from the original Austrian officialese or, rather, the use of language as influenced by it.

The miracle rabbi, Izsák or Isak Grinfeld, then had a son by the name of Marcus Grinfeld, who became the teacher of the first local Israelite school, a young man of prodigious knowledge who spoke a variety of languages, and who was afforded the title of professor by Emperor Joseph II's decree pertaining to parochial schools. I'd be hard put to believe that the miracle rabbi or his son, the erudite teacher, could have been as easily persuaded to change their name as my innkeeper great-grandfather, even if this German family name, this clan name, continued to mean little to the Jews. What counted was the proper name, the father's proper name, and let us not forget, they are all descriptive names, names that indicate whose son you are; what's more, your name also indicates the character your parents wish you to have, not unlike the Christians, who borrow the names of saints, offering the newborn babe into the saint's protection. I knew from my parents, from whom else would I have known, that the name of the city is a mightier name than the name of our family, meaning the German or magyarized German name of our clan. It encompasses the surrounding neighborhood, the houses in the neighborhood, its apartments and the families living in them, and the families with the individuals with their first names, this is how we become part of the city, along with all the others. We hail from Sátoraljaújhely, Tiszasüly,

Szolnok, Nyíregyháza, Austria, Germany, Czechoslovakia. And the city also includes the organs of public administration, the decrees pertaining to the city, the streets, the street names, the sewer system under the city, as well as the electric tramlines overhead, and also the streetlights, each and every tinkling tram, the grocer in Dembinszky Street, and also his notebook with its marks indicating goods bought on credit, and the baker Glázner on Lipót Boulevard, the ice-skating rink on the corner of Sziget Street, and along with so much else, the city also includes the city sparrows, whereas they could freely go some-place else at any time, yet prefer to chirp in our city ears, and so I was aware of this worldly superabundance at a very early age, the formida-ble might of Buda and Pest with the Danube flowing between them, its legions of chirping sparrows and pigeons, and I respected them just as I respected the people with their proper names.

Although I had no idea what it meant, I liked *karpaszományos*, I was impressed by my father's elegant-sounding military rank, because of the *paszomány*, or trimming, I should think, and a *karpaszományos* he remained until they called him up for labor service, that is, and wanted to drag him off from Szombathely. I didn't understand this, either, this dragging off. I didn't understand it for a very long time, for decades. I tried to make sense of it through moving house, meaning dragging off furniture. They're dragging someone off, like a wardrobe, they're trying to get the wardrobe around the bend on the landing. He explained *karpaszományos* with recourse to his graduation from commercial school. When I asked him why, he said that the *kar-paszományos* youth came from the ranks of fresh graduates. He had a high school diploma, he had a diploma in commerce with, what can I say, lamentable results. His grades from the subjects in which he had to graduate: Hungarian composition and literature with László Lévai, satisfactory. History with Dr. György Kurucz, satisfactory. Introduc-tion to law with Dr. Ernő Lajta, satisfactory. Introduction to econom-ics with Dr. Ernő Lajta, satisfactory. Geography with Mór Földes, satisfactory. Introduction to commercial goods with Mór Földes, sat-isfactory. Commercial arithmetic with Dr. Elemér Bálint, satisfactory. Bookkeeping with Dr. Ernő Lajta, good. Office correspondence with

Dr. Ernő Lajta, satisfactory. Why he was good in bookkeeping of all things I can't begin to imagine. German language and correspondence with János Böhm, satisfactory. French language and correspondence with László Lévai, satisfactory. When he had to speak German or French with them around, his brothers and sisters invariably made fun and corrected him. I felt ashamed, as if I were he, as if it were me having to be corrected all the time. Of course, they were right, it wasn't correct like this, but like that, he used the wrong tense, a faulty article, a mistaken idiom, and so on. Compared with his older brothers and sisters, his knowledge of foreign languages may have been lacking, but then, none of them was especially adept at speaking a foreign language. They lacked the ear, they were annoyingly tone-deaf, down to the last man. It was embarrassing the way they could not sing. They suffered at concerts or the opera, and preferred to give the great musical events a wide berth. Simply put, music left them cold. At the opera my father's head kept falling. He was so bored, he fell asleep. Despite the best efforts of their language teachers and governesses, their intonation remained Hungarian. Their spelling was also atrocious. By all odds, the teasing and the correction of his mistakes became my father's lot because he was the youngest of the siblings. They had already felt ashamed that there were so many of them, and then came their little brother. The older ones, as is usually the case, used him to exhibit their own linguistic inaptitude. Their dissatisfaction with themselves, and this strange family characteristic, the lack of a good ear. Besides, when they were together, it was like a barnyard gone berserk. They lost no time in setting up a pecking order, a hierarchy defined by age. They pecked away at my father with their beaks, they *slashed* into him, made belittling remarks, lectured him, put him right, made fun of him. From time to time Eugenie, the prettiest, the oldest and prettiest, would take her little brother under her wing, but only so she should get at him herself. Some notes my father made have survived. They were written in two languages, and he must have made them during one of his official trips abroad; he sometimes wrote in French, at others in German when he attended some telecommunications meeting, but he must have been very bored, because he made notes about all sorts of other things in these foreign languages, and from what I can tell, they were nearly perfect. His grades in the other subjects of upper commercial school were no better. Religion and ethics, satisfactory. Natural science, satisfactory. Mathematics and political arithmetic, satisfactory, though I can't begin to imagine what political arithmetic could have consisted of. Possibly statistics. I will have to look into this, too, sometime. Shorthand, satisfactory. Penmanship, satisfactory. Physical education and practice, not too enthusiastic and not too skilled. My poor dear father, who was so proud of his skills as a gymnast. Health education, satisfactory. The outer appearance of his written compositions, tolerable. Dated September 30, 1927, Budapest. Baron Géza Braun, Ministerial Commissioner, Chairman of the Examination Committee.

Some of his explanations had me confused for years. I couldn't keep track of the amazing conceptual transformations. With the explanation of his impressive-sounding though worthless military rank he very nearly got me to think that graduation and the military are somehow intimately related, while with a Bachelor of Commerce degree, you're basically doomed. As a result, I spent at least two decades trying to find the essential link between the concept of commerce and military rank, to no avail, need I add. As soon as he spoke about commerce or the gradations of military rank, I slipped up. I couldn't bring the partial concepts, which were miles apart, under one roof. And then at some point the penny dropped, to wit, that the *karpaszományos* were called *karpaszományos* because they wore their *paszomány*, or insignia of rank, not on their lapel, not on their shoulder, but on their sleeve, or *kar*. In which case, it would have been wiser to take this compound apart twenty years earlier, after all. And also, in that case, language doesn't follow the system of logic that, in accordance with wise counsel and strict rules, I try to follow, not that I succeed.

The pontoon bridge, I knew what a pontoon was, I knew what a bridge was, a compound was being constructed in front of my very eyes, it started at the beginning of Sziget Street, from the quay in Pest that had survived in relatively unscathed condition, it swayed gently, it trembled under the weight of people's feet; we reached the other side in front of the collapsed dome of the Lukács Baths, on the quay over in Buda marred with blasts and shell craters. For a long time, for a very long time, until the late fifties, traffic did not start on this quay, there was no traffic on the upper quay and there was no traffic on the lower quay. When they carted away the debris in the early sixties, I stood agape at the sight of the completely intact road of the lower quay under the bridge laid with square basalt blocks. Something that was left to us from the time before the siege, and every one of its basalt squares, cut and polished by human hands, gleamed. I even took a picture. But at the time the heavy broad-stones that had tumbled from the collapsed supporting walls were still lying around in heaps. When we reached Buda over the pontoon bridge, we had to climb up over this rubble. The people holding on to the sharp edges of the broken blocks left diverging paths. I couldn't see out of the desert of barren stone. The stench of urine and feces wafted up from below. Later, bushes sprouted from the many fissures in the rocks, and after several years, a veritable little forest. The sight of gentlewomen in turbans and city furs, their clothes pulled up and their heavy underpants wrapped just under the knee, their white backsides briefly showing among the ruins, was by no means unusual, or the urban gentlemen in furs passing water behind the shelter of a tree. It was not proper to stare. I was a well-meaning child, on the borderline of being overly credulous, and I willingly observed the rules of etiquette. If I mustn't, then I wouldn't. I was naturally curious to catch a glimpse of the various body parts of these strangers, but I did not stare. The effort of not staring made my neck ache. You need to know that city furs are made of wool on the outside, a dark gray or a lighter brown, and they're fur on the inside, and generally, a wide fur collar falls over the shoulder. In the months and years following the siege, everyone was on the go, everyone walked, pushed, hauled, pulled, or carried something on their shoulders, carried something on their back or in their suitcases and bags packed to the bursting point. In the city reduced to rubble, the people were headed somewhere for long hours at a stretch, half a day, they passed urine or feces everywhere, and for a long time, for years, in fact, it was a great burden to me that my nose was incapable of not sensing the stench. I couldn't turn it off. If I held my nose, I was told not to be a sissy. If there was a stink then there was a stink, my squeamishness was no reason to hurt other people's feelings.

On the bright side, we could pound on the boards with our feet. When the pontoon bridge was up, I could pound on the boards to my heart's content, except I couldn't let go of my parents' hands. The pontoon was just like a barrel. In the amazing underground labyrinth of my Uncle Pista's chemical plant, there were lots of barrels. There were also chemicals that stank to high heaven, but I didn't have a problem with that. There were empty barrels, too, and barrels filled with chemicals or finished products. You must roll barrels on their hoops, and then they make a booming sound. My Uncle Pista also had me memorize what oxygen was called before the Hungarian language reform, and what hydrogen was called, and what sulfur was called. Sulfur, for instance, was called brimstone. Which made us laugh. When he laughed, he neighed like a horse. It didn't even bother me when he showed me what brimstone smelled like; he lit a strip of paper soaked in sulfur, which he used for sulfuring wine barrels. And I should note the color of the flame. It had a stench that made you back off. Except in the stinking city there was nowhere to back off to. We're rolling along, we're rolling along, pounding on the pontoon, boom, boom, boom. Nothing could have been more natural, everything was fine, just as it was. The stench was the great exception; though I reproached my nose, or I don't know what, I couldn't manage to accept it for what it was. Possibly, the stench of urine and feces challenged my instinct for survival; my instinct for survival was challenged by it on every street corner. They held my hand tight on the pontoon bridge lest I should tear away, because I bristled, promptly and vehemently, against the slightest constraint. If I understand that I mustn't be running around helter-skelter, why are they holding it so tight. They understood that I understood, but after a while, they held on to it just the same. Though I understood their lack of trust, it offended me. For a long time, the bridge lacked a railing. Under the feet of so many people, its shaking and trembling was terrifying; the bridge, so to speak, had to find its tectonic coefficient in the measured pounding of all those feet. Besides, I wouldn't have let go of their hand anyway, because despite all my pounding on the boards and all my frenzied yearning for freedom, the pounding scared me, not the pounding of all those feet, but my own. After all, I was adding my own lesser sound to—let's face it—the terrifying rhythmic pounding of all the other feet. I was terrified, there's no better word for it, but I had to keep my terror, too, under strict control.

We could see the rushing water between the gaps in the boards. But I couldn't scream to my heart's delight from fear, or scream about my fear. For all practical purposes, complaining was not to be tolerated. At every wider gap between the boards I wanted to stop, I wanted to fall on my belly to see what frightened me so, what was so terrifying, what was the thing that I should come to terms with despite my fear. The water's mass, the water's force, the nearness of the mass of water was what terrified me. If I remember well, and why shouldn't I remember well when the mind stores and retains every tiny fragment of our sensations, only twice did they allow me to lie on my belly on the boards warm from the sun's rays, so I could look down through the gap. Yes, twice. The mighty force of the river was miraculous twice. But then we had to go, because we were always headed somewhere with something or for something, or because of someone. In literature, the Polish poet Miron Białoszewski knows the most about this wartime constraint to be perpetually on the go from here to there or from there to here, he knows it from the time of the Warsaw Ghetto Uprising. We were pushing something in my deep old stroller, my sports car. Sometimes they put me in it, too. I knew it was best if I didn't whine, wanting them to put me on top of the stuff and push me. If they felt that the child had had quite enough of all the walking, or they wanted to go faster, they'd do it anyway, but in that case I had to put up with being bounced about atop all that sharp and heavy stuff. But if I asked, if I whined that they should pick me up, they should put me on top, I could be sure they wouldn't do it. On the other hand, if I asked them to take me out, because I'd rather walk, they did as I asked. I pounded on the boards to show them how brave I was, how worthy of their love, but the intriguing closeness of the yellowish gray current rushing at us and surging heavily past wasn't the only thing that terrified me. The days were getting longer, we would venture farther afield, but still, we had to be back before dark, no matter where we'd been. The general dread was hanging in the air. What if we don't make it back in time. This, too, frightened me. I was afraid I was making too much noise; I was afraid of this throughout a lifetime. Someone at the bottom of the cold river wouldn't approve, and in those days there were lots of people tarrying under the water. I must walk more gingerly, without making a scene, I knew that. But my fear couldn't keep me from pounding with my feet. Let them see how brave I am.

The people of Pest called the pontoon bridge Manci, the diminutive name of its older sister, Margaret, which blew up, or was blown up on purpose, during the noon rush hour on November 4. It is still impossible to know for sure what happened on November 4. The remnants of the bridge on the Buda side were blown up later, when Margaret Island surrendered on January 29. But the annihilation of the Pest side of the bridge in November haunted people for years, and became a subject of hearsay. Somebody had to do it. The Germans. The Arrow Cross. Illegal Communists. You don't mean that. Sabotage. Jewish resistance. You can't be serious. The Zionists. Honest. Come off it. You're talking rubbish. The Zionists, in the plural. I remember that after the siege it was in this connection that I first heard the word *Zionists*, always like this, in the plural. I didn't know what to make of the word. Apparently, Zionists came in groups. Except I couldn't imagine who these Zionists, whose name people pronounced as Cionists, could be. It sounded perilously akin to cyanide. In the days and months following the siege, people used it to fumigate their homes. I heard that we'd have to have our home cyanided, too. Zionided. But from what I could gather from the talk about them, the Zionists had nothing to do with cyaniding homes. Still, I decided that they must have had something to do with it. Cyanide was a gaseous substance, the gasman carried it in a big metal box, and the Zionists were also being carried someplace, people wanted to gas them, while those that remained, that was the word for it, *remained*, were heading in large groups to a far-off place called Palestine. Something or someone protested inside me. My feel for language protested that I mustn't let *Zionist* come into too close a contact with *cyanide*, because in that case I would never understand these words, nor the connection between them, nor the distance between them, not to mention Palestine, despite the fact that to this day I'd be hard put to say what a feel for language or a sense for language might entail. Until you find a secure place for something in your conscious mind, you are forced to create subsidiary connections between the various areas of consciousness, you make a connection between the morphology and possible meaning of the word in question and open a temporary storage space for it.

At the time I couldn't have known either that Ernő, the republican younger brother of my great-grandfather Mezei and a respected journalist, was carrying on a correspondence with Theodor Herzl, the father of the Zionists, and was at loggerheads with him. On March 10, 1903, Herzl wrote to him that he'd gladly give up on the Hungarian Jews if only he could be sure that their patriotism would spare them anti-Semitic misery. He wrote his letter in Vienna and addressed it to Budapest, which at the time was still bilingual, specifically, to Nagykorona Street, where Ernő, a notorious bachelor, lived in the apartment of my great-grandfather, who was fifteen years his senior, until he got married, that is. *Auf die ungarischen Juden möchte ich sogar verzichten, wenn ich wüsste, dass ihnen das antisemitische Elend durch ihre Patriotizmus erspart bleibt.* And that he's not a speculator in misery, Herzl wrote. *Ich mache keine Elendspekulation.* But anti-Semitism will strike Hungarian Jews brutally as well, *es wird auch über die ungarischen Juden kommen*, and the later, the harder, *umso härter je später*, and the more brutally, the more powerful they will be by then, *umso wilder je mächtiger sie bis dahin warden.* There is no salvation. *Davor gibt es keine Rettung.* And Theodor Herzl was right. He didn't even need to be a prophet. The political alliance of the Jewish *haute bourgeoisie* and the aristocracy stood on perilously weak footing, I now say. In fact, four decades on, with the exception of the wealthiest Jews, barely anyone escaped. When the time comes, you can take your patriotism and celebrate Shabbat with that, Herzl wrote in his justified anger to Ernő Mezei, the adamant champion of independence and, seen in retrospect, a man of touching patriotism. But when I tried to translate this sentence, I was baffled, because like this, you can take your patriotism and make Shabbat with that, it means nothing in Hungarian. *Dann können Sie mit Ihrem Patriotizmus Schabbes machen.* It was clear that the sentence did not mean what it meant literally, in short, that it bears with idiomatic meaning, Yiddish jargon, surely, but for my great-grandfather's younger brother and his patriotic cast of mind, its meaning must have been devastating, profoundly disdainful. And now as I am engaged in my research, I see that a footnote in Géza Komoróczy's monumental compilation *Sources and Documents* appended to *The History of the Jews in Hungary* also cites the sentence in word-for-word translation. But regardless of which dictionary or lexicon I consulted for the secondary meanings of Shabbat, Shabbat was Shabbat everywhere, I didn't find the solution, Shabbat remained an untranslatable reference. Months passed. Possibly a whole year. Meanwhile we, Theodor Herzl continued his own Zionist say in his letter addressed to Ernő Mezei, we, whom you make fun of, remain active, because we are building a domestic house even for the benefit of those, he writes in his anger, who will have nothing to do with us. Not yet.

From this agitated exchange of views it seemed to me that Palestine is less than a country, but for them, meaning these Zionists who are always in the plural, it's something left over from ancient times that they must get their hands on.

When Herzl wrote his letter explaining why he was forced to give up on the Hungarian Jewish patriots, why instead of the law-abiding views of liberalism he had chosen the blood-tie views of Jewish nationalism to confront the blood-tie views of European anti-Semitism, he may not have been familiar with the parliamentary speeches delivered by my great-grandfather's younger brother regarding a variety of subjects. But even if Herzl knew nothing about this, he was surely familiar with the interpolation that Mezei had made fifteen years earlier, on November 15, 1882, addressed to Tivadar Pauler, minister of the interior, in the matter of the investigation into the charge of ritual murder of a Christian girl supposedly committed by the Jews of Tiszaeszlár. Because of its subject, if nothing else, the effect this interpolation had has survived in the public consciousness.

Needless to say, the Mezei brothers' onetime position is still of concern to me. Their position with respect to Jewish nationalism and the various forms of European anti-Semitism, along with the hallowed naïveté of Hungarian Jewish patriotism, is part and parcel of what we might call the intangible mass of my family heritage. For a long time, a very long time, perhaps half a century had come and gone in my life, and I still did not realize that with my Hungarian patriotism I was whistling in the wind. Those intent on a brighter future shoot their dick into an empty sky, the poet Petri writes. A tradition that for the most part has vanished. No one understands it, or hardly anyone. It fails me every time, but I can't admit to the failure. And if with my Hungarian patriotism I've slipped off the wall yet again, it just prompts me to try again, to find detours and attempt hair-raising and hopeless stunts. My life would have taken a much easier course had I managed to back up into one of the populous families of Hungarian or Jewish nationalists. Because of the firmly anchored mass of my mental inheritance, I find both repugnant. This is the only question in which Ernő Mezei of the left-wing Independence Party saw eye to eye with his brother, my great-grandfather Mór Mezei, who was fifteen years his senior, and who was more highly regarded than he, and many times wealthier, too, and who sat on the opposite side in Parliament, on the right side, in the benches of the freethinkers and rigorous liberals, meaning with the staunchly uncompromising government party. I couldn't have been more than four when these two men had already made a great impression on me, one with his serious speech defect and frenzied love of freedom, the other with his calm and unerring feel for power. People quoted them and told one another anecdotes about them. They followed their customs, manners, and precepts. For example, that at the table a well-bred person does not engage in political arguments, or what is even worse, family arguments; at the table, one must talk only about neutral topics. Such arguments are conducted before a meal or after a meal, and preferably in the smoking room and not the salon. I realized very early on that they couldn't keep to these rules themselves. Once Ernő managed to sneak in a delicate issue, and though those sitting around the table held out for some time without reacting and just gazed furtively at their father and grandfather, meaning my great-grandfather Mór Mezei, who was a master at pretending that he hadn't heard anything, Ernő would try his hand until someone at the table reacted after all, and then all hell broke loose; this rarely happened, but it happened then, it came to pass that to the consternation of my aged great-great-grandfather and my great-great-grandmother, the brothers raised their voices as they spoke, they yelled at each other at the table, called each other names, and Ernő, because of his speech impediment, even pounded the table with his fist.

They didn't know, how could they have known, that the tradition of Hungarian-Jewish patriotism was viable only when the country was fighting for its independence, and under conditions of a freethinking and mature liberal democracy. As freethinkers and champions of independence, how could they have suspected that the days of equality were drawing to a close, and in what manner they were drawing to a close. Later on, I at least should have learned the lessons to be gleaned from the abject failure of the Jewish patriotic tradition in Hungary. But I did no such thing. First, I would have had to discover in which layer of my conscious mind it was stored. The structure of the intellectual faculty with which I make sense of the world simply does not function without it. The truth is that even though I am fully aware of it, I cannot accept that my need for equality and my Hungarian patriotism might be the two most blatant mistakes of my life. As they saw it, European history could no longer ignore the basic principles of liberalism. They were wrong. As for me, I had nowhere to advance and nowhere to retreat with the tradition of liberal values I'd inherited, nor with my Hungarian Jewish patriotism. On the other hand, were I to excise these two building blocks from my conscious mind, the entire structure would collapse. Without the mistakes they represent, I would be an intellectual nonentity.

For a long time, for a very long time, I did not even realize that the notions of equality and patriotism are my great-grandfather's ingrained intellectual legacy to the family and to me, and have remained so despite the fact that they were of precious little use to us in either of the two autocratic regimes that followed in quick succession. It was dead knowledge.

Throughout a lifetime, I have nourished an inherited Hungarian patriotism that exists only in my own mind and in the mind of my homeland in a very limited way, provided that a homeland has a mind at all.

But what Shabbat could have meant in this derogatory sentence from the pen of the father of Zionism, one that dismissed out of hand and on the basis of blood my inherited patriotism, piqued my curiosity. When I drew a blank with my search, I turned to my dear colleague András Forgách, in an e-mail. He is an exceptionally obliging person, kind and courteous. There is no period or linguistic style he is not familiar with or can't imitate at the drop of a hat. He is an exceptional stylist. He can read and speak in almost any language; he knows Hebrew, and surely Yiddish, too; his gift for empathy is impressive, and he is a born mimic. Yet his mimetic kindness is not infinite. When it reaches its end, it suddenly becomes clear that he's been hiding his infinite stubbornness, obstinacy, pigheadedness, and the fact he's a law unto himself behind that boyish and charming smile of his. He does it merely to oblige. At times he asks me very nicely, merely to oblige, if I would give him advice about one thing or another. I don't give him advice, since I'm at a loss myself, but I am glad to share my experiences with him. In one ear, out the other. Stubborn as a mule. There's no stopping him. But this time, he answered me promptly. In a nutshell, and basically word for word. I can translate Herzl's sentence for you, he wrote, as follows: Shove your patriotism up your you know what. Quite by coincidence, I am just reading about Theodor Herzl and Max Nordau, he continued, for the money, I'm fixing up a short series of scenes, the play is about their meeting. They were both highly successful writers, he explained. In both, clear-sightedness is combined with perverted fin-de-siècle decadence, journalistic superficiality with prophetic foresight. The Dreyfus affair gave both of them food for thought. Both of them lied right and left, yet they were right. They were both Hungarian, but achieved world fame as Germans. It's a fascinating story. Up till now I made a point of giving them a wide berth, except, of course, when I was recently strolling along Nordau Boulevard in Tel Aviv, Forgách wrote, relating his story for me in the e-mail, because in my family Zionism was an object of scorn. I grew up in an anti-Zionist tradition. No wonder that it was an object of scorn, I thought as I read the letter, no wonder you grew up in an anti-Zionist tradition yourself, seeing how your parents were old Communists, just like mine. And the old Communists did lots of stupid things, but at least their universalism rejected nationalism out of hand. By the way, in your translation I think you should feel free to use love of country instead of patriotism, Forgách advised, in the interest of informality, he added by way of an aside. In which case, the sentence might be more accurate and more tactful as follows: Go make Shabbat with your love of country. Though I can't resist repeating: Go Shabbat your patriotism, he insisted. But all right, another option is: Spend Shabbat with your patriotism, and not with me. If we look at the original Herzl sentence, I think that *damit, davon, daraus* are in fact interchangeable, as it turns out from Hans Peter Althaus's excellent Yiddish dictionary, see the entry full of juicy, modern examples on the attached page. The title of the book is *Chuzpe, Schmus & Tacheles: Jiddische Wortgeschichten*, and he attached the relevant entry. Wanting to decide for myself, but more to the point, so I could solve the task of translation, I immediately ordered the book on the Internet.

Die Redewendung mach Schabbes davon *bedeutete um 1860, "lass es dir die Kosten einbringen, welche ein Sabbat erfordert";* around 1860 the saying meant that in that case, pay the cost of the Shabbat. *Nach Tendlau wurde sie gesagt,* according to Tendlau they said it *wenn das in Rede Stehende vollkommen uninteressant war,* if what the person had to say was of no interest. In which case, Herzl's opinion of Ernő Mezei couldn't have been too flattering. A nothing, a *niemand,* a nobody, his opinion is neither here nor there, my Tauber grandmother, born Cecília Nussbaum of Hasidic roots, would say of such a person. *Wein-*

berg hat die Wendung daher als Ausruf der Geringschätzung bezeich-net, and so Weinberg considers the saying a sign of derision, *der "nun wenn schon! Was kann ich damit anfangen" bedeutete*, so what, what am I supposed to make of that, it meant something like that. *Das Ver-ständnis einer derartigen Wendung erschließt sich oftmals richtig erst im Kontext.* The meaning of such expressions is provided by the context. Thanks to Forgách's explanations and Althaus's examples, my doubts about what Herzl had written to my great-grand-uncle vanished.

Stick your patriotism behind your ear.

Something I could have said to myself as well throughout a life-time of years.

Except I had even less to do with the Shabbat then Ernő Mezei. For me, there was nowhere to retreat from freethinking. Nowhere to retreat to this day.

Mezei delivered the address in which he pointed out the prepos-terous irregularities of the Tiszaeszlár blood libel investigation in the House of Deputies in mid-October 1882, and on this occasion he also addressed an interpolation to the Minister of the Interior, wrote Mór Szatmári, Ernő Mezei's former colleague in the House; this was half a century later, when he recalled his own career as a representa-tive in his book, *Twenty Stormy Years in Parliament.*

Except he was mistaken about the date; Mezei delivered his in-terpolation on November 15, 1882, and he addressed it not to the Minister of the Interior but to his former professor the internationally renowned expert on criminal law, just then minister of justice.

It was a beautiful speech. Mezei put his heart and soul into it. I was present at the session, Szatmári wrote.

The liberal-oriented party suffered it in dead silence, while on the extreme left, the anti-Semites made themselves heard. Mezei's speech was not met by any other demonstrations of sentiment, neither from the right nor from the left.

In Szatmári's memoirs this isn't quite correct either. Still, Me-zei's predicament as he delivered his address reminds me of my own. The ghost of the family's midway position hovers over it. More often than not, I, too, feel as if I've committed some colossal impropriety.

However, in this case, not only was Ernő Mezei's opinion at odds with everyone else's, a cause of embarrassment, but so was his serious speech defect, the nationwide tension, and the international uproar pursuant on the Tiszaeszlár blood libel. There were riots in these weeks, in Pest as well as the countryside; the rabble took to the streets, setting things on fire, looting, destroying everything in its wake, beating up Jews, crying out for Jewish blood. Prime Minister Kálmán Tisza, who offered the summary opinion that there was no Jewish question, he knows of no such thing, was so insistent on his fundamental liberal principles, the principle of equality, the principle of the rule of law, the principle of the separation of powers, principles that he considered unequivocally universal that in fact, he was somewhat tardy in taking action. Liberal thinking is founded on truthfulness and trust, which also happens to be its first serious boomerang. Thanks to his liberal, trusting nature, Tisza realized too late that the police and the gendarmerie were helpless against the rabble not because they were poorly organized, but because they felt an affinity for and were fraternizing with this same rabble. The liberal Hungarian state has no laws for Christians, it has no laws for Jews, it has only broad-minded liberal laws; there is equality before the law, there is freedom of conscience, and no one may violate the law with appeal to religious affiliation, Tisza had commented earlier in response to interpellations by certain anti-Semitic deputies. But as things stood, and with the powers invested in him, he was now forced to declare a state of emergency and martial law in a number of towns and counties while, in the same breath, he spoke about the Usury Act then before the House, the law about compulsory civil marriage and the industrial law, also under consideration, the purpose of each and every one of them being, he shouted over the objections of the deputies, to ensure, in both the economic and social spheres, that such violent acts should never again take place. At which point Gyula Verhovay, who would soon leave the Independence Party to become co-founder of the National Anti-Semite Party, interrupted by shouting that the highly esteemed prime minister can say whatever he likes, all of this is sure as hell the Jewish question.

Which got the prime minister fuming mad.

While I am speaking, the highly esteemed deputies are having their little fun by shouting that this is a Jewish question, and that that is a Jewish question, he retorted. But the uproar in the House prevented him from continuing. We hear you, we hear you! Desist! Meaning, desist and stop talking.

So it would seem, gentlemen, shouted the prime minister over the roar, that there is no passing a law in Hungary at this point in time that would apply equally to Christians and Jews.

Yes, that's right, the deputies shouted from the right, while on the far left there was general restlessness and cacophony.

Except, this country has both Christian and Jewish residents, the prime minister went on; consequently, there is no matter that is not equally a Christian question and a Jewish question.

Unrest in Pozsony, Nyíregyháza, Pest, martial law and a state of emergency in Nyitra and Szabolcs counties, screaming and shouting, utter chaos in the National Assembly building in Sándor Street which the Speaker's bell was helpless against.

And then, as the morning session drew to a close and the deputies were worn out, there appeared a small, fragile man with a pronounced speech defect who couldn't be called well-favored by any stretch of the imagination. According to the records of the House sessions, the deputies, who had repeatedly engaged in disputation with Ernő Mezei, now offered the comment that although they have paid close attention, they can't be sure that they heard their honored colleague's words correctly, and regardless of their earlier indulgence toward him, now that he stood up to speak, they began shouting, of which the court notary recorded only the let's hear! let's hear! Which, as the family tells it, did not mean that they were eager to hear him speak, but that he should speak more clearly. And also, that the last thing they needed just then was a man with a speech defect.

Honored House, began Mezei, who despite his speech defect was not a timid man, just pronouncedly reserved, I must admit that when the first bits of information surfaced about the Tiszaeszlár affair, even I wondered whether there might not be secret traditions in the circle of Jewish worshippers of which I am ignorant, and which I couldn't have even imagined. However, this line of reasoning sidetracked me only for a moment, he went on. Though he personally did not receive Orthodox religious education, nor did he gain especial proficiency in it from religious texts, he nevertheless had a sufficient number of Orthodox acquaintances to inform him on such matters. If a man hopes to see clearly but cannot rely on his own knowledge, he can always take advantage of the knowledge of others. And he personally must see clearly, because he has received more than his share of letters from Orthodox circles laden with the most strident personal invectives, or as we would say today, sharp attacks and enraged outbursts, asking why he does nothing to shield them against such unworthy and absurd accusations.

I will further admit, highly esteemed House, he went on, that had this been the first time that the accusation of ritual bloodletting has been made, I might not have thought it so absurd, I might have conjectured that some crazed Jewish rabbi might conceivably have believed that he is doing a service pleasing to God when he sacrifices a Christian girl. Except this is the same accusation, esteemed House, that has been brought against the Jews throughout the centuries and which, like an old wives' tale, has survived as part of popular lore, but which, when it was brought before a bona fide court of law, has proven to be unfounded, each and every time. The accusation is patently absurd. It stands in opposition to the religious laws of the Jews. The teachings of the Talmud can be excessive, they can be foolish, but there cannot be among them things that stand in opposition to the Law itself. Well, let me say that it is the abhorrence of blood and dead bodies that gives the Jewish religion its special character. It is this abhorrence that marks, for a Jew, the dividing line between the pure and the impure. It is every Jew's bounden duty to look upon murder and blood as an abomination. The present affair, however, is already before the court, and so public decency demands that no person prejudice the court's judgment or proceedings. As for the present speaker, it would be unnecessary for him to do so in any case, for he entertains no doubt that the Jews of Hungary have always had full trust in the administration of justice. Except, let us be clear about what I call trust, he shouted as best he could, considering his speech defect. By trust I do not mean that passion or the spirit of prejudice might not possibly rule over the lesser forums of law. Possibly, there are those in this House who look upon Hungarian justice and the judiciary as being without fault.

But even if they were without fault, it would be ill-advised to entertain such an opinion about them. For there are few things in heaven and earth that are unblemished. Judges can make mistakes, and the system of supervision is there to identify them, and the function of the higher courts is to rectify them. What I call trust is the circumstance that the Hungarian court system contains all the indispensable guarantees for juridical conscience, the superior courts have at their disposal all the guarantees of strict revision, and the administration of justice guarantees the freedom of the defense. However, there are those who would put a different interpretation on the independence of the courts. We are all familiar with how the investigation into the Tiszaeszlár blood libel began. In spite of the law, in such a grave case the Nyíregyháza court appointed not a bona fide judge, but a junior notary of the court, whose imagination was absorbed with the thought that the celebrated affair he was sent to investigate would direct the attention of the entire world upon his person. If he could now uncover a centuries' old secret, then all the acclaim of a future age and all the appreciation of the present would be his. As soon as the anti-Semites realized this, they considered the principle of judicial independence contingent upon guaranteeing that the examining magistrate Mr. Bary's person remain sacrosanct and untouchable by the very controls that the Hungarian legal system itself had created. Never before has the verdict of the court been so prejudiced, never before has it proceeded so aggressively, never before has it allowed such incompetent people to influence the course of events. It wasn't even Examining Magistrate Bary who brought the verdict, it was the newspapers that held a court martial over the accused. They launched a fatal shakedown against all those who might have exercised legal influence over the proceedings. To start with, they attacked the counsel for the defense. I, who am personally acquainted with the initially delegated defense counsel, can safely say that I was aghast when I heard the accusations that had been brought against him. I have first-hand knowledge of the severe personal vexations to his person. In Nyíregyháza, the delegated defense attorney could no longer appear in the circles he used to frequent. He was forced to relinquish his post as defense attorney and was, furthermore, charged with finding nationally recognized defense attorneys to replace him, with sufficient prestige to ensure that the court of Nyíregyháza and, indeed, the people of Nyíregyháza should respect them. But the influence of the anti-Semites did not end here. They lost no time in clamping down on the new counsel for the defense, heaping opprobrium and dirt upon them. Gentlemen, this is what became of the right to defense, a right that every civilized nation willingly honors. Here, however, the defense was treated as if he were part of some secret conspiracy, as if it had tried to derail a just sentence through unlawful, deceitful, and underhanded means. I have never before heard such an opinion about the defense. Presenting the defense counsel as a corrupt individual, calling him a double-tongued crony, insisting that he is part of a conspiracy, nowhere else would anyone have thought of doing any such thing. Civilized nations hold the freedom of defense in high regard, if for no other reason than because infringements that might adversely prejudice the interests of the administration of justice are not likely to originate with the defense.

But in this circus, after the defense, it was the turn of the prosecution. We have heard accusations in this House to the effect that the public prosecutor not only intends to get rid of the evidence of the crime, and not only is he attempting to clear the criminals of the accusation against them, but is in fact attempting to put incorruptible judges in jail with false witnesses on trumped-up charges. Gentlemen, this is the path to absurdity with absurdity heaped atop absurdity. The absurdity starts with the Jewish *shohetim*, who are supposed to kill people for Passover, it continues with absurd accusations against those who defend them in court, and ends with even more absurd accusations against the prosecution. In Nyíregyháza the rabble threaten to kill the royal attorney, who is afraid to leave his room, and when at last he leaves the town under the greatest secrecy, he is attacked on the street. What is this, greatly honored colleagues, my lawyer ancestor with the speech impediment asks, if not the unrestrained outpouring of irrational rage. What is this if not a blatant attempt to wipe out lawful guarantees, an attempt to ensure not only that the agitators writing for the papers should lord it over the administration of justice, but that the rabble should do so as well. We have seen the rabble triumph over the government of a nation, but that the rabble should direct the course of justice, that it should practice overseeing rights over private lawsuits, I am not aware of this ever occurring before now.

My esteemed colleagues, I ask you: what can be accomplished by resorting to absurdity. Murder by law can be achieved. The heightening of agitation can be achieved. But by no means justice. If you think that no other religious group has yet suffered murder by law, you are mistaken. You need not look far afield. Barely twenty years before the French revolution, Protestants were sentenced because of their alleged religious murders. No lesser man than Voltaire took the persecuted under his protection. It was with respect to this that he wrote his famous sentence, *J'ai fait un peu de bien, c'est mon meilleur ouvrage.* I have done a bit of good, it is the best of my accomplishments.

I wonder if you are familiar with the case of Jean Calas, Pierre-Paul Sirven, or Montbailli, to mention just three. In all three cases, the courts brought a sentence of death, because they set out from the belief that Protestants are bound by religious law to kill those who wish to convert to Catholicism. In some Protestant families, no one could die suddenly without stirring up popular suspicion. Voltaire called upon all of Europe for help. He turned to the sovereigns of Europe, and refused to smile again until he procured the revision of the relevant laws. Led by philosophers, public opinion in the eighteenth century regarded work in the interest of others as philanthropy, noble thinking, and wisdom, while by the late nineteenth century, public opinion, which came under the influence of demagogue instigators, has come to regard it as the concealment of sin, it has called it complicity, and it has called it corruption.

Honored House, I am fully aware that there are those who do not repeat the accusations of the Middle Ages out of bias. Even among my friends there are some who, precisely because they are enlightened and condemn religious fanaticism, are fully prepared to believe anything about religious fervor.

At the time, this is surely liberalism's second most serious boomerang, exorcising Satan with Beelzebub, curing the missionary zeal and fatal demagoguery of the various religions with atheist demagoguery.

This passage of Mezei's speech went against his own comrades, those who championed independence, among whom there were not only such adamant anti-Semites in the benches as Verhovay and Géza Ónody, but also one of his closest political friends and allies, Lajos Mocsáry, the leader of the Independents, whose raw anticlericalism and enlightened views prevented him from taking a clear stand. He regarded the religious fanaticism of the Hasidic Jews emigrating from Galicia with profound aversion, not to say repugnance. He was not alone in this. The contemporary press called them riffraff. They killed the young peasant girl Eszter Solymosi, no doubt about that, so their *shohetim* could collect her blood and bake it into their matzo for Pessah. Even the truly tolerant Kálmán Mikszáth evidenced obvious disgust toward them when he reported on the court hearings for the papers, while in his memoirs, the examining magistrate József Bary talked about the filth in their homes as well as in their ritual bath, the *mikveh*, the likes of which he'd never seen before.

At the time, party discipline as practiced later on, when the deputies were more than willing to go against their own conscience in the interest of their party, was nonexistent. On the other hand, there existed a significant requirement among people of culture, namely, the coherence of personal opinion, or at least a striving to achieve such coherence, a requirement that went hand in hand with the striving and wish for the reconciliation of coherent opinions. This is one reason why it took such a long time, years, in fact, for the independents to force the anti-Semites from their ranks. In Mocsáry's eyes, the unconditional freedom of the right to your own opinion may have seemed more important than the principle of equality, and this is how liberalism's third and most serious boomerang struck back. Fixated on freedom and fueled by instinctual self-interest, liberalism is incapable and unwilling to acknowledge that the mutuality of brotherhood and equality is a prerequisite for political freedom. Lajos Kossuth had to send harsh words from his emigration in Turin, Dániel Irányi, the respected head of the Independence Party, had to interpolate in no uncertain terms at the Sándor Street assembly building before the independents came to their senses and ousted their own anti-Semites from their midst, so that hand in hand with the anti-Semitic deputies who were ousted from among the freethinkers, a year later they should oganize their own National Anti-Semite Party with Győző Istóczy at the helm.

Honored House, continued Mezei, I allow that, indeed, profound darkness reigns in the heads of the Jews of Tiszaeszlár. I allow that they are not sympathetic. I allow that they are far removed from the customs and morals of our century.

The fact that with this gesture he drew a line between himself and them was not merely due to the accepted *bon ton* of the era, it was also something with which a thinking man had to contend. Even the most influential anti-Semites of the times, Istóczy, Ónody, and Gyula Verhovay, did not equate domestic Jews with the Hasidic groups pouring in from beyond the eastern frontiers of the Monarchy, groups that were at odds even among themselves.

Have the rule of law, truth, impartiality, and justice ceased to be the norm in this land, he asked. Are the noble principles that have hallmarked Hungarian public life a thing of the past. Does incitement of the masses and hatred enjoy exclusive entitlement. When I hear the statements that Speaker Pál Somssich has made in this House today, when I read the statements that Kossuth is making today, when I reflect that they constitute two poles of political life, I am beset by the sad doubt that the democratic transformation that the previous generation has effected has ended up liberating raw instincts and brutal passions, giving them right of way.

He respects the independence of the judges, he continues, that goes without saying, and he wouldn't want the minister of justice to interfere in investigative procedures, but things are happening that do not fall within the jurisdiction of the courts and which the minister of justice should not have countenanced. In the face of the agitation that has brought aggressive passions to the fore and which, furthermore, is attempting to weaken lawful guarantees, there would have been urgent need for the voice of reason to ensure that in Hungary the administration of justice remain a sturdy dividing wall that passions cannot breach. The minister should have let one and all know that the guardians of justice are securely in place, in short, that Hungary has a minister of justice.

The fact is that the court of Nyíregyháza is responsible for multiple outrageous breaches of the law. The first was the violation of procedural law, which prescribes that in serious matters a judge must be delegated every time. When in a matter whose social and political significance calls for the utmost vigilance they appoint an immature young junior notary, one suspects, as I have suspected and experienced firsthand on my visit to Nyíregyháza, namely, that from the start the president of the Royal Court regarded the entire matter as a ridiculous figment of the imagination, one undeserving of serious attention. But once the motives involved became clear, the minister of justice should have felt it incumbent upon himself to ensure that the investigation be conducted by experienced professionals.

But the court of Nyíregyháza has committed the following breach of law as well. At the start of the investigation, the examining magistrate handed a thirteen-year-old boy, who had never been accused of complicity, into the custody of the notary. The notary managed to squeeze some evidence out of him, whereupon the court kept the boy in custody as a witness for months. Should not the minister of justice stand guard over the credibility of the law, he asked.

As for the third, he went on, the minister of justice should have prevented the agitation of the press from influencing court proceedings. Needless to say, he is fully aware that he cannot demand anything of the minister of justice for which there are no lawful guarantees. It is not the office of the minister of justice to decide whether the examining magistrate is prejudiced or not. Nor can he prevent the examining magistrate from being on friendly terms with the newspapers. But surely he should not have allowed the examining magistrate to place himself at the service of agitation and publish secret information in the newspapers pertaining to the investigation. If in this House there is an interdiction against the galleries demonstrating their approval or disapproval of the speakers lest they influence the speakers' feelings, what are we to make of a magistrate who is courting the approval of the press, and who is hoping to receive said approval from the very same people who are using this approval, too, to fire up wild, unrestrained passions against an appreciable segment of the population. The minister of justice is surely conversant with the ongoing polemic between the deputy prosecutor and the examining magistrate. And from this it does not seem to me that the prosecutor is of a different opinion than the magistrate, though the jealousy stands out clear as day, namely, that like Themistocles, he is setting his sights on Miltiades's laurels.

Fourth, I must make mention of Examining Magistrate József Bary's proceedings. The weekly paper *Egyenlőség* published information that one can read only with the utmost indignation. I do not wish to present anyone here as a monster. I do not believe in born monsters, whether the individual in question is the *shochet* of Eszlár or the examining magistrate of Nyíregyháza. Still, from what has been published, I see what can become of an otherwise decent individual when whipped-up passions place him at the mercy of his own ambition without lawful control. Having been published in the papers, such scandalous information can no longer be swept under the carpet. It must be proven true or else the papers must be sued for libel. Let it suffice for me to point out a couple of things. The examining magistrate subjected Mr. Vogel, one of the rafters of Máramaros, to the most excruciating torture. On his orders, they tied the rafters together and poured water into them.

I am ashamed to copy here what the court clerk reported, but he wrote down that on this November day, the deputies in Sándor Street considered this information a source of general amusement. Perhaps they were laughing at the words the speaker used. I am familiar with several versions of the torture of the Jewish rafters of Máramaros. I found nothing amusing in any of them. They were either held down or tied down, their mouths were pried open, and they poured water into them until they vomited, or until they literally burst, until they wet their pants or defecated, or in fear of this happening, they confessed sins of which they were innocent.

Mezei continues as if he has taken no notice of the amusement in the House. Bary promised fifty forints to a teacher if she kept quiet about what she knew. He promised money to other witnesses if they kept quiet about the torture, and he promised money to still others if they gave evidence against the Jews. The Guardian Spirit of mankind hides his face in shame. It is absolutely necessary that these things come before the court. And if they should prove fallacious, those who have made them public should be punished. On the other hand, if they are true, then the examining magistrate might very well achieve what he craves, the admiration of all of Europe.

What has happened to us, Honored House, he shouted in his peculiar manner caused by his speech impediment. As a child in Újhely, meaning Sátoraljaújhely, he had been stung by a wasp, which brought on an allergic reaction, and the doctor who rushed to the scene had no alternative but to attempt a partial tracheotomy, which in itself would not have been a problem, had the wound not filled with pus, and had the fester not spread to his vocal cords. At the time, there was no effective treatment for wounds infected with pus.

I believe that all sides concur that an open hearing must be held, he continued. The royal attorney himself said in the newspapers that he will ask for an open hearing. With respect to the mood of the public and the general unrest in the nation, he considers it imperative.

And at this point in his speech, Mezei asks his audience whether they should not consider such a statement by the royal attorney of significance in and of itself.

Where will it end, he asks, if in consideration of the reigning trend it is acceptable to plead the principle of *salus rei publicae*, the public good, not only in politics but in the dispensation of justice as well, in the lawsuits of two parties; in short, is it acceptable to plead the principle of *salus rei publicae* and, in spite of the law, to keep certain individuals in custody and subject them to choice indignities in order to pacify public opinion.

I have nothing against the public good. Certain gentlemen need not worry, the Jews are not averse to a public hearing. However, one thing is essential. The public hearing must be conducted by those who will guarantee the objectivity and independence of the court. With regard to this, I would like to ask the highly esteemed Minister of Justice the following: Does the Nyíregyháza court hold out such a guarantee. About the local situation I do not wish to speak in detail, but I do wish to mention that the court of Nyíregyháza has committed so many mistakes to date, it is so thoroughly implicated in the course of the proceedings, that it can no longer be regarded as unbiased. What is more, the Nyíregyháza court cannot lawfully bring judgment. A judge who has participated in the investigation cannot participate in formulating the sentence. The court has not only delegated an examining magistrate, five of its members also participated in authenticating the records and questioning the witnesses, and thus, these five members, according to the law, may not participate in the public hearing.

In short, the court of Nyíregyháza cannot escape the accusation that it was swept along by the current. This current has swept aside the props of the administration of justice, it has suspended the guarantees needed to discover the truth, and it did so without us, the National Assembly, having brought special laws to legitimize its actions.

The truth must come out. The truth must come out not in the interest of the Jews and certainly not in the interest of the *shohetim*, but in the common interest of the rule of law and of mankind. The nineteenth century has been granted the noble task of liberating truth from its religious character. There is no Catholic truth, there is no Protestant truth, there is no Jewish truth, there is but one truth that must be generally honored. I believe that no one understands this better than the Honored House. This is why we have modern state institutions, this is why we have a Parliament and a responsible government, and this is why our responsible government has a minister of justice.

And now I ask the Honored House to allow me to read my interpolation.

After it was over, Speaker Tamás Péchy adjourned the session at 2:10 in the afternoon.

As for the explosion, it took place soon before the Soviet army was to systematically surround Budapest. These were busy days in the life of our family. We had just sneaked back in mid-September with our forged papers, because in Bácska, perhaps at the Biebers', I don't know for sure, but I do know that the soil was getting hot under our feet. The Biebers also thought it best for us to leave, the sooner the better. Then as soon as we got back, my mother had to leave for Szombathely, so that with yet more forged documents she should help my father, who'd been transferred there from Szentkirályszabadja with his forced labor battalion, escape from labor service, something that, needless to say, I found out only after the siege. The siege itself was full of sudden changes in location, events, tidings, but at the same time, it was filled with profound silence and nondisclosure. Hours passed in the basements, long days in the dark, by candlelight, yet we were always short on time. The news that they were transferring the labor company from Szentkirály came from comrades through an illegal Communist channel. Even after the siege they did not say who, just through a channel, which meant the underground movement, which meant comrades. It seems to me that Ani Tóth had brought the news; she was a pleasantly plump young woman, Károly Tóth's wife, who at the time may not have been his wife yet. They worked in the military section of the resistance. This wisp of information, the name of the messenger, her figure, has survived in my mind, because my mother felt gratitude of an unfamiliar nature toward her. Ani must have brought the news in the twenty-fourth hour. My mother's gratitude was silent, circumspect; surely she had to be careful not to let her feelings get the better of her; she preferred to satisfy the ascetic dictates of her emotional life, her heritage from her father.

My mother headed for Szombathely the afternoon of our return from Bácska. The train had to stop repeatedly because of air raids, the passengers had to disembark on the open tracks, hide in ditches or run to the bunkers built outside the fences of railway stations. The pointed mushroomlike structures of the bunkers stood around for decades. As for the plural of *comrade*, comrades, it served to stop people from asking who brought news of what. I could tell that this plural, *comrades*, had a different function from the plural *Zionists*. Some words were so tightly bound to the conspiratorial setting that they could not be freed from their confines, then or later. As far as I could tell, and even given that at the time I wasn't clear about certain things, the plural *Zionists* did not square with this conspiratorial character. At most, I could see my parents' reserve in the face of the overwhelming enthusiasm of the Zionists, which is one reason I would have liked to know what we were being reserved about and why we were reserved about it in the first place. Besides, the Zionists were on the outside, far removed from the members of my family, more like in opposition to them; they barely scraped against the outer limits of my family's sphere of interests.

Even today it is not always easy to discover who is behind the code names used in the movement. But I understood the conspiratorial logic of the maneuver of the purposeful uninterpretability very early on. If a man is subject to torture, then in his pain he's willing to confess, thus endangering the lives of others. They called it squealing. If I don't know somebody's real name, I can't squeal on him. It's got to be hidden, so the pig can't squeal. The silence stops the squealing. In the most unexpected place not knowledge but the lack of knowledge bore significance. Get rid of him or her, they've been squealed on. Except I couldn't understand who had been squealed on and who became compromised thereby.

In November, at the time of the blast, my father must have been down in the basement with the others for the past two months. Besides Pug Nose, their senior liaison, only three other people in the city knew about this, my mother, Klára Tauber, my aunt Magda Nádas, and her husband, Pál Aranyossi. A man had looked him up in late

September or early October, a man called Rácz whom he'd known from before, and whose identity I have not been able to ascertain for sure from reading my aunt's memoirs. Meanwhile, my mother, on one of these September days, September 10, to be exact, helped my father escape from Szombathely, I don't know how; his code name was Jupi, short for Jupiter, and on orders from Pug Nose he immediately disappeared in the clandestine lower depths of the chemical plant of my uncle István Nádas, whose code name was Keeper of the Seal; the forgery workshop and the printshop of the illegal Communist movement had been set up there. As for Aranyossi, he began secret negotiations with the man he'd known in the past. The less you know, the less they can beat out of you, this was the conspirators' first rule, and they held themselves to it even after the siege, and when it came to delicate matters, they continued to wrap themselves in silence, even in front of one another. They had a special look to accompany this silence. Even the open refusal to ask a question or to answer it was forbidden. They looked the other in the eye, they did not blink, which meant, don't ask. I won't answer even if you ask. According to my Aunt Magda, in such cases, silence was the most emphatic answer.

As a child, I spent years expecting to be tortured and agonized over what I would do to keep myself from squealing. So people shouldn't squeal on me, and I shouldn't squeal on them.

Also, I wanted to know everything, and I do mean everything about all the uncleanliness that might conceivably happen in the world because of squealing, betrayal, and informing.

I kept a sharp eye out, I picked up my ears, I marked and observed, going unnoticed, I eavesdropped, I was there, I took mental notes. Later I read every piece of paper I could get my hands on without delay, or at the very least, I gave it a cursory look. I searched among their confidential papers. I was sure that I would not squeal. After all, my father didn't squeal either.

Minister of Justice Pauler did not answer Mezei's interpolation until the 140th National Assembly, held on November 27, 1882.

Honored House, the minister of justice began, Deputy Ernő Mezei has addressed certain questions to me regarding the Tiszaeszlár affair.

How can I justify that in the Tiszaeszlár affair the Nyíregyháza court appointed a junior notary and not a bona fide examining magistrate, and how could I allow this to happen. How could I allow the court to keep the boy Móricz Scharf under detention for several months, when he had not been accused of complicity nor was he among the accused. How could I allow the examining magistrate to make the course of the investigation prey to passions and hot temper by making public the information pertaining to the investigation. He asked why I have not taken steps to ensure that the public prosecutor bring a suit in the matter of the article published in *Egyenlőség* that seriously compromised the examining magistrate, and lastly, after what has happened, is it my intention to appoint another court in the so-called Tiszaeszlár affair.

I wish to respond to these questions as follows. In accordance with the law of the land and the temporary rules governing criminal procedure, the examining magistrate is appointed by the president of the Royal Court. As a general rule, the president appoints the person of the examining judge from the ranks of the judges of the criminal court, in lesser cases, from among the notaries. The president must appoint the investigator after consideration of the contents of the impeachment papers or the prosecutor's proposal. As is well known, the investigation in the Tiszaeszlár affair began on the basis of the transcript of the interrogation of Eszter Solymosi's mother by the municipal magistracy, presented to the court on May 7. Since one of the examining magistrates was ill, and the other whom he could have assigned to the case was away, he assigned the junior notary József Bary to head the investigation. When I approached him and asked him to justify his choice of a junior notary, the president of the Royal Court stated that he considered the denunciation so preposterous that at the time he personally considered it of little consequence. But when the public began to show interest, when the matter assumed unforeseen proportions, he said that he could no longer hand the case over to someone else, not only because the particulars of the investigation were already in Bary's hands, but also because, had he handed the investigation over to someone else at that point, he would have laid himself open to the most serious allegations.

Whereupon there was lively approval in the chamber.

Furthermore, I wish to submit, Honored House, that the appointment of the junior notary was necessitated by the fact that there are several individuals among the judges who never or only rarely engage in investigation themselves. Also, the president of the Royal Court had to ensure that a sufficient number of judges be kept in reserve for the public hearing. But be that as it may, I wish you to keep in mind that in case after case, the examining magistrate has given outstanding evidence of his expertise, circumspection, and unquestioned reliability.

At which sounds of approval could once again be heard from the extreme left, a demonstration of sympathy for Examining Magistrate József Bary.

The president of the Royal Court has further stated that having spent nearly thirty years in the service of the law, surely he is capable of judging a man's capabilities and is willing to take the responsibility on himself.

At the hearing of which, approval could be heard once more from the extreme left, where the anti-Semites of the Independence Party sat well apart from the others.

Under the circumstances, Honored House, I see no justification for interfering in the practice of the law assigned to the president of the Royal Court. Nor do I see justification for interfering, to whatever extent, in the appointment of the examining magistrate. As for the president of the Royal Court, I had still less reason to hold him accountable because, apart from the reason I have just mentioned, I have received no complaints against the investigative magistrate either from the local royal prosecutor's office, nor from the delegated deputy chief prosecutor, nor, finally, from the defense attorneys who, after having been named by the accused, what's more saw no reason to lodge a complaint; though they lodged a number of complaints against the examining magistrate, in the petitions and statements addressed to me as well as the court, which were made public in the papers, they did not request the appointment of new examining magistrates, lest the possibly favorable conclusion to the investigation should be attributed to this change.

The other question was how I could countenance the court's breach of the law whereby they kept Móricz Scharf in custody for months even though he was not accused of complicity. With regard to this, I wish to point out that although he was not suspected of complicity, Móricz Scharf was suspected of connivance. It was not the testimony of Móricz Scharf that had implicated certain individuals, but the testimony of his younger brother. This is why Móricz Scharf was put in the charge of the local authorities for a few days, and this is why it was deemed necessary to remand him in custody from May 22 to 27. Thus, it can't have been months, just a couple of days. I further wish to draw your attention to Para. 13 of the decree pertaining to detention in jail, which stipulates that if because of his youthful years, physical disability, or other reason, a prisoner should require the care of the court, the civil courts or some other political authority must place him in an institution or else in the care of relatives. The court took the necessary steps in this regard. They turned to the subprefect of Szabolcs County, requesting him to attend to the boy's placement. And until the subprefect could take the necessary steps, with the approval of the royal prosecutor, and not as a prisoner, nor with the enforcement of prison regulations, he was kept in the courtyard of the jail, where the prison guards are quartered. Having no place at his disposal, the subprefect looked up the prosecutor's office, requesting that the boy, in the interest of his personal safety, as he put it, might be quartered there. He stayed there until, thanks to the royal chief prosecutor's initiative, the subprefect, under whose supervision he is even now fed and quartered in the county hall, took him in. This being the case, I could not countenance any action of the Royal Court of Law, because this decision was not for them to make, and so there was no action to be countenanced in the first place. Jail supervision falls under the jurisdiction of the prosecutor's office. Afterward the defense attorneys protested against this, but having questioned the boy's parents, they accepted the decision of the prosecutor's office.

The third question of the interpolation was how I could countenance that the examining magistrate should make public rulings and examination secrets, thereby making the proceedings, so to speak, prey to emotions. On the basis of the unequivocal statement of the president of the Royal Court of Law of Nyíregyháza, I may safely say that the examining magistrate did not make the findings public, nor did he publish documents pertaining to the examination.

At this point, the representative Imre Szalay interrupted the speaker by shouting that the royal prosecutor's office had made it public. The interruption was followed by noise and chaos that prompted the Speaker to use his bell once again.

Szalay was an interesting person, loud, corpulent, with training in law, a landowner, a world traveler, and a popular writer of hunting books. He was extremely radical in his views, but he had humor to go with it, humor that tended toward the cynical. The immunity committee had its hands full with him, because he was not only a notorious interrupter of speeches, but an infamous hero of duels as well. Either he was engaged in a duel himself, or else he was accessory to the crime as a second, forcing the prosecutor's office to request a suspension of immunity.

As I said, he neither published nor let slip any such thing, the justice minister continued, having raised his voice somewhat. How and in what manner that news got out is extremely difficult to determine, especially if we consider that the reporters who appeared in Nyíregyháza and Tiszaeszlár, essentially conducting their own investigation in the wake of the examining magistrate, questioned the witnesses themselves.

According to the National Assembly reporter, this was followed by lively cheering in the chamber, which had just now been called to order.

Whenever any such act could be ascertained thanks to the name appearing with the newspaper article, the appropriate prosecutorial measures have been taken with respect to these unauthorized questionings. I have personally requested the president of the Royal Court as well as the royal chief prosecutor to take action ensuring that the information pertaining to the examinations should not be made public before it is time. The president of the Royal Court rightfully insists that Examining Magistrate Bary, who stands accused of resorting to unlawful means in order to guarantee the success of the investigation, meaning in the interest of furthering his own aims, would in fact have aborted the outcome he desired had he made public any such information before it was time. According to the honorable deputy Mezei's interpolation, in face of a current tendency in a certain undesired direction, it is in the utmost interest of truth that both the investigation and the court procedure be protected from falling under the influence of undue passion. I could not agree with him more. Except I wish to go one step further. The public prosecutor, the examining magistrate, the sentencing judges as well as the defense, must all be protected not only from one current, but all currents of influence.

He has barely just finished the sentence, and the chamber resounds once again with lively approval and a standing ovation.

No one is sadder than I that because of the things that have been made public, the course and success of the investigation have been seriously compromised. But I never had at my disposal any means of influencing the free press and thus preventing anything of the sort from happening, nor do I have any now, nor will I have any in the future.

The extreme left evinces loud agreement.

To the question of whether I have taken steps to initiate a libel suit against *Egyenlőség* because of the compromising statements that have appeared in its pages against Examining Magistrate József Bary, I have the following to say:

Don't bother, don't tire yourself unnecessarily, Justice Minister, Imre Szalay interrupts once again, which is followed by shouting in the chamber. However, not letting himself be unnerved, the minister merely raises his voice above the chaos.

To be perfectly honest, I do not approve of calling the apparatus of the juried court into action every time one or another newspaper publishes an accusation or a charge, thereby endowing with significance something that is of no significance by itself.

Which was followed by the sounds of general agreement in the chamber.

If, on the other hand, whenever a judge, a clerk of the court, or a royal prosecutor comes under attack and that attack undermines the integrity of court procedure, I am always willing to authorize the initiation of a suit. I will take the necessary steps, all the more so because Examining Magistrate Bary himself has petitioned me to authorize judicial requital for, as he asserts, the unfounded charges and slanders aimed at his person. As for appointments, the honored deputy's question with regard to it was whether, after what has happened, I intend to appoint another set of judges.

Honored House, one of the fundamental laws of this country prescribes that no person shall be deprived of the judge appointed to him.

The sentence is followed by lively, prolonged cheers from the far left.

Incontrovertibly, there are cases when, in the name of His Majesty, the law authorizes the minister of justice to appoint new judges. This can occur in cases of bias as defined by law. In the case of criminal procedings, the law does not define these, but the court rules do, and in criminal cases, it is on the basis of these that the justice minister proceeds *per analogiam*. Besides cases of bias, the law also authorizes him to delegate judges, should considerations of expediency so require it. I, Honored House, have not as of yet found any reason with respect to the court of Nyíregyháza that would indicate bias, and thus I do not see the necessity of delegating.

This statement is followed by general and animated approval from both sides.

As for the principle of expediency, I have concluded the opposite. Whether I consider the interest of objective jurisdiction, the interest of the accused, or the social interests emphasized by the deeply honored interpolating deputy, I deem it expedient for the procedure to remain with the court where it was originally initiated. Thus, my answer to this question is unequivocal. I have no intention of authorizing an *ad hoc* delegation.

Honored House, from what I have said, you will perhaps be convinced that I have not failed in anything that is within my sphere of authority. I have practiced my supervisory rights between the limits and boundaries prescribed by law, but have abstained and shall continue to abstain from interfering with the sphere of authority of the courts as prescribed by law.

The minister's words are followed by general spirited approval, even cheering from both sides of the chamber. However, in his exemplary style, the minister does not react to the celebration of his person, even though the shouts of approval bring his speech to a momentary standstill.

Because it is my conviction, he shouts, that the free and independent practice of the law between legal boundaries is the mightiest guarantee of social order and freedom.

The statement is followed by prolonged general agreement on both sides of the benches, the deputies leap to their feet, with lively ovation coming from the far left.

The minister is now forced to pause a while to finish his speech.

Let those in question live with their lawful means. If the deeply honored deputy said that it would have been necessary to demonstrate that in Hungary jurisprudence is an impenetrable dividing wall that passions cannot breach, then may I be allowed to take the liberty of voicing my conviction that our courts will, indeed, prove that in Hungary jurisprudence is, indeed, an impenetrable wall that neither passions, nor bias, nor any other manner of undue influence can breach.

His last words are followed by boisterous agreement and accolades from the extreme left, as if the Honored House were celebrating its own *judicium*, the state's consciousness of the law, its own revolutionary liberal consensus, of which hardly anything remained by the time I was born, but moving along mysterious paths, of which I persistently give account on these pages, it nevertheless became part of my intellectual heritage along with the conflicts that the parties waged with each other in the protection of *judicium* and liberal consensus.

Ernő Mezei lost no time in asking for the floor, the Speaker granted it amid the loud ringing of his bell, and when he began to speak, with his wheezing consonants and barely audible vowels, there was silence once again on both political sides of the chamber, the kind of aversion-filled silence I am all too familiar with from my own public appearances.

Honored House, I will respond to the honorable minister of justice's answer point by point, just as he has done. The honorable minister of justice's answer to my first question is that when delegating the examining magistrate, the Nyíregyháza court proceeded according to the rules, because initially it had no one else at its disposal except the junior notary, while subsequently it could not recall the junior notary Bary without prejudicing the credibility of the president of the Royal Court.

I understand that perfectly. In my eyes, the court of Nyíregyháza stands vindicated. Or if it does not, it is at least on safe ground. I could find excuses for these procedures myself, a hundred if need be. But I can find nothing to vindicate the minister of justice's actions. Here, in the House of Deputies, in his first interpolation, the honorable deputy Győző Istóczy asked whether the government has done anything to prevent Jewish money from bribing this court. I could have brought with me to this House the articles of those newspapers, along with the letters written to the editors, that gave clear warning at the very outset of this affair; to wit, that if the Nyíregyháza court should acquit the accused, it would surely elicit public suspicion. Under these circumstances, what should have been the obligation of the minister of justice? Under such conditions of crisis, was it not the obligation of the minister of justice to offer moral support to the Nyíregyháza court? Perhaps the minister of justice was waiting for the defense attorney and the prosecution to request the appointment of another examining magistrate. But the defense and the prosecutors found themselves rowing in the same boat as the court. The minister of justice, who is the supreme guardian of the dispensation of justice, and who is not exposed to the influence of local interests, should have felt it incumbent upon himself, he should have felt a sense of duty. Paragraph 25 of the ordinance published by the honorable minister of justice provides that in the event that the denunciation is addressed to the court, in more important cases the president of the Royal Court must appoint a judge, while in lesser cases, a clerk should be appointed to head the investigation. I allow for the court not having kept itself strictly to the ordinance when it appointed a junior notary, but I cannot allow for the honorable minister of justice ignoring the infringement of the law and taking no steps, whether the attorneys and prosecutors had requested it or not. In keeping with the aforementioned paragraph, at this point, the honorable minister of justice should have taken steps as required by his office, especially when he saw that this was called for.

Unrest and agitation filled the chamber, but it lasted only while the speaker paused for effect.

The minister of justice's answer to my second question was that Móricz Scharf was kept in custody not as a witness, but for complicity, and as soon as he was proven innocent, he was released. I hope the Honored House will excuse the expression, but I must say that this boggles the mind.

I was told the authentic version of what happened to Móricz Scharf's younger brother. When Examining Magistrate Bary appeared in Tiszaeszlár, he took the four-year-old child on his lap, stroked him, and asked him what he knew, whereupon the boy said, we got the girl to come in, my mama put her hand on her lips, Móricz held down her hand, my dad slit her throat, and I held the bowl to catch her blood.

Which was followed by agitated movement and subdued amusement in the chamber.

Honored House, whoever told this story, I consider it rather curious. Neither as an attorney, a deputy, nor as a journalist can I imagine what sense it could possibly make or what use it could be to anyone. And now I hear the minister of justice say that it was on the basis of the alleged testimony of a four-year-old child that his older brother was kept in custody.

The commotion and amusement in the chamber is followed by shouting.

Hear, hear!

Imre Szalay interrupts once again.

First he's got a problem with them being nice to the boy, then he's got a problem with them beating him.

It boggles the mind that the minister of justice handles all this as fact and not only does he confirm it, he presents it as a matter calling for sanctions. It pains me, but to this presentation by the minister of justice, my former teacher, the renowned professor of criminal law whose lectures I once listened to in awe, I have nothing to add. But then, I cannot talk about the trustworthiness of our judiciary with the majestic equanimity we have just now witnessed.

To my third question the minister of justice responded that he ordered the Royal Court of Nyíregyháza to prohibit the publication of the investigative secrets, and furthermore, that Examining Magistrate Bary averred that he never made public any such secrets. Still, I might ask, Honorable Minister of Justice, how the transcripts of the autopsy could have appeared in *Függetlenség*, before any of its contents were made known to the defense and the prosecution.

At this point Gyula Verhovay shouts that he wants to answer this question instead of the justice minister.

Which is in theory justifiable, because Verhovay is senior editor of *Függetlenség*, so he should know how the paper came into possession of the transcript.

However, Mezei continues as if he hadn't heard the interruption. In the face of Verhovay's and Szalay's methodical interruptions, this unblinking equanimity puts him in good stead to uphold his dignity; furthermore, it is justified by the circumstance that these two are sitting in the same party benches as he, except his Independence Party comrades have sequestered themselves on the outer recesses of the left wing so they shouldn't have to find themselves sitting near the Jewish deputies whom, in defiance of the principles of their own party, they do not consider their equals; on the contrary, they want the House to repeal the law of 1868 pertaining to the emancipation of the Jews, a question on which Verhovay and Szalay are even more radical than the leader of the anti-Semites, the liberal Istóczy, who sees the primary cause of all the maladies and decay of the world not in the character of the Jewish race, but in modernization. He sees historical reasons, and consequently he wants to convince the Jews of Hungary to turn their backs on the erroneous direction, disown modernization, and most of all, not throw in their lot with the Eastern Jewish riffraff flooding into the country.

His fourth question, Mezei continues undaunted, was whether they have initiated the lawsuit against *Egyenlőség*, but he considers the honorable minister of justice's answer in this regard satisfactory. He appreciates that the minister of justice did not wish to act in haste, and especially that he did not wish to hinder the progress of the investigation with yet more procedural intermezzos.

Yet it is clear why he is nevertheless bringing it up in his rejoinder. He is a senior correspondent of the newspaper himself, the most-read organ of Jewish emancipation, and only the outcome of the libel suit brought against it could make the multiple irregularities obvious before the law, the scandal that the minister of justice is clearly hoping to avoid.

There remains the fifth and most important question, namely, whether the minister of justice should not be appointing another court. The minister of justice's answer was an unequivocal no. I understand the minister of justice's firm stand in this regard. I would think it over a hundred times myself before I were to express any suspicion with regard to a Hungarian court of law. Honored House, if it were just a matter of the accused of Tiszaeszlár being acquitted, we could safely trust the proceedings of the court of Nyíregyháza. I believe that it will acquit them. Or if it does not acquit them, because they have in fact committed a crime, they will receive their just punishment. But this is not what is at stake, Honored House, rather it is that the public calm down. Why else are we calling for a public hearing, why else would the relevant authorities agree to a public hearing? Because to the last man, we are all hoping to calm public opinion. But to order a public hearing without ensuring that it produce the desired outcome is, simply put, a farce.

These final words are met with unrest in the chamber.

As we know, there is only one witness to substantiate the first accusation, that of murder, a child who gave his confession under the supervision of the constable, and as for the second fact regarding the sneaking of the corpse to Dada so they could exchange the ritually murdered girl's body for another body in order to get rid of the evidence, the court itself issued orders for the corpse to be exhumed. Well, what else is the honorable justice minister waiting for? He does not believe that the court is biased. Nor does he believe it expedient to appoint another court. But isn't what the minister of justice himself said sufficient, namely, that the president of the Royal Court could not delegate another examining magistrate to discover the truth because he was afraid of how the public would react??

At which point the stirring and restlessness degenerates into noise and shouting.

That's enough!

That's enough of that!

I would consider my remarks exceptionally misguided, were they to give anyone the impression that they are motivated by bias or the least denominational self-interest. I merely wish to voice my legal concerns, I wish to express that I do not understand the government's proceedings.

The minister of justice had decided to embrace the principle of noninterference in the sphere of the court's authority.

At which deputies from both sides of the benches loudly approve the principle.

Honored House, I cannot accept the justice minister's reasoning. The minister of justice says that the court of Nyíregyháza must be spared not only the influence of passions, but all other influence as well. Well, I have not seen any evidence of him taking steps in this regard.

Or else your memory is exceptionally poor, someone on the extreme left shouts.

I have seen only with what indifference the minister of justice looks on as justice is derailed in Nyíregyháza, aimed exclusively at finding evidence for the ritual murder, which in and of itself is patently absurd. I have seen only with what indifference the minister of justice is looking on while barbarous manhunts are being organized in Tiszaeszlár, Tiszalök, and Tiszadob.

At which, the sounds of loud amusement accompany his words in the House.

I have seen only that the Jewish residents of three villages are now living under a state of siege, without having given the least cause for it. I can say only that the honorable minister of justice is looking on with indifference all the while that the calm, peace, and honor of six hundred thousand souls is at stake.

Loud disapproval, writes the Assembly reporter.

He has been looking on with indifference, whereas all this concerns the safety of Hungarian society, of law and order, the law and order of the Hungarian state.

The honorable minister has, indeed, looked on all this with indifference. The honorable minister of justice should have at least noticed that his actions are made to appear as if, indeed, the minister of justice, along with the court, and despite the conviction of the prosecution to the contrary, were convinced of the charge of ritual murder. All this is a mere pittance in the eyes of the honorable minister of justice, and so he has found no reason to interfere. I do not believe that the mission of the minister of justice is to sit here in his red velvet chair like some embalmed pharaoh.

Infernal noise fills the chamber, shouting and yelling.

Order!

Desist!

Order!

I beg your pardon, but I will accept a call to order only from the Speaker. I believe that the question of order in this country happens to be the question of anti-Semitism. The honorable prime minister proved it by ordering a state of emergency. It is my conviction that many things would not have happened in Nyíregyháza if only people had seen that the law has not been put on hold.

At this point the Speaker's bell is helpless against the commotion in the Assembly hall. Shouts are heard.

That's enough!

The Jews deserve no better!

Down with him!

Desist!

I was so disgusted by what has been happening, that the three months I spent abroad, when I did not have to read the Hungarian papers, felt like a veritable blessing. It looks as if the law does not pertain to the accused Jews.

Stop it!

Desist!

I am asking for nothing more than justice for the Jews. I am not asking for unlawful decrees, I am not even asking for a state of emergency. I am asking for nothing more of the Jews themselves either than to practice the self-respect to which, as the free citizens of a free state, they are entitled. They should not have to seek protection with the high and mighty. This entire procedure suggests to me that the government is showing forbearance with respect to the causes of this agitation and will act with the greatest determination only once the most dangerous consequences of the recent events will have materialized.

According to my Aunt Magda's recollections, during the last days of September 1944 or possibly in early October, Regent Horthy sent his man to Pál Aranyossi, with Vilmos Lázár acting as intermediary, his man being a certain Rácz or Rátz, after it was too late, after British diplomacy had rejected his intention to launch negotiations and initiate talks with the Russians. Taking advantage of illegal channels, Aranyossi was to go to the Russians on the double. It is more than likely that this meeting between Aranyossi and Rátz or Rácz took place prior to October 11. Horthy's intention was clear. If a Communist he was persecuting were to be included on the list of members of the delegation, his commission would carry more weight in their eyes. Or possibly, the go-between was one Endre Rácz, the minister who, in the resistance, was in touch with Albert Bereczky, the minister of the Reformed church on Pozsonyi Street, and who, in turn, with my mother's mediation, was in touch with István Nádas, the Keeper of the Seal. The second possibility is more likely, in which case the person was not Rácz, as his name repeatedly appears in my aunt's memoirs, but a certain Rátz, his full name being Kálmán Rátz. This Rátz must have been one of the most original characters of the period between the two wars. Besides, this wouldn't be my aunt's only mistake or mistaken spellings in her memoirs and handwritten notes. This Rátz was an officer of the hussars, who at the outbreak of the First World War was sent to the Eastern Front, where he was repeatedly wounded, taken prisoner, and ended up in the POW camp at Tomsk. He himself bragged that he fought on the side of the Reds against the Czech legion. On the basis of their archival research, Ágnes Renfer and Attila Seres, who are researching this period, feel that because of the closeness of the dates, this is hardly credible. At the same time, they say that the works Rátz later wrote about those years provide evidence of intimate familiarity with the Red units. Be that as it may, during the last months of the war, he managed to escape from the POW camp with several of his mates, was caught, escaped again, had an adventurous journey home via Finland and Sweden, and arrived just in time for the Michaelmas Daisy Revolution, though he did not join the Reds, nor did he join the bourgeois democratic followers of Count Károlyi, soon to be appointed prime minister of the short-lived First Hungarian Republic; instead, he joined the Whites, and hand in hand with others, promptly founded one of the most important organs of the anti-Bolshevik forces, the pre-fascist Defense Association, meaning the Hungarian National Defense Association, of which he became a member. On February 13, 1919, he was arrested, and was released only in August, after the Republic of Councils had collapsed under pressure from the superior Entente powers. In all likelihood, he must have been one of those individuals who can't do without championing one ideology or another and showing devotion to radical causes. Still, I don't believe he was a political adventurer. He attempted to find a foothold in the narrow confines of his special political ideas, within which the two extremes of bourgeois thinking, the ideologies and methods of the National Socialist movement and the Communist movement, merged. This is where he hoped to discover the gateway to his political utopia.

Having been profoundly disappointed in the Communist movement, he offered the poet Attila József, who by then had been largely abandoned by his friends, a position and money if he were willing to be co-founder of the National Communist Party with him. He offered him the position of secretary, which would make him the second in command of the party. At any rate, this is how Judit Szántó, Attila József's longtime companion, recalled the Communist poet's brief flirtation with national socialism before her own death. Judit Szántó considered Rátz, who loved Attila József's poems, a man of impressive erudition. Rátz was of the opinion that we were on the verge of a great war and the mission of the national Communist parties at the moment was to save at least their own nations from the clutches of imperialism. Which, as conceived by the Marxists, meant that they could save mankind from the nightmare of the inevitability of war. Rátz saw a possible solution in the cooperation of the two very different movements, which were nevertheless grafted from the same anti-imperialist branch. With the new movement the two of them would awaken the Hungarian people to their own national consciousness, this is what he hoped. They must be spared the war before they could become international. At least, for the duration of the night while he penned his "National Socialism" manifesto, Attila József was also convinced of it. The eminent scholar András Lengyel says that this night was sometime in the spring of 1933. When he got up in the morning, Attila József handed the manuscript to Judit to read, and Judit confiscated it. As long as you are living here, meaning with her, in her apartment, where she paid the rent, this writing will not appear. Attila József would have had nowhere else to go. And though posterity has no love for the stern and abrupt Judit, she had their interest in mind, and Attila József loved this stern and abrupt Judit, and not the upright literary scholars of the future, for the time that he loved her, if he loved her at all. Or as long as they shared one bed. From personal revenge and wounded pride you cannot betray those to whom you belong. And in this Judit was right. National communism is a contradiction in terms. Judit was right in this as well. Their arguments over this went so far that Judit would not speak to Attila for six weeks. She must have also refused him their shared bed, and so, after six weeks, Attila József's flirtation with national socialism came to an abrupt end.

But Attila József was by no means stupid, and he saw the problem with the international Communist movement better than Judit did. He realized the difficulty of an internationalist movement directed from Moscow in accordance with Greater Russian interests. Members of my own family also locked horns over this question, first with Béla Kun's adherents, then with the Party functionaries of Moscow, until they came to grips with the hardline Muscovites. They were even at odds with their own views. In the illegal Communist movement, they were adherents of Jenő Landler and had no intention of leaving the terrain of local or national givens; they did not want the rug pulled from under the feet of their own party because of Moscow's interests; but at the same time, they did not recognize the difference between Stalinist great-power politics and the needs of the international Communist movement, whereas back in the 1930s Mihály Károlyi had already brought it to Aranyossi's attention somewhere in the Swiss Alps, where the two families were spending a couple of days in each other's company. It is also part of the story that because of this, sooner or later my relatives drew the shorter end of the stick, their numbers dwindled, they left or were expelled from the movement, even though, from pure self-defense, at times they tried to seem more dogmatic than the next. Considering the inquisitorial system of the Communist movement, their resistance was not without danger and their concessions were understandable. Once I asked my mother what this pulling the rug from under one's feet meant, and why people say it. In a split second, I was lying on my back on the bare floor.

She actually pulled the rug from under my feet. That's what it means, she said, laughing as she stood over me.

In short, Kálmán Rátz's attempt at reconciliation failed, Attila József did not become a national socialist, and Rátz did not force the issue. Besides, three years later he was again on the opposite side, having become a parliamentary deputy of Prime Minister Gyula Gömbös's National Unity Party. In 1941, when his first book about Russia, *The History of Pan-Slavism*, appeared, he came into conflict with Ferenc

Szálasi, the leader of the Arrow Cross, left the Arrow Cross Party, and set up the anti–Arrow Cross Independent Hungarian Socialist Party.

He arrived at the Aranyossis' when the major work of his life, *The History of Russia*, had been out for a year, which made him generally known. My Aunt Magda considered the work muddled. But whether it was this Rátz or the clergyman Endre Rácz, or even some other Rácz, I can't understand how he could have found them in the city, when the Aranyossis had been living undercover for months by then.

Regent Horthy wants a separate peace, he wants to send a delegation to Moscow within twenty-four hours, and he wants a Communist in the delegation.

As far as that goes, Aranyossi was a Communist, a surefire Landlerite, not only an adherent but a friend, too, of Jenő Landler, People's Commissar of the Republic of Councils, but even if he'd known this anti–Arrow Cross Rátz or else the Protestant Rácz from before, they might have known each other from the Eastern Front, they might have been lying wounded in the same lazarette, Aranyossi did translations for Kálmán Rátz's publisher, the Grill, and so they may have met at the publishing house; be that as it may, I also don't understand why, upon hearing the message, it didn't occur to my uncle that they had sent a provocateur to him.

How could this Rácz or Rátz prove that he was really sent by Horthy.

I have no documents pertaining to this.

They had chosen him, explained Rátz or Rácz, my aunt told me, because, after all, Aranyossi was a nobleman, even if he was a Communist, and so Horthy found him acceptable, at least in this emergency.

But regardless of him being a nobleman, when it comes to the proper spelling of my uncle's name, I'm at a loss. At various stages of his life, at times he spelled his name Aranyossy, then Aranyossi, or even simply Aranyosi, not to mention the various names he used to sign his newspaper articles, his code name in the movement, and the names on his forged documents. He was an exceptionally intelligent and sound individual who kept changing his name all his life. On his birth certificate he is Aranyosi, but in 1919, after the demise of the short-lived Republic of Councils, for a time he went into hiding, then fled from the sure prospect of arrest, and in November of the same year he crossed the border into Austria as Károly Szolcsányi. Szolcsányi had been a friend of his youth, and from what people have told me, as well as from Szolcsányi's own correspondence, it seems to me that he must have been a sharp-witted, charming good-for-nothing who nursed the friendship of their former college years in Paris, and who had a photographer take a picture of him with glasses on in which he masqueraded as Aranyossi, and then had a passport issued to him with the picture at the Hungarian Royal Interior Ministry. For his part, in Italy Aranyossi went around with a passport made out in Szolcsányi's name. His wife followed him with her old passport that bore her maiden name, Magdolna Ida Nádas, and so during the six months they spent in Florence, according to their papers, they were not married, except they happened to have a child by the name of György, whose existence was not indicated in either of their passports, and so they had no way of proving it. My uncle was expelled from Italy under the name of Szolcsányi, but by then he had acquired a Spanish safe-conduct pass in Rome that bore a Spanish name safely tucked away in his pocket, and this safe-conduct pass indicated that he had a wife, though without the indication of her name, but it did not mention a child either. This is the most the Spanish consulate in Rome could do for him. When they reached the Austrian border, this was the safe-conduct pass he showed the Austrian border guards. My Aunt Magda's passport, made out in her maiden name, was later taken in hand by a Hungarian graphic artist by the name of Göndör, who changed her maiden name to her married name so that along with their child they could acquire a Swedish visa and continue on to Luleå, where, after a highly adventurous journey, her husband had arrived on a cargo ship illegally the previous week. In Stralsund, which many years later I visited myself, he was told to look up a certain comrade in the harbor. The comrade was a sailor. He'd already been informed that a comrade would come from Berlin whom they must sneak aboard a ship headed for Sweden. Under cover of night, they snuck him into a cabin that quartered the rank and file, which, considering his blatantly intellectual appearance, was no easy task. They could have taken him for many things, but never a sailor returning from a night at a bar. But if he took off his glasses, he tripped over his own feet. The men in the cabin were stokers, they worked in shifts, and as the boat sailed on and on over the Baltic Sea, he had to lie down in whichever bed had just been vacated and pull a stranger's blanket over his head. He had to pull it over his head because anyone might come into the cabin at any time. And they did. Sometimes they gave him a friendly but stiff pat on the back, and said something in Swedish or German. They made a short stop in Stockholm, where he was supposed to look up the radical socialist poet Ture Nerman, and Zeth Höglund, who at the time was editor in chief of the *Folkets Dagblad Politiken*, but they moored the boat in broad daylight, just long enough to unload and reload, and the Communist sailors were unable to sneak him off the boat. They shared their own food and drink with him, but were forced to take him along still farther. They stopped in several places along the Gulf of Bothnia, sometimes for a longer time, but in none of these places could they sneak him safely ashore. They took him all the way to Luleå, the northernmost part of the gulf, which was the last stop, and here they did manage to sneak him off. He stood with his small bag in a very foreign place, barely fifty kilometers from the Arctic Circle; however, thanks to his good nature, he was not terrified but started walking instead along a relatively busy road that he hoped would lead him into town, which at the time had a little more than ten thousand residents. But he had hardly taken a couple of steps when, struck by the way he looked, a policeman on patrol asked for his papers, arrested him, and took him to the city jail, where he had to stick it out for days. For the first time in its history, the country had a socialist prime minister, so he decided that he had no reason to hide anything. He hadn't even finished with his confession when his interrogators brought him breakfast, and then not only did the police captain release him under the most formal of circumstances, but along with a small group, personally accompanied him to the Storgatan, as if it were a triumphal march, and there they lodged him at the best hotel in town, the Stadshotellet Luleå; what's more, he was given the second-floor suite reserved for the most distinguished visitors, he, the communard, the emigrant Communist, the editor of the *Red Banner*, who was headed to Stockholm to speak with his comrades but ended up in their town, and whom all of a sudden everyone wanted to see and hear tell the story of the rise and fall of the Commune. He was glad to oblige, and in less than an hour the town's mayor was also on the scene, and he began from the beginning, so they should know what they must do and not do.

In Stockholm, my aunt and uncle lived under their own name, but with their earlier forged documents, which they later used to move back to Berlin. When in the winter of 1924 my Aunt Magda was sent by her party on an illegal errand to Budapest, in order to lend credence to the fiction that she was going to visit the family, she had to take her five-year-old son with her. But for security reasons, they didn't want to send her on her way with a forged passport, and she was given a forged certificate of statelessness made out to her own name, a so-called yellow slip, to which the Hungarian embassy in Berlin set its seal without a second thought. But seeing such an elegant young woman with a yellow slip in her hand, the good-looking young Hungarian border guard asked, rather indignantly, why don't you have a proper passport, madam. Sir, my Aunt Magda responded with a heavy sigh, this is just another instance of what Trianon has done to us. The officer nodded and did not pursue the matter any further. Above my aunt's head rested in the luggage rack the suitcase made of the finest calfskin that her grandfather had given her in her youth on a trip to Switzerland, and which later came into my possession until my friend Miki took it, who after all sorts of adventures ended up in Sweden, with or without it, I don't know. Mór Mezei liked spending his summers in the Swiss Alps. The suitcase had been altered by a comrade of theirs called Károly Garai in Berlin so that a large envelope that my Aunt Magda had to take with her to Budapest could be hidden inside the lining. Naturally, she didn't know what was in the envelope, nor did she know who it was meant for. They just gave her an address and a password, so she'd know who to look up at the given address. And also, what code word the person had to say in response.

For the first two weeks she was told to restrict herself to visiting members of her family, her uncle, the banker Pál Mezei, her aunts Erzsébet Mezei and Anna Mezei, her cousins Ilma, Mária, Anna, and Edina, the latter of whom was married to the respected physician Henrik Benedickt, chief counselor to His Grace, the Regent Horthy, while Anna was married to Aurél Egry, legal advisor to Archduke Joseph; but above all, she was ordered to visit her grandfather and check if she was being followed. Few people today know who my great-grandfather Mór Mezei was, but at the time, the memory of the conservative liberal world that had fallen victim to the recent world war had not yet paled, and of that world, he was a notable figure. She did everything as she was told; first she visited her family, one by one, but after two weeks, when she was sure that the air was clear and she was not being followed, when she could not remove the brass screws hidden between the folds of the silk lining of her suitcase to retrieve the envelope from behind it and take it to the address in Pest that she had been given, she had no choice, she asked her younger brother István to help, and that's when it came to light that brother and sister were veritably rowing the same boat. After the demise of the Republic of Councils, István was active in the illegal Communist youth movement, and soon became secretary of the Hungarian association of the Young Communist International, but when Moscow demanded things from them that could not be carried out without risk of them being found out and the local chapter of the association being eradicated, he resigned from his post. At which point they threatened him. At which point he said he was leaving the illegal party. At which point they threatened him with death.

But now he put his sister's mind at rest that he did not cease his activities altogether, it's just that he would not have them put him on a leash. For her part, Magda told him that eighteen months previously, they had gotten themselves embroiled in a similar conflict in Stockholm when, having fled Hungary after the Hungarian Republic of Councils, Béla Kun gave the absurd order from Moscow that those who had left Hungary should return home, which was tantamount to him saying that they should return to Budapest and give themselves up. Pali's instructions were to pass on the order, but Pali refused. He also refused to pass on those issues of the *Red Banner*, published in Moscow, that included this absurd call to action, and which they shipped, along with other things, on a smuggling boat over the sea from Soviet Russia to Sweden, where they loaded the boat with medicine, bandages, food, illegal postage, and sent it on its way back to Russia, which was under a blockade. When a year later Gyula Lengyel, who headed the Berlin legation of the Soviet foreign trade agency, sent the two of them to Paris, my Uncle Pali was given the passport of a German journalist ten years his junior, while my Aunt Magda was handed the passport of a certain Stella Seidler, ten years her senior, but first it was altered, making their son, György, a year younger, so he wouldn't need a passport of his own. This was how they reached Paris, a twenty-eight-year-old man living in cohabitation with a thirty-nine-year-old woman and a six-year-old child, who in fact was older than seven. They laughed a lot over that. The child started school in Berlin, then in Paris. Later in Paris, Aranyossi edited the left-wing illustrated weekly *Regards*, under the pen name Paul A. Faluche, even though he was living under his own name once again by then. My Aunt Magda became Mrs. Aranyossi again, but her Hungarian code name was Auntie Falush. The movement needed this duality so Horthy's police should realize as late as possible that one of the most important French weeklies of the time was being edited by a Hungarian Communist, while his wife was editing the left-wing illustrated magazine *Femmes*.

Aranyossi's family hailed from Aranyosgerend, in Kolozs County, and their title of nobility was the same as their family name, though according to family legend they originally came from Armenia, which left a visible mark on their countenance for generations. In Budapest, the Arrow Cross were forever on the lookout for Jewish characteristics, and they grabbed him more than once and dragged him into drafty entranceways, where he had to drop his pants and show his penis, to see if he'd been circumcised. They saw what there was to be seen; he had not been circumcised. By all odds, the spelling of their name was changed by Pál's father, Gyula, who one fine day, when he worked as a city clerk in Kolozsvár, turned on his heels and became a wandering actor, and in the spirit of the age he felt that a more noble-sounding name would carry more weight on stage. Or else his first stage director thought so when he sent the poster with his new name to the printer. His journalist son kept this spelling until he came into close contact with the Communist movement and worked for various papers, namely the *Nagyváradi Napló*, the *Pesti Hírlap*, and *Világ*. One of his beautifully written love letters reveals that just before they were married, the noble gentleman wanted to start a button factory from the dowry of Magda Nádas's grandfather. I have no idea why a button factory of all things, but a button factory it was. The noble mademoiselle, Magda Nádas, on the other hand, would have liked to open a tree nursery and a garden center on her parents' estate in Gömörsid, her way of remedying my grandfather's outdated management of the estate. But then, a couple of weeks later, at József Kelen's apartment on Városmajor Street, the groom, who had been sympathetic to left-wing ideas for some time, became a founding member of the Communist Party, a decision that altered the course of both their lives. Still later, when the subject of the button factory or the garden center came up, they had a good laugh over it. Pál must have literally begun to hate the letters in his name that indicated his nobility, and must have left off at least the *y*. Then after the siege, he also left off one of the two esses in order to reinstate the plebeian and, according to his birth certificate, only authentic form of his name.

I once asked him why he writes it one way one time and another way another time, and what prompted these changes in the spelling of his name, whereupon he gazed at me from behind his horn-rimmed glasses, and in his charming way he only said, how interesting, I never noticed. Which of course is the response of a bona fide aristocrat who does not feel bound to account for his actions.

In any case, his wife consistently wrote it as Aranyossi.

He was a bohemian, often impulsive, I often saw him with Oszkár Orody and Oszkár Solt, his bohemian friends, but when it came to bohemianism, they couldn't measure up to him.

As if life could never be a problem for him. What he said or did wasn't necessarily coherent, but he was charming and disarmingly elegant. On his birth certificate as well as his baptism certificate, they wrote their son's name as Aranyossy, and he remained György Aranyossy until his death, though in France he became Georges Aranyossy, the books he wrote in French were published under this name, and the French administrators put this name as such on the birth certificates of his four French children. On the other hand, the first file of the "B" dossier in the Historical Archives of the State Security Services, filed under number 10–69.138/1951, in which he signs on as an informer and which is written by hand in French and is dated October 19, 1951, Paris indicates an interesting variation on his name. *Je soussigné, Aranyossi György, déclare me mettre au service du Államvédelmi Hatóság, pour toutes les missions qu'il désirera me confier.* In short, when he offered his services to Hungarian State Security, he left the *y* off his name and replaced it with the more plebeian *i*. Also, in the top-secret report dated October 22, 1951, and typed in duplicate, the subject of which is the recruitment of one "Imre Lukács," Miklós Bauer, State Security major and head of department, writes that he had successfully recruited György Aranyossi in Paris according to the recruitment plan. In what follows, the report uses the new recruit's code name and provides a detailed report of the circumstances of his recruitment.

In the family we called him by his French name; he was Georges to everyone, and Georges he remained, which everyone pronounced Zhorzh. Exactly twenty years later he published his memoir, *Ils ont tué ma foi*, with Robert Laffont in Paris, but in this book with the plaintive title, according to which they had killed his faith, he makes no mention whatsoever of this important episode in his life. On the other hand, he gave the well-sounding and meaningful title *Préface aux silences* to the first part of his book. Indeed, there was perhaps no one in our family surrounded by as much silence and secrecy as he. But he lived his tragic life with good cheer. Physically, Georges took after our grandfather, whom he knew; he was tall and slender, but in his emotional makeup he took after his own father, and was a great bohemian, just like him, though his bohemianism had an ease and playfulness about it, thanks to which he managed to avoid just about all profundities that could be called intellectual or emotional. He was a witty man, he was known as a great practical joker, he could keep an entire company at the table amused indefinitely, he gave their diaphragms a thorough workout with his puns; his storehouse of puns was inexhaustible, in Hungarian as well as in French; there was always a wave of laughter around him, I can bear witness to that, one joke following upon the next; he was an excellent cook, the techniques and tricks of French cuisine were at his fingertips, so to speak; he drank with pleasure and abundance, and he never gave the impression that he had anything on his mind. If now and then he nevertheless decided to say something profound, quite out of character for him, he turned maudlin, banal, and kitschy; he was moved and would often weep at his own depth of feeling. Sometimes he tried to alleviate these awkward moments with a joke, but in this one thing, he lost his sense of humor.

At the time of his recruitment he managed the news office of the Hungarian embassy in Paris, which in those days had its quarters in a building on rue Saint-Jacques. Major Bauer writes in his report that Comrade "Modra" called Comrade "Imre Lukács," saying that the Comrade Ambassador would like to speak with him. Comrade "Lukács" showed up at the embassy approximately thirty minutes after the call. At the embassy, Comrade "Modra" told him that before he went in to see the ambassador, a comrade from Budapest would like to speak with him first.

Since I had met Comrade "Imre Lukács" during my last trip to Paris, he writes, I did not need to be introduced.

Using the excuse that we did not wish to bother Comrade "Modra," I conducted Comrade "Imre Lukács" into another room at the embassy, I took him to the military attaché's room, which stood empty at the time, and where I conducted the meeting with him. The meeting took appr. an hour and a half, we protected ourselves from possible bugs in the room by keeping the radio on. I told Comrade "Lukács" at the start of the meeting that I was in Paris as a representative of the State Security Service and it was in this capacity that I wished to speak with him. I told him that the work against the enemy has to begin outside Hungary's borders and that we are counting on his help in this matter. It seemed to me that Comrade "Lukács" understood right away what I was telling him and he immediately said that we can count on his help in everything, and he is very happy that we turned to him with such a request. He considers it a very great honor from the Party, and our news couldn't have pleased him more. He made it clear that before we discuss the details of his assignment, he wants to state that he intends to help us to the best of his abilities. After that I told him about the tasks in whose realization we are counting on him. I told him that through his regular job he hears lots of information of value to us and meets several individuals who might be of interest to us. After this, Comrade "Lukács" told me that he'd been passing on the most interesting articles that appeared in the French papers to Military Attaché Sárközi, and when necessary, he also translated them. I told Comrade "Lukács" that he should continue to translate news of a military nature for Comrade Sárközi, but that in the future all information of a political nature he should pass on to us, and that he must make no mention of his contact with us to anyone else, not even Comrade Sárközi.

With respect to the work ahead, Comrade "Lukács" brought up a couple of concerns. His first concern was that in the main, his present circle of acquaintances is made up of intellectuals and journalists who belong to the Party. After I told him that he must enlarge his circle of acquaintances to include non-Party intellectuals, he asked whether he won't get into trouble if he should make contact with vacillating individuals who cannot be fully trusted.

To this concern I answered that we cannot promise any sort of advantage to him for his work, but we can assure him that he cannot suffer any disadvantages either.

"Lukács's" next concern was that his present salary will not make it possible for him to do the work we require of him and to enlarge his circle of acquaintances.

I assured him that we will always cover his expenses with respect to the work he does for us and will do our best to help his finances in this regard as well.

At this point two pages are missing because, with an appeal to György Aranyossy's personal rights, the Historical Archives of the Hungarian State Security blanked them out. Sensitive material, the young woman working in the archives told me, a woman whose features were set in stone, a young, pale woman into whose care the Historical Archives in Eötvös Street had entrusted me. Her conduct was conspicuously hostile and dismissive, but I made a point of ignoring it. I asked her what would happen if she and the other staffers were to find the State Security files pertaining to me, which is why I'm actually here, and which they can't seem to find for the life of them, even though I'd found information in other people's files that clearly indicate the existence of my own. Would she also black out the personal information relating to me in these files in order to protect my personal rights, I asked.

Yes, she said, and her lashes didn't even quiver, yes, she must black out all personal information. From which it became painfully clear to me that they'd been watching me for decades, had opened and read my letters, and had attempted to derail my life from its appointed course; furthermore, their operatives had gone through my papers and manuscripts, leaving traces of what they'd done behind on purpose; they'd stolen letters with intimate content and other carefully guarded batches of papers off my desk, including a love letter from the red briefcase of the woman I loved; they'd also had people write anonymous letters and they engaged in spreading disinformation about me, and they are doing so to this day. I have no right to the information pertaining to me. They are continuing their activities in the third Hungarian Republic basically unscathed. They are laughing in my face and along with their high-handed ways will outlive me.

After a discussion of these concerns, I informed Comrade "Lukács" that Comrade "Modra" will be his liaison in the future, he will give him the orders from headquarters and he must report on the progress of his mission to him. Comrade "Lukács" was obviously pleased, he said that he liked Comrade "Modra" very much, and he was happy that with Comrade "Modra" there would now be two of them representing State Security in Paris. When our meeting ended, I told

Comrade "Lukács" that he must put the substance of our talk into writing. "Lukács" exhibited no sign of resistance, he merely asked that because of his poor knowledge of Hungarian, he be allowed to write his statement in French.

His case officer spoke French, and so the reports he wrote in French became a problem only after his case officer was given another assignment within the Security Service. On orders from the Service, Georges had to learn to write in Hungarian and was in fact grateful to the Service for it, and repeatedly mentioned his gratitude in his reports. He was promoted to secret agent and the Service changed his cover name to Imre Almádi, but because of his total inaptitude as an informer, on May 28, 1957, in the wake of a drawn-out conflict, he was discharged from the Service.

But to return to our story, at the juncture when Regent Miklós Horthy wanted to send Aranyossi to Moscow, the anomalies in the spelling of his name were not important. What was important was that the secret delegation should depart before the Russians crossed the country's frontier. Rátz or Rácz said that we could pass through the front lines in safety through the estate of a landowner close to Horthy, because it was situated near the border.

Aranyossi was willing to leave immediately, provided two of his conditions were met. Horthy must release the jailed Communists, for which twenty-four hours should be more than sufficient. The anti–Arrow Cross Rátz or the Protestant Rácz or a third Rácz told him to produce a list containing no more than thirty names.

You shall have the list.

He couldn't very well compile the list on his own, he first had to find his senior liaison, Pug Nose, but he couldn't very well tell Rátz or Rácz this.

There's no time, answered Rátz or Rácz, you must compile the list immediately. Meanwhile, let's hear your second condition.

Include Regent Horthy's son Miklós in the delegation.

I can't say who the other members of the delegation might have been, and my Aunt Magda couldn't answer the question either when at night I sat by her bed in my great-grandmother's armchair under her life-size portrait. Nor could she answer the question between June 2 and August 31, 1970, when the historians of the Party History Institute, who were her colleagues, plied her with questions on eight separate occasions about their former lives, then routinely filed the typed transcripts of the sessions in the institute's archives. The two stories, the one she related to me and the typed version, do not always coincide, while some of the details of both are clearly at variance with the details in my aunt's memoirs published in 1978 by Kossuth Kiadó. With respect to the variability of the truth, I consider what she told me in person the most reliable; after all, she had no reason to distort or censor her memories or to lie outright to me; on the contrary, she wanted to pass her real life on to me; she shared her experiences with me with a passion, and though I know what one is like with one's own memories, still, I trust my own memory, meaning my memory of what she told me, which I carefully round out with information from the Archives transcripts and her published memoirs, which in turn I use to check the accuracy of my own memories, and not merely in this one instance.

Why is it important, asked Rátz or Rácz.

Because otherwise the delegation may walk straight into a trap on the landowner's estate at the frontier.

At this, Rátz or Rácz pretended he didn't understand.

If they catch us and the Germans arrest the delegation, Horthy will wash his hands of us and tell the Germans that this is a Communist plot and they should do with us as they like, he has nothing to do with it. On the other hand, if his son is part of the delegation, Horthy must take full responsibility for the negotiations.

He can't give an answer on the spot, answered Rácz or Rátz, but I should take a slip of paper, compile the list of names of those the Regent should release.

My uncle succeeded in compiling from memory the names of thirty arrested men and women, and according to my aunt's recollections, the name of László Rajk, meaning Firtos, Fiertos in Spanish, which was also his code name in Kirghiz, stood at the head of the list. He and Aranyossi had been fellow prisoners at Le Vernet detention camp in the Pyrenees; in fact, it is more than likely that they made their escape together. My Aunt Magda told me that she helped them escape. Using the vocabulary of conspiracy, she said she helped them escape along with other comrades. But she would not say how or with whose help she helped him escape. What I mean is she furnished a detailed account of the circumstances of the escape, but said nothing about with whom, how, and why they organized it the way they did. When I insisted, she just laughed. She kept silence in line with the rules of the underground. They had to come back home on Party orders. She accomplished the task with other comrades. It doesn't matter who, I wouldn't know them anyway. On the other hand, there are several written versions of the escape story in which, according to my aunt, Pál Aranyossi escaped on his own from the internment camp at Les Milles, and in these there is no mention of László Rajk. And although there are a number of versions in circulation, I couldn't find reliable information about Rajk's escape either, whether he escaped on his own or was assisted. But if anyone reads the paranoia-infused materials of Rajk's show trial meant for the public along with the secret records and in them Rajk's confession pertaining to his stay at Le Vernet and how he cooperated there both with the Gestapo and the American Secret Service, it sheds light on how, at a given moment, two other versions of the story of my uncle's escape could have materialized that are not identical with the one my aunt told me. These versions had to distance Aranyossi as thoroughly as possible from Rajk and Noel Field, an American accused of spying for the CIA, and altogether from the camp at Le Vernet.

Be that as it may, Aranyossi and Horthy's secret agent agreed to meet within two hours at a certain place, I don't remember where. That would give Rátz or Rácz enough time to come back with his answer without jeopardizing their departure time. Aranyossi, too, needed time to inform Pug Nose about the list and obtain the Party's permission for the trip. Except he couldn't find Pug Nose anywhere in the city.

As for me, I can't begin to guess how this Rácz or Rátz could have found them in the first place, with or without Vilmos Lázár acting as a go-between, because, in line with Pug Nose's orders, they'd been out of their own apartment in Damjanich Street for months by then and were under strict orders not to go back to the apartment, where my mother and I were staying, for so much as a handkerchief. Day after day, they had to wander from one night's residence to another, using the forged documents made out in various assumed names, documents that thanks to the slew of new decrees went rapidly out of date. They had stayed with Oszkár Solt, they had stayed with Oszkár Orody, both of whom were Aranyossi's bohemian friends from the old days, although neither of them had anything to do with any sort of illegality or any movement; on the other hand, they were both physicians, bohemian and brave with a sense of social responsibility; next they stayed with the Lomboses on Garay Street, and also with Stefánia Sugár, István Dési Huber's widow, in the apartment on Ipar Street crowded floor to ceiling with the paintings by her husband and by Andor Sugár that she had inherited; in fact, by that time, Kata Sugár's photographs also had to be there, or at least, those of her photographs that she neglected to burn before she committed suicide. Decades later, I saw these photographs and contact prints myself in Stefi's apartment on Ipar Street. At the moment in question, the Aranyossis were staying in István Nádas's summer house on Testvérhegy above Óbuda, which, with survival in mind, my Uncle Pista, the Keeper of the Seal, had bought and remodeled nearly ten years previously. My uncle was a man of foresight. He had bought the plot from his own aunt Erzsébet Mezei, who owned great patches of wooded property in this area just outside of town, but when, during the Great Depression, the family's fortunes declined at an alarming pace, Záza sold off her woods. And then, when Aranyossi couldn't find his senior liaison even after several hours, whereas he'd looked in Semmelweis Street, the Casino, even City Hall, where there was a loosely organized yet effective resistance group among the staff, he had no choice, he had to tell his wife about what had happened, hoping she'd know where to find Pug Nose.

My Aunt Magda went out looking for him, and found him, too, because she had a security address where she could leave urgent messages.

Pug Nose, whose real name came to light only after the siege, shrugged when he heard out my aunt. Your husband can go on his own initiative, if he wants. My aunt, who spent her whole life attempting to control her tempestuous nature, which was really the tempestuousness of her father and grandfather and so on, now let fly at him.

In that case, she said quietly, her tone foreboding, nasal, as befits a lady to the manner born, but then she quite unexpectedly began shouting, in that case, kindly tell me. Since when have we done anything on our own initiative. Tell me that. Either Aranyossi receives his orders, in which case he'll go to Moscow with the delegation, or he does not receive his orders, in which case he will not go to Moscow with the delegation.

Whenever she put someone in his place, she blurred her *r*'s even more than usual; she spoke as if she were scolding a servant, and as we know, that's something that is just not done.

She never used that tone of voice with me, but having inherited an impressive store of it myself, I am all too familiar with it, and have also attempted to hold in check this inclination to scold, an inheritance from Grandfather Neumayer, all my life, and from time to time, I actually succeed. At other times, I let go on purpose. If I had a mind to, I could even count how many times.

Pug Nose had a round, friendly face, a gentle look in his eye, but his nose was in fact pug-shaped, which annoyed my aunt every time they met.

How could the comrades choose such a descriptive cover name. A descriptive cover name must never be obvious.

She should never have asked. The Party knew what it was doing. The Party was always right.

Though come to think of it, László Rajk also had a descriptive cover name. With his square jaws and narrow eyes, he could in fact just as well have been Kirghiz.

Accordingly, it is strange that in his memoirs György Markos says it was my aunt who'd come up with the Pug Nose cover name for him.

How could someone give her own superior contact his cover name, she asked.

And yet, it is more than likely, this is what happened. In which case, the version of the story that she told me does not agree with the version that György Markos committed to paper, nor with the version she herself wrote in her memoirs, thoroughly censored by her comrades though it would have been. In the book she writes that her senior liaison introduced himself as Karcsi Jászberényi, but between themselves, she and Gyuri Markos called him Pug Nose.

My aunt's lady to the manner born style did not surprise Pug Nose, who kept shrugging his shoulders, which according to my aunt's upbringing was just not done, and she lost no time in telling him, don't you shrug your round shoulders at me, do you hear, which, considering the way she rolled her *r*'s, must have been a source of amusement.

With surprising candor Pug Nose told my aunt that he was indifferent to her news and unwarranted indignation because a similar delegation had already crossed the border (we now know that it was led by Colonel-General Gábor Faragho, and the Communist in the delegation was a certain Imre Faust, the respected publisher of the journal *Kelet Népe*, and they were already in Moscow, which means that Pug Nose must have passed this information on to my Aunt Magda on October 6 or 7, because the delegation had arrived on October 5), and things being the way they were, he couldn't imagine why Horthy would want to send yet another delegation after them. But if they're really going, Aranyossi should go with them.

Rátz or Rácz came to the meeting in the Inner City bearing the message that Aranyossi's first condition would be met but he must write another name at the top, because Rajk can't be on the list.

Why on earth not, my uncle retorted, hardly able to control his rage.

Because Rajk has been released.

Which is how Dr. Emil Weil ended up at the top of the list.

On the other hand, he can't answer Aranyossi's second condition at the moment, said Rácz or Rátz at this afternoon meeting, but in any event, he should ready himself for the trip. The political prisoners he'd named would be freed within hours.

It was logical that the senior liaison had to be informed of everything under all circumstances, while the junior liaison knew only what concerned him directly. This way, should someone be caught, the circle of those who might have squealed on them remained relatively intact. This way, the network could be controlled and, if need be, the individuals who fell under suspicion could be split off from the hierarchy of the movement. The splitting off had to be done posthaste. The viability of the network was at stake. This expression, split off, which was part of movement jargon, could at times signify something fatal, they never said what, but in some instances, even murder. This exceptional action was expressed in the plural, we saw to him. Or in its other version, the boys saw to him. In her nightly monologues, my aunt repeatedly used both variations of the verb. The verb carried such a psychological punch that even I could imagine as, under cover of night, the boys saw to the traitor, the murder becoming the collective object of their pride. It was the Party that had effectuated it, and not they personally. And as I discovered in her confession stored in the Political History Archives, my aunt also used the fatal plural, we saw to him, in connection with Marcel Gitton, a well-known French Communist. My aunt gave it in writing, she gave it in her own hand.

After the German-Russian pact had been signed, Gitton, who had originally belonged to the extreme left wing of the Party and who was in contact with the Aranyossis after they went to live in Paris, followed the lead of the other disillusioned comrades and in his anger turned his back on the French Communist Party. He had earlier been a representative of the Party at the National Assembly, and the inspection of the Communist unions was in his purview. Along with Léon Blum's socialists, he and Thorez founded the anti-fascist popular front, the Front Populaire. According to my aunt, during the German occupation, it came to light that Gitton was working for the police. The plural verb phrase familiar to me from her late-night narratives is there in her own handwriting, on the last page of the transcript of the confession she gave on July 17, 1970. Then the comrades saw to him. Before signing this latest testimony she gave of her life in the movement, she felt it incumbent upon herself to do this, to add this information in her own hand.

Today we know that everything happened the other way around. His own comrades accused Gitton of being an informer in order to give them a reason to assassinate him.

In his outrage over the German-Soviet Nonaggression Pact, Gitton had indeed gone to extremes when he turned against the Communists; he cooperated with Jacques Doriot's fascist movement, the Parti Populaire Française, and was a regular contributor to the movement's paper, *Le Cri du Peuple*. But he was not an informer. I feel it incumbent upon myself to mention here that before he joined the fascists, Doriot had also been a Communist, and in fact came from the highest echelon of the French Communist Party. Gitton was killed by his comrades on September 5, 1941, in German-occupied Paris, on the corner of the rue des Lilas and the rue de Bellevue. We also know that he was assassinated in broad daylight by Marcel Cretagne, who, as a member of the action group, bore the code name Focardi. Gitton's assassins may or may not have known, but it is typical of the dramaturgy of the movement that a couple of days before his assassination, Marcel Gitton had saved Jacques Duclos, General Secretary of the French Communist Party who had taken over for Thorez, then living in hiding, from being exposed, which would have meant certain death, and he did so despite the fact that he had resolutely turned his back on the Party two years earlier.

On that fatal Saturday in November 1944 when the Margaret Bridge collapsed, down in the bowels of the two-level basement my father and the others lived through some dramatic moments. They adhered to a strict schedule. Magda Róna, whom all my life I called Auntie Duci, had just finished making lunch for them down there, but hadn't yet called them to the table. She improved the leftover flour with cornstarch, added water, and was just cooking the flat cakes on the small stove. They still had some preserved vegetables and meat, but they had to use them sparingly, if for no other reason than because some of the preserves were made by István Nádas using his own methods of conserving food, and not all his methods proved equally felicitous. Some of the food he preserved did not actually go stale, but because of the pungent flavor or odor of the preservatives, it was highly unpalatable. Still, *Für alle Fälle*, they put these carefully aside for an emergency. In keeping with their daily schedule, my Uncle István and my father were just busying themselves forging documents in the upper level of the basement, where they had a carefully stocked small cabinet. They had to clean and iron the documents making sure that the paper wouldn't thin out where it had been chemically cleansed of writing, nor wrinkle in response to the various liquids. Members of the Arrow Cross and the police who had been specially trained to recognize fake documents held them up to the light and could spot the clumsier efforts with ease. Their uncompromising sense of precision made my father and his older brother eminently suited for this delicate task. Meanwhile, all the pipes of the huge building complex trembled repeatedly in the wake of the explosion. They were afraid that the pipes would burst and the water would flood the basement, or else the sewage water or the gas, or all three at once. For a moment the light actually went out. They were afraid that fire would break out, because the electric cables in the walls had been damaged. They expected another explosion, but only the ground trembled, and with it trembled, creaked, and rattled the huge building complex.

Thanks to their foreign sound, *pontoon*, *razzia*, and *sabotage* may have been the first foreign words I could actually remember and comprehend. But by the time I learned what it meant, even *Brückenkopf* was already familiar to me from war films. *Der Brückenkopf, der Brückenkopf*, the bridgehead, the fleeing Nazis shouted to one another as they leaped on their motorcycles with sidecars. At the age of four I was already mesmerized by certain words, sounds, and gestures, the sight of the rushing river, the speed of the mighty mass of the thick yellowish gray emulsion, its mighty strength as it swept everything along. This everything, my own little everything, swept me along and took hold of my imagination forever, not mimetically, but empathically. It wasn't I that took possession of the words, the information, the emotions or phenomena, it was the other way around, the words and the phenomena took hold of me. They fenced me in, they devoured me, they absorbed me, and I let them, I let them do it, they could devour me whenever they wished, this was how they penetrated my faculty of comprehension. If I had one, if I have one, in those moments they freed me of my ego. Information that came through other channels I couldn't make heads or tails of, I couldn't comprehend.

Surely, I must be slightly autistic, except for a long time, a very long time, until the threshold of old age, I didn't realize it. I ignored the fact that the character of my apprehension differs from that of others.

The experience of the loss of the self was mind-boggling. A person's ego, meaning the sum total of his characteristics, is like the slightly cool, thin layer of earth under which there smolders and rumbles the pure, physical realm of magma.

This is no longer the person, but his physicality.

Which more than suffices to occupy a child. The icy depths hid the dead, the dead of the quay and the dead of the bridge, and I knew this, too. I was the icy river and its dizzying current, the swelling water as it engulfed me. For decades to come, I didn't understand that I wasn't the dead of the icy depths. On the other hand, I knew that relentlessly rolling along, the Danube runs down to the sea, and that the sea is a huge body of water, it reaches as far as the eye can see, even farther than that, that's how big it is. It's where the seagulls come from. For a long time, a very long time, I wanted just one thing, to see the ocean. As my parents and I stood by the rails on Újpest Quay disfigured by shrapnel from land mines, they showed me where it was and how immense it was. It must have been something amusing, because as they showed me how big it was, making circles with their arms, it's this big, they couldn't stop laughing, and I couldn't help but laugh along with them.

And it was indeed a miracle when years later I saw the sea for the first time. Leaving the others behind, I walked on and on over pathless paths in the wake of the sound. Whereas I had never heard the sound before, I knew that this was the sound of the sea, the sound of the waves as they crashed against the shore. I hadn't even seen a film with the sea in it. On the other hand, Yvette, my cousin Georges's daughter, had told me about their summer vacations many times. For her, the word for vacation, *vacances*, meant the sea. I sank ankle deep in the sand among the dunes, every step exacting more and more effort, and though I heard the sound of the sea as I approached and for the first time in my life felt its scent in my nostrils, and the gentle breeze, too, yet it was nowhere to be seen. Good Lord, where is the sea. At the age of seventeen, I ran toward it, and before I realized, I was standing in the water with my shoes on, frantic with joy. I'm standing in the sea. The next instant the water crashed against my waist and then I felt the salty spray on my lips. And then, in the pretty little Polish seaside resort of Międzyzdroje that the Germans call Misdroy, in the milky-white morning fog, for the first time in my life I saw, or rather, for the first time in my life, I did not see the sea.

With its quaint seaside promenade, quaint pier, and wooden-porticoed villas, with all the pompous stylistic hallmarks of the *Gründerzeit*, the German fin de siècle, the small town survived the war relatively unscathed. The salty fog dispersed only an hour later. On each and every blessed summer's day, it dispersed at precisely ten thirty, and even then not in a way to draw attention to itself. Until the day I die, or even beyond, this meteorological phenomenon, the fog as it lifts, is transformed in my mind into the sensation of the suntanned body of a woman, the light imprint of her two-piece bathing suit covering her lap and her breasts. Being autistic, I sense the outside world in terms of images rather than concepts. The words accompanying the concepts I understand only years later, or not at all, words that other people understand immediately. With the sea and the lifting fog, it was all like a backdrop to a theatrical performance in which I was participating as more than a mere viewer. A cool body, it emitted soft sounds, it moaned, and it had as much scent to it as it had retained from the day before. This Polish woman, Danuta, whose family name, despite my best efforts, I can't recall, although I've looked among my old letters and papers, she was as lively as a loach, cheerful, shrill, slim, sunburned, irresistible, though at the time I knew nothing about this, nothing at all, nothing about this irresistible, about the unexpected lack of my own resistance, in short, wherever she went, she took the grains of sand stuck to her skin along with her, and actually, with her short blond hair and small breasts there was something boyish about her, everything around her having taken on a grating quality from the sand, an office girl from Warsaw on holiday with her lazy girlfriend, probably slightly mad, high-strung, and her lazy girlfriend wasn't all that sane herself, and before I realized, I was doing something I had no intention of doing, and next thing I knew, she was part of my life. I don't know how they came to be there. The house belonged to a friend of a friend. She spoke rapidly, mixing French with German. At ten thirty, when the fog lifted every day, in the well-appointed German room where the sand-strewn floor creaked under our feet and we were surrounded by the objects of piety left over from previous German vacations, she initiated me into the physics of emotion-free love. Standing by the window, our bodies went in search of the interlocking points of contact. Nothing else, just the interlocking points of contact. Her willingness to help was just like her, a cool yet cheerful operation that a lady surgeon was conducting on me. The Creator might have seen us through the window, but surely, no one else. Out of the blue, I now remember her family name, but I'm protectively stuffing it back in its place all the same, relegating it to oblivion. And suddenly the fog had lifted, and there was the glistening sea. I was glad that we'd done it, because if I wanted to be a writer, I had to find out why others consider this certain act so interesting, seeing how I couldn't understand either myself or her, or why I'm feeling as proud as a peacock, which disturbed and unsettled me. Then out of the blue Danuta dropped me for another boy slightly older than I, and let's admit it, far better-looking, too. It hurt, even though I couldn't help but approve of what she'd done. I'd have done the same in her place. It took just a couple of days, and I interiorized her whole being and could see others through her eyes. Something hurt that I didn't know existed and that it could hurt like this. Which had nothing to do with her. It was the loss that hurt. The loss that had nothing to do with her.

I kept my eyes open. I wanted to discover which visible or invisible aspect of physical love she appreciated the most in him. This boy, perhaps two years older than I, slept right near me, our beds were two arms' lengths apart, no more, and I'd have liked to see him naked, to find out what advantage his nose, his skin, his limbs, his muscles, his movements, the waves in his hair had over me. I wasn't interested in comparative physiology, I was scrutinizing him through the eyes of Danuta, who by all odds scrutinized nothing, or was impressed by one thing or another only on occasion. At which point a trapdoor sprang open, and had I accidentally fallen into it, I'd have remembered one of the definitive erotic experiences of my early childhood. But I didn't remember it, I didn't remember the trap, and so I couldn't very well remember my early childhood either. For years, possibly decades, everything remained unexplained.

I waited impatiently for the older boy to come back from Danuta. If in the middle of the night or in the early hours of the morning I was startled awake, thinking he was back, he'd come back after all, he fell into bed in his clothes on; he kicked off his underpants just once in the early morning glimmer, but then he stood with his back to me. All I could see was that he was white as snow. A white, silent boy. He carried a weight even greater than mine. He kept to himself, though I noticed that he didn't look at the girls with the same belligerence as he looked at the boys. But as a rule, he didn't answer the girls either when they asked him something, he looked right through them; he thought they were morons, dimwits, and in this he was mostly right. On this summer, possibly the last summer of their girlhood, these girls, who were studying art in vocational school, were indeed absurd. They were always ironing, rearranging their clothes on their hangers and shelves, fussing about, exchanging dresses, polishing their nails and combing one another's hair; they were wholly taken up with their ridiculous appearance. Which amused me, and I ironed along with them, arranged their curls, and helped dress their hair in rollers. Seeing how I'm underfoot, I might as well help them with their rollers and curling irons. This boy played handball and basketball, he was nimble on his feet and never once did I hear him shout. He was going to be a glassblower. Nothing ever agitated him, nothing frightened him, though nothing excited him either, for that matter.

When two weeks later we ran into each other on the pier, Danuta called to me. She was standing among the screeching seagulls with this more prepossessing, silent boy, with whom she couldn't exchange a single word because he couldn't even speak Russian. They were standing there intertwined, knee between knee, their fingers interlaced. She was leaving tomorrow, she shouted to me in the seaside wind, and she'd give me her address. But she never did. On the other hand, she wrote to me once, possibly half in German, possibly half in French, but as far as I can remember, she didn't give me her address, it wasn't even on the envelope. I looked for her letter, I am looking for her letter now, too, but I can't find it, whereas I remember keeping it, or possibly I just meant to keep it.

When after the siege, as I clung to my father's or mother's or some other grown-up's hand and attended to the excitement and gestures of the men and women who were just then lowering their voices or, on the contrary, were shouting to each other over the din, and I listened, frightened, to the erupting shouts that cut into the sweep of their sentences, I became as excited as they. The excitement made me happy, its dangerous current swept me along. They had no idea why I was shouting and acting berserk at their feet. This excitement was awkward all around, but it was most awkward for me, I just wanted them to know that I was excited because of them. Wallowing in their discarded excitement. Which didn't belong to me. Still, I didn't dare ask them what happened to the dead under the water. Their strange excitement made me uneasy. There were questions I wouldn't have dared to ask, and this torments me to this day, as if they could have given me the answer to things that because of my negligence or timidity I dared not ask. Perhaps, when a person asks or neglects to ask, he is looking for his own pace, and it is already a success of sorts if he fails to find his own pace in others because, after all, they are too fast or too slow compared with him, too daring or else more timid and distant than he.

I stopped worrying about such things only when I could sit perched on the lookout, around my father's neck. That's what he called it. I liked that word, *lookout*. He held my feet, I held his ears, afraid I might tear them off, or else I wrapped my arms around his neck; I preferred wrapping my arms around his neck, but in either case, it was up to me to keep my balance. Being around his neck had its risks; if he were to let go of my feet, I might fall backward, and so I held on even tighter, and my fear was not unfounded, for now and then he'd unwittingly release his hold on my ankle or the tip of my shoe as he grabbed something with one hand or shook someone's hand, for instance. But sometimes he'd let go on purpose, so I'd feel the weight of my own responsibility. But it was a majestic position all the same, gazing at the world from a lookout, it was worth the risk. Once we walked up to the Jánoshegy lookout like this, which was one of the greatest events of my life. The lookout stood on top of the hill. We were standing on top of the lookout, but sitting around his neck, I was even taller than the lookout. Seen from up there everything took on a different aspect, the quay, the balustrade of the bridge, and the water, too, looked different, it was more exciting than being with the people below noisily going about their lives or being in the river with the ice-cold dead. Sometimes as we walked along I would yell at their feet, but they didn't understand, I failed to reach them with my emotions, while they looked indignantly down at me, why was I interrupting, whereas I just wanted them to know that I was there. This happened when I couldn't keep up with them in their strange excitement anymore, the cup ran over for good, this is what I felt, that I must take leave of them for good, to politely indicate to them that I would now leave their circle, to indicate in some manner that I must now cast them out of myself one way or another, and tooth and nail, protect myself against the nauseating strangeness of their presence inside me. One of my recurring dreams contains the metaphor of this unavailing struggle, the vast expanse of stone along the riverbank stinking of urine and excrement, and me, holding on to the rubble, desperate not to fall behind, not to slip away from them, whereas I'd already fallen behind, fatally, I could feel myself slipping away, I've slipped away, all the time that with their unending chatter they're burdening my intellectual faculties beyond despair, the vowels and fragments merging, and I can't make sense of it, and I am slowly slipping back along the sharp edges of the stones and the edges of their vowels, and suddenly the pathways are deserted, they have left me to my own devices. The feeling produced by the dream sequence or the daydream got stuck inside me in the shape of the ever-present threat and nagging anxiety that they would now never again reach out to me, but leave me to my fate in the stench among the ruins.

This was the riverbank in Buda, the other side, where for lack of understanding or comprehension a person finds himself in a flash an easy prey for death.

Also, it was interesting for me to realize that the excitement often referred to something or someone of whom or of what I had no previous knowledge and couldn't have had previous knowledge, and as for my newly acquired knowledge, I had no place to deposit it, nor did I have the time, because the next bit of knowledge was already elbowing it aside. Once the question had been raised, namely, whose interest it served to blow up the Margaret Bridge and why they did it, there was no skirting the issue, because you either stepped over it or tripped over it, to wit, is there or could there conceivably be an interest or conspiracy that causes greater damage than the amount of good it brings to the conspirators, the Arrow Cross, the Communists, the Germans, the Zionists, or what have you. Who is led by what calculation of proportionality. The question was not theoretical. I actually saw the foot of destruction as it trips over, steps on, or passes over us. I can still see the foot, it originated with an early daydream that has persisted in my mind as the explanation for the visual link between death and destruction, intention and outcome. The foot heads in one direction but lands in another. Destruction wore men's shoes. Destruction wore handmade shoes with toe caps, yellow, I can clearly see before me that former image of a gentleman's shoes, and not the ankle boots that we wore during the siege and in the years to follow, practically all of us. You couldn't make your way among the ruins any other way. Everyone wore ankle boots or at least lace-ups, and even those ladies of breeding who didn't own long pants and ankle boots, not even sturdier shoes, pulled on all sorts of thick knotted knee-highs over their silk or cotton stockings.

If they didn't understand something, then in their excitement people would start yelling, come now, that's really too much, you're taking too many liberties, my good woman. The person in question had gone too far yet again, or as they put it, she plucked the strings too heatedly. I had a small bow, I had small arrows, all made of colonial reed, but I was not allowed to aim at any living thing, and so it scared me. Beautiful shoes, though, were another matter. My grandfather had a fine pair of made-to-order yellow gentleman's shoes, but I never saw him wear them. Whenever he had an important meeting, which by all accounts meant that he was going abroad and using great-grandfather's expensive suitcase to pack his things, my father would ask to borrow these shoes. Grandfather Tauber had inherited all of his finer belongings, vested suits, coats, hats, and shoes, from the wardrobe of his sister's fabulously wealthy husband. I liked this fabulous wealth, too, riches making someone fabulous. What fabulous tits, people said. This fabulously wealthy man owned the jewelry shop on Dohány Street, as well as the workshop on Holló Street.

As for me, I had a small pair of Bata ankle boots. The small ankle boots were the spitting image of the big ankle boots the grown-ups wore, their exact likeness. In the indistinct times before the siege, Bata may have been the be-all and end-all in shoes and ankle boots. My small pair of Bata ankle boots were too big for me, so I wore them with several layers of heavy socks. I was especially proud that I had inherited this pair of small Bata ankle boots, just like my grandfather, who had inherited all his best clothes from Janka's husband, his fabulously wealthy brother-in-law. The happiness lasted as long as a pair of heavy socks fit into it and we didn't have to pass it on to Márta. This passing on was a great loss; I can safely say that it was the loss of a lifetime. I knew that it should have made me feel good, because it should have made me feel fabulously wealthy, but it didn't feel good at all.

Having to pass those boots on taught me the meaning of the word *loss*. It made me realize, for the first time, that some objects do not last forever, or else their everlasting life can shift outside my field of vision. Whereas I just grew out of them. For long years to come I pondered how I might have avoided growing out of my small Bata ankle boots or, to put it another way, whether there's a guarantee for eternity. How can I stay small for my small ankle boots when I want to grow big, as big as those others, the grown-ups around me. Maybe we could have cut off the toe of my small ankle boots. Or if I'd been more disciplined. If I hadn't complained that it's pressing on my big toe, it's rubbing my heels, they wouldn't have deprived me of those boots and they wouldn't have passed them on to my cousin Márta.

I couldn't imagine, for the life of me I couldn't imagine what was to become of me without my small Bata ankle boots.

The truth of the matter is that Raoul Wallenberg yelled at anyone who wasn't wearing ankle boots of some sort, and I knew that. Surely, this knowledge was among the earliest bits of knowledge in my own little universe, like this, bound up with the name of the Swedish diplomat Raoul Wallenberg. His name and his orders were perhaps the first absolutes, a practical warning of a type that has not been refuted to this day. The name of the other great savior of the people of Budapest, the Swedish-born Carl Lutz, stuck to this knowledge like an outer shell, and so, for the rest of my life, the thought of Switzerland became inseparable from his name, just as the thought of Sweden became inseparable from Wallenberg's. Consequently, when I first learned that my great-grandfather Mezei had a special fondness for summering in the mountains of Switzerland, his decision made full sense to me; after all, all the forged as well as bona fide letters of safe conduct had come from there. They can't very well save people in patent leather shoes. My parents had said this or, come to think of it, it was my resolutely anticapitalist mother who had said it. Which gave poor patent leather shoes an irrevocably pejorative cast. And so I was later surprised by the matter-of-fact way Géza Ottlik used these three words, *patent leather shoes*, in the short stories he'd written before the siege. As if history had no effect on his patent leather shoes, and as if he doesn't use the concept to signify a social class; if anything, it signifies the frivolity of youth, a young man heading off to a dance or a game of cards. After all, what else can he do when the world around him is in flames. In the evening, the hero puts on his patent leather shoes, it's as simple as that. What else could he do. It never once occurs to Ottlik that patent leather shoes might be the polar opposite of ankle boots. Still, in the short stories he wrote after the siege, he no longer mentions patent leather shoes. They belonged to the past. Mándy, the master conjurer of the language of Budapest, would have said, a pair of patent leathers, what an idea. What was he thinking of. Or if anybody in the city had patent leather shoes, he had to keep them under lock and key, because only wicked imperialists and people who hid or hoarded illegal amounts of merchandise wore patent leather shoes. On the other hand, even the most inveterate imperialists and black marketers wouldn't have wanted to appear evil and imperialist in other people's eyes, and so they didn't wear patent leather shoes in public either. Nevertheless, when I was twenty-something, though closer to thirty, I gave way to my subversive leanings and, flying in the face of the universal condemnation of polish, lacquering, decorating and decoration of all kinds, in short, the condemnation of frivolous appearance, I bought myself a pair of black patent leather shoes that I spotted in a dusty shopwindow in Pest. I was poorer than any proletarian, poorer even than a church mouse, but I bought them because, although I wouldn't wear them, it gave me a chance to luxuriate in my admittedly linguistic resistance; it was my chance of flying, with the symbolic redefinition of words, in the face of my own historically determined knowledge and attendant outlook.

Today I say that I did the right thing. In the interest of better understanding, I had to rise up against the well-oiled contents of my own consciousness.

But two years after the siege, my greatest concern was still how, if anything happened, I could be saved without my ankle boots. I couldn't. Without ankle boots I'm exposed to danger, I'm putting my life on the line. During the last days of the siege, the Russians dragged Wallenberg off from Budapest so they could kill him in Moscow or somewhere in the Gulag, and we still don't know why they did this or when, perhaps it was just the historical routine of killing; and as for me, for decades to come, I felt anxious if I didn't have a pair of ankle boots, because, without them, how would I be saved, whereas when, at the age of twenty-nine, in rebellion against my own consciousness I bought that wretched pair of patent leather shoes, it was clear as day that my survival had no value or meaning whatsoever. By then, the question that had been nagging at me for years was not whether it might not be better to kill myself, the question was where and in what manner I should go about it. With these nearly three decades weighing on me, it also became clear to me that there is no reason motivating the elemental urge to survive. It is situated outside the system of causality, while the urge for suicide functions within the system of causality. Suicide is determinism's final argument. This is how we lived on within the short circuit of determinism with Wallenberg's dictates.

Buy, acquire, get ahold of a pair of ankle boots for yourself. If you don't, then *kann ich Ihnen sicher nicht helfen, gnädige Frau*, there's nothing I can do about it, dear Lady.

I waited impatiently for the older boy to come back from Danuta. The pain I felt and whose source I could not understand kept me from remembering his name. But this was the hidden substance of the science of physics, the fact that the boy stayed away for the night. With me, Danuta didn't do this. She just sent her girlfriend off and gave me part of her sober mornings until the fog lifted, because we then hurried off *au plage pour baigner*. We left the unsavory remains of breakfast out on the veranda table.

And next thing I knew, there I stood, in October 1956, smack in the middle of the revolutionary upheaval, without ankle boots. Because much before that, perhaps in '54, I grew out of my hiking boots, which I was given to replace my excellent small Bata ankle boots. Though, truth to tell, by then we didn't go hiking anymore. My mother was dying, she knew she would die, I knew she would die, everyone knew, though for our sake she pretended, poor dear, that she was getting better. See, I'm getting better. I didn't have my ankle boots by then. I will get better soon, she kept saying as we left her hospital bed, but so softly, you'd think she was revealing some great secret, just for my sake. But I saw that she would not get better now, except at the time

I didn't know what would follow. Your troubles continue to prey on your mind. There I stood in January 1957, on Lipót Boulevard, which had been shot to bits once again, on a long line in front of a shoe shop, its display window partly boarded up, because they had ankle boots for sale, what luck, so now I'll have ankle boots again. The line stretched around the corner from Sólyom Street. I hated standing on line. Anything might happen on a line, horrible things happened between people on lines; besides, by then I'd spent years standing on lines. I stood on line for flour, I stood on line for coal, wood, sugar, milk, butter, and of course bread, and also cooking oil, and I stood on line for yeast, because my grandmother said she had flour, and if only she had yeast, she could bake something; I stood on line for potatoes, I even stood on line for watermelon, without a second thought, because my grandparents wanted watermelon. Why must they eat watermelon, of all things. I stood on line, fuming inside, why, why, why.

In the summer of 1952 the heat was relentless, the drought devastating, but the watermelon thrived, the only thing that thrived; it stood in huge mounds, and it was sweet as honey. I didn't understand this either, this sweet as honey.

Unless they're his own, the mature human animal shows no mercy to the children standing on line. He elbows them, he shoves them out of the way; after all, he has it easy with them, and meanwhile he even yells at them and berates them, he casts aspersions on them, and on occasion even strikes them. When it comes to judging human nature, neither Zola nor Dickens was mistaken or had overstated his case.

I didn't have ankle boots. Years later, in preparation for an illegal border crossing, Miki, an older friend of mine, took the very fine ankle boots I'd bought in Sólyom Street from my wardrobe, or possibly the ones I bought next. He also took the tote bag I used when I went to the Lukács Baths for a swim, and he also took the small calfskin suitcase I'd inherited from my great-grandfather. I also had a small vulcanized fiber suitcase that we called the volcanic fever suitcase, but that's not the one he took, damn him, and he also took the two most fashionable pieces of clothing I owned, my black shirt and my black tube trousers, the indispensable pieces in which I went for the five o'clock tea dance with Erika Delikát at the gentile Astoria or the noisy and profoundly plebeian Emke Café, where the men frequently came to blows over the women. Before that he'd taken my pointy gray shoes that went with my gray slacks, and after a couple of weeks he wore them down so badly with his crippled feet that I couldn't have worn them again. He later remembered only the tote bag, and he seriously thought that I was mad at him because of a tote bag. I didn't argue the point. Truth to tell, from all the ironing and wear, from all the five o'clock teas and dances, the seat and knees of the black tube pants I'd had to wriggle my way into were shiny with wear by the time he took them.

Anyway, because of Miki's stupid flight, there I stood again, without a pair of ankle boots to call my own.

But I wasn't mad at him because of the boots. After all, I knew what he was up to, it was clear as day. He'd already made two unsuccessful attempts, and there were plenty of signs to indicate that he'd try to get out of this prison, our homeland, again, the idiot. He was obsessed. As chance would have it, he met a Viennese girl who came from a wealthy family, he began courting her, he was determined, not so much because of the girl, but because she marked out a direction for him in which to proceed. This cheerful freckled girl was going to save his life. Which was understandable back then and is understandable now. Yet despite all my friendly feelings and best wishes, I couldn't stomach the fact that he had bound his intention to a single living being. He was learning German as well as English so they could correspond, and also so he could make his way in the big wide world.

I wasn't mad at him because he was leaving the country either, because he didn't let me in on his plan. His disappearance came as a surprise. I was actually grateful that he hadn't burdened me with the details of his planned escape. The country's borders were hermetically sealed all around, and those who were caught attempting to cross the border illegally were apprehended, beaten, and sentenced, or worse, were shot as they attempted to make their escape. Miki was just eight when he found himself alone. His father was a bookseller in Orosháza, where he'd bought Nina Pless's bookshop. Like all the booksellers at the time, he also sold paper goods, because you couldn't make a living in the countryside from just selling books. His mother had gone up to Pest, suspecting nothing, when in April 1944 decree 1.270 M.E. came into effect, restricting Jewish travel. It stipulated that a Jew who was obliged to wear the yellow star may not use a private automobile either for travel or for transporting goods and may not travel either on passenger or limited-passenger trains, nor ships equipped for public transportation, nor on buses used for public transportation. Considering that Jews living in the countryside had to be barred from travel to make their herding into the ghettos easier, to be conveyed from there to labor camps and extermination camps, this administrative decree made a lot of sense. Miki never saw his mother again, and when, as a survivor, he thought about her, he failed to conjure her image.

I had it easier, because my memory did not delete my mother, neither her gestures nor her words, nor her figure. Sometimes I saw her on the street and I took off after her. I saw her on the street too often, and it took far too long until I stopped seeing her. One summer, I must have been twenty or so by then, it was a gloomy, cloudy day, I was walking along Üllői Street not far from the clinic where nearly ten years before she had died behind a second-floor window, except I was walking along the opposite side of the street in front of the Institute of Pathology where the sidewalk widens, and that's when I saw her. I ran after her as fast as my feet would carry me, so that this time she wouldn't get away. But it wasn't her once again, it was someone who looked nothing like her. Which was the last time I saw her in the flesh.

They set up the ghetto in Orosháza on two premises of a timber merchant called Dér on May 10, writes Randolph L. Braham, the noted researcher of the attempt to annihilate the Jews of Hungary. Miki knew both lumberyards, but didn't understand what was happening. He also knew Dér. They were herded into Dér's lumberyard in front of the eyes of the people of Orosháza. Besides the Jews of Orosháza, they also brought there the Jews of Gádoros, Pusztaföld-vár, and Szentetornya, nearly six hundred people in all. In line with

Eichmann's conception, a committee of five Jews was appointed to oversee the ghetto. This conception had its rationale. Responsibility was conferred on the Jews at a time when, in the interest of establishing a thousand-year empire, the very notion of responsibility and the bearing of office had been suspended. This was why it could be transferred to the Jews.

Miki marched into the Orosháza ghetto in short pants and sandals, and since his father didn't think that a state of emergency such as this could last very long and, besides, must have been a foolish man, he didn't pack warm clothing and proper shoes for his son. They could not leave the ghetto without permission, but a couple of days later the gendarmes, who'd known him for a long time, let Dér senior out so he could bring some warm things for his son. Especially blankets. The nights were cold. He found the house empty, they'd broken in and ransacked it. Whoever they were, they had taken everything, all the underwear, all the furniture, all the blankets, all the pictures, all the nails from the walls, and also the upright piano. They left only an armchair, who knows why. All the same, any mother worth her salt would have found warm clothing in that damned fucking Orosháza. Miki had no long pants until April of the following year and apart from his one pair of sandals, he had nothing else on his feet. It was a terrible winter. If he could get ahold of it, he swathed his feet in newspaper and bound them with string.

The foot wearing the handmade yellow shoe stepped over me the way we stepped over the corpses on Újpest Quay in the snow. Anyone wanting to get from here to there or from there to here, something that in wartime everyone hopes will ensure their survival, has no alternative but to step over corpses. It was as simple as that.

Miki was deported to the concentration camp at Strasshof, and had he known that as soon as they arrived in Auschwitz the others were immediately sent to the gas chambers, he could have felt himself lucky at the age of eight.

I have always been particular about the aesthetic quality of men's shoes and have taken care to wear the best, but my real interest has always been women's shoes, and it still is. A feel for shoes is a very peculiar thing, a true mystery. It is as rare as an opera singer's gift. Of the women I know, I can think only of Gitta Esterházy and Karin Graf who have a feel for shoes. If I so much as look at them to see what they're wearing on their feet this time, my knees buckle under from the onrush of joy that shifts back and forth between the erotic and the aesthetic. The women's ankle-high tie-ups that some women wore as a substitute for ankle boots had slightly elevated heels, and this sufficed to make me happy. Watching them walk in those elevated heels. In their pumps and the wedges that were in vogue at the time, they went to extremes, they wobbled and swayed, and I loved it, I worshipped their affectation. I couldn't get enough of it. You're going too far, dear madam. The way they're putting on airs, dousing themselves with perfume, the way, all tricked out, they hold their noses up in the air. I adored the affectatious nasal sounds of the ladies of Pest and Buda, especially when they were engaged in running one another down. Seeing, touching, and smelling the primal, animal scent of the leather, the maddeningly soft and silky leather linings, slipping my foot inside a shoe recently abandoned by their feet, immersing myself in their silk-stockinged being, and in imitation of their feminine movements, rising up high on this wondrous buskin. To be higher. Not just a lady but an honorable lady, not just an honorable lady but a right honorable lady, not just a right honorable lady but a gracious lady, and so on, your eminence, your majesty, your holiness. I wanted to be a woman. Or the Pope. Of the men I know, only Richard Swartz has a feel for shoes, and wouldn't you know, his grandfather manufactured shoes, even though there may not be a causal relationship between the two things, a feel for shoes and their manufacture. I was convinced that being a woman is of a higher order, my own calling is to be a woman. To turn into a woman. I studied books to see what I needed to be like a woman. And only decades later did I realize for the first time how, with his constant make-believe and primping the little boy called Péter that I was or became or am with my feel for shoes must have seemed in the circle of grown-ups. Good Lord, given my natural playfulness, how I must have differed from everyone else in the family. Needless to say, I had to curb the mimesis because of them. They looked askance at what I was up to, they whispered behind my back. It took a decade and a half before I understood the reason for their apprehension, the thing they were afraid to discover in me. Of course, my bent for mime had nothing to do with femininity or masculinity, it had nothing to do with the social injunctions about the dual exclusivity of gender identity, the thing that, sensing the malleability of its borders, people are most ready to protect; it had to do solely with empathy. I needed the mimesis in the interest of my empathy, and because of my propensity for mimesis, I needed to give myself over to something that is obviously not me, to experience something, to understand something that I don't understand, and be capable of something for which I lack the physical and hormonal requisites, to find the path leading to it, to go in its wake and identify with it, to be prepared, to be prepared for freedom, to step over and across, to go one better. With two lost world wars, with the stench of corpses in my nostrils, how could I have not thought of the feminine as something of a higher order, and if need be, to find the most preposterous version, so I could stretch the limits of my perception and understanding; in the years following the times of devastation, this was and has remained the essence of my gnostic passion. Political freedom is merely a subcategory of the universal yearning for freedom.

In the months following the siege, the streets of Pest were steadily crowded with people, the pedestrian bridges, the boulevards all jam-packed, just like all the trams at all hours of the day. The trams began running in May, but the number 15 tram that went along Pozsonyi Street was already running in mid-March, when they put up flags on the ruined streets once again. Jam-packed. That's what they called it. In every sense of the word, the people and events overlapped, they crowded in on one another. Grown men hung from the steps of the trams like grapes on the vine. There was no way of getting inside, because with the exception of the trams running along the boulevard, they consisted mostly of just one carriage. The men, if they were polite, let the women with children get on first, they helped them force their way in. On the other hand, there was no forcing your way out. At every stop, getting on and off became a veritable war game, a drama, and the confusion of human voices, the yelling and the belligerent shouting threatened to turn into a real fight every time. The older boys sat on the car's bumper, where they had more room. In Hungarian literature, no one describes this phenomenon better than Péter Lengyel, nor have I found a description to match it in the literature of any other nation. They bummed a ride so they shouldn't have to force their way in, and also so they shouldn't have to pay; in short, they bumpered a ride, this is what people called it. I couldn't imagine ever being that brave once I grew into a big boy and stopped being such a painfully good child.

I never wanted to be that polite. I'll become a rebel, an anarchist, a resistance fighter, a troublemaker, I decided. At the same time, you couldn't stay outside, because even though you tried to steady yourself on the platform, the people pushing to get on shoved and elbowed you in, and then afterward you couldn't elbow your way back out, and consequently people got stuck inside, shouting as if they were fighting a battle with the other passengers, begging for their very lives. But they were fighting a losing battle. They rang the bell. If people got off a second too late, they could easily find themselves under the wheels. Hey, they rang the bell, are you deaf, can't you hear, what the hell are you shoving for, you're pushing me off. You should be ashamed of yourself. Have you no shame, how can a man be so wicked. It was like an aria, a duet, a trio, or the chorus of the Furies. The tram carried them along with their cries. They pulled on the bell cord, will you stop, stop already. Sometimes the tram dragged its victims along as strong men attempted to pull them back, or hold them steady on the steps. Or something of theirs got stuck in something, it got caught. At the time many people wore ankle boots with holes or loose, flapping soles secured with strings or leather straps, but the steps of the trams were grated. I never saw it with my own eyes, fate had spared me that. But once I saw someone who managed to let go, she had a lucky fall between the rails, but her bag, her bag. We took her bag along, stuck between some passengers. Will you stop. Stop. Every week the tram would cut someone's leg off. Or one of the boys bumming a ride ended up being run over by a car. They jumped off the buffer of the moving tram just before it stopped so they wouldn't have to run away from the ticket inspector and were caught by the wheel of a car. But just as often, the ammunition they'd managed to collect despite their parents' strict orders to the contrary killed them when, driven by their taste for adventure, they tried to disassemble it. Or else a fight broke out in the crowded car because somebody persisted, no, no way, he doesn't want to go inside or else he doesn't want to get off. Fistfights became the sole means of settling the issue. I could count myself lucky if I didn't end up in the middle of one of these fights. The grown-ups had to pick their children up in their arms, even the children of others, otherwise they'd have been trampled underfoot to the accompaniment of frightful verbal abuse from both sides. What're you, blind, can't you see I have a child with me. Why can't you pick up your own child, why. It's beneath her dignity, ma'am, believe you me, it's beneath her dignity. Can't you see she's a lady. Ha, some lady, don't make me laugh, I'll show you a real lady. She won't pick up her own child, but she's sure got a mouth on her, the cow. Can't you see I'm disabled. You should've thought about that before. The nerve, talking about a cripple like that. A poor disabled war orphan, and don't you forget it. You got your nerve, talking to me like that, me, the widow of an army officer. Have you no shame, putting a poor, distressed war widow through this. And so on.

Why are you taking the tram if you're the widow of an army officer. Take a cab, that's more your style.

With children in their arms, they could neither hold on nor stand their ground against the crowds pressing in on them. In this congested mass of humanity surging over the ruins, my parents knew a lot of complete strangers. They kept bumping into complete strangers. We stopped in the middle of the surging crowd, I got shoved around, and for what seemed like a long time I was lost among their coats. Someone would suddenly break free of this throng of strangers, he would call out of its depths, shouting from the other side of the street, Jupi, Jupi. Jupi was one of my father's cover names in the resistance. Jupi, Jupi, for a minute I thought you didn't hear me. His other cover was Jancsi Nagy and they used it less often, but when they did, this plebeian Jancsi Nagy would sometimes make them laugh, except I had no idea why. I later learned that Jupi was short for Jupiter, while his other cover was actually not the plebeian-sounding Jancsi Nagy, but János Nagy, although for years after the siege they'd still pointedly call him Jancsi, because his cover names contained, in no small measure, the sarcasm or dismissal of my father. In their eyes, my father was a well-mannered and well-spoken headstrong know-it-all of the genteel class given to fits of rage and melancholy, this was how they saw him. He was not of their world, he was not one of them. On the other hand, they loved my mother, her high spirits, her proletarian shrillness mixed with humor; they loved her, they adored her, and surely, this was why they put up with my father. Even decades later I met elderly people who spoke lovingly of my mother, but thought little of my father.

Klári, Klári, Klári dear, oblivious of everything else, they ran toward each other, they clung to each other, they fell into each other's arms and burst into tears, and the strange woman was suddenly one of her acquaintances. Whereas I didn't even know her. The flapping wings of the coats and city furs posed the greatest danger. Sometimes these battered coats had an acrid smell and hid me from view. Sometimes my mother held my hand, but even so, she couldn't find me among the coats. But instead of doing her utmost to find me, she just laughed, wouldn't you know, that child is lost again. Actually, the wicked phenomenon held me in thrall. Though I didn't understand what was going on, I kept turning my head every which way, I kicked, I bit, I protested, because I was stuck inside those coats. I was terrified that after a while they'd declare me missing, too. I will live, but I won't be able to break free of the vast jungle of coats. Basically, they will know that I exist, they will wait for me, but I will never again come out of there, and then I will be declared dead. No matter how hard I try, I won't be able to reach them before the declaration is made and I will join the ranks of those they mourn, those they are looking for in vain, I'll find myself among people who are strangers to me. I didn't understand this either, for a long time I couldn't understand this disappearing or this being declared dead either. Leonhard Frank wrote the most haunting and shocking short story about people like that. I understood being dead, how could I not, when in the days following the siege my father and I carted the frozen dead on the sled he had as a child. It was his sled from Gömörsid, a sled appreciably wider and longer than usual, the joint masterpiece of a village carpenter and a village blacksmith. They made it big enough so you could hitch a pony or a donkey to it.

I don't think that they took me along out of anything except necessity. By all odds, they found no one to watch me on short notice. They had to take the frozen corpses to Szent István Park and dump them into the shallow snow-covered pools. I remember the scene vividly, so vividly that for decades to come I could see the dark mass of corpses, whereas the pools were empty by then. Since they had cracks in them as a result of the bombing, they were not filled up with water again. But in spite of this, the being declared dead I could not understand.

Why couldn't they wait a day, why couldn't they wait.

Some of the strange-smelling strangers even kissed me, whereas I'd never seen them before. They laughed because I couldn't remember them. Can't you remember, can't you remember. As if they were trying to prompt me, as if indeed this could make me remember. My problem was that no matter how hard I tried, I couldn't remember something that I couldn't remember. I didn't understand this either, I didn't understand what they wanted with this constant remembering and their that's-not-very-nices. I didn't understand what they expected of me, what is nice, what is not nice, what is the past that was. Naughty little boy, you're picking your nose. On the other hand, the words *jam-packed* and *city-state* thrilled me, they mesmerized me, they hit home; even though I couldn't find a place where I could deposit it in my consciousness, for a long time *forum*, too, remained magical. Jam-packed. The forum is jam-packed with Greeks. Or is it Creaks. But I couldn't understand what made them creak or where the wind was blowing from so they'd creak like the wheels of a tram. I listened to the wheels creak as they rolled along. Roller bearings of any kind were in great demand among the children, and even among the grown-ups.

If you had four identical roller bearings, you could make a small car or a rolling board for your crippled relative whose leg was chopped off by the wheel of a train or cut off in the military hospital at the front. If a word was not self-explanatory, like in the jam-packed tram with the people jam-packed inside it, then there I stood like an oaf in the middle of the knowing crowd. Sometimes I repeated the words silently to myself, hoping to understand them better, and so at a very early age I caught on to their musicality. I'd have liked to find a creaking wheel so I could dismantle it, except I never got to do it, because I didn't know where to look for one. The dazzling quality of the words couldn't make up for the lack of their meaning or the confusion of meaning, and so their aesthetic, their sound, their melody remained their sole tangible meaning for me. Guided by their melody, I tried to fit them inside some meaningful systems.

Or else the person in question looked down her nose at me, what a horrid, spoiled little boy, meaning me, how could I not remember her. It's not very nice, when it's been less than six months since I was so happy playing with her. Well, she's not going to play with me anymore, that's for sure. Both versions made me feel awful, being offended and offending someone else. Besides, why should I bet my life on anything, put it at risk, when she just told me she wouldn't play with me anymore.

As a matter of fact, I really was spoiled, not that anybody spoiled me; on the contrary, they were very strict with me. But they loved me. Two people who loved each other loved me, and though they loved each other unconditionally, they had enough love left over for me and later even for my little brother. I could think of nothing else for days, even weeks. What have I done, oh, what have I done, not recognizing Zsuzsa Leichner. It wasn't very nice of me, because not only did she X-ray me—according to the X-ray film that has somehow survived along with the records from the hospital, this was on February 2, 1944, when, at the behest of Dr. Elza Baranyai, this Dr. Leichner X-rayed me at the X-ray Institute of the Hospitals of the Israelite Community of Pest, and when they arrested her husband, Emil Weil, and she was forced to go underground, she hid herself in our apartment for weeks, anyway, after the siege she wrote a testimonial, I don't know for whom and why; the typed draft that has survived, with copious corrections marked in pencil, lacks the addressee as well as her signature.

In response to your question, I have known Comrade István Nádas since 1919, she writes, I was on comradely and friendly terms with his entire family. He had a small chemical works with several comrades in the basement, on a comradely basis.

The second sentence reveals at a glance how, in her innocence, Zsuzsa Leichner, whom I, the sinner, did not recognize on the street in June 1945, gives reality a twist. She intends to acquit my uncle of the sin of ownership. A Communist cannot be an owner. If someone has a small workshop in the basement that he runs on a comradely basis, it is to be understood that he is running it in line with charitable or comradely considerations, in short, out of pure self-sacrifice. The workshop was located in the two-level basement of the building at 7 Újpest Quay, and there was also a smaller one across the way in the extended basement system that could be approached from Palatinus Court at 14 Pozsonyi Street. My uncle used the latter of the two premises to store raw materials, because in the case of a chemical plant, it is advisable to keep the two premises separate. According to the documents at my disposal, he did not own the extensive system of basements, he just rented them. But in these rented premises, he ran his workshop on a business basis and not a comradely basis. He couldn't have done it any other way; he had his parents to support and he had to put his younger brothers, Miklós and László, through school; he had several people working for him who did the accounting, acquired the raw materials, and sold the finished products, and he had to pay their wages; and my father's first workplace was there as well, in this workshop; furthermore, he employed chemical experts, so-called druggists, and at his highly profitable drying and heating company, unskilled laborers. They delivered and put in operation the buckets of coke at construction sites or those clever little stoves that they used at the sites even in the sixties of the last century. They called these the Nádas-type drying stoves or simply Nádas stoves. These stoves dried things not just with heat but through a chemical process. In the other, chemical section of his workshop, my uncle manufactured light chemical products whose production did not emit significant steam and smoke, floor polish, floor wax, soaps for industrial use, especially lubricating soap, and also the black, blue, and violet powder, or indigo, used for the manufacture of carbon paper and typewriter ribbons, as well as various liquids and solvents.

He did this in underground premises with their characteristic smell and exhaust-ventilation ducts. Of course, today the troublesome question arises, namely, where did the exhaust fumes go. I can't answer that, but I remember perfectly well that Palatinus Court, enclosed by seven-story apartment buildings, almost always smelled of chemicals, at times stronger, at times weaker, and this smell, so comfortably familiar to me, always hovered in the air; sometimes you could even smell it in our upstairs apartment as it seeped through one of our windows that looked out on the court. This must have been on foggy winter afternoons, when the western breeze blowing in from the Buda hills did not sweep it along with it. For years after my uncle's workshop was nationalized, we still used his floor polish and his small cubes of floor-maintenance wax that fit so comfortably in the palm of one's hand. My uncle inherited the part of the workshop dealing with the drying out of buildings at construction sites and the impregnation of building materials from his father, but the chemical plant was his idea. The workshop impregnated canvas, and my uncle had tubs made of cast stone as well as drainage pipes in the parts of the plant where they dried the impregnated canvases. In his chemical works he had a silent partner who, as a matter of fact, was his comrade. His name was Ferenc Róna.

The first couple of lines of Zsuzsa Leichner's testimony that can be conceived of as an acquittal leave no doubt that the report was written at the request of a political screening committee in the Communist Party. These committees investigated the activities of members of the illegal Communist Party, ferreting out the ideological, political, and ethical transgressions in said activities with the rigor of the Sacrum Officium. In István Nádas's case, such an investigation could not have gone smoothly. He was a highly headstrong, we may safely say self-propelled soul, but he was always ready to make sacrifices, even at his own expense. Today it seems to me that besides Mór Mezei and György Nádas, he was surely the best qualified member of my family, the one with the most cerebral convolutions, a curious piece of humanity who stood out of line with his self-effacement; also, he was a Georgist, a follower of the social teaching of the American Henry George, and not that of Marx. Needless to say, the Marxists were quite right when they insisted that you're either a Georgist or you're a Communist. I don't think that István Nádas had a penchant for extravagance, but he veritably hoarded the various -ists. He was an inveterate pacifist, another pill the Communists could not swallow. Given half a chance, they much preferred to shoot. He was also a vegetarian, though at most, this rubbed only my family the wrong way. Pista, dear, a bit more meat, they loved saying to him. For his part, he answered them as courteously as if this were the first time he's told them that he did not eat meat. A true Communist proletarian is satisfied only if there is meat on the table, at least on Sunday. *Pot-au-feu.* But where were the proletarians among the Communists in my family to be found. Nowhere. Also, Pista was a nondrinker, which gave his family yet another reason for making fun of him. The groups of the Hungarian temperance movement were organized by two prominent physicians, József Madzsar and Emil Arató, who by the late thirties became quite influential, and my uncle was an enthusiastic member of Madzsar's group and made handsome contributions to the movement, while our mother was on close terms with Arató, who was not only the founding president of the Workers' Temperance Coalition, but the physician of the Hungarian Gymnasts' Club as well. Pista, I put some rum in your tea, my Aunt Özsi, who was never known to smile, not even when she was joking, said when she handed him the cup. Thank you, Özsi dear, in that case I'd rather not. Pista, I didn't put rum in your tea, my mother said, handing him the cup, whereas she'd added a good helping of rum, I saw her do it. Pista took the cup, thanked her for her consideration, thank you, Klára dear, and whether he tasted the rum or not, which shall remain one of God's little mysteries, he drank it as calm as can be. He drank it because thanks to an operation he had as a child, he could no longer taste anything. Meanwhile, the others screamed with laughter. Which he didn't notice. Or else he didn't mind. Or else, with his self-conscious and obliging smile, he followed their laughter, while he didn't understand them at all. My mother had studied gymnastics and eurythmics with József Madzsar's wife, Alice. Pista was also an Esperantist. And as a young man, a nudist. He danced, played ball, and ate with naked girls and naked boys, while they all pretended that it was the most natural thing in the world. They took pictures of one another. All of which was too much for the outside world. Since the cultural movements he preferred were not organized with class considerations in mind, these things made him suspect in the eyes of the Marxist Communists. Even though these activities had strong ties to the emancipation movements of the European left, and at times directly to the Social-Democratic Labor Movement or avant-garde art movements, and later to the anti-fascist movements, still, as far as the Communists were concerned, such activities lacked class consciousness, they were elitist, they did not adhere to the plebeian character of the proletariat and were thus considered decadent. Their intellectual background was suspect. A bit of misunderstood Rousseau, in its adoration of nature a touch of *Blut und Boden*, and something of the stuffy insularity of the *Burschenschaften*. My uncle had his head in the clouds. Inspired by God only knows what branch of nudism, when summer came, he shaved his head completely bald. My uncle was a minimalist, a reductionist, a true ascetic.

The Marxists saw Georgism as the last great intellectual experiment devoted to saving capitalism. *Das Kapital*, published in Hungarian in 1921 in Vienna, was translated by Antal Guth, who later appended it with copious annotations. Along with other works on sociology, it came into my possession a couple of years ago, when his daughters, my cousins Katalin and Judit, gave it to me. The annotations indicate at which points and to what extent their father criticized Marx in accordance with George's ideas. In several places he corrected the printer's errors in the mathematical formulas and, amusingly enough, even Marx's assumed mistakes in calculation along with his formulaic mistakes.

He may have been right, I'm no judge of that. But I can judge the sharpness of his intellect. Following the system of his references marked with page numbers, I can judge the nature of his objections. My uncle was a dissident, an accusation that few Communists got away with and lived to tell the tale. He became acquainted with the Communists while he was still a professional atheist and very young, and he felt that it was only right that he should resign from the Jewish congregation. It was the honorable thing to do. A comparison of dates indicates that out of like considerations, he had urged my father to do the same. In any event, on August 28, 1928, he accompanied his nineteen-year-old brother to the street of the goldsmiths, where the Office of the Rabbinate of the Israelite Congregation of Pest was located at 4 Holló Street and where, as the records indicate, László Nádas made an official declaration of his intention.

The clerk at the office recorded his intention and took down the required information. He told László Nádas that he had two weeks to reconsider. On September 17, 1928, the Nádas brothers, who at the time were still bachelors and lived on Pannónia Street with their parents, repeated their visit to Holló Street, where yet anew, or as the clerk wrote in keeping with contemporary spelling, a-new, László Nádas announced his intention to resign from the Israelite congregation and requested a written attestation to that effect. The clerk at the office acknowledged his decision and made a record of it, but according to the official records, he refused to issue a written attestation, reasoning that László Nádas had announced his intention to withdraw in front of live witnesses both times. István Nádas's signature stands at the bottom of the document to verify the fact.

In the midtwenties, my father's brother was secretary of the illegal Communist youth movement, since after the fall of the Commune, the Communist Party was outlawed. He took over his post from Pál Demény. Demény was also a chemist who for a while worked for István Nádas's construction drying company, and who from his earliest youth was considered the preeminent, meaning the most stubbornly defiant dissident member of the Hungarian Communist movement. As he writes in his memoirs, he set off every morning to oversee the workings of the Nádas stoves at the Újlipótváros and Kelenföld building sites. For a while my uncle belonged to his oft-anathematized group, but his relationship to it was typically marginal. He shared Demény's distaste for nationalism in all its guises. As far as I can recall his ongoing arguments with the Marxist, though not Muscovite, communists in the family, he wasn't even a Hungarian patriot like my mother, for instance, who held strict patriotic views. All the same, even as a young Communist, my Uncle István vehemently opposed the Bolshevik manners of the Hungarian Muskovites with their respect for the considerations of great-power politics.

It was by no means a question of style. By the midtwenties he and Demény were convinced that the illegal Communist movement must function in line with local conditions and not the directives of the Moscow-based Hungarian emigrants that had no relevance back home and could not be effectively carried out in any case. Along with Demény, he came to the radical conclusion that the lines of communication with members of the diaspora living in Vienna, Berlin, and Moscow must be severed. If I were to speak clearly, calling the arguments of the fifties to my aid, I would say that my uncle was protesting, in no uncertain terms, against the Bolshevik actionists and the prevailing Bolshevik paranoia, a political mindset that sprang from Pan-Russian nationalism and which, despite their best intentions, the members of the Hungarian diaspora living in Vienna, Berlin, and especially Moscow had internalized. In Moscow they lived sequestered in small rooms at the Hotel Lux, which was declared the official residence of the Communist International. They spied on one another, they formed factions, and they denounced one another for forming factions. By the thirties, this had become the prerequisite for their survival; they decimated their numbers, they were out to cleanse the Party of one another, while in fact they were all suffering from the same thing. Smack in the midst of the Stalinist purges, they resorted to ignominious means; one by one, man against man, they were fighting for their mere physical survival. This was not accidental, nor was it historically inevitable; it was a psychological system malfunction. Demény wrote in his memoirs that in his own Marxist ABCs he could find no acceptable explanation for their factionalism. Perhaps Freud or Adler could find a clue in the near meatless meals, the dreariness, the lack of money and lack of sensual stimulation that was their lot in the Hotel Lux in Moscow, where they lived with a chronic lack of women; perhaps they could find a clue in their yearning for their lost desks at law offices, editorial offices, insurance companies, and union organizations, or the devil only knows what. One thing is certain, Demény writes with plain simplicity that three years after the fall of the Commune, they became desperate men with the rug having been pulled from under their feet, men who, for lack of an enemy, lurched at one another's throats. In their peaceful hours, in the depths of smoky cafés, they thought they'd seen a mirage and took off after it, and they urged their adherents to do the same, and if they stumbled and fell, they urged them to clear themselves by putting the blame on others. As I said, they spied and were spied upon. But paranoia is not only, and certainly not exclusively, the trademark of the Bolshevik movement, which functioned in isolated groups.

The women and men gathered around Demény, many of whom had returned from POW camps in Russia, had discovered early on the differences in disposition and organization that divided the continent's eastern half, living under a Byzantine system, from the continent's western half, living under the Roman system. It constituted a massive dividing line that is cultural, religious, and geo-economic all rolled into one. And they didn't want it not to divide them. Whether they were living undercover at home or had moved to the West, it would have made no sense for them to honor the Byzantine system of guidelines. They did not execute pointless orders and in fact made sure that these orders, heavily tainted with psychosis, should not reach the members of the illegal movement in Hungary to begin with.

But the illegal Hungarian Communist movement had its home-grown fault line as well, one that divided the Communists who had stayed at home every bit as dramatically as those who had been forced to emigrate. This fault line was made up of the followers of Béla Kun, called Kunists, and they did whatever they had to do in line with the Byzantine-style system of directives; in short, they became orthodox Stalinists because, whether they realized it or not, they were serving Pan-Russian nationalism and its internationalist slogans, or else they were the adherents and followers of Jenő Landler, or Landlerites, who conducted their actions in the movement in accordance with the Leninist principles of democratic centralism and, despite all their respect and worship of the Soviet state and Generalissimus Stalin, gave primacy to local conditions and national particulars, the particular over the general.

These groups had been engaged in a top-secret war, a mortal combat for decades, those who lived at home as well as those who had left the country, but without either group knowing this about each other. And as for investigating committees, they were active and vigilant at home as well as abroad. The law of group psychology was at work more thoroughly and at deeper levels than either Demény or even Freud could have imagined.

Demény, who like my uncle later put his knowledge of chemistry to use with his own small group in the antifascist movement, was arrested right after the siege because the Communists who'd returned from Moscow were convinced that he must have been a police informer all along. They had no proof, but they needed an excuse to take their revenge on him. He was sentenced in 1946, and when he was supposed to be released in 1953, he was interned at the infamous Kistarcsa camp without the authorities even bothering to sentence him again. But those who'd been living undercover at home were no strangers either to covert cleansing activities, and they conducted inquiries and brought sentences not only in response to the encouragement of the Muskovites, and not only on orders from the Bolsheviks. Which is only rational. Without filtering out police informers, the various illegal Communist networks would have suffered immediate collapse. They had to find the informers in their ranks, except without the paranoia that marked those living in diaspora. Sometimes the Byzantine and Roman-based methods are identical, or at least similar. At times, they even had to eliminate individuals they had pronounced guilty.

It is thanks to Dr. Leichner's admirable gesture of friendship or else crazy naïveté that the draft made its way into the family archives at all. Surely it is by pure chance that it survived at all, because the person under investigation was not allowed to know anything about the investigation, much less about the contents of the written report. At most, he suspected what was happening behind his back, what was in the offing. The only thing he could be sure of was that something was happening. His party is busy conducting investigations, and this time around, they're testing his own reliability. A man's life is a series of party investigations with no end in sight, in which case it is plausible, they reasoned, that there exists a party with a capital *P* that stands above individual interests, and that with their service, sublimated to the point of the impersonal, they are contributing to its success. As a child, I shared in their condition and this made me feel fortunate, it gave me a chance to observe firsthand those being observed and watch their mounting suspicion and anxiety. Simply put, they considered it their intellectual and moral duty to live in the midst of constant refutation and contention; and even if they were Landlerites and served their party according to anti-Byzantine, avowed patriotic convictions, they were convinced that their party demanded it of them. It was my great good luck that I retained my sanity and that my sanity put the brakes on my zeal. Still, they were surprised every time they received a summons from the Central Supervisory Commission in Akadémia Street to appear as witnesses or defendants. It was tantamount to guaranteed exposure. No one was allowed to know about it. I noticed that, too. Whether they had to act as witnesses or to clear themselves of some accusation, they invariably broke the strict rule of silence. They spoke to one another about it, and they spoke to others about it. I had a trump card in my hand that could have been turned against them. From time to time, they were not just expelled from the illegal movement, they were given a death sentence due to those who had betrayed the movement, which meant that their comrades would render them harmless, meaning that they'd be assassinated.

If after the siege the commission summoned someone, it already had such a huge amount of information at its disposal, hashed and rehashed time and again, that the person under investigation could hardly have had a chance to correct it on the spot. Just like during the Spanish Inquisition, people had to count on being accused at any moment, ready for the questions pertaining to possible heresy, and ready, too, with their answers, even though they knew beforehand that the questions would always come from a place they had least expected. Life invariably comes up with the unexpected and does not verify prognoses born of fear. Reality moves along one track, speculation along another. On the other hand, I do not think that my Uncle István was afraid of being arrested. He was a consistently calm individual, highly sensitive, yet he never batted an eye, but by the early fifties, he'd wrapped himself in profound silence.

At times, people would have had to account for themselves in matters that reached back several decades, matters about which no records had been kept, nor written documents found, and about which they had no notes of any kind in their possession. Under the circumstances, and because of the strict rules governing conspiracy, they stood disarmed in the face of the damning, confidential evidence furnished by anonymous witnesses. It required extremely complicated procedures to document or certify anything, while in the case of friendly witnesses, the mere suspicion of mutuality rendered defense effectively impossible. Such witnesses were suspected of partiality and in turn these witnesses suspected the witnesses for the other side of the same thing, and consequently, the witnesses themselves could not avoid the charge that on the occasion of one of their prewar arrests, Péter Hain and József Sombor-Schweinitzer, the two notorious chiefs of Horthy's secret police, had recruited them. That goes without saying. As for Doctor Leichner's attestation, it could have been declared invalid for a number of reasons out of hand. After all, her younger sister, Lonci, meaning Ilona Leichner, was the great love of my uncle's life. Their love was legendary within the illegal Communist movement until during an Arrow Cross raid Lonci was caught, dragged off, and killed.

My parents talking about such extremely delicate matters under their breath was the most thrilling but also the most worrying experience of my early years. I was pleased that I could discover signs indicative of the workings of the clandestine system but, at the same time, the insight I craved caused me more than a little anxiety. I was afraid I'd hear something that I'd be obliged to report, and I wouldn't be able to plead that I'm just a child; I would have to denounce them. And so, for a while, the law of group dynamics had me in its grip. For instance, my parents and Aunt Magda knew that Lonci was first taken to the Arrow Cross building on Andrássy Boulevard, and that she was then tortured in the Margit Boulevard prison; they even knew what had been done to her, but they couldn't tell Pista, who thought Lonci had disappeared, and after the siege, he waited for her for about three years. For a long time, for years, they'd talk to one another about what had happened to Lonci just to keep themselves from talking about it to Pista. Still, after a while, they had to tell him something of all the horrors, because they feared that the futile waiting would kill him. One way or another, they had to let him know that there was no one to wait for.

As soon as they realized that there was a witness to their conversation, my parents lapsed into silence, or else they scurried off, taking their story with them to talk about it elsewhere. They merely dangled the carrot of their secrets in front of my nose, but they left the key words behind just the same, sentence fragments, some of which gained meaning only years later. Also, when they couldn't keep their secrets from each other any longer, when they couldn't resist the urge to talk about them, they'd go for an evening walk or retreat to another room, the hallway, the hall, or the bathroom with them, though they'd started relating it on the way. I had to sneak up behind them, making sure I went unnoticed or, to my shame, I listened through closed doors. Sometimes they took a bath together and they'd discuss things sitting in the bathtub. I trembled all over, my body trembled and my soul trembled, I don't know why, considering how overwhelming the urge to know was.

If my calculations are correct, this psychosis took its toll on me for about two years and ended once and for all in July or August 1947 on a Sunday stroll with Sándor Rendl.

It was the raw desire not to be excluded altogether from their tight alliance that made me engage in this silent eavesdropping. Their alliance had an overwhelming power to it, and I was bent on driving a wedge between them, because it left no room for me. There are married couples like this, they live in symbiosis. I sat in the dark hall, I shivered and listened, and I had to take care that my teeth shouldn't chatter too loud. My curiosity clearly impaired their shared aura. I took it into my head that they were just deciding about something of vital importance, which means that they're deciding about me. In which case, I have the right to know. I have the right. Psychologically speaking, this was a paranoid fixation, hypertrophy directed at details. I can't be left out. As if some people were deciding about my life without me.

The unrelenting constraint to observe and the fixated fear of observation have undoubtedly left a physiological imprint on my brain cells.

Sometimes a lengthy silence would ensue in the bathroom intermittently broken by the splashing of the water, squelching sounds that were accompanied by all sorts of unwarranted noises and sighs. Isaac Babel writes that between three and five in the afternoon, the sighs of love lift cheap little Parisian hotels into the air. I didn't understand these either, these escaping sounds. I am committing a sin against God even if in our family there is no God. For at least two decades I didn't realize what I had heard coming from the bathroom, nor did I realize what had happened in their bed. I snooped, I followed the scent, but to no avail. Which means that they activated the very same animal instinct in me that they were trying to keep at bay. Or else they were so taken up with their private discourse to begin with, they had grown so thoroughly deaf and desperate from fear and anxiety, that they ignored my presence. They counted on my not understanding. After all, they didn't understand either. They're going to stop now, really, but they've got just one more thing to tell each other. They recited things for each other's benefit in whispered outbursts that had no beginning and no end, and without a beginning and an end, there is no temporal structure of any kind. They thumbed their noses at convention.

Nonetheless, I understood a great deal of the details anyway, and not just facts, but the emotional drift most of all.

Except I had nothing to which I could attach the details I understood, and that's the truth; for long decades to come, I couldn't see the system that could accommodate the details as an entity. They'll just say this one last sentence, it's crucial, except there was no last sentence as they continued panting and whispering. But no one should console themselves by thinking that I'm referring here to the aberrations of the political system known as communism. No political system or intellectual movement exists that is free of aberrations, or in which conviction does not go practically hand in hand with physical urges. The attraction and repulsion of proximity is a biological given, and until there is worthwhile collective reflection about this, societies and political movements will unwittingly and without exception indulge themselves in the recurrent, erotically charged and nourished excesses most characteristic of them.

Or else at certain moments, they'd send me out of the room, the kitchen, the bathroom; they'd send me out of everywhere; they'd sent me out politely, that is true, because they followed the tenets of socially accepted liberal-democratic thinking, I hand it to them. Would I please leave them alone for a while, because they need to discuss something eye to eye. They appealed to my reason, without which there is no liberal-democratic thinking. Or else, with her harsh proletarian humor, my mother would say that I should go look for them elsewhere, in the kitchen or the children's room or out in the hall.

I hated this eye to eye, not them, not their eyes, but the polite yet brutal linguistic formulas that constituted their request. They seemed not to have minded that I was still there, that I was paralyzed by anger, and that I sometimes stayed just to spite them. They lowered their voices, but after a couple of soft-spoken words, the intensity of emotion or the profundity of their misgiving that they had nothing concrete, no proof whatsoever, would make them raise their voices again. Once and for all, they are locked in the caisson of their former illegality, carried over from the time before the siege, and now there they are, entangled with it. They had no idea that they were entangled like that, that they were locked in, whereas the difference in pressure told them of the mental and physical danger to themselves, and through them, to others. Fine, but how can you prove it. Nice and slowly, paranoia snuck up behind them and fenced them in. Who would testify on their behalf. At times it caught up with them and gobbled them up. Nor did it spare me. The situation was made worse by the fact that several of their comrades in the underground had been killed and could not testify on their behalf; they died when they were tortured or force-fed by the police, or else killed outright, executed or shot at a police station, the gendarmerie, or one of the Arrow Cross buildings in Zugló or on Andrássy Boulevard, or Lipót Boulevard. I have kept in my possession a sketch of the interrogation chambers of the Arrow Cross building on Lipót Boulevard with key words appended to it. Or else their own comrades hanged them or beat them to death. In the ten or thirteen years following the siege, for that's as much time as I was allotted to spend with them, they recited for each other's benefit the various episodes of my father's numerous arrests, the details of the tortures he'd been subjected to, and in even more detail, those of others. In the final analysis, the latter, the torture, which was by far the most shameful for all concerned, remained an act that could not be shared. Interestingly, my father left it out of nearly all his short autobiographies. He was not the only one. The torture, the forced feedings are the most critical junctures of an interrogation, the physiological and ethical end-stations of life, one might say; after all, theoretically, from the point of view of the movement, it is at this juncture that the interrogated person is most likely to squeal. When he is on the threshold of pain, his interrogators turn him inside out. More's the pity, at this point the considerations of the political police and the political movement coincide, overruling and suspending all political concerns, or else place the person outside such concerns. So naturally, in front of his comrades, meaning publicly, my father wouldn't have wanted to brag that he was tortured but held his ground. Let us be the judge of that, let us decide if you held your ground, his comrades would have said, even if he had not bragged. They had no choice. They had to be sure. The torture made him a likely candidate for squealing, so naturally, the Communist movement had good reason to investigate. Whether he had squealed on one or more persons knowingly, of his own free will to put an end to this whole unbearable torture, to bear the unbearable physical suffering, to bear the humiliation, or he might have implicated someone unwillingly, but willingly or unwillingly, from the point of view of the movement it amounted to the same thing. Jean-Paul Sartre wrote an exceptional story about this phenomenon, a novella of some length from the time of the Résistance. They're questioning you and you lie steadily or you deny everything, but as you search among the information stored in your mind, your lie or your denial is not capable of choosing anything but what seems most realistic in line with the laws of probability. Reality forms the most cogent image of itself in the imagination. At this juncture, psychological experience and existential theory are truly as one; in short, the psychological setup cooperates more pronouncedly with your presentiment than your heroic intention of denial would expect.

Or possibly you blurted out something, something slipped out, some information that can put your interrogators on track slipped out unintentionally. During the decades of the counterrevolutionary regime, detectives of Horthy's police became experts at this type of interrogation. They spent an improbably long time asking completely inconsequential questions, they got bogged down with these; meanwhile they collected information, they hoarded information. The subsequent Arrow Cross takeover enraged these cultivated experts of their profession. The Arrow Cross reintroduced brutal logic into the system, the logic of the rabble that feeds on revenge and free plunder which they, with an end to the White Terror and in accord with Prime Minister Bethlen's politics of consolidation, had abandoned, thereby crushing to bits the fine mechanics of the interrogation methods that Horthy's police had perfected over the years.

Coupled with the most deep-seated imperatives, chance does not merely create the illusion that you've squealed but, despite your best intentions, that you actually did squeal. No wonder. By that time you were no longer your own master. You may not have meant to, but you said it. You may not even have realized what you've done. You made a mistake. You could no longer see through the detectives' questions, you could no longer suit your lies to their needs. You realize you must continue to think logically, except the detective knows what you're up to, and he also knows that your attempt is doomed to failure. Your suffering has made you blind to the traps they've set for your attempt at logical thinking, and by this point a simple negation might have put them on track, it gave them ideas. Or else you gave them an idea with your adamant refusal to speak, because it indirectly pointed out the direction the interrogation must take. This is why the profession-ally apt, conscientious detective had to get bogged down for hours or days with seemingly irrelevant questions.

When they tortured my father at the Hadik barracks, they used not only physical, but psychological methods as well. They detained him but did not arrest him. As if they were saying that they had noth-ing definite to go on. There was no doubt that he duplicated leaflets on a mimeograph machine he kept in his apartment and helped spread them. That's what the special vocabulary of the movement called it. But they didn't find the mimeograph machine on any of their various searches of the apartment in Pannónia Street. To be honest, despite my assiduous research, I don't know what to make of the fact that a member of the Workers' Physical Training Association that func-tioned under the direction of the Social Democrats, who had been discharged because of his Communist activities, a young man out of work, a telephone technician from a good family who at the time was living with his widowed mother in a bourgeois apartment house that had seen better days, should be interrogated in 1934 by the mil-itary police in the Hadik barracks. In another place he writes that he was interrogated by the military investigators of the Ministry of the Interior. The only plausible answer is that although the law that qualified Communist activities as espionage had not yet been passed, it must have been under consideration; we know that it had been ap-plied much earlier. Contemporary Hungarian security considered Communist activity as part and parcel of the general Soviet political effort, part of the Communist aspiration to become a world power, something that the defensive subdivision of the Hungarian chiefs of staff had to prevent at all costs.

My father's expulsion was the inevitable outcome of the internecine struggle between the two workers' parties, the legal Social Democratic Party and the illegal Communist Party. The illegal Communists regularly, and in large groups, stormed the Social Democrats' legal institutions. Also, he wasn't the only one who was expelled; they expelled the entire intractable group, my mother, the beloved leader of the association's gymnastics club, among them. Today they'd call her a trainer. The association was used as a training ground for the Communist movement, that goes without saying, and why shouldn't the Social Democrats put up their defenses against them, if they didn't want the political police to disband them on the grounds that they, too, were engaged in illegal Communist activities. My father joined the Social Democratic Party in 1927, but because of his Communist activities, three years later he was expelled. In 1934 he joined again, but continued his Communist activities, and of course, he was expelled yet again, this time for good. It is possible that they had reported him to the police, or that they, too, had reported him. Be that as it may, it is unlikely that my father had gathered intelligence for the Soviets. Where would this young man have gathered intelligence, and what would he have gathered, coming as he did to the illegal Communist movement from a sheltered middle-class life. He had previously worked for the American Eliwest-Priteg telecommunications company, but at the time of his interrogation, he'd been unemployed for nearly two years. But even if he had been gathering intelligence for the Soviets, who were under technical and scientific embargo at the time, and which, by the way, would not have been contrary to his convictions, even then, for lack of sufficient evidence needed for a formal arrest, they wouldn't have detained him to begin with. According to the rules of the game, the secret service would have first opened the way to blackmailing him or would have swooped down on him at some secret prearranged meeting place. There is another possibility, though, namely, that they wanted to recruit him in the

interest of reconnoitering or spying on the Moscow links of the illegal Communist movement in Hungary. In theory they could have
considered him for such a commission, but I have no information to
indicate that he had connections of this type, not to mention the fact
that he, along with other members of the family, was clearly antago-
nistic toward the Moscow wing. Besides, he was not a sufficiently important member of the movement. He distributed flyers at night, or,
as they said among themselves, he went on a roll. He mimeographed
leaflets. He attended illegal political gatherings and protests. He practiced gymnastics in a sports club. He went rowing, and from time
to time participated in gymnastics exhibitions. He collected money,
warm clothing, and books for Red Aid, the Communist aid society.

Then, from one day to the next, they released him along with the
injuries he'd suffered during his interrogation; let everyone in his surroundings know what had happened, his family, still intact and rather
well-off, and his comrades, too, and as for him, let him think that he
was now scot-free. A couple of days later they conveyed him back to
the barracks and the whole process started all over again. At irregular
intervals, for about a six-month stretch, they kept their hands on him,
as if their intention was to make this youngest of the brothers, whom
his nursemaid, Miss Júlia, had spoiled rotten, turn Communist, seeing how, with the exception of Özsi and Miklós, his siblings were all
Communists. But even Özsi took part in the movement insofar as,
ignoring Sándor Rendl's interdiction, she regularly dipped into the
household money and, ignoring the regulations pertaining to foreign currency, supported her younger sister Magda and her younger
brother Endre, *qui ne sait pas dire dormir*, with handsome sums since
they were living abroad without funds, and often found themselves
in dire straits. They took him back to the barracks at the most unexpected times and gave him a thorough beating. They interrogated
him about things he knew nothing about and also about things he
knew about but would not divulge. He allows himself only a half
sentence about this, and even then, only in one of his many short
autobiographical sketches. To this day his silence outrages me. What
I overheard by chance as a child, just barely, but still, or what they

blurted out, let drop in relationship to some other subject, was more than enough to make my hair stand on end for a lifetime. Once when we were rowing on the Danube and I was sitting on the bottom of the boat watching his legs slide back and forth on the footplates of the sliding seat, I noticed two scars on his shins. I asked where he got the scars. They'd broken his legs during interrogation. In the brilliant sunshine and with the regular rhythmic splashing of the oars in my ear, I couldn't get the question out for some time. How. With an iron rod. I also don't understand why he writes in his short autobiographies that his interrogation lasted a month. I remember it being half a year. On the other hand, this time determination originated not with him, but with my mother. Possibly my mother exaggerated, while my father unwittingly shortened the time span.

As if my mother had meant to prepare me for something quite matter-of-factly, something that a person can hardly avoid in life, interrogation under torture. This intermittent half a year included electric shock to the genitals, electric shock in water, which I remembered very well, because I didn't understand it, but my father explained in detail how and why certain materials such as the mucous membranes amplify electricity and how the body can be made to conduct it, how the positive and negative poles of electrical energy function; it was Sunday when he explained it; and also beating the shoulders and the head with truncheons, and then the so-called *talpalás*, the beating of the soles of the feet, the knocking out of the teeth, being spread-eagled, being hung up, the repeated and deliberate ripping open of scabby wounds, standing you up against the wall, and so on. So that I'd understand electric circuits, he even had electric current strike me. Let it be said in his defense that back in those days they hadn't amplified the voltage to 220 volts yet, though the 110 volts gave me quite a shock, too. In the autobiographical sketches he wrote for the benefit of his comrades, perhaps he held off revealing the temporal lengths and means of his interrogations under torture because by relating the story of his physical trauma, he'd have called attention to the helplessness of his situation.

Theoretically, I should have been proud that my father remained such a strong man, tough and unyielding. They couldn't force anything out of him, and I do mean anything, or at least he hoped so, but he passed the burden of his cringing fear of his fellow comrades on to me, and from then on, until I was thirty-three years of age, I was not afraid of being tortured, I was afraid of fear itself.

Besides, in her testimonial Zsuzsa Leichner went further than anyone had a right to according to their own rules. Had the Holy Inquisition gotten hold of it, the paper itself could have served as the *corpus delicti*. Not only did she hand the draft of her testimonial over to my uncle, the person under scrutiny, she obviously talked it over with him, and even left written traces to that effect. Or possibly, she may have talked it over with several people, possibly, they talked it over at our place, in the former artist's studio that we used as our living room. Parts of sentences are crossed out in pencil, other phrases are corrected with the same pencil, and in spots words are inserted by other hands.

At my request, István Nádas made, among other things, the chemical compound called dimethylglycine, with which for years Emil Weil made the secret Party correspondence invisible. Comrade Nádas also made the developing liquid required for making the correspondence visible again. In the basement I had a chance to meet illeg. comrades. With Comr. Nádas's permission I set up a meeting here between András Szalai and another comrade.

Everything that they did in the thirties and forties, meaning, as I reckon time, before the siege, during the German occupation, or during the months of the Arrow Cross terror, the underground Communist movement or the antifascist Hungarian Front, they referred to as *illeg*. They used the abbreviation exclusively among themselves, as a sign of their initiation. It was as good as a password. Which, when one is familiar with the general rules governing conspiratorial activities, also reveals at a glance that in the hierarchy of the illegal movement, Szalai was Zsuzsa Leichner's senior liaison, whose real name she presumably did not know, just as she did not know the real name of the third person whom Szalai met through her mediation. In the same way, the Keeper of the Seal, meaning István Nádas, had good reason to remain ignorant of the identities of the people meeting in his workshop.

On the other hand, Zsuzsa Leichner's mere mention of Szalai's name makes it immediately clear that she must have written the testimonial before May 1949, because in May 1949 András Szalai, who was the head of the cadre department of the Communist Party, meaning that he was the senior personnel chief of the Party, and thus theoretically in charge of selecting the members of the Supervisory Commission, and whom we once visited with my mother in the Akadémia Street headquarters of the Party, was arrested by his comrades so that, in line with the logic of their movement, they should then use the story of his life and his activities in the Communist underground to fabricate the fiction of his betrayal.

From the summer of 1946 to the spring of 1947 my mother served as secretary to László Földes, András Szalai's predecessor in the cadre department of the Hungarian Communist Party. At the time of our visit to Szalai, Party headquarters and the cadre department were no longer located on Tisza Kálmán Square, where she had worked for Földes, but in Akadémia Street. This building of humble proportions subsequently annexed the adjoining buildings one by one, until the Party apparatus gobbled up the entire block between Nádor and Akadémia streets. For some reason, my mother was highly indignant when she spoke to Szalai, but Szalai didn't let her feelings rub off on him and continued smiling, and when he put a word in, he tried repeatedly to disarm my mother with some courteous remark, all the while remaining seemingly unperturbed by whatever it was that had upset her. It seemed to me that he wanted to keep his opinion to himself. Later, as a principal witness in the Rajk trial, András Szalai was sentenced to death. According to the indictment, he had committed the following crimes: war crimes, disloyalty, orchestrating an action to overthrow the democratic state, and on September 24, 1949, the special council of the People's Tribunal headed by Dr. Péter Jankó found him guilty on all counts. On October 15, 1949, the death sentence was carried out.

From then on, it would have been ill-advised to mention his name in this type of testimonial.

And there on the street I saw a round-faced, pale, freckled, extremely lively, elegantly dressed, and decidedly forthcoming woman, but I could not remember any Zsuzsa. My mother tried to save the day, because this heavy and heavy-freckled Zsuzsa, this stalwart champion of the illegal Communist movement, this bulky X-ray doctor familiar with psychology got offended because a three-year-old child couldn't remember her. She saw her affection and the gratitude she felt for my family go up in smoke all because of me. She had wasted her feeling on an unworthy child. In which not only the symptomatic lack of a feel for psychology, but also the fact that before the siege children were looked upon as small adults clearly played a part, because these small beings were expected to owe allegiance not to their own nature and character, but to the social standing of their family. Grown-ups had nothing against child labor either. I was only twelve when during summer recess I worked in the photo lab of the Workers' Movement Institute for a month in total darkness, at most in lamplight, in the basement of the pompous building of the former Supreme Court on Kossuth Lajos Square. The following summer, after our mother had passed away, I spent a month in the gloomy Király Street warehouse of Pharmaceutical Industry Headquarters.

A child such as I had to remain courteous under all circumstances. If I don't remember, I don't remember, what I remember is my business, but I shouldn't have said so out loud. I felt the weight of responsibility, from which even my mother couldn't save me; what's worse, I didn't know what I was supposed to do to remedy the offense I'd committed against the freckled lady. Seeing how I can't remember the X-ray. I can't remember anything. I couldn't even remember that an X-ray doctor by the name of Zsuzsa Leichner had stayed with us, and how happily we played together. It felt as if I'd been locked inside some reverberating space with my wretched doubts, a place where I am expected to feel responsible for the times before my memory kicked in, a space where I should at least lie or else engage in a heroic attempt to remember. Whenever I was in big trouble, I always ended up inside this reverberating space where all proportion ceased, everything was equally gigantic in size and rumbled and reverberated, and I could feel my hands and feet grow to gigantic proportions and they were no longer in their accustomed places. I couldn't stop them from growing. Also, in this interior space, sounds had a hollow ring to them.

Your name, say your name. My father had explained echoes to me when we were in Tihany. I was allowed to shout my name into the vast Balaton landscape, I could shout anything into the distant surface of the water. And now it actually came back, my own first name, syllable by syllable.

Today I remember being X-rayed, and the room, too.

I could describe everything in this twilight space in detail. Authentic memory images appear only in response to a related system of associations; at will or on orders, all you get is fiction. They did not draw the heavy black curtain all the way, and the doctor or her assistant sometimes crossed the blinding ray of light or the darkness blinded by the light, and right away, I wanted to be a radiologist. I liked the smell of this vast and echoing space. My own candy box, I decided, would one day be filled to bursting with silk candy, it would be swelling with light, color, and stripes, because in the hospital, good children were given silk candy. Here they called the silk candy pillow candy, and I decided I'd also give one to every child who didn't make a scene in the X-ray room. They didn't give you more, just one at a time. If only they'd give me another. I didn't dare say so, but then, it's only fair, if I were an X-ray physician, I'd give myself only one, too. This is how I consoled myself. Today, I can remember this, too. And also, that if, while turning the candy around and around in my mouth, I managed to bite it in two, it flooded my mouth with sumptuous flavors, several at once. Meinl on Pozsonyi Street near us sold silk candy. But we didn't buy silk candy there, we didn't buy it anywhere, because according to Harald Tangl, candy is physiologically harmful, even for grown-ups. Harald Tangl's book gave advice on nutrition for the benefit of several generations, but as I see it now, though our parents used him as an excuse, the strict prohibition on candy did not originate with him. Only our grandmother in Péterfy Sándor Street would give us silk candy, while my Aunt Bözsi in Dembinszky Street gave me money for it, go get yourself a bag of silk candy from the grocer's. But I had to make it last a week. Aunt Bözsi preferred to suck candy with alcohol inside it, and when she bit into it, the alcohol poured out on her tongue. By the end of the week, the seventh silk candy got stuck to the bottom of the paper bag. The delicious stuffing of the silk candy was made from sugar and sunflower seed. You will now feel some cold, but you will not yell, you will not wriggle, you will not move, you will not breathe. And keep the air inside. Several tastes came pouring out at once from the striped outer shell of the candy. Raspberry, lemon, peach. What can I say, Zsuzsa Leichner was pretty impatient in the X-ray room; she kept pushing and shoving me every which way, keep your breath in, keep it in, I said. She said it as if I didn't want to keep it in. I tried to behave myself and do as I was told, but still, I was afraid of her, afraid of this freckled Zsuzsa Leichner. Then they put me on a higher bed, where it was more difficult to be a good boy because they kept contorting my arms and legs. Zsuzsa Leichner worked on me with another woman, they arranged my limbs, then no, that won't do, let's try it like this, and they wanted me to hold still and not breathe. I urged myself to keep it in, for God's sake, keep it in. But back then, on the street, I didn't remember any of this, and also, I couldn't shake off that scene on the street, and that I had hurt Zsuzsa Leichner's feelings, and now she would never forgive me. I was at a loss, and through time, this feeling fixed itself more and more thoroughly in my mind, and I could not shake it off.

The small workshop with the Alfa Chemical Works sign over the door where they made the floor wax was eminently suited for illeg. meetings, because anyone could go in to buy something, and it had so many secret rooms and passages that anyone could hide there and anything could be hidden there. As far as I know, for years it served as the secret depository of the *Social Review*. I also used it as a hiding place for the papers and printed matter that Emil put in my care, and I continued taking things there even after he got caught (*Imprekor*, *Kommunista*, etc.) that had reached me through illeg. routes. A 1919 Communist, even after the fall of the Republic of Councils István Nádas remained true to his convictions. I believe that through his connections to the illegal Communist aid society, the Red Aid, István Nádas offered substantial support to the Party, with hefty monthly contributions, sums that far surpassed his means and his family's finances. In 1944 he gave me 1,000 pengős, so that Comrade Weil's prison sentence should be reduced by a third. The full sum (10,000 pengős) was delivered to the lawyer Dr. Endre Szöllősi (who later defected), but the action failed, because in the meantime the Germans came in. In March 1944, when the Gestapo's men came looking for me in my apartment, the Nádases hid me in theirs, which was doubly dangerous for them, because they themselves lived in the building, adjacent to the basement, and they must have been under suspicion themselves in the eyes of their neighbors. I met the Aranyossis at their place. Then, on October 4, 1944, Emil Weil was released from prison with Comrade István Nádas's assistance. In this way Comrade Aranyossi knew about the friendly and comradely connection that was in evidence between István Nádas and my husband until his arrest.

Emil Weil was also a radiologist; he seemed much older to me than his wife; he was a corpulent, grave man; after the siege he became general secretary of the Public Health Workers Union and later ambassador to Washington, and for a while, Zsuzsa Leichner and her freckles disappeared from our lives.

Some people they were glad to see, with others they cried on each other's shoulder, which was more my mother's style, this outburst of emotion. In his physical remoteness my father was averse to dramatic scenes. You might say that he preferred to keep his distance. At most the corners of his lips trembled when he saw my mother's emotional outburst, or else his eyes were overcast with the characteristic silent, suppressed horror that could also be seen in the eyes of his four older brothers. Their father, Adolf Arnold Nádas, had beaten his sons relentlessly and kept them under constant surveillance; they had nowhere to flee his, my grandfather's anger, but despite all visible signs of their fear, the other half of their souls remained withdrawn. Surely, this seeming calm was in the genetic code of their mother, my Mezei grandmother, the only protection they had from the paternal rigor. They had no physical shelter to protect them. At best, their governess or nursemaid would whisper words of encouragement in their ear, or sneak them a bite of something to eat; their tutor, Mr. Tieder, was even more helpless than she in offering them comfort. At times my grand-father would keep them on water and dry bread. At times they received two or three days' punishment along with their having to stay in their room, an ordeal after which words of comfort could hardly calm their trembling bodies. Their father would beat them with a leather strap, a stick, or a dog whip, whatever was at hand, and as for their mother, Klára Mezei, she'd leave the room without a word, leaving them de-fenseless. Just like Mr. Tieder. The governesses as well as the servants were helpless against scenes such as these.

There was a small scar running across the curve of my father's up-per lip; from time to time I felt what the scar was like with the tip my finger; it was smoother and brighter than the lines of his lips. He even let me distort his features and laugh at him as I did so. My mother would not allow it, and Grandfather Tauber wouldn't allow it either. No, son, we don't do that to other people. I suggest you stand in front of the mirror and do it to yourself. My Aunt Magda let me, though, she even made scary faces to go with it, and sometimes this scared me, or more to the point, I was scared that because of our game, she'd stay like that forever. When she realized what scared me, she started moan-ing that she can't, she can't possibly rearrange her features back to what they were. You ruined my face. She was so good at this pretense that as often as not, I believed her. Now it will stay like this forever. I should fix her face up this instant, since I was the one that ruined it. But when I tried to fix one half of her face, the other half would go awry. It started out as a game, but then it became deadly serious. How could I do this, how could I do this, my poor aunt cried, what's to be-come of her now, she will now have to live like this for the rest of her life. My Uncle Bandi, properly Endre Nádas, whom his siblings called Dajmir because as a small child he couldn't pronounce the French verb *dormir* any other way, *Dajmir, tu dois dormir, s'il te plait*; he was so against me rearranging his features, he'd smack the back of my hand. Although he was the apple of Adolf Arnold Nádas's eye and the only one of the brothers his father didn't beat, Dajmir had a horror of physical contact and the other children in the family hated him because of it. He was small, but strong as nails. Sturdy little fellow, his father said proudly. He'll grow up to be a real man. Not a sissy like this big lout, Gyuri, and not a scaredy cat like Pista. If something got my father upset, if for instance, he was mad at me because I didn't do something, or else because he didn't catch me fibbing, he caught me telling an outright lie, because in his eyes the smallest confabulation or amplification for the sake of style counted as a lie, the scar on his lip would turn white.

He must have been about the same age as I am now, he climbed up on the spiked iron fence of their summer house in Pesthidegkút, slipped, and got stuck on a spike. For goodness' sake, what are you telling that child, my mother cut in. Which didn't mean that he should spare me the bloody stories; it meant that I'd understand a really bloody story, too, and he might as well tell me that the cut on his lip came from the buckle of his father's belt. I must have been five when he told me the true story. For two days his father wouldn't let them call a doctor, and when they did, they called Béla Mezei, so the incident should stay within the family. He was born there, in the house in Pesthidegkút. His brothers and sisters were also born in various vacation homes or summer places around the country. György Nádas was born in Balatonkenese, where my grandfather bought his first estate, which in a couple of years he mismanaged and brought to ruin, and according to his daughters, this debacle made him so cocksure of himself, he lost no time in acquiring an even larger estate in Gömörsid. Endre Nádas, meaning Dajmir, *qui ne dormir pas*, was born in Szentendre, though it's too late now to find out why Szentendre of all places. Even though the belt buckle was the real culprit, from then on I regarded spiked iron fences with a certain horror, even though the belt buckle was the culprit, and I can't look at the buckle of a belt today, including my own, without thinking what it can be capable of in the hands of a father.

My father remained unperturbed, he'd have gladly taken me along into the vast universe of family lies, and it is my great good luck that he didn't have enough imagination for that, and so, when called upon by his wife, he related the true story to me without batting an eye. As far as he was concerned, everything was concrete, there was no imagination, only lies. He'd show me their house with the iron fence, he said. As if that iron fence could have afforded me a glimpse of the obscure garden of family lies.

We'll walk from Testvérhegy to Pesthidegkút on Sunday and look for it.

No, it's not our house anymore, your grandparents had to sell it.

Your grandfather was a bad manager, he squandered his entire fortune.

All his life he dreaded going broke, and did so more than once.

For one thing, there's no escaping the cyclical crisis of capitalism, he explained, and when it comes, some entrepreneurs run scared and crash drive their businesses, but in fact your grandfather went bankrupt because he bought frightfully expensive machines on credit that worked well on the flat English countryside, but not on the Gömörsid estate.

The Great Depression came, construction ceased, his construction company could no longer produce profit, and he couldn't pay back the bank loans on their due date.

He couldn't pay them back because from one day to the next his expenditures outstripped his returns, and his bank wouldn't grant him further loans on his expected income.

No, I don't mean that it was his bank. He didn't own a bank.

The machines were designed for flat terrain and on the hilly Gömör uplands, after a couple of years the machines needed repair, and there were no mechanics to be had, there was no one who could repair them properly, and they were ruined.

And so was he.

He couldn't bear it any longer.

When his nerves couldn't bear it any longer and the overseer in Gömörsid couldn't bear him any longer, and he came and said, either Your Honor leaves or I leave, and I'm not coming back, you can bet your last farthing on it, then after a heated exchange of words in which our poor mother took the overseer's part, he up and left your grandmother to manage the estate, whereas our poor mother had never done anything of the sort before, she knew nothing about farming or finances, she had never talked with field hands or servants. He left our poor mother alone with them, saying he had to go to Pest to save his drying company. Which was true. Uncle Róna, who ran the company, looked up our poor mother several times in secret. For God's sake, Your Ladyship must do something, we're in trouble. For months we've been spending more than we earned and the bank won't give us another loan.

By now our father couldn't get a family loan from Grandfather Mezei either, who, of course, is your great-grandfather.

He'd already mortgaged off your grandmother's jewels and engagement gifts so he could pay back the loan on the machines that were of no use to anyone anymore.

Your grandmother knew nothing about her jewels having been mortgaged off. It came to light at a Sunday lunch at your great-grandfather's.

Our poor mother said nothing at the table, but we saw from the look on her face that your grandfather hadn't told her.

Our poor mother, this is what her children called her, and as if they couldn't say it enough, this remained her *epitheton ornans* even after she died. Only my Aunt Magda resented their poor mother's conduct, why didn't she stand up for herself, how could she be so sheepish her entire life. Why did she engage in this comedy, why didn't she leave this irresponsible, squandering, and bullying man.

I see from her letters that she didn't leave him because she loved him.

Our poor mother was first left to fend for herself in Gömörsid with her two youngest children, Miklós and László, our father, in the fall of 1914, when the war they called the first was already raging out in the world. The older children had already returned to Pest. Eugie was attending the Industrial Drafting School, she was studying to be a goldsmith, and an internist by the name of László Mándoki was courting her, he was a close friend of Pál Aranyossi, Magda's future husband, who would soon be introduced to Magda, with whom he'll be starting a correspondence. György was a second-year student at the College of Engineering, and his two best friends, Lajos Ember and Endre Lovas, both ardent pacifists, were already at the front, which for him was more than a tragedy, and Magda was attending the Budapest School of Economics and Domestic Science, she had to take the tram every morning from Pannónia Street all the way to Zugló, where the school had a huge horticultural depot on Egressy Street. She wanted to become a gardener so she could take over the management of the estate from our poor mother and go about it a bit more rationally. The two big boys, Endre and István, were attending the high school in Markó Street, and they were looked after by Miss Júlia, while Miss Jolán was in charge of what you might call their intellectual, moral, and linguistic development. She may not have done a good enough job, though, because István was already following his older brother György into the Galileo Circle of high school and college students, something your grandfather frowned upon, but following in his brother's footsteps, he became an activist of the pacifist movement. It was not without danger, because back then patriotic feelings were still running high in Budapest. The saber rattlers, who approved, and the pacifists, who did not, even came to blows over it. Of course, our poor mother in Gömörsid knew nothing about this. She wrote letters to her husband, Adolf Arnold Nádas, the beloved monster, every single night, and she wrote to her children every single night as well, sometimes to more than one, depending on when they answered her own letters.

My dear Magduska, she wrote in the early spring of the following war year, because as soon as spring came, she had to oversee the spring preparations in Gömörsid, you are the most industrious correspondent among the children, and your recent examination mark of 2 can take nothing away from this industry. I have already consoled myself and you should do the same. This 2 cannot detract from your knowledge, nor can it stand in the way of your future prospects. I have finished the cleaning here to good effect. Today and tomorrow I am having work done in the garden. I am leaving on Sunday.

Our poor mother first had to drive to the neighboring Fülek by coach, where she boarded the train, the bumpy train took her to Miskolc, where she transferred to an express train that took her to Pest. If her uncle Ernő Mezei happened to be in Miskolc, she visited him and had lunch with the old bachelor.

Some things are doing very well, she wrote, the beans, for instance;

you had bought the seeds, Magduska. It is already in full bloom, which given the weather conditions is an impressive achievement. The rye and the oat is also satisfactory. But the other plants haven't even sprouted yet. I had four liters of seed onions planted in the vineyard, of which four stems have sprouted, if that. Everything is perilously late this year. The parsley and the carrots have not appeared yet, it is to be feared that they won't sprout in time, and then the heat will ruin them. I don't know what to do. The fruit trees will also bring limited yield. Your hunch about the gooseberry was correct, all the stems and branches have mildew on them. Find out from your school if we should cut the stems all the way back in the fall. At least, that's what the local women advise. Will it help? Currants will be plentiful, they can withstand anything. The boys are well, their constant fighting lets up here, they don't beat each other the entire day, and they're also bored less. Laci doesn't ask as much either whether I love him.

If only someone from here would take him in, but as things stand, I will take him with me to Pest.

When summer was over, the older boys went back to Pest. Miklós was attending the small village school by then. Our poor mother was very strict. Though Miklós begged her to have someone hitch up the cart, he's not feeling well, his leg hurts, our poor mother just laughed. Miklós limped to no avail, he had to go and come back with the children of the field hands, and as a result, he walked about eight kilometers every day. At best, our poor mother had the sleigh hitched up when a lot of snow fell, and then all the children went to and fro on the sleigh. They even put bells on the horses' bridles.

Sometimes the countryside was already white with frost in mid-November, or the first snow had even fallen by then.

From September of the following year, my father, whom everyone in the family referred to exclusively by the diminutive Lacika, also walked along with them. The older boys would sometimes pick him up on their back and carry him, except he kept sliding off, even though he held on as best he could. He always came back alone, sometimes as much as half an hour late, weeping, because the others kept throwing him down or kicking him down and then they left him behind.

My dear Magda, our poor mother writes at the end of that month, our farewells were said in such haste, I forgot to congratulate you on your upcoming birthday. Thus, I am doing it now, if belatedly. I daresay that I did not forget the importance of this day; on the contrary, I thought of you all day. You see, I meant to buy birthday presents for you and Eugie from the apple money, but I have just started the apple harvest today. I went out to the *puszta* at nine, and we came back at five. We brought back a horse wagon and a donkey cart laden with apples. While I was away, the cook harvested the fruit here in the garden. Yesterday afternoon, we potted your flowers. It seems that the old gardener knows his business. Your father will probably be in Pest ahead of this letter. For the time being I am not sending you money by post, but if I have to postpone my trip, which could easily happen, I will send some on Monday. Eugie, that proud Spaniard, said in advance that she is not going to write to me. So please write instead of her as well, even if no more than a couple of lines. Hugs from your loving mother, Klára.

And in fact, she couldn't leave for Pest. On Monday she sent the money that she must have received for the produce she'd sold, perhaps the apples. Then on Tuesday she wrote again.

My dear Magda, to my chagrin, it rained all day yesterday. I am sitting here and the work is not progressing. I have still not finished with the apple harvest, even though we go in the morning, and we come back only in the late afternoon. I have become quite accustomed to riding on the yoke cart. But I would rather not send apples to your friend Irén. It takes 6–7 days even for the express produce to reach Pest. Verespatak it wouldn't reach even within 2 weeks. By the time it would get there, half of it would surely be bruised. Transylvania is the best apple-growing area, I can't believe that Irén Pontó and her family can't get apples in the vicinity of Verespatak. If your father is still in Pest tomorrow, please write and tell me how he got on with Lukács. You can imagine how impatient I am to hear the news. And yesterday, of all days, the mailman brought no letter. In your next letter, send me two small skeins of no. 5 embroidery yarn. During the summer I neglected to mark with my initials the new dustrags and sponge cloths that I'd brought back with me. I will do it now during the long evenings. Embraces from your loving mother, Klára.

Lukács was the banker, and Irén Pontó was Magda's best friend among her numerous friends; at least, this is what the tone of the surviving letters would indicate. There is also a letter from a friend called Klára that carries an even more affectionate tone.

I don't know why it is, our poor mother writes to Magda on October 15, but from time to time one is not in the mood to write letters. It is my only excuse for not having written. In answer to your special wishes, I am very sorry to have to say this, but under no circumstances will I send Irén Pontó apples. For one thing, I have no apples for sale, and this first reason exempts me from having to mention the other reasons. Once, a long time ago, when we were around six or seven, we plagued your Aunt Záza by telling her that the customers were already standing in droves in front of her shop, demanding that she open up. And see, it is not all that absurd. When I brought the apples back from the *puszta*, I had hardly gotten off the cart, and the buyers were already there. And when I got up in the morning, I hadn't even washed yet, and the buyers were already waiting by the porch. And now, when the apple harvest is over, I still cannot go along the village street without one or another of the women stopping me, asking me to give them at least another bushel.

Of what is left over, I really cannot spare any. Of course, I must also take into consideration that every other week you consume 1 quintal at least. I am not sending any to you either for the time being, but will bring some with me as personal luggage. It is a much faster means of transportation. I hope that you will not lack for food without it, considering all the packages that I am constantly sending you. If I were to listen to your father, I should be sending twice as much. He is constantly worried that come tomorrow, all of us will starve to death. Just today I sent a basket of grapes, an indication that the grape harvest is also finished, and with it, I am again a step closer to going home. I think we can safely dispense with the question of the blouse and the costume until my return.

The big news here is that we are getting Russian prisoners again.

Needless to say, not thirty, as we had requested, but for the time being just two. They're from the Madarassys' disbanded group. They will probably show up here on Monday. Hungarian servants are not to be had these days, and even of those who are left, some are sure to give notice. They've started behaving like cocks on a dunghill. They know how indispensable they are. I have no more paper, nor things to write, so in God's name I embrace you and your brothers and sister. Your loving mother, Klára.

Then on a Monday in September of the following year, our poor mother writes to her dear Magda that one letter in the morning and one letter in the evening is as much as can be expected of a poor mother.

She knew that behind her back her children referred to her as poor mother, and from time to time, she played along with them in her letters, a gentle hint that they had no reason to feel sorry for her. But I get your lines like clockwork every day, of course, and I wish to pay back your precision with mine. Also, I wish to inform you that Bandi is arriving Friday night at 8, and Pista must not forget to wait for him at the station, because he is traveling alone and with lots of luggage. He will need Saturday to see to his textbooks and school supplies. We have already packed the apples and will send them off tomorrow as express freight, and they should be there in 3 or 4 days. In case you are not home, see to it that there's money to pay for them. If there is no money and they take it back, it will cost three times as much. Although I did not count how many there are in the crate, you can let Róna's children have 30 or 40 pieces. As for the rest, take them out and lock them away. Fruit is very expensive in Pest now, and besides, I don't take pains picking and crating them for the sisters, the sister-in-law, and other relatives to make off with them. But I'm not saying that Irma shouldn't have any. I am also sending a basket for Micike, Péter, and Feri. Please see to it that the empty baskets get back to me in time. Down here, the threshing isn't finished either. We were hoping to be done with it tomorrow, but it started to rain again this evening, so it is uncertain whether we can work tomorrow. Gyuri writes that he's leaving Széplak on the fourth, which means he should be in Pest by Sunday or Monday.

I do not think he'll come to Sid again in the fall.

Write to me about everything in detail; also write about the state of the eggs when you get them. Is it worthwhile to send more, perhaps with Bandi? I wish Pista would write!

My embraces to him and to you, too, your loving mother, Klára.

But Friday still finds her in Gömörsid, which the locals call Sid.

My dear Magda, your last letter was truly exhaustive, worthy of praise. Yes, I'll be satisfied indeed to find a bright and clean apartment, seeing how, after God only knows how many years, it will be the first time that your poor mother will be spared the delights of a thorough housecleaning. And I will have you to thank, Magda dear! When you have Bandi and his luggage safely in hand, unpack the latter right away, because it is best for the foodstuff if it is not standing there tightly packed. Irma should cook the chickens tomorrow, otherwise they might go bad. They are too big to fry, so have her make stew from them or have her roast them. I think it will be more than sufficient for the four of you, with some left over for a snack. At the moment I can't send Ilus apples, I don't have any baskets. Write to me when yours arrives, and also in what manner and how much you paid. We would have finished the threshing by noon today, if only the rain had not started to fall last night. It has now let up somewhat, but there is still a drizzle. The Russians are just sitting around comfortably, disparaging the food, whereas the cook has truly outdone herself.

I am impatiently waiting for Pista's letter; he should inform me of the result as soon as possible.

I hug you both, your loving mother, Klára.

In the next surviving letter from Sid, dated July 1916, she thanks Magda for at least sending her a postcard, because the others didn't even send as much as that to their poor mother. She doesn't know that Eugénia has been secretly engaged to László Mándoki, who is serving at the front, and she doesn't know that Mándoki's friend, who was brought back from the front wounded and is presently being cared for in the royal palace in Gödöllő, had earlier made the acquaintance of Mademoiselle Magda Nádas, with whom he is carrying on a passionate exchange of letters. Do not expect, she writes to her innocently, that I should write that your excellent report card came as a surprise. Although I expected as much, it did nothing to diminish my joy, except it is not focused on one thing. I was happy with the results of your efforts, I have been happy for three whole years.

About myself I have nothing to write. Apart from work, I cannot say that all the uncertainty and the considerable annoyances are too pleasant.

Hugs from your loving mother, Klára.

From this point on, the maternal letters grow shorter and shorter, because the dramatic turn of events is closer and closer.

My dear Magda, your letters are arriving more frequently now, what's more, you are now my most diligent correspondent. If I do not answer every one of your letters, the main reason is that life here is even more monotonous than yours in Zugló.

To Laci's delight, his birthday package arrived today. He and I think that the *Spritzmalerei* is a present from you.

I will write more in the future, for now I send hugs and greetings, your loving mother, Klára.

She writes the next letter from Gömörsid on September 10.

My dear Magda, I received two letters from you today, except you forgot the dates, and so I have no way of knowing which one was written first, and which second. But I have no cause for complaint, because in the meantime, the boys have also written. Please tell Bandi for me that he should improve his penmanship as well as his spelling, because his second letter is full of mistakes.

You are sure to find Miklós's report card in the salon, probably in one of the two writing cases. By the way, I am going to Pest with Miklós on Sunday night. I don't know what Laci will say when he finds out that he is staying behind. While I am there I want to mend your underwear, so write to Gizella Herzog and tell her to be there on Monday. Róza has her address.

Gizella Herzog was the family seamstress and Róza the maid. When the two fastidious young ladies had a problem with their toilette, Róza was sent to fetch her.

Gyuri must not worry, I will bring his tuition fee with me.

One last thing. After staying a year, the Russians left last night. They finished the threshing. The machine is back in the shed, but there is still some reaping to be done. If the rain had not interrupted, we would have finished that as well. It is a great load off my mind, but we will feel the lack of manpower for some time to come all the same.

We will now hire the ranger's father to watch over the vineyard and the garden; this way nothing will remain unattended. But there is hardly any hope that the vine dresser will come back from the front again.

We know that the rain finally stopped and by the following day the sky above the hills of Gömörsid were clear, but in September they couldn't very well count on the hayfield drying up. It was no use waiting, and three days later they mowed it down. Then the harvest had to be diligently tossed, then carried into the shed, the sooner the better, and gathered into pyramid-shaped stacks. Our poor mother was just about to come out of the kitchen with a cup in her hand when she collapsed, as if her legs had slipped from under her, as she later put it, then she fainted. When she fainted for the second time, Miss Júlia sent the coach to Fülek to fetch the doctor. But before the doctor arrived, she fainted several more times, and it was more and more difficult to slap some life into her, to spray water on her and fan her. They then carried her into the bedroom, laid her on her bed, but this ordeal made her faint again. The doctor said her ladyship is exhausted and anemic, but her heart is fine. She must lose no time in going to the baths. He administered sedative drops, which put his patient to sleep. Miss Júlia had the doctor taken back to Fülek, but she first hurried to the pharmacy, then sent a telegram to the family in Pest. The telegram turned out to be more ominous than was absolutely necessary, because the boys and the servants lost no time in looking for their father, but could not find him. When he showed up all unsuspecting late at night, Róza handed him the telegram. Adolf Arnold Nádas's chest heaved like a man who'd just been stabbed, and then for long minutes he couldn't stop howling. He wanted to set out right away and gave orders to hitch up the horses. He forgot that he'd just sent the driver away. Well, then, they should run after him. Eugenie, who rarely lost her composure, managed to calm him down. She said that it was no use hurrying like that, the last train had left, but early next morning, she would go to Gömörsid with him.

But he'll never survive the night.

This sentence actually calmed the children somewhat, because although the howling had really come from deep down, the sentence about him not surviving the night was all too familiar to them.

Our poor mother wrote her next letter sixteen days later, when she was recovering at the Lukács Baths in Buda.

My dear Magda, imagine, I am so lazy here, I am writing this letter sitting up in bed. Even you and the others don't do that. On the other hand, I do have one excuse, namely, that it is very cold. But I don't mind the cold, because it means we will have a lovely bright day. It rained all day yesterday, at night the stars came out, and today the sun is shining. I won't even stay in bed until 9:30, but as soon as I finish this letter and have breakfast (it is now 8 o'clock), I will get up. For one thing, I want to have a closer look at the facilities. But I will not let them give me a massage or a shower, I will be satisfied with a simple civilian bath. The women here are surprised that I am not taking advantage of any of the cures. The doctor better not think of forcing any such thing on me. I'd rather deny that I was sick to begin with. But enough of my chatter and, coming to the crux of things, I am sending my best wishes along with the promised one hundred crowns for your birthday tomorrow. Most of all, I wish that having passed your twentieth birthday, you will always be sober minded, that you will always be smart. A person has great need of both. Sober thinking can save a person from many bitter disappointments.

Magda dear, don't be angry if I don't write more now, but it is difficult to give an account of such a monotonous life. If the weather remains this pleasant, come to visit me, you know the way now. If you and the others come, bring some towels. What they give me here is so small, at most it will do to dry one's hands. I hope Gyuri will bring me my thimble, without it I would even be deprived of the pleasure of darning. I hug you, your sister and brothers, your loving mother, Klára.

Which, however, was merely the first act of the drama. As we have come to expect of any bourgeois drama worth its salt, Act II unfolded a couple of weeks later at the grandfather's house in Nagykorona Street, during the usual Sunday dinner, when in the midst of the profound silence Záza commented ever so softly that a person doesn't do a thing like that. Meaning that a person does not mortgage off his wife's jewels without his wife's consent.

Whereupon, beside himself, your grandfather began shouting as, dumbfounded, your great-grandfather listened and glared at this strange bellowing man who was our father.

He shouted never again, never again, as if he couldn't stop, never again, he'd rather go broke, never again, he'd rather drown himself in the Danube before he'd take a single fillér from any of the Mezeis.

Never again.

You didn't take it, Arnold, Záza said sharply, you asked for it. Every time.

He's had it up to here with the whole arrogant and stuck-up Mezei family. They haven't the faintest idea about business or running an estate. They never ran a farm. Money, that they know how to make, barrels of it. Well, they should just go on sitting on their money chest, for all he cares.

And with much ado he stormed out, slamming all the possible doors behind him, so that we had to take his coat, hat, and umbrella after him. Except he took the coach, which he neglected to send back, so our poor mother had to ask Planck to fetch another posthaste.

We bought a coach, this is what they said instead of we hired a coach.

Our father was a likely candidate for a stroke or a heart attack. Back then if someone was suffering from high blood pressure, they bled him. Our poor mother was afraid for him and came with us after him as we veritably trembled in the midst of the huge family commotion, in which even the grown-ups went white with fear. Gyuri, giddy with fright, was literally supported by his sisters.

My head was in a whirl. Though I didn't know how they came about, I understood the word *mortgage* and I understood *bankrupt*, but I was in the dark about their relationship, and I was especially in the dark about what all this had to do with the English farm machines and the English flatlands and capitalism with its cyclical crisis, and the hilly uplands, and the loans.

To this day, every time I think about it, I see an abandoned tractor against an empty horizon, and the coaches standing all over the place, waiting for someone to come and buy them, along with the horses.

But on Sunday we didn't go anywhere, neither to Testvérhegy, nor Pesthidegkút. We didn't go anywhere else either, because my parents always had somewhere to go first. They went without me. Or else they had to make a quick visit someplace, to run off for a spell, or, on the contrary, they had to go on a long errand where they couldn't very well take a child along, and so on. Something more important always came up, something that excited them, and when they got excited, they forgot about me.

Years later, when I had forgotten the story and we were returning from a longer tour, maybe on our way back from Zsíros-hegy, the two of us, my father and I separated from our group and went looking for their former summer house. My heart skipped a beat. So he hadn't forgotten about his promise after all.

Terrifying dogs were barking behind the terrifying iron fence, and this scared me. I wanted us to leave right away, let's move on, I no longer cared about the spiked fence and his bloody family secret, or his birthplace. But my father ignored me, as if he hadn't noticed how frightened I was, and waited until a man came from the depths of the garden to answer the bell. The large house with the wooden porch that my grandfather had built and which he squandered could just be glimpsed among the trees. They had to shout to be understood, because though this man tried, though he told the dogs to be quiet, the dogs would not stop barking. But the moment he cordially opened the gate so we could enter the setting of my father's birth, childhood, and injury, instead of biting me, the dogs licked my face and pranced merrily around us.

There were some people whom my parents recognized but gave a wide berth, and there were others they did not recognize because they were all skin and bones. Everything about this man was lost inside his ragged cloak, and I looked at him in his ragged cloak with fright and aversion. He'd lost everyone, and I do mean everyone, and I felt ashamed that I should find adversity and the unpleasant coat smell of people suffering from adversity repulsive.

When they met, people lost no time in talking about the living and the dead, who had spotted whom the last time and where, what had happened to certain individuals and where, or what might have happened, who had news of whom, or who had run into whom. I couldn't understand why grown-ups talked so much about adversity. Who was declared dead or missing, and why. For me this declared was and has remained the most serious thing of all. With their questions and answers they wove a web around the city, they wove a web around the country, and so on, a web around the unfamiliar world outside. Which is where we were looking for my cousin, György Mándoki. My Aunt Özsi advertised, searching for him out in the vast universe. We were also looking for Eugénia Nádas and also my uncle Miklós Nádas; he was sought after by my Aunt Bözsi, Erzsébet Tauber, who, with near manic precision, clipped notices out of the newspapers that dealt with the fate of the forced labor units of the camp at Bor, as if she were trying to piece together the fate of her husband, who had been declared missing. This being declared missing was legally necessary before they could start searching for him, but even though it would entitle her to a widow's pension, she refused to accept it. She was not frustrated but continued her search and waited with manic confidence. Surely, the dread I feel today at the thought of someone going missing or being declared missing or dead can be traced back to my mute identification with her.

His wife asks the comrade-in-arms of Miklós Nádas 101/163rd technical forced lab. bat. to provide news of him. Mrs. Miklós Nádas, 37 Dembinszky Street, I. 9.

As many versions as the number of carefully filed newspaper clippings.

Her husband of beloved memory started out on his last journey from Bor on October 8, 1944, with the 101/322 labor battalion, and arrived at Kiskunhalas, the scene of the tragedy, on October 11. Lipót Vorsatz, a German with Hungarian sentiments who hailed from Sopronbánfalva, and against whom no complaint was ever lodged, was the company commander. On this fatal journey, however, the commander was not with his company, because he had to go to Budapest on official business. In Kiskunhalas, they split the train in two. The wagons that had transported the guards remained on the outer confines of the station, and they intended to move on with the wagons crowded with prisoners, when an air raid warning was suddenly issued. Some of the prisoners started jumping off the wagons that stood across from the station, leaving the doors open. Just then, one of the infamous sergeants of the skeleton camp staff at Bor came staggering out of the station dead drunk, and cursing wildly, threw a hand grenade through the open door of one of the wagons. The hand grenade did not explode. One of the prisoners still inside the wagon grabbed the infernal contraption and flung it out of the wagon. The hand grenade blew up and wounded the drunken sergeant.

Hearing the explosion, the members of the SS detachment just then at the station came running outside, formed a skirmish line, and opened fire on the wagons. When it was quiet in the wagons, they dragged out the survivors, had them dig a grave, and buried the dead. A bit later they shot the survivors as well. Of the company, only seven men survived. One of the young men, who in civilian life had been general manager of a large company, died when they laid him on the tracks and beat his head in with a hammer. When Lipót Vorsatz, the commander, heard that his company had perished, he wrote a report about the event to the Ministry of Defense. A first lieutenant took the report and read it, then with a wide smile flung it on his desk and patted the commander on the shoulder.

Thank the Lord, he said, there are that many fewer of them. As for you, you'll get another company.

More than ten years later it came to light that Miklós Nádas was last seen on a forced march in the same column as the poet Miklós Radnóti, except Miklós Nádas never even made it to the mass grave at Abda. Perhaps it was his blood mixed with mud that had dried on the poet's ear in one of his last poems.

I once asked my cousin Vera, who remembered Miklós Nádas well, why his brothers and sisters would have nothing to do with him.

He was the meekest of them, she said.

But that's no reason to be shut out. He must have been the most obtuse as well.

No, he was not obtuse in the least, but I had never met a person as meek as he. Neither then, nor later. It's more like they looked right through him. They took him for air.

Thanks to the assiduous research of a historian called Daniel Blatman, we now know what happened on these roads to these sick, thirsty, and starving men during the last months of 1944 and the first months of 1945, when they were led on forced marches from camp to camp to escape the approaching front, driven into annihilation. According to his calculations, on these forced marches approximately 250,000 prisoners perished on the roads of Europe. My Aunt Irén was looking for the aged parents of her father-in-law and mother-in-law; my maternal grandmother, Cecília Nussbaum, was looking for her older brother, Ármin Nussbaum, with his four grown-up children and his two young grandchildren; they searched for them in newspapers, they searched for them in advertisements. My Aunt Bözsi's collection of clippings from the papers survived, but only the articles, the dates and the names of the newspapers were missing. Like a maniac, she snipped off everything that was not of consequence. She even snipped off the margins of the newspaper sheets and the lines separating the columns. Which says a lot to me today. As I look at these carefully cut-out newspaper articles and announcements today, I see my mother's always smiling and loud older sister again, the far from meek wife of my father's meekest brother with her scary gums, whose fate and silent search and refusal to divest herself of her laughter and her strident ways despite all the tragedy, affected me so profoundly that in order to lessen the isolation into which the family had tossed her, I resorted to the magic of words.

Once I called her mother, and when she pinned her questioning gaze on me and laughed, I said that I was almost her son.

I wanted to comfort her. After much reflection I realized that our family ties had crisscrossed each other. My father's older brother, Miklós Nádas, married my mother's older sister, Erzsébet Tauber, and so in a sense they could almost be my parents. In a sense Miklós, who had been declared missing, could almost be my father.

When she understood, she let out a terrible cry, she hugged me and howled as she wept, she laughed like one demented, she laughed and cried as if one emotional state had merged with the other without transition and with no end in sight; she hugged me, and to this day I feel her lap, its heat and sturdiness, she pressed my face to it, she pressed it everywhere, and she wouldn't let me go. I don't like remembering this episode because we were alone in the apartment on Dembinszky Street, and after a while I wanted to be free of her arms, her unfamiliar breasts, the feel of her unfamiliar lap, her crying out, which soon subsided into tears one moment and a burst of laughter the next.

I imagined, though I couldn't imagine, what the world would be like without this almost. What would it be like if instead of what happened, something else had been what happened.

I was later repeatedly, compulsively drawn back to this subject, agonizing over what it would have been like, and I was glad that what had happened is what had happened and so my aunt didn't become my mother after all but remained my aunt completely, because with her constant strident laughter and her overaffability, she got me all confused. There were just too many things behind her harshness that I could not accept. I pretended to love her just as stridently as she loved me so we could get it over with and not offend her or cause some unforeseen complication, but I couldn't stand her strident cheerfulness, though it was not her cheerfulness but her overaffability that was the bad omen, something that my parents confirmed in their secret conversations.

On the other hand, that's why I wanted to comfort her. Poor Miklós had to die because of Bözsi's cowardice.

Between them they said that it may not have been Bözsi's fault, because Miklós was the bigger coward of the two.

Miklós could never say no to anyone his entire life. No forged documents, not for him, no fake name, no fake date of birth, not that. Going underground, no way. This was the only strident refusal in his life. And Bözsi always agreed with him, whereas of the two, Bözsi was the more intelligent. But one can understand Bözsi. Her all too obvious dislocation of the hip would have made a life underground even more complicated for her than for Miklós.

All the same, the family could not forgive her. They said that they understood her, but they did not. It was the first time I saw anything of the sort in my life. They would have nothing to do with her, whereas they'd rejected the both of them a long time ago. They communicated with her through me, and I had to suffer the viscous and slobbering and clammy affability behind which she hid her suffering, the hopelessness of her search, and her waiting game.

Világ has recently published an article about the trafficking and dragging off of so-called commanded forced laborers to Germany, Jews in the ranks of the military, who were nevertheless deprived of weapons and uniforms and forced to wear a yellow armband, went one of the articles we found among her old clippings. But with the exception of this one objective article, many of the other writings that have appeared in the recent past have not provided a true picture of the situation of the forced laborers under Szálasi's government. The author of the present article has been commissioned by the Jewish community and for years was in charge of the welfare problems of forced laborers.

Since Bözsi clipped everything superfluous from around the texts of the article, there was no way of knowing who wrote this article and where else his findings may have been published.

I have forwarded the complaints and grievances to the Ministry of Defense, he continued. As painful as it is to say this, but with the exception of four or five officers in the ministry, the majority of the officers viewed the suffering of the forced laborers with hostility or, in the best of cases, with cold indifference. This went so far that the complaint threatened not the member of the skeleton staff responsible for the atrocity, but the person lodging the complaint. Every complaint the committee deemed unfounded was passed on to Department XIII, and the person lodging the complaint was given a harsh sentence.

To mention just two examples, the journalist Jenő Lévai, the former brave opponent of Arrow Cross subprefect László Endre, who forwarded the grievances of the forced laborers appended with his full signature, was conveyed to the detention center on Margit Boulevard, where he was tortured and sentenced to several months of imprisonment. Or I might mention a female relative of the outstanding writer Elemér Boross who had been suffering in forced labor for a long time, and who was likewise given a six-month prison sentence because the accusations she lodged were declared unfounded.

But the Marányi-Bartha affair reveals the mood best. In August 1944 the affair caused quite a stir at the forced labor department of the XIth administrative command. When Colonel Ede Marányi, known as the Bori Executioner, arrived in Budapest, he bragged to his fellow officers that the greater part of the Jewish men under his command were dead. At this, László Bartha, lieutenant colonel of the river forces, burst out, offering the comment that the duty of a Hungarian officer is to take responsibility for the men under his command, and he will never again shake hands with a man like him. Initially, Marányi wanted to demand satisfaction, meaning that he wanted to have a duel, but later changed his mind and reported László Bartha. Next, Major István Fehér handed in an eight-page memorandum to the Ministry of Defense in Bartha's defense and against Marányi, in which he offered proof that Marányi had committed a grave breach of duty. He accused Marányi of murder. Ministerial Counselor István Oláh, personal secretary to the minister of defense, suppressed it and did not pass it on to the minister.

However, let us return to our main subject, to wit, the heinous crimes of the Szálasi regime, as a witness allow me to supply the following data concerning the sneaking of the protected and dispatched forced laborers out of the country.

On November 27, 1944, every forced labor outfit stationed in Budapest received immediate orders to call back all its men who had been dispatched elsewhere. There was a secret order in effect that in the early morning of November 29, all the men must be entrained at the Józsefváros railway station. I was also given my orders. After a while I convinced my commander to make an exception in my case and he said that he would let me know later what I was to do. I got the concession I wanted. He said that in view of my exceptional military situation, I need not present myself at my company, but could go for entrainment straight to the Józsefváros railway station at 6 a.m. on the 29th. I did not accept this favor. Instead, we took immediate action. The question was how we could arrange for the ministry to reverse the orders for the immediate recall of all dispatched forced laborers.

I first looked up the Ministry of Defense. On this official visit to Brigadier General Fábián, I was accompanied by István Békeffi. To our utter surprise, the following notice greeted us at the gate of the ministry: "In view of a government decree, from this day forth matters pertaining to forced labor will he handled by the Ministry of Domestic Affairs." This was the worst possible scenario. At long last, Colonel Vitéz Hibbey received us, but he announced that his hands were tied, all matters pertaining to the forced laborers were now under the jurisdiction of the gendarmes. We then looked up Colonel Gátföldy, chief of the 43rd department, only to learn that on October 20, this field officer, who had always conducted himself in the spirit of humanity, had been relieved of his office by Szálasi's men. Major István Fehér tried to do something but to no avail, he said that they even took the seals pertaining to forced labor affairs away from him.

In the end we looked up Lieutenant Colonel Rajmund Both, of whom it was also known that he never rejected a petition by a forced laborer. His name was known in all the labor camps. He went from one place to another all day on October 28, but without success, whereupon he gave us one piece of advice. Anyone who can should escape. I will provide everyone with some sort of paper, he said.

Meanwhile we managed to find a contact in the Interior Ministry. Sándor Ujváry, who headed the joint office of the neutral nations and who was just then ministerial counselor, spoke so firmly with Lieutenant Colonel Ferenczy of the Gendarmes that this bloodhound granted permission for the forced laborers assigned to the Red Cross to stay in Budapest, but with the proviso that they must move into the ghetto. Part of the group assigned to the Red Cross, which at the time was still equipped with cars, spent days sneaking out those who'd been herded into the brickyard, thus saving the lives of several hundred Jews.

At the time, Captain László Ocskay of the Hussars successfully arranged for his company, which was also waiting to be entrained, to remain in Budapest. This upright Hungarian man, suffering from high fever and typhoid, got up from his sickbed and obtained permission for his own company to be taken to the Jewish school on Abonyi Street, illegally raising its numbers with the escaped forced laborers and their families to 1,600, meaning that he upped their numbers to the equivalent of seven companies, thus saving them all.

The gendarmerie put the protected as well as the dispatched companies on trains, most of them never to be heard of again.

While relatives, acquaintances, and strangers were talking to one another on the street or at home, in our house in the studio, they drew up virtual maps of their search and the devastation, they marked the possible sites of the devastation, and jointly tried to appraise the harm to men and goods. They all went in search of their own lost relatives. They were busy collecting information. Later, on the basis of the extant information, documents, and testimonies, Daniel Blatman marked out about 110 routes for us. He perished, people said when any further search for a missing person would have been of no use, when they found no more traces and death gained final surety.

They arrested one of the bloodthirsty commanders of the camp at Bor. Géza Bánhegyi ended up in the prison of the political department of the police. It is typical that Bánhegyi, whose mournful activities included the annihilation of several hundred forced laborers, later not only forced his way into one of the democratic parties, he was also given a post on the political screening committee of the Electrical Works. But we should know that as the commander of the 110/59th camp labor company, in June 1943 Bánhegyi reached Bor with two thousand forced laborers. At Bor the forced laborers were assigned to various subcamps. Bánhegyi became commander of the "Berlin lager." As aide-de-camp of Lieutenant Colonel Marányi, he did everything in his power to see these men dead. He gave despairing speeches to the unfortunate men standing in the scorching sun in which he kept repeating that no one will get out of there alive. Being strung up and the brutal exercises meted out as punishment were everyday occurrences. Bánhegyi placed anyone accused of trying to escape in underground cells and kept them there on bread and water. Most of the food was stolen. What they could neither sell nor eat they fed to the pigs on Bánhegyi's orders. On September 17, 1944, Bánhegyi received orders to return to Hungary with his forced laborers. The marching column, which consisted of 3,500 men, set off with Bánhegyi at the helm. Bánhegyi ordered anyone who leaned down for an ear of corn, anyone who tried to drink from a puddle, to be shot on the spot. Now he is saying in his own defense that he gave no such orders and that the skeleton staff is responsible for these deeds. He was marching at the head of the column, he couldn't have seen what was happening behind his back. Besides, he has flat feet, he couldn't very well run after the skeleton staff from the front of the column all the way to the back.

Sometimes my parents would invite people for tea, even though we had neither tea nor sugar. They laughed, because at least we had plenty of lemon substitute. A bit of talc, a bit of tartaric acid, it's no big deal, Pista doesn't just make soap and floor wax, he makes lemon substitute as well, loads of it, he is responsible for the veritable worldwide overproduction crisis in lemon substitute. This was so much the case that even ten years later, in the mid-fifties, we drank tea, lemonade, and goose champagne with his lemon substitute, we used the unscented soaps made in his chemical works for bathing, we scrubbed the floor with his soap paste, polished it with his polish, and waxed it with his wax; we attached a floor brush to our feet or used a brushing machine he'd just put together, and which my father had to render operable again every time. Something was always missing, the brush disk was worn down, or the carbon rods in the carbon brush were worn out. You couldn't buy anything. Pista, on the other hand, still had everything or, if he didn't, he figured out what he could substitute for what, and how.

Needless to say, the drink was lemonade in name only. There was no lemon anywhere on the horizon. As for the goose champagne, nothing could be more horrific.

A couple of weeks before, the article went on, the police arrested Imre Apáthy, a thirty-nine-year-old merchant living in Budapest, who from June 1943 was a member of the skeleton staff attached to one of the labor units in Bor. His harassment of the forced laborers was sadistic. He took part in torturing them, in plundering them, he misappropriated their food, as a result of which many of them starved to death. When the liberating army was approaching, they drove 3,500 forced laborers escorted by gendarmes from the Bánát to Crvenka. The forced laborers arrived at their new camp drastically reduced in numbers, and once there, the skeleton staff executed 1,200 more of the men. Apáthy had been informed about the planned mass execution twenty-four hours before, and although he could have prevented the massacre, he did nothing in the interest of those about to die. People's Prosecutor Dr. Jenő Sámuel has just prepared the bill of indictment in the criminal case of the mass murderer and the People's Tribunal will hold the public hearing shortly.

My father, who was interested in healthy eating and who gained his knowledge firsthand from Harald Tangle, the distinguished Swedish doctor living in Hungary, explained why the frequent drinking of goose champagne is detrimental to one's health. It was made from bicarbonate of soda, lemon substitute, and a bit of sugar. While the lye was reacting to the acid, it bubbled like crazy and poured down the side of the glass. If there was ice, they made it with ice water. It was sour and sweet, cold and hot at the same time. Just yesterday, Pista even came up with the perpetuum mobile, and is now busy working on his hair-splitter. *Poil à quatre.* He can cut it in two, but not in four. No way. They often said no way. He can't make English too either. No way. They said no way all the time. They called some people

Mr. No Way or Madame de No Way. By all odds there must have been something about them that warranted the use of this strange-sounding expression.

But not only was there a crisis of overproduction in lemon substitute, and not just in our family, there was a crisis of overproduction in witticisms as well. Up until the end of the sixties, everyone made fun either at their own expense or at the expense of others. These city dwellers who had survived the siege now burdened one another with their witticisms. They meant them as a distraction, an obliging gesture; they offered them to one another by way of recreation, they mutually offered them up as a sign of their vitality; in order to keep themselves on the surface of the centuries-old rubble heap where everything has to be built from scratch again and again, they resorted to witticisms as proof of the constancy of their good cheer. They argued, they reasoned, they flung their arms about, they kidded one another compulsively, they shouted, they laughed, they kissed and squeezed the daylights out of one another; for at least another four decades they made fun to the point of exhaustion, and much too loud. They didn't realize that they were resorting to it as a substitute for intelligent discourse. The compulsive banter and the inclination to speak down to people became part and parcel of their shared mentality. Or else they refused to talk to so and so, a miserable scoundrel, because he behaved disgracefully during the siege. Which was worse than cowardice. A coward is a coward, cowardice comes from God. But this other expression, that during the siege someone behaved disgracefully, for this there was no excuse. *Disgracefully* was another word that accompanied me for many years and to many places until I finally came to understand the temporal structure of their experiences and with it the system of the abominations they mentioned.

They had questions at the ready to check how a person had behaved during the siege.

He behaved disgracefully. He behaved honorably.

With my parents, as with others, a person could pass muster only after repeated and complex background checks.

Later, this strict stance on their part found them in considerable and repeated conflict with the so-called screening committees. It was the cause of their first serious conflict with their own party, the Hungarian Communist Party. They couldn't comprehend why their party should legitimize Arrrow Cross mass murderers or, if once they were legitimized, why the Party as a whole did not protest against such procedure. Instead, their party went further, and knowingly put the egregious scoundrels on the Party screening committees. They couldn't understand it, they couldn't accept it, and they fought tooth and nail against the erroneous or arbitrary decisions of these committees.

Needless to say, these screening committees had nothing to do with the silent interior screenings of their own party. At least, not for a while. When the Communist regime began to liquidate its own adherents and was paranoid enough to see enemies of the regime in every nook and cranny, of which there were plenty and their camp kept growing, the two screening systems merged into one, and in the years immediately following the siege, their decisions had to be posted on the walls of the apartment houses. Also, there was a chance to appeal and a deadline for the appeal. According to the documents in our family archives, in the months following the siege, a person was assigned to one or another screening committee depending on his place of residence or his workplace. Each committee had four members and a president, and its activities were regulated by Prime Ministerial Decree no. 1080/1945, the democratic sense of which would have been that no one's fate should be decided arbitrarily.

On the other hand, no citizen could escape being screened.

The copper mines of Bor in the southeastern part of Serbia were made infamous by the shocking suffering and death of 6,000 Hungarian forced laborers, the writer of the article in *Világ* went on. Of those taken there, only 1,600 starved and ragged men returned, many of whom died soon after. László Rózsahegyi, the well-known young journalist and the only son of Kálmán Rózsahegyi, member for life of the National Theater, was among those who died of starvation and exhaustion soon after his return. The court dealt with the horrors of the labor camps at the copper mines of Bor for the first time when the People's Tribunal of Szeged brought charges against Cadet Károly Szaulich, the second in command of one of the Bor labor companies, accusing him of crimes against humanity on five counts. During the hearing, which lasted nearly five hours, the accused, who was questioned by the presiding judge, Dr. Ferenc Bozsó, repeatedly denied the crimes of which he was accused and in answer to the charges said in his defense that he was following orders from his commanders, Lieutenant Colonel Marányi and Ensign Frigyes Torma, but that in contravention of their orders, he did what he could to mitigate the suffering of the forced laborers. On the other hand, according to the testimonies of the former forced laborers, municipal officer Dezső Zabos, baker's assistant Ármin Herczeg, and city clerk Vilmos Weisz, shocking details of the atrocities perpetrated in the copper mines of Bor came to light, such as being strung up for hours, which was nearly as bad as being hanged, the forced labor itself, and being starved to death. After a closed hearing, the People's Tribunal sentenced Károly Szaulich to fifteen years of penal servitude, the suspension of his political rights, and the confiscation of his property.

There is a seemingly innocuous name among the Hungarian list of war criminals, a certain József Dadasev. Yugoslavia asked for his extradition because of the inhuman acts perpetrated by him in the labor camp at Bor. The police, who have been looking for him for a long time, have now caught him thanks to happenstance. Dadasev ended up in Bor as a forced laborer, but he soon became an informer for the Gestapo. For a long time the other prisoners had no suspicion of Dadasev's vile actions. He got wind of their attempts to flee and reported them to the camp's commander. In order to avoid suspicion, he took part in the attempts himself, all of which came to a sorry end, needless to say. The prisoners who attempted to flee were caught and executed, except for Dadasev, who was being moved around from camp to camp. He won the trust of the Serbian patriots, because he spoke Serbian well. When people in the camps realized that he was working for the Gestapo, he had himself transferred to Hungary, where he continued his vile activities. He informed mostly on Serbians, which is why the Yugoslav authorities were looking for him. Dadasev is at present a prisoner of the political police. His fate has not yet been decided.

On October 5, 1945, Screening Committee No. 1 of the Electrical Works of the Capital of Budapest gave my father its stamp of approval.

On September 26, 1946, my mother was notified in a letter bearing the letterhead of the United Electric Bulb and Electric Joint Stock Company that she must look up the company's Works Council forthwith in order to pick up and fill out the forms she needed to submit at her own hearing. She wrote back the same day, asking the Works Council to hand the required papers over to her husband because she was otherwise engaged. I may have had whooping cough, scarlet fever, or chicken pox. I was not a sickly child, but there was no infectious children's disease in the entire world that I did not catch. A comparison of the various dates indicates that at the time my mother was working at Communist Party headquarters on Tisza Kálmán Square as Department Chief László Földes's secretary. She must have filled out the forms, but the letter from the Budapest Screening Committee asking her to appear at her hearing bears the much later date of December 26, 1947. We also learn from this letter that with his signature and stamp the building warden verified that on December 17 the notice of the person to appear before the screening committee had been tacked to the noticeboard of her residence and would remain there until December 26, 1947. He then had to hand the signed statement over to the person to be screened so she could take it with her to the hearing.

The notice was tacked to the noticeboard even if the person ordered to appear before the screening committee had moved in the meantime.

This may not have been my mother's first screening but the second, because the screenings came in waves. She had to show up on December 22, 1947, at 3:30 p.m. in conference room no. 132, second floor of the building at 25 Markó Street in the Fifth District.

The notice also calls upon all those who possess information pertaining to the individual to be screened that may be or might have been detrimental to the interests of the Hungarian people, for example, if they know that the person held forth views favoring the Germans, proclaimed extreme-right ideology, or was a member of the Arrow Cross Party or any other fascist organization; they were to report it either in person or in writing to the Budapest Screening Committee, preferably while the notice was still on display. The notice also let the residents of the building know that their written statement would be considered only if it included the name and address of the informant; in short, if it was not anonymous.

In keeping with their social utopia, our parents would have liked to see the list of names of those accountable for the recent mass exterminations and the national devastation to be made public. To snatch ignominy from the jaws of anonymity. They demanded as much of their own party as of the coalition parties, because unless they appeared before the People's Tribunal, these individuals would be forgotten along with their personal accountability. By the late forties, when Klára Tauber and László Nádas understood that this phenomenon was not the outcome of erratic mistakes but was in fact the well-considered decision of the executive committee of their own party or of some intraparty agreement, in short, a systemic malfunction based on deplorable calculation, an odium, an Arrow Cross task force was already virulently active not only within the state apparatus, but their own all-powerful and all-knowing party as well. The Party denounced the innocent while its secret cells sheltered the guilty. This Arrow Cross task force within the Party was still active at the time the Berlin Wall collapsed; they were active until the dissolution of the Party. But at the time, this calculated move by our parents' party was well-considered, because in this way it could not only significantly enlarge the circle of those indebted to them, it could also take advantage of the Arrow Cross's network of connections, while the upper Party echelons could see into the network of their personal connections, and through the language and medium of social demagoguery and other means, the middle level could unobtrusively merge with them. In 1989, this path, laid out on unstable ground, determined the establishment and functioning of the democratic parties.

For years to come, I saw the man who'd acted disgracefully walking along in our street in his impeccably tailored coat, pencil thin, on his head a shiny, soft rabbit skin hat, sometimes brown, sometimes anthracite; he owned many hats, and many coats, too, and for the rest of my life I just barely avoided equating disgraceful behavior with being a discerning dresser. He was always alone, and he looked arrogant. Despite all the protest, he was cleared of all charges against him. My parents did not intervene in his case, but I remember clearly that they intervened in other cases, though unfortunately, nothing pertaining to this has survived among their papers. For a long time I was under the impression that this man's arrogance had something to do with him being disgraceful. I also knew that he was a certified public accountant and a ministerial chief counselor, though I didn't understand what *certified* meant or what the public had to account for, and also, what he gave counsel in, like my father, who gave counsel in technical matters, or my Uncle Sándor, Sándor Rendl, who gave legal counsel to Minister of Finance Károly Olt. Just like this disgraceful man. As far as I can remember, with one exception, my parents and their friends got nowhere with their interventions at any level of their party.

One of my Aunt Özsi's advertisements in which she was looking for György Mándoki, her son from her first marriage, appeared in *Magyar Nemzet* on November 24, 1945. A week later the mailman brought her a letter sent to her by a certain Dr. Móric Máyer.

My dear Lady, in response to your advertisement published in *Magyar Nemzet*, I wish to inform you that I was with a fellow sufferer by the name of György Mándoki in Dornach, the camp near Linz, until August 1. Whether he was in labor service or not I have no way of knowing. He was young, tall, and handsome, with exceptionally good manners. When last I saw him he was in very good health. I started for home on August 1, but I do not know where he may have ended up. I would surely recognize him on the basis of a photograph.

It would give me great satisfaction if I could put you on his track in this way.

My Aunt Özsi visited the doctor from Hajdúdorog to show him the photograph of her son from her first marriage, and basically, he fitted the doctor's description. The young man with the exceptionally good manners was twenty-four, tall, and handsome. Surely, the doctor recognized his fellow sufferer in the photograph, because my aunt jotted down on the envelope an address the helpful doctor had given her. Mrs. Dezső Holczer, 3 Ferenc Boulevard, perfumery. In turn, Mrs. Dezső Holczer wrote another address on a slip of paper. Ernő Beer, 7 Péterfy Sándor Street, apt. 3, 3rd fl.

She must have visited there as well, because there is another slip in the envelope, and it is in her own handwriting.

István Mayer, Zalabaksa.

It was all the more difficult for me to understand *counselor* or *council*, because during the siege the Jewish Council acted disgracefully, too. The miserable wretches. At home and in the circle of my parents' friends, these two words became staples to describe the Jewish Council, and they referred not to the hopeless state of the conscience of its members, but to their impaired intellectual faculties. The members of the Jewish Council were not on speaking terms with their own intellects; at most they were conversant with their own interests. Whereas they knew in good time where the trains were headed. Well, they can now go explain their deeds as best they can.

They sent the Jews confined to their care to the slaughterhouse.

The doddering fools.

A bunch of cowards.

Idiots.

What idiots, criminals.

Doddering fool sounded the least offensive, it meant a man who had lost his reason. But as a judgment, it was the most severe.

They were playing for time with the collaboration, that's why they kept it quiet. They had no other choice.

They believed in the mitigating power of cooperation. Apart from the Almighty, what else could they believe in.

These were the well-meant but somewhat hypocritical counter-arguments brought up in favor of the Jewish Council.

They believed in a bunch of rubbish, that's what they believed in. They believed that His Serene Highness Vitéz Miklós Horthy de Nagy-bánya would come on a big white horse, or the horse's ass, more like it, and bestow his personal favor on them.

Wouldn't you know, they're taking the others, for the time being they're being spared themselves, along with their nice little families.

They knew perfectly well where the trains were heading.

Not before June, they didn't.

They most certainly did.

Bereczky in the Reformed church on Pozsonyi Street knew back in April, he talked about it, he'd heard it from Török, and if Török knew from the letter of the chief rabbi of Pozsony and the documents attached to it that Kasztner had brought from Zsolna, then how could they have not known. They knew. Sándor Török was a member of the Jewish Council. And you think he didn't tell the others. Who are you kidding. Or if not him, then Kasztner.

How can you tell six hundred thousand people the truth.

You can't.

Even that half-baked Milán Füst knew.

And he told Anna Bán, Duci's sister.

Like it or not, you knew, too. Everybody knew. Only those didn't know who didn't want to know.

You must've heard Hitler speak.

Our parents were not fair to the members of the Jewish Council. As if they couldn't understand or else they couldn't accept that, like it or not, there are critical situations when people seldom follow the dictates of honor, and their survival instinct makes their decisions for them. No situation exists in which you won't find willing collaborators, no act of ignominy without its enthusiastic collaborators. The survival instinct and the collaborative disposition are present in nearly all of us. You can always doctor your memories later.

Good Lord, if only I had known back then. I didn't know, how could I have known.

Our parents didn't like either Milán Füst or his writings; they thought he was shrill, prophetic, and ironic at the same time, and because of him they were extremely reserved with Anna Bán as well. But decades later, Milán Füst's last diary entry, written just four days before the German occupation and dated March 15, 1944, confirmed their former conviction, namely that only those didn't know who didn't want to know. What's more, in Budapest, Milán Füst even knew about the gas chambers that apparently no one knew about in Germany. The people of Weimar didn't know, when the stench of burned human flesh must have stuck in their throats at night, and in Berlin the praiseworthy Wilhelm Furtwängler and the even more praiseworthy Leni Riefenstahl didn't know, Martin Heidegger didn't know in Freiburg, and when he did, he ignored it, Winifred Wagner didn't know in Bayreuth, and so on; even Albert Speer didn't know, because he was too caught up in his foul Nazi architecture.

My parents spoke as if each person were capable of making well-considered, honorable decisions, and if he nevertheless failed to do so, then in the interest of improving mankind, he must be punished. They maintained that there is no situation in life in which a person can't make an honorable decision. Our parents used a peremptory tone when speaking about what the Jewish Council did or failed to do or, as the case may be, about the all too conspicuous egotism of its members. Needless to say, the council included adventurers among its ranks, and criminals and scandalous cowards, too. That goes without saying. Only decades later, when I first read Hannah Arendt's report on the Eichmann trial in Jerusalem, did I finally understand our parents' partly romantic, partly heroic stance, radical and accusatory, which in some measure demanded too much of humanity. Arendt's preface to the German edition carries the same accusatory tone, as if she didn't know what sort of creature man is, what anthropological traits he is composed of; on the other hand, she knows what he should be like. Her tone when chastising her American critics' views on ethics springs from her conviction that people can't be expected to turn their backs on temptation. That if someone points a gun at your chest and demands that you kill your best friend, you have no choice, you kill him. People were outraged because she refused to equate Eichmann with Satan, she characterized his ethics as springing from banal indifference, and she considered the Jewish Councils equally banal, especially the collaborative inclination of the Budapest Jewish Council; she deemed its inaction, the result of its collaboration, guilty, thereby basically criminalizing them.

Our parents' thoughts and actions were motivated by the ethos of Communist resistance, while Hannah Arendt's were motivated by the ethos of Zionist resistance. While their manner of expressing themselves was by no means sententious, they considered their activities in the resistance as normative, a possible measure of ethics, and it is strange that Arendt did not catch on to this small analytical hitch. They called people to account after the fact for not having been in the resistance, people who tried to ensure their survival within the scale of values contingent on everyday life and in line with personal interests. If under the circumstances I am not in the resistance, then practically speaking, I am not interested in the fate of others. At most, my own family's. Which amounts to a very real and major difference between one man and another. They were right, of course. Except, no person has the right to demand self-sacrifice of another person. At most he can demand it of himself. Even while she was fleeing, in the last possible moment, Arendt was still battling Nazism. She had to flee Germany, then she had to flee France. Her book draws its inner strength not so much from the intellectual clarity and impeccable attention to detail of her analysis, but this stance of resistance tied to her being; this is what endows her ethics with strength. Like our parents, she did not acknowledge extreme circumstances, while others did, some willingly, some apathetically.

Not that the idea of resistance does not appeal to me. On the contrary, I have followed my parents' exacting standard of ethics all my life. I avoided even the proximity of collaborators. No one is as boring as a collaborator. I was always a lot more interested in the perpetrators. Nothing interested me so much as appearance and reality, the conditionality guiding human judgment that is positioned between comprehension and acceptance. I had also adopted their habitually modest, antiheroic use of language. Except, after a couple of decades, it was my own squeamishness and my own antiromantic use of language that made me realize there's something here after all that's not quite right.

Adhering to my parents' rigorous ethics, I had to make too many decisions to the detriment of my own interests, and I had to put up with the consequences of my decisions and renunciations without a word of complaint. Which is fine as far at that goes; one doesn't inform on one's friends or shoot them, but that's no reason to permanently banish the desirable, the ideal, the romantic, and the sentimental from language. At one time this became my most serious professional problem. I followed in their wake, but funny as it may sound, I didn't become a Communist because I followed them, but because they didn't follow themselves. The series of renunciations made it quite clear what constitutes the set of conditions required by opportunism and collaboration, what the sentimental use of language is a substitute for, and what it is meant to hide behind this spellbinding sleight of hand. To hide and reorchestrate, through the manipulation of language, offenses against others in the interest of preserving one's desirable self-image. And when I reached this point, it became clear to me that their ethical rigor, based on individual resistance, is not quite without fault from an anthropological perspective either. Their stance of resistance, whether our parents' or Hannah Arendt's, does not shed light on the relationship between the masses of Jews or those unexpectedly designated as Jews who were incapable of resistance in the face of certain death, and the Jewish Council on whom Eichmann had so graciously conferred legal status.

Everywhere in Europe, the Jewish Council was a fiction of the Nazis, and I can evaluate it only as fiction.

Lacking political representation, those who at that moment were Jews or who, despite their intentions, suddenly counted as Jews, found themselves up against an armed and bureaucratic apparatus that would not tolerate or acknowledge representation of any kind. A nation, too, is also invariably the fiction of others.

When despite all logical counterarguments and deliberation, the members of the Jewish Council nevertheless swelled the ranks of doddering fools and idiots in our family vocabulary, my parents made and perpetuated an error in thinking, they equated the reality of fiction with the reality of free decision-making, free action and pursuit, and I subsequently had to correct this mistake. On the other hand, they significantly expanded in my mind the scope of the concept of ignominy and mental deficiency, and to this day I am very grateful to them for it. From then on *ignominy, mentally deficient, doddering fools*, and *idiots* referred not only to specific individuals, but organizations and institutions as well. And consequently, this functioned in my mind like a proper boomerang with relationship to them, and it was the same with any relationship to their party, which, in theory, should have been as infallible in my eyes as it was in theirs. And so very early on, exceedingly early on, I began to see how fallible they were when it came to their party.

The siege was just behind us but the show trials had not yet begun, when with their opportunism and penchant for collaboration they took things in stride that could not be reconciled with their principles, the sum total of their individual traits, and the intentions or rationale of their previous actions. During the siege they came close to representing the image of humanity that pleased them, but after the siege, they became further and further removed from it.

Their fate had been decided by Rákosi's political chess move when, upon his return from Moscow, he delivered his so-called Whitsuntide speech in which he labeled the Hungarian Communists, meaning all those who had not come back from emigration because they had not emigrated in the first place, sectarian, an expression familiar to one and all from the history of the Catholic Church, and not just the Landlerites, but the Kunists as well. Side by side with *revisionist, police informer, Trotskyite,* and *Menshevik, sectarian* became the Communist movement's strongest word of abuse, while its most dangerous psychological gesture was classification. Sectarians were all those who did not serve universal interests; instead, they wanted to force the views of a sect grouped around some arbitrary opinion on the Church on the one hand, and the Communist movement on the other. Something the Party would not let them get away with, that goes without saying, and so it excommunicated them.

Needless to say, the accusation had some basis in fact. Gerő and Rákosi knew perfectly well what political considerations demanded of them. They heard it straight from Stalin. In the Hungarian Communist movement, the Landlerites and not the Kunists were in the majority, and served the interests of the Great Russian Empire. The polemic reached back to the 1920s when, in the wake of the defeat of the Republic of Councils, Béla Kun fled to Moscow, where he presented his plan for an all-out offensive against which not only Jenő Landler and Gyula Alpári argued in word and writing, but Lenin as well. His offensive theory, according to which the Hungarian Communists must return to Hungary and emerge from illegality even if faced with the prospect of summary justice, met with outrage from his comrades, who suggested that he try the method out on himself first, but he went even further when he demanded that the social democrats on the left boycott Parliament and turn against parliamentarianism. Which brought Lenin's wrath down upon his head. But now, with frequent references to Lenin, Rákosi saw his chance to rid himself of the sectarian Landlerites and the followers of Béla Kun in one blow, who in the meantime had been put out of the way.

On the other hand, in his speech the Party chief, recently returned from Moscow, used the word of abuse to maximum advantage, a masterstroke, because the only way to avoid the charge of sectarianism was for the person accused of it to sever his relationship with those members of his group who shared the same convictions. In short, he had to eschew contact with his friends and alter his views.

From up close it looked like this: the two of them were constantly seething, they expressed their indignation about their assumed or actual sectarianism to each other, but could not share their anger even with their friends. They played it safe, but with all their circumspection, they either remained too cautious with respect to their friends, or else their friends made sure to avoid them; what's more, cautious or not, they couldn't prevent people from considering them sectarians who should be kept at a safe distance. Who knows, they may be in the service of some big underground movement, possibly a conspiracy manipulated by foreign powers. And this was only the second slap in the face that their party had in store for them. You couldn't help noticing how they're avoiding the usual subjects of conversation with their friends, how they and their friends are becoming estranged from each other, while their party has already merged with the Arrow Cross movement, and how, in their mutual awkwardness, the muscles responsible for their smiles keep twitching around their lips. There was no avoiding the third and fourth blows either.

I had to grasp all these relationships and words indicating relationships, all these circumstances and complications, at an age when a child is by no means ready for theories and critical thinking, he's still busy with all the whys. He's at a stage in life when he doesn't know yet where he should be looking for information, and of what kind, in the systems of causation that stand in conjunction with one another, nor does he know where he should store such information in his conscious mind.

Before he can understand the system of causality, a child needs to grasp the general order of existence, which is surely situated outside of causation. And so he will even ask about the legs of a table why a table has legs, and if it didn't have legs, would it stay up in the air, and in that case, why don't we have four legs so we can stand more securely and not fall, and why aren't we tables, and why don't we fall, and where do little tables come from, and why do they call *why* why; in short, following in the footsteps of St. Thomas Aquinas, we would like to give a name to the nominal and substantial content of individual names.

And so, I couldn't imagine the substance of group or individual ignominy. For a long time, a very long time, ignominy remained an empty concept. On the other hand, it became as clear as day that the observant man with his religious books and the Jewish Council did not do something with respect to some people that they should have done, or didn't do everything and, purposefully or not, even denounced others,

Neglect or betrayal for personal gain.

They couldn't spare the time for reasonable explanations, they couldn't attend to me, and so I had to fall back on my own understanding and store whatever I understood somewhere in my consciousness. The billowing ebb and tide of their own emotions had them in thrall. The moments when my father explained something for my benefit, moments stolen from his life, were exceptional, and I did everything, and I do mean everything, so it shouldn't end, and of all my urgent whys, each should be followed by the next. When they were with friends, they were deaf to the world along with them, as the drama of the siege was immediately followed by two other dramas, the drama of the various parties and the interparty fights, each topic of conversation pushed aside what came before it, and was itself pushed aside by the next.

I have a recurring dream related to this push-shove experience, in which I am standing in front of the empty shopwindow of the big, well-lit pharmacy on the corner of Pozsonyi Street and Rudolf Square, at the spot where the sidewalk and the road rise, forming a pleasant curve and merging with the entrance to the Margaret Bridge. I am standing by the lit-up pharmacy, watching as the number 15 tram pulls into its last stop. For decades, it always pulls in, time and time again. For a long time, the ruins of the bridge abutment and the bridge house were surrounded by a tall plank fence, and the plank fence was covered with slips of paper tacked or glued to it. On these slips someone was looking for someone, or someone offered something for sale. I learned the letters of the alphabet early because it bothered me that I couldn't read the notices and I didn't know who they're looking for or what they were offering for sale. My parents would linger in front of the fence for a long time, sometimes reading the slips out loud for each other's benefit. They were looking not only for Miklós Nádas and György Mándoki, but their lost friends and acquaintances as well. When the Margaret Bridge was reopened, I had difficulty getting used to the plank fence not being there, wondering where people would be looking for those who were lost and where they'd be offering stuff others couldn't do without. As I stood there by the lit-up pharmacy, someone at the stop must have recognized someone in the crowd getting off the tram, because a woman cried out, and then a man, and the gentle spring twilight was suddenly filled with shouting and yelling.

Don't move. Stay where you are.

My parents had already left the corner where I was more than happy to remain by this well-lit pharmacy, where later on there was no pharmacy to be seen. It was first nationalized, then it was walled in, it disappeared, possibly such a beautiful pharmacy never existed there in the first place, the kind that I later saw in Vienna and London with their deep brown, brightly polished coffered wood panels; possibly, it owed its existence only to my recurring dreams.

My parents had run off to prevent the lynching. This was neither a dream nor a daydream, it was part of wretched human reality. It spews forth questions of continued relevance.

Someone must have ended up on the ground and people were kicking and stomping on him. I will never know if this is in fact how it was or what happened exactly. But the Rudolf Square of my recurring dreams with its brightly lit pharmacy is silent and peaceful. There's nothing but a lit-up tram as, in the crimson Danube nightfall saturated with reflected light, it pulls into the Rudolf Square terminal with its one lit-up car. In my recurring dreams, there are no crowds and there is no mass hysteria degenerating into a fight because people are even beating those attempting to separate the people who are beating each other. The tram is empty, the open platform is empty. By all odds, the horror had frozen in midair, just like in the moment of a blast. Meanwhile some people ran away, but not in my dream, mind you; they ran away on the evening of the first warm post-siege day in March. They were running for their lives. There must have been some light still over the Danube, because they ran across Lipót Boulevard, shot through with deep crimson light and marred by ruins. As if the twilight had burned itself into the pediments of the ruins. The shadowy figures of others took off after them, desperate, yelling, catch them, catch them, and there came a scream, the scream of an elderly woman in a much higher pitch, murderers, murderers.

We were past the so-called decisive year, past the Communist takeover, which is an exceedingly temperate name for the Communist putsch, the all-out liquidation of democracy, when you could often still hear the call to arms on the streets of Budapest, catch him, catch the thief. The person in question, who was really a pickpocket, a cutpurse, as they were called in those years, worked with a modified razor blade or razor. With these he could not only get into inner pockets, he could cut off the bags women wore on their arms, and with a single slash he pulled out the men's wallets from their back pockets, then made a mad run for it, knocking over anyone in his way, knocking them off their feet, pushing them out of the way with a single sweep of the arm. Decades later I found myself face-to-face with a man like this. He was deathly pale as he ran toward the ground-floor exit of a Paris department store, I think it was the Samaritaine. I could have stopped him, but to do so I would have had to get a tight grip on him, I'd have had to lock him in an embrace. He was a young man, skinny, pale, unkempt, with straight blond hair reaching to his shoulders. As he ran he pressed his precious stolen goods to himself, a battered, simple leather case, a nearly flat, old-fashioned briefcase. A briefcase like this couldn't have belonged to a wealthy man; there might have been money it in, he must have taken it from a poor elderly person. His pale tongue hung out of his gaping mouth like a dead dog's and his two huge eyeballs protruded from sheer terror. I was panic-stricken. I could have stopped this man, a total stranger. I groped for the feeling, the conviction, anything that would allow me to meddle in his fate, or rather, something inside that would activate my sense of justice so I could take off after him. But I could find nothing of the sort. His paleness had unsettled me. He was like a man who in the blink of an eye comes up against the ceiling of his physical powers, but with his animal strength he knocks that ceiling down. This sufficed, this brief reflection, the crisis of conscience, for him to find a loophole of escape, dodge the department store crowd, and even hit a woman on the forehead with the heavy swinging door, causing her to lose her balance. As the surprised victim tottered, some people came to her aid, and this bit of time once again proved sufficient for him to run outside to the sunny rue de la Monnaie.

Back then, the cutpurses and the dips were actually caught now and then; it was a great mystery, this dip, they beat him with umbrel-las, briefcases, handbags, sticks, crutches, iron poles. They beat his head, they beat his back, they beat him anywhere they could get at him, and there was no reprieve, the beating didn't put the brakes on their passions but fired them up even more, the fact that they're beat-ing a live human being, they're beating him with whatever they can grab or whatever is in their hands. We found ourselves stuck in the middle of scenes like this more than once. These iron poles were at-tached to the side of the sandboxes at the last tram stops or bypasses. The driver got off at the crossing to turn the switch, he then freed up the iron pole and walked over to the switch while the passengers waited patiently in the tram. I remember this in detail because at one time I wanted to be a tram conductor, and so I was intent on studying my future. He hurried only when it rained. He hooked the end of the iron pole into the switch and turned it in the required direction. He sauntered back to the sandbox, fixed the iron pole under the strap, got back on the tram, and pulled the leather cord just above his head to sound a small bell. The tram was then ready to continue down its line. This was the iron pole they used to beat the thief, they had ripped it from its place and swung it at him.

That's taking the law into your own hands, it's taking the law into your own hands, my mother yelled, desperate, because she didn't want to see people take the law into their own hands, ever again. Her voice and anger were great. She elbowed everyone out of the way so she could reach the fighting core, the human coil brimming with passion, but needless to say, her yelling was to no avail, and the others ended up shoving and tearing at her, beating her with their fists. It was not the first time nor the last that she had called for the rule of law, and my father hurried after her. Not that he could have stopped her. They beat my mother, she's got some nerve, trying to protect that scoundrel. Whether they caught the thief or they didn't catch the thief, whether they beat him to a pulp or didn't beat him to a pulp, passions ran high, and instead of relieving the mass hysteria, the act of beating him fired it up, and the city dwellers, angelically meek just a moment ago, and despite their wartime privation well-dressed and well-mannered, panted and screeched *en masse*. Beside herself, my mother screamed along with them, beating and pounding them with her fists. Budapest has retained this erratic temperament to this day; its fever rises in a flash and it is always ready for a lynching. We know from Krúdy that its fondness for lynching reaches back to the turn of the nineteenth century, when Budapest grew into a big city and people beat up Jews with their bare hands.

I am in the habit of cautioning smug individuals who come up to Budapest from the countryside about what to expect. Hardly had a month passed after the siege, and the people of Pest stirred up and went on a lynching spree. Then ten years later, in its revolutionary fever, it lynched again without so much as assigning special significance to the lynching. To this day, if you bring up the lynching, most people will say that lynching belonged to the revolution, whereas it belonged more to the changeability and fragility of the revolution, the chaos of the revolution, and you're casting doubt on the purity of the revolution, whereas by distancing the actions of the rabble from the revolution, you are protecting its purity. Enthusiastic as I was, during the last week of October 1956, I saw what I saw. And what I saw belonged to the typical actions of the urban rabble let loose on the world, and not to the revolution. Once there is freedom, or when this many people want freedom at the same time but can't manage to organize it right away because public pressure is too great while the organizers are too weak, then in a matter of days the urban rabble wakes to its own sense of freedom. I will never forget the man strung up with barbed wire, his black tongue hanging out and his artery split open. But he was still alive. I will never forget the crowd's raging expression either, or their movements, like marionettes. The separate groups of those taking active part in the lynching, and the bullies thirsting for revenge, egging one another on. The unconscious choreography of their mutuality. The onlookers who, despite what any of them may have thought personally, collaborated by providing an audience for them. I just gaped. And to avoid being a gaping collaborator, I, the coward, ran away from scenes like this. Or a bit farther off, on the corner of Szófia Street, from the book burners, frantic, choking from the smoke and their hatred of the written word.

The rabble tries to gauge the daily allowance of socially acceptable anarchy, all in the name of freedom. It legitimizes its actions with recourse to the concept of revolutionary anarchy, all the while that the revolution is concerned with the ways and means of eliminating political anarchy, with the new forms of order, which are two very different qualities. Confusing them or mistaking one for the other is lethal with respect to the future, to any sort of future. The rabble wants to bring into sync the elimination of anarchy with its own anarchy, and invariably find a solution that is more anarchic than revolutionary anarchy. It will not settle for less. I had a good look at the Russian soldier who was burned in his tank, I didn't run away, and I don't want to forget it. They not only dragged his body out of the tank, they separated his charred head from his body, and on the corner of Népszínház Street and József Boulevard they placed the head between the tram rails, exhibiting it, as it were, and repeatedly violating it amid the triumphal shouts of the cowardly masses.

Meanwhile, the truly foolhardy headed for the border hoping to try their luck yet again.

I felt ashamed because of my mother's shouting. Here she is, panting and screeching, just like these madmen, and she's beating people, too, even if she doesn't approve of beating.

I couldn't have said why it is not acceptable to stop a lynching with one's fists. I certainly couldn't accept it from her. As if I were getting a glimpse of the insoluble and inescapable ethical problems of my own future life, whereas I accept as a matter of course that ethical problems are insoluble to begin with, because our ethics generally follow in the wake of events. It can't be any other way, because this is not an individual but a general human characteristic. Or else, I realized something very early on. To my eternal shame, I was more concerned with the futility of her screeching and panting than the futility of that lynching, even if I knew, I knew then and I know now, that I am not fair to her. If the lynching must take place, then let it take place, this is what I thought at the bottom of my heart. Not that I approved of the lynching. But I can't ignore the fact that these people who look so innocent and who are, at times, impeccably dressed, mimicking obligatory good manners, do an about-face from one moment to the next and can't do without killing. They want to kill. They don't want to calm their feelings but to fire them up even more through their shared hysteria. When Nadine Gordimer says that the only thing that pacifies man is murder, then, on the basis of my own experience of human nature, I would like to add to her observation that man would even like to violate his victim once he is dead. And it is not a personal but a ritual need.

It seems that at the age of four or five I felt ashamed because my mother couldn't assess her situation realistically, whereas her obstinacy got her nowhere. She couldn't see it for what it was. When faced with these realer-than-real individuals on that realer-than-real street, she couldn't gauge the actual place and specific weight of her notions and convictions. She is trying, I thought, to alter the expected outcome of events with her convictions. Whereas the sweep, the shared fever and panting of the crowd was so simple, the logic of the popular dispensation of justice so obvious. It concentrated on the done deed and the person who had done the deed, and to that extent, it was objective. Usurped goods must be repossessed, the crime avenged. From the point of view of the angry mob, my mother's attitude was incomprehensible. Why would anyone want to prevent the great public dispensation of justice. Actually, I understood. At the boiling point of public passion, she opposed their excess in the name of the biblical commandment and the rule of law. Considering the situation, it was a heroic undertaking. Except it made no sense at all. In the language of chemistry they'd say that the element in question has formed a weak bond, meaning that its bond to the structure of the compound is weak. When exposed to light and heat, it begins to disintegrate, and the elements, freed of their bonds, bind themselves to other, more stable compounds. But a blow remains a blow. If she delivered a blow to someone, even if she did so in the name of justice, it was still a blow. As if she were guided not by justice, but by something more elemental, a senseless wish. Her blows were messianic, her punches missionary-like; she delivered her blows in the name of the future, so that these individuals, fired up and ready to take the law into their own hands, whether individually or collectively, shouldn't be the way they were, and under the weight of her blows, should renege on the collective offense they were about to commit.

Such are the laws of the Inquisition, such is the reason for the cleansing flames. Communist conviction and Christian faith meet along the identical blind spot of an ethical crossroads, and given their consciousness of mission, can't seem to get out of each other's way. Neither is willing to renounce their faith in the redemption of human nature. In the interest of achieving their aim, they either attempt to put the instinct to multiply under their guardianship, or else the survival instinct, or both at once. So there should be order at long last. A couple of weeks after the siege and the Arrow Cross terror, no one could have engaged in a more hopeless task.

We do know, however, that in the same place, on November 4, 1944, during the noontime hours of that fateful Saturday, the sappers of the occupying German forces were busy undermining the bridge, while above them the busy Saturday traffic headed from Lipót Boulevard in Pest toward Margit Boulevard in Buda, and also from the direction of Széna Square in Buda toward Berlin Square in Pest. Pedestrians crossed the bridges of Pest in droves well into the late sixties. Before the siege, tram tickets were expensive. Saturday was a workday. Market day. Most state offices closed their doors at noon and the children were let out of school, but everyone else worked in the afternoon as well. After a couple of years, I learned to appreciate our Saturday escape. When the church bells rang out at noon and we scrambled through the school gates, we were frantic with joy. Back then, the girls came running out of their own gate, and the boys came scurrying out of theirs. Physical contact was allowed neither during classes nor during our mad rush through the gates. Like the bright light of the sun, our shared freedom was waiting for us outside, and the entire long Saturday afternoon **and** all of Sunday, until Monday, without end. But the sappers were just then fixing the explosive charges to the structure of the bridge. They say that these were already connected to the detonation fuse. According to one version of the investigation, the tram's current ticket collector came in contact with the fuse placed next to the electric cable, thereby causing a short circuit, and this led to the explosion; according to another version, the gas seeping out through the loosened seal of the gas pipe was ignited by a cigarette stub someone had cast away, and the gas explosion activated the explosive device. The public felt that both versions were blatant lies meant to hide the ugly truth.

The explosion was not big. On this one point all experts agreed. I have memories of the explosion myself, it is not surprising that I should, after all, it happened near us; what I don't remember is how, at that moment on that memorable day, we ended up there. I have no available information. My memory stored not the acoustic experience of the explosion, but the surprise of the sensory experience, its unexpected appearance. You can't help but pick up your head at something you hear from the outside, and so my consciousness stored the shady image of everything that happened inside the apartment. I was probably sitting on the floor in the studio. Something trembled, something shook, something rattled. I had to be familiar with the din of the aerial attacks by then, the effect of the air pressure, the roar of the cannons as the Russians aimed their artillery at the city while the British and American airplanes bombarded it at regular intervals. It was the experience of surprise that rendered the images of this strange event permanent in my mind. The surprise that makes you pick up your head in order to see. But the not too big explosion caused such major stress on the bridge's structure that the first arch on the Pest side of the bridge, between the first and second pillars, collapsed. The stress then spread and ripped the structural elements from the second and third pillars, veritably distending them. This must have been the unusually high pitch, the grating sound as the metal screeched, the plunging, the rumble and roar that shook the heavy blocks of the Palatinus houses. Then the superstructure collapsed between the third and fourth pillars and plunged into the cold current.

I remember that there must have been several people in the

apartment, and I remember these people running helter-skelter between the rooms, since they don't know what had happened either. I remember it clearly, my memory has the immediacy of the present. Possibly, Zsuzsa Leichner is among them. My mother, though, is not there. Perhaps I can best exemplify the structural workings of memory with the aid of this sentence. I see the hall, but nothing in it, and the cool light from outside through the cathedral glass of the front door. I may have looked out because she had left through there and should have come back through there, I now say somewhat baffled, somewhat distrustful of my own memory images. At the same time, someone must have surely opened a window looking out on the street, because I can feel the penetrating noise of the street. The people on the street are running, carrying their screams with them, though I have no similar sensory experience in my consciousness from an earlier time. As if in a given moment, as I am looking out into the hall, someone were forcing the street filled with the sounds of screaming men and women into some chamber of my mind. In the blink of an eye, the Danube swallowed up a hundred people, six hundred people, according to a later report, possibly a thousand, along with fifty German sappers, the trams and automobiles.

And if the survivors in Budapest were used to life like this, if when the church bells rang out at noon, everyone and in spite of everything wished to return to the order that prevailed before the siege or even to the times before that, to a time when the fabled order of the Monarchy still lingered and there was peace and happiness under the blue skies and life was not as expensive and you could eat a hearty breakfast for two *krajcárs*, and they gave you rolls, two soft boiled eggs in a cup, honey, tea, then how could I, as a small child, think that life could be any other way. Everything was like this. When during the first summer after the siege the iceman came with his two handsome horses hitched to his abundantly dripping cart every morning and he rang the bell on his dickey and shouted, iceman, the iceman is here, buy ice, and when he stopped somewhere and the two horses snorted, and one of them must have surely neighed and they shook their manes the color of straw, and they wanted to move on, to go, to pull, they were merry horses, the ladies of the house, the servants, the assistant superintendent, the restaurateurs, and the pub keepers came hurrying out with their buckets for the ice, or else the icemen, strong as oxen, hauled the long, heavy blocks of ice resting on the oxhide or jute sack protecting their shoulder to the butcher, and for extra remuneration even up the stairs, they brought it to us, too, on the seventh floor, and I wanted to be like that, too, this strong, like an ox, so I could carry the ice up to the seventh floor myself, then what reason would I have had to question that everything had been like this in the world, and surely would remain so. The world is in ruins. The decaying corpses lying under the ruins and the damaged sewers fill the city with putrid currents of air. When they're taking me along the sunny street, through the jungle of burned-out and collapsed houses, in my head I hear the lively chirping of sparrows everywhere. How could it be otherwise. The iceman pulls the block of ice from his cart with a grappling hook. The stench of decaying corpses is just barely less offensive than the smell of the desiccating human excrement and the other materials decaying in the sewers as it rises from the battered pipes, it all depends, and why shouldn't a small child like me decide for himself what the world is like through his sense of smell, given that there is a difference between the two smells. The main characteristic of the stench of a corpse is not that it is sweet; people describe it using this conventional adjective because its characteristic sweetness refuses to let up, it refuses to disappear. A person yearns for the sweetness of a mother's milk, its fatty scent, but not the sweetness of unburied human flesh or the flesh of dead animals. The stench of putrid sewage, the stench of withering shit and stale urine stay with you until you pass through them and reach the other side of the street. A few more seconds, and you can shake off the smell of other people's urine and excrement, the sense of transcience. But the corpses of others you must take with you wherever you go; decay with its characteristic scent, its particles, its materiality, what else, settles not only on the hairs in your nostrils, because the smell of a person's corpse is material, matter, what else, it settles in heavy layers on your fingers as well, your shawl, your teeth, your tongue. It doesn't settle there figuratively speaking, it's always a concrete corpse settled there with its concrete stench, someone who is a stranger to you, someone whom someone still loves and is waiting for their return, someone you can't ignore or declare missing. There is no declaration. There is no washing of the hands to dismiss the sense of its intrusive presence. For quite some time you can't get rid of it by rinsing your nostrils and gullet. You eat it, you drink it, you kiss it off the other's lips with your love.

This vast difference constituted such a self-evident reality in my consciousness, that though ten years on it no longer made sense, it had no function and no significance, I might have just as easily forgotten about it, like the plank fence with all those slips, the lynching, or those who had disappeared for all time, my uncle and my cousin and Uncle Ármin, whom I never knew, along with his four grown-up children and two small grandchildren, whom I never knew, or the frantic cries of catch him, catch the thief. In the recess of my mind where their absence dwells, the formula of this difference has nevertheless survived, and though not forever, still, as a point of reference for sensory perception it will remain with me until my own death. In Europe we are all war victims and the descendants of war victims, and this holds true if we accept it, and it holds true if we would rather ignore it because we are contemptibly stupid and wish to remain contemptibly stupid.

The iceman is coming. This information occupies an all-powerful if small place in my consciousness, along with some brief marginal notes that can be extracted at any time. After all, it had to do with one of my possible future professions. The iceman hauls the block of ice into the butcher shop, adroitly slips it from his shoulder onto the lined icebox, easing it down onto a riveted tin plate, I paid close attention, nothing escaped it, when I'm an iceman too, I will do the same, he's been holding it with the grappling hook and now he is breaking it up with the grappling hook, the splinters gleam, the larger pieces fall straight into the container, the rest he sweeps together with the hook, and so on. Whereas no icemen will ever come again anywhere, and theoretically it makes no sense storing the image of the iceman and the information pertaining to his trade adhering to the images.

In memory of the victorious Battle of Belgrade against the Ottoman Turks, and on orders by Pope Callixtus, ever since 1456 Catholic churches have steadily been sounding their bells at noon. If, however, there is an air raid, there is no ringing of the bells, because the man who rings the bell has gone down to the bomb shelter. What else could he have done. It might be worth ringing the bells when there's a storm, but when there's an air raid it's pure madness. The ringing of the bells is replaced by the shrillness of the sirens. Bácska, Baja, air-raid warning, beware. This was the first sentence I could say intelligibly in my mother tongue. The absence of the noonday ringing of the bells also has its secure place in the consciousness of the survivor, which from then on functions like an alarm. There is trouble, great trouble, we don't know yet what sort of trouble, but the bells did not ring at noon. The bells must ring at noon. Come rain or shine, Sunday at noon at Grandmother's we must sit down at the table, and no excuses. I wanted to be an iceman. My father explained in great detail all about the ice factory, ice-making, the ice rink, natural ice formations, ice pits, ice crystals, the process by which ice crystals are formed, and the proper way to store ice in a pit. He left nothing out, while I understood almost nothing. I am diligently following in the wake of the sentences, but I keep slipping off their edge, whereas the last seven decades have indicated that everything was in fact carefully stored, my consciousness has preserved it, and not just his sentences, but all the small, characteristic intonations of a didactic nature with which my father spoke them. When a couple of years later we were going on vacation to Balatonlelle and my father and I were standing at the open window of the train, he suddenly cried out, look, there's an ice cellar. And in fact, the ice cellar with its thick thatched roof was just as he had described it earlier, just as he'd seen it in Gömörsid when he watched it being built. A survivor takes everything in, he remembers everything that might aid his survival. I also made a point of remembering the ice cellar and ice-making. Nothing is irrelevant when it comes to survival, whether the look of an ice cellar or the technique of building an ice cellar, and also, you're proud, see, my father is never mistaken, because the ice cellar in Gömörsid is just like the one in

Balatonfőkajár. The sense of wanting to survive is to be sought only in the wish to survive.

You won't find Gömörsid on the map by this name; the Treaty of Trianon annexed the area to Slovakia, and the town is now called Sid. The *Révai Great Lexicon* of 1913 still says that Gömörsid is a small town in the Rimaszécs district of Kis-Hont County, it has 748 Hungarian inhabitants, a railway station, and the nearest post office is in Fülek. When in the evening my grandmother wrote letters to her daughters or sons in Budapest, the next morning Miss Júlia would take them to Fülek with the coach driven by a liveried coachman. And when she was alone in the bright yellow manor house with the two youngest children, Miklós and Lacika, Lacika being my father, she wrote to them frequently, sometimes daily.

You must greet your neighbor with utmost courtesy, on the balcony, the stairwell, the street, everywhere. The survivor must know this, too. I wanted horses with straw-colored manes from Muraköz as they start off and strain with pleasure. But the younger person must always greet the older person well in advance. After eight in the evening, playing in Grandmother's yard is not allowed. And not only is it not allowed there, it is not allowed in our house either. With a discreet bow of the head, the man must let the woman through the door first. On the other hand, in the theater, the movies, restaurants, or cafés, the man must go in first, so he can see where he is taking the lady with him. God forbid they should hit the lady over the head with a bottle and not him.

My mother kept making comments about my father's obsession with etiquette, she made fun of it, saying it all depends. But in vain.

With his proper middle-class upbringing, my father minded his manners against all odds. This, too, belonged to his proper middle-class upbringing. There is no world outside of our world. And if there should be one, it is surely not a sensible world, it is a world not worth talking about, *nicht der Rede wert*. And surely, he passed everything on exactly as his mother or Mr. Tieder, their tutor, or Miss Jolán, their governess, who spoke with them sometimes in French, sometimes in German, or the young girl, their nursemaid, a certain Miss Júlia, whom the children affectionately called Kisa, short for *Kisasszony*, the Hungarian equivalent for Missy, had taught them. Kisa must have been thirteen or fourteen when she came to us from a poverty-stricken family in the countryside, this was in the Hold Street apartment, then she went along with them to the Báthory Street apartment, then to the Pannónia Street apartment; she went along with them to Balatonkenese and Pesthidegkút and Gömörsid; she went to Tiszasüly, she went everywhere the children went, and all of a sudden she was past marrying age. To make a long story short, she ended up staying with the family until the seventh child, my father, grew up, by which time she was an old maid, perhaps thirty-three, and she went to America, where, wouldn't you know, she quickly found a husband, a well-off widower in the Bronx who married her, a man by the name of Papanek, and so, past the age when you wouldn't expect it, she brought a baby boy into this brave new world, whom she brought up decently along with the little girl of the widower, who was much older than she, and according to family lore, this is how she became Papanek.

Needless to say, a man must watch his every move. It is not proper to point. His handshake must be firm, but the grip must not be too tight, it must not be too forward. Also, he must make sure not to misplace his grip. The survivor must know this, too, he mustn't relinquish his knowledge of etiquette for a single moment; he must even put the brakes on his own survival instinct.

All seven children, my father's two sisters, four brothers, and himself, worshipped Kisa unconditionally, but let us add that they worshipped her in their own caustic, antisentimental way, and they passed their caustic worship on to us, their children. And not just this. They also passed down to us the emotional key to the relationship between irony and worship. Papanek veritably flooded the family with her names. In our family consciousness, Papanek is an oracle. After the siege, Papanek, because among themselves, members of the family mostly called her Papanek, sent her very first fabulous parcel from America to us on Pozsonyi Street, because my father had been and remained the youngest in line. Still, I was baffled, how could a grip be forward, why is my father saying such things, my father, whom Papanek spoiled perhaps even more than Pista, the smartest and most helpless child and her favorite, and whom she protected from my erratic grandfather like a lioness. Indeed, his father never again spanked Laci's bottom after he'd unwittingly beaten him to a pulp with his leather belt. I didn't understand this either, though I accepted it, accepted that I don't understand a palm being too forward, although later I understood it. I even understood why I couldn't understand it earlier.

If the lady doesn't offer her hand to the man then there is no handshake, I hope you understand, and make sure to remember it. Also, I hope you know that you can't call everyone by their first name.

I knew.

Among men, shaking hands is also governed by strict rules.

One photograph of Papanek, taken in New York, has survived among our family papers. *To Pista from Kisa*. This is what was written on the back of the photograph.

And so, this ancient Kisa with her charming smile and long life also has a place in my consciousness; with her nippy love and the name of her husband, whom she married late and lost early, she is planted smack in the middle of the family storehouse of legends; they laughed at her, they made remarks, they quoted her and teased her because they loved her, or the other way around, they loved her because they could make fun of her without restraint. Making fun of her all the time may have been the precious pawn of their freedom of thought. Their mother, Klára Mezei, couldn't be the pawn of freedom, because she did not stand up to her despotic husband. Emotionally, she was the stable pawn of bourgeois cruelty. Kisa took the children under her wing, or at least comforted and pampered them. Everyone else just made demands on them that were difficult to satisfy. In the photograph, good old Kisa is resting her elbows on a table with an open book in front of her, possibly a very old book printed on ragged sheets of dipped paper. Two of her letters have survived. She wrote the first on November 23, 1946, and, according to the stamp, she mailed it at the main train station in the Bronx on November 27, 1946, at 8:30 p.m. As I imagine it now based on my own experience of New

York, on this evening, in the small-town calm of this part of the city, she must have walked to the post office of the main train station in the Bronx, located less than one subway stop from her home. If she nevertheless took the subway at this late hour, she first had to walk to the corner of Longwood Avenue, but as I know from the habit of New Yorkers, it is not likely that she'd have taken the subway one stop and then walked back a half, or that she'd have taken the subway for just one stop to begin with. No, New Yorkers wouldn't do that. Or maybe she asked someone to mail the letter for her, since he was going that way anyway. A young Black man lived in their house, a Negro, as they said back then, she mentions a Frank in her letter, possibly it was Frank who had mailed it. She took him in when he was just a child and was fleeing a riot, seeking shelter with her.

My very dear Magduska, Júlia Papanek writes in a large scrawling hand without bothering with paragraphs or commas. Her letter is like a heap of porridge, with no beginning and no end. She addressed it to Her Ladyship Mrs. Pál Aranyossi, 42 Damjanich Street, fourth floor, apartment 5, where we lived with our mother during the siege, though it might be more correct to say that we lived through the siege, though it might even be more correct to say that we experienced it and survived it, more or less. She gives her address as 873 Bruckner Boulevard. She lived in her own house. The house is the third building from the corner of Tiffany Street and Bruckner Boulevard, a three-story, semidetached house of red brick, its facade in keeping with the Dutch tradition New York has preserved in its architecture. At the time of her emigration, this area was inhabited by the reliable lower third of the Jewish middle class. Stairs lead up to the main entrance of the building, and so the ground floor is above street level, just like almost everywhere in New York. Trees line the sidewalk. The street would still have a provincial feel if only the houses across the street had not been demolished in the meantime.

Where the houses once stood, there is now a highway resting on awful cement pillars. The area booms and echoes from it something dreadful.

I wouldn't like to make Papanek's letter from the Bronx seem other than it was; at the same time, I wouldn't like anyone to laugh at her manner of writing and have their attention diverted by her spelling mistakes instead of the significance of what she had to say. She couldn't have had much time to attend school when she was a young girl, and by the time she was thirteen or fourteen she was living with my grandparents in a strange town and in strange surroundings, and in the ensuing three decades she may have even forgotten the rules. She uses language as she sees fit. Also, she has a way of slipping back and forth between her mother tongue and American English, which she learned at a ripe age. And thus, from sheer reverence, I will follow each one of her sentences with my own, as if I were translating them, or where her idiosyncratic use of words or the awkward yet lovely meaning of a sentence demands, I will leave her own words as they stand.

Your letter proves that you are the nobler of the two of us, she writes to my Aunt Magda, you are the more faithful and I can hardly say how dear you are to me. Magda was the prettiest of the children, a real beauty. Then in her teens everything about her changed, her proportions, her lines. This caused her great suffering. As a young woman the others felt that yes, Magda is quite pretty, but she must take care how she dresses. I was very anxious thinking who has survived among you. The members of your family were always as close to my heart as if they were my own. When I learned from our Rózsi that you are alive, I laughed through my tears. Though she writes that due to your many tasks my fate does not interest you, I like to wait it out, I make no hasty judgments and so I was not overly upset that you did not hasten to write. Once I knew from a reliable source that you and the others survived I didn't even care if you have forgotten me. This was enough. I waited and hoped because I knew you would write. And then when your letter came I was near hysteric with joy, this is how she writes it, hysteric, as if she were French, *hystérique*, I ran up and down the house hysteric and I was so proud I told complete strangers that you wrote me. Magduska wrote me. A woman of sixty-five, I felt like nineteen once again,

There stood before me your dear mother, my idol, and then comes

268

a sentence I don't know what to make of, or I'm afraid I may be taking it amiss. There stood your father, my friend, Júlia Papanek writes, whereas in a decent home it was not customary for the nursemaid to be friends with the master of the house, especially if she idolized the lady of the house the way she did.

It is also possible that she translated her memories into American English with its democratic roots, learned in the meantime, it is almost unavoidable, then she translated the sentence back into Hungarian from the democratic transcription in her mind. Americans say about everyone in the world, whether a man or a woman, that they're friends. As for emigrants, they very often navigate between two languages and the cultural conditions of two languages, as it were. She must have been thirteen or fourteen when she first stood in front of her future idol and her friend, meaning my grandmother and grandfather. People didn't take in a nursemaid older than that. And so, on the photograph she sent Pista, she may have been as old as seventy-two or seventy-four and not sixty-five. Be that as it may, Júlia's statement, according to which my grandfather had been her friend, to some extent modifies and tempers the picture she drew of him, sometimes with anger, sometimes with scorn.

After the horror you have lived through, she writes, for the first time I was completely at peace. I am grateful that you have survived. It is very strange that she does not mention to whom or to what she feels grateful. This lack in her sentence is like an open wound in the flesh. Every cliché in the letter is in place, but the missing concept of Fate or God is offensive, especially considering the list of obligatory clichés needed for a letter. Or, possibly, she couldn't write down at least one of these words because of the terrible lessons she'd learned from the recent war; and also, the end to the Second World War brought a great antipathetic change in the use of the various European languages.

But it is even stranger and more grave that she makes no mention of those who have disappeared, neither György Mándoki, the first-born son of Eugenie Nádas, meaning Eugénia, whom everyone called by her nickname, Özsi, and whom she may not have seen as a baby or a little boy, nor Miklós Nádas, the meekest of the other boys and who, from the moment of his birth, was confined to her care just like those born before him, or my father, who was born last in line. If this certain Rózsika gave her a faithful account of the fate of our family, it is out of the question that she should have been uninformed about the gaping absence of these two, or that she didn't know that on the list of every possible search service and aid service they were indicated as having disappeared.

If much of your goods have perished, don't let that worry you now, dear Magduska, she writes to quickly cover up the want of the persons who have gone missing, I now have everything at my disposal to help you. Write me if you need money, clothes, food, anything. I can send you 500 dollars right away. Not just you, but anyone who needs it in the family. I mailed a package to you yesterday. When you get it, I hope your happiness will match the love with which it was sent. I realize that the first parcel should have gone to the older children, but your letter came at a time when I felt dejected. The usual dejection, she writes bashfully, this is how she refers to her recurrent depression. If you pick up her picture to study the lines of her face with this in mind, you will clearly see the signs of serious depression. But you also see her self-control. Her bright glance, the merry look in her eye, gives nothing away. Júlia has beautifully shaped eyes, her glance radiates warmth of heart. Perhaps she keeps silent about Gyuri Mándoki, whom Eugenie is looking for, and Miklós, about whom she'd have plenty to ask, out of the goodness of her heart. In case you have not yet heard, she writes, I will now tell you. Our Jani's family has perished. My brother Ármin's two sons and daughter with all their children, they have perished to the last man. So her family also had an Ármin who had perished along with his three children.

She then changes the subject.

My Magduska, and this time she writes her name as if it were a prayer, I would like to ask you something after all. Please write me and tell me what you need and I will send it without delay. It is the least I can do for you. How is Aunt Elisa, she asks. And how is the ever-smiling Aunt Anna. The associative leap is easy to understand, for with this she is extending her offer of help to the family as a whole, the two idolized younger sisters of my grandmother, whom she also idolized. And is Pista married yet, she asks. You wrote that Bandi has returned from labor service, but what is my Bandi doing, she asks. Kisa couldn't have learned in the Bronx that Bandi had in fact returned from labor service, but he did so illegally, he escaped and came back to Budapest, where he found a safe refuge in the illegal basement. I will pull Pista's ear if he doesn't write me. He could have written with confidence and tell me what he needs. Here the mention of Miklós should follow, but instead, only the glaring absence of his name follows. She doesn't mention Lacika, my father, either, but she'd sent the first of her packages to him, and my father answered right away to thank her. The parcel contained powdered milk, canned milk, canned meat, sugar, chocolate, cocoa, unroasted coffee beans, tea, soup cubes, all precious commodities in a starving Budapest immersed in pitiful but lifesaving black-marketeering. I remember every single labeled American package, tin, paper box, the tastes and the smells, most of all the persistent taste of the unfamiliar spices in the soups made from cubes. My tongue searched for this taste for a full decade afterward, until it reappeared from the aid parcels after '56. It may have been wild marjoram, or possibly peppergrass, or possibly some tarragon with lots of black pepper. The package also contained warm underpants, warm scarves, warm gloves and sweaters, all the things that a package like this should contain, and as a bonus, not just a low-cut evening gown of bright apple-green silk and tulle, and not just two pairs of worn silk slippers with extremely high heels, one a light purple, the other turquoise, but as the *ne plus ultra* of presents, two men's ties of hand-painted silk, Black slaves like monkeys on one, one of them climbing up the trunk of a palm tree on the slant, the other flinging a coconut from a branch to his white lord, who is standing smugly in colonial costume, khaki shorts, a military-style short-sleeved shirt, and a cork hat under the palms, watching the efforts of the slaves with a hand shielding his eyes. This was a light blue tie, the sky above didn't have to be painted, just the fleecy clouds, laid on thick. On the other tie, which went from green to red to black, the moon was up above the branches, a boat bobbed up and down on the blue waters of a lake enveloped in the dark of night, in it a pair of lovers, but that's still not everything. The package also contained two pink bras of a considerable size, and on them two black hands, probably Negro hands again, as they grab these impressive boobs from behind.

There sat my parents on the ground next to the open cardboard box screaming with laughter, and for days, for weeks, our relatives, acquaintances, and friends came to gawk, they showed the apple-green gown to one another, several of them even tried it on, they couldn't get enough of it in the city that stood in ruins. As for me, I toddled and tiptoed, putting on airs around them, the neckties of the slaveholders around my neck, on my feet the finest silk slippers lined with calfskin.

I know full well, Papanek writes in her letter, that for the unselfish friendship that was my lot among you, for all the good things I enjoyed in your circle, my gratitude can never be complete. Your letter is a masterpiece. You wrote about everyone, which is a great gift by itself, and I thank you. The next sentence, which must have been written in response to the last lines of my Aunt Magda's letter, I once again have difficulty understanding without feeling a certain sense of unease. About me I can only write that the time will come. Perhaps she is thinking about benign death. Perhaps she is thinking about the death wish plaguing her, the profoundest strains of the depression dogging her, perhaps she finds consolation in the thought that sooner or later death will come for her. Then without transition of any kind, she writes that she has a seventeen-room mortgage-free house with three kitchens. One part of the house, with seven rooms, is occupied by her older sister Lujza, who rents out four of the rooms, which is the extent of her income. My own apartment has six rooms, she writes. The six rooms and three kitchens are fully furnished. I rent out three furnished rooms on the upper floor. If it's the top floor, I can see in the mind's eye these spacious rooms with the so-called American kitchen and the light streaming in through a skylight. There also has to be a sleeping alcove next to the bathroom, even if it has no window. The three rentals pay for the expenses of the house, she continues. I live well off of 25 dollars a week. I have sent 32 packages so far to strangers in Europe. I am just putting a package together for Özsike. Whatever she doesn't need she should pass on to those who can use it. I can't tell you how much I would like to see all of you one more time. But I don't think it will happen. My son Gyuri is teaching at the university. Elzus, Mr. Papanek's daughter from his first marriage, will turn 34 the day after tomorrow. She has a 10 year old daughter and a 7 year old son, he's a veritable lad. They are lovely. The little girl is even well-behaved. And my son-in-law not only earns a good salary, he seems to attract money. All in all, he is a good man. I am not worried about my daughter-in-law either. She studied to be a lawyer. She finished last year. As for me, I've become a 170 pound woman to be reckoned with, you wouldn't believe it if you saw me. When I reflect on the course of my life, I always think I must enjoy the years that I may have ahead of me, if any. You write that your dear mother has passed away. It is good like this, she did it in good time, this way she doesn't have to know about all the immeasurable bad things that have happened to us. She is standing in front of me now, weeping, because I know that she is feeling what I am feeling. She loved Gyuri just as I loved him. This woman, who appeared so stern, was all heart. Nobody knew me, nobody understood me like your sweet mother. Nobody ever exerted a greater influence on my life than your parents. I hope I will hear from all of you more often from now on. Magduska, my darling, my sweet, I was very angry with your father. After this surprising revelation what follows in Papanek's letter contains such awful temporal mumbo-jumbo, such ethical and linguistic nonsense, that I have a hard time making heads or tails of it.

This is what must have happened. Old Josefina Neumayer, meaning my paternal great-grandmother, asked her to take an antique shawl to America with her for her daughter-in-law. Apart from this one reference, I know nothing about my great-grandmother's daughter-in-law. The elderly Mrs. Neumayer, who at the time was past eighty and a widow, lived on her estate in Szolnok, while her firstborn son, Lajos Neumayer, ran a farm in Tiszasüly, at some distance from her own. Josefina also had an apartment in Pest, on the third floor of the house at 16 Vörösmarthy Street. By all odds, Josefina must have asked

Papanek to take the valuable shawl to America when Papanek went to pay her a farewell visit. As far as I can make out from her letter, by all odds she took her leave of my great-grandmother in Szolnok or Tiszasüly, because she writes that she brought a shawl up to Pest with her. Had she stood face-to-face with my grandmother earlier in Pest, when she was mourning her son György Nádas, who had committed suicide, and if she mourned the loss of the beloved son as deeply as my grandmother, and she couldn't have felt differently, because ever since he was born, she was Gyuri's, meaning György Nádas's, nursemaid, she wouldn't have left our family, and she couldn't have emigrated before 1917.

After he had passed his end of semester examination, on April 24, 1917, at dawn, the twenty-two-year-old man shot himself through the heart on Margaret Island, but the bullet, instead of reaching his heart, mangled his lungs. They found him in the early morning, and he was still alive. They called the police, a doctor came with them, but strangely enough, instead of taking him to the hospital, they took him to Pannónia Street and up to the fourth floor on a stretcher. His mother, who had turned to stone, had just enough presence of mind to order Miss Júlia to call the two family physicians, Béla Mezei and Henrik Benedickt, the latter of whom later married Edina Krishaber, the daughter of Anna's younger sister. Just as he was, they moved the wounded man from the stretcher to his bed, which lay unmade from the night before. No one knew where he'd spend the night. The doctor who'd come with the police wanted to say some words of comfort to the devastated woman. He will recover. He'll pull through. He'd extracted the bullet. They don't have to do anything except give him water every hour, taking care that it shouldn't go down the wrong way. And they should change the bandages tomorrow. Except he mustn't speak. Not a single word. Hearing this, the young man opened his eyes and seeing the face of his mother leaning over him, driven by some animal pain coming from deep down, he began howling with all his might. When the blood gurgling from his throat forced him to stop, he was happy and he smiled, his face was radiant with joy that he would now suffocate and could finish what he had set his heart on.

Those standing around him didn't get a chance to warn him or hold him down. He didn't want to live anymore. The blood came pouring out of his mouth, and after a couple of minutes of bloody suffocation, he fell silent forever.

During his final semester at the university, he took an astonishing number of courses. He began his university studies in September 1913 at the engineering and architecture faculty of the Royal József Technical College. During his first semester he studied analytics and geometry with József Kürscsák, descriptive geometry with Béla Töttösy, chemistry with Lajos Ilosvay, geology with Ferenc Schafarzik, drawing with Árpád Schauschek, English with László Grisza, he already knew French and German, and a year later he was also admitted to the faculty of the humanities, and from then on, parallel with the faculty of engineering, he studied Hungarian stylistics with László Négyessy, differential and integral calculus with Manó Beke, function theory with Lipót Fejér, higher algebra with Gusztáv Rados, experimental physics with Lóránd Eötvös, laboratory practice in experimental physics with Jenő Klupathy, experimental chemistry with Gusztáv Buchböck, and so on. During the fatal semester he added new layers of knowledge to his already impressive storehouse; he took up national economy and financial studies with Farkas Heller, whose seminars he attended, Hungarian common law, financial common law, the history of economic law and public administration law with Ernő Friedmann, commercial statistics and banking with Gyula Mandelló, transportation with Kornél Zelovich, workers' insurance and social policy with Dezső Papp, industrial plant accounting with Kálmán Méhely, the Hungarian credit system with Aladár Edvi Illés, mining industry policy with Farkas Heller, political and commercial civil law with Károly Goldziher, agricultural and industrial engineering with Pál Lázár, and patent law with Zsigmond Bernauer.

But it seems that this did not suffice to fill up his life. He came into the world after my Aunt Eugenie, he was the second child, the boy his parents had prayed for. The heir apparent and future apple of his father's eye, he was born prematurely on August 10, 1895, at the Balatonkenese estate, and when they packed up all the transportable or preserved produce of the estate on a huge dray and a buggy filled to overflowing and moved back to the apartment in Hold Street, there followed a whirl of celebrations. Lunches, dinners, afternoon parties, and afternoon teas came in quick succession until mid-October. On occasion, the table was set for thirty people. At such times my grand-mother had to borrow Zsófi, my great-grandfather's celebrated cook, for a couple of days because such celebrations were too much for their own cook, Mari Vastag, to manage on her own. She announced that she'd rather give notice than cook for this many guests. But she didn't quit, and amid loud altercations, she and Zsófi engaged in a furious round of cooking and baking. There came the populous Mezei rela-tives from Nagykorona Street, first and foremost our great-great-grand-father, the innkeeper from Sátoraljaújhely who after the death of our great-grandmother Eugénia Schlesinger moved to Budapest with his wife to live with his eldest son so Little Mother, my great-great-grand-mother, could take care of the five orphaned children, but especially the newborn Béla. But by the time Gyuri was born, Little Mother had died, too, and from then on our great-great-grandfather was at-tended to by his nurse, and in Hold Street the servants carried him up to the third floor in a wheelchair; then came our great-great-grand-father's two sons, the firstborn, our great-grandfather Mór Mezei and his younger brother, Ernő Mezei, who, insouciant to his pronounced speech impediment repeatedly spoke up in Parliament, as has often been mentioned before, in the former National Assembly building in Sándor Street designed by Miklós Ybl in the neoclassical style, then came my grandmother's younger sisters and brothers, Erzsébet, who was the handsomest of the lot and also the brightest and the founding member of the first Hungarian feminist society and who, for some mysterious reason, remained an old maid her entire life, except back then they called it self-sacrifice; after all, she managed her father's populous household, she kept it going, you might say, and there came Anna from nearby Duna Street, who followed in my grand-mother's wake and was conventionally married, she married a Vien-nese banker called Krishaber, and she was also the first who, thanks to our great-grandfather's position as a lawmaker, was able to get married in a civil ceremony. Our great-grandfather was the first in Europe to champion the law making civil marriage possible and to have the House of Deputies accept it. Pál Mezei came, too, from Frankfurt am Main, where he studied law, and so did Béla Mezei, who studied medicine in Vienna, both of them students who were about to graduate and were as yet unmarried. There came the Schlesingers from Vienna, the relatives of their mother who died in childbirth when Béla was born, Josefina and József, the Neumayer grandparents, came from their estate in Tiszasüly, there came the girlfriends of Klára, Anna and Erzébet, and their former friends from boarding school also came from Vienna, Basel, and Zürich, most of them married, the former nurses, nannies, tutors, and chambermaids also came to see the newborn child, friends and acquaintances of the family sent telegrams of congratulation or at least friends and acquaintances of the family paid their respects during the morning visiting hours, leaving their visiting cards, even if not as many of them and not in such a wide circle as three years previously, at the wedding of Klára and Arnold on May 19, 1892, which the upper class of the time attended, or at least congratulated them in letters, telegrams, or left their visiting cards, but especially the newly entitled Jewish nobility, and those who had been raised to baronial rank came. Which, needless to say, was not so much a sign of joy over the nuptials of the young couple or the birth of their son, no, by no means; it was addressed to the prestige Mór Mezei enjoyed in those years as lawyer and lawgiver in a city engaged in a building fever fired by conservative liberalism and striving to become a true metropolis. However, seeing the development of his child in Hold Street, the sources of the father's inordinate joy very quickly dried up. Not that the baby wasn't developing; the females of the family were awed by his size and strength. But he was hardly two, and his father was already dissatisfied with him. He was barely three when his father was already beating him. He was a quiet child, not in response to the beatings, but in spite of them, doing his best against the headwind, because he really did his best, but despite his best efforts, he couldn't be as perfect as his father had expected of him. He was perfect in his own way. He was interested in so-called girlish things such as cooking, they kept finding him in the kitchen, and also embroidery, reading books, and the sciences. Basically, he was interested in everything. As far as our strict-minded grandfather was concerned, he couldn't do anything that you could call manly. I'll put the fear of God into you. He had to bathe in cold water every morning, and neither Miss Júlia nor Miss Jolán, not even his own mother was allowed to lend a hand. It is not proper for women to be present when a young man is bathing. I'll make a soldier of you. If you're going to be like this when you're a soldier, they'll string you up, take it from me, tie you to the whipping post, put you in irons. He bought a dog whip and from then on he beat him with it to turn him into a real man and a fine soldier of the realm. And he meant it. He, Adolf Arnold Neumayer, had been sent by my great-grandparents from the manor at Tiszasüly to a Bavarian boys' boarding school, where, with the written consent of their parents, the teachers beat the boys from good families with a dog whip. But while József Neumayer, my paternal great-grandfather, was a man who knew his own mind, Josefa was cruel and merciless, and not just with the servants and the farmhands. If they didn't like something or bristled, she sent for the hajduks or the gendarmes, and had them beaten in the servants' quarters. And they were not the only ones she treated like this, she treated everyone like this, the rabbi, the cantor, the children's tutor, even herself. If in midwinter they were reminded of their paternal grandmother, her grandchildren shivered with fear at the thought of spending the summer with her. As for my paternal grandmother, Klára Mezei, whom the entire family idolized, this ice-cold and goodly woman, as Miss Júlia had characterized her in the letter she wrote Magda after the siege, she left the room without a word and did not protect her son from the dog whip. She preferred not knowing what was happening. She didn't believe in God either; in our family there was no spirituality and no soul. All the same, it is clear from the photographs that the unfortunate little boy grew into a brilliant young man who after his botched suicide attempt howled himself to death. With the wistful fear in his eye that had become more pronounced with time, he was better-looking than his younger brothers, who, with the knowledge of their older brother's self-inflicted death and that bloody howl, had to go on living with the same parents. Children have no choice but to go on living with their sadistic, fascist, pedophile, or Communist mass murderer parents. They're the ones God had shoved in their faces to love. From among my Gyurika's books. This is what my grandmother, whom the family idolized for her unabashed ways, meaning her self-discipline, meaning her *contenance*, wrote in the books he'd left behind. From among my Gyurika's books. She wrote it in ink, in her round, regular, glaringly inhibited letters.

Contenance. Composure.

If anyone lacked discipline at the table, all they said to him was *contenance*.

Or a bit louder, *Fassung bewahren*, maintain your composure. Do not lose your bearing and dignity, no matter what.

When I was young we had several of Gyurika's books with my grandmother's timid handwriting in the margins, mostly works on sociology and literature that, without my realizing, had a profound influence on me. These included the best of the Hungarian liberal democratic thinkers of the early twentieth century, because in spite of his insistent protests and prohibitions, when he was still in high school, Gyurika became a member and later secretary of the Galileo Circle, and he took his sisters Özsi and Magda and his schoolboy brother Pista along with him. I don't know what became of these books in the course of all our moving about, but one remained, Anna Lesznai's *Poems of Return*. It was published by *Nyugat* in 1909, the year my father was born.

When our brutal and hot-tempered, dog-whipping, and probably morbidly homophobic and profoundly phallocratic grandfather Neumayer, who had by then changed his name along with his children's to the Hungarian-sounding Nádas, learned from Miss Júlia of his mother's intention to send a present to America, which, according to various sources, must have happened in 1918, but certainly before the proclamation of the Republic, in short, when he heard about his mother's intention to send an antique shawl to America, he came up with the crazy idea by no means alien to his nature, petty-minded and generous at the same time, that Miss Júlia shouldn't just take the antique shawl to his sister-in-law in America, but also a shawl of newer provenance. She consistently writes *antique*, and if the shawl was in fact antique and not just old, it must have been valuable. My great-grandparents dressed with utmost reserve, but being familiar with the quality of the objects that have survived from them, we can't discount the possibility that they might have had a couple of valuable shawls at home. Be that as it may, along with the shawls, my grandfather instructed Júlia to give his American sister-in-law the new shawl, sell the more valuable antique piece, and send what she got for it back to him in Pest. I am trying to follow Papanek, but the whole thing remains confusing, because apparently, my tightfisted yet generous grandfather also told Papanek that if the sister-in-law should choose the antique shawl, she should keep the new one for herself. The entire affair would make no sense, and I would hasten to relegate it to the category of one of our incomparable family nightmares if only I were not more or less familiar with the emotional politics behind it.

There was nothing in the family that Adolf Arnold Nádas did not stick his otherwise noble, aquiline nose into, nothing he did not interfere with, or did not wish to interfere with. He must have been a colossal domestic tyrant, Harpagon and Croesus rolled into one, a monster, a demon, whose terrible mood swings brought deeds of evil as well as deeds of charity in their wake. His pathological compulsion to be on top of everything made his family and servant suffer every hour of the day that they spent with him. He famously wanted to know even about things that did not interest him at all, but when offered, he ignored the answers. He was exceptionally handsome as a young man, his hands were the hands of an exceptionally handsome man, with unusually long and well-shaped, finely articulated fingers. You're devouring your food like animals, bellowed this handsome man with the large physique when his children forgot about his presence and for a carefree moment ate with hearty appetites. Otherwise, Özsi hardly ate, Gyuri and Magda ate, provided their father's raging fury did not prevent it, you're eating me out of house and home when I'm working my fingers to the bone for you. There is no knowing what kept body and soul together in Pista, because he could hardly be made to eat at all; for his part, Bandi couldn't have cared less, come rain or shine, he shoveled it in with gusto while the two youngest brothers, Miklós and Laci, looked on wide-eyed at what was happening around the table, and barely ate anything themselves. But when they didn't eat, their father screamed, you'll be licking even the dry bread crumbs from the tablecloth, because you'll never amount to anything, ever. Nothing. You'll end up in the ditch, like paupers, you'll rot away under a bridge. Members of his family said that the beauty of his hands was of the forbidding kind. Ivan the Terrible had beautiful hands like his, his daughters said. Later, when this handsome man had lost his original shape and had grown inordinately obese because he was a glutton, he stuffed himself in the kitchen and he stuffed himself at the dinner table, while everyone suffered from his chomping and the smacking of his lips, the sound of his lips and tongue and teeth, and when they were invited somewhere, they suffered from shame, because even there he'd hardly hold himself back, he picked up the bone to chew the gristle off it, the sauces dripped down his large mustache onto his vest, there was no getting away from it, there was no way to plug up their ears, and if he saw that they plugged them up with the bread pellets they surreptitiously rolled between their fingers, his handsome hand turned into a huge, fat paw. Children must not roll bread pellets. And he struck out. You have desecrated the bread. The boys knew a thing or two about how hard he could strike with his big, handsome, ringed hand. He struck with the full force of his suspicious nature, his crazed need to be in control, and his persistent discontent. His tyrannical bent drove him on; he may have suffered from an overabundance of testosterone. Yet he was also soft as butter, infinitely beholden to his wife, obliged, for she not only put up with him but, in her own infinitely cold and sharp manner, loved him. Also, in a public display inclining to kitschy sentimentality, he often cried, he howled, even at the table, no doubt enjoying his spectacular sadness. He could be moved to extremes by himself, his infinite goodness, his infinite generosity, the considerable bulk of his body trembling from the might of his love of mankind, and how there is nothing he wouldn't do for his family, and how they repay his love with wickedness. All is wickedness, the world is wicked, there is wickedness everywhere, his family is wicked, and the Mezeis are the wickedest of the lot, not to mention the wickedness of his one and only beloved mother, no wonder he is forced to shed profuse tears of woe. Which frightened his children at least as much as his tantrums and furious outbursts. But they'd laugh behind his back, too, that's a tyrant's fate; they laughed at him for everything. People are terrified of him, they said, but they do not respect him. Even half a century after his death, his children made fun at his expense, asking one another what Adolf Arnold Nádas would have to say about one thing or another. They didn't say my father, or our father, or our dear father, or our dear departed father of blessed memory; they said, what would Adolf Arnold Nádas have to say. Like this, contemptuously, with his full name. They said it so they could laugh at him, even after he was long dead. He was a troubled soul, I couldn't say in what way or why; he was troubled in keeping with the times. He never missed a chance to revenge himself on his beloved parents, because this is how it had to be said and written, demonstratively, theatrically, parents had to be beloved, this is what the etiquette of the great bourgeois era called for; in short, he never missed a chance to take his revenge, at least symbolically, on József and Josefa.

Which was another reason the children laughed at their perpetually whimpering, shouting milksop of a father, who was cruel and sentimental at the same time, behind his back. By then they also put up much better with their fearful grandmother. Though she was rigid and heartless, monstrous and irrational in her cruelty with the domestic servants, the farmhands, and the day laborers and had little affection for her grandchildren, she, at least, did not go into fits of rage. After finishing a Bavarian boarding school, their second son, my grandfather, studied at the agriculture academies of Berlin and Eindhoven, hoping to take over the estate from his father at some time in the future, but he did not finish his studies. For some reason that is shrouded in mystery to this day, he picked himself up and headed for Marseille, where he had two photographs taken of himself, two handsome miniatures; he sent one home to his parents with an inscription written on the back in German and gave the other to Aurelia Rosenzweig on March 15, 1885, in Budapest. It is apparent in the first photograph that this outstanding piece of humanity, this young man with the perfectly shaped limbs, had not washed in at least three days, did not comb his thick shock of hair that stood up off his scalp, because he must have visited Lacour's photo studio on the rue Saint Férréol after a night out on the town, and by all indications he'd slept a couple of hours without bothering to remove his clothes, neither his trousers nor his vest nor his jacket. In the second photograph he looks a bit more orderly because at least he placed his hat over his thick shock of hair; he is holding his overcoat thrown leisurely over his arm, and in the same hand he is holding his kidskin gloves, while in the other, just as casually, he is holding his silver-handled walking stick between two fingers. But he did not marry Miss Rosenzweig, and as was the custom, the mother of the bereft young lady packed up all the letters and souvenirs, tied them with a string, and returned them to the sender. Something like this was a deed of great consequence; a young lady of good breeding, even if she was beautiful, lost her chances of ever finding a husband, her fate having been sealed by a dubious character such as he.

The estate at Tiszasüly was not sizable, it was just 499 cadastral holds. But it was fine soil, the best soil; the Neumayers at first rented the property, then bought it, and in the surviving photographs, my great-grandfather and great-grandmother from Tiszasüly look nothing like the owners of a vast estate. They were just prosperous farmers, well-off peasants, and even though some of the photographs were taken in Szolnok and Jászberény, and still others in Karlsbad, they are shown wearing simple, much-worn clothes. However, some of the photographs were taken at Strelinsky's, the celebrated photography studio in Dorottya Street in Pest, and in these they are dressed for the occasion, and in keeping with their means. József Neumayer also had a wheat business in Szolnok with six granaries located at some distance from one another. Be that as it may, they owned 499 cadastral holds of this good soil along the Tisza River, and my great-grandfather considered my grandfather, his son Adolf Arnold, unfit to run it. It was as simple as that. He may have studied what he says he studied, but he hasn't got what it takes, it's not in him, he has no feel for the soil. And since it's not in him, his son can take over the wheat business, but he's got to learn it first. The running of the estate, though, is out of the question. He wouldn't be able to find the right tone with the farmhands, nor the day laborers. Such were the arguments against him. But he wants to manage the farm and not the wheat business. The matter is settled, Great-grandfather Neumayer said. I've just put the dot on the *i*, he said when about ten years later they confirmed his rational decision at the notary public's office in Jászberény. As was only right and proper, his older brother, Lajos, took over management of the estate. They paid Adolf Arnold off and let him go in God's name and take his bad nature with him. He never forgave them for this profoundly rational intrigue and refused to take over the wheat business even when his father was ready to entrust it to his care. After my great-grandfather's death, he wanted to buy the Tiszasüly estate from his brothers and sisters, but the hard-as-nails Madam Josefa wouldn't hear of it. Well, he'll bring them around with his offers. But his brothers and sisters, Lajos, Ida, Regina, and Miksa, who at the time was living in Pozsony, had no intention of selling off their shares. In which case, he felt he should at least get his hands on the price of the antique shawl. He should at least do everything in his power to thwart his beloved mother as long as she's alive and frustrate her intention in all things.

It is rare for a male child to hate his own mother, to despise his one and only beloved mother, Josefina. But in this convoluted shawl story, Papanek may have also lied or distorted the truth a bit. One gets lost in the labyrinth of other people's families, not only his own. In any event, my grandfather's sister-in-law, Miksa's wife in America, chose the newer shawl over the antique, just as, knowing his sister-in-law, my grandfather had predicted. But when Papanek gave him the news, according to her, my grandfather didn't believe it. He doubted it. But I don't understand why he should have doubted it, and what he doubted, considering with what good instinct he had expected

284

precisely this outcome. He flew into a rage, saying he does nothing but good for everyone, nothing but good, and yet everybody cheats him. But surely he'd have flown into a rage even if it had happened the other way around. He accused Papanek of wanting to kill him, this woman is trying to send him to an early grave, she's bent on cheating him. Whereas the good Papanek just wanted to know how things stood, to find out from him whether she should really sell that damned antique shawl.

From that time forward, I didn't write him anymore, I wrote only your dear mother, she continues. The antique shawl is yours, of course. Write me please if you want it, I will send it, it's been in mothballs since 1921. I think she must have sent it back, because I had seen this shawl or one like it as a child. It was a huge black silk shawl embroidered in lilac and gold, by all signs baroque or even older, and when they took it out of the tissue paper to have a look at it, the silk was already threadbare and falling apart. I have no idea what became of it.

And then, without preamble, Kisa goes into the following subject of interest to her. I saw your husband just once, but right away I thought he'd be a good man for you. From this observation, too, it would seem that she must have left Budapest with the shawls in 1917 or 1918. Magda Nádas married Pál Aranyossi that year, while her older sister had married László Mándoki just months before. The two sisters didn't even wait for the year of mourning to end after György Nádas's suicide. They wanted to get married so they could get away from their father, the sooner the better. By now the devastated parents barely had the strength to raise their voices against a penniless doctor and a penniless journalist marrying the girls, whom, in theory, at least, they should have bestowed on men of equal rank so the family fortune would increase and not decrease in value. The aunts and uncles nevertheless continued to bristle a bit at the Sunday dinners in Nagykorona Street, saying this is a *mésalliance* and that is a *mésalliance* the family must not countenance. A scandal. Until Mór Mezei ordered his sons, daughters, daughters-in-law, sons-in-law, and grandchildren to silence, and in order to lend emphasis to his approval of the girls' decisions, he offered each, as he put it, *zusätzlich*, an additional thirty thousand crowns for their dowries. Which may not have been a vast sum in this family, but at one time in Vienna, he himself had married Eugénia Schlesinger, a woman far wealthier than he, out of love, and the world did not come to an end. He was not unnecessarily prodigal, though, nor tightfisted either, for that matter. He was thrifty and did not like ostentation.

Where is your son and how is he? If he gives me his address, I can send him a couple of things that are difficult to get a hold of in Paris right now. Send me instructions, Magduska dear, I wouldn't like to seem silly and send things all over the world, things that the family doesn't need. But please don't think I am trying to show off either. I am not a wealthy woman who throws money out the window. But I know what I owe you. Even more so, what you deserve. I won't stand by while you lack for anything, even for a moment. And with respect to this, I hope you will understand, I must clear something up. Your mother once gave me 10,000 crowns. She gave it to me as what you might call a long-term loan, this is what she came up with so I shouldn't feel bad about it. That I should have it until I am in a situation in America when I can give it back without a problem. And so, Magduska dear, please write me what I want to know about the family. Meaning, she wanted to know who needs what. In Kisa's name as well, the 170 pound ancient Júlia sends you lots of kisses.

Always the older one, and among the older ones the one who enjoys the most respect offers his hand, and it is up to him to start talking to the other on a first-name basis.

Why.

Because that's how it's done.

I acquired my knowledge of table manners and etiquette not so much from Júlia as from Miss Jolán.

You do not put a finger in your mouth, and not just at the table. You never put a finger in your mouth. You do not put a finger in your mouth even if you have washed hands before a meal. You do not put a finger in your mouth for a variety of reasons. For one thing, it is simply not done, it is not nice, no one is interested in seeing what is in your mouth, and for another, we do not let germs get inside us voluntarily.

My Aunt Magda relates the same germ story in her *Irregular Autobiography*, published by Kossuth Kiadó in 1978. At the age of two, she shared her croissant out on the balcony of their home in Hold Street with Aunt Fritz's sandy-haired dog, even though her mother repeatedly explained why she mustn't do it. Aunt Fritz was the widow of an army officer who lived with her sandy-haired dachshund downstairs in the small courtyard apartment on her humble life annuity.

If she gives the croissant to the dog and then takes a bit herself, germs will settle in her mouth and worms will grow in her stomach. Except she couldn't think of any other way of sharing the croissant with the dog. She didn't know how to tear her croissant in two. She put it in the dog's mouth, the dog bit into it, and that's how they ate it, taking turns. Rolls were a different story. Sometimes they gave her a roll. Her brother Gyuri taught her what to do; he was a big boy by then, three years of age. Gyuri stepped on the roll so that half of it should slip from under his shoe, then he pulled on it. He showed her, see how easy it is, the roll is torn in half right away, you can go, give it to the dog. Which is when their father happened to come into their room and he began shouting, what have you done, what have you done, you accursed children with the bread, may all be damned who do this even once, I'm cursed, having children like you, and where is Miss Jolán, why did she leave the children to themselves again. Jolán paved the way for the crime, letting them do this to the bread, to the life-giving bread, the precious bread. And where is Júlia again, what's keeping her. Jolán has gone to the kitchen. Why has she gone to the kitchen, when he's paying her not to go to the kitchen but to keep an eye on the children. She went to the kitchen because Pista's milk had gone cold and had to be warmed up. And where is Miss Júlia. I'm paying two, why can't one of them watch these good-for-nothing children. Somebody call Júlia this minute. You must not step on the bread. Why can't this simpleton of a boy get it through his thick skull.

Gyuri, the dotard, my aunt writes with derision even in her old age, he put up with the humiliation without a word, mutely, he put up with his father calling him a simpleton and beating him, whereas she threw a fit and screamed because of the obvious injustice, whereupon hearing all the excitement, their mother reluctantly came in from the bathroom.

Germs settle on the doorknob, the balustrade, your hand. Why. Just like the sparrows and the pigeons. You can't see them with your eye, only under a microscope, but germs are also looking for food. It wouldn't be felicitous if they were to find their food in your mouth.

It seems that in our family, such pieces of hygienic wisdom were passed on from mouth to mouth.

You do not sit down until you are offered a seat. You do not take someone else's place. You do not pick your nose. My father was especially adamant about this nose-picking. He told me repeatedly that I mustn't pick it, even in secret, even if no one sees. I had the feeling that he hadn't quite finished the sentence, and so I didn't dare ask why I couldn't pick it in secret. I came upon the other half of his unfinished sentence only decades later. There was a Hungarian monk, his name was Tihamér Tóth, who ruined the lives of generations of growing boys. In his severe sermons and books, this Tihamér Tóth asserted that those wicked little boys who enjoy picking their nose will take to masturbation more readily than the others, and their fingers and noses, and even their penises must be smeared with hot pepper so they won't end up suffering from venereal disease later in their lives. Throughout his long life, the monk Tihamér Tóth racked his brain to find ways and means with which to distract the attention of little boys from their own penises. He prescribed rigorous fasts, cold showers, the strict segregation of the sexes, physical punishment for the repeated offenders, and also biblical curses.

Until the lady of the house or the oldest lady at the table unfolds her napkin, you will stay put. Your hands remain by the table setting, lightly, only the tips of the fingers and the sides of your palms touching the table, meanwhile your elbows are pressed to your side, but not too tight. You do not swing your arms, you do not lean on the table with your arms or elbows. Your back is straight. Let your shoulders hang loose, that makes for straight posture. Not too stiff, though, not too rigid. You mustn't think of the rules as an unpleasant duty. Loosen up. Until the oldest lady or the lady of the house begins to eat, you do not eat either; do not rush, you are not catching a train, you do not pick up the knives or forks either.

But where was the oldest lady or, for that matter, the lady of the house by then. My mother's legal status was that of wife, she was married, but she was never the lady of any house, ever. There was no house and no residence. And no estate. I realize why my father did it. He wanted me to learn the rules still current at the time. He passed his knowledge on to me. Do not clatter, do not munch, do not slurp. We do not bang the cutlery against the porcelain. Whereas in Péterfy Sándor Street, Grandmother Tauber didn't even have porcelain. Each plate bore a different pattern. Put less food in your mouth. We do not chew with our mouth open. We do not put a finger in the soup. We do not pick at the food. Do not leave anything on your plate. What you like or don't like is your own affair. Before you drink, wipe your mouth with the napkin. Why. Because otherwise you will leave a fatty smear on the rim of your glass. Others find it *dégoûtant*. After you drink, wipe your mouth with the napkin again. Why. I don't know, I can't say. Just do it.

It was a rare pleasure to experience moments when my father was himself surprised that he didn't have a rational explanation at hand for something.

Do not sniff your nose at the table.

He shouldn't sniff it, if you don't mind me saying so, anywhere, not just at the table.

Do not stare under the table, and if you must, don't do it like an oaf, don't fiddle with your fingers. The napkin ring is not a toy, don't roll it around, it's there so you'll find your napkin tomorrow, too.

Do not fumble with your weenie, do not scratch the base of your nose, do not shout across the table.

We'd better check the child's stool, he keeps scratching his behind.

Wouldn't you know, he's got tapeworms again.

In the years following the siege, it was not advisable to go out on the street after dark; people could have done so, but it was not advisable. On the other hand, there were no more blackouts. There came a moment when the streets were deserted, this was what they called nightfall. Earlier, this was when the blackout came into effect. For the rest of my life, nightfall remained something sinister. The streets were deserted, the city was forsaken. You had to reach home before dark or stay the night at someone's house. For many years to come, I remained anxious for us to make it home on time, to hurry and not have to stay the night at the home of strangers. And also, that our footsteps shouldn't echo along the empty streets.

We didn't have to black out all the windows anymore and anyone could switch on the light as he pleased, or as his finances permitted. There were no more blackouts. The bombers didn't fly overhead anymore. Anyone could sleep with the windows open, if that's what they wanted. For long years after the siege, I couldn't get enough of all this uninhibited freedom. For me, for a long time, for many long years, the lack of the blackout, the total blackout of the city, remained my most pleasant experience, that as much light could escape into the dark of night as there was of it. I couldn't get enough of the beauty of the city lights either, that the nights would never be dark again. And yet nightfall remained sinister. The lights were burning in the streets. Which meant not only that there wouldn't be an air raid, but that air raids were out of the question. Air-raid warnings, shrieking sirens, bombers flying overhead were a thing of the past. The first sentence of my life was forgotten for decades. And yet, on these peaceful nights, the silence that would suddenly fall over the deserted sidewalks and roads seemed ominous and all was not right with the night after all, and it wasn't advisable to turn on the light. Or so I felt. I could have, but it was not advisable. Names of places both distant and not so distant were laden with horror and dread, burdened with hearsay and events. It is risky. Lövölde Square by no means, Királyerdő, Margaret Island, not for anything in the world. People's Park, Városmajor, the Horváth Garden, City Park, pure nightmare, murder, sudden death. At night, the cries for help shattered the silence of the city ruins, the shrill cries of the women and the guttural cries of the men. Being startled out of your sleep to someone being struck down, robbed, or killed on the streets down below was disorienting, to say the least. On the basis of what I had heard in post-siege times I can safely say that in extreme situations the men scream, beg, whine, and whimper, just like the women. Or else they sink the knife in someone's back, and from the way he is shouting you can hear the soul leaving him, leaving a total stranger who is just like you might be in a similar situation, but no one rushes to his aid, people are more concerned about their own shitty little lives than about saving the lives of others. Even my brave Communist parents were not ready to make such a sacrifice. Next thing, you hear the sound of running on the street and the silence of death. The murderer got away, and the silence issues from the dead man; there is so much silence in the body of a dead man, it reaches all the way up to the seventh floor. There were two murderers. No, the murderer was alone. Among the Palatinus houses or Sziget Street, on the empty corner where a house had been hit by a bomb, and where they later fenced in the empty plot with a plank fence and then opened an ice-skating rink in its place, and where the victim had surely tried to escape, or under the trees on Pozsonyi Street, it always happened the same way as in Péterfy Sándor Street or Dembinszky Street or somewhat later on Teréz Boulevard. Three decades later I was startled awake by the same screaming on the corner of Twelfth Avenue and Thirty-eighth Street in the Garment District in New York City on an extremely cold January night, I was startled out of my sleep once again, and at the height of eighteen stories it was once again clear as day what had happened on the street, they have stuck a knife in someone, and his soul is leaving him. And the same thing happened the following night, on two successive snowy and icy January nights. Which again made me feel disoriented, I didn't know where I was, and it made me feel that my life is one long nightmare, no matter where I go with it.

When this happens in Budapest, all the people in all the apartments, the entire street, the entire neighborhood from the ground floor to the seventh jump out of bed, dash to the window, and the lights come on. In New York nothing and nobody. I tried it. From the eighteenth floor you can't see down to the sidewalk without the risk of falling out the window. What happened remained an auditory drama, as if it weren't really happening. In Pest, if people spotted the screaming victim and the thief down below, they're running that way, they shouted from their windows for all they were worth. Sometimes the chorus scared off the thief, in which case the victim was in luck, he sang his luck on the street, Let us dance the Carmagnole, long live the sound, long live the sound of cannons, at other times we heard the sound of gunfire, but no one dared go out on the street. No one went, either to rejoice along with the singer, who was retreating into the distance by then, nor to help him. For years the town was up in arms, where are the police when you need them. The front doors of the buildings were under lock and key. The victims knew that they had nowhere to flee. The front doors were handled by the superintendents, no one else had a key. A veritable eternity would have passed by the time the ringing woke the superintendent asleep in his apartment in the courtyard or mezzanine and would put on a cape or a coat and in his slippers shuffle to the gate across the yard. For a long time the fear that I have nowhere to flee haunted my dreams. For two years after the siege, marauding bands of thieves plundered the streets of the city; they knocked down, stripped naked, and robbed of all their possessions those hurrying home in the night. It was no joke. If they weren't knocked down and they weren't killed, then there they stood naked in the cold night in front of the gate of a strange house, ringing the bell in vain. They could count themselves lucky if their attackers didn't take their panties or let them keep their underpants. They came from work, my parents explained, or they were headed to work, the city works at night, too, otherwise the city would have no light and no water and no bread at the bakery the next day, and the newspaper vendor wouldn't get the latest papers, and then there'd be no news. Still, people did not run down to the street to help. No one did. After about two years, order of sorts was restored, and after his many dreadful deeds, they even caught up with Copper Dönci, the solitary city guerrilla who for some time managed to give people the impression that he was a sort of Robin Hood, after the fortunes of the rich. He was eventually sentenced and hanged, but for a long time, a very long time, perhaps into the late fifties, Budapest's public lighting remained defective and faint, and at night the streets and squares retained their sinister character. Rape combined with homicide became the norm, a circumstance to which Copper Dönci's history had served as a mere prelude; but following the siege, lesser parasites were also on the rise, and a veritable crusade had to be waged against the onslaughts of bedbugs and cockroaches, tapeworms, fleas, and lice, not to mention rats and mice.

It is no wonder that in the late fifties Miklós Mészöly should have written a short story entitled "Report About Five Mice," in which he examines close up how the ignominy of war lives on in the hunt for mice in a pantry, how the memory of the manhunt has survived in the operation against the mice. I didn't have fleas, I didn't have lice or scabs either, but despite all their hygienic precautions, my parents discovered in my excrement long white tapeworms feeding off my intestines. Our heroic struggle against the bedbugs and cockroaches was not easily won either. They kept mentioning fumigation, that we'd have to fumigate our apartment, that we'd have to leave for a while, because our apartment would be filled with cyanide. They seal all the doors and windows and fill the space with cyanide gas. They calculate the cost by cubic meters. A cubic meter is the result of multiplying the length and width and height. I first heard about cubic meters or that there's such a thing as multiplication in relation to the upcoming fumigation. I liked this sort of multiplication a lot. On the other hand, when I was told about the tapeworms, I was terribly upset, not to mention the upset in the bathroom. The tapeworms had to be driven out of me, so far so good, except my rational self couldn't come to terms with the fact that there were other living beings inside me, and not just me.

Such a serious breach of my physical integrity formed the outer limits of rational thought. They showed me, I looked and I saw, there they are wriggling in your feces, they live off you, they can take all your partly digested food away from you, they need to be gotten rid of. Theoretically, I should have been grateful for all the things they had to do yet again for my sake. Fumigation against bedbugs, too, is effective only for a time. My father explained things persistently and very intelligently, he made sure that in all cases, the information pertaining to the subject should reach every nook and cranny of my intellect, and consequently, in the interest of ennobling my intellect, our joint assembling and repairing of things, our walks and conversations took on a dry, rigorously objective character. On the other hand, when faced with a commotion that took a toll on all his sense, he stood aside; he was not really interested in the commotion as such, because he couldn't explain it. When in the interest of my body's integrity they had to violate my body's integrity, he watched the operation in alarm, he was alarmed at all the things happening to his son, but he helped my mother helplessly, unfeelingly, and awkwardly, as if the unexpected physiological disorder inside me shocked him as well, and as if, in the appropriate section of his intellect, he could find nothing to explain it.

Later, Grandfather Tauber just shrugged and nodded when I told him what I'd been through.

The tapeworms have to live off of something, too, son.

Which was like being doused with a bucket of ice-cold water.

Grandfather showed no sign of sympathy at all; instead, he shed light on the situation from the perspective of the tapeworms when I was facing yet another enema at home. Against which I protested with elemental fury. Although I didn't mean to, I kicked and bit, I screamed and flung my arms about, I don't know why, it was involuntary, I kicked the bulging bag of the kit out of their hands, or else the rubber tube came loose, and everything in the bathroom around them was swimming in enema fluid. I didn't mean to. I was beside myself, I swear. They held me down as, ignoring the voice of reason dictated by my own intellect, I fought for the self-determination of my body; I screamed for all I was worth, and my mother was screaming, too, but she was also laughing fit to burst; she was laughing at me, she was screaming with laughter. My father, at least, didn't dare laugh at me quite so blatantly. He laughed along with my mother, that goes without saying, but at least his gaze was full of fear and his lips trembled. At times they even had to give up their struggle momentarily because of their common laughter or the water that had spilled out and flooded the place. I kicked and flung my arms about, I squealed, don't stick me up, don't stick me up. Oh, Mother dear, sweet darling Mother, don't stick me up, I beg you. Which made them scream with laughter once again, they beat their own thighs and each other's thighs, too, in their merriment. These mother dears and sweet darling mothers and I beg yous cut no ice with them, nothing that was affixed to words as so much stuffing, because they used words in line with rational rules, they were not about to be duped by words that marred the rational import of their sentences with petty bourgeois sentimentality. Exaggeration was all right, in fact, they always reacted to exaggeration with delight, but the exaggeration had to be ironic to prevent it from being sentimental; their tears flowed, they held on to the doorjamb or to each other, the towels, the bathrobes, what an idea, we're not sticking you up with anything. With great burst of laughter, they later told the story to anyone willing to listen. Péter wouldn't let us, whereas we wanted to stick him up on purpose. Because I felt that if they weren't doing it on purpose, I could maybe forgive them for sticking me up. We wanted to stick him up with the nozzle on purpose, but he wouldn't let us. He wouldn't peddle his ass. I came upon this sentence again decades later in Romain Gary's novel *The Life Before Us*, which he published under the pseudonym Émile Ajar. I haven't seen or heard this sentence, which in the book the dying Jewish survivor Rosa bequeaths to the little Arab boy Momo as an eternal moral truth, ever again. After she dies, he will be left to fend for himself. Do what you want, just don't peddle your ass. She passes on the absolute taboo at the hour of her death. Hearing my heroic deed, that I wouldn't offer up my backside, everyone screamed with laughter along with them. But luckily, as far as my honorable backside was concerned, they kept quiet about my greatest shame. While they laughed, I trembled, my whole little soul quivered, lest they mention it.

They had enough brains not to.

Which meant that even they set limits on violating taboos and did not tell their friends what happened next.

Because after a while they pulled themselves together and resumed their struggle. Hold down his arm. Hold down his leg, I said. If you don't hold down his leg, he'll tear it out again. But when we were done with the terrible humiliation and they'd inserted a long Bakelite tube that they first carefully smeared with cream up my anus, my rectum, my asshole, and they opened a small Bakelite water tap into me without ado and everything was back to normal and we were over the ordeal of them sticking me up because it slipped in nice and smooth, though then it smarted something awful because they let the entire foul-smelling, lukewarm contents of the douche bag up my backside with no room for appeal and flooded my insides with the bestially stinking liquid to drive the vermin out, and then they even experimented with the pressed juice of one whole garlic bulb so that not only these nasty vermin but their eggs should also leave me, oh, I can't take it anymore, it hurts, Mommy, it smarts, Mommy dear, it hurts so, and she said, you must put up with it some more, if you can't take it anymore that's good, let it strain, it can't hurt all that much, don't be so squeamish, don't be a wimp, if it stings, sting it back, the bag is nearly empty, just hold still, that's it, hold still, and I had just decided that since I hadn't been a good boy, I'd be a good boy now, but that's when disaster struck and the ultimate humiliation came, because when my ordeal was over, just so they'd be in the right and so we should put an end to the necessary but unjust and shameful events by keeping silent about them together, they made me admit that actually, no, you couldn't even go so far as to call it disagreeable, no, no, we're over it and no harm done.

But you mustn't do it to me again. Promise me you won't do it again.

But first we have to scrape the shit off the ceiling, my darling child, we must first scrub this whole damnedly shitty bathroom down with Lysoform, but let us agree that everything is in the best possible order, nothing could be in better order than this, though alas, we cannot make you a promise like that, because we will do it as often as it should prove necessary.

My father would have never let a thing like that pass his lips, that

I shitted all over the bathroom, and he'd have been the first to faint dead away in face of the threat that, if necessary, they will do it again, if they have to, they'll stick me up, only my mother was this unsparing, my one and only beloved mother.

You are quiet, you are timid, you are reserved, you pay attention, you make no sarcastic comments about people. For his part, my father, my one and only father filled my head with sentences such as these. At the table you make small talk only with your immediate neighbors, you do not shout across the table at those sitting at a distance from you, you keep in mind that they must also chat with their neighbors, you cannot monopolize people. You never say *bon appétit* to anyone, they must always say it to you, the man or the lady of the house must say it, at most you thank them for their good wishes. We, for instance, don't wish our guests *bon appétit* at the table. This is not an unfriendly gesture on our part, it is just another established custom. We keep ourselves to this other established custom. And so on and so forth, with no end in sight to all the rules and established customs, all of which he knew. On the other hand, ask as I might, he did not explain why it is not the custom at our house to say *bon appétit* at the table. Seeing how customs exist side by side and must exist side by side, if they overlap and are not in force on all occasions and in all places, how am I to know when and where a custom is in force. I couldn't solve this problem on my own either without at least posing the question pertaining to it. And also, one question prevented me asking the next.

They didn't understand and just wondered, wide-eyed, what on earth I was up to. For a long time they were afraid I'd end up stuttering and stammering like Pista, Bandi, and Miklós, my father's brothers.

At one time I readily accepted their fear and was afraid that what had happened to Pista, Bandi, and Miklós could just as well happen to me, that the task waiting for me in life would terrify me so much that I wouldn't be able to speak. A good thing that I don't have a lisp. Magda had a lisp. Özsi had a lisp, too, except not as pronounced.

When I have to speak in public, their former fears sometimes appear from behind the wings, and in order to get the better of their fear, even after so many years, I begin stuttering on purpose, by way of preemption. Let's get this interior stutter over with. Let's turn our insides out. Let's put its contents on display. Ours is no different from yours. Stuttering and stammering and searching for words always makes a good impression on the audience, who are happy to discover how fallible the speaker is. Their dead souls live inside me with all their stuttering. At such times I show the audience their physical being through my own physical being; I show all those total strangers that the story of my family is the story of speech impediments and fallibilities. They see me searching for words, struggling with them, and I am not ashamed; rather, I am thinking about my own personal fallibility, which is part of my family's fallibility. I have no ready-made formulas at hand. They see that my independence is merely the striving for independence, but that I take this striving seriously. I am striving for an optimal result, for clearly articulated, properly intoned sentences, but even before the most prized audience, I have no guarantee that I will ever reach the desired optimum I am aiming for. I am limited by my own limited abilities, not to mention my esteemed ancestors' mistaken guidelines and tailor-made limits. This intentional advance on stammering and stuttering helps me sidestep my own anxiety over their former mortification, except that won't get us out of our present predicament.

The fundamental problems of independent thinking are so much in the here and now that, try as I might to ever so cleverly preempt my ancestors' anxieties, I begin to stammer and stutter myself, not as a joke, and not to preempt the problem, but in dead earnest. There I am, falling into the pit I have dug for myself. I have a pretty clear view of the situation into which, thanks to the questions I've been asking myself and the associative lines leading to them, meaning thanks to my complex reflective drive, I am stuck for life. I can see that at certain well-defined structural points of the contents of consciousness, at the junctions of motivistic and material correlations, of similarities or identical phenomena, the beginning of my life comes into contact with the end of my life, or else gets so thoroughly entangled with it that it is impossible to distinguish one from the other. If I get tongue-tied, let me get tongue-tied. If a short circuit is the result, so be it. If I have nothing to say, I might as well keep silent. If I am contradicting myself, then let it be clear to one and all that my esteemed thinking is struggling with its contradictions.

Or else their assertions clashed head on, and again, I didn't know what to make of it, or what to do about it. At times the subjective observation clashed with the objective observation. I observed something, something showed two faces simultaneously, for which I had no words or explanation, if for no other reason, because with near hysteria those closest to me attempted to come up with one single explanation or metaphor, a mathematical formula, a chemical equation into which the phenomenon in question can be made to fit without leaving any room for doubt. Their assertions and analyses must leave no room for contradiction. They'd rather lie to themselves than allow such a thing to happen. Contradiction was one of the greatest specters and boomerangs of modernism. They strove for a world free of contradiction, and if the world today is not yet that lucky, they will see to it that come tomorrow, they will free it of contradiction.

Decades passed, and I was still profoundly humiliated if anyone said that for one reason or another, my assertion is contradictory.

Good Lord, so my assertion is contradictory. So what.

How could it be otherwise when the thing itself invariably contains its own contradictions, and not just one but seven, ten, and if that's the case, why shouldn't I reveal the system of contradiction with my sentences. It seems that these fools don't want to follow the contradiction along its path, they don't want to admit that one thing is never just one, or else they do not wish to understand it but, for the sake of convenience, they would rather exile the contradictory fact, worlds that manifest themselves simultaneously, from their consciousness, so that what exists shouldn't exist. Which is the object of a great polemic, the mighty polemic of modernity with itself. But solely with itself, because a fundamentalist is not concerned with his own contradictions. He couldn't care less. The world is what it is. Or else the world shouldn't be like this, but something entirely different. But in relationship to what should it be different. It is best not to notice certain phenomena; what's more, I shouldn't notice either what I notice, or else I should change myself, thereby bringing about a change in what I notice. Fine. Give me a fixed point in the universe. The fixed point, of course, should be me. Me, me, me. Or if that's not feasible because in that case we'd end up face-to-face with relativity or the ascetic striving for the loss of the self, then at least let's not talk about what we perceive but rather of what we deem desirable, because that won't stand in the way of contradiction-free comprehension, it will not stand in the way of the ancient striving to create a contradiction-free universe. Let us wipe out the undesirable contradictory elements one by one, let us cut off one or another part of our body because it does not fit someone's modernist worldview.

Always, my parents will be the ones who tell me what does not fit. Nothing must stand out, be an eyesore. I would have gladly gone along, I even made an attempt each time in the interest of peace, but try as I might, I couldn't understand why this was good for them, why they demanded it, why they engaged in manipulation, and many decades had to pass before I more or less understood the modernist logic of the utopian ignorance that pertains to contradiction. Or to be exact, for a long time, a very long time, I did not understand my own stubborn inner resistance to normative thinking. Just because. I flew into a rage, I flung myself on the floor, I writhed in pain, which made both of them laugh, of course. But when I fainted from rage, they were forced to do something sensible. They made a phone call. She didn't pick up. They ran. Down from the seventh, across Pozsonyi Street, up to the fourth, that Elza Baranyai should come and do something about me that was within her power as a physician. My younger brother did the same thing, right before my eyes, and each time they did the same thing to him they did to me. Only a protracted fainting fit had any effect on them. My brother has dark skin, which made him turn blue more easily for lack of air.

For a long time, a very long time, the established custom of the family also remained a great mystery. Good Lord, I have nothing to decode it with; who established it, and what was it they established. And if it was established, I wondered, why wasn't it established in our own home. All the same, the established custom became so en-trenched in me that it has required great effort on my part ever since to wish my guests, or anyone, *bon appétit* at my own table, I'd rather not do it, though the older I am, the clearer I see that in keeping with their own strict unwritten laws, my guests are waiting for me to do so, because they have accepted another, a much more current established custom. If I find a gap, a way out, an exit, a detour, a loophole, if I spit on it, if I have shed it years ago, I nevertheless have to admit that every one of their accepted customs has mesmerized me and held me in their spell my entire life.

Once on an excursion to the Pilis Mountains, where the paths seemed endless and we walked on and on in the woods somewhere between Dömörkapu and Pilisszentkereszt and there's no knowing why we're walking and why we're heading downhill or heading uphill in these mountains and why they're not picking me up and hoisting me around their necks and why they are so silent and why we children aren't allowed to shout, wait till we reach a clearing, a meadow, there you can shout to your heart's content, because the established custom is that one does not shout in the woods, one does not disturb the birds and wild animals, and while still at a good distance from the tourist lodge where we spent the night in a big, ice-cold room with the whole company, children and grown-ups alike, they also taught me that I am never cold, I am never hot, I am never thirsty, I am never hungry, I am never tired, I am never sleepy, but most of all, I am never bored, and I'd better not forget it. And I didn't. I liked all these nevers. And for another thing, I mustn't burden anyone with my physical or emotional needs. And that includes themselves. We will keep going until we get there, and not before. If I am bored, that's my problem. Only sim-pletons are bored. If I'm a simpleton, that's my own affair. I'd better not say I'm bored ever again, they don't want to hear it. You certainly didn't learn it from us. We never said anything so stupid to you. The world is a whole, the interval and the rest are also part of the music. I have no right to be bored. And I shouldn't count on them picking me up on their shoulders and carrying me and drinking more water from the flask than I'm entitled to. They told me how many sips, and no more, and I better make sure not to go over the limit. You must not shortchange others to please yourself. This is all the water there is, there it is on the map, the next spring is still at a good distance.

Repeat it after me.

In this vast, dense forest where the shadows came streaming down on us along with the light, I was on the verge of fainting from hunger, or more to the point, from the abject terror that I might feel hungry, and strangely enough, at three in the afternoon this feeling comes over me every day, as if I were pronouncing a death sentence on my sweetest physical privilege once and for all. I am not cold. I am not hot. I am not tired. I am not thirsty. I am not hungry.

And what is it, they asked, that we do not say out loud, just so you don't forget.

But when I wanted to say it, because I didn't forget it, they laughed and said, oh no, don't you say it, you'll be boring as hell if you do.

I also understood perfectly well that the prohibitions you address to yourself are much more effective than the prohibitions you merely repeat, they're not about being thirsty and they're not about feeling, they're not about such passing sensations, rather, that we are trespassing on something once again, we are stepping over something, I am stepping over something with them, the foot in the yellow shoes with the toe caps is stepping over the corpse, we are loading the corpse on top of the sled from Gömör and we haul the corpse to the depot, but we are trespassing something once again, we are stepping over something with them and this phenomenon intrigued me as well. We are putting the seal on something now, we are confirming it, something that I know to begin with, I always knew, I know it before I even say it. Someone needs to clear away the dead. There's something that is final and fixed for all time. One might say that they weren't passing their knowledge on to me, they were making me aware of what I already confirmed for my benefit of my own knowledge about Creation. And all the while that I was repeating what they said as, interrupting each other at every turn, they had me repeat the heroic catechism of the limitations they had imposed on themselves, enjoying it, screaming with laughter at their own words, they held on to each other as they laughed, I enjoyed it every bit as much as they, I enjoyed their bodies convulsed with laughter, and I enjoyed myself as well, I enjoyed my eager and dangerous childish eagerness to learn, and I was as happy as they were with me. They will now beat it into me once and for all. With their demand for self-control and the negation of the self, they will now override my animality, much stronger than I. They weren't laughing at me or my childishness, they weren't laughing at my expense, they were laughing at their shared animality, which, needless to say, survived unscathed in its original form despite having been sublimated by the intellect, an eternal contradiction incomprehensible to the intellect.

They were laughing at the impossibility of their endeavor, laughing because they knew that without this hopeless modernist endeavor, everything would be even more hopeless, if that.

After this there was truly no court of appeal where I could turn with my complaints, which, let us admit, fills one with a certain sense of satisfaction and implacable calm.

Another time, with respect to something, I happened to say to my mother that I was entitled to it.

As far as that goes, you are entitled to nothing, she said quietly, shit, that's what you're entitled to.

The memory of various customs and rules of conduct survives way beyond what the numerous historical upheavals and world wars would have us to think. Customs, even if they have lost their reason for being, outlast the historical conditions in which they are rooted. Day in and day out, my maternal grandmother, Cecília Nussbaum, gave sufficient proof of this, because she adhered to her own special rules of conduct as relentlessly as the hands of a clock to the numbers on its face, or the year its change of seasons.

Which, among other things, taught me that there are people like that. Always and in all things they insist on doing everything exactly as others do them, and if anyone, my grandmother knew what had to be done, and when. When the church bell rang out at noon, the boiling hot soup had to be on the table. My maternal grandmother was a simple woman, small, round, forbidding, with glasses, infinitely headstrong and tyrannical. At her table we didn't have to pull the napkin from the monogrammed silver napkin ring, because there was no silver napkin ring, nor damask napkin, and as for monograms, there were none to be seen on the horizon. And also, I could put my hands wherever I wanted on the kitchen table, which was covered with checked oilcloth. My grandmother's demands were of another, possibly even more exacting kind. In her house there was no room for middle-class pretensions, good manners, or an appearance of meekness, because my grandmother was a brutal woman, loud and aggressive even in her oozing sentimentality, nor was there room in her house for rebellion or anarchy, all the things that, going against the rules of etiquette and established custom, only my mother, the eternal rebel, allowed herself, but no one else. According to her, my mother didn't act arrogantly only with her, she was arrogant to begin with, an *ausgesprochen azesponem*. She brought her into the world, but that's not her fault. By no stretch of the imagination. How anybody can be such an *azesponem* is beyond her. Except for her, there has never been such an arrogant person in the family. I managed to put the others right, but not her. I'm not surprised she can't hold you in check. I'm not surprised at anything, and I do mean anything, anymore. Your behavior doesn't surprise me either.

The truth is that if her sense of justice called for it, my mother would kick up a fuss anytime and anywhere without a second thought. It's her radical sense of justice that must have guided her through life, the street, the tram, the workers' physical fitness club, the illegal Communist movement, and her various places of employment, anywhere, as I later learned, even at the highest possible level of government negotiations. She'd make a scene. When there was too much lying and hypocrisy, she caused a scandal, it came on her like lightning out of a blue sky. She was an anarchist at heart. She used her fists. She blew things sky-high. Whether pale or lobster red, she enjoyed the scandal; wide-eyed, she watched the scandal she herself had created. She enjoyed banging her head against the wall. Burning her bridges. And she did burn them. Okay, Lord, let's see what you and I can do. At the age of forty-six she was dead, as if she were doing it on purpose, hoping that for once she could really create a clear situation, all the liars should have nowhere to retreat, and then she would put everything in its place in the chaos she had herself created. For the sake of appearances, for the sake of peace in the family, her older and younger sisters always succumbed to the brutal maternal rules of conduct, they were shamelessly sentimental, like her, oh, my one and only, my darling, my precious, my dove, I could eat you all up, my little angel, never has the big wide world seen anyone as sweet, such a darling, smart little boy, what adorable thighs he has. Here's some more cake. If you're a good boy, we'll buy you ice cream. Or would you like some honeycomb toffee, a balloon, cotton candy. If you're not a good boy, there's no ice cream, but a spanking on your behind. I'll get the carpet beater and beat you with it. But not her. She disdained her sisters for their lifelong hypocrisy, but despite all her disdain, she stood up for them in the face of their mother's tyranny, and they in their underhanded manner expected it, Klári, Klári will come to their aid, and then, calling all the flowery words at their disposal to their aid, and there were plenty of them, they would continue feeding the radiant, eternal fire of their hypocrisy. For a long time, a very long time, I felt that this was pure arrogance, my mother acting as an accomplice to their hypocrisy. She used her arrogance to protect the two sneaky women, Irén and Bözsi, to protect them from themselves. No matter how stupid, calculating, and base they may be, one quietly, the other harshly base, she had to protect them come hell or high water. By now I am familiar with this expression and, if need be, I use it, albeit with caution; I even use it in foreign languages, and I use it in writing; yet should the occasion arise, carefully and in the greatest secrecy, I need to look it up in my trusted dictionaries to check its meaning, or whether it doesn't mean something entirely different than what I imagine about it based on my grandmother's interpretation of it.

And indeed, it means something different and not the self-sacrificing shielding of the sneaky and the cowardly. Understanding and misunderstanding became irrevocably intertwined. I have a number of such intertwined words in which the original meaning, the misunderstanding dominated my adult life. But my grandmother's stubborn, fated implacability is understandable, by now I understand this, too. Thanks to her marriage she found herself in an entirely different world than the one she grew up in, and in this new environment, the morphology of the words and their semantic content as she knew them did not correspond. Theoretically, she was called upon to reconcile three different forms of the rules of conduct in her life. Which was too much for a feeling heart. Besides, three different modes of behavior can't be reconciled to begin with. Not that she was ever a party to reconciliation; this was the hitch, the philosophical hitch, one might say. She wanted to assert her own knowledge in the face of everyone, and in spite of everything. She wanted to break through with her knowledge, she had to break through with it, even through the Great Wall of China, because this stance of being in the right constituted the foundation of her knowledge.

She could not afford to entertain doubt. She could not afford to launch into explanations. She could not give in. She could not resort to reason. Surely, the abandonment of being in the right was as much an imperative for her as complaining was for me.

It is not easy to accept that you are entitled to nothing, at most, to complaining to no avail. That you can't even ask for as much as you give, because in that case, you're flaunting something that should be natural. If man were not exceptional, an animal different from all other animals, who always insists on getting more than he is capable of giving, such a gesture would be natural. To give nothing, but rather to take, to steal, to tear out, to sweep in, to gather up, to gobble up, and on top of it all, to show off with such an accomplishment.

This is what is natural, the animalistic is natural. The humane is merely for show. As for Kant's ethical imperative, it doesn't work at all, because ethical considerations do not precede action but follow in its wake. It defines what is desirable instead of describing the practice. Of course, the desirable is nevertheless present.

Besides, what's a man to do with several simultaneous promptings within.

Still, from time to time I managed to make my grandmother lose her sure footing; this occurred when without raising my voice, gingerly, switching into a statement mode, coolly, dispassionately, I managed to confront her with different rules, with our rules, the modes of behavior of the paternal side of the family. I hardly ever succeeded, but the vivid outlines of these moments have survived in my memory. These were my minor triumphs. That, after all, there's a path leading to the desirable, even in the face of the most obstinate animalistic individuals. Because we could see by her expression that she couldn't manage to force us out of her own pluralism altogether, she couldn't force all living things out of it, she couldn't remain quite so isolated with her own older sister, Szerén. This happened when I managed to penetrate the border of her consciousness and bring with it the realization that there's another set of rules, another set of established customs that is also part and parcel of the family. For instance, at home. After all, Péterfy Sándor Street was not really my home. They're shipping me back and forth between the parental and grandparental homes, but when all is said and done, my home is on Pozsonyi Street. Always, it was no more than a fleeting moment in her consciousness, no more than the raising of an eyebrow, some fleeting irritability, some aversion, a twitch, the barely perceptible restructuring of her features. But that was enough for me. I saw that she didn't even reflect on her confusion, because her mistrust of everything and everyone would immediately come to the fore, getting the better of everything else, depriving her of her own common sense, propelling her words and actions; or else she lacked common sense to an extent that I, due to my rational upbringing, couldn't begin to imagine. I was reduced to gauging by the expression on her face that no, no, there are no concessions, no exceptions, there will be no change, and that she will continue to insist on her fundamental knowledge at all cost and against appeals of all kinds.

As witnessed by the only surviving early photograph of her, when she found herself in the midst of my grandfather's family, and for the first time in her life, had her picture taken, my grandmother must have been a beautiful young girl. Her corseted waist was nearly as tiny as that of Empress Elisabeth, whose doings she related in great detail, she talked about no one else but her, neither about dwarfs nor giants, just Sisi, but that without end. She showered exuberant praise on her delicate hands, her snow-white breasts, her lips, her arms, her wispy waist, her clothes, her entourage, her corsets, her veils, her figure, and her slippers, she indulged in fancies only about her, because she idolized her. I don't know where she got such detailed information about Sisi, because although she could read, she could never make the sense of the text reach her own senses. On this old photograph my grandmother's pretty face was like a delicately worked jewel, her wild dark hair a sea of surging waves. It was my keen impression that her dark, Moorish beauty had so enslaved my grandfather that he remained her faithful servant even once her beauty had faded. By the time I was born there was no trace of this beauty left, her skin had taken on a decided pallor, her shock of curls had greatly thinned, had straightened out and turned gray. She had her hair cut boyishly short, or else she twisted it into a practical little knot at the nape of her neck and fixed it with a bunch of her ugly hairpins; but even so, my grandfather continued to serve her in silence. There were hairpins all over the house, under the chairs, stuck in the towels, and they somehow retained the scent of her hair.

She spent a lifetime trying to adjust to her new surroundings; my grandfather was her guide and he made excuses for her, which must have been the most difficult part of his conjugal duties. He translated Grandmother's words, Grandmother didn't mean it like that, that's not why she said it, she must have meant it otherwise, just so he could exonerate her. But even so, Grandmother would sometimes fly into a rage, saying that Grandfather better not make her out to be a liar.

Papa, you're making a liar of me.

Don't make a liar of me, Papa.

My grandfather also had to protect her from her own daughters, because Grandmother couldn't find the right tone with them either, with either of them. Unheeding and insensitive, she launched into endless monologues or would suddenly call out from inside her lifelong interior monologue; she'd snap at people, she'd scold anyone at the drop of a hat. She scolded the ticket taker, the shop assistant, the coal man, the market women, the butcher, the mailman, the assistant superintendent, the neighbors, because they tried to cheat her, to hoodwink her, to shortchange her, they were out to confuse her, they wanted her to pay twice. Well, she's going to teach them a lesson they won't forget. But given the chance, she also lashed out at those who were below her in the social hierarchy. Basically, she was cantankerous because she was timid, she was always at the ready with her anger in the face of a world order unfamiliar to her. Her garrulousness functioned as a protective wall, she filled the air with her words to stop others from speaking. Or as she said, to stop them from putting her down, maligning her. People keep putting her down, maligning her. The whole house does it. She didn't say that the neighbors put her down, though in fact they did, but that the house puts her down and maligns her. The house is maligning me. She was a villager through and through, and her starting premise was that the village is of this or that opinion, the village is saying this or that, and so on, while these others, they were born in Pest and they think they know everything better, whereas they know nothing, nothing at all. They get everything muddled. *Der riah zoldie trefn.* The devil take them. *Der Teufel soll die holen.* She grumbled the whole day long, she grumbled in Yiddish, she grumbled in German, she cursed, she chafed; a true daughter of the countryside, she was programed for all-out self-defense, everyone against everyone else; she struggled with a spirit world, and she spoke loud and nonstop in the name of this spirit world; at times she would even talk to the objects around her, at other times with them, animating them, while at still other times she let her inner monologue loose on the world around her.

When she was thinking, she made sure people heard. She used her words to affect the body, not the mind. She lived in a waking dream, she gazed out at us from there, and so the simplest things would shock her. In her waking dream we represented the call to arms of that other, real spirit world that apart from my grandfather, basically no one in the family understood or was familiar with. She could neither translate her own rural omniscience, the unassailable knowledge of the collective individual, nor replace it in favor of urban knowledge, which is invariably the system of partial results open to revision. People are wicked, everyone is wicked, base, vile. I can't begin to imagine just how vile. May I never know how vile. Don't tell me, don't even mention him, he's a base fellow, a vile fellow.

When faced with a situation she didn't understand, this is how she reacted. As far as she was concerned, the world was an assembly congregation of villains and criminals.

How can people be so base. And don't think the Jews aren't like that, the Jews are worse than anybody. They're jealous, they cheat right and left, they'd cheat their own mother if they could, those good-for-nothings.

With her constant yammering, she was nothing but a small, rotund, crazy old woman. It took me sixty years of experience to understand her somewhat, if only in retrospect.

The Sunday soup, too, she put in it only as much as was absolutely necessary. When she described what beef soup was like in the happy peacetime years, and she missed no opportunity of doing so, it was soft, it was tender, the knife cut through it like butter, it melted on the tongue; needless to say, she wasn't talking about the time before the siege but the time before the First World War, the time of the Austro-Hungarian Empire, the time of her infancy and childhood. Those were the real peacetime years. Later, everything became prey to decay, to annihilation. *Prey*, this was one of her favorite words, don't be such prey already. Meaning that I should be thrifty. To be precise, as far as she was concerned, these bona fide peacetime years lasted only two decades from the time she was born, which more or less encompassed the political history of the Austro-Hungarian Empire. In Austria, Count Eduard von Taaffe was prime minister, in Hungary, Count Kálmán Tisza. During their long terms in office both men attempted to curb or at least moderate, as best they could, and in the interest of the aristocracy and the Catholic Church, the strivings of the bourgeoisie for liberty and equality, but without curbing industrial and commercial modernization. But they made sure that there should always be less political equality than the logic of modernization dictated.

Also, Grandmother didn't say that I shouldn't be wasteful, shouldn't be a spendthrift, instead she said, don't be such a waster. He's a waster. He's a big waster. Which as she used the word meant that the individual in question threw money out the window, while a great big waster in turn meant a squandering rich man, someone who had enough to squander with plenty left over, yet his wastefulness is unethical. Sometimes I had difficulty imagining what she might be thinking, because in any case she was thinking of things that were unfamiliar to me; I had neither seen nor heard about them, and so I knew nothing about them. Where were the true peacetime years by then, the tradition and heritage of the conservative-liberal world order, after two world wars had trampled them underfoot. World conflagration. That was the expression for it. Two world conflagrations. When she spoke about the peacetime years, in my mind I paired her accounts with images that I had stored during our summer travels, a field of wheat stretching to the horizon under a blue, cloudless sky as the gusts of wind sweep over the stalks, making them tremble.

My mother taught me how to store images. For instance, if the sunset is important to us for some reason, we don't need to borrow anyone's camera. My father owned a camera, an ancient foldout Voigtländer with a crank shutter, a wonderful little contraption, he had a tripod to go with it and a self-timer, he especially liked pictures taken with the self-timing release, he wound up the shutter release, he worried whether he'd manage to step back into the picture in time, but when he used a cable release there was no need to hurry; all the men in my family liked taking photographs, they even had some knowledge of the lab work involved, they must have used a self-timer, I bet. They'd use a cable release, but releasing the pent-up tension in their manhood was out of the question. I knew that one was recommended while the other was prohibited even before I knew what it was that I should know so I could understand the difference. I knew that self-gratification would make me suffer from serious anemia, they also called it autoinfection, but that didn't make it any clearer, I'd become pale, sleepy, and weak, and finally the marrow in my bones would shrink, I'd grow dumb, except for a long time to come I didn't understand what I would have to do to be like that, and what the relationship was between the cable release and this infectious linguistic mystery.

We were out on the Danube, in sweltering heat, rowing, the summer was so hot you couldn't bear it either on the pebbled shore or anywhere, except in the water. There was always a light breeze on the water, a light, cool breeze. They were avid rowers, avid hikers and campers. Keep your eyes focused, do not turn your head, do not blink, just take it all in nice and easy, don't strain. The light bridge over the water, let that nasty light bridge settle in your eye. Mother liked the word *nasty*, she used it to balance things out. The sentence had to make it evident that when all is said and done, and even though she can't ignore it altogether, she considers this beautiful light bridge sentimental bourgeois nonsense, kitsch. Close your eyes, but don't squeeze your lids down too tight, let the small flashes of light, the circles and little stars and what have you settle. The *what have you* also served as a means of alienation. If you squeeze your eyes tight, the little stars won't settle down, or if they settle, it'll take time. When it's calm inside, and it'll be calm in a minute, you will then retrieve the image.

She asked if it's all settled inside the dark. Not completely. She asked if the image had come back yet, can I see the water and the light bridge now. Yes. In that case, you can open your eyes again and check if you remembered correctly.

You will look again, so you can correct the mistakes in recall, then you'll close your eyes again, and wait, wait for it to appear.

She asked if it's calm in the dark now.

It wasn't calm, because the red, expanding and retreating circles kept reappearing, and also, there were sparks in the dark, but I said that it's calm in there.

I couldn't wait, I couldn't control myself because of the excitement. I wanted to see if my memory worked the way she said it would, if the workings of one person's memory are the same as the workings of another person's memory.

You will now conjure it up again. Ask for the light bridge. Let's have that nasty light bridge. I also liked *light bridge* very much, the combination of these two words, and I didn't think it was mean at all. The light inside felt good, and the bridge inside was comprehensible.

If you do it twice, it will stick.

We were on the train. But if we're on a train, I couldn't do it twice, not even once, because the first image had hardly gone and the next was already there. This was a challenge I had to face on my own, I wouldn't sit down, they couldn't have dragged me back inside the compartment from the corridor. There was no way of properly letting in a world that was in constant motion. I wanted to find the key, a way of choosing moving images with my eye and retaining them.

It kept passing, I turned in its wake, but whether it was approaching or passing, it was impossible to arrest the image. There was no knowing ahead of time what else would come, and also, how I should choose an image and with respect to what.

They took me to the movies for the first time about two years later, I think, but before that they took me to the theater and the opera. I had no firsthand experience of the moving image except for the train, the boat, and the tram, images of which for two years at least I was the sole, select center and only optic, I constituted its vanishing point and its focal point. This is how, for a long time, actually for a very long time, possibly until I was eight, I stood smack in the middle of my visual world, whereas for some time by then, I had been standing in a world of which I was by no means the center.

If anyone thinks that it's easy for a child to understand and follow the idea of one point perspective and the visual relationships pertaining to it, or one point perspective and motion, he is very much mistaken.

The memory of the rhythmic chugging of the locomotive has remained with me. I even remember the scent of the rhythmic chugging, the scent of the summer field as it fills up with the rhythmic chugging. If I give this chugging free rein, then from this acoustic memory the images, the image fragments, come back in their barely remembered state. They appear to the memory of the rhythm in which, seeing the infinite wheat field, I turn my head in sync with the rhythm of the chugging locomotive. Life in the Monarchy was as if we were standing in this sweltering summer, on the breezy train, inside the chugging. The bona fide peacetime years floated expansively over the sweltering air. Which was true to some extent, this expansiveness; after all, that's when the country's railway system was constructed, that's when the country's hospitals and schools were built, that's when the country's granaries and storerooms were filled up for the first time, even though a third of the country's population was forced to live in abject poverty and the law gave the landowners and the gendarmes the right to beat the farmhands and the servants. Concretely, this association of ideas, my thinking of the countryside, probably originates with the fact that not only did my paternal grandfather own an estate of appreciable size in Gömörsid, but even his father, my paternal great-grandfather, owned one in Tiszasüly. Initially he just rented the land, as I was told, but when my other great-grandfather, my Mezei great-grandfather, my lawyer great-grandfather, drew up the law regarding the emancipation of the Jews with Baron Eötvös, my great-grandfather, my Neumayer great-grandfather, József Neumayer, the son of Lázár Neumayer Freystadt, who'd come from somewhere in Germany or Austria, from Freistett or Rosenheim, was free to buy the lands he was renting, and thus became a landowner. These were supposedly very good fields. Early each summer, but definitely before harvesttime, because the threshing reached into the fall, they took a trip to Karlsbad or Baden with their children for a couple of weeks *für Sommerfrische*; and later they took their numerous grandchildren along, and in the afternoon in Baden they could all see the emperor. My father's brothers and sisters saw the emperor, of whom my maternal grandmother gave an account. I didn't understand this whole familial and historical complication. The two of them, the two great-grandfathers, weren't acquainted yet back then. Klára, the great-grandfather's daughter from Pest, couldn't have met Arnold Adolf, the second son of our great-grandfather from Tiszasüly. Back then József Kiss was paying court to Klára. He was a poet whose poems my grandmother loved, and she respected the upright elderly gentleman, but Klára liked the Neumayer boy more. They met at a charity ball. They were brought together on purpose and took to each other right away, except what they knew about each other they couldn't say out loud. I understood this complication right away. I behaved the same way in just about everything. For a while they had to keep their mutual attraction a secret, even from each other. Also, the Neumayer boy first had to break up, as carefully as possible, with the beautiful Aurélia Rosenzweig. Some suspicious souls in the family said that Adolf Arnold found Klára's appreciable dowry more attractive than her person, while her own daughters said throughout a lifetime that at this ball their mother decided to fall head over heels in love with him on the spot, and once she launched into it, she played out this romantic comedy until her dying day.

Adolf Arnold Neumayer married Klára Mezei on May 19, 1892, and as the surviving documents indicate, the wedding was a big social event in contemporary Pest; even the newspapers carried the news that this Adolf Arnold, who hailed from a family of landowners, married Dr. Mór Mezei's eldest daughter. The wedding was attended by everyone who was anyone, some of whose names are familiar to us from history. For instance, we went to Falk Miksa Street, named after the writer and politician Miksa Falk, who had been Great-grandfather's friend, or so I was told, but I didn't understand any of this, I swear. But as we traveled on that train, I felt that this must be the ancient order of things, the key to all secrets. A person should own a big estate in Tiszasüly, or an even bigger one in Gömörsid, he should manage it, sow wheat, which should then sway *en masse* over the infinite fields, and the train should chug along it to a merry rhythm. Except he mustn't buy English machines on credit, for God's sake, anything but that. While we looked out the window of the train, or at the stations where we had a long wait and we could get off, because they were refilling the locomotive with water, my father would explain things, for example, he pointed out and explained where the firebox is located in the engine, what burning is and what heat is, what the steam is driving, what the feed pump is and what the regulator valve, what the gear and what the power transmission, what coal is and how it differs from coke, what thermal value is and what the difference is between thermal values; to be sure, I was a curious child, but at times I'd had enough of all the details, I'd have been curious about other things besides what thermal value is and why, as a result of incomplete burning, we smell the stink of the devil's brimstone in the smoke. The stink is from the sulfur dioxide, not the devil, meaning that the oxidation of the sulfur is insufficient, and so one part of it does not turn into sulfur dioxide but sulfur monoxide, which has no smell and under certain conditions discharges fairy lights. *Elements. Valence. Free valences.* Almost all of these words I first heard from him. These are the laws of physics and chemistry. The devil and his brimstone thunderclaps, that's just so much superstitious rhetorical nonsense. What oh what is rhetoric, and why non-sense and not sense, rhetorical sense. I didn't understand, I stuttered and stammered, I would have liked to ask what these laws of physics and chemistry mean or, to be precise, I didn't understand what he wanted with it, and where I was supposed to store so much stuff.

There were questions my father understood even when I couldn't manage to ask them, I just hemmed and hawed, I couldn't keep up with him, he waited it out and looked on, and at such times I thought he was handsome, and his answer made me understand what I was really thinking, what I was struggling with. No wonder I considered his knowledge extraordinary. He effortlessly filled up the words that existed inside me as empty forms, but as empty forms they really did exist and were waiting to be filled in with words and explanatory comments. Impatiently waiting to be filled in, to be filled up. Filled all the way up. You sure stuffed your belly full, son, good for you, that's what'll make you grow into a big boy, all those vitamins. I wish I were a big boy already.

It simply did not occur to my grandmother Cecília Nussbaum that there could be anything else on Sunday except for beef soup, this, too, belonged to the order of things, just like the noonday ringing of the church bell. If there was no beef, then in an emergency, she would fall back on mock soup. It looked like beef soup, except Grandmother cooked it from pumpkin brains, making sure the stringy pulp and the seeds should release their full flavor and make the soup as thick as jelly, but without the strings turning the liquid murky, the secret of which was cooking on a slow fire. The preparation of this mock soup and the tricks involved in making it mock took longer and demanded closer attention than the preparation of real beef soup. To make real beef soup, Grandmother placed the ingredients in a big pot, added water, covered the pot, and lit the flame under it. Why is the mock more difficult to make than the real thing, this would have been my question, if only I knew how to ask. I kept finding myself timidly circling around some lack or some question that I didn't know how to ask. But I also had questions I didn't dare ask anyone, as if the questions themselves could disturb them, and this self-imposed prohibition has remained with me to this day. There are questions we do not ask. There are truths we do not voice. We do not make other people's lives any more difficult than is absolutely necessary. We do not scare off our fellow men. So far, so good. Except, try as I might, I couldn't understand what caused my fear, because in order to understand it, I'd have had to understand, at the age of three or four, their own complex system of views of which my fear was surely a by-product.

I enjoyed watching Grandmother cook. She was quick, thorough, and systematic, she always made everything the same way, and it is thanks to her that I learned the proper order of the steps needed to make a particular dish. I never saw anyone cut parsley with such intelligence, either then or later; she seemed to be extracting the oil from the parsley, careful to keep the extracted oil together with her knife and fingers. If only I knew where she learned to do this, I could glimpse into the depths of time and, following this lead, find my way back to the many unfamiliar places of our origin, to Podolia, Galicia, and I don't know where else. Then she pressed the liquid from the cooked stringy pulp through a sieve, the sieve had to be made of horse hair, she was adamant about that, it couldn't be a copper sieve, then she cooked the soup greens she'd first chopped up in the thick yellowish liquid. She left the onion whole, but cut the celeriac into thick slices, then she cut the turnips and carrots in two lengthwise, then in two again, thus quartering them, she cut the cabbage in two, but she only put one wedge in the soup. Never any other way. Then the following day or the day after she used the three leftover wedges and, with the addition of potatoes, made stewed cabbage.

On the other hand, in case of need, in an emergency, on Sunday she might make chicken soup with roux. I didn't understand this roux, there were many things I didn't understand, regardless of how hard I tried. Roux brought nothing to mind, there was nothing I could relate it to, and I certainly couldn't see it in the soup. But what puzzled me even more was how a soup could be mock, because if a soup is mock, if it's not real, then it's bad soup and it should be thrown out the window along with the soup bowl. Or if it has meat in it, why does my grandmother call it roux soup, because roux, whatever that may be, is certainly not meat. Or was it the thickening agent, a mixture of lard and flour, that she called roux. There was also the whisking, which reminded me of whiskey but was not identical with it. How can a soup be whisked, when all the other soups are cooked or prepared, and also, the soup made from pumpkin brains isn't called brain soup but mock soup, even though it's not mock but is made of real pumpkin. In short, what are the considerations on the basis of which people make up words and concepts. That was the big question. How do they differentiate between true and false, real and mock. This would have been my question if only I knew how to ask. Many decades later I was still preoccupied with trying to understand the meaning of words and concepts, or else I tried to find a place in my consciousness for them, only to find that there was no such place. My contemporaries already knew everything about the world, they made use of their knowledge, they were happy to put it in practice, they walked in and out of one another's minds, meaning that they understood one another's hidden thoughts, they could read one another's thoughts, while I understood nothing of these matters and procedures, nothing at all. Not a word. Possibly, I may have asked too many questions, I may have expected to understand too many details. Or possibly my father explained too much and in too much detail, and so he planted the nagging suspicion in me that I know too little to know anything at all. As a consequence, I couldn't launch into anything or comment on anything with as much determination as I should have possessed and which other people clearly did. Or possibly, with its objects, materials, and actions, and from the interpretation of all these, I expected more from the world than it had to offer. I headed in one direction and ended up in another. I was waiting for the fulfillment of knowledge, or at least some insight into its metaphysical scope. I didn't understand but I admired children my own age with their exceptional abilities, first and foremost, the ease and speed with which they learned things. How on earth could they acquire knowledge so fast and with such confidence. Who could have tipped them off. Or if they don't know either, how did they dare attempt it all the same. Because whether they understood something or not, they didn't shilly-shally, they launched into it, they practiced it, they understood it to suit their purposes, in short, they made sure that the ways of the world would play into their hands. And it did. Or else they bent and forced the ways of the world to submit to their needs, and if the ways of the world refused to bend, then it refused to bend, and they gave up without a second thought. Or else they resorted to fisticuffs over it. I, on the other hand, found it difficult to give in before I understood something. Two of my classmates were blown up, one died, the other had his arm ripped off by a mine, which marred his face, too, for a lifetime. They didn't come to school after that. In the years after the siege, my contemporaries couldn't wait to dismantle the mines and hand grenades so they could barter the explosives among themselves or blow up selected objects with them. As for me, I couldn't understand what good was or what I was supposed to think of as good, considering that everything is good just the way it is, for the simple reason that it couldn't be otherwise. Also, I didn't understand what I was supposed to do to change things. Or maybe I didn't understand who I was, the person for whom some things should be good and others bad, and also, what this certain person should do to make the world submit to his needs.

I will now add some greens, my grandmother said of her beef soup, because not only was she always busy, she also pampered all her movements, she coddled and caressed them, she took possession of them with words of endearment. I couldn't understand why she had to talk like this, and why to the pot and the soup of all things. In my inordinate shame I thought that others didn't have grandmothers half as crazy as mine. She talked to no purpose because no one, and I do mean no one, would talk to her, my taciturn grandfather least of all. As best I can recall, in my grandfather's family being taciturn must have been mandatory. Exaggeration was not to be countenanced, they had to express themselves with economy, they had to banish anything extraneous from their thoughts. Which left no room for anything extraneous in their sentences either. Which, all told, meant that they had to do most of their thinking inside and for themselves before they spoke. They might acknowledge events, but would not comment on them. Day in and day out, year in and year out, Arnold Tauber spent his long life listening to Cecília Nussbaum speak. It makes me shudder just to think of it. I don't know how he put up with it. He hardly ever raised his eyes to her, but he did listen to her, he listened as if this time he really meant to hear her, as if this time he meant to understand her. His eyes veritably penetrated his effort at listening, he offered no comments or objections, he wouldn't have wanted to cut short what my grandmother had to say; he smiled timidly and devotedly as he listened, all the while he was absorbed in his own listening. His listening may have been identical to his love. Still, he wasn't smiling at Grandmother but at himself. Or God knows who. He was satisfying the obligation that someone had meted out to him, and so with this silence or listening, or his love, his marriage, his ears, he stood obligingly at Grandmother's service; after all, she had borne him his daughters; he sustained his patience or love with his smile, he sustained his marital fidelity, but that was all. When Grandmother asked him anything, his answer was brusque and to the point, so much to the point that his answer no longer contained his personal opinion. It seems to me that my grandfather's attempt at self-annihilation had been a complete success, or else he'd been born like this, lacking a self. Which, strangely enough, did not seem to upset my grandmother; on the contrary, this brusqueness, akin to rejection, seemed not to reach her. She couldn't be unselfed, because her self was situated in a ritually regulated plural, and her only task was to navigate the rules of this ritual. For instance, in her lifelong ritual monologue, greens didn't just mean greens, and I couldn't understand this either, but carrots and parsnips, celeriac and parsley and onion, all the ingredients that went into the soup, and also all the ingredients that weren't green at all and which, in other parts of the city, bore proper collective names such as vegetables or soup vegetables.

I will now add a dash of black corn to it. Not peppercorn, just corn, and not just any which way, but by counting them one by one; she counted the number of peppercorns as if they were so many gold coins she was adding to the soup, one, two, three, possibly seven in all; but at least they were black, at least she got the black right. There was no keeping track of Grandmother's words. Or else I understood the words, but not the sentence. When I asked her, listen, Grandmother, whereas I knew that we do not start a sentence like this because we do not address anyone like this, listen, why do you call pepper corn and the carrots greens, and why do you say that it's chicken soup with roux, do you mean that if we eat your famous soup, Grandmother, we'll rue the day, and so on, with more and more edge to it, tormenting her on purpose.

Why are you making us soup that'll make us rue the day, Grandmother, why are you so mean to us, Grandmother.

I took pleasure in tormenting her. And I didn't even have to shout impermissible, nasty things at her, I was quite capable of hurting her just by asking questions persistently.

It was as if with each of my little questions, far from innocent, to be sure, I were challenging the integrity of an unfamiliar world based on ritual. There's a world we all know, but that's not her world, her world is different, and I know nothing about it. It's located someplace else. For all I know, no one is familiar with it. I didn't just want a horse with a blond mane, I didn't just want to be an iceman or a grain merchant, a miller, a tram conductor, or a landowner, I wanted to be a discoverer, too, in the act of discovering something, because everything I could think of had already been discovered, but I'd have liked to discover something for myself. To set off and discover something different, this other world that would afford me a glimpse of the limits of my own sensations and perceptions. My grandmother put up obstacles in my way that no one else but she could have, because they didn't know me half as well. I understood, of course I understood, but the minute I spotted it, the structure or the outline disintegrated, this is why I wanted to set off and explore the inevitable legitimacy, the way things work, the concept surely familiar to others, but I drew a blank. I didn't know which way to head off in order to track it down. I couldn't commit the fleeting structural images to memory by shutting my eyes tight like with the light bridge or, as in Dobogókő, when we found our bearings with the help of a map and compass, so we could go on this way or that with their help and not lose our way. She trembled, her huge bosom heaved, her voice quivered, that's how upset she got from every little question, the slightest opposition or objection. Will you stop tormenting me. Objections irked her most of all. Would I stop tormenting her already. I'm tormenting her again. One way or another, everyone's tormenting her. What has she done to deserve this tormenting of her person.

You're tormenting me to an early grave. She didn't mean me, or anyone in particular, she was referring to the world at large. She used words I'd never heard before. She'd repeatedly call things by new names, she'd heap names on top of names; she created veritable word thickets. This also made me rack my brain. She sometimes shouted that she couldn't bear this constant tormenting of her person anymore, this vexation of her person that she had to put up with. Don't go vexing my person. She supplied words and phrases unfamiliar to us with Hungarian helping verbs and suffixes and so we could more or less understand what she was saying after all. She beat her chest with her two small fists, meaning the bone above her two huge, round breasts, the stones of the beautiful rings that her most faithful admirer, my grandfather, had made for her shooting off sparks. This really made it appear as if she were living in another world, and not in her own home, in a world that I'm not yet familiar with. Because the place where she lives, people don't torment her. We're not occupying that space. We were never there, we never will be there, in the world where people don't doubt her.

She never said that she's going, or that she was there the day before, or that on Sunday we'll go there together, yet at times her world would nevertheless reveal itself to me.

My grandfather never tired of trying to reconcile her to the world that was in the here and now, her apartment, her neighbors, the city, us, objects and procedures, strangers, their customs and use of language, all the things that we, the others, the unfortunates and infinite fools imagined to be a unified and genuine world. When we, myself or her daughters or my father, the mailman or the superintendent of the building in Péterfy Sándor Street were no longer in hearing distance, quietly, exhaustively, with long pauses, he explained to Grandmother how things really were, who said what and why they'd said it and why they couldn't have thought it any other way, why people say this or that. Surely he must have tried to open Grandmother's eyes for decades, but he could only count on making some headway when he finally lost his patience and raised his voice. When, ominously and brusquely, he called his wife by her nickname. In critical situations he had no choice but to do it even in front of strangers.

Cili.

At which, as if there existed some sort of understanding between them with regard to this, my grandmother fell promptly and readily silent. She attempted a smile, but given the circumstances, it didn't suit her, because being startled or backing down was not in her nature. My grandmother was a first-rate cook, she kept the house in impeccable order, her preserves were famous, and she made delicious *Kugelhopf* and apple pie. *Kugelhopf* was the emperor's favorite, she told me so herself. She embellished the food she made with words, she endowed it with adjectives, she sprinkled it with diminutives. Eat, sugarplum, eat some nice little *Kugelhopf* with your *café au lait*. Go on, my child, take some more of that nice little apple pie, I sprinkled it with lots of sugar because I made it from delicious little apples just right for pie, and they're nice and sour. Had he so much as touched it, meaning the emperor, he would have surely found my grandmother's *Kugelhopf* and cinnamon apple pie deliciously mouthwatering. But that Sisi, what a horsewoman she was, she rode her horse like lightning, and she didn't even ride in a lady's saddle, but she couldn't bake anything, the emperor never got *Kugelhopf* from her, believe you me. Though why would she have bothered, they had plenty of cooks and pastry cooks. Katalin Schratt had to get up every morning at dawn to make a proper *Kugelhopf* for the emperor. That Katalin Schratt, she was no better than she should be, some baggage she was, attending the highest court circles, a nothing of an actress like her, and look at the way she climbed the social ladder. The emperor thanked her every morning, but then one morning he didn't eat what Katalin Schratt placed in front of him. He loved the scent of freshly baked *Kugelhopf,* he liked that plenty, if I say so myself. But the bean coffee with milk he accepted. Grandmother could get my goat with this bean coffee every time. To her, bean coffee was the be-all and end-all of life.

Well, it's either bean or coffee. Or if it's not real, then it's not bean, and it's not coffee. Why can't she make up her mind. Also, she called ersatz coffee made of malt or chicory black coffee, whereas one was brown, the other, the chicory, was definitely yellow. She said coffee, but there was no knowing what she was thinking, was she offering malt or chicory or whatnot.

I couldn't stand the vertiginous confusion of concepts that came in the wake of her words. It was like her coffee. She poured the bean coffee and the ersatz coffee together, and she said, proud as a peacock, this is how I save, and Dad doesn't even notice how much of the household money I save.

When my grandfather called my grandmother by her nickname, her annoyance and the intention behind her awkward attempt at a smile afforded a glimpse of their most secret lives. She may have smiled to acknowledge the little smile that was always perched on the corner of my grandfather's own lips, she may have been attempting to partake of Grandfather's inner cheer and thereby to understand his intentions better, so she could be as tolerant toward my grandfather as my grandfather was toward her, though by all indications, this sort of mutuality did not exist between them. They lived side by side, but not in osmosis by any stretch of the imagination. They were irrevocably separated, isolated from each other, but in their state of isolation they nevertheless found each other. I wouldn't have wanted to see their most secret partnership. As I child I was even curious about things whose existence I couldn't have known about. But this I was not curious to know. Perhaps as a child, you can differentiate between the various qualities of the knowledge you lack. Which again points to the fact that you first gain familiarity with the structure of knowing and only afterward do you collect the material needed for reflection. I was reluctant to acknowledge or understand, to whatever extent, the signs of their secret lives. Only decades later did I understand what I didn't want to acknowledge and understand as a child. The happiness they shared must have been grave, determined, almost bitter. Surely, they were not heading toward the light; rather, they were out to vanquish the darkness.

The conceptually unselfed, rational world came in contact with the poetics of the ritually unselfed world.

My grandmother was not a woman given to smiles. She was constantly in opposition. Unsmiling, she was up in arms against conceptual reality, big-city existence, the worldly. To her everything in our one and only, perfect world remained foreign. Everything. And everything that was foreign was bad. I had no idea where the other, the world that satisfied her was located, the good world in which she felt at home, whereas it was simply in her past, in her family's past, which meant in my family's past, in her secret life bound up with my grandfather's own. I was not far from the truth when I wanted to set out to discover this other world, unconfined by space. At times she yelled, she rolled her eyes behind her small horn-rimmed spectacles like a madwoman, she tore her dress, saying I'm just like my mother, that *chutzpah*, I'm hardly out of the ground and I'm already tormenting her to an early grave. The Almighty will strike you down, don't you worry, He'll punish the both of you for all the things you have done against me.

Don't you worry, He won't leave anything unavenged.

The hour of retribution will come.

And also, why did He punish her with us, why must she be such a *meshugga*, why must she put up with us. Why her. She can't figure it out. What has she done, why is she being punished like this, this is what she'd like to know, seeing how she'd sacrificed her entire life, the best years of her youth, for our sake. Why can everyone torment her her entire lifetime without punishment, why this bunch of nobodies, the entire *mishpocheh*, drive her insane. You're a nobody, understand, she shouted, a nobody. I don't even hear her. I don't even pay attention. In my eyes you're a great big zero, a great big nobody. I look right through you. I consider you air and nothing more. And for the sake of emphasis, she kept repeating this in various languages. Which was yet another thing I didn't understand, because if I'm air, why does she get herself all worked up. A nobody. A nothing. A *niemand*. A *nebbich*. Ad infinitum. That such a great big nobody, a big *niemand* like me, a *nebbich* like me, should teach her a lesson, such a nobody, such a great big zero, a *niemand*, a good-for-nothing.

She screeched. You little shit. How can it happen, how can such a little shit do this to me.

I'm done with you. You're my grandson no more.

I'm disinheriting you. You're not inheriting my turquoise ring either. I'm leaving it to Mártika. I'm disowning you and don't you forget it.

You will get nothing, do you hear, nothing.

I'm disowning you once and for all.

She sobbed and rent her clothes at the breast, then suddenly sober, she turned on her heels and went about her business or went to complain to my grandfather about me in a sneaky, underhanded way.

I didn't know what this whole dramatic scene with her wailing, disowning, and underhanded punishment, this driving her insane, death and the great big nobodies could have meant, if they meant anything at all, but I found it highly amusing. In the language she spoke, the pantry was the *Speis*. Also, I was glad that I was such a great big *nebbich*. Such figurative speech made me happy because even at the age of four or six I was very small, pint-sized for my age, a little shit indeed. When I started school, I was always the smallest in the gym line. Always the second or third from the back. Which had its advantages. The taller boys, who stood at the head of the line, always came to my aid when the boys from class A or C wanted to have a go at me. We were class B. For years I felt lucky because I was in class B. I don't know why, but being in this class was considered special. His mates from class B wouldn't let a boy be beaten up. They didn't want to beat me up because I did anything against them, it's just that the big boys from class A picked on the boys from class B at random. In turn, they got as good as they gave. The boys from class B saw me home every day, sometimes they even saw me through the gate in case the bigger boys from class A or C should lie in wait for me in the stairwell, or if they did lie in wait for me and flung stones or snowballs at me, or snowballs with stones hidden inside them, which I feared more than the stones because of their treacherous character, they'd put their heads together and come up with new plans against the boys from class A and C; they gave the little boys from A and C a thorough beating, while they embraced me, the little one, the weak one, who must be protected in the name of brotherly love; they gave me all sorts of things to comfort me, whereas I never complained about anybody, I never asked them to protect me, and I never asked anybody for their apple. I was ill-suited for the role of victim, or for that of the sheltered victim, for that matter. They shared what they had with me, though for that matter, I also shared what I had with them. They shoved it in my hand, they stuffed it in my pocket, so others shouldn't see and hear how they were making an exception of me, though they used words of endearment with me openly and loudly, as if they were my older brothers.

This continued even through high school; I could have had my choice of one of the two roles even then, I could have been a drag on them or an eternally whining victim of fate; on Thököly Street and in the Petrik Lajos School for Chemistry the bigger boys called me Cutie Pie, because I never reached beyond medium height. Cutie Pie this and Cutie Pie that, they called me Cutie Pie even among themselves, guess what, Cutie Pie didn't come swimming yesterday, Cutie Pie is playing hooky again; because the truth is that after our parents died, I played hooky from school for six months running; Cutie Pie, why won't you have lunch with us. They enjoyed this Cutie Pie even more than I, as if they owned me, a piece of cake they shared fairly among themselves. I'm not saying that they enjoyed this game at my expense, because they didn't go as far as that, they were really sweet and kind, charming, their strength and size protected them, but they took playful advantage of the attracton they felt all the same. In which the real sympathy they felt played a part. I was an orphan. None of my schoolmates ever asked me about it straight out, I just had to let them keep me out of harm's way and spoil me, the poor orphan. Though at times it proved to be a burden, though at times it was balancing precariously on the borderline of humiliation, I didn't protest. They enjoyed my humiliation. Also, they tormented me all the time; we were older by then, we had hair on our chins and were full of unsightly pimples; they twisted my arm until it hurt, they squeezed my knee between their thighs, and I could see and sometimes feel them getting an erection; in this big camaraderie, they wrestled me to the ground and rode on top of my chest. These fights and wranglings gave their bodies an excuse to rub against each other legally and without fear because, needless to say, all physical contact was strictly forbidden among them so they shouldn't feel toward each other what they felt, or what others felt toward them. This feeling was the secret of secrets, and no one ever spoke about it, and in its way this Cutie Pie of theirs gave vent to and legitimized the thing that stood under the strictest prohibition, a feeling of attraction that they not only would not deny themselves, but the interdiction and their silence rendered it all the more intense. They enjoyed the resultant tension, this is where it drew its depth, and they were bent on amplifying the tension, and their pricks stood as straight as a flagpole, while I didn't want more, nor something else, for that matter, even this was too much, a burden, and I needed at least two decades of experience to more or less understand the order and logic of this rite.

But when I heard Grandmother's words, I often burst out laughing, for goodness' sake, what is my grandmother talking about, it's really amusing the way her passions, the depths of which were unfamiliar to me and black as tar, sweep her along with them.

In my father's family almost everyone laughed like this, there was no animosity or disdain intended, we laughed when we were surprised or scandalized. If we felt that rationality had suffered a defeat, that someone was going against the rules of logic, or spoke in line with the premises of rationality while acting against it, we were inordinately surprised and thought it highly amusing. I realize that in the eyes of others they laughed out of line, but my father did it, and so did his older brothers and his sisters, my younger brother does it too, though as for me, for years I've been trying to hold this reaction of mine in check.

Needless to say, it was so much fuel to the fire. In my grandmother's eyes, laughing at someone was one of the most grievous of sins. And she was right.

Basically, my grandmother didn't just call it looking down on someone, she called it maligning.

That I'm maligning her.

You better not malign me, boy.

I'm not maligning you, Grandmother, I said cocksure of myself, and sarcastically, too, though today I'm more than willing to admit that in the name of rationality and the Hungarian language, I did indeed malign her. She used the expression correctly, I now admit. We have no other expression for what she was protesting against. I laughed at her when something was not rational, in short, when I couldn't make her brand of rationality suit the system that I considered rational.

Don't you mock me, boy.

I don't even know how to do that, Grandmother.

There you go again, mimicking me, eyeing me up.

But Grandmother, if I don't know what eyeing up means, how could I be doing it.

You're glaring at me, giving me the evil eye, that's what it means. You're casting an evil spell on me, the way you glare, there you go, you're doing it again. You know perfectly well what you're doing with your eyes.

Don't you look at me like that, boy, you're glaring at me again with your two eyes.

I have two eyes, Grandmother, but I'm not glaring, I'm just looking with my two eyes, trying to understand.

You all glare at me, you look right through me, an old woman, why must I be subjected to people glaring at me, turning what I say against me. You, son, are turning everything I say against me. You all know perfectly well what I'm saying, you understand it well enough. I can't even breathe in this place without you turning my words inside out. An old woman, and you're turning me inside out. All of you.

We're taking her for air, we're taking her for granted.

And she won't survive it.

I enjoyed the repeated sinning, taking her for air and turning her words inside out, turning her out of the only wealth she possessed, even though I sometimes laughed not because I was mean, but because she took me by surprise. Honestly. I honestly didn't mean to laugh at her and turn her words inside out, and malign her least of all. Definitely not. Still, I laughed at her repeatedly, and it was no use me knowing that as far as she was concerned, this was a wicked thing to do. Had I known beforehand what she was about to say, and I almost always knew which locution would inevitably follow in a given linguistic situation, I'd have beaten her to it and I'd have said it instead of her, and when I did, saying it two seconds before her made me feel inordinately happy. Which got her dander up.

That I'm mocking her, in short, that I'm watching for the effect and enjoying it, that I'm aping her, I see through the sieve, I'm exposing her, this was my wickedness, and not when I laughed in spite of myself.

God Almighty will pay you back so you'll live to regret it, all of you, He'll pay you back, don't you worry.

You'll live to see my dying day, but it'll be too late. You'll regret this bitterly, just you wait and see.

I will not forgive you.

You'll be sorry. Who is going to knead dough for you on Sunday, that's what I'd like to know. Who.

Nobody.

Even though I wasn't familiar with the expression, I knew perfectly well what she wanted with this dying day of hers. I'd never heard anyone else having a dying day, except for her.

Your mother, you can wait till doomsday before she'll knead dough. A roast duck will land in your mouth first. You'd think she was Queen Elisabeth personified. Baking is beneath her dignity. She can't even make proper soup dumplings. That's why you have a maid. Let the maid do the cooking, let her clean up after you. What's money to you. There's no wealth you can't squander. Your mother can't even cook, she can't bake a cake, even though I showed her, I taught her how to do it, but she looks down her nose at housework.

Grandmother was the only one in the family who didn't say cotton fabric, but cotton fiber, and she didn't pay the chimney sweep, she paid him off, and she didn't say go, but be off. What could I do if I didn't understand, because in the midst of her laments and shower of invectives I was so taken by the force of her strange use of words that even if unwittingly, I became their faithful slave for life; but for the time being, her words made me lose the thread of what she had to say. Very early on, I was at the mercy of the exceptional, it pulled and tugged at me, diverting me from everything else, it jump-started my fantasies. There was always something out of the ordinary in her use of words, however slight, in her syntax, in her intonation, that I got caught up in and couldn't pay attention to anything else, just this, the unique, the singular, the different along with all aspects of this different, and how the details of these details might be related to other more familiar details.

Don't you look through me. Even when I wasn't.

She did it again, she wasn't talking to me, she was talking in a plural of indeterminate outlines, and for a very long time I couldn't understand why she was talking like this when it was just the two of us, as if I weren't the one looking through her. Which means that I exist for her in the plural, and also, she's hooked into some unfamiliar plural that I can be a part of only through her. She estranged me from herself, meaning that with her use of the plural, she let me know that we were estranged from each other. I was a stranger to the ritual community in which she had felt at home as a child, and where people have the sky cave in on them more than once in their lives. And also, I'm just like my mother, except I don't know it yet. And we have conspired against her. We're the foreign element in the family, not letting her get a word in edgewise in her own home. And the Lord will rain cats and dogs down on us for it. We can rest assured. I also didn't understand what the tormenting of her person meant. What I mean is of course I understood. Except I refused to accept it as a synonym for vexation. I also understood scrubbing, come spring people all over the city got on their knees and scrubbed the floor of every apartment in town with boiling hot alkaline water, they wiped it dry then colored it, this was the color agent, a yellow powder in a small sack that they dissolved in water, though this I didn't understand, this color agent, I understood the color, but not the agent, then they waxed it, this I understood because there was plenty of wax in our home to rub on the floor, floor wax that they applied to the floor with all their strength using the floor brush that they attached to their bare feet, I understood this, too, though there was a catch to it, they made hump-hump sounds as they worked, which gave the innocent activity an obscene tone, later on I scrubbed and waxed and polished myself, but what does that have to do with vexation.

When the pediatrician Elza Baranyai, whom I loved affectionately, came over from the other side of Pozsonyi Street, I especially loved the birthmark above her lip, a little dot, a beauty mark that the gods placed just in the right spot on her face, and I dreamed that in that case I'd rather not be an iceman or landowner or a locomotive driver but a doctor, like her, I'd become a gynecologist and marry Elza Baranyai because I loved the smell of chloroform issuing from her skin, she already had a husband, someone by the name of Gyuri, a very handsome man, a sportsman, but that couldn't stop me. Besides, they didn't have children. As I looked at this Gyuri with his long locks falling over his forehead and his long limbs that somehow reminded me of a lazy cat, his muscles, his shapely buttocks, I could imagine him being my father. Which meant that I'd have liked to be Elza's husband and child at the same time, so I could be Gyuri's son or lover. Her scent constituted Elza's sex appeal, the sterility, the hospital, the smell of disinfectant and ether, and when she was examining me she asked the nurse, as if by way of an aside, what the child's stool is like.

Time and again I would have liked to get a firm grip on how grown-ups form words and from what, words that they then not only exchange among themselves, so to speak sharing them, words that they have no trouble understanding. For instance, the theological logic of Grandmother's sentences remained an eternal mystery. I took off in its wake so I'd understand it, but the jungle became darker and darker and more and more impenetrable. Someone would punish me for my sins, that was clear, someone we can identify with the heavens or the supreme heavenly dweller, since he is obviously superior to me in all things, and so, come rain or shine, I am bound to respect his invisible existence every moment of my waking day, except in that case, why does my grandmother say that I shouldn't be afraid. Why shouldn't I. Of course I was afraid. Or if I shouldn't be afraid, is it this certain individual I shouldn't be afraid of, or heaven, or perhaps my grandmother, who asks the heavens to punish me for my sins, although this certain preeminent someone has punished her plenty with our mere existence. Also, if this preeminent someone can punish someone severely, then surely he can punish him lightly, too, if he wants, except apparently, he doesn't want to. In which case, what's the difference between severe punishment and light punishment, this was also one of the cardinal questions of my childhood and I agonized over it for many years. Meanwhile, my grandmother was agonizing over an insoluble theological problem of her own, because in line with the expressions current in the language of Pest, she kept saying God's name in its various forms in vain, whereas with such frequency and in such an unworthy linguistic environment she shouldn't have done so. Perhaps it was the Hungarian vernacular of Pest, this variation on the Hungarian language foreign to her many times over that led her onto this misguided path. The truth of the matter is that God made an all-too-frequent appearance in the sentences of the people of Pest. My grandmother was thinking in terms of clichés and figures of speech, she fixed linguistic stencils to each other, and so she couldn't very well have avoided God's name or expunge it from the typical sentences of Pest. Perhaps she preferred to speak Yiddish in order to avoid committing this particular sin.

I have no way of knowing now, but by all indications, Yiddish was her mother tongue. Every single time she spoke the name of God out of turn, she'd slap her small fist to her mouth, the one that bore her rings.

If I said something blasphemous, she'd sometimes slap my lips, too, with the hand that bore her rings, from which I learned firsthand the pain it causes to take the Lord's name in vain. If she held her fingers apart, and she did it on purpose because of my blasphemy, her rings would come in contact with my lips that much harder. Once she split a lip with her turquoise ring, whose stone kept turning, an act that resulted in a loud altercation that lasted several weeks, because my mother wouldn't stand by and not say anything, while my grandfather made vain attempts to come between them.

You have no right to hit my child, Mother. No one has the right to hit a child.

You ruined our childhood with your rings. I'm fed up. You have ruined all of us psychologically. You even hit poor sick Margitka, you had the nerve to strike a gravely ill child.

Who. Me. Me. Margitka. How can you say a thing like that, me hitting my one and only darling baby. How could I. Have you no shame, saying a thing like that. You say this to me, me of all people. You say this to me, my own daughter accusing me of such a vile act.

You must have forgotten, Mother.

Me. Talking to me this way. What was I supposed to forget.

You want to forget.

My own daughter accusing me. How can you be so base, why did I bring such a monster into the world. What have I done to deserve this. You talking to me like this.

I will not sit back and let you ruin my child psychologically as well.

If only I told you how mean, how vile, how wicked your darling little child is, you'd be surprised. But I'm not telling you. I won't tell you anything. I'll keep it to myself. Put up with it. All my life, I must put up with everything. Well, from now on I will keep everything to myself. Everything. I'm not talking to you ever again

You even beat Bözsi like dirty linen, not just me, you beat her with

334

the coal shovel, you beat her on the head. Of course, you had an easy time with Bözsi, Bözsi couldn't run away.

And then thanks to this name all hell broke loose, not because of Bözsi, because nobody loved Bözsi, but as a delayed reaction, because of Margitka. Which is not something I like to remember. As if the mention of Bözsi and her limp had released from some recess of her mind the infinite pain Grandmother felt over Margitka's death.

As they gave vent to their crying and shouting and screaming, I saw how alike they were and realized how many things my mother had to keep in check in her own nature so she could be the enlightened individual that she imagined herself to be.

Days later she must have felt bad about the small accident. Meaning my grandmother. But I was sorry too, sorry that I didn't keep my wounded lip a secret from my mother. Or why didn't I lie. Why didn't I keep it to myself, because in her great humiliation Grandmother unexpectedly announced that after they place her in a cold grave under the ground, because thanks to us her days are numbered, but at least it'll be over and she'll find peace at long last, in short, I am going to inherit her turquoise ring, me and no one else, it's already in her will, because I'm her only darling little grandson, and leaning over the hot stove, she started crying and whimpering.

But I'd better be careful, I'd better be on my guard, she cried bitterly, or else Bözsi will get her hands on the ring. At which point let me say that Bözsi did get her hands on it. Grandmother hadn't even died, but the ring was already on display on Bözsi's finger. Because Bözsi always wheedles everything out of everyone, she coaxes it out of them, Grandmother sobbed. But we must forgive Bözsi, Bözsi is handicapped, a wounded soul, Bözsi is an unfortunate human being. I brought a monster and a miserable cripple into the world. A cripple. Why did God punish me with a miserable cripple like her. I asked nothing else of the Almightly all my life, just this one thing and nothing else, that He should tell me why He is punishing me, what have I done to deserve this.

This is how my grandmother prepared me for my inheritance, my future, the ring with the turquoise stone, with these sentences. Which in fact put a prompt end to my devil-may-care sadism, my laughing at her, the pleasure of maligning her.

She wants to do what she accuses everyone else of doing, she wants to bribe me, she wants to make me feel indebted to her with her turquoise ring.

I didn't want her ring, but I didn't say so. There were lots of things that I managed not to say by then, and even more things that, try as I might, I didn't understand.

Don't you worry, Bözsi will take the food out of your mouth. If Bözsi wants something, she respects neither God nor man.

My grandmother was determined to conspire with me against Bözsi, and in order to succeed, she proceeded to bribe me with the promised inheritance.

Most of Grandmother's sentences pertaining to the future had something horrendously offensive about them, some anticipatory ill will. No matter what I came up with, I couldn't stand in the way of this ill will. If it wasn't in the unfamiliar verbs, *wheedle, coax, bribe*, take the food out of your mouth, and so on, then it was in her intonation, it was in the structure of her sentences. She prefixed a person's names with a definite pronoun, the Bözsi, which stylistically functioned just as it was meant to function, as a stylistic element, I use it myself when I write. She must be indulgent with people, in this case with her own daughter, after all she's handicapped, she was born that way. She gave her birth, she brought Bözsi into this miserable world with a dislocated hip. There wasn't a doctor who could've helped her, whereas she took her to every doctor she knew. I won't believe this, but they even deprived themselves of food, just so they could take her to old Doctor Bókay. Not the young one, because he's not worth anything, not him, but the old man, to examine her.

And I'd better believe it.

There was no helping this unfortunate cripple.

She cried, or better yet, in her rage she pretended that she was crying, crying for herself; with her spectacular weeping she put her innocence on display, she put her untimely death on display, which made her feel like crying in earnest, but she wouldn't give this free rein either, this crying, not entirely, all the while that she made a spectacular show of holding her sad faith in check with her last remaining strength. However, this had precious little to do with self-control, in which we were supposed to set an example, though we didn't succeed all the time either. It wasn't her crying, she couldn't afford to cry, but now and then, instead of her, she nevertheless had, so to speak, to cry her despair out of herself. She invariably launched into this demonstrative crying at the most opportune moment, the most suitable dramaturgical moment. I never saw her cry in earnest, not even when we buried my mother, then my grandfather, and finally my father. Not even when I saw my grandfather die. I even touched him. She wouldn't have touched him, not even when he was dead, or when he was dying, which couldn't have lasted more than ten minutes; it repelled her, she stood by the window and watched my grandfather's dying agony from there. And as soon as my grandfather died, when the body's spastic, desperate struggle for air, for one last full breath, had ceased, she began screaming, yelling for me to go fetch a doctor. Go on, what are you waiting for, get your clothes on and go, I said, go. It was obvious that it didn't make sense to call a doctor for a dead man, but I quickly threw my clothes on and went for the doctor all the same. Throughout a lifetime and for greater effect, she turned her ritual complaints and ritual accusations into ritual wailing, it was part of the rite, she stretched her words out until she really cried for lack of air, and then she'd abandon her imperfectly accumulated fragmental sentences. This is how a person's own early childhood calls out from within, though not once and for all, because she invariably recovered herself from the silent weeping, the wailing, the infinite mourning felt over her own death, her selfishness and sadness, and then, choking from tears, she reverted to her accusations, her self-accusations, her complaints, this is how she disciplined and checked herself, this is how she kept herself on the surface of intentionality and ritual signification, all the while that she nevertheless kept forcing the sound from her chest, steadily amplifying the intensity of her woe.

It was clear to me from these loud scenes that I'd be better off turning to my forbearing and taciturn grandfather with my questions, and most of all, that I should stop pestering my grandmother about her hopelessly confusing use of language. Let her use it as she sees fit. I'd be better off not tormenting her and not taking advantage of her weak points. And I should try to be more understanding. My grandfather's admonitions went no further than this. I did my best, because I saw his point, I knew that I shouldn't annoy my grandmother, but I succeeded in my effort only in rare instances, because to my surprise I'd either laugh at her against my will, or else feel annoyed because of her.

But I could have just as easily felt annoyed with myself, or with my parents. Why did I let them lead me so far astray with the worship of reason. I had no way of knowing that these ritual tirades that came in loud bursts, all the screeching and supplication, the many senseless apologies and lamentations are not a game, though they should not scare me either, because they're a dead end leading nowhere, and even in their most glaring manifestations they mean nothing; they're nothing but so much trimming and embellishment, so much somber background noise; their only worth is self-worth. They are no more than rhetorical curiosities, variations on a theme, and should be taken as such, and it's no use attributing special meaning to them. They are the imprint of ancient emotional rituals and standardized emotional outbursts, and it is their modulations I am witnessing and hearing, and their only significance is historical, ethnic, and etiological. They are not personal and they are not familial; on the contrary, they remove the familial from the personal, because by its very essence the tribal won't tolerate personal and familial characteristics; rather, they bring news of the conventional language of the ghetto, its established customs, intonations, and gestures. My grandmother's language is the language of a clan, a characteristically rural language, an emotional inclusion that, along with their experience of the regularly recurring pogroms, the constant fear, and the insufferable shame of survival her ancestors had brought with them about 120 years previously from Podolia or Galicia, Poland or Russia; because of the current administrative complications, it is impossible to discover just where.

It is curious, but for a long time, a very long time, a surprisingly long time it never occurred to me that my grandmother's ancestors are also my ancestors and consequently, that I might have something to do with her family, her religious undertones and her use of language. Even now I have to force myself to acknowledge this tribal relationship, to accept that indeed it was not her ancestors but our common ancestors who had brought this special tribal mentality with them from beyond the Monarchy's frontiers, a mentality that was not familiar here, or else it was not familiar in this shape and form. I therefore find it positively painful to get the better of my inner protest by calling to my aid the regard I have for objectivity, because to this day I find it strange that my grandmother should be an empty tribal loudspeaker, and no more. My grandmother's family remained strangers to my grandfather as well, but at least he was still familiar with the convention and understood it, and surely, he could come to terms with the strangeness of this Eastern European Orthodox xenolith. On the other hand, regarded from the perspective of my father's family, it was like viewing an object through the wrong end of a pair of binoculars. They could not find a path leading to it, no one could find a path to it as they looked on courteously, though with a touch of aversion.

When I think about it, they didn't even attempt to understand, and in fact there was nothing to understand; they passed indifferently over it as over a phenomenon that exists but has no bearing on their own lives.

When my grandmother spoke, my father seemed not to hear; you could tell by his expression that he'd switched off. In order for him to understand, he first had to let each of my grandmother's words in one ear and out the other; this was his way of isolating all that flotsam and jetsam, all that embellishment from the essence. At such times my grandmother would go on speaking to him at length, because she could see that there was no impediment to her flood of words, though she also saw that she could not expect an answer.

Meanwhile, my father remained as courteously interested in her say as if he were with a complete stranger.

Yes, Mama, that's right, Mama, that's exactly right.

Or else he found some transparent excuse not to answer but turn his back on something of which he never understood a single word, and quickly go on his way. Though the truth is that he would often demonstrate at close range the same attentive aloofness that was so much part of his makeup for the benefit of his two sons as well.

But at the time that is the subject of my present discourse, I was still an only child, and I saw my mother, my father, my grandmother, and my grandfather as an only child. Also, they hadn't moved in with us yet, they hadn't moved from Péterfy Sándor Street yet. My little brother hadn't been born yet, we couldn't use the plural together and say our mother, our father. I was all alone with them.

When my grandmother let loose, only my mother would speak up, annoyed, as if every single motherly word had hurt her to the quick. There was nothing Grandmother could say that didn't get my mother's dander up, all the while that she tried to be meticulously careful not to be like her, not to show her annoyance in the same manner as her mother, not to be the living mirror image of her eternally disgruntled mother. To make sure she won't fly off the handle. Won't make a mountain out of a molehill. Since she regarded the tribal conventions of the maternal side of her family as worthless, dismissing them, even in her gestures, she had to keep her emotions in check with the conventions of the paternal side of her family, except she possessed neither the equanimity of her father nor his discernment and dignity. But then, this is what's exciting about inherited traits. I'd like to follow one of the two, my mother or my father, feeling as I do that I am just like the one or the other. But I can't follow just one, because the other dwells inside me as well, and I am the third those two together make. I want to follow the one, but the other lives inside me with equal force. At times I discovered the same struggle on my own mother's facial expressions and gestures; I saw her turn crimson from the effort as she adamantly refused to allow the ritual reflexes she'd inherited from her mother to surface by calling the rationality she'd inherited from her father to her aid, to hold the unwanted reflexes in check with the liberal reasoning that she must remain liberally tolerant at all costs. Which proved to be next to impossible.

And as for me, I'm ashamed to admit it, but when they took me to

my maternal grandparents for a few days, or else my maternal grandparents took me with them on vacation to the Danube, to Dömös,
Dömsöd, or Göd, my curiosity repeatedly drove me to provoke my
grandmother's fits of passion. I want to see how she mimes and holds
her real anger in check, how she makes her chagrin swell, how she
transforms her ritually shaped emotions into theatrics, how she brings
her momentary passions and transient emotions into the world order
whose nature has evaded her. To watch, a hundred times a day, if possible, the fixed order of the scenes, the rhythm of the rituals she performed. At the same time, I worried what these ritual outbursts might
do to her. I caused her fits of rage, then looked on in trepidation,
waiting to see what would happen next. But I showed no mercy, small
children especially have no mercy, or God knows, I wouldn't want to
excuse my own sin by calling the sin of others to my aid, perhaps I
alone was such a cruel little boy.

The next generation comes, and as it stands atop the mountain of
corpses, once again understands nothing of what is happening.

It has learned nothing.

I enjoyed not understanding her, I followed in my mother's wake
in rejecting my grandmother Cecília Nussbaum, who despite her husband's repeated protests wickedly beat her own daughters all her life.

I never knew my paternal grandmother, Klára Mezei. By the time
I was born she was dead, but we respected and celebrated her even in
death. Still, and it comes as no surprise, for me my maternal grandmother impersonated the concept of grandmother, and so, on this
small, sensitive family surface, our valued rational world nevertheless came in contact with the mythical, lyrical, and irrational world.
They could not be reconciled. With its linguistic signs and emotional
traces, the unfamiliar history, and with it the story of the Eastern
European Jews, the story of their ritual persecution, the story of their
special brand of isolation, the story of their individual lives and their
use of language came streaming in through this small side door, in-
advertently left open. Their escape from and their escape to, their religious, linguistic, and social segregation, their voluntary isolation and
their lack of a homeland in their new homeland. The story of their

expulsion and tragic separation from their roots in which, on behalf of rational progress, the respected members of the paternal side of my family, my paternal great-grandfather Mór Mezei and his younger brother, Ernő Mezei, had played a significant historic role.

Their actions came to represent the ideal of progress in the family, this is what they hoped to emulate, the liberalism, the ideal of independence and enlightenment, the quantity and especially the carefully checked quality of knowledge, the objective observation, the dispassionate acknowledgment of things, the scientific stance, the encyclopedism, their belief in precision and not privilege, not that, but personal worth, character, and moral bearing, yes, but not hierarchy. If they said of someone that he was a strong character, then that certain someone had won their respect. During the one and a half centuries I was able to survey, they measured everything in their own families by these basic standards, by honor and strength of character. This value system, this *valeur*, this is what we became, and in the interest of this plural, they had to pare down their individual selves, veritably unselfing themselves. Surely, my deeply honored great-grandfather Mór Mezei and his younger brother, Ernő Mezei, could have come up with something different, something more imaginative, they could have done something more worthy, more sober, and more just, though I couldn't say, even now, how they could have acted more reasonably in face of the tribal orthodoxy of the refugees from Podolia and Galicia. Their actions were pragmatic. In the name of the Jewish communities of Hungary and Transylvania they elaborated a system of rules pertaining to a unified organization that would have made their unified political representation within the parliamentary system possible, since it was to be feared that without such representation, their voices would not be heard. In December 1868 they had Parliament pass the so-called congressional statute that the congress approved, the government introduced, and the king sanctioned, but the greater part of the Orthodox Jewish communities rejected. The Orthodox religious communities were not interested in political equality, it did not interest the immigrants belonging to the various Orthodox religious movements, nor did it interest the Hungarian Orthodox Jewry, who did not wish to be represented in this manner. They didn't even want to know what political representation was all about. They were grouped around rabbis, their religion was rabbinate, and as far as they were concerned, that ended the argument. They rejected free-thinking as a hideous sin, and the government was later forced to acknowledge their independent existence in a special decree. What my great-grandfather and his younger brother were campaigning for, what they hoped would be unified political representation, never ma-terialized as unified, because in questions pertaining to religion the Jewish community itself was not unified. Practically speaking, in the face of two different orthodoxies they elaborated a unified neology, in short, they gave the great inner schism of Jewry an institutional face. They came up with a unity that, through no fault of their own, could not accommodate other unities. None of the branches of fundamental orthodoxy could be channeled into the riverbed of their liberal prin-ciples, nor were they amenable to regulation by them. At the same time, they realized that traditional orthodoxy or Hasidic orthodoxy would pull them in an undesirable direction and would work against them. It would have led them into a fundamentalism they were unfa-miliar with. It was not conceived in their own past, they had nothing to do with it at any time whatsoever. In Germany, the Czech lands, and Austria, from where they had come to the Kingdom of Hun-gary a century and a half earlier, this type of Jewish orthodoxy was unknown. There were Jews and non-Jews, there were Sephardis and Ashkenazis, which meant disparate systems of established custom, but their ideal of the universal was urban and not rural in character, and thus fundamentally different. Their wisdom and philosophy was not based on the exclusivity of religion or of place, nor was it based on the wisdom of their rabbis, if for no other reason than because Jewish religion had a sturdy freethinking current that was born in opposition to traditionalism and was nourished for about three thousand years in the face of traditionalism. They knew that traditionalism meant to hold in check the politically regulated current of life, and it is in the face of this that they were freethinkers. In their worldly lives they wanted to be adequate to social progress, the principle of development as such, the ideal of progress and liberal thinking that they believed in, and not their religion. As far as they were concerned, their religion was not the embodiment of the universal, just a part of the universal relegated to their care. And that is an appreciable difference. One results in tolerance toward the religious conviction of others, the other results in indifference and impatience. Only through an insight into these historical differences can we understand why these factions could not understand each other. These Jews were adherents of the Enlightenment, of cosmopolitism, of science, of multilingualism, the ideal Hegelian progress of history, empiricism, the objective approach to things, they were adherents of commercial interest, the industrial revolution, the great liberal change and current in European political history, the concepts that Locke and Montesquieu held of the individual and the common weal, and not the wisdom of the local rabbis.

There I stood at the age of four or five, barely two or three years after the greatest fiasco, regression, sin, and catastrophe in human history, among those struggling with the death and disappearance of their loved ones, in my grandmother's spotlessly clean kitchen, where the copper chandelier was twinkling and glittering once again, and so were the copper kettle, the two beautiful copper plates of the kitchen scale, the Turkish coffee grinder, the Turkish copper tray, the copper candlestick, and the black sheen of the black stove plate and the red sheen of the red copper siding of the stove, there I stood as if nothing had happened, refusing to acknowledge that she is also me, trying to make my very own racist ignominy fit my very own system of exclusion, refusing to acknowledge that an individual is made up of the conventions of various traditions, and this is so even if he or she chooses among them or has been forced to choose among them because of the happenstance of the place and time of his or her birth and the social conventions that he or she inherited along with them.

My curiosity had an animal vitality to it, a vital force barely susceptible to control, and no matter how we look at it, it is part and parcel of our anthropological heritage, it is part and parcel of the history of humanity kept under a very tight, ritual cover. My own animality gave the appearance of naïveté, but in the meantime I made sure that taking advantage of numbers, I curry favor with the majority, the silent judgment and will of the family. I am not an opportunist by any means and I willingly crossed people all my life, at times in ways surprising even to my friends, but mind you, it wasn't because I wanted to annoy anyone, or because I wanted to call attention to myself with my extravagance, but because the animal simplemindedness of people living in a herd has nauseated me ever since I can remember, their prefabricated sentences have made me laugh, they have offended me profoundly; and yet when I was around my grandmother, despite the opportunity that offered itself to the contrary, at the age of four I was a bona fide opportunist. I decided that we had nothing in common with her unpleasant style and intonation, her language and exaggerated gestures. And as a matter of fact, we really had nothing in common with her, we had nothing in common with her brutality and nothing in common with her sentimentality either, but then, this is what piqued my curiosity. But I valued the perspective, the plural, our ritual plural, our historical mode more than the unreflected subject of my curiosity.

To be on the safe side, I tended toward it, toward the will of the majority, I preferred the warm, comforting feathers of the mother hen. I told myself that we are more enlightened than that, we are more genteel, more forward-looking and modern. We do not polish or else we do not have others polish our copper objects quite so bright, because we see no sense in it, it's a sign of compulsive behavior and not of respectable poverty or cleanliness, nor do we pretend, day in and day out, for the benefit of each other. We are not taken in by the beliefs of others. We are temperate. Our collective brain functions in a higher gear, it does not bog down in material things, the singular, the single number, the singular case. Our intellect does not judge, it registers. What's more, it abstracts. It remains aloof in the face of everything and just about everyone, or at least attempts to, and our spirit, too, is descriptive in character. It takes stock of identities, differences, and similarities. It isolates, it establishes relationships, it is not content remaining on the surface, it looks beyond the jungle of masks and disguises, it does not concern itself with singular characteristics, it does not panic, it does not disparage, it does not find pleasure in the sins of others. It prefers to engage itself with causes, and not be bogged down with the effects. It identifies problems and solves them. Needless to say, I had no way of knowing at the time that thanks to all these liberal bourgeois admonitions, especially the last one, I'd repeatedly find myself in situations of conflict that I wouldn't be able to disregard.

With her strikingly different mental makeup, my grandmother must have been very lonely in this other populous family. How could I have understood her. What my family did to her involuntarily and, of course, in a more courteous manner, I repeated with intent to provoke. While other children tore off the legs of frogs and grasshoppers for want of anything better to do, I practiced exclusion on her. At the same time, just as unaware, meaning in spite of myself, I learned a great deal from her. From who else would I have learned the language of the eastern ghettos, their system of gestures, the logic of isolation, even if I did so at the price of committing serious ethical offenses, because I learned these things in the course of the series of conflicts that I had provoked.

Many kinds of Jews lived and continue to live in various districts of Buda and Pest, but invariably mingled among the rest, or wedged in between other ways of life, or else lost in the crowd. In the centuries between the early Middle Ages and the Arrow Cross terror, there were no ghettos either in Pest or Buda, and consequently, there existed neither a language nor a system of gestures typical of the ghettos. Pest spoke Hebrew, it spoke German, it spoke Hungarian, it also spoke Slovak, it spoke Greek, it spoke Serbian, it spoke Armenian, it spoke Romanian, it spoke Romany, it spoke Yiddish, it spoke Ruthenian, but regardless of what language it spoke, it always spoke in several languages; what's more, it mixed languages and it especially mixed the music of these languages. In the city, Hungarian became a point of reference only in the early nineteenth century. Even Buda was multilingual; it spoke German before it spoke Hungarian, not to mention the use of Latin in its initial official dealings, which was replaced by the language of Austrian administration only after the Turkish occupation of the country. Thus, thanks to my grandmother,

I was taken back to the distant times and unfamiliar cultural terrains of the lives of the Eastern Orthodox Jews that I couldn't have known otherwise, how could I, and which they pilfered and destroyed, wiping it off the face of the earth, it would seem once and for all. People whose names we know did it in the name of Nazi ideology, but they did not do it alone, nor in isolation, nor in secret, they did it with the knowledge and approval of the big wide world. The representatives of thirty-two nations sanctioned it in July 1938 at the Évian Conference. Two millenia of anti-Semitism convinced the national delegates that regardless of what would happen, they need not take in Jewish refugees. Arm in arm with the Nazis, the representatives of these nations declared war on four centuries of humanism. They did not agree to anything outright, but their tacit agreement sealed the fate of millions of human beings and put the stamp of shame on their own ethics. To use the language of psychology, the moment they gave up their humanity, they regressed and plunged right back into the mythical and magical worldview of the times before Copernicus and Galileo.

Four years later, on a Wednesday in October, in the early hour when on Pozsonyi Street my mother felt her first birth pangs, with the tacit agreement of the world a German task force, police battalion 101 deployed from Hamburg, was just readying itself to destroy the ghetto of Mizocz. Concretely, this meant that on orders from Captain Hoffmann, on the day I was born, they drove 1,259 people out of the city to the nearby stone quarry, where, on this Wednesday, they separated the women and children from the men. On this Wednesday, they had to strip naked, as naked as my mother was when in the maternity ward of the Jewish Hospital in Szabolcs Street, the renowned gynecologist Imre Hirschler helped me come into the world.

In the final analysis man is nothing but water, a certain amount of mineral matter, hair and nails.

They had to place their clothes down at their feet.

On that Wednesday, in Budapest at least, it was very warm, as warm as if it were summer.

My mother later told me that she took the tram to the hospital wearing a light silk dress. They called it pure silk. My father explained

347

how to grow silkworms, he knew that, too. Having slightly altered it, she continued wearing this noteworthy pure silk dress for some time yet even after the siege. But it never occurred to her to take a cab. She got on the number 15 tram on the corner of Sziget Street, got off at the last stop on Váci Street, walked to Lehel Street, and from there one more block to Szabolcs Street, though I don't know which gate she used.

They first herded the naked men into a narrow valley. While on that Wednesday the number 15 tram rolled along with my mother, they were felled by machine-gun fire, thereby preventing the occurrence of any further scenes, shouting, or attempted escapes. I was intimately familiar with the route; I walked along it later when I went to the technical school located on Thököly Street. The city had another chemical school where, to use the antiquated expression current at the time, they trained druggists, light chemical engineers, who produced mainly cleaning compounds and cosmetics. I could have been a druggist for all that, because in the summer of 1955, the summer following my mother's death, I spent three weeks of summer training at the Király Street laboratory and warehouse of Pharmaceutical Company Headquarters. At the time the gigantic neoclassical building was the bastion of the druggists in Budapest. During these three weeks I learned all that could be learned, because assisting in laboratory work was right down my alley. But my chemist uncle considered the other school where they trained industrial chemists superior. And indeed, our teachers were masters of their craft.

At the last stop on Váci Street, I waited for three of my classmates who came from Angyalföld. The tram started from the corner of Botond Street and Angyalföldi Street, it was the number 74, it was always jam-packed, and we had to go on from there. First it turned into Aréna Street, this is how I passed the Szabolcs Street hospital every morning, with these working-class boys from Angyalföld. I knew that before the siege the senior government counselor Henrik Benedickt had been the executive medical director of the hospital, and he was related to the family, he was a college professor, a serious scientist, and he was primarily engaged in research on the pathology of metabolism, the pathology of the nervous system and the heart and, as they called it back then, pathological chemistry, and had written about fifty books and articles. As we passed the learned doctor's hospital, surely, I must have remembered that this was where I was born, or to be precise, I was looking at the building and the tall brick wall surrounding it like one used to the idea that this was where he was born, and where at one time a relative had been the director. Not that I ever mentioned it to them. The boys I was really close to at the school came from elsewhere. Gyuri Kiss came from Partizán Street in Kispest, Krasznai from Dunaharaszti, and Lajos Mag from Csepel, but as far as I can remember, I didn't tell them, either.

Why should they know where Cutie Pie was born.

Oh, he was such a cutie when he was little. He was so cute when he peed and shit in his diapers. They shouted stuff like this as they stuffed my head under their pungently odorous armpits, or between their thighs. With his equanimity and natural distance, Lajos Mag was the one exception. As I headed for the school every morning, thinking that I'd be a chemical engineer and might even make it to production engineer, the place of my birth had precious little significance.

In the early hours of that warm, sunny Wednesday morning, while my mother was walking along Aréna Street and, to tell the truth, was hoping she'd reach the hospital in one piece, as she later said, because she couldn't be sure that she'd make it, because she still had the big sunny yard to cross ahead of her and the upper floor with its long balconies, up in Buda's Sándor Palace, the Hungarian prime minister, Miklós Kállay, was just signing the decree whereby the Hungarian government regulated the official proceedings pertaining to Jewish tenant farmers renting land from other Jews. According to the new decree, Jewish tenant farmers were obligated to maintain the property along with all its constituents, appurtenances, and livestock, all goods and chattel belonging to the farm with the scrupulousness of a proper farmer, yes, that is what the decree said, with the scrupulousness of a proper farmer, in the state they were in on the day the decree came into effect, and to attend to all the usual agricultural and forestry chores, the preparation of the soil, the sowing, the planting, and the care of the animals and plants with the scrupulousness of the rightful owner, yes, with the scrupulousness of the rightful owner, this is what the decree said, to see to all the chores of the farm in accordance with the custom of the farm until it should pass into the ownership of the state, the credit institution assigned by the minister of agriculture, or the natural person who would come into ownership. The Hungarian prime minister based his decree on a law passed a couple of weeks previously, according to which the Jews constituted an element of the population which, from the point of view of the life of the nation, was barred from ownership of Hungarian lands of significance to the state, to wit, lands and forestry lands under labor. The decree said under labor, the dialectical and antiquated variant of cultivation.

At the same time, in keeping with contemporary military custom, the Hungarian Royal Army worded its Wednesday morning communiqué in a plural that excluded me even before I was born. With the aid of German fighting units in the Stalingrad area and the front line at the Don, we nipped all Bolshevik offensives in the bud, says the Wednesday morning communiqué, just like this, in the plural. In the northwestern part of the Caucasus we successfully encircled and annihilated a belligerent power group. In other places, with effective artillery fire we thwarted preparations for attack by Soviet troops. To the south of the Terek River, the enemy's counterattacks, supported by tanks, remained unsuccessful. German and Allied planes on both sides of the Volga bombarded the enemy supply centers and transport columns. At the crude-oil center in Grozny we further fanned the flames with our aerial attacks carried out at night, the newspaper writes. On this Wednesday morning in October, as my mother was heading for the hospital on the tram, in Bordeaux, in Le Fort du Hâ built of yellow sandstone, seventy prisoners were taken down to the yard one by one, men and women, for relocation to a forest near Paris, the Fort de Romainville, commanded by the Germans. They had been arrested because they were active in the Résistance. There was a young woman among them, a seamstress, the mother of two, Georgette Lacabanne. We know that she was born in a southern suburb of Bordeaux, she was one year younger than my mother, her father was a coppersmith, her husband a pipe fitter. Georgette had hidden Résistance fighters and helped them escape. They lived in Bègles, the southern suburb of Bordeaux, this was where she had been arrested in her home. At the time of her arrest, her son was nine years old, her daughter nineteen months old. The following day the little boy was taken in by his aunt, the baby by her grandmother. Her husband volunteered for work in Germany because someone had told him that if he did so, they would release his wife without delay. Not only did they not release her from the Fort de Romainville, but along with the other prisoners transferred from Bordeaux, she was kept in solitary confinement for weeks. Georgette's registration number at the fort was 939. One of her fellow prisoners, Yvonne Noutarine, was able to sneak a message out with the help of a resistance group working at the post office. This was on November 19, and the message said that there were nine of them, they communicate through signs, and she mentions Georgette as one of the nine. We also know that on January 22 they were transported to Compiègne, and apart from Georgette's name and the date, there stood the words, *nach Compiègne überstellt*, transferred from Compiègne. Two days later, she was taken from Compiègne along with 230 other women. The women had to get into the last three cattle cars of a train. The train was transporting 1,450 prisoners. They were first taken to Halle in Saxony, from where the men were taken to the concentration camp in Sachsenhausen, and the women to Auschwitz. They arrived on January 26. They could not get off the train until the morning, they sang the "Marseillaise" on the ramp, and this is how they were herded to Birkenau, singing. Georgette was registered as number 31717 and they immediately tattooed the number on her left arm. Which is as much as we know about her fate. By all odds, her bunker was first in block 14, then in February in block 24 or 26, but it is possible that she had to lie under the open sky with the other dying prisoners in front of the block. Her death was entered in the camp records on March 8, 1943.

On the same October morning, on Wednesday, when my mother is still on her way to give birth, whereas it would have surely been better for me had a car hit her or if a tram had run over her, in Amsterdam

Anne Frank and her family are peacefully weighing themselves on a scale and note that Margot weighs 120 pounds, Mother 124, Father 141, she weighs 87 pounds, Peter 134, Madame Van Daan 106, Monsieur Van Daan 150. On Prinsengracht, where they were hiding in a secret annex, this was what they weighed on the morning of October 14, 1942, just when the German ambassador handed Martin Luther's memorandum to the Hungarian Foreign Ministry in Budapest and when, rather carelessly, I might add, I came into the world alive, and as such I later visited Prinsengracht several times, because that's where my favorite though exorbitantly expensive hotel was located, and my wonderful Dutch publisher, Van Gennep, was just a short walk away.

On this morning, in the name of his government, the German assistant state secretary for foreign affairs called upon the Hungarian government to come up with a definitive, meaning final, solution to the Jewish question. They wrote that the Hungarian government must adhere to the German model in all respects. They must compel the Jews under their authority to wear the *numerus nullus* sign and the Hungarian government must start planning their mass deportation. As for the expulsion of the Jews, it is in the interest not only of Germany but the whole of Europe, they wrote in an official, circuitous German, which they'd have been well-advised to hand over to an official stylist beforehand, in short, *das es sich nicht um ein deutsches, sondern um ein gesamteuropäisches Interesse handele, die Juden zu vertreiben, und dass die grossen Anstrengungen, die Deutschland auf diesem Gebiet mache und vor der Welt verantworte, illusorisch gemacht würden, wenn in einzelnen Gebieten Europas die Juden weiterhin Möglichkeiten der intellectuellen und wirtschaftlichen Einflussnahme in Verbindung mit dem uns bekämpfenden Weltjudentum besässen,* meaning in a somewhat more fluent and accessible translation, those mighty efforts that Germany expands in this regard, and for which it bears responsibility in the face of the entire world, can easily become illusory if the Jewry of the world that they are vanquishing retains its intellectual and financial influence in just one territory of Europe.

The naked male places his open hands in front of his genitals, lowers his head slightly, and remains silent. It's the only choice left to him.

Thanks to the American historian Christopher R. Browning, we also know that wholesale massacre has a firmly established, logical choreography. It had, it has, and surely it will have, because along with its own rigid staging, wholesale slaughter basically dictates its own procedural order and transactions. The compilation and subsequent confiscation of the property of Hungarian Jews, the inventory and redistribution of said confiscated property, the preparation for the deportation of the dispossessed Jews and the deportations themselves, all in line with Hungarian interests and German demands, required the participation, for years, of 287,000 registered Hungarian Christian public servants who ordered, commanded, endorsed, corrected, read, signed, and sealed the necessary orders and who, if they did not wish to come face-to-face with the nature of their actions and be at odds with their Christian beliefs, expediently put their Christian ethics on hold, and must have surely brought up all their little children in the same spirit, more than one of whom is nursing this curious concept of Christianity to this day. Consequently, while the murdered individuals continue to live on in silence and in very great numbers, their murderers can't die either without bequeathing their group consciousness to the generation that will outlive them.

They knew that unlike the women, the men will accept their fate in these situations. At most, they will place their hands over their genitals.

From Browning's research we also know the names of the reserve police detachment, the story of their actions on that Wednesday; we know their mental makeup, the course of their lives, and last but not least, their professional problems with respect to the mass executions.

Until the end of September, though he kept away from the wholesale slaughter, the infamously strict Captain Hoffmann was in charge of service tasks with his unit, but the moment he was supposed to conduct one of these massacres and, basically, come face-to-face with the great task of mass murder done by hand, he suffered from grave abdominal cramps and acute diarrhea. He was diagnosed with vegetative colitis and had to absent himself from the missions themselves. Tuesday night, the night before I was born, he issued orders, telling his men in no uncertain terms that they must have no scruples and shoot all those who can't walk and thus cannot be driven out of the city in time wherever they are found, including small children; but on Wednesday morning, the morning of my birth, his vegetative colitis acted up again, and so he absented himself from the mission at Mizocz. His subordinates suspected that his diarrhea was of psychological origin, a fact they discussed among themselves but did not mention in front of him. The reason was obvious; there was no way of preventing the people waiting to be executed from panicking. Browning documents that the order pertaining to the summary execution of small children remained a subject of contention among the men for some time. Their objection to their orders was not ethical in nature. Rather, they did not consider it sensible; in short, they felt that it went against the dictates of reason, and so members of the units or the unit commanders themselves did not always follow them. When they did, they had to tear the little children from their mothers' arms one at a time, which involved the unpleasant circumstance that the people waiting for their execution panicked and began to protest. It's an anthropological given. The human animal will protect its young even under the most desperate of circumstances. Nearly all the members of the *Einsatzkommando* from Hamburg had families of their own and the task took its toll on their nerves, *nervlich*, as it stands in the original protocol. We may safely acknowledge as a law of human nature that mass exterminations are bad for the nerves of the male members of the species. *Nicht geistig, nicht emotionell, nicht spirituell, nicht sinnlich, sondern nervlich.* But factually speaking, another anthropological given must have been the cause of the short-circuiting of their nerves, and I can say this without reserve, setting their mistaken assumption right even after so many years: their empathic predisposition short-circuited their nerves, which is a characteristic all mammals also have in common.

Struggle as they might against it, it was like shooting their own children.

Orders were carried out without a hitch when the Germans had the collaborating rabble tear the small children from the arms of their mothers and grandmothers, Ukrainian and Polish men whom, with their greater German superiority, they considered more brutal than themselves; in such cases, they didn't have to be confronted with their awkward anthropological endowments and could safeguard, to some extent, their group consciousness from their individual consciousness leaning toward empathy. Thanks to the increase in their pálinka allotment, these Ukrainian and Polish men carried out their orders without protest, they tore the small children from the arms of their mothers and shot them one by one and flung them away, then fired rounds into the naked, screaming, and protesting crowd. Still, this method had one serious drawback. By the time the members of the collaborating Polish and Ukrainian rabble carried out their orders, the spirit of massacre and the alcoholic haze freed them of their anthropologically given inhibitions and the dictate of empathy, and they began shooting one another. They could not stop the killing, they could not be restrained. Which is not an unknown phenomenon, it's called killing fever, it works even without increased pálinka portions, which is another archaic anthropological trait authors rarely mention. The only authentic report of this phenomenon was written by Hans Christoph Buch from Africa, the testament of an eyewitness about a force that swept him along with it. It sweeps those along with it who are not under the influence of alcohol or are just witnessing the slaughter. Which is also due to empathy. I see and experience what others are doing and, being a human animal, I am naturally, I repeat, naturally, with those who are engaged in the killing. After all, they are stronger. I, as an eyewitness and a member of the horde, must go along with the strong. Even my hands and my feet move in response as the shared joy of the wish to kill beckons me. The feeling of camaraderie beckons me. When this happened, the members of the German units had to shoot them for their own safety, or else a close combat developed alongside the uncovered ditches and pits that demanded German victims. Before they could fill them up, in response to the difference in pressure the groundwater slowly began to rise in the pits and ditches and the shoulders of the ditches and pits turned slippery from all the brains; after all, that's part and parcel of being shot in the back of the head, the sudden pressure splits open the scalp, at times the scalp opens up along the suture, and the brain has a high fat content, all of which had to be taken into account. If they had shot a lot of men in the back of the head previously, Mother Earth turned slippery around them, the brains splashed all over their clothes and faces, the dead and the wounded were floating on top of the water, not to mention the fact that the men lined up along the side of the ditches waiting to be shot very often peed and couldn't hold back their excrement from fear, and from time to time even members of the Hamburg unit, fastidious about their physical appearance, would slip into this infernal human concoction.

As the records say, they had to be fished out.

On that particular Wednesday, the day I was born, the members of the unit once again did not follow Captain Hoffmann's orders pertaining to method. On the other hand, there was unanimous expert agreement that the naked men had to be shot first. That's what made sense. Insofar as they wished to follow the rules of reason and the dictates of past experience, it followed from the situation. They invariably shot the wailing women and their screeching children only after they'd finished with the men.

After they were done with the grown men, they didn't have to worry so much about the grown women anymore.

On this particular Wednesday, the day I was born, despite Himmler's strict orders, a member of the unit active in Mizocz couldn't resist and with a newly pilfered Leica he took pictures of the group of women lined up for their execution as they hugged their little children to their naked bodies, then he took pictures of the same women and children as they lay lifeless, strewn on the ground, while his comrades, standing over them, shot a couple of women in the head. They must have still shown signs of life. In the language of photography these are called phase photos; phase photos show a process, but without the meaning, cause, or purpose of the process itself. I know from Imre Hirschler, the obstetrician who strangely enough remembered the circumstances of my birth even decades later, that when this was happening, I came into this world of promise with ease, I behaved most considerately, he didn't have much to do, he said twenty-eight years later, snapped his fingers in acknowledgment, and patted me on the back.

The fact that he recognized me as I walked along a hospital corridor and even remembered the circumstances of my birth was nothing to wonder at; after all, he'd known my mother, to whom apparently I bore a close resemblance, from before I was born; they had been comrades, which in the illegal Communist movement meant less than love but more than friendship, and for years they worked together for Red Aid.

Their work was not without danger for either of them. Arrest meant beatings without delay, detention meant torture. They wanted names. The political police were hell-bent on eliminating this Communist aid society, but never succeeded. Thank God, despite all their efforts at folding it up and all the bloodshed, the web continued its work unabated. They knew what they were doing, the dangerous game they were playing. My father was caught several times, he was repeatedly beaten by the police and tortured by the detectives of military intelligence at the Hadik Barracks on Horthy Miklós Street. I couldn't discover how long he was held prisoner there, or at what intervals he was set free, only to be arrested yet again, and how long the physical and mental torture to which he was subjected lasted. Basically, I must fall back on my mother's accounts, a couple of my father's gestures and sentences, in short, my memories. The written sources are no more reliable than my own memories. My mother reverted to the topic time and again, she reverted to it fanatically, always adding some new detail that my mind was barely capable of apprehending, and yet was willing to store.

I stored the information without knowing what I was storing or what I was supposed to do with it.

Decades later, the memoirs of various authors confirmed the reliability of their accounts. My mother talked about it as if she were reporting on the state of things exclusively for the benefit of her older son, so I should know how they search a home, how they apprehend and arrest a person, how they conduct a person to the Hadik Barracks through the deserted streets of the city at dawn or during the dark hours of the night, how the detectives squeeze him between the two of them on the back seat as they look rigidly ahead, not talking, not answering one's questions. Exactly as her own comrades were doing at the moment she was describing it to me. Perhaps this was why she spoke about it with such lack of emotion. She entrusted me with the story of my father's repeated arrests, but she depersonalized it, sharing it with me as general experience. Which couldn't have been difficult for her; after all, at all times, the police go about these things according to a strict ritual. But it would have never occurred to me to ask why on earth I needed to know. Obviously, parents prepare their children for their own fate even if they're hoping that they will have a better life.

The Hadik Barracks on Horthy Miklós Street, which in earlier times they called Fehérvári Street and now call Bartók Béla Street, is not one building but a huge block of buildings from various times, it was rebuilt many times over, with annexed wings that open into each other, the whole block located between the narrow Zenta Street and the wider, tree-lined Bertalan Street. The windows of its eastern wing give out on Budafoki Street, more precisely, on the lecture halls located in the park of the University of Technology. At one time it had been the barracks of the Imperial and Royal 3rd Hussar Regiment. The regiment was named after the greatest Hungarian hussar, Field Marshal András Hadik, commander in chief of Buda, for all time to come, as the official announcement read when the barracks received its name. Empress Maria Theresa endowed Hadik with the rank of count and made him a rich landowner, bestowing on him vast estates in Czernowitz and Futak. In order to enhance his glory, a couple of years later Emperor Joseph II raised him to a further rung on the ladder, and in 1777 made him Count of the Holy Roman Empire. As sprawling as this repeatedly renamed complex may be, it is certainly devoid of aesthetic qualities of any kind. Fortunately, its facade is hidden behind old plane trees. To this day, its huge, rambling inner courtyard is closed to the public and is strictly protected, so much so that from the outside there are no signs of just how strict this protection really is.

It was freezing cold, a snowstorm swept along the streets, Imre Cherépfalvi, the prestigious publisher active between the two world wars, writes in his memoirs. He was taken from his apartment in Váci Street on January 18, 1942, around the time I was conceived. But in his case it is understandable why he was taken to the Hadik Barracks, the main headquarters of Hungarian military intelligence in Buda. György Páloczi Horváth, one of his best authors and an editor at his publishing house, was an agent of the British secret service. By all odds, the Brits sent word that his situation was perilous and he fled to Ankara through Belgrade, where he continued his secret service activities against the German-affiliated Hungarian government. The Turkish ambassador brought Cserépfalvi a letter from him, though the letter may have been written by military intelligence in order to provoke Cserépfalvi, thereby liquidating Palóczi's intelligence network, I have no way of knowing. I know hardly anything. I know only that intelligence is part and parcel of the life of a state, which doesn't make its activities any more ethical, not by a long shot, just as the frequency of unethical actions does not render a thing more ethical. The detectives did not speak on the way, they didn't even speak among themselves. After our arrival, they led me up to the second floor in silence, Cserépfalvi writes in his memoirs entitled *The Notes of a Publisher*. Eight years previously, my father had also been conducted to the second floor. This was their established custom. Then in another building and over another staircase, they conducted him down to the ground floor. Cserépfalvi makes no mention of this other building, but our father was conducted along a long corridor to a room whose two barred windows looked out on a huge cobblestone courtyard, and not the street. On the other hand, both described the underground prison of the barracks where they were locked up. Tall trees stood in the yard, I seem to remember that they were not planes. Perhaps they were maples or sumacs. And then the four or five detectives who were there threw themselves at me and beat me up, writes Cserépfalvi. Our mother said of our father that the men who were engaged in a peaceful conversation in the room with the barred windows leaped to their feet when they entered and beat him within an inch of his life. The detectives who had conducted him from Pest to Buda he didn't see again until, to his mother's consternation, they appeared in the door of their apartment in Pannónia Street to take him to the barracks once more and to beat him within an inch of his life once more. I remember it because the expression occupied my mind for many years. I didn't understand what within an inch of his life meant. What it must be like. And why is it in this order. They probably have to beat him first to an inch before they can get at his life. Also, I knew nothing about being beaten yet, because my parents didn't slap me until much later. Still, I felt compelled to figure out how a long time ago my father could have been beaten in this way. In the meantime they were shouting incoherently, of which I understood very little, writes Cserépfalvi, and the same thing happened not only with my father, but also Béla Szász, who was detained by his own comrades on May 24, 1948, after his mother's attempts of twenty years before to prevent him from joining the Communist movement, this time during the light of day and not at night, in the corridor of the Ministry of Agriculture, before he could enter the office of Secretary of State Mihály Keresztes. Except Keresztes had not summoned him. Secret service activities are composed of carefully chosen appearances. Anyone working for the secret service must know that in life, appearances occupy a much larger territory than reality. Béla Szász's protest was in vain, too; once they were out on the street, they shoved him into a big, curtained Buick and wanted to cover his eyes with a table napkin, whereupon he asked them in conversational tones what sort of game they were playing. You should be glad we're covering your eyes, because it means that you might come back again. The logic behind this ritual sentence is admirable. It constitutes a threat and a betrayal at the same time. Then they fell silent. As for him, he had plenty to think about.

When they started beating my father, they screamed the same thing they'd screamed at Cserépfalvi, you'll get what's coming to you, you filthy bastard, you rotten Communist pig, you traitor. Ilona Kojsza was taken from her apartment in Galamb Street at dawn, way before the others, on one of the first days of May, and she asked the detectives where is the joyride to, Comrades, if you don't mind me asking. At which one of the comrades brought his fist down on her head. Wouldn't you like to know, you cheap whore. Meanwhile, in the back seat of the curtained Hudson, the other hissed, you, you filthy baggage, you no longer have comrades. Which put an end to the conversation in this automobile as well. They covered her eyes too and drove with her at a maddening speed. She said that when they turned a corner, the wheels squealed. There is also an account of squealing wheels on the corner of Istenhegyi Street in Béla Szász's memoirs entitled *Without Constraint*, in which he writes that he judged where they were by the sounds and the air coming in through the half-open window.

Kojsza was slated to be the great Yugoslav spy in the trial just then under preparation. In the spring of 1941, she was supposed to have convinced Noel H. Field to travel to Le Vernet d'Ariège and recruit Rajk, who was in internment, either into the CIA or the Gestapo. In this initial, preparatory phase of the trial, as Kojsza told me two decades later, the accusations were not yet set in stone. The version they would choose depended on the results of the interrogations that were being conducted simultaneously. They didn't care what she admitted to as long as she admitted to something, and then they would tell her what else she must admit to for the sake of appearances.

But even though he tried, he really tried to understand what good this entire sham was to them, he couldn't oblige them, not with the best intentions in the world.

Which means that two people were left in the history of the international Communist movement who, despite the torture and beatings, refused to play along.

She protested that she won't, no, she won't, it's all so open to misunderstanding. She said no not despite the torture and humiliation she had been subject to, or because of the torture. If she does it, if she admits to something of which not a word is true, if the same henchman beats the truth out of her now who had beaten her at the Horthyite political police so she'd betray her comrades, she could never again consider herself a human being. She told me the proper civilian name of this henchman, but more's the pity, I can't remember it. You can't admit a lie, she yelled. She didn't think they'd let her live. She didn't want the stamp of shame to adhere to her after she was gone. No, not that. She refused to join these dishonorable men in their lies.

Would I believe that by then this Horthyite thug, this henchman had the rank of lieutenant colonel.

Comrade Lieutenant Colonel, the other said to him.

During the first weeks of her torture she wouldn't believe it, she thought that this must be some fatal mistake. She must do all she can to clear herself with her comrades, but not this henchman. And when this didn't help either, her not believing it, she wanted to die, she wanted to kill herself in the most unlikely manner.

I asked her what that manner was.

But she didn't want to tell me.

She felt ill, she actually retched, she had to go to the bathroom.

Then a couple of weeks later, on one of our regular strolls in the neighborhood, she finally told me. Though she found it difficult to talk about it, I could see that her code of honor required that she tell me. She wanted me to know. In the twenty-fourth hour. She couldn't believe that they wouldn't take her away again. She couldn't believe that one fine day they wouldn't be responsible for her disappearance.

She fought her party so they'd get rid of this henchman, put him out of circulation.

Whose real name I can no longer remember, alas.

I must have been twenty-two and she perhaps past sixty when we took casual strolls in Óbuda.

She lived one might say lethally alone in a small apartment in one of the prefab housing estates of the neighborhood. I have tried to trace the fate of her former Serbian companion, whose name I have also forgotten, but so far have found no trace of a quietly executed Serb. Apparently, they beat him to death in the adjacent interrogation room so she'd hear what was going on and in her fear admit to what they wanted to put in her mouth. She can't talk to her guests in her apartment, because they're listening in twenty-four hours of the day, she said in the small apartment loud enough for them to hear, let the pigs, those tapping her, hear, those disgraceful henchmen, her comrades. The probability of which was very slight, but still, the possibility that they were in fact wiretapping her twenty-four hours a day could not be ruled out. She never gave up her fight for the full legal rehabilitation of the persecuted, and so in principle it was in fact in their interest to keep a close watch on her, and as her notes now make abundantly clear, she was right; in the years we'd meet and she talked to me, she was in fact under surveillance. She was still beautiful, and this scared me a little. She had the air of a born aristocrat about her, but she was born into a populous proletarian family somewhere on outer Váci Street, smack into the middle of big-city poverty. All told, she had twelve brothers and sisters. Once she began to whisper in her soft voice, in her polished manner, about what she'd lived through, always in full sentences, always without emotion or undue emphasis, there was no stopping her. The chronology propelled her forward, her associations drove her on, and in this she resembled others who in those years, in the early sixties, broke their long silence, the wounds opened up, and they began describing their experience in the concentration camps. Even the most laconic among them. I asked them something, they began to talk, and once they began, they couldn't stop, because some detail was always left out of what had to be told, what couldn't be kept to themselves. Something that they felt the world must know, if only the world were not averse to accepting reality and did not think so little of it. In which case, they would at least tell me.

It was cold that May, the early mornings, the nights, and when they dragged her off, she took her overcoat with her, just in case. She took it from the hook in the hall and quickly put it on, then they shoved her into the black car, she thinks it was a Buick, so they should lose no time in shedding light on what they called the truth.

She said that they broke down her door in the early hours, because the ringing of the doorbell didn't wake her.

She was still wearing this beige overcoat two weeks later, but she couldn't say any more to how many places they had taken her. A light, beige Burberry. They beat and interrogated her in this coat, there was dry blood on the collar, it smelled foul, she had to sleep with the dry blood, they didn't give her a blanket and they wouldn't let her clean herself up. In one place where they moved her, there was an overseer, a woman, and it was no use begging her either, she was worse than the men, and then she pulled off the cover of the straw mat, she soaked it in the slop pail, in her own urine, because they wouldn't remove the slop pail for days on end, but they made sure to take the lid away, she rolled up the cover of the straw mat and tried to hang herself on this rope, but the weight of her body tore the sheet from the bar she had tied it to.

She was past knowing what she was doing.

She hadn't known for some time what day it was or what was happening and why. She slipped out of her overcoat, ripped out the lining, she soaked it in her urine as well so it would hold, the other had been an old, used cloth, but she knew that real silk couldn't be torn. This was real silk, thick woven silk for the lining. While it was wet she rolled it tight, looped it around her neck, and she pulled at the two ends with all her might so she would choke.

I couldn't follow, it made no sense, she had to show me, so I could understand what she had done.

We laughed on that deserted street in Óbuda. No matter how much strength a person has, no matter how strong he is, how could he strangle himself with a wet, twisted silk rope.

Fifty years passed, yes, half a century passed after this stroll, when a couple of months ago I accidentally came upon the testimony of a man by the name of József Kiss. He wrote it about his own case. He started work at six that morning. He made the rounds of the cells to check up on the prisoners. Instead of peering through the hatch, he had to open each cell and do a thorough inspection. He found Kojsza writing on the floor, these are the words Kiss used, *Kojsza, writhing, on the floor.* She'd ripped out the lining of her spring coat, had soaked it, twisted it up, tied it around her neck, and was jerking her head in the hook, her whole body was jerking on the ground so she could suffocate. I yelled, I kneeled down next to her, untied the rope, sat her up on the bunk, and meanwhile I said to her, Ilona, for God's sake, don't try this nonsense again. If anything happens to you, I'm done for. You can't die like this anyway. These people make sure that you all survive. Only then did he notice that a wet handkerchief was laid out on the bunk bed, carefully smoothed out, and Kojsza had written on it with indelible pencil, dear Comrade Rákosi, what you are doing to us here is terrible. With beating and threats they are trying to force us to make incriminating testimonies against our best comrades. They want to make us say we were fascists, undercover men, and we came back to Hungary only to disrupt the Party from within.

Sándor Cseresznyés, the press secretary of the Ministry of the Interior, and Colonel Gyula Oszkó attempted suicide in the same improbable and impossible manner, Kiss writes in his testimony. One of them broke his glasses and tried to cut his main artery with the broken glass, the other hooked the wire of his glasses into his artery, and tried to tear it out.

They broke both of my father's shins, but I don't remember this exactly either from our mother's account, or they cracked them, the traces of which he bore until his death. Two clear-cut scars, two dents on his shins, which were either blue or red, and they rarely blended into the color of his skin.

It may have been in the building, in one of the rooms on the ground floor where a couple of decades later, as a private in the army, I was doing specialized duty in photography. When my basic training ended, they transferred me here from the Ságvári Barracks on Budakeszi Street. The transfer was a simple operation. Soldier, stuff all your things into your sack, and I do mean all your things, don't leave anything behind, and show up at the company office in five minutes. The same stout, hairy junior officer, strong as a bull, a prizefighter, issued the order who every blessed morning bellowed for all he was worth during our calisthenics exercises, run, soldier, run, like an animal, if you don't run, soldier, if I catch up with you, I'm gonna fuck your ass.

The sentence was not addressed to me but, morning after morning, to all of us. Morning after morning, all these different men were as one in his eye.

On the other hand, they never caught my mother. She was quick and resourceful, or just plain lucky.

Imre Hirschler maintained his elegantly appointed obstetrician's office in the Inner City through cross-financing. He used the high prices he charged his wealthy patients to support his poor and destitute patients. Which meant not only that he did not charge them for his services, but he even gave them money for food and medicine. Red Aid was an organization of the illegal Communist Party, it collected money to help the families of Communists and union activists who had been arrested or fired for political reasons. My mother had been sending women in need of Hirschler's services as a gynecologist or obstetrician for more than ten years by then.

But on the day I was born, on that eventful Wednesday, for some reason they did not make the Jewish men dig ditches or pits first, they lay on the barren ground in Mizocz, massacred while I was born. Concurrently, Jan Karski, the secret messenger of the Home Army, or Armia Krajowa, arrived in the Pyrenees, he arrived that Wednesday to convey news of the state of the Polish resistance to the Polish emigrant government in London, to give eyewitness evidence of events in the Warsaw ghetto and one of the subcamps of Belżec in Izbica Luberska. On this same bright and sunny Wednesday, the Radzyń ghetto, which had been cleared out once before, was cleared out yet again, this time of its approximately three thousand Jews. In the early hours of the morning, they were first herded together onto the marketplace, then they were packed onto a hundred horse-drawn carts and taken to nearby Międzyrzecz, and from there to the extermination camp at Treblinka. In the selfsame hour of that Wednesday morning, Minister of Defense Vitéz Vilmos Nagy of Nagybacon left Budapest for the Eastern Front to personally inspect the equipment of the Hungarian army or, to be exact, its lack thereof. Also on this Wednesday, October 14, the morning papers wrote that the radio speech of the Most Eminent Magda Purgly, wife of the Most Eminent Regent, in which, in a voice repeatedly failing from emotion, she called upon the citizens of the nation to donate all the winter clothes they could do without, brought outstanding results. The paramilitary *levente* corps in charge of collecting the donations gathered enough winter clothing, men's and women's furs, fur linings, fur-lined leather, yarn that could be used as raw material, wool, wool debris, as well as other materials that could be ripped apart and reused to fill up approximately two hundred railway cars. During the collection for winter clothing, the paper said, besides the well-to-do social class and white-collar society, the working class and the masses of simple people also gave heart-stirring evidence of their love of the homeland and their appreciation of the Hungarian army. They made contributions that veritably exceeded their means so that, with this sacrifice, they could protect the physical health of our soldiers facing the harsh Russian winter. The material thus collected is presently being sorted and processed by the pertinent organizations so that before the early Russian winter should make its appearance, the winter clothing should be in its proper place, and safeguard our fighting men from the freezing cold who, if called upon, will even sacrifice their lives for our sake.

Needless to say, on this October Wednesday there were other, more exceptional events as well that in accordance with army protocol, had to be entered into the records and reported. Major Trapp, commander of the 100th Hamburg reserve police battalion, had learned just a couple of days earlier that Captain Wohlauf, commander of the 1st Hamburg company, brought his new bride with him straight from their wedding in Hamburg. In her puff-sleeve, fine-print silk dresses, her elegant tailor-made overcoat, and a perky little hat on her head, the attractive young woman wanted to see with her own eyes how they went about emptying the ghetto or how they conducted the hunt for Jews with her husband at the helm. The expression itself must have fascinated her, the hunt for Jews, the *Judenjagd*, the Jew hunt. That's what they called it. Because, needless to say, there were fugitives as well as groups of fugitive Jews who were reported to the authorities or else hidden by Polish and Ukrainian peasants. Seeing how all the urgent work kept them from going to Sorrento, the lovely young newlyweds decided to spend their honeymoon hunting Jews. The fugitives have a truly wonderful writer, his name is Aharon Appelfeld, himself a survivor, in short, an eyewitness. But all the same, it is not difficult to imagine how maddeningly exciting it must have been for them to bring the manhunt, the handcrafted killing, and the lovemaking under a common denominator. Their nights could turn into day. Appelfeld describes the fate of an eleven-year-old girl, Tsili Kraus, starting with an unspecified day in the month and year of my birth, when her parents left the little girl home alone, perhaps on this particular Wednesday, to watch the house, but this is fiction, and an unspecified commando swooped down on the village, perhaps on the morning when I was born, and killed all the Jews they could find, though this is just a novel. They burn down all the houses. The little girl manages to slip through the ring of the manslayers and flees all alone. All of world history is the product of the writer's imagination. My God, what exquisite delight beyond measure these Wohlaufs, the newlyweds, exhilarated as they were by the shared thrill of the manhunt and manslaughter, must have given each other. If only their names were not descriptive, or else bore a more innocent meaning.

I read Appelfeld's novel in French, but surely, the pet name of the fleeing little girl in Hungarian would be Cili, like my grandmother's, Cecília Nussbaum's, whose family, by all odds, also fled from this region in the midst of a previous pogrom, which however, was not fiction in the least.

Major Trapp was fuming mad. He was outraged.

He should have had Captain Wohlauf court-martialed. But he acted like a true gentleman with the newlyweds. And so on this Wednesday, the day I was born, Wohlauf could not be present either, to witness the important mission with his young wife. The beautiful honeymoon was over. *Die schönen Tage von Aranjuez sind nun zu Ende*, as Schiller would say. By the way, on this particular October day, his unit liquidated the Łuków ghetto and not the Mizocz ghetto without him. Then after the successful massacre in Serokomla, which lasted several days and which the excited young woman was fortunately able to see for herself, on orders from Major Trapp, the captain had to accompany his attractive and elegant wife back to distant Hamburg. On the afternoon of the same Wednesday when, at a fever pitch of love over the massacre, they were holding hands on the train, in Budapest, where the temperature was summery, at the Sándor Palace, the Hungarian Council of Ministers met to approve the decree signed by the prime minister earlier in the day, according to which a Jew could no longer rent nor own Hungarian land, while at Vichy, along the banks of the Allier River, with due ceremony Marshal Pétain, head of the Vichy government, received the representatives of the French prisoners of war who had been released by the Germans as a token of goodwill. Needless to say, pictures were taken at the reception. Marshal Pétain is standing on the left, smiling inanely as he presses the hand of a mustached gentleman. Standing next to them are three other men with the well-mannered demeanors of the subjects of a collaborating head of state, waiting their turn for the honor of shaking Pétain's hand. One of them is the young François Mitterrand, who, as the representative of the grateful prisoners of war, is waiting to shake the old marshal's hand, and meanwhile he is staring vacuously into the eyes of the marshal, who in turn looks as if he were in a state of suspended animation. A couple of years later General de Gaulle forbade his minister of the interior to use this picture in the election campaign against the socialists, and the photograph disappeared from the political scene once again. From an ethical standpoint the prohibition was justified, because in February 1943 Mitterand joined the Résistance, where he was active under the name of Morland, a circumstance of which, in her *War: A Memoir*, Marguerite Duras offers an insider's view with the unflinching honesty that served as one of the models for my own book. On the other hand, in the afternoon of the same memorable Wednesday when the young Mitterrand could at last shake the hand of the old traitor to his nation and on which I was born, in far-off Dresden the Romance languages scholar Victor Klemperer, who by then had been stripped of his college professorship and was supported by his Aryan wife, wrote in his diary that his fingers were stiff with autumn cold. All meat and white-bread coupons are to be withdrawn from Jews, he wrote with his stiff fingers. Jews will not get white bread anymore for their bread ticket. As for the latest decree on handing over metal, it is so unclear that the Gestapo will have a hard time, so wrote Klemperer in the Dresden cold, if they want to pin sabotage on anyone. The incorrigible Klemperer, who in the midst of the human catastrophe would have liked to examine everything according to the rules of reason, found the decree pertaining to mixed marriage equally unclear. According to the decree, the property of the Aryan wife must be susceptible to proof. But for the love of God, Klemperer asks in his diary, after forty years of marriage, how is one supposed to provide documentary proof as to a wife's property in a household, that something is not the property of the Jewish husband but of the Aryan wife, or else the other way around. Then during the afternoon Klemperer also describes how a certain Fränkel, who shared the Klemperers' apartment after he'd been rousted out of the villa he and his wife had jointly built, and who was prompted by the same idiotic, rational thinking as his own, insisted on checking various objects in the apartment with a horseshoe magnet, lest something be left out of the obligatory objects to be surrendered.

As far as Fränkel was concerned, there was no law he would not abide by with the help of rational means. With the help of a magnet. For once, how a magnet works, magnetic fields, and the earth's magnetic field were explained to me not by my father, but my Uncle Pista. Thanks to the magnet, they finally handed over a small lead box Klemperer had used for postage stamps, a brass ashtray, and a nickel-plated letter clip, all on the day I was born, objects whose use at the time of my birth and prior to it are now, for most of us, shrouded in mystery. The valet or the maid used the clip to take the visitor's card in to the lord or lady of the house and to convey the letters they had received. It was an insane tool that at best served to thoroughly humiliate the servant with its preciosity, thereby making the insane master and the insane lady and insane young lady and the insane young master of the house happy.

When I think about it, it doesn't even console me that the servile servants would sneeze and spit into their master's soup.

But by the time it grew dark and my worried mother took me

to her breast for the second time that day, devoid of their load, the hundred horse-drawn carriages had returned to the deserted main square in Radzyń. In Budapest that evening, lights had to be out by eight o'clock. Generally, a person is ignorant of the oh-so-romantic things that happen on the day he is born. He won't be interested in it later on either, because he lives his precious life in the belief that on that exceptional Wednesday, Friday, or Tuesday when he was born, the central event in the world was his arrival. Later he holds magnificent celebrations, so that in the company of his friends he should joyfully commemorate the anniversary of the wholesale slaughter in Radzyń, Łuków, and Mizocz. Whereas not only the candles on the cake are burning to the accompaniment of the idiotic happy birthday song lacking all musicality, but the same day the oil wells of Grozny are also up in flames, happy birthday to you.

But on this particular Wednesday, in the course of the first breast-feeding, it also came to light that my mother wouldn't be able to nurse me, because my sucking caused her such pain. It wasn't Dr. Hirschler but an elderly nurse who examined her. The milk coming from her breast was mixed with blood. You won't be able to breastfeed, my dear, don't even try, your nipple is turned inward, the nurse announced. A couple of hours later, as a result of my mother's insistence, they had another go at it, but the few drops of milk that she was able to squeeze through her inverted nipple, hoping that she could nurse me after all, again contained some blood. Meanwhile, one of my father's brothers came in and started taking pictures. My father had no way of knowing that he now had a son who has plenty of everything, a mouth, eyes, weight, arms, a penis, and is already so intelligent that he can sleep unaided and can scream unaided, except nursing him won't be quite so simple. From July in the year I was born through February of the next year, my father was conscripted into labor service. At the time I was born, he was in Szentkirályszabadka with company 109/16, on specialized service duty. This was his first time in forced labor. He was working on the expansion of the communications network at the military airfield, he was a pick-and-shovel man, but from time to time he was allowed to engage in professional work. In the photograph my mother puts on a brave face despite the pain, which, to add insult to injury, she saw as a serious personal defeat. I couldn't breastfeed you, she kept repeating even years later. My mother had been a sportswoman, an athlete, head trainer of the worker gymnasts, an agile and very determined woman who relished competition of all sorts and was inebriated by the smallest victory, and so she was naturally not used to failure. We couldn't even squeeze milk out of me. She died thirteen years later of breast cancer with metastasis of the liver. She was already ill four years before she died, she underwent surgery, they maimed her, she had difficulty recovering, she went for radiation therapy, my father took pictures of her; he knew she would leave us, I also knew she would leave us, but we pretended we didn't know. The old, agonized woman looking back at us from the last photographs is a stranger to me. My father also collapsed under the weight of her illness. She was weak, her skin yellow, radiation therapy made her hair fall out, her body was bloated and swollen with water, but laughing, she kept repeating that she's fine, really. Even as she lay dying, this is how I saw her. She'd never been so spoiled, she got a new nightgown every day. But her laughter has remained. Except she'd like to eat something delicious, a carefully peeled balloon, for instance. I cooked for her, I made her beef soup, I baked for her, I took sponge cake to the hospital. She was bursting with pride that her eleven-year-old son cooked and baked for her. She kept showing the other women in the ward. She could hardly taste the food, but for my sake she put on a show, how wonderful, excellent, perfect, and she'll eat it when her visitors are gone. I didn't believe it, but I accepted it. My first sponge cake was nice and fluffy. The second turned pasty because I was so impatient, I opened the oven door too soon. I couldn't bake another one, because we ran out of eggs. And not only did we run out of eggs in our home, there were no eggs to be had anywhere. Only when they'd be handing them out again, as people put it. It still hurts that I took that pasty sponge cake to the hospital. She laughed at this, too, as if she were glad that the sponge cake turned pasty. But the next visiting day, there I stood again by the window of our dining room looking at the garden, the roses, the trees, our dog the color of bread crumbs, and I couldn't keep myself from cooking and baking again, from what was on hand, from what they had handed out. From what I was able to get standing on line. I really did learn to cook and bake, I had to, because our grandparents, seeing the approach of the next major catastrophe, became helpless, our grandfather suffered from bouts of asthma and for days he'd be so weak, he could barely rise from his armchair, while my grandmother chose the only solution left to her and fell prey to dementia so she wouldn't have to face anything ever again. Grumbling, dragging her feet, she saw to the two of them with the cheer of senility, but only the two of them. As if she wasn't even aware of our presence or my mother's absence. There was no one to take care of my father and younger brother. Someone had to keep the house clean and the fireplace working and do the cooking. My rational upbringing lost part of its validity. We hadn't had a maid for two years by then, I did the cooking, I did the laundry, I even washed my mother's nightgowns with my own hands, and I did the ironing every day, too, so my father could take the freshly washed nightgowns to the hospital. After her surgery my mother's wound did not heal, it oozed, surely as a consequence of her radiotherapy. My mortally afflicted father had been dismissed from his workplace, proceedings had been started against him, we were poor in the unheated Perczel villa on Svábhegy. He bought half a kilo of cheap 2 *forint* and 2 *fillér* sausages for my birthday. It was a real celebration because he could have bought the 1.80 sausage, because at the time there was such a thing, but proud as a peacock, he bought the more expensive one. I loved it very much, it had lots of garlic, paprika, and fat, too, though as far as that goes, it had precious little to do with sausage. When I took the present out of the paper soaked through with fat, it took all of my childish self-control to keep from crying. It wouldn't have been right to trouble them with my tears. Or ruin my brother's yearning for the sausage with my tears. We ate it with mustard and bread. It served as our dinner. I laid the table as it should be laid, with damask napkins and silver napkin rings. On October 14, 1953, this was my last birthday. All the rest that was to follow my afflicted father had forgotten, and he was right to do so. I remembered it myself only a day later, my, oh my, I'm past yet another birthday, but even remembering it after the fact had no significance whatever for me. They operated on my mother a second time, but by then the surgeon had nothing to do. He opened her up, took a look, showed the medical students the cancerous liver, then sewed up the abdominal wall. My idiotic mother in her altruistic manner even liked that, the fact that the professor had invited a group of medical students for her operation. Can I imagine, all those nice young men having a look at her sick abdomen. I still remember what I imagined. Exactly the same thing I had seen earlier on the color illustrations of Kirschner and Nordmann's six-volume *Chirurgie*. Why we had this work and how we had acquired it I have no idea. I have no idea about this either. A couple of days later, it was on a Sunday, she died at the clinic on Üllői Street. May 15, 1955. When I go to Ferihegy Airport or come back from the airport, I can't stop myself from looking up at the second-floor window.

The weather on this day in May was cool and cloudy, the blood beech was in full bloom. The breeze passed through it, and then it passed through it yet again, and the huge blood-red top of the tree trembled in majesty.

Fifty-six years later I received an e-mail from Tusi Szabó, who still lives there, in that former superintendent's apartment, a small separate house in the one-hectare garden, saying that the wind had ripped the huge blood beech out by the roots, it had been chopped up, carted away, and only the mound formed by its dead roots remained.

When our father came back from the hospital and stepped out on the veranda where I'd been waiting for hours, possibly since early morning, for confirmation, I don't know why, but I already knew, surely I must have been psychically linked to my mother's being and existence and so had known for hours that it had come to pass, she was gone. Our father didn't say anything, no word passed his lips, he was a demented man staring openmouthed into space, a skin-and-bones human wreck with stooped shoulders wearing a threadbare suit, then out of the blue he began to howl and cry, then just as suddenly, he stopped. But at the time it seemed to me he'd choke from all the accumulated self-control. And he never recovered either, ever again, from the shock of losing the person he loved, whereas he tried, he really did everything within his power, there was no behavioral cliché or life strategy he did not retrieve from his consciousness so he could recover and bring us up.

For this reason and no other.

By the time he returned with the news it was afternoon.

And as for me, I turned back to the tree and watched the majestic swaying of its crown.

Not only could my father not see me on this Wednesday, the day I was born, he couldn't see me a month later, on November 15, either. On this day in November he wrote on a postcard bearing the censor's stamp, my dear Klára, the November visit will be on the 22nd. It hurts me too, but I must tell you in all earnestness that you must not attempt this trip in the interest of our little Péter. I hope that you will conclude the same. I will be happy to see anyone else visit me. They must take the same train you took last time. The briefing at Szentkirályszabadja station is at 12:30. I am allowed two visitors. They must bring their IDs. As far as I know, they can return the same day at four thirty with a transfer at Veszprém and Székesfehérvár stations. They should dress as if they're going on an excursion, it may possibly involve a bit of walking. I am making a point of this so you should talk your parents out of this trip, I would like to see them too, but this trip is not for older people. I continue to be well. The parcel arrived, and today, so did the money. The warm clothing came in handy. I'd like to ask for the winter coat and the blue sweater as well. I was happy to receive news about our little Péter, continue to take good care of him. With kisses, your husband, Laci.

Then in a postscript he adds that he'd be grateful if my mother could make him an abdomen warmer and send him a couple of flat batteries, though I have no idea what an abdomen warmer was like, what it was for, or why he needed the flat batteries. He might have had a flashlight to read under the blanket.

When laughing at her own complaining my mother told me, she told me repeatedly, that try as she might, she couldn't breastfeed me and she couldn't pump milk from her breast either, she couldn't have known yet that whether she fed me with her bloody milk or occasionally with the clear milk of a stranger would have made no real difference. So they brought me up on Zamakó and Ovomaltine. Later she didn't nurse my younger brother either, and Rózsi Németh and I brought him mother's milk from András Kepes's mother, who lived nearby, and so my brother and András Kepes became, in the vernacular of the day, milk brothers.

This expression, for instance, I understood right away, I took to it right away, I accepted it without a second thought. In my mind, milk brother took its place right next to milk tooth, because that's when my milk teeth had to be pulled out, one by one. Once Rózsi Németh and I took the tram to Böszörményi Street in Buda to get mother's milk. It was a Sunday, possibly a Sunday in September. I'd been going to school for a couple of days by then, which was a great event in my young life. It meant that I could now learn everything for real, under ordered circumstances. The autumn sun shone beautifully. Böszörményi Street was nearly deserted. We found the District Mother's Milk Collection Station across from the modernist brick building of the Mayor's Office.

I couldn't understand this either. How can they collect mother's milk at a station.

I asked Rózsi Németh.

She said that it was the other way around. It's not the mother's milk that they bring to the station, it's where the mothers come to be milked under sterile conditions, and that's how station should be understood.

They use a machine to pump out the milk, she added.

What sort of machine.

An electric machine.

But why do they pump it.

If they don't pump it, if the mother's breast fills up with milk, and if the mother's breast is not pumped, if the mothers have more milk than they need for their babies, it feels tight, it hurts, it gets inflamed, and that's why they milk mothers.

This is what she said, that they milk mothers, whereas I'd heard the expression only with relationship to cows. This literally struck me in the head. It feels tight, it hurts, it gets inflamed. She struck me in the head with these words as well. How could a mother's breast be inflamed. For a long time, a very long time, this was beyond my comprehension. Also, I could sense that they used the verb *milk* differently when they talked about women than when they talked about cows, but I could not understand how they could allow the two senses of the same word to approximate each other in this perilous manner. This is my first distinct memory of why, from then on, the problematic interplay of the human and the animalistic preyed so precariously on my mind. Could this be the only difference between the female of the animal species and the female of the human species. I also asked her, because disingenuously, I wanted to test her knowledge, why the Mothers' Milk Collection Station stayed open on Sunday, but her answer, instead of calming me, made me all the more upset. She said, or else she said something like this, that a mother's breast does not stop milk production on Sunday, and that's why the station has to stay open. It would feel tight and hurt on Sunday, too. With that she struck me in the head again, as if she were saying that there's no point of respite where the vegetative, the animal, and the human meet. There wasn't a single soul in the corridor, I didn't see a single mother being herded along in great haste with her bulging breasts to be milked, so they shouldn't hurt. In Dömsöd I stood by the open gate every morning when the cows ambled out of the barn, and I stood by the open gate every nightfall and watched them amble past me as they headed back to the barn. The cows knew where they were going, and they knew where they had to return. I was full of awe thinking how intelligent cows are, every bit as intelligent as we are, because we can both find our way home. Because of the silent corridor, I concluded that the women waiting to be milked must have already arrived. I also understood milk tooth; it pleased me that my milk teeth were just then being pulled out to make room for my permanent teeth.

While Rózsi Németh went inside with her coupon to bring the mother's milk allotted to us, because you had to have a coupon, just like for cow's milk, flour, semolina, and sugar, which I didn't understand either, this whole coupon business, but be that as it may, while she went about her business, I had to wait out in the corridor. I was so profoundly lost with this whole obscure business about mothers' milk and mothers' breasts and the milking and the breastfeeding and my own mother, who could not breastfeed me and now couldn't breastfeed my baby brother either, it brought on a veritable fever. How could they know beforehand that András Kepes's mother wouldn't have enough milk today, and anyway, why did we have to come here and why don't we leave already. An infernal metaphor haunted me on this quiet, sunny, early autumn corridor, and I couldn't find an escape route. I can still remember the image. My brother was born in August, on August 24, and on this Sunday he was less than a month old. This was not my first metaphor, but in all probability, it was the first metaphor that gave me food for thought, this milking of the breast, this milking of my mother's breast. It haunted me with its raw brutality until at long last, as a grown-up, I finally understood the process of milk production and breastfeeding, and then at long last it left me in peace, taking its horror and phantasms with it. Still, even later, for a long time, for an inordinately long time, the points of contact between the human and the animal continued to terrify me. Every life phenomenon that situated man in the vicinity of the animalistic terrified me, the image, the notion, the sensation of human bodies locked in an embrace, the uniting of body masses, their mutually felt weight and resistance, or even filling up, eating, chewing, swallowing, munching, slurping, and then the unloading, the artery and the varicose veins, the sight and system of their sensations, all this terrified me, the cabins of public toilets, where people shit and fart within the hearing of others, and boys and men with their shared, intimate, ritual passing of urine, the openmouthed dreamers, the odor of their mouths, the sight and smell of oily hair, the uncleanliness, the smell of asses, the lethal odor of the night's excreta, the snoring, and also the animality of the frightened awakenings in the middle of the night in the shared bedrooms of tourist lodges, children's camps, and the bunk beds of barracks. When I was an adolescent, a couple of girls told me when they were expecting their periods, when they would menstruate, or that they were menstruating just then, and at such times their smell really changed, for one thing, the smell of their sweat, and for another, the raw smell of the iron content of their blood, which also hovered around them, but this just called my curiosity into play along with my propensity for identifying with others.

Which is why they said it. That I should join them in this exceptional trouble of theirs.

When I opened the door, it was as if I'd caught them at it, women were sitting around a tub, at least five of them were sitting around the tub, bending over the tub, strange hands, huge hands whose owners I couldn't determine rhythmically tugged at their full breasts, first one, then the other. Steel hands, mechanical hands, hands tied into a single electric circuit. Dead hands. My imagination when I saw this must have been jump-started by the tugging at the bell on the trams. Needless to say, my father hadn't spared me the explanation of how electricity is generated, how the poles work, how they are related to lightning and storms, how electricity can be stored, what transformation means, we fixed the switch together so I could see how the electric circuits work, and also what happens when we break them, he even took me to the Electrical Works on Váci Road, where we headed for the big switch room, we headed for the dangerous, terrifying, humming transformer house hermetically sealed off from the outside world. But still, this made my head whirl. Several times before, Rózsi Németh had taken me along with her by train to her home in the village of Törökszentmiklós, where I had to stay still by the stable door and watch them milk the cows in the half-light. Cows kick. Once the milk bucket tipped over and almost all the milk came spilling out. The hands veritably tugged at the breasts above the bucket, just like the tram's bell or the teats on the cow's udders. The milk turned into mud, which worried me, but they ignored it, stood the bucket up, patted the cow's shank, ran their hands over her flank, and continued milking her. Real milking was anything but pulling and tugging. The bell that was situated above the door of the deck was pulled at by a leather strap. My father explained that when the leather strap is pulled the spring mechanism cuts off the electric circuit, and that's what makes the bell ring. In the stable, too, you had to go up close to see that this was not tugging but pulling followed by the application of pressure. I was allowed to watch from up close how goats were being milked, I climbed up on a log and could look over the pen. Rózsi Németh's mother not only pulled on the teats of the goats with her hand, she also gave them a fine, quick squeeze, and then the milk came splashing in loud sprays into the bucket she held tight between her knees. I saw no sign that the goats or cows minded. I think they kicked because of the flies, or because they were getting impatient.

The leather strap was located on the ceiling of the tram, and when the ticket inspector was on board, he just had to reach above the heads of the passengers and tug at a leather handgrip. He rang down the tram, this is how people said it. Stop ringing it down already, don't ring it down yet. They will continue doing it, they will tug at the full udders until the bucket is quite full. Breast. Teat. For a long time, a very long time, these two words, *breast* and *teat*, made me shiver. My mother had breast cancer. Still, I couldn't help connecting the two, and this kept alive the infantile terror I felt over these animallike phenomena. Sometimes the interpretation of words and the interpretation of existence slip dangerously one into the other. But the bucket wasn't full yet, the bucket was nowhere full. Until it is full, Rózsi Németh won't come back to rescue me. I'd have liked to get away, just as I had repeatedly set off as a small child to head for the big wide world, though I couldn't tell you why, not even now. In the countryside, I set out from Leányfalu, I took food along for the road, determined to go over the mountains and never come back, and I also set out from Dömsöd, but I didn't get very far from there either, because the hands on the melon fields fed me melon then took me back to Grandmother Tauber, and I also took off from Budapest. I once sneaked away from kindergarten on Lipót Boulevard, I went down the stairs, crossed the street in the morning traffic, I must have been five, I think, but in this one case I knew perfectly well why I was doing it. I wanted to buy ice cream at the cake shop on the corner of Rudolf Square and Lipót Boulevard. But when I went up to the counter, it turned out that I needed money to buy it. Which surprised me. And I had no money, but the lady selling the ice cream was so amused, she gave me a scoop anyway; I also remember that she gave me strawberry, except she asked me not to walk away with the ice cream but to eat it there, and she'd find someone to take me back to the kindergarten. I stood inside by the glass door of the cake shop, licking my ice cream and watching the cars and trams pass by and onto the bridge. I don't know what I found so compelling, but the next moment, and in spite of all the warning, I took off. The sidewalk was jam-packed. I was just nibbling the side of the cone with the melting ice cream slipping down it when I stepped off the sidewalk, heard something, turned my head in the direction of the approaching sound, and there it was, a huge bus heading straight for me. For some reason I knew that this was the end, it would run over me. At that moment a man's hand grabbed my collar and with immense strength and in the moment after the last, it grabbed the seat of my pants as well, veritably hoisting me up, pulling me, and he started screaming at me for all he was worth, then he deposited me on the sidewalk so I squeaked. Amid earsplitting screeches from the bus and screams from the bystanders, the bus came to a stop somewhere on the corner of Falk Miksa Street. Everyone was cursing. In the blink of an eye the traffic came to a halt and I thought that these people, drunk with joy and outrage, would now lynch me for sure. Meanwhile, the man who'd pulled me back continued on his way as if nothing had happened. But then a young woman somehow saved me from the screaming and the commotion, which, needless to say, was filled with the sound of reproachful questions and relieved answers, joy, wonder that he'd seen it too, that it can't be, it boggles the mind, and where is the man who'd pulled me from under the wheels, while the young woman picked me up and began running with me across the road to take me back to that damned kindergarten where the kindergarten teachers, wouldn't you know, pay no attention, they just chat and polish their nails and have a good time among themselves.

She waited for me to go inside, but she didn't come with me. This was good, I was glad, because to this day no one has ever found out what I've just related.

I loved Rózsi Németh so much that I thought she'd be up to saving me even from my own notions. As if by magic, the feeling of love renders the other omnipotent. She'll save me. This, too, was among the discoveries I made for life, that no one can know what I am thinking, and that's good, though no one can save me from my notions either. And these notions had a way of always coming in through a side door, a window, the wall. Something began to grow and it grew more complex in my head. I felt that without her, my legs won't bear me up anymore. I couldn't leave, whereas I wanted to leave, to go out into the world, so I shouldn't be here and shouldn't see the breasts of the mothers. But my feet refused to obey me. I didn't understand, I couldn't get it through my head why these women, strangers to me, let themselves be milked, considering that they didn't know my baby brother. I didn't understand the world, nothing, no matter how hard I tried, I understood almost nothing of it.

Come, come, you're not going to faint, are you.

Will you pull yourself together.

She slapped me, two light slaps, I don't know who she was, a woman wearing a kerchief, and as a matter of fact, I didn't faint. But by then there were many of them standing around me, shouting and very angry, all of them women, that this little boy is about to faint here, he's fainted, hurry, bring some water.

Water.

This water slowly faded from my consciousness, because this time I fainted for real.

But on the Wednesday I was born, not only my mother's milk contained blood, but in the eyes of the existing or nonexisting God, who saw the empty horse-drawn carts return without their load of Jews, my birth, too, lost its reason for being. Reason first faded then it was absorbed, and later even my own exertion on behalf of rescuing something of the theological meaning of life with the help of this existing or nonexisting, dead or just recently massacred God proved to be a miserable failure. I was nourished with the milk of strangers, though mostly with formula, and true enough, I survived, and true enough, I became the living advertisement for Zamako and Ovomaltine in the family, they even loved me, but still, there was no sense to my survival, either then or now. At most, it was real and it was shameful. But neither its reality nor the accompanying shame accomplished what the Hungarian and the German languages promise. These languages gain meaning and they create meaning. And so it would be logical if they were to gain it from something. But I could not find this something.

I can further relate that on this particular October Wednesday, the day I was born, Miklós Radnóti was taken to forced labor. The Radnótis lived on Pozsonyi Street, today I know that it was just a stone's throw away from us, on the odd-numbered side of the street. The poet had been herded into a wagon at dawn the previous day, on Tuesday, but he had no idea where they were taking him. They've been standing in Szolnok for hours, he writes in his diary on this Wednesday. The news got around that they were going to Hatvan to gather beets. But then they were allowed to get off and go to the toilet. Here in Szolnok, Radnóti writes, the sign that it's a latrine is written in German, it's a German goods transfer station. Then he sleeps through the night. They're sleeping in the wagon like sardines. Even as they were trying to find a place for themselves, they were laughing fit to burst, he writes. On this evening, Jan Karski took off on a bicycle so that a Spanish young man by the name of Fernando should guide him over the passes of the Pyrenees. The road was shrouded in darkness. There was no moon, no stars, and for the sake of safety, their bicycles had no lights. Amid all the merriment, one of their comrades shouted for a shoehorn, writes Radnóti in his diary, another comrade for a toothpick to pry the toes of a certain Lambi from between his teeth. Take your ankle from my hemorrhoid. Radnóti provides an objective record of these typically manly witticisms, aids to survival, and also that after a while his comrades were heavy with sleep that engulfed them, along with their childish pranks. At least, thanks to Radnóti, who was buried in a mass grave in Abda, I know what the first night of my life was like just before dawn on Thursday. Though no one can say for sure that the body they found in the mass grave in Abda covered in his trench coat was really Radnóti. His wife, Fanni Gyarmati, could not identify the exhumed body as that of her husband. But it is certain that the poems and a message written in five languages found in the pocket of the trench coat were his last. Lager Heidenau, above Žagubica, in the mountains. This small notebook contains the poems of the Hungarian poet Miklós Radnóti. He asks the person who finds it to get it to Hungary and deliver it to the address of the university lecturer Dr. Gyula Ortutay, Budapest, VII., 1 Horánszky Street. Then in Latin letters in Serbian, then German, French, and finally, English. By the time the notebook was retrieved from the grave, the request written in French and German was fragmentary, but the name and address of the person survived in all the languages. *Prière de vouloir faire parvenir ce cahier*, followed by a line and a half that is illegible, *d'écrivain hongrois Miklós Radnóti*, then something illegible again, but the name and address of the person are legible. At dawn the following day, they were still standing in Szolnok.

We also know from the surviving notes of an anonymous victim that on the first early morning of my life, at dawn on Thursday, in the relocation camp in Lublin, he woke to a pogrom. When the person in question jots down his notes, we don't know why and we don't know for whom, the camp is still burning, smoldering *dans ce meilleur des mondes possible*, as Voltaire would say. He doesn't know who among his mates have survived and who have perished; for our part, we don't know who wrote the Lublin notes; he perished, leaving no name, only his report survived him. I also know from the research of others that at a time that can probably never be ascertained, Radnóti was transported to Bor not from eastern Hungary, where the train was headed the day I was born, but from a place near the western border, he was transported to Bor from Szentkirályszabadja, the poet was transported from the spot where, while they were gathering the men for the forced march, my mother helped my father escape in September. They were taken to the copper mines in Bor, where my uncle Miklós Nádas was also taken, then they were herded back in a forced march. But regardless of what had happened and regardless of how it happened on this Wednesday so meaningful for my mother, and also on the first Thursday of my life and in the course of the following decades, if I had to rely on reason alone, on causality, the rational thinking of my family, what's called the philosophy of history, lexical knowledge and the knowledge one gains in college lecture halls and fabulous university libraries, in short, without familiarity with my grandmother's anecdotal, poetic, and ritual knowledge, surely I'd have had a more difficult time trying to decipher the infernal logic of destruction and survival.

Needless to say, I saw clear as day that on each occasion my grandmother submitted to dangerously potent emotional impulses. She submitted to them because of me. We are entering a forbidden zone, but theoretically, being made an exception of is my right, I deserve it, this is what I thought, that secretly, I deserved it. For one thing, I deserved it because I was her adored little grandchild. A boy. The future course of my life stood so clearly before her, all I had to do was to follow the path. I would follow in my grandfather's footsteps, I'd become a goldsmith, I'd take over the wicked and wealthy Janka Tauber's workshop in Holló Street and her shop in Dohány Street as well. I deserve it. We deserve to be rich. Because I won't be nearly as timid and helpless as my grandfather has been all his life. A washout, people can't imagine, except for me, meaning my grandmother, and no one else, what a washout my grandfather is, a pitiful bungler. A pitiful bungler, right and left, everybody cheats him. Still, what the possible relationship between his being a pitiful bungler and his eternal little smile gave me food for thought. There's nobody that doesn't cheat him. Yet his smile, it never leaves him. His own sister cheats him, leads him up the garden path, she's done it all his life, cheating him, leading him up the garden path, yes, just as I say, she denies it, of course, but she wormed everything out of him. But he just smiles unperturbed, he smiles at everything. He's a fool, he falls for her tricks every time.

That she should order us around, that a lowlife like this Janka Tauber should call the shots.

My grandmother was nevertheless weary of Janka Tauber. No wonder she was weary; after all, for decades, their lives, their future depended on her, so the girls could at least learn a trade. Because Bözsi, this poor unfortunate cripple, we had her take lessons, she learned music and playing the piano, she might as well have something to fall back on, seeing how she can't walk properly. The truth is that my aunt had a pronounced limp, and though this did not prevent her from walking, my grandmother considered her her flawed daughter. It wasn't easy, we had to rent an upright for her, we skimped on meals to do it, it was no petty sum, we made sure she could attend the Music Academy, but that didn't leave much for the other two girls, neither Irén nor your mother. But your mother, she's no better than she should be. She could've made something of herself, if only.

She never finished the sentence, but it meant that my mother never amounted to anything and never would, the reason being my father, and consequently, she eyed her one and only little grandchild with misgiving from the moment he came into the world. Consequently, I even had to study my own dubious little existence from various angles if I wanted to understand her.

Not only what she said, but also what she left out of her sentences.

She could afford to say many things about Janka, but that Janka is a nobody, a big *niemand*, a great big zero, a *nebbich*, like just about everyone else, surely, this she'd have never dared say, nor even think, for that matter.

As a matter of fact, my grandfather received meager wages from his older sister, my mother confirmed it, in times of crisis she didn't pay him at all, for eighteen months during the Great Depression nothing, nothing whatsoever, sometimes food, foodstuffs, flour, so okay, she sent the girls some apples, what can I say. Whereas my grandfather had to work extra hard so they, he and his sister, would muddle through the Depression somehow, to save the workshop and the shop. It was not an unsuccessful undertaking, they survived. The business survived two world wars, until the Communists came and nationalized it. But meanwhile they had nothing to eat, and that's a fact, they were reduced to renting out a bed. Janka never had to make such a sacrifice. Ever. Granted, she always lived modestly, she skimped on herself. As for my grandfather, at least he didn't lose his job, he was even insured throughout, his retirement pension was insured, and he had health insurance, too. Janka rented the upright for Bözsi, another thing I learned only indirectly. Your grandmother remembers wrong, she may remember wrong on purpose, Janka rented that pianino. And when, outraged, I called my grandmother to account, cool as a cucumber, she simply said that that was true, what's her due is her due. Her composure made my jaw drop all my life. But even then, she refused to say Janka's name. What's her due is her due. Because a rich relative had certain responsibilities toward the poor or fallen members of the family, but the wealthy's responsibility did not include sharing their personal fortune or business capital in any shape or form, possibly jeopardizing it because of a poor relative, whether they loved the poor relative or disdained him, whether they disdained him because he was poor, for being such a washout, or they disdained him because of the real or imagined flaws in his character.

On the contrary. The general accepted and inviolate law dictated that the fortune be left intact, no matter what, and could not be shared.

Still, no day passed without her making some derogatory remark about Janka, whose fortune she nevertheless held in awe. You'll never get to see for yourself with your own two eyes how much that woman's got. What she managed to salvage. Meaning her gold and her scrap gold. You, you can't begin to imagine. Regardless of the situation, the self-propelled sentences issuing from my grandmother's lips were related only and exclusively to the speech situation, but the sentences bore no logical relationship to one another, and she meted out their truth content according to the emotional or temperamental content of the situation at hand. About which my mother made a very short and sobering comment. That and its opposite. She used it not only to characterize my grandmother's manner of speaking, but as a general guideline as well. Behind it lay her own correlative compulsion. I can't say cold and kind at one and the same time, whatever I say, I should be able to justify it. In my grandmother's manner of speaking everything was in flux, a compliment could mean abuse, abuse a compliment, but she also had a set of sentences, some said, others implied. For instance, she and her sister-in-law mutually shied away from meeting anywhere or at any time. But no one ever said so outright. Janka did not interfere in their lives in any way. She was even more sparing of her words than my grandfather. Unless my mother provoked them, there were no open confrontations in the Tauber family, nor secrets, and so all the family wounds were always open, more or less. Janka never once made mention of my grandmother in front of me. When we paid her a visit, she didn't ask, tell me, Ernő, because the family called my grandfather Ernő whereas his name was officially Arnold, Arnold Tauber, as it stood on his birth certificate, tell me, Ernő, is Cecília well.

On the other hand, without the least intent to provoke, Grandfather dutifully and repeatedly brought up Cecília.

Had he not obeyed his sense of the golden mean, Janka couldn't have had such an outstanding goldsmith.

Cecília.

Janka Tauber consistently responded to this name with silence. I had to accept this as well. Given the chance, she ignored Cecília Nussbaum's existence altogether. Her silence was so eloquent that even my own ears could pick up its meaning. It gave me vertigo. It was as if even after several decades, she were saying to her younger brother, it's your affair, Ernő, it's your affair, you married that penniless, dim-witted woman. I won't ask what her father was. I don't have to because I know. A nobody, a feather Jew. And in fact, that's exactly what he was. My grandmother explained in detail what kind of a Jew a feather Jew is. He goes around the countryside, even traveling great distances once the snow melts, he'll go even as far as Orosháza, he goes with his small bundle, he goes to the farms where they plucked feathers all winter and are waiting for him to show up, and the bundle he carries gets bigger and bigger, they wouldn't think of selling the feathers to anyone else, then two bundles, then three, all bulging with the feathers, as much as he can carry. Waiting for the Jew Nussbaum to show up. There were no two ways about it. With her dispassionate delivery Janka was, every time, bringing a merciless sentence on behalf of the family. Someone whose father had been a feather Jew can't be expected to enrich the family coffers. A reasonable man does not marry a woman like that. Not only did Janka not smile, she had no expression at all. I could never detect anything on her face, ever, not for a moment. At most there was the nothing, that was all I could see on her face and nothing else, ever, not for an instant. With which she was saying that she didn't think much of feelings. She'd learned this from her own life. The truth is I found this compelling and it served me as a standard of conduct throughout my life. Only later, much later, did I realize how much she had not said about her emotions with this nothing.

When my grandfather got married, marriages of the heart were considered exceptional. In traditional communities throughout the Monarchy, and hardly anyone could live outside of them, the head of the Jewish family decided the fates of the young Jewish women and young Jewish men recommended to him by the matchmaker, and even then, only after lengthy consideration of mutual interests. By all odds, Janka's fate was not decided by Janka either when, basically still a young girl, she was given in marriage to a filthy rich jewelry merchant thirty years her senior, who lorded it over her for fifteen years before he did her the favor of dying. When she was given in marriage, her only capital was her youth and her modest dowry, and by the time she became a widow, she couldn't have thought very highly of the thing she'd known only from hearsay, but had never experienced firsthand. For a long time, I didn't understand this custom, which we have mostly dispensed with by now, and to tell the truth, I still don't.

It would mean that man, an intelligent being, is created capable of copulating with anyone, something that animals are incapable of, because they follow their instinct for natural selection, and not some prescribed rite.

In which case all of us descend from beings not native to the animal world.

I will be rich, she can tell by looking at my eyes, she sees it by looking at my nose, I needn't worry. When she told my fortune, she always leaned in close and spoke in a whisper. Her whispered secrets were encouraging and threatening in turn, but be that as it may, they were based on knowledge I could never have gleaned from my father's books. I'll get back what Janka took from us throughout a lifetime, but why is she saying took, when it's robbed. She robbed us of all we had. She spoke softly so what she said in the kitchen shouldn't be heard outside on the balcony. Weather permitting, the upper windows were kept open to let the steam out, otherwise everything, and she means everything, would go bad, even in the pantry. And we're not as rich as Janka, to go and replace everything all the time. That Janka, she's a bad sort. She's got no shame, that woman, no shame. Base. She's a base sort, how can anybody be so base, so wicked, like that Janka. Wicked to the core, robbing her very own brother every blessed day. No shame, no shame at all. *Mishpocheh.* Which in her language didn't mean family in general, it meant that with this word she was making short shrift of a specific family. It erased the Taubers from the ranks of the living. Although there was no keeping up with the long list of objections she had to my person, in her eyes my existence guaranteed the family's survival, which, in her mythical and antirational universe, must have been identical with the meaning of life. My golden flower, my bright little star. This I understood, because it was like something from a fairy tale. My one and only. Whereas she had another little grandchild, Márta, who committed the capital offense of not being born a boy, not to mention the circumstance that she came into the best of all possible worlds in August 1944, when Romania, until then allied with Germany and thus Hungary, declared a unilateral ceasefire with the Red Army, and thus at a time even less opportune than mine.

There's no one I love more than you. Take my word for it. I was not her one and only. I didn't want to be anybody's one and only, the very thought of being anybody's one and only disgusted me. Besides, Márta was much closer to her, they talked and bickered as if they were friends, sisters, while I caused her nothing but chagrin, nothing but annoyance, you're nothing but a nuisance, she cried, you make my whole life a trial, I've never been so disappointed in anyone before, which could be heard out on the balcony, nothing but a nuisance, she yelled, sadness, pain, but Grandmother, they can hear out on the balcony, but now it's what she seems to be after, to have everyone share in the pain I'm causing her, because ritually, although I was the cause of her great disappointment, she had to love me because I was a boy.

If only I didn't have to be disappointed in you.

Every hour of every day I pray to the Almighty to spare me such disappointment.

I'd rather die.

I couldn't bare it if you ran amok, like Elemér.

Elemér was an exceptionally handsome young man; Grandmother showed me the family photographs so I'd see and learn. Elemér was this handsome, and I'd better not be this handsome. Not for anything in the world. See, this here is poor Elemér, and don't you follow his example, he's a bad sort. We do not speak about him. Not a word. I'm showing him to you just this once. See, this here is also Elemér. On one of the photographs he was standing with my mother and other attractive young men and women in the wintry landscape looking very elegant in his soft, unusually light-colored coat with a fur collar, they were standing arm in arm, you could tell that they were a genteel group who felt at ease with one another, they were all very elegant, in furs, while in the third photograph it was just the opposite, he was wearing perilously small bathing pants, he was on a boat excursion, a pair of bathing pants couldn't have been smaller, this, too, is Elemér, in Göd, as he's pulling the bow of the boat out of the water, because to give him his due, he was as strong as a bull.

But no matter what my grandmother whispered to me about what I should be and what I should not be, I wanted to be like him. I wanted to be as perfect as Elemér once I was a grown-up.

A snorting and stampeding bull as he runs off with Europa.

He became the family's great shame. That's why we didn't talk about him, we didn't even mention him. Under no circumstances. Not even his name.

You know who I mean. Just don't say his name.

If I so much as opened my mouth and she saw that I was about to say Elemér, she turned on me.

Don't say it.

When someone mentioned Elemér Street to her, that they were

walking along Elemér Street, or they said to her that they were going to enroll their child in the Elemér Street primary school, her mouth went into a ritual spasm.

Elemér was Grandmother's nephew, her oldest sister's son the same age as my mother, who one fine day tore off all his clothes, everything, and I do mean everything, and ran out to Csepel Island from Kálvária Square, which is a distance of at least ten kilometers as the crow flies, that's where they caught up with him, but only because he collapsed and then they wrestled him to the ground, but he continued to rage and bite even then, foaming at the mouth like a mad dog.

For a long time, a very long time, I understood neither the story nor the interdiction that went with it, but the truth is I didn't really believe it to begin with.

Something must have happened that was no less dramatic, but not this, this is not what happened, Grandmother is exaggerating.

I don't know where I got the daring not to believe her, whereas my mother corroborated her story, yes, that's how it happened, poor Elemér, yes, he was mad, in every way and with everyone and all the time, a man that ran amok, yes, he ran to Csepel as naked as the day he was born.

To this day I insist on my stubborn conviction that something else had happened to Elemér, and not like this, but in some other way, something that they're hiding behind this extreme legend. By all odds, the antecedents hold the key. By all odds, they caught him in flagrante with another man, it got out, he may have been blackmailed, it may have come to the attention of the police, the other man may have been the great love of his life, the one who threw himself out of a fifth-floor window because Elemér cheated on him, left him, Elemér must have been charged with his death, the charge was justified, and possibly he even had to face the fact that his family did not stand by him, even his mother was against him, and his aunt was against him too, who was my grandmother Cecília Nussbaum. The mental short circuit that grafted the frenzied rage he felt in face of the human wickedness and stupidity he saw around him onto the fatal desperation he felt over the nature of Creation could drive him to tear off his clothes and try to exit this vale of tears.

I love you so much, I could eat you all up. I heard these cannibalistic manifestations of adoration for the first time from my grandmother, and no one else, either before or after. Luckily, nor did anyone else say later on that I'm their bright star and golden flower. Meanwhile, with her perilous love Grandmother thought me perilously handsome. I was blond, I had blue eyes, my hair tended toward curls, and only decades later did I understand why she kept an eye on me the way she had. Terrified, she kept a close eye on me, won't I be like this poor Elemér, won't I be the shame of the family, like him. And she wasn't the only one in the family for whom my appearance and mannerisms were a problem of the same sort. She feared that indeed, that's what I was, a germ, dead ground, barren, stunted, yes, indeed, I'll be just like that, there's an Elemér stirring inside me and when it's discovered, I can run for all I'm worth, breathless, foaming at the mouth, they'll drag me off to the insane asylum, like him, where in the name of sacred medical science and all of enlightened humanity they will torture me as long as my heart can hold out against their loving care.

And then you'll get what's coming to you.

When a person dies, he gets what's coming to him, and those he leaves behind get what's coming to them, too. In my grandmother's eyes, death was what was coming to you. When she was angry, she lost no time in announcing that I was just like him, I was the spitting image of the person we do not talk about. Which affected me just as she had intended. Though I protested against it, it latched itself onto me like an incomprehensible curse, a prophecy; she painted the devil on the wall; in the language of psychology, it was projection, meaning that she assigned something to my future self that she herself was afraid of, she bequeathed it to me, and surely, her fears were not unfounded. People are not bound to their gender emotionally. On the other hand, their sexuality is tightly bound to their emotions. My grandmother was enamored of Queen Elisabeth's waist, she imagined that her alabaster breasts were her own, whereas hers were at least twice the size, breasts shaped like two apples, in her youth, her own breasts were surely very beautiful as well; but to my great good luck, for a long time, a very long time, until I was about thirty years of age, I had no idea what she was talking about, and what the object of my bewitchment was supposed to be. For lack of sensual incentives, as far as I was concerned, the sentences, similes, curses, innuendos, and ritual prophecies surrounding Elemér's figure were not open to interpretation, and this was so even in high school, when I fell in love with the other boys possessed of elementary, vital, and attractive traits; I waited for no one's approval, I had no moral or emotional qualms, and as for them, they were in love with me, there could be no doubt about that, and it felt very good. At times I had an erection. I didn't give it a name, I didn't say that in that case I'm in love. At times they had erections as well. Which did not stop me from loving some of the girls. And it didn't stop them either. Not in the least. Also, I never loved girls as such the way that, in obedience to certain magic rites, boys are supposed to do. I just stared like an oaf, wondering what they were thinking. I loved certain girls. I loved Lívia Süle and Hedvig Sahn, and with all the bitterness, it was good just as it was. Besides them I also loved a mildly hysterical, blond, dark-skinned girl, their classmate, with whom we'd hardly exchanged more than a couple of words. When Hedvig entered the scene, she went into hysterics because of it. That I mustn't love that certain individual, whose full name I've forgotten, surely in response to her strict admonition. And Éva Juhász, I mustn't love her either. And Margit Leba, the same goes for her. They also gave me an erection. I never felt embarrassed because of it, after all, it was mutual, it was just the two of us, another reason I didn't think I should talk anything over with anyone, or share what had happened. For me, this was Creation itself, or the Creator's mute manifestation, and it should be understood in the theological sense of the word. This is what I think. It's a gift or a given that needs no commentary. One first had to understand the hunger and passions of the body and the pagan guiles of a society applying pressure through disdain and exclusion before one could be strong enough and wise enough to withstand the infringement of others, even to the extent of a single word, on his feelings and sensual urges. For a while, for a time, for a long time, perhaps I was protected by my autistic naïveté. But how could handsome Elemér's understanding heart have withstood the siege. They tortured him until they succeeded in killing him, all the time that, surely, it would never have occurred to the members of my deeply honored family that it was they who had killed him. The Nussbaum family mustn't have their shame parading about like that.

After György Nádas, he was the second person my honorable family had put out of the way.

About ten years had passed between the two ritual murders, then another ten, and when another ten years had passed, not only my grandmother, but my Aunt Magda also set her sights on me. We'll skewer him, yes, that's good, we'll slowly roast him, then have him for dinner. My Aunt Magda kept an eye out, listened, and in an erotic fever whispered in the ears of her relatives and steadfast friends; first and foremost, she whispered behind my back with Vilma Ligeti, now that I think back on it, and she must have whispered with Jolán Kelen and Stefi Dési Huber as well; some misguided curiosity continued with Jolán Kelen, with Stefi Dési Huber some misguided sympathy that puzzled me; as if they'd put their heads together and had come up with a story concerning me, I sensed it, but could not understand it, the outcome of which was that Magda Aranyossi, my favorite aunt, when she became my guardian, took me, along with her story, to a child psychologist; she consigned me to a doctor's care, perhaps hoping to get rid of me with the help of science, something that at long last, at the age of sixteen, I finally understood.

But the extent to which people will go in their ritual scheming in the hopes of regulating others' emotional lives and sensual urges, I've come to understand only now, after about six decades, thanks to the surviving family correspondence, even if I wouldn't go so far as to claim that I understand it in all its details.

Yet I remember perfectly well where I was standing, at the age of about twenty-two, in the story of the girlfriends and their ritual concern. I was standing by the open window of Vilma Ligeti's apartment in Fő Street. The weekday morning street below was rumbling and stinking. On this weekday morning I had bought Vilma some wild-flowers to cheer her up. We had to raise our voices to be heard. She wanted to know what had weighed on my mind of late, she reproached me for not sharing my problem with her. Except, I had no problem I could share with anyone, her least of all. Vilma, or Vilmuka was rather dull upstairs. Nearly every hour and moment of my life I was occupied with how I might kill myself. Surely, I know that there's nothing I can't tell her. It's called compulsive suicidal tendency. She's surprised, because people tell her everything, and she means everything. This was my burden, there was nothing about it I could share. This burden let up somewhat only when I could be with Magda, Magda Salamon, a woman eleven years older than I, the mother of two sons. Both of us worked for the weekly illustrated magazine with the largest circu-lation in the country; she was a journalist and I was a photo-reporter trainee, and so sometimes we would go on an assignment together. As soon as we set eyes on each other, in the editorial offices, the street, in her apartment, in a hotel without heating where the police held nightly raids, in her bed, anywhere, at any time, in the blink of an eye my passion drove my temptation to commit suicide from my conscious mind, but when I was alone once again, it reappeared fully armed. It was temptation, a malfunction of the psyche urging me to swallow the poison, to fling myself into the depths, to hang myself. How could I get my hands on a gun. I didn't talk to her about this either, I didn't talk to anyone.

Magda didn't want to leave her husband, the father of her children, she couldn't do it, and I had no right to aggravate her painful decision with my demands. If she decides to leave him, it shouldn't be because of me. When I was standing in front of Vilma Ligeti's noisy window in Fő Street, we'd been tormenting ourselves over this for three years, and there lay several more years of torment ahead of us; we tormented each other, we upset the children, but we couldn't get the upper hand over our passion; in short, our torment was not just our own, nor was there an escape route for either of us. It was a scandal, we had become scandalous, whereas we thought that with our self-restraint we could keep our affair to ourselves. A long and by all odds rambling love letter containing some highly indelicate details that I had written to Magda disappeared from the red briefcase that she had left on her desk at the office. The local agent of the secret service had taken it. Some weeks later, Irén Németi, the magazine's editor in chief, a friendly and sympathetic woman, asked Magda to come to see her and cautioned her against the dangerous affair because of the difference in our ages. Magda asked her not to worry about her. Next, Irén Németi quoted my aunt Magda Aranyossi, who'd come to see her and said what an exalted individual I was. For months, we laughed and laughed. What an idea, exalted, what an idea, an individual, and besides. It was a grand joke, it came in handy for the loving couple, neutralizing the infinite stupidity of the outside world by clinging to each other with their naked bodies and kissing each other's lips. Still, we tried to put an end to the affair again and again and again. It felt like a terrible personal debacle, a failure that must be acknowledged. We couldn't bear it for more than a week. Once, we were able to stretch it out for three weeks, thanks to her, but not longer than that. A glance, a slight gesture, a cliché meant to be a sign of courtesy was enough to make us scream with laughter, as if we were waiting for this to happen, our laughter ousting from our bodies the useless attempt at breaking up. Down with stupid social clichés. What will be will be. This is the point I had reached in my own life when I was standing between the open panels of the window in Vilma's apartment holding the wildflowers I'd picked for her, but she and my aunt were down a different path in the story of my life, and as I now see from the letters I found, they continued weaving their wicked dream concerning me for years to come.

After she became our official guardian, Aunt Magda lied to me when she told me that I must see a child psychologist in my brother's interest, because it was high time she learned why the child couldn't read or write. Which I willingly believed, because I couldn't get my brother to read or write either. He wanted to play, to run riot, not to read or write, he wanted to go skiing and sledding, to fight with the other boys and play football. I believed that I had to go to Szondi

Street twice a week because of my brother's inability to learn. It was a bleak building with iron bars on all its windows. When I looked at my Aunt Magda's face, I could tell that it was not true, except I didn't know what was not true. But it became clear soon enough that they were getting at something with their tests, trying to bring something to light, gathering evidence against me, that they wanted to bring something out into the open, wanting to cure me of something of which, for another fifteen years, I remained ignorant and hadn't the faintest inkling of what it was about. And in order to free myself of the burden and in the name of my right to self-determination, I decided to lead Imre Hermann, the celebrated psychoanalyst who, in accordance with the current practice of child psychology relied on tendentious questions and humiliating tests, in short, I determined to lead him astray, even though I had no idea what I was leading him astray about.

For a while he suffered it, he suffered it for weeks, he must have seen through the logic of my tricks. But then he lost his patience because I saw that he saw and so changed my tactics for fending him off. With his tests, repeated ad infinitum and his stupid cross-examining, after a couple of months he came to resemble a distraught clerk who can't find any of his files on his office desk.

Which told me that I was on the right track.

I missed one appointment, then another, and the next time I went, I wouldn't give him an explanation for the missed appointments. I watched for his reaction. He must have been in a state. He had to come up with an acceptable explanation, a solution, something banal with which he could close this affair once and for all, because he wouldn't have liked to say to my aunt that the problem is even worse than you thought, dear Magda.

Dear Magda, the child is mentally ill.

At best Hermann could have added, Comrade, take your charge over to Psychiatry, our methods are inadequate for the treatment of schizophrenia.

They wanted to screw up my life, and I was not about to let them.

I stopped going. When my aunt called me to account, I shrugged and threw my hands up in the air as if to say it wasn't my fault. She asked if Imre Hermann had offended me in any way. I threw my hands up again, as if to say, what an idea, I'm thick-skinned. She wanted to put the blame on Imre Hermann, whereas it was clear as day that she was the one behind Imre Hermann with some intention unclear to me, and that's why I was not about to go back to him. As for her and her grande dame manners, she dropped the subject, as if it had never come up in the first place.

Except I couldn't imagine what they were up to. I found out only half a century later, when I read one of Miklós Mészöly's letters.

Though she kept hounding me with questions, I was a lot more lenient with Vilma, a lot more permissive than with my aunt; though she kept at it, I was more lenient because she wasn't a member of the family but a stranger who gradually became almost totally isolated. She came to loggerheads with whomever she could. I felt sorry for her. During the revolution she was at the headquarters of the Writers' Association in Bajza Street; she couldn't have gone home to Buda anyway; she translated newspaper announcements into French, she acted as interpreter for foreign newspaper reporters on the battle-ridden streets of Pest, she collected the odd printout pertaining to the revolution, organized food supplies and supervised their distribution, she wrote appeals and protests, later she organized boycotts and strikes, for which, though she was not taken to prison, she was under a full publication ban, and there was no knowing if the ban would ever be lifted. She found herself without an income. She wanted to go to New Delhi to her older sister, who was actually her younger sister and the wife of a well-to-do Indian banker. Until she died, Vilma always doctored her age, which is why she turned her younger sister into her older sister. Her passport request was denied. She gave French lessons and piano lessons, which was barely enough to keep her going and to pay her bills. Sometimes her shoe had a hole in it for months on end, she had no money for the tram, she had to wear stockings with runs in them, and at times she had nothing to alleviate her hunger. She kept cheap tea biscuits at home. I had to take care not to eat them all up. She was a cheerful person. She didn't complain. She was in need of solidarity.

And I shouldn't be so dismissive with her, she said that morning. My solidarity, however, had nothing to do with love, it was political in character. Stuck for an answer, I said that indeed, I'm not in a good mood, though I'm not morose, at most I see a grim future ahead, though not necessarily my own. And that one fine day I am going to sell my soul to the devil. If I have to, I'll draw up a blood pact with him.

I was reading Goethe's works at the time, one after the other, and also Thomas Mann's *Doctor Faustus* with its fine Palestrina scene in which, in exchange for writing his great musical compositions in the Casa Manardi, Adrian Leverkühn sells his soul to the devil. Which means that I was interested not only in the idea of a world with two essences, the nature of good and evil, I was also interested in the physical presence of the powers of darkness. In those years I couldn't discount the possibility that at any given moment they might turn into air, at another they take on a human aspect. At times they leave the world of men, at others they return.

The world of phenomena is nothing but endless metamorphosis.

But what I said, hoping to be evasive, had a strange effect on Vilma.

I hope it's not syphilis, she said after a long and suggestive pause.

I laughed and said no, it's not syphilis, but as a matter of fact I had no idea what she was getting at. Her round, heavily freckled face reminiscent of a Japanese doll turned reflective, then you know, she said, it doesn't speak well of your aunt, but I'll tell you anyway. We were sitting out in the garden in Leányfalu and you were playing theater with the others, you monkeyed around, putting on airs, impersonating a woman, I guess, and Magda broke out, look, I'm willing to bet anything he's going to grow into a pederast, *il est complètement pédé, une vraie pédale.* And I to her, come now, Magda, how can you say a thing like that of a small child, can't you see he's playing.

I didn't know what relevance this bore to our conversation, why she was telling me this.

But to be perfectly honest, at that moment I couldn't have cared less what my aunt had thought of me ten years before; Vilma and I both loved her, but we held her in disdain because of her horrendous political opportunism.

The only sense I could make out of the episode she'd just related was that she wanted to say something defamatory about my aunt, and that with this episode, which seemed authentic enough, she wanted me to know that I can trust her, I can tell her everything, anything at all, I can even tell her if I have syphilis, for instance, after all, she'd taken me under her protection when I was just a small child.

But in fact, she wanted me to own up. She'd meant it as a parable. To get me to speak. So far, so good. Except, try as I might, I couldn't find anything inside, either inside my head or in my heart that would have resonated with her story. Of course, I could have told her about the real reason for my sullenness, and about my real emotional and erotic life, but I have always lacked the impulse to deliver accounts of this type.

Also, compared with their fiction, it would have been disappointing, because reality is always weaker than fiction.

It was the same with my grandmother. Whenever she put body and soul at the service of one of her grand scenes of adoration or hatred, unconditionally and without the least touch of irony, I might add, I had no way of knowing, ever, where this frenzy of language and emotion was taking us. It could be laughter, joy, it could be weeping, the sudden stoppage of the heart, wailing, excommunication, and eternal damnation. Even murder. Why not. Or why couldn't it be some mystery. This ritual playacting had no religious or rational content, that was the whole point behind it. All its content was prereligious, meaning, magical; it was not archaic, that is not the earliest layer of human consciousness, and not mythical, which is a later layer of human consciousness, rather, it came from the thousands of years that passed in between. In short, magical. They joined forces and killed their own with the strength and joy of their magical regression, and they didn't even have to confront themselves with their religion, which had faithfully retained magical elements, because their religion prescribes their duty to kill people of this sort. They have to stone them to death. Something that a couple of millennia later, Christianity had most conscientiously and, let us add, with not a little enjoyment, taken over from them, in each case deciding, as it were, what a faithful Christian must do and when in the interest of killing others.

Will it end, this was my frightened childish question, or will it stay like this forever.

This question aimed at the nature of life made my entire wicked little being tremble, because at times I had the distinct impression that in her ritual grandmotherly emotions my grandmother would not only end up disgustingly biting and kissing me, but exactly as she had promised, she'd tear me apart with her dentures, which at night she removed and placed in a cup of clean water; she'd chew me, swallow me, make me disappear inside her.

I felt equally apprehensive when she merely hugged me and pecked at my cheeks.

With Vilma, too, I balked at the slightest physical contact.

She also used eau de cologne, she got hold of her classic lavender-scented 4711 that was made from lavender oil and not synthetics. My grandmother used the same cologne. When she kissed me and bit my cheeks, I couldn't think of anything else except that I don't love my own grandmother. And I didn't. Because I thought that you have to love your grandmother, regardless of what she smelled like. And if you love her, then you have to hate Elemér, hold him in contempt, just like her, in short, not be hoodwinked by Elemér's radiant beauty, and while you're at it, disdain Creation itself so that you may satisfy the ritual aversion that a nomadic people who lived five thousand years before felt against Creation.

But when all is said and done, I loved my grandmother. No one could ever exasperate me as she had, and by all odds, no one ever exasperated her as much as I had either.

But it was pouring forth from every part of her.

The odor came pouring forth from her clothes, it was odor, not scent, an odor that stood in the way of love. It poured forth from her wardrobe, it poured forth along with the scent of her authentic cologne, as authentic as they come.

When the dictatorship had reached the point where it wouldn't put up with lavender and you couldn't get your hands on a bottle of proper eau de cologne anymore in the whole city and the whole country, Grandmother switched to Molnár & Moser's cloyingly sweet and by all odds synthetically produced smell, but this just accentuated the smell of her body. It may have been ambergris or musk, a chemical hodgepodge, of course. I kept sniffing, wondering where it came from, which part of her body, which gland, what the thing was that even the cloyingly sweet scent could not mask, it merely corralled, held it in check; there's no two ways about it, it was my grandmother's body, the smell of her functioning glands.

The truth is it was issuing from between her labia.

As fate would have it, during the last years of her life, I was charged with visiting and nursing Vilma in the hospital. She died in my arms. I had to take hold of her, hold her with both hands, so that my body, a living body, could help her in her death struggle. Sometimes Magda took charge of the nursing, but only when it couldn't be helped; because Vilma hated her, even though she hardly knew her. Though Vilma was cheerful as a lark, she could be furious and spiteful. I'd known this side of her from before, but the depths of her hatred remained mostly hidden from me for about another half century. When she got wind of my close friendship with Miklós Mészöly, she tried to talk me out of it by resorting to professional arguments. As a writer, he's mediocre. The statement contained the type of hatred that those in the same profession have a way of entertaining for each other. I didn't even argue with her. Ever since a couple of years previously the filmmaker Miklós Jancsó had handed me Mészöly's *Dark Signs*, here, read it, I had no doubts about Mészöly's quality as a writer. But Vilma, who couldn't have been satisfied with the result of our little chat, made up a story with my Aunt Magda and passed it on to Miklós, asking for his help. She said that I'd entrusted her with the great secret of my life, according to which I'm waging a terrible struggle against the attraction of homosexuality, because I consider it ethically unacceptable, what's more, repulsive, but I can't fight against it, and this satanic urge is ruining my relationship with women. In the hallway of the writers' retreat in Szigliget, she asked Miklós to help ease my relationship with women. Though he must have had his suspicions, Miklós nevertheless believed Vilma's story for a while. I remember him asking me about Vilma, but I had no idea why he'd be interested in her. It is to his credit that he did not do as he was charged, he did not support me in anything and he did not doubt anything. On the contrary, whenever he had the chance, he gave me the books of known gay writers to read. He gave me the works of James Baldwin, Hubert Fichte, and Jean Genet, I remember this perfectly, he'd brought them from Berlin and Paris. I must get to know them, along with Cavafy. But in those last months when at times I'd take Vilma to the hospital or bring her out, at least Vilma made friends with Magda. She had no other choice on her deathbed. At times I had Magda visit her instead of me. But at times, when the nurse, for whom Vilma's younger sister paid through a London bank account, hadn't come for two days, I had to sponge her down so she wouldn't get bed sores, and at such times, thanks to the peculiar mix of the two odors, the 4711 and the labia, I finally understood where my grandmother's smell that could not be reconciled with her eau de cologne had come from.

At the height of her frenzy or adoration, one would think that my grandmother was in the act of transforming the ordered universe. Chaos entered the scene along with her physical being. I felt sorry for her and I was afraid of her; still my sense of adventure remained dominant. Just as for a while I didn't play hooky from the prestigious child psychologist professor's office hours either, I visited him regularly twice a week, whereas I realized pretty quickly that we were not concerned with my brother, I was the one on the autopsy table, but I watched, I wanted to see how far I would go and how far they would go. It took great self-restraint on my part to put up with my grandmother, but that just made me obsess over her all the more, I obsessively plagued her, I provoked, hated, and disdained her, I wanted to decipher the riddle of her strange being, find the source of the scent or the smell while, for her part, she was hell-bent on saving me from perdition, she wanted to teach me all the regressive rites, to make me understand the duality of the body and the soul and internalize the methods by which my body would be devastated but my soul saved before it was too late. In short, to force myself to feel the frenzied love that I didn't feel for her nor would I, even though I'm aware of the existence of such love. Or if this sort of love does not exist, there is a stylized version of it. What's more, I wanted to learn not to be unfair to her. My grandfather grumbled, come, son, leave your grandmother be with your never-ending questions, but in vain.

He said no more than this, he didn't discipline me, at most, he cautioned me.

Still, with this cautious sentence he managed to check my developing sadism.

When once in a while Grandfather spoke up, the din of the family or friends settled down because they could all be sure that they were about to hear something apt and amusing, and the mischievous, boyish smile on his face mirrored his intent.

On the other hand, I barraged my grandmother with questions that she answered with undisguised annoyance. Or else I put up a fight, I refused to follow, I ranted and raved, because she was hell-bent on a model that was innately unfamiliar to me, the hatred, the adulation, the humility, and the disdain, her lack of moderation and her manner of presenting these were all strange to me. She followed a different pattern, every one of her words and gestures was subordinated to an unfamiliar standard. She didn't need to be authentic with respect to her beliefs, only her mimicry needed to seem authentic. She aimed for effect, she performed to mislead, she seduced you with rewards that were not forthcoming, something that the others in the family would never do. She watched from behind her ritual mask to see if she had coaxed the desired effect from you. At times she nearly put me off guard, the presents she promised nearly put me under their spell. It was pure theater and it took its toll on her, because she would sometimes take the four- or five-year-old child that I was or still am seriously, she took herself and my resistance as seriously as if we were equals, as if we had to come to grips with something, as if Creation itself were at stake. She caused not a little pain for herself with these performances. I got to witness with my own eyes what ritual pain means in a person's life, all the things that even five thousand years could not remedy, all the things for which there will be no remedy to the end of time. For which there is no forgiveness. It was a constant reminder of something we no longer remember. It was a universalized pain she used to aggrandize and deepen her minor, momentary pains. She used the burden of this perpetually evoked and perpetually whipped-up and heightened pain from the past to add gravity to my daily transgressions. Perdition shall strike us again because I have not tied up my boots properly. She treated the silliest little mischief or omission from a biblical perspective, with recourse to the words of the prophets. The effect was ludicrous. She couldn't say or present anything without immediately exaggerating it. Oh, bring me a drop of water, I'm about to die of thirst. Which simply meant that she was thirsty and would like a glass of water. Once I actually took her a drop of water. Hunger is gnawing at my stomach. Which just meant that it was time to sit down at the table. Ever since Margitka has left us, my darling little angel, may her name be inscribed in the Book of Life, I am among the walking dead. You won't believe it, but I'm dead. And I didn't. This is not life. My heart is broken, dried out, I'm dead. Why don't you place my miserable body in the ground already. My grandfather made no answer to sentences such as these, but his faint little smile revealed a strange imperturbability. Whereas my grandmother meant what she said. With Margitka's death her heart really did break, and with time, it dried out. With his smile, my grandfather tactfully bucked against all the things that my grandmother expressed or evoked in her theatrical manner, all the while that he paid close attention he was on the alert, prepared for any eventuality, including the dire consequences of magical regression.

My grandmother would go pale or turn purple at the drop of a hat; with her wild gesticulations she sometimes knocked off her own glasses, at other times she had a coughing fit, I'm choking, water, oh, I'm choking. Without her glasses she couldn't find her glasses.

Oh, my God, find them, I can't find them, can't you see, without my glasses I'm as good as blind. Oh, Lord, why did you afflict me with blindness in my old age, she cried as she felt for her glasses. My God, that I should live to see the day. That I should have to live to see this. Which just meant, will you please help me find my glasses. And because of God, she then lost no time in striking her lips with her ringed hand. Because of you. Meaning that she sinned against the Almighty because of us, this is why she must cause herself pain, and this is why the Lord has rendered her blind and plagued her with thirst. We won't even help her find her glasses. We won't even bring her a drop of water. If only you'd bring me a drop of water. The Lord will punish you for your wickedness, he'll punish you good and plenty. For her the Lord had a close physical reality, on her lips theological concepts received a weighty physical cast. As for the plural, first and foremost it included my mother, then me, her two other daughters, the loud and brutal Bözsi, Erzsébet Tauber, the pianist, and the neurotically meek, profoundly intimidated Irén, Irén Tauber, the little tailor's cutter with her celebrated sense of the line, but just a little bit it also included her own husband, my grandfather Ernő, meaning Arnold Tauber, though he least of all. I think he was the only person she loved. At any rate, she didn't expect him to find her glasses or bring her water. If nobody went to look for them, sooner or later she found them on her own anyway. In her, ritual reflection and a realistic sense of things ran in parallel yet connected courses. Probably, she wasn't even thirsty; rather, in line with the dictates of some magic rite she had to keep her family in perpetual motion around her, just as, thanks to the two hours of her afternoon nap, she kept herself in perpetual motion, too. As if this whole unnecessary ritual construct that she kept in operation alongside her sense of reality was meant to guarantee that she should be able to keep up her way of life, that her energy should not slacken, and that through it, she should be able to keep depression at bay.

After lunch she scrubbed the kitchen floor again, whereas she'd scrubbed it during the morning cleanup, and also the hall, and twice a week the balcony in front of the door and the shared toilet out on the landing, and only then would she take her nap.

She left only one person out of her use of the second person plural, their dead daughter, Margitka.

Who was an angel incarnate.

She used the notion of the angelic to sustain the idea of a world wholly devoted to self-sacrifice. After all these years I might as well admit that, to some extent, she sustained it in me as well. The utopia of the existence of angelic beings. Or if they don't exist, then there must be or should be angelic people at least. Certainly, this notion had more radiance to it, it was more attractive than my parents' social utopia.

We'll put up a fight, he can't get the better of us, he can't be allowed to have exclusive dominion.

Indeed, she got up at dawn so she could put our Sunday soup on the stove in time. But with the possible exception of the ambition tied to our Sunday soup, every one of her words and gestures amounted to ritual mimicry.

As for Margitka, with the fine lines of her little face and her golden-blond, curly hair, it was easy to imagine her as an angel.

Even in the city that stood in ruins, my grandmother would go anywhere for the meat and vegetables needed for the soup, she'd pay any amount for the meat on the black market, because it had to be loin of beef. Sometimes my grandfather grumbled. Kindly add the bone, she told the butcher. Meaning that he should throw in some bone for free, and also some gristle, in short, that her butcher shouldn't forget that a good customer enjoys certain rights. She couldn't imagine anyone not cheating her. Not every butcher gives her soupbone for free, because they're all scoundrels, cheats, leeches, goys. With the exception of her own butcher, of course.

I wish I knew why I didn't go to my regular butcher. He'd be up in arms. Meaning he'd be deeply hurt if he knew that she'd been to another butcher.

She was passionate about her purchasing decisions.

Come now, Cili, my grandfather said, if there's no meat, then there's no meat, you could've made some other soup. Sometimes she was Cecília, at other times she was just Cili, at times they used the familiar form of address with each other, at times the formal. Their daughters used only the formal mode with them.

I didn't understand the black market either, I didn't understand it for a long time. It was like fishing in murky waters. Grandmother and I went to the market, we walked along the length of Péterfy Sándor Street, except when we got there, I saw nothing black about the Garay Square market. Everything changed hands just like anywhere else. My grandmother bought the meat for the soup, she paid out a lot of money for it from her purse, whereas she knew that this meat was not that meat. If you buy it under the counter, why are you surprised. There's no good meat to be had these days. As if she'd bought it under the counter, meaning the black market, from people fishing in murky waters, just so she could make this observation. The last time she bought proper meat, Franz Joseph and Queen Elisabeth were still on the throne. But why bother trying to explain to an ignorant world what meat was like in those happy peacetime years. They wouldn't understand. Of course, knowing good meat from bad, she should have never bothered buying meat for the family. When still dazed from the previous night's sleep I staggered from the room, the soup was already bubbling on the stove, she was ladling off the foam with angelic know-how, so it shouldn't be murky. The soup had to be crystal clear. This was a point of pride with her. See, I put the soup on the *sparhelt* in plenty of time, and the dough is properly in the *rerni*. What a sentence. Nothing short of a miracle.

I understood her language, how could I not have understood that *sparhelt* meant the stove and *rerni* meant the oven, and *dough* meant cake and *buksza* meant wallet, but this didn't help me understand the essence of the thing, why she had to give everything strange names, and why she had to attach such highly charged adjectives to them. She put the soup on the table separately, then came the cooked meat with the vegetables, with which she served goose sauce or sour cherry sauce. But why can't she say gooseberry instead of goose. If she asked what sauce she should make, I invariably said sour cherry, just to stop her from saying goose. Or instead of tin, why can't she say tray. All right, so she put the tin in the *rerni*, but why does she have to say that she put it in properly. She couldn't have put it in improperly, could she. I didn't accept, I refused to accept this goose and tin business. She first made the big matzoh balls for the soup, these she sometimes called *knédli*, and needless to say, no one could make them better than she. They were light and fluffy, yet had a firm bite to them. She took a spoon and carefully placed the *knédli* or the no-less-tasty semolina dumplings, which she called *haluska*, on the plate, then she carefully ladled the soup over one or the other, making sure they remained intact and did not turn the soup cloudy. If she managed to buy a nice fatty hen and make some nice little chicken soup from it, she cooked the hen's liver in the hen's fat, she had a separate iron pan for it, a battered old thing, and then we ate the nice little chicken soup with the nice matzoh balls and the nice liver.

Five years later how could I not have known how to make soup for my sick mother. Basically, I felt, if I do it well, if I make sure to do everything the way I saw my grandmother do it, our mother won't die. In accordance with this inner conviction based on word magic, I made her food she couldn't even eat. I learned to cook from my grandmother and, despite all my protests, I learned the magic of words as well. That you don't make chicken soup but nice chicken soup with which, in this particular case, you will save your mother. Whereas I could hardly bear it when she'd say, again and again, all right, I'll make some nice little stew. Still, I made some nice little chicken stew for my mother several times just like Grandmother had made it, with roux, determined to save her from the thing no one would talk about. An adjective, an emphasis, a gesture, something invariably urged me to harass my grandmother, especially because of the stew that she made with roux. I harassed my grandmother from earliest childhood until, at the age of nineteen, I saw her for the last time. Grandmother, why do you say you're making some nice little chicken stew, Grandmother, why do you say there will be some nice little matzoh balls in it and you're adding some nice little liver to it. Why are you saying again that I'm making some nice little meat pilaf and I'm adding this nice little giblet. She didn't understand what I was getting at. It's just the way she spoke. This was her language, these were her words. Even when she spoke Hungarian, she used key concepts from Yiddish along with the expressions and antiquated syntactical rules of the Great Hungarian Plain that she brought along with her when she came to Budapest with her older sister, Szerén, meaning Szeréna Nussbaum, to work as a maid, but ended up as a polisher in a silversmith's workshop in Dob Street, and my grandfather soon married her. She must have been a fragile young woman with an hourglass waist but, even as a young girl, full-blooded nonetheless, and I bet that it was she who hooked my grandfather for herself.

But it wasn't just the unfamiliar expressions that rubbed me the wrong way. Not a single sentence left her mouth that wasn't a horrendous cliché. Others didn't speak with their own sentences either but with clichés hooked into each other, they spoke idiomatically, which in Pest could basically change district by district. But despite all my experience with language, my grandmother's ritual use of language got my goat. She'd say, I'm buying some nice butter. As if she would buy not-nice butter. I'm making some nice little bean soup. When no one will make not-nice bean soup on purpose. I'm making a nice roux for this nice little shredded pumpkin, and I'm adding lots of nice dill to it. I wanted something from her that I couldn't put into words, because I lacked the language for that as well. Not only her ready-made sentences, not only the lack of personal linguistic manifestations, not only the constant outpouring of locutions and idioms, not only the peculiarity and antiquity of her language, but its logical impossibilities drove me up the wall. If the liver were not nice, surely she wouldn't add it to the matzoh ball but would give it to the wicked cat of her wicked goyim neighbors. She didn't just hate her goyim neighbors, she hated their goyim cat as well. On the other hand, the cat was in the habit of leaving its stinking calling card on her threshold. I even have to clean up after the goyims' cat. Also, if the chicken soup were not nice, surely she wouldn't serve it to us on Sunday. Or why would she make a not-nice chicken stew with roux on purpose. In short, why would she use adjectives unnecessarily. And what does she mean by roux when she talks about chicken stew; with my autistic, meaning visual, conception of things, I couldn't make heads or tails of this roux either. Mark my words, you will rue the day. Are you planning to cook the day, too, Grandmother. Whereas she didn't use adjectives unnecessarily, she used them ritually. Every time and with every gesture, she felt compelled to draw a ritual difference between good and bad, nice and not nice. Exaggeration was her poetics and she had set the bar high to begin with. She didn't reach the heights of exaggeration through gradations, she started at the rhetorical peak and then, as the orator, she watched, curious, to see how she would enhance that darned sentence, how she could give its emotional spiral yet another upward twist. Whereas I wanted her to use words functionally. After all, she was my grandmother. She should use them the way we use them, without all sorts of poetic exaggeration and rhetorical embellishment. I wanted her to speak like the others, like us, each and every one of us.

But she was not us, she was not part of our plural. Or even though she lived with us, our plural excluded her. When I slept at their place in the thick of town, on the divan at their feet where the angelic and consumptive Margitka passed away in the middle of a horrendous septic shock due to infectious meningitis, in that more humble than humble apartment in Péterfy Sándor Street where my mother and her sisters had grown up, sometimes in the company of an alternating series of bed tenants, early in the morning I had to wash in a basin placed on top of a stool in the middle of the kitchen, my grandmother poured hot water into it, but I'd better not make a *gezerah* out of it again. Throughout my childhood I shuddered at this *gezerah*, I was terrified beforehand, anticipating when she'd say it again, say that I'd made a *gezerah* again. She shouldn't be saying it. If only she wouldn't say it ever again. But no matter how careful I was washing myself so we could avoid it, she kept at me with this *gezerah*. She said all sorts of other things, too, a man she respected was *schneidig*, another was a *kvetsh*, a *yammer*, a *kolboynick*, a *schnorrer*, a *schlemiel*, a *niemand*, and a *nebbich*, but these words I liked, they didn't bother me. I understood them because of their context. But her *gezerah* scared me. At home on Pozsonyi Street, the grown-ups spoke a different Hungarian, though I'm not suggesting that I understood everything they said. Only my grandfather spoke in a way that left no room for doubt or ambiguity. Accompanied by a little smile, he spoke in unadorned, dry, simple sentences. Everything was clear, everything was apt, his sentences hit the nail on the head.

My grandfather didn't smell even when he took off his pajamas; at most the air stirred around him. On the other hand, the air around him was at times cool, at other times warm.

At home, everything smelled different. The wind and the light swept over Pozsonyi Street. In the thick of town, many things stood in the way. At home I could at least hope that one day I would understand the words, that I would understand them in the sense the grown-ups used them, but the smells, unless we happened to be smelling the stench of the corpses or the stench of the open sewers, were mostly pleasant. These smells came from the Danube, the Danube had a summer smell and it had a winter smell, and these changed from day to day; they came from Margaret Island, the scent of lilacs and jasmine, and also, there was the Julius Meinl shop with its yellow tiled display window, where every time someone opened the door, the smell of coffee from the red copper coffee roaster came pouring out, while another dangerously attractive smell wafted out from under the stack of smoked fish covered with cellophane, and also it came wafting from the licorice and the silk candy. The women brought with them and they took with them the penetrating scent of their perfumes, nail polish, face powder, and lipstick, each of which I loved separately. I virtually caressed those feminine scents, I was ready to lose myself in them, ready, always, to go in the wake of still newer and newer scents so I could inhale them and weigh their value in the balance.

Guests brought the smoke of their fine cigarettes and with the cakes on paper trays wrapped in white tissue paper, the sweet and creamy, coffee and tobacco-smoke scents of the best cake shops in the neighborhood.

In short, what in her home my grandmother called *gezerah* and nothing but *gezerah*, here, on Pozsonyi Street, meaning the center of the universe, everyone else called a rumpus, a melee, a circus, a free-for-all, and so much else.

But why would she have said it.

She didn't say it.

At most she wiped it up.

She wiped it up.

But then, in our home we didn't wash ourselves like this anyway, not in the middle of the kitchen, and not in a basin.

All the while, I could tell by her tone that in her language, Grandmother's *gezerah* bore several other meanings as well.

It is a Yiddish word of Hebrew origin and it means a big to-do, a circus, chaos, pandemonium.

In the case under discussion, in my grandmother's language it meant that I should wash myself properly and not spare my neck, my shoulders, my back, my underarms or my arms, but at the same time I shouldn't splash the water all over the place, I shouldn't make a mess, I should make sure the kitchen floor doesn't get all wet, because she has so many other things to attend to. She must finish the Sunday lunch by the time the noonday church bell rings. For decades no day passed without her making breakfast, lunch, and dinner for her daughters and bed tenants, if they had also paid for meals, and especially my grandfather, who took his meager lunch to the Holló Street workshop in a small pot, but on Sunday, she stood in her kitchen like a great actress suffering from stage fright. Won't the meat be tough, won't the semolina dumplings be harder than they should be. But in her language *gezerah* in a figurative sense could mean reluctance, postponement, what's more a reference to some especially egregious impropriety. Very often, my grandmother spoke to my grandfather in Yiddish, except my grandfather couldn't speak Yiddish, so he answered in Hungarian or German. He spoke to my grandmother in grammatically correct, properly formed German, though let me add, in the language of the Monarchy. When over two decades later, in June 1968, I went to see Ida Kamińska's doomed Jewish theater in Warsaw on two consecutive nights, and in the moment after the last I even saw her in person on stage, I was surprised to discover that thanks to my grandmother, I more or less understood Yiddish.

But back then in Péterfy Sándor Street, this great big *gezerah* was not an unfamiliar word, just sinister and inexplicable. In the original Hebrew it doesn't mean splash or splatter at all, but a decree or ordinance. On the other hand, with a surprising twist, in the Yiddish of Galicia and throughout Podolia, it became synonymous with pogrom. The Polish aristocratic hordes came and the dashing Cossacks on their horses came so that with lynching, fire, and murder they should wipe the burden of their IOUs off the face of the earth for the greater glory of God. As the wise rabbi Tamás Raj writes in his Yiddish dictionary, in this part of the world, the 1905 pogrom in Kishinev was not the first big *gezerah*. In Ukraine, Bohdan Khmelnytsky, who led a terrible pogrom against the Jews that began in 1648 and spared neither the children, virgins, or the aged, throwing them on pyres or putting them to the sword, is still celebrated as a national hero, and year after year, the inheritors of his spiritual and intellectual heritage followed his example ritually, as it were. The change of meaning in Yiddish is not gratuitous in the least, but refers to a commotion and upheaval that is repeated with a certain preordained regularity. By all odds, the original Russian meaning of *pogrom* has also contributed to the change of meaning. As a noun, it means thunder, tempest, devastation, while the verb that comes from the root means devastate, destroy. This meaning became so embedded in the local Jewish consciousness that in midsummer, meaning the twentieth day of the month of Sivan, the Jews of this wide Polish, Russian, and Ukrainian territory hold a day of fasting, which was later observed even by those who managed to escape and pass to the other side of the borders of the Monarchy.

I could have known about pogroms at the age of four, but I didn't.

I lived through the Holocaust; thanks to the bravery of my parents and relatives and their Communist self-respect I am its humble survivor, but two years after the Holocaust, as they washed themselves in my grandmother's kitchen, no one thought that they'd lived through a holocaust. Not yet. For a long time after the siege, the people of Pest had another word for what had happened. In Budapest, you died during the siege or you survived the siege. With the use of this word, the people of Budapest veritably placed the war and the genocide, in short, the mass extermination of an entire group of people, in the category of natural inevitability. The siege. This served as the noun and the cover name, too, for what had happened. I didn't know about the *gezerah*, I wasn't aware of the changes in meaning it carried, brought about by history; still, the way my grandmother said it, there was no ignoring the sinister undertones of the word.

For a long time, a very long time, in the language of Budapest the siege was the umbrella term used to signify a historical watershed. Irrespective of religion, party affiliation, social standing, or the role people may have played in the siege, they could characterize the event in what one might call a neutral manner, thus negating the need to mention the murderous Arrow Cross or the aggressive Russians. This, too, was part of the deal. With recourse to the word *siege*, people could refer, under one breath, to the events they'd survived, the scope and significance of which had not yet been fully explored or understood, while at the same time they could avoid venturing into a territory in need of further scrutiny. Those who used the word *siege* had lived through the siege, and to the last man experienced it as a catastrophe that wreaked havoc on the urban order of things the likes of which Europe had not seen since. People living outside Budapest did not use it, because they had not lived through the siege and couldn't have known what the unrelenting human catastrophe of the 102 days of the siege entailed, just as they did not know what the reconstruction might mean, even though this more or less eighteen-month-long but never completed operation was closely related to the siege. Though it never regained its best aspect of ten years before, by 1947 the city was basically livable again. People in the countryside didn't know either that this was a catastrophe from which, despite the best-meant efforts, full recovery was not possible. At most the street names remained as they were, but as a result of the siege, the character of city life suffered a sea change. Possibly Buda had experienced something similar under Ottoman rule, the part of the city that has remained silent and tongue-tied ever since.

After the siege the character of city life suffered a sea change if for no other reason, because after the catastrophe, Hungarian society became newly stratified. The peasantry was given a role it did not have previously, but at the same time, it was deprived of a role for which it could find no substitute, and when as a consequence of the two big influxes of the early fifties and the mid-sixties, the numbers of those coming from the countryside grew by leaps and bounds, the concept of the siege gradually lost currency. To the newcomers deprived of their lands or else chased off their lands, the word meant nothing. At the same time, there was no other mutually agreed-on word for what had happened, and the 102 days of the siege fell prey to oblivion.

In our home on Pozsonyi Street we washed ourselves standing by the sink or sitting in the tub, and if I made a big puddle, worse comes to worst, I had to wipe up the stone floor after myself. Actually, it was not stone but black-and-white tile, so-called mettlach tile; I didn't understand this either, why did they say mettlach if it was stone. But they were so insistent that I clean up after myself, and it went without saying that no one else would do it for me, that it didn't really matter whether they were consistent in their use of language; this wiping up was so inherently part of Creation and the universal order that I did it before I knew what I was about. And so it is to this day. I have never left a puddle for others to clean up, not even when I was ill. Maybe just once, but even then shamefaced, I said to Magda, calling her by her pet name, Pony dear, for once I'm leaving it just as it is.

Also, at home on Pozsonyi Street, we didn't have to do our number one or number two sitting on the potty, like at my grandmother's home, because the toilet was not outside on the landing; we didn't share a toilet with others; the potty belonged to my earliest childhood. I was safely weaned off the potty very early on, and so we didn't keep a chamber pot even under the bed. We didn't have immediate neighbors either. We lived on the seventh floor, there was nothing else there except the laundry room and the mysterious, huge attic behind a big wrought-iron door. This was my profane place of worship, this deserted, several-stories-high art nouveau attic, where the lights delivered their first lecture, my introduction to metaphysics and theology. At my grandmother's, the shared toilet was situated on the landing between two floors, where she had to take the chamber pot filled with the previous night's contents that she'd carefully covered with a copy of *Népszava*. Whenever she railed, for all she was worth, against the dirty goyim, meaning her neighbors, with whom she'd just been billing and cooing out on the balcony, we could be sure that she would have to wash the stone floor after them again and scrape their vomit off the wall again. They left it, let the Jewess clean up after them, may their hands dry off. For a long time I didn't understand this either, this goyim, who according to my grandmother stink from alcohol night and day and who are not human beings but murderers. They're going to kill you. They're our murderers. But don't take it to heart. They were born murderers. They haven't done it yet, we're still here, but don't you worry, they'll get you tomorrow. In our own home on Pozsonyi Street, there were no Jews, there were no goyim, there were no murderers, meaning that it never occurred to me that there might be, or that anyone might stink from alcohol, because I don't remember anyone talking this way about others. At least, I don't remember anything of the sort from the first ten years of my life. I will gain close acquaintance with these words and emotions only when I turn eleven and we will move to Svábhegy, up in Buda. But once there, I'll get my share of the most perfidious Jewish persecution possible with its entire glossary of terms in tow, though I won't understand it because in my own autistic manner I hadn't understood my grandmother's previous references to it either. In my early childhood years, these words were tied to the house in Péterfy Sándor Street, and later to the mental image my mind retained of the houses in Dembinszky and Damjanich streets, but they remained expressions, my grandmother's peculiar expressions. I considered them incidental, local peculiarities, in short, an indication of the abundance of language at variance with the norm and the desirable. When my grandmother spoke in the plural, it never occurred to me that I might be part of this plural.

For a long time, for a very long time, I was convinced that these strange beings, these goyim, breed only in these houses or around our neighborhood, in Chicago, this is what the locals called this part of town. This was their language, the language of Elemér Street, Hernád Street, Bethlen Square, and Nefelejcs Street, but first and foremost, it was my grandmother's language, and I was under the impression that people don't talk like this anywhere else. I kept a close watch, I kept an eye out, but even so I couldn't tell who might be a goy, in short, who might be my potential murderer, or who might not be a human being. The city was brimming with marvelous and frightening verbal flourishes. But this particular flourish oppresses me so much, I didn't even dare ask my grandmother how she knows, and what makes a goy a goy. Goy. A goy is someone who is not Jewish. This much I understood, but nothing more. I didn't understand Jewish either. I kept waiting for Grandmother to tell me. That's one ugly goy, take it from me. But even the better-looking goyim, even the handsomest of them, she called ugly. There was something about them that prompted her to call them ugly, but I couldn't see what she saw. She hid what she saw behind the words she used. My grandmother was a proper racist, but some time before this obvious fact, born of firsthand experience, penetrated my conscious mind as, with her racist conviction, she easily went one better on the dictates of aesthetics and ethics. She held everyone in disdain who was not born a Jew. But she disdained apostate Jews even more than the goyim. If she had had her way, she'd have liked to step over their dead bodies. But considering that she had to let them live, she'd have at least liked to look right through them, as if through a glass pane. They're not Jews. Which meant that from birth, these Jews boil milk in the same pot they use for making their fatty soups, they stuff themselves with *khazer*, pork, the most repulsive cold cuts, patés, bologna, mortadella, salami, you name it.

My grandmother did not mince her words. You live like pigs. Meaning us. Meaning her apostate daughters, all three of them.

Not that she believed in anything. She believed in nothing. She had some remnant of the concept of God in her, but there was no coherence in the way she used the concept. Before the siege, Grandfather would go to the synagogue on major holidays, but never my grandmother. Sometimes she even showed a preference for variants of the Christian concept of God taken from the slang of Pest, and so now and then even the Virgin Mary would make a guest appearance in her sentences, while at other times she'd resort to the Hasidic variant of the Orthodox Jewish concept of God, taken from Yiddish. No wonder I couldn't understand this religious, ethical, social, and racist hodgepodge of concepts. People said that so-and-so is a great Christian, all the while that curses and maledictions came pouring from between his lips. Just like my grandmother. In this regard there was no visible difference between Christians and Jews. If a young person took a good look around, he couldn't even discover two variants of hypocrisy. There was just one modern-day variant, a shared mental variant rooted in some magical consciousness. She, too, resorted to racism, hatred, and self-hatred to fill up the void left by the absence of God, just like those who resorted to hatred in the name of Christianity or the Magyar nation, then as well as now.

From time to time, we had ham in my home; there was a big slaughterhouse on the corner of Rudolf Square and Lipót Boulevard, they always had mortadella, which I liked, if for no other reason than because of its sound; the slaughterhouse had three entrances, one on Lipót Boulevard, the other on Rudolf Square, for me a source of elemental joy, going in one door, out another; the third entrance was a sort of service entrance, it was generally left wide open because there was no other way of airing out the place, and it was through this door that they carried the sides of pork and the sides of beef, and it was through there that the iceman hauled the blocks of ice over his shoulders, but in this part of the city I honestly never experienced disdain of any sort toward anyone at all. I now know that in this respect my immediate family was the exception, which is one reason I didn't come up against these expressions and racial prejudice, and this is why I could remain deaf and blind even toward my own exclusionist bent. The weak signals that nevertheless reached my consciousness even in this milieu I had no way of deciphering. My mind ordered or systematized this subunit of the material I stored, the concepts that remained unelucidated, along with their frequently used expressions, only much later, on the basis of more recently acquired experience. At home, the Hungarian words they used did not carry a strong emotional charge. First and foremost they carried meaning, and their meaning contained their emotional charge, and never the other way around.

I adopted the family's approved way of creating meaning before I could construe the general meaning or the special use of words, and by all odds, I must have imagined that this is the only mode of creating meaning in the world.

I had to find a way of keeping the worlds I came to know in balance, which was no mean feat, because they did not overlap either linguistically, emotionally, or structurally, nor could they be placed on an equal footing with recourse to the principles of their own systems. A system that strives for exclusiveness will not tolerate the striving for equality, and my parents strove for exclusiveness, though it was an exclusiveness that, to be sure, surpassed the exclusivity that characterized racism. When I tried to use a word in line with my grandmother's racist recipe, a word that to her meant something inconceivably different, I did so in order to please her, even flatter her. Or maybe I wanted to force her to show her hand. My grandmother had said that her good kosher butcher was on Garay Square and we were in fact standing on her storybook Garay Square at her good kosher butcher. Except this good kosher butcher of hers wasn't easy for me to understand because the good kosher meant something ritual, and rational thinking can't comprehend the ritual. Which to me meant that the good kosher on Garay Square is ceremoniously separated from the bad kosher. And if it's that obvious to Grandmother, I might as well say to her, for all to hear, let's buy some good little mortadella. Because at home, on the corner of Lipót Boulevard, we must have been buying bad mortadella. This was my point of departure. That we don't have a good kosher butcher, and the good kosher mortadella is sold by the good kosher butcher. Which made them laugh so hard that Grandmother's good kosher butcher very nearly buckled under behind the counter along with his big kosher knives. Good mortadella. What an idea. He sharpened his knife by scraping it against another knife. Before he cut the meat with it, he always sharpened it first. Which was another thing that scared me. *Butchered* was one of those rare words I never had a problem making sense of. A butcher is someone who butchers the animal, and he has a butchery they call a slaughterhouse for cutting up the meat, this is where he sharpens his knives, and his knife slides through the meat as if it were butter. Sometimes they sink the knife into a man's flesh, they butcher him, like they do a helpless animal. The great mass of small differences and relationships made your brain spin before at long last you understood, or once and for all misunderstood them, in which case you had no more problems with them. My family's love of the rational dictated that no difference can be small enough to be ignored, it couldn't be small enough for me to ignore, and I must make sense of it and understand it. Accordingly, it would have been difficult for me to accept that the poetic, the anecdotal and the ritualistic, all that my grandmother's mind operated with so freely, could not be translated into something rational.

The two conceptual functions have different structures and have nothing in common. In her lexicon, good did not mean some universal good, but what was good for her, some particular good, which is due only to the Jews from the God of the Jews. And there's the rub. Because in our home on Pozsonyi Street, or at the homes of my father's sisters on Teréz Boulevard and Dobsinai Street, or at the homes of my father's two brothers on the odd side of Pozsonyi Street and out on Verpeléti Street, or at my father's aunts' homes on Benczúr and Duna streets, it's not that they didn't err in their thinking or that they were not narrow-minded, but that they did not cultivate the language of racism or even the language of antiracist racism. You'd think they were inoculated against it, all the while that postwar Europe veritably wallowed in the joy of racist antiracism. I had to get my bearings among my father's five surviving siblings, two dead siblings, and the husbands, wives, widows, aunts, and cousins, but I never experienced prejudice or scorn of a racial hue, they did not practice racial discrimination against anyone, not even against themselves. In this milieu, being Jewish bore no special significance because it had no significance to begin with. In our family, no one considered every single German a Nazi, whereas no one had closer ties to the legal as well as the illegal antifascist movements than they. Unintentionally, meaning indirectly, even those members of the family had ties to the antifascist movement, which was a political movement and not a racist movement, who tried to distance themselves from ideologically charged political movements of all kinds. But they couldn't have considered every single German a Nazi anyway, because they had German comrades who as antifascists were risking their lives in their own German homeland. There were also others who were neither Communists nor antifascist; there was Bach, Goethe, Thomas Mann, and Beethoven, and you certainly couldn't say that they were not German. I first read *The Book of Songs* as an older child, but it took several more attempts and several decades before it occurred to me that Heine was a German who was also a Jew, or a Jew who couldn't have been more German had he tried. By the same token and in line with the dictates of rational thinking, I couldn't have imagined that Molière or Shakespeare were anything but Jewish.

I could never have formulated an emotionally compact, lucid universe in my mind on the basis of racist principles, because I lacked the concept of racism for it. On the contrary. For a long time, possibly for a criminally long time, I was unaware of a universe coordinate with racist vernacular. For a long time, I was not aware that there were people for whom the existence of an exclusively racist universe was a given. In the countryside, this works more like a tribal or family universe. Not that the people around me did not know about this real, functioning racist or tribal universe. But they didn't share this knowledge with me, not because they wanted to save me from it, but surely, because they understood the world they shared with the racists on the basis of another dictionary, and it had been like this and continued to be like this in the family, generation after generation. Hand in hand with its full storehouse of significations, all the expressions tied to racism were included in the dictionary of liberal thinking, but these expressions had no effect on the system of thought and ideation of liberal thinking and thus did not affect the system of ideation either.

It is nearly certain that a child comprehends the structure of ideation much earlier than the various words and their dictionary meaning. As for the children around me, they did not share the definitions in their own racist dictionary with me. I would remember it. They either lacked such a dictionary themselves, or else they had one, but because of my relatives' liberal-minded, civil-rights-oriented thinking, for a long time I was unreceptive to it.

If I wasn't confronted with racist thinking at home, it wasn't because my parents and relatives tried to hide their racism behind the language they used, and it wasn't because they were so afraid of it, they didn't even dare mention it. By all odds, they wanted to continue their lives where they had left off before the siege, and at the same time they wanted new lives for themselves. They would have considered it unworthy to engage in discourse about ancient beliefs, tensions, and social policy movements in the language of those beliefs and the intellectual level that belong to them which, thanks to various new scientific methods, they would soon get rid of and progress beyond anyway. This is what they are striving for, this is what they are about at this very moment. They are interested in causes and effects. The conservative liberal, or the liberal democratic perspective was one of the traditionally preferred attitudes in the family; in short, the abandonment of the idea of exclusion in favor of the principle of free choice and equality before the law; the other was the Communist ideal of equality, meaning the introduction of the ideal of absolutism in the form of proletarian dictatorship based on class principle, but in the interest of eliminating class principle. Though these were not reconcilable models of renewal by any means, each being functional only within its own system of logic, still, in the interest of the rationality they held in common, the Communist, liberal democratic, and conservative liberal members of my family shied away from conflict both within the family as well as outside of it. When they avoided calling the prolis trash, the Slovaks dull, the Vlachs hair-footed, the peasants stinking, the whores dirty sluts, the bourgeoisie decadent, the Communists filthy, the Blacks repulsive, and the gypsies odious, just as they avoided casting aspersions on the Christians, the Jews, or the Hottentots, they were rejecting the emotion-charged epithets of racist vocabulary. It goes without saying that my parents were atheists; they considered religion the opiate of the masses, and undoubtedly, they did everything they could to help eliminate the various churches; I even have documents to that effect, but they did not revile the various religions, or the priests of the various churches and religions; in short, they did not engage in verbal religious warfare.

Not that they were angels; on the contrary, they wanted to take religion, which they considered misconceived, by the roots and eradicate it, pull it from the soil that had nourished it, and in order to achieve their aim, they did not even shy away from unlawful means to achieve their end. If someone made racist comments, my grandmother, for example, who tried to moderate herself in their presence, they would put her down without fail, they called her to order, or treated it as a joke, or spectacularly let it in one ear and out the other.

Such were their versions of dealing with verbal prejudice.

I became acquainted with the endemic perverse, racist outbreaks of Jewish and Hungarian self-hatred only at a much later date.

Until I was eight, I didn't even know that in the spirit of the Nuremberg Laws, rooted in anti-Semitism that went back thousands of years, I should regard myself as a Jew. It wouldn't have made any sense anyway. I couldn't very well think of myself as someone I was not. As a small child I wasn't concerned with my origins not because I was told that I shouldn't be, or because I was feeble-minded; it simply meant nothing to me. My parents didn't think that the intention behind the Nuremberg Laws applied to them, and possibly, I followed them in this respect rather more severely than ethics would have called for. They didn't say that they were Jewish, even as a form of verbal self-punishment. They were Communists, and that sufficed for them. Without conditions and restrictions attached, my mother was a Hungarian patriot, and the two things got along just fine inside her. When at the age of ten I would have liked to go to a Russian-language school, she cut me short with a single sentence. A Hungarian child should learn Hungarian literature. Which did the trick. She was not a Jew who also happened to be a Hungarian patriot, and she was not a patriot who was also a Hungarian Jew, it's just that, being a Communist, she did not accept the racial theory based on the misconception that a person carries his origins in his blood or cells along with all the characteristics accruing to it. My father, on the other hand, had his reservations about Hungarian patriotism, just like he had his reservations with respect to all manifestations of emotion. At the age of eight, when I said that I hated Jews because they crucified Jesus Christ, a statement I didn't realize was racist, I was the one who, with this statement, forced them to stand me in front of the hall mirror and confront me with the fact of my origin.

I was a Protestant, I attended a Protestant Bible class, and I took this sentence of Christian anti-Judaism home with me from Bible class. After all, I considered them truth-loving people, and the crucifixion bothered my sense of justice.

If I hate the Jews, I should look in the mirror, I'll see a Jew there, I can hate him all I want.

But instead of making me realize that I was Jewish, this shocking confrontation just made me realize that I must be more circumspect with my statements concerning my sense of justice, the things I know about, as well as the things I know nothing about. And so, in that mirror in the hall it was not the Jew that I recognized in myself but the anti-Semite, the narcissistic gut reaction of the anti-Semite to mete out justice, the feeling of revenge and murder. In short, they called my kind attention to the fine mechanism of reflection. First we gather the information, and only then do we formulate judgment. We verify the feelings and impulses with facts, when there I was, outraged at what the Jews had done to the Son of God, giving my outrage full rein, hoping to please them. When I looked in the mirror, it was clear to me that injustice had definitely been perpetrated, but the perpetrator was definitely not me. For one thing, I wasn't even born yet, and for another, several people were involved, and I'm not several people, just a single individual. In the mirror my mother confronted me with a problem of epistemology, and not necessarily the one she was hoping to confront me with. She would not allow normative judgment, and it was along these lines that I later found myself confronting not so much her personally, as her Communist notions. Nor did I have to wait long; nor was the confrontation what you'd call tame. Also, it was no less inevitable that in the wake of this confrontation I should come face-to-face with enough Jewish racism to last me a lifetime.

From all that I heard Grandmother say about the Jews it didn't follow logically at all that apart from my lineage I was the same kind of Jew as my grandmother, because my grandmother's anecdotal, lyrical, and ritual Jewish knowledge did not square with my grandfather's knowledge; what's more, every one of her ritual sentences or ritual gestures suffered a shipwreck on the rock of my grandfather's knowledge and ascetically rational use of language. I never saw or experienced anything that might have reconciled their dissonant knowledge and sense of the world, unless it was the fact that presumably they loved each other; earlier they may have even loved each other with a passion, even if to an outside observer it as often as not remains a mystery how two people who are as different as they could love each other to begin with.

And in that case, in this cataclysm of the senses and the understanding caused by our mere existence, what might be the standard or law of love and hate.

Be that as it may, in Péterfy Sándor Street, before our Sunday stroll, I had to put on my formal attire every time, my so-called Sunday best, my white shirt, my blue knee-length pants with the suspenders, and my white knee socks. Which in our home bore no significance either, even though we were familiar with the expression, Sunday best. His parents had my friend Laci Tavaly, the son of the superintendent, put on his Sunday best when they took him to church on Sunday. Linguistically, this Sunday best made Grandmother sympathize with Laci Tavaly more than her own family. I wasn't dim-witted, just autistic, I knew that there were several churches in the city, but that we didn't attend any of them, either on weekdays or on Sundays. Which wasn't quite true, because I'd go to church with Rózsi Németh. Still, logically, from the point of view of my atheist parents, it nevertheless followed that for those who do not go to church, a church has no function, and so they need not own a Sunday best. I didn't have one either or, put another way, everything I owned would double as my Sunday best, meaning that whatever my Tauber grandmother considered suitable became my Sunday best. There was a Reformed church on Pozsonyi Street, a rather imposing structure that suffered some

damage during the siege where, without my knowing what was happening and why, I was properly baptized at the age of six, and from
then on Rózsi Németh was not only our maid, she was also my god-
mother. There was also a very mysterious synagogue hidden in the
backyard of a house in Csáky Street where Weiss's mother did the
cleaning, and I don't know why, but sometimes when Rózsi Németh
came to pick me up in my kindergarten on Lipót Boulevard, we'd take
Weiss there to his mother, and then, at least once, Mrs. Weiss gave me
some leftover baked beans, what they called cholent. This delicacy
whose taste was new to me was very thick, and since I couldn't store
its name in any other section of my mind, from then on, cholent to
me became a subcategory of bean dishes. There are many kinds of
bean dishes stored there, just as there are many kinds of stairwells. By
the time I got to taste this bit of leftover bean dish, they had probably
eaten the smoked goose, the shreds of beef brisket, and the hardboiled
eggs, but fortunately, the barley retained their taste. As for Weiss, because of their baked beans or for some other reason, he decided that
we were friends. Maybe because they told him that I was Jewish. But
I already had Laci Tavaly for a friend and I didn't want anyone else.
Also, try as I might, I couldn't make the connection between cholent
and friendship. On the other hand, Weiss had told me that only Jews
eat cholent, and I didn't want to give that up, so I was hoping that I'd
be taken to their church again, which they called a synagogue, and
that I would get some more leftover cholent again. I wanted to stay
in the vicinity of their thick baked beans, which included not only
beans, but also puffed-up barley, which, when you bite into it, scrapes
the roof of your mouth in a pleasant way. In an utterly selfish manner,
as a true egoist, I approached their Jewish existence through my taste
buds. I also liked this expression, roof of the mouth, the idea that the
mouth has a roof. Mother even said that if I touch the roof of my
mouth with the tip of my tongue, I will even feel the tiles. Be that as
it may, for a long time, for a very long time, until I was at least thirty,
I was under the impression that a person has only one friend. Maybe
girls have more than one at a time. And my friend goes to a Catholic
church. Also, I couldn't stand Weiss. I avoided him because he had

a runny nose, though I saw no compelling argument for associating this awkward happenstance with the synagogue, the Jews, myself, or anything else. But the cholent tied me to him, the hope of getting more, and in the interest of getting it, I even put up with his runny nose. I don't remember ever eating cholent at Grandmother Tauber's. After she died, my Aunt Bözsi, Erzsébet Tauber, called me and said I should come over, because she's finally made me some really good cholent. We'd been looking forward to it for some time, and she didn't cook it, but baked it, the way it should be done. It had everything in it that should be in it, smoked breast of goose and brisket of beef, barley and eggs baked in the shell. If they had eaten it, my grandparents would have eaten it on Saturday, but I remember nothing of the sort, even though on weekends I spent quite some time with them in Péterfy Sándor Street.

Also, the synagogue in Csáky Street was full of wonders. It was gloomy, mysterious, with many corners, and it had an obscure brilliance thanks to the colorful stained-glass windows. Of course, this was not the first time I saw glass windows that shed a dark brilliance. I knew that the heavy ornamentation with which the synagogue people prevent the light from coming in and piercing the gloom was supposed to be beautiful. The eclectic architecture of Budapest entertained a special fondness for stained glass and used it in the most unexpected places, in the staircase landings of the private residences of the haute bourgeoisie, in their curtained-off anterooms, winter gardens, dining rooms, and even in their bathrooms. The fashion for stained-glass windows lasted for at least fifty architectural years. Having held its own even through the so-called historical styles, the neo-Romantic, the neo-Gothic and the neo-Renaissance, it enjoyed a revival in Art Nouveau and Art Deco architecture, and was even present in the neo-Baroque and neo-Classical styles that were in fact profoundly pagan, even if they considered themselves Christian. In Budapest, stained-glass windows, domes, and roofs had a grandmaster in the person of Miksa Róth, who could play the scales of all these periods and styles. He left behind many followers ready and eager to work, and they received plenty of commissions. The citizens of Pest, rich and poor alike, loved this colorfully filtered light, which to them was synonymous with luxury, and which architecture committed to practicality could not abide. The adherents of stained glass with its unabashed ornamentality were hoping to emulate church architecture, but instead, they imbued profane architecture with a spiritual touch that the stucco-embellished landing of an apartment house in Nefelejcs Street had as little of as the bathroom of a wealthy luggage manufacturer. All the same, they were at the height of their profession when the siege of the city interrupted their endeavors.

At the time just before the siege, Miksa Róth was already training the third generation of stained-glass makers. The master was seventy-nine, he lived and worked in Nefelejcs Street in an imposing house and workshop in the heart of the busy city he had built to his specifications. He was the recipient of every conceivable prize, he was addressed as Your Grace, he was chief state counselor, he made the stained-glass windows of the country's public buildings, including Parliament, but all the same, he was not among those naïve people who were blind to what was about to happen in the world. He wanted to round off his life. He wrote and had his memoirs published, and in the following year, in January 1944, he wrote his last will and testament. In this he appointed not his children, neither his two daughters nor his son as his heirs, but his older sister's son, Artúr, Artúr Elek, the distinguished writer and art historian, and himself no longer young. Elek, a man of many accomplishments, received his forced labor summons on April 23, 1944, at the age of sixty-eight. The following day he wrote to those professional friends of his who were so-called Christians but in fact were profoundly pagan, and who were spared his fate. To Lajos Fülep, a well-known colleague who was wholly insensitive to the lives of others, he wrote that he has accomplished what he came to do on this earth, he does not wish to experience any more than he already had to experience through no fault of his own, and he is ending his life in protest at the dehumanization of the world, the wearing of the yellow star, the ghettos, and the deportations. At dawn the next day, he made good on his promise.

Last night I mused over the date of Artúr Elek's voluntary death and I mused over the date of Miksa Róth's own death. I asked Tibor Fényi, the director of the Miksa Róth Museum, if there is a connection between the two dates. Simply put, he wrote in an e-mail just a couple of hours later, Artúr was Miksa's best-loved relative. His two daughters and his son had no feel for the arts. From the moment he learned what had happened to Artúr, he took to his bed and never got up again. The family feared for his life; they knew that his title of chief state counselor would not protect him. Their father wouldn't even be saved by the fact that in 1897, on the day before he married Josefina Wall, a Catholic of Moravian descent, he was baptized under the stained-glass windows and mosaics he had designed in St. Steven's Basilica, which at the time was still known as the Leopold Town Basilica. In the summer of the previous year he had already asked the rector of the basilica for forged documents attesting to his parents' baptism, but in a letter written in no uncertain terms, the rector rejected his request. The forged baptismal certificates were later issued by the rector of the originally Gothic Roman Catholic church of Keszthely, rebuilt in the baroque style in 1747 and decorated with the stained-glass windows Róth had designed and made. But the family was nevertheless afraid that the forgery would not help them. Indeed, they were far too well known throughout the country for the forgery to be of use to them. A doctor acquaintance of theirs admitted Róth, who was by then a shrunken old man who had refused to speak for a month and a half after Artúr's death, to his hospital on Balassa Street, which was also decorated with his stained-glass windows, until it was hit by a bomb, that is. Róth hadn't yet died in his hospital bed when the cartographers of the Wehrmacht appropriated his house and workshop, until the cartographers of the Soviet army moved in, that is. After Miksa's merciful death, his son József succumbed under the weight of recent events. József had graduated from the renowned Fasori Lutheran Secondary School, whose church had also been decorated by his father's stained glass. He received his Ph.D. in economics, but he never again left the one room the Arrow Cross assigned to them, and even after the siege he just sat quietly in a chair, staring into space, and he never spoke to anyone, ever again, until his own death a couple of years later.

Indeed, why would I have thought that I had anything to do with the secret synagogue with its mysterious lights located in the murky depths of the yard of an apartment building on Csáky Street, when my nose wasn't running, a dirty handkerchief wasn't hanging from the suspenders of my pants, and though my mother was undoubtedly also a woman, she was not a cleaning woman in the Csáky Street synagogue; at most she cleaned along with the servant, who in our home was called a domestic, whereas in our building on Pozsonyi Street, women of such low birth and menial position were invariably called servants and were addressed strictly by their first name. Servants were not entitled to family names. Gentlemen's drivers, cooks, tenant farmers, and field hands were not entitled to family names either. Or else it was the other way around. My great-grandfather's valet, Planck, for instance, was entitled only to his surname; it was his first name they had deprived him of. Only Rozália Németh, who worked for us, retained both her names, Rózsi, who on Sunday went to the Reformed church on Pozsonyi Street with her book of psalms and, with the approval of my parents, took me along with her. There we met her older sister Juliska, who'd been serving at Doctor Szemző's home on Visegrádi Street since before the siege.

My Aunt Özsi had two best friends from when she was a girl, they graduated high school together, then they attended the Industrial Drafting School together, where my aunt was studying to be a gold- and silversmith; strangers called one of her friends Mrs. Szemző, but to her friends she was Topi, while the other of her two best friends they called Margit Gráber, but throughout her long life her friends affectionately called her Médi; she became a painter, not a significant painter, but a reliable one, the wife of the painter Csaba Vilmos Perl- rott, far better known than she, but both belonged to the first big wave of modern Hungarian art known as the Nagybánya School, as well as the Kecskemét School and the Szentendre Schools, and both their paintings hung on the walls of our apartment on Pozsonyi Street.

Just three paintings on the whitewashed walls, nothing else. Two of them have been my steady companions. The third, the most mysterious, a beautiful pastel by Gráber, is hanging on the wall of my brother's living room. I couldn't take my eyes off the house standing in the depths of a garden that lacks a door and has only a blind window. The minute they'd brought me back from kindergarten, or when I came home from school alone, I would go look at it; I never grew tired of its muted, fractured colors.

Juliska Németh, who served as a maid in Doctor Szemző's home, was always sitting in the pews already, having reserved places next to her for the two of us, her younger sister and her younger sister's godson.

Those who'd worked in our home before, Irén Turi and Rozália Kiss, as well as those who came after them, Eszter Horváth and Szidónia Tóth, also had surnames, we didn't deprive them of their surnames, because in our home they were not servants. My father taught me that sometimes things accrue to words that won't leave them ever again, even if, for the most part, the words themselves are innocent. For instance, in the past *domestic* didn't mean someone who helped keep house, it meant child, a person who belonged to the family. And so we didn't have servants in our home, we had domestics.

If Apáka and Mamáka don't mind, because in line with what I called them, Rózsi Németh called them the same, Apáka and Mamáka, I will now take Péter along to church. She also said, Petyonka and I are going to church. Petyonka and Petyusha were leftovers of my mother's Russian studies from before the siege. Rózsi laughed a great deal, all her words and gestures were ironic, sharp, she placed everything between quotation marks, she never tired of playing. She couldn't keep herself from doing it, she kept challenging the narrow limits of language, she confronted clichés head on only to pass beyond them. She was a hefty woman with glasses, altogether lacking in charm, but everything that she said or did was clear, direct, to the point, open and cheerful. Her actions had no frills attached. For simplicity's sake, today I'd say that she was a warmhearted person who hijacked every one of her sentences to prevent herself from sounding sentimental. Her clothes were puritan to the extreme, a strange mixture of country style and city style. She didn't wear kerchiefs, but she didn't wear hats or caps either. She insisted that she's not Hungarian but Cumanian. That's why her hair is like a beehive. These bones and this hair, they're Cumanian. Cumanian to the bitter end. But this Cumanian was more like a game. She's a stiff-necked Puritan, a stiff-necked peasant. Her raven hair resisted the comb. For her, there was no other church. Her infinitely patient, persistently cheerful, round, red-cheeked face with the round glasses bore the traces of great bursts of laughter. Why wouldn't I have gone willingly with Rózsi Németh, who always smelled of soap, to her church, and why wouldn't I have liked listening to the minister whom my parents had known during the siege, and who gave them blank forms to forge papers or, to resort to my parents' use of words, he was a decent man. So I went.

Once the worshippers were seated, they made a lot of noise in the pews, they felt around, looking for their hymnals. Rózsi Németh didn't have to feel around because she brought her own with her. They cleared their throats, they coughed, they made scraping sounds on the black-and-white floor with their shoes. The sunken panels of the coffered ceiling were painted sky blue and the edges of the latticework night-blue, and the silvery stars shone on these. The light came from up high, along the length of the walls of the nave, through the ten tall, narrow windows situated above the galleries that in the language of architecture they call lancet windows. The light entered in wide shafts, revealing the floating particles of dust. In the shade of the galleries, in this continuous dance of light and dark, in the continual appearance and disappearance of light that was itself laded with refracted light, after the singing had stopped, it was quiet once again. Let us not forget, we are on the flatlands of Pest, barely a stone's throw from the mirror surface of the waters of the Danube, where the winds coming from the hills of Buda veritably waft over us as they move the clouds along with them. A bit more scraping, shifting about, coughing. As the minister approached the pulpit in his black robe, the stairs creaked, but there was plenty of room left in the general reverence for the creaking. The order of the universe, if indeed remnants of it had survived at all in the city that stood in ruins, regained its dignity thanks to its ordered Sundays, as far as I was concerned, at any rate, just like Grandmother Tauber's steaming soup that she served promptly at the ringing of the noonday bell after Grandfather Tauber and I returned from our walks in City Park or our visits to Janka Tauber. I also liked the lack of decoration in Rózsi Németh's church, and I liked the voice of the minister, too, the congregation as they sang, the meaning of the hymns sung in an antiquated language used nowhere else, and the way the black marble columns articulated the interior whose whiteness and darkness couldn't have differed that much from the white and black tiles of our apartment's floor on Pozsonyi Street.

The rationality inherent in renunciation and asceticism, what the modernist architects of the period aptly called rational form and which they pitted against the mannerisms of the various stylistic schools, was already imprinted on my retinae. The two old aunts from Duna and Benczúr streets, Anna Mezei, meaning Fat Baby, and Erzsébet Mezei, meaning Záza, were the great exceptions in the family, whereas a couple of decades earlier, at a time when Záza's pink salon served as the family's be-all and end-all of good taste, they must have been the arbiters of style. I even knew why this salon was pink. It was pink because Lipót Strelisky, the celebrated portrait photographer of the age, photographed Erzsébet Mezei's mother, who was born in Vienna as Eugénia Schlesinger and who died when Erzsébet was still a child, took her photograph wearing a pink evening gown with a décolletage and yellow roses pinned in her hair, and later Vilma Parlaghy painted her full-length portrait in the same gown. Subsequently, Záza used this color for the tapestry and upholstery of her salon. Now, as they retreated behind the stuccos and vestibules of the shell-shocked facades of their homes, they attempted to save what could still be saved by parading the seeming abundance of their eclectic frippery, velvets, silk wallpapers, upholstery, and drapes, even though the need to keep up socially sanctioned appearances was gone. The bearer bonds of the Capital City of Budapest, made out in Hungarian and German in crowns, had lost their value along with the Hungarian Trans-Nubian Electric Company's portfolios, whose handy, easily detachable coupons promising a 6.5 percent yield were a thing of the past, as well as the Trieste-based Assicurazioni Generali's property insurance securities made out in gold pengős and bound by strings representing the national colors.

The apartments of my father's sisters and brothers, on the other hand, were furnished in line with the dictates of simplicity, austerity, and functional aesthetics; in short, in line with rational forms. Accordingly, for a long time, for a very long time, as far as I was concerned, this style represented the only option for the future.

I'm not implying that people didn't have their own individual style within our family's strict functionalism. In our own apartment, for instance, a confusion of styles prevailed. Among our strictly modernist furnishings that, in line with the strictures of the interior designers of the Bauhaus, combined black and white with terra-cotta, there stood the huge neo-Romantic pieces elaborately carved of ebony from the dining room at the manor house in Gömörsid that ended up with us, God only knows how, and even more surprisingly, the two baroque armchairs from Erzsébet Mezei's pink salon in Nagykorona Street that came down to her from great-grandmother's salon, nearly all the furniture from Grandmother Mezei's so-called informal salon, the miniature armchairs, sofa, and small tables from Pannónia Street. It was referred to as the green salon. In such cases, pink or green had to dominate not only the furniture upholstery and the drapes, but the wallpaper as well. In a proper bourgeois home, the smoking room opened from the living room, this was where the men removed themselves after meals so they could smoke their cigars or pipes, and from where you could see the study, whose door was left open only on special occasions. While the men smoked and drank cognac and argued over politics or discussed matters of business, in short, engaged in bragging, the female guests generally retreated to their hostess's salon and engaged in small talk about very prosaic matters. This room generally opened from the formal salon on the opposite side of the dining room. The study, the smoking room, the dining room, the formal salon, and the informal salon had to look out on the street and had to open from the reception room, whose thick, heavy drapes kept out the light, which was provided by a chandelier and sconces, and which faced the inner courtyard. When these conditions were met, people said that their apartment had six rooms. Which didn't even count as an haut bourgeois residence. The haut bourgeois residences were located on Stefánia Street, Vilma királyné Street, Sugár Boulevard, meaning Andrássy Boulevard; in these, besides the just-mentioned rooms, the mezzanine apartments also had a library, a picture gallery, a small separate room where the lady of the house wrote her letters, paid her bills, and so on. On the other hand, the proper six-room bourgeois home had other rooms as well that lay adjacent to the smoking room and the informal salon. After all, besides the rooms facing the street that were used when there were guests, there were bedrooms that faced the inner courtyard, and also the children's rooms, the bathroom, the governess's and the nursemaid's room, the linen room with its huge wardrobes, the chests for the tableware and all the things needed for the twice-weekly ironing that lasted a full day, and there was also a pantry and a kitchen, and farther down the maid's room permeated with the smell of constant cooking, and in more genteel homes where they also had a valet, possibly a butler, rooms for the domestics. In her own memoirs, when she wrote about the apartment in Pannónia Street, my Aunt Magda reticently admitted to six rooms. According to contemporary custom, only the rooms looking out on the street were considered proper rooms, the rest were there just because they were. Generally, people didn't even bother counting them. But in her devil-may-care manner, my Aunt Magda belies her bashful self when she provides further information. She writes that in such a big building there were only eight apartments, two to each floor. The rooms that went uncounted encircled the inner courtyard, sometimes a double courtyard.

Also, you knew that the next moment the voice of the minister, Albert Bereczky, would fill the hall, and this voice, trained in the delivery of rhetoric, further contributed to my post-siege sense of security. I loved Rózsi Németh at least as much as my mother. Regardless of the situation, I felt safe by her side. My mother was a lot more erratic. Sometimes she disappeared for weeks on end. She went to the countryside. We must not forget that after the siege the Communist women were responsible for rebuilding the system of socialist welfare. They raised social welfare out of the occasional acts of charity connected to the churches or women's associations, and as a consequence immediately found themselves in confrontation with the churches and the women's associations. But I stand as witness to the fact that getting the better of their abhorrence, holding their noses, so to speak, they did their utmost in the interest of cooperation. As a first step, they healed wartime wounds and organized a children's welfare service and a people's health-care service. They didn't want starving or orphaned children wandering about like stray dogs or misfits, whether on their own or in groups. They didn't want children to grow up with rickets, or women with goiters, or women squatting over washbowls forced to get rid of unwanted fetuses with knitting needles. They founded institutions to save children, though not in line with the visions of the various churches or women's associations, needless to say. They organized winter and summer camps for children, school lunches, summer day camps, one on Margaret Island, the other in Csillebérc, they organized a network of school physicians and the system of compulsory inoculation against childhood diseases. They organized health-care convoys, mobile clinics of sorts that set out from Budapest and went first and foremost to villages and isolated farmsteads with doctors, nurses, midwives, and they were fully equipped, including a laboratory and X-ray machines. They went to places where the people of the former large estates had been living on the level of medieval serfs and had never encountered such care in their entire lives. They set up an institutional system for curing endemic diseases, first and foremost, a nation- and countywide network to care for those with eye diseases and lung disease, trachoma and tuberculosis. In their eyes, the dramatically high child mortality rate and illiteracy were also endemic diseases. In the villages, the outlying farms, and the servants' quarters of the former large estates, they organized the teaching of writing to grown-ups. They organized a library network for schools and villages, they organized night schools and, in fact, the entire system of adult education. They set up a national and county-based network to care for infants and feed the children, they set up the network of trained health-care visitors, and since it was immediately evident that there were hardly any trained midwives and nurses, that the number of trained kindergarten teachers was practically nil, they set up a training network for them in just two years, and so on. All this took place after the siege in front of my very eyes, in about five years' time. Sometimes my mother took me along. Needless to say, time has buried all this underneath; in short, despite the fact that the networks and institutions are functioning to this day, the anti-Communist regressive gut instinct wiped out the memory of these social welfare pursuits.

Also, I trusted Rózsi because my mother, who was perpetually absent because of these things, loved her. She left me in her care for weeks on end without a second thought. Of course, she had no choice. She thought highly of Rózsi Németh's intelligence, though they probably never talked about such things. She first came to see us on a Sunday afternoon; she came for a visit to have a look at the family and, so to speak, to show herself to us. As soon as she walked down the hallway and as, still slightly self-conscious, she entered the living room, she and my mother came to an understanding. I don't know what happens at such times between people who do not know each other. Both had beautiful singing voices, sometimes they sang together, sometimes they had me sing along with them. Sometimes they had my father sing, too. Let's hear Apáka, yes, let's hear the counselor sing along, and they laughed so hard, their tears began to flow when, pleased by their request, Apáka joined them in their singing. Like his sisters and brothers, he had as much pitch as the deaf earth and as much of a singing voice as a cracked pot. Their relationship continued so untroubled that before the increased dose of morphine she was given to dull the growing pain had fully incapacitated her, my dying mother wanted to match them up. She asked Rózsi to marry Apáka, meaning our father. It would be the obvious solution. She tried to convince the two of them, and if only they had said yes, she would have surely passed away with a lighter heart. But her passing was difficult, made even more difficult by the act she put on for the benefit of her two sons, pretending that she was on the way to recovery. But both of them, Rózsi as well as my father, shied away from her suggestion.

This was the case when they stood by my mother's hospital bed alone, and this was the case when they stood there together.

Sometimes they would laugh for minutes on end, pushing and shoving each other, two immature adolescents chatting and singing as they carried the wicker basket home from the Lehel Square market, creaking with each step under the weight of the tomatoes and peaches for making jam; and they laughed as they carried the wash up to the attic, taking me along to help hang it out, or else they suddenly started talking about something over the heap of dirty clothes, and they were so engrossed, they sorted the clothes with less and less care, the whites go here, the colored there, the light wash was separate and the big wash separate, and as for me, they enjoyed sending me down to the living room to see if I could find them there. In which case, what objection could I have had against her church. None whatsoever.

This church is an exceptional example of Pest's architecture. Of which, for a long time to come, I had no idea, of course, even though my eyes and sense of proportion were as lively as they are now. Architect was thus added to the long list of all the things I wanted to be. The design of the church combines Imre Tóth's ideas of placement and Jenő Halászy's design for the bulk of the building. The cornerstone for the church was laid on April 25, 1937, and it was consecrated by Bishop László Ravasz on December 6, 1940. The siting of the church and its shape were dictated by the special geological characteristics of the site. One hundred years previously, before the Danube was constrained within bounds by heavy broad-stone ramparts, the Danube widened on this windy, flat area between Vizafogó and Újlipótváros, while its floodplain was even larger than its muddy and alluvial bay. Due to the winter and summer floods and the current that crashed into the tip of Margaret Island, the water formed a kind of elbow. The muddy floodplain was covered by sedge and bulrush. The area was reclaimed from the river not in accordance with the demands of city planning, but slowly, at the commodious pace with which steam mills were built at the end of the nineteeth century and with which the part of the city known as Újlipótváros was developed in the early twentieth century. They used the soil extracted during the ground-work to push back the floodplain. It was not economically feasible to build a structure of great weight on this reclaimed, barely just settled quagmire. In my child's eye, there was nothing but a desert behind the modernist blocks of houses of Újlipótváros. Not a bush anywhere. The area was so barren, you could see all the way to the Gödöllő Hills thirty kilometers away. They built the solitary church in this waste-land. When the number 15 tram with its single car passed beyond the last houses of Pozsonyi Street, even the road paved with yellow clin-ker tiles came to an abrupt end. The tram continued for at least five minutes along the meandering earth roads into this wasteland until we reached Dráva Street, where a very different city began, the pro-letarian district dotted with manufacturing plants, the extreme pov-erty crammed into desolate-looking city houses and huts. Between Tutaj and Vág streets there was a bypass, and there was also a tram stop, though I never saw anyone get on or off, for that matter, but we waited a long time in the wind coming off the Danube, at times it whistled, the wind whistled a musical tune on parts of the tram car, until the tram coming from the opposite direction arrived. On the two sides of the streets on the outskirts that bore deep grooves from the horse-drawn carts and trucks, there was nothing but industrial buildings of various sizes abandoned fifty years before, now standing waist-deep in weeds. Farther off, possibly on the edge of Váci Street, you could see a long line of baroque-style industrial buildings that had burned down. But in this outlying district, one huge building nevertheless stood like a ghost, the roller mill in Tutaj Street, the only one of the spectacular mills that had survived the great depression and the siege. The remnants of the other mills had been carried off to be used on construction sites. I never saw a single soul anywhere near it. It was out of commission.

Halászy situated the monumental, raised mass of the church on the periphery of this wasteland, away from the modernist blocks of Újlipótváros, between the empty Pozsonyi Street and the empty Újpest Quay. He raised the solemn main facade facing the Danube and Margaret Island half a story above street level so he could build an assembly room for the congregation under the church nave the same size as the nave itself. Regardless of how good the waterproofing was, they couldn't situate the underchurch below Danube level. As a result, Halászy in fact built a Greek temple. The substructure raised the superstructure out of its surroundings. The portico with its pediment rests on two square-shaped pillars and six Ionic columns. Because of the possible weakness of the subsoil, the architects didn't want to further burden the church with a bell tower, so they stood the elegant tower accentuated on the upper third of its body by arcades at some distance from the nave, and connected it to the nave with a covered arcade. They connected the offices, the council chamber, the parish offices, the rooms for caring for the poor, and the foyer that opened from Pozsonyi Street in the same manner, and the spacious residences of the minister and the assistant minister on the northern front, which were also thus connected to the bell tower.They built a clearly articulated complex of buildings that encircled a large atrium, but because of its row of arcades, it was open to the Danube, the changing lights and the constant wind.

At most, Halászy subjected the spiritual space to the forces of nature, the water and the wind, which enhanced the Greek or pagan character of the building. In January, the row of arcades was damaged by grenades. Two columns were torn from the pediment by a bomb or possibly atmospheric pressure. The carved ashlar base and the elegant plasterwork were also damaged by street fighting, but the structure of Albert Bereczky and Rózsi Németh's church escaped damage. And as we climbed the stairs on Sunday, I had to take a close look at the damaged columns that lay in the knee-deep weeds atop the fallen parapet. I also had to take a close look at their original places, high above where they'd been torn. I don't know what I was hoping to see, and why. I also had to touch the broken surfaces every time. For many years, the smell of the siege floated on the wind, the unsettling mixture of the sweet smell of corpses and of human excrement. The corpses that had been buried just under the surface were exhumed only in the early 1950s.

However, I felt an aversion not only to the smells, but the building as well. I've never been able to find a connection between Halászy and the neoclassical architects of the Italian Novecento, but there had to be a connection. I couldn't find Halászy's name in the records of the Hungarian Academy in Rome, and thus we can safely say that unlike the painters of the Hungarian neoclassical school, whose style was dominant at the time, he had not received a grant to stay at the Palazzo Falconieri. When he designed his neoclassical church, the monumental designs of Marcello Piacentini, Mussolini's star architect and the recipient of every possible and impossible Fascist rank and title, must have led his hand. It was a hot June, and meanwhile three decades had passed from my life, when I wandered around the deserted squares and paths of the Esposizione Universale di Roma, EUR for short, its architecture as dead as its spaces, and I said to myself that I know this grand architecture smelling of corpses from somewhere. I know it from somewhere. Stalinist architecture also flirts with classicism, but it does so in a much more awkward manner. It is awkwardly symmetrical, it thinks in terms of blocks, it feels best close to the ground, and it uses Doric columns instead of Corinthian. Piacentini's buildings have three trademarks that art historians recognize, which are also in evidence on Halászy's building. When in a row of arcades or colonnades Piacentini contains the Ionic columns with their classical base and volutes between square cross-sectioned pillars, then these square pillars, standing humbly on the sides, serve as frames that in part enhance the use of classical Ionic columns, and in part hide the static function of the square pillars. The square pillars serve to support the roof. In an aesthetic sense, this is how the Fascist Piacentini processes and makes use of modern architecture with its reliance on rational form; like a bona fide thief, he incorporates functionalism into his ideological monumentalism. For his part, Halászy makes use not only of the offensive ideological appropriation characteristic of modernism, he also adopts Piacentini's third trademark, monumentalism, without questioning it; he raises the mass of the nave, conceived in the classical style, meaning that it is reminiscent of a Greek temple, half a story above ground level, as if he were placing it atop a pedestal, thereby giving it far too much prominence, this in line with his Italian master. In effect, he articulates a modernist structure and the structural problems it entailed in the classical style. The Ionic columns with the voluted tops support nothing at all. The air pressure could have just as well torn four from their place. The roof and the pedimented portico are held up not by the columns and pillars but by the elements of the ferro-concrete structure, which for the sake of support are joined to the monumental buttresses on the side of the nave.

For a long time, a very long time, I felt that this is how it should be in this best of all possible worlds, the world did not exist for me without Rózsi Németh or her church, for which I felt a strong aversion. Yet I now see from various documents that only three years passed, from February 1947 to September of 1950, the time that Rózsi lived and worked in our home. But in those three years, now lost in the depths of time for me, I had no reason to think at all, ever, that this church was not my church. Although its outward appearance bewildered me, still, along with the bewilderment I felt respect for it, and its God became my God. How else would a child accept what exists in the world, if not along with the aversion he feels. Rózsi and our mother bore a physical resemblance as well. They possessed the same strong bones, the same thoroughly worked, muscular abdomens, wide hips, and the same physical strength. Our mother must have been about ten years older and she felt responsible for Rózsi, though I doubt that it was the responsibility of an older person for a younger; she just thought highly of her, she thought that she was destined for better things. The two women were equally intelligent, headstrong, cheerful, and stubborn. But my mother kept at her to further her education, she must further her education, she can't spend the rest of her life in other people's homes, among strangers; she kept at her until Rózsi Németh agreed to train as a kindergarten teacher. But first she had to break down her family's resistance. I remember perfectly well that Juliska held the same opinion as their relatives from Törökszentmiklós, meaning, the opinion of the village. They had saved a portion of their earnings so that they could buy some land for their old age, I am going to marry the daughter of Rózsi's younger sister, we will put some money aside too, and we will also buy land and breed rabbits. I liked the plan a lot, in one way or another, I wanted to get back the Gömörsöd estate my grandfather had squandered.

Rózsi remained with us a while longer, though; her training began in late August, they had barely just finished making tomato preserves, and in fact she may have stayed with us until the end of September, when she moved into the dormitory in Nagytétény. She couldn't have gotten up early enough to get there in time. I visited her a number of times, and as far as I can remember, the residence of the teachers' training school named after Amália Bezerédj was first situated in a wing of the baroque palace in Nagytétény, then subsequently in one of its more humble baroque-style farm buildings. Surely, my mother had suggested the place for the school and the dorms. Alice Hermann, a highly trained psychologist and the wife of Imre Hermann, who was a child psychologist and analyst, was appointed chief superintendent of kindergarten affairs, and our mother had organized the kindergarten system with her. She wasn't working as László Földes's secretary at Party headquarters by then, but was first made head of the department responsible for organization at the Democratic Alliance of Hungarian Women, then she was appointed secretary to its Budapest wing and worked in its headquarters located in one of the small mansions on Múzeum Street. Ever since Rózsi Németh had left Törökbálint to serve in our home, in my mind the two women were as one. Besides, this was the time when our paths with Mother parted, one might say once and for all. When I think back on it, by the time I was five, I hardly ever saw her, and I saw my father even less. It is not a pleasant thought, because it makes it far too likely that this is why I adopted the excessive aloofness I practiced with respect to myself, I learned it from myself, and possibly a bit from our father, and perhaps a bit from the code of behavior that my father's family held dear, but I had to find a way of protecting myself against my mother's absence and the pain that came with it. But even so, I felt the stress of our mother's absence less than my brother did later on. It took exertion, it took a toll on my emotions, no doubt about that. Without Rózsi Németh's Protestant objectivity and warmheartedness, I probably couldn't have managed to survive unscathed. I never blamed them, I made peace thanks to a certain kind of empathic approval; it became a spiritual exercise in sociability, the adopting of a sober attitude to the circumstance that they were engaged in work that would benefit others. What is of benefit to many is surely of a higher order than what benefits a single individual. At any rate, this is what I concluded on the basis of Rózsi Németh's Protestant ethic.

Also, I was probably extremely lucky that Rózsi Németh was physically so much like my mother.

The two of them were nourished by an energy source of unknown origin. It's called inner strength. A love of the comic and aversion to the pathetic. Their puritan rigor was coupled with a strident love of life that each blessed morning kept melancholy and doubt of all sorts at bay, if for no other reason than because of their shared convictions. My father needed time to slip out from under the covers, and even then he'd putter about under a cloud of melancholy for some time, sitting by the side of the bed, scratching himself with a vacuous expression, his mind occupied with some abstraction conceived in the charmed circle of the exact sciences. On the other hand, the two of them had hardly leaped out of bed and right away they were inordinately happy. Rózsi Németh washed, got dressed, grabbed the small basket, and went out for milk and freshly baked rolls to the big grocery store on the corner of Sziget and Pozsonyi streets.

What exception could I have had to Rózsi Németh's God.

At last, we have something my parents don't have. I got the drift of what our minister said from the pulpit well enough. Bereczky was not especially prepossessing, but his voice rang loud and clear in the silence of the nave. There he was, a man who during the siege did not act disgracefully.

Of course, it might help to recall that besides the copy of the report that Rudolf Vrba and Alfred Wetzler, the two escapees from Auschwitz, wrote in German and which made its way to Budapest via the Bratislava rabbi who handed it to Rezső Kasztner, another copy, also written in German, made its clandestine way to Dr. Endre Soós, one of the leaders of the illegal resistance movement of the Hungarian Front. He then passed on the document containing the exact description of the operation of the concentration camp at Auschwitz along with its blueprint to József Éliás, president of the Good Pastor Committee, which was in charge of saving and exempting Reformed persons of Jewish origin. Éliás's secretary, Mária Székely, translated the document into Hungarian and English, and the Hungarian Front sent orders through Soós that five copies of the Hungarian text should be passed on to important public figures and the English-language copies should be given to the ambassadors of the neutral nations. The document need not be sent on to His Grace Miklós Horthy, Soós was told, because His Grace as well as other members of the government have already been given the German-language version of the document through another channel. Then Éliás gave one of the Hungarian-language copies to Bereczky, and Bereczky passed it on to Bishop László Ravasz, director of the National Synod of the Reformed Churches, but to this day we don't know, or at least can't be sure when all this transpired.

As I reconstruct the past events of my life, I can see before the mind's eye Bereczky sitting down to his desk in the unheated room of his quarters in the Reformed church on Pozsonyi Street, this was in January, just a couple of days after we moved back to Pozsonyi Street from Damjanich Street, and just a couple of days before the Arrow Cross and the German units attempted to break out of the Royal Palace in Buda, having been forced to seek shelter there; at the time they were still bombarding Pest from Buda, and my parents were pulling frozen corpses along Újpest Quay on the sled from Gömörsid, and if my memory serves me right, they left me behind in charge of strangers, saying go along Pozsonyi Street, because it's safer there, and we'll meet up in Szent István Park. They may have left me in the care of older children, I don't know, I remember only that they were strangers and I was afraid of them, and so I tried to behave the way a small child is expected to behave. Like a good boy. I remember us walking along a war-ravaged street blanketed in snow. These post-siege streets would later constitute the core of my dreams about looking and not finding my way. When I need to find a solution to some daytime question, in my late-night dreams I go looking for it in a ravaged city and, naturally, I can't find it. It may have been Péter, Péter Róna, or possibly Erzsi Róna, but in any case, there were several strangers. Erzsi Róna remembers nothing of the sort, but she says that I probably joined a group of children gathered up by the Children's Aid Service after the siege, because she remembers that my mother had a part in setting it up and was in constant touch with them. I also remember that these strangers on the street were too noisy, but I was afraid to say anything, I couldn't have explained to them why they shouldn't be so noisy. I struggled with not being able to say something that was vitally important. My parents weren't alone either; they pulled the dead along with others using various conveyances. They went back and forth between Újpest Quay and Szent István Park several times; I seem to remember that they brought the dead from Rudolf Square as well, and also that they put their burden down in one of the empty, snow-covered neo-Baroque fountains in the park. I remember watching them from a distance, and meanwhile my mother keeps turning in my direction to see if I'm still with the strangers, and in the midst of these strangers, I feel very grateful for her attention.

Surely, Bereczky must have wanted to commit his testimony to paper without losing time. What the government has committed against the Jews, and thereby against God's eternal law, must be condemned by all true Magyars and Christians without reservation, he wrote by way of a preamble, as it were, what is more, they must show repentance for all the things that were committed in their name and in their sight. There is urgent need for repentance, the sincerity of which is revealed in the willingness to make amends. Then he commits a parenthetical remark to paper. If he were writing for the Jews, he'd have further things to say. But we would never get anywhere if everyone were to repent the sins of others. That would not be repentance but accusation. At which point he closes the parenthetical remark. The corpses lay in a crisscross pattern in the empty pool, on top of each other, this is where they were dumped. The soil beneath the snow was hard as rock. Who would have had a pickaxe, a spade, a shovel.

People said that the Russians would cart them away.

In his testimony, published in the spring of the same year by the ecclesiastical publisher Tractatus and entitled *Hungarian Protestantism Against Jewish Persecution*, Bereczky reconstructs two conversations between Bishop Ravasz and His Grace Regent Horthy that had taken place in April. He based these on Bishop Ravasz's own notes. Fortunately, we know the dates of these conversations. We don't know how Bereczky came into possession of Ravasz's confidential notes; possibly, the bishop himself felt the need for historical testimony and gave them to him. On the other hand, we know that when he read the Auschwitz Report, Bishop Ravasz took to his bed and was ill for months. Sándor Török's memoirs contain a passage pertaining to this. It was already summer when he visited the ailing bishop at his sickbed, and when he wanted to give him Vrba and Wetzler's report on the order of operations at the camp in Auschwitz, the bishop sat up in his bed and said that alas, he's all too familiar with the report and started sobbing. He kept shouting that this is not what he wanted, he didn't want this. It must have been quite clear to his contemporaries what he was thinking. Along with the head of the Hungarian Catholic Church, Bishop Ravasz also signed the first two Jewish laws, but he didn't sign them so that others should then commit these horrendous crimes in his name, something that Bereczky explained in his book, he had signed them so that they should prevent an Arrow Cross putsch through lawful means and, along with it, the Final Solution advocated by them.

Bereczky comments that the bishop notified only Zsigmond Perényi, Speaker of the Upper House, and Jenő Balogh, retired minister of justice and chief warden of the Calvinist diocese of Transdanubia, of the conversation he conducted on April 28. The previous morning, on Thursday, April 27, Perényi informed the bishop in person that in the counties of northern and eastern Hungary, the gendarmes were driving the Jews from the ghettos and herding them into corrals set up under the open sky by the railway junction, and that the gendarmes told them that they were being taken to work along with their babies and grandmothers, and that they were being kept prisoner under disgraceful conditions. Perényi asked the bishop that in the name of humanity he should persuade His Grace to put an end to these shameful conditions. On the basis of Bereczky's description, it is more than likely that he handed the Auschwitz Report to his bishop on one of these days, possibly that very day.

The following day, on April 28, 1944, when Ravasz went for an audience with the regent, he already knew what, according to other sources, the regent also knew.

The regent had special ties to the bishop; after all, he was a member of the Reformed Church himself, and so the bishop was his bishop, although according to secular protocol, as regent, he stood above him. In any case, during the audience, Bishop Ravasz ignored the protocol dictated by secular hierarchy and insisted more resolutely than ever that the regent, whom according to his own records he had already approached earlier, should in no way be responsible for the atrocities committed against the Jews, that whatever he can prevent he must prevent, because deeds are being committed in the name of the people of Hungary, the odium and responsibility of which they will not be able to clear themselves of before the Judgment Seat of History and all of civilized humanity. At least, these are the words with which Bereczky recorded the bishop's words. I have little doubt that these are the words that were heard by the regent at the audience, in the course of which each of them kept silent about what at that moment they both knew, yet about which they nevertheless spoke in an abstract manner. Still, Bishop Ravasz must have detected the antipathy settled upon His Grace's increasingly hard features, but he had to take the chance. He was bound to follow the hierarchy of conscience as countenanced by God, and with the accompaniment of the strictest words of warning, handed the regent the information that Zsigmond Perényi, the Speaker of the Upper House, charged him with.

When he learned about what had happened at Nyíregyháza, the regent answered, he lost no time in telephoning the minister of the interior and screaming bloody murder, as a result of which they immediately dispatched two state secretaries for domestic affairs, and they told him that the scandalous conditions had been put to an end.

Even if in fact this is how it happened, let us quickly name the two state secretaries that the interior minister was supposed to have sent to Nyíregyháza to restore order. László Baky was one, László Endre was the other, and, fully aware of the Final Solution and hand in hand with German ambassador Veesenmayer and special envoy Eichmann, they were in charge of the ghettoization and deportation of the Jews. We have no reason to underestimate the logistical and organizational scope of their task. Be that as it may, His Grace attempted to put an end to the awkward conversation with his bishop by explaining that with regard to the military situation, the Germans were demanding forced laborers and he could not deny their request, and so a couple of hundred thousand Jews would be taken out of the country, but no harm would come to them.

And then His Grace added, just as no harm has come to the hundreds of thousands of Hungarian laborers who have been working in Germany since the outbreak of the war.

At which point, writes Bereczky, in a very low voice and with the greatest regret, the bishop commented, as if speaking to himself, that in that case, His Grace the Governor has been sorely misled.

Today it is especially sobering to see proof of their gullibility in print. Neither of the men, neither the bishop nor the minister, assumed that the regent, who according to his own admission learned the basic fortés of high diplomacy at the Viennese court as Emperor Francis Joseph's adjutant, would blatantly lie in a matter of such crucial importance to his bishop, who was also the head of his Church. Historians have not been able to document with absolute certainty the exact dates either, but by all odds, Horthy must have received the Auschwitz Report from the resistance movement a couple of days before the bishop of his Church paid him a visit; in short, at the time of the audience, both men were familiar with the facts of which neither of them dared to speak openly in front of the other.

To put it bluntly, His Grace Admiral Horthy lied through his teeth, while in line with the contemporary codes of conduct pertaining to hierarchy, the bishop kept his peace.

Sándor Török, who dreamed up the two fairy-tale dwarfs Kököjszi and Bobojsza along with other enchanting children's stories, gave another copy of the Auschwitz Report to Countess Ilona Edelsheim-Gyulai, Horthy's daughter-in-law. The two of them put the time of the exchange at a much later date. In his memoirs, Sándor Török writes that it was in the summer, but provides no particulars about the month and the day, while in her memoirs, Countess Ilona Edelsheim-Gyulai writes that the date was July 3, information based on her diary. The first train for Auschwitz left Sub-Carpathia on May 15, and between mid-May and the middle of July, and as we know from various sources, during that time several institutions as well as men of goodwill had informed Horthy about the real aim of the big journey as well as its real destination. As for Horthy, with the code of behavior he learned at the Viennese court, he pretended each time that it was the first time he'd heard of the horrors and was deeply troubled, but needless to say, he had taken the necessary steps already.

On one of the chaotic days following the German occupation, meaning in the days after March 19, His Grace received the same information from József Cavallier, who, as head of the Hungarian Holy Cross Society, worked hand in hand with József Éliás's Good Shepherd Mission in an effort to save people. Neither of them had any doubt that the German occupation would entail the annihilation of the Jews, and they informed not only His Grace the Regent, but also the bishops of their respective Churches, of their fears. Bishop Ravasz had also been handed a report by Bereczky, the details of which may have shocked him, the data and the maps, if that, but not the subject of the report.

In the days following Bereczky's delivery of the Auschwitz Report, he cooperated with my parents in falsifying certificates of baptism as well as marriage certificates, and he did so despite the fact that he must have suspected that he was not cooperating with the underground resistance movement in general, but with the Communist resistance in particular. Supplied with official seals and fee stamps, my mother brought these documents from the minister's office of the Reformed church on Pozsonyi Street so that in the walled-off basement Duci, Magda Róna, should affix the necessary data with the ink that my Uncle Pista, meaning the Guardian of the Seal, had concocted. On the other hand, even my mother learned only after the siege that while she moved back and forth between the Reformed church on Pozsonyi Street and the basement of the house at 7 Újpest Quay, hopefully without being observed, Bereczky was hiding several Jewish families in the laundry room of his church.

How could I have misunderstood what Albert Bereczky was saying in the pulpit, I understood it perfectly. He said that our God is everybody's God.

The Tavaly family worshipped everybody's God at the church on Lehel Square. It was comforting to know that everybody's God had his dwelling in every church of every religion. In Rózsi Németh's village, the church of everybody's God was nothing like ours. It was completely empty, too, with snow-white walls, and in the silence even the steps of the ornately carved pulpit creaked the same way, and yet it was different. If on Sunday morning everybody's God can be present in several places at the same time, and I had no problem understanding that, then he's a God who doesn't expect special treatment for himself and could easily be reconciled with the freethinkers around me. Once I even visited this church, Laci Tavaly's Catholic church. He insisted on showing it to me. He was proud that his church was so ornate and sweet-smelling. He was explaining something about frankincense to me, but I couldn't make linguistic sense of it. I couldn't hold myself back from deconstructing the word. But when I did so, it turned into a call to arms. Frank. Incense. The Frank hordes are incensed. Run for your lives. We sneaked off one afternoon, at any rate, that's how the grown-ups saw it, that we had sneaked off, and when we got back home to his place, they yelled at us and they slapped him, and his mother even promised him a thorough beating later that night. When your father comes home, you'll get what's coming to you. In Németlad, where they came from, mothers were not allowed to beat the boys, in theory, anyway. At most they could slap them. As Laci Tavaly would say, he got slapped around. But he didn't say that his mother had slapped him around, he acted as if he were basically immune to his mother's slaps. Mothers were allowed to beat their daughters as much as they liked. But boys were beaten by their fathers to teach them a lesson they would not soon forget.

I'll teach you a lesson you will not soon forget. I'll put the fear of God in you.

To reach their church, the two of us tripped over the cavities and abysses of the damaged road as we made our way, just the two of us, from Csanády Street to Lehel Square. During the siege, Csanády Street had been badly damaged by bombs and cannon fire, and it remained damaged for a very long time, possibly for years. I didn't want to tell him that I didn't like their church, so I let him go and explain things to me. Their church still bore traces of damage. We had to get on tiptoe and press our faces against the pane of the swinging door so we could see inside. We could only go as far as the entryway of their church, the heady smell, the smell of this linguistically mysterious something, I should just press my nose there, it comes through the gap in the closed swinging doors. I had read the Bible and was familiar with it when I finally saw a piece of frankincense and understood what it was that they were burning. I thought that the window of the synagogue was much more beautiful and brilliant because of the stained glass, and what a shame that was hidden in the courtyard of that house in Csáky Street, so that only those could find it who knew that it was there to begin with. I was quite happy with the thought that everybody's God, who according to my parents was invented to dull the brains of the people of the world because people had no other consolation except for this distant God, resided in such very different churches. For me the two conceptions of God, the theist conception and the atheist conception, were nowhere as obscure as many other matters of common knowledge that I couldn't understand at all, and even decades later failed to understand.

One thing is certain. On Sunday morning, before they went to their Catholic church and we went to our Reformed church, we were not allowed to play to our hearts' content. Laci Tavaly stood over me in his short pants with the suspenders and snow-white knee socks, his legs spread apart. He obeyed the prohibition against playing before church and he wouldn't kneel down, because his parents would hit the roof if his knees got dirt on them. He gave me orders from up there about what I should do with my building blocks, my Marklin, or my badly worn colored wooden train. I had marvelous building blocks. Ocher and terra-cotta and smooth, with traces of grease from my fingers. My uncle István Nádas gave me these building blocks, and even their boxes with the sliding tops were marvelous, because if I packed them with care, the smooth blocks with their slightly rounded corners fit the boxes just so. I had to pack them with care, making sure that the pieces of various sizes, colors, and shapes should form a close-knit unit when placed in two rows on top of each other. Which in itself sufficed to stir my imagination. As I was building something with my blocks, I had no doubt that when I grew up I'd become an architect. I could even build the Reformed church on Pozsonyi Street from my building blocks. The set contained columns and triangular roof shapes, these would serve as the pediment. The grown-ups around me said that they had played with this set when they were children in Pannónia Street. I enjoyed building things, this in spite of the fact that for many years I couldn't imagine a time before I was born. Still, the building blocks provided evidence of a time before me. I was playing with an earlier time, as it were, which made me respect my building blocks all the more. I also inherited my father's incomplete Marklin set. It consisted of dark gray perforated metal profiles, head screws, female screws, screwdrivers, and screw wrenches of various sizes. He told me the name of each part and had me repeat it. For some reason he didn't want me to forget the female screws.

But in that case, why aren't there male screws.

He looked at me for some time, then he looked at the Marklin set with the screws inside. I had him there. Then he picked out a head screw and showed it to me.

This is the male, the head screw.

I persisted that, in that case, why don't they call it a male screw.

He gave a soft laugh, which was more like a short cough. Then with the other hand he picked out a female screw and showed it to me as well.

See, they fit into each other, I can place one inside the other, and

I can screw the two together. One has a head and a body, the other holds it with its grooves.

He laughed at this, too, but again, it was no more than a short cough.

On Sunday, we'd sometimes play with my building blocks for hours. Laci Tavaly stood over me and told me what to do. He gave me instructions in everything else as well. If we got too absorbed in the game, his mother would shout from the ground floor, which we didn't hear in the children's room, but Rózsi Németh heard in the kitchen, that it's time to leave, and when he was gone, we also got ready to go to Rózsi Németh's church to meet Juliska Németh and hear Bereczky's sermon. It often happened that Laci Tavaly's underpants peeked out of his best Sunday pants, and from under his underpants not only the tip of his white shirt, but his whistler hung out as well. I tried to look up at him so I wouldn't see this complication. It wouldn't have been proper to bring it up, whereas he being my only friend, in principle I should have called this anomaly to his attention. I didn't have a suitable sentence at my disposal. Whereas it bothered me that others might see his whistler too. People will see it, this is the expression they used in kindergarten and later on in school. But it's not his whistler I was worried about, it was the anomaly. I thought that it was all right for me to see it because I'm his friend, but strangers mustn't. Such a thing must not happen. This was one of the principal rules of life, and so I'd remember it, they told me that no one had ever seen my great-grandfather improperly dressed, they hardly ever saw him even in his dressing gown. Not his daughter, not his sons, not his grand-children, no one. At most Planck saw him, the valet who helped him dress all his life. Still, how could I tell Laci Tavaly when he wasn't a relative. Surely everyone is responsible for his actions, his appearance, and thus his whistler, too. We do not interfere in the private business of strangers. We do not make comments related to physical character-istics, and above all, we do not make fun of such things. We do not say that someone's gotten fat, we do not say that they've lost weight, we do not ask why they look so pale. I came up with an aesthetic explanation for why I couldn't say anything to Laci Tavaly. A man's whistler is not a pretty sight. This is why we don't talk about it, this is why others mustn't see it, it's best not to talk about the fact that we have something so not nice. Whereas Laci Tavaly's whistler as it hung out of his pants interested me for aesthetic reasons; I could provide a precise description of it even today, if such a description had a place in this text. Yet despite this, or along with this, for three decades I saw the penises of boys and men alike as inordinately ugly. Apart from my linguistic helplessness, there was really no impediment to my warning him. He made no bones about grabbing it, taking it out of his pants, and he also took a good look at mine. He took his out even when he didn't have to pee. In Németlad they look at one another's. For a long time I felt that such things are among the secret assays of friendship, though I never initiated anything of the sort myself. I couldn't transgress the liberal prohibition, because I'd have had to go against my better sense. Besides, I felt no impulse to do what he did. I even considered the whistlers of those boys and men whom I loved with all my heart as ugly. On the other hand, if I honored the liberal prohibition on any mention of physical characteristics, much less make them the butt of jokes, we do not touch strangers or hug them, we leave them alone, we do not touch them and we do not scratch our privates under any circumstances, then I couldn't very well satisfy my duty as a friend, and this troubled me a great deal.

At most, they occasionally dressed me with more care than usual, but they endowed neither the act itself nor the clothes with exceptional adjectives. In our home nothing was festive. At the same time, I didn't understand why we must always differ in our expressions and customs from others, even if just a bit. At times I felt embarrassed, at others annoyed, though I wasn't sure who I should be annoyed at. Why don't I have Sunday clothes. Am I unhappy with what I have. No, I'm not unhappy. A good thing, because we can't afford to buy you other clothes anyway. Something was always missing, if just a bit, but I quickly grasped the advantage in it. I had no Sunday clothes, but at least there were no unpleasant comments that go with them, kissing, like at my grandmother's, oh, aren't his little pants cute, what cute little thighs he has, look how cute his little shirt is, oh, my, what a handsome boy he'll grow up to be, because his grandmother dresses him in his best clothes. Just look at him. My grandmother used her words to endow my clothes with a festive air. At most, when they took me to her, my mother made concessions to my grandmother by packing freshly washed, carefully ironed clothes into my suitcase, a white shirt and a pair of white knee socks. For the sake of peace. See, Dad, how *fess* he looks, a sight for sore eyes. He'll grow into a *fesák*, a pretty boy. A *svihák*, a dandy. I hated this *fess*, *fesák*, and *svihák* at least as much as the *gezerah*. It gave me the shivers; I got goose bumps from the fear of hearing it and also the effort to keep myself from saying something. To let sleeping dogs lie. I mustn't be a *fesák*. My grandmother mustn't see how every one of her words turned my stomach. Sometimes she said I was *adrett*, dapper. As far as I was concerned, this *adrett* crossed the line. It was worse than the *gezerah*, worse than the *fesák*. It was as if she were hitting me on the lip with her open palm on purpose again, because there was something slick, something equivocal in her words, the *fesák* and the *adrett*, as if my grandmother meant to treat me the way she treated her alcoholic goyim neighbors, those murderers that will murder her in her own home one day, they'll leave me drowning in my own blood, just you wait and see; all sweetness and charm, she fawned on them but was always wanting to say something wicked at the same time. Which, needless to say, her neighbors knew. Why wouldn't they have known what Grandmother thought of them when in their eyes Grandmother was a fucking old Jewish whore, and seeing how many they'd burned, it was really a shame to have spared this one. As if with the *fesák* and the *adrett* Grandmother were saying that with my pretty-boy airs and dapperness I'm a swine and she can only hope and pray I won't be like her first nephew. She always made a point of it, that he was the first. And that my mother wanted to marry him, her first cousin, just imagine, what an abomination. Whereas the chauffeur was paying court to her by then, oh dear, what was his name, a *fess* boy, the chauffeur of a great gentleman, what was his name, oh. She expected me to understand the function of this first in her sentence. But the swine she never actually said. What an idea, my mother falling head over heels for her own cousin. It would have been better had she said it. Had my grandmother not been so devious. Now I know that she avoided saying it not because she wanted to spare me; her intention was more complex. Her not saying the word meant that I'm destined to become a great big swine just like her nephew. She sees it coming. An even bigger swine. But in my grandmother's deterministic dictionary this great big swine didn't have a concrete meaning, not even a deferred meaning, it had a ritual meaning, she used it in its impure sense. But for now, she loves me. For now, my impurity is just that of a child. I'm not even aware of it. But if I end up doing anything like that Elemér, who almost married my idiotic mother, she's going to stop loving me. If I have the audacity to do something like that, I can run all the way to Csepel, like him. I'm going to collapse, there in Csepel, I'm going to shit bare-assed in Csepel. In Csepel my saliva will drip, my mouth with foam, yes. But if it should come to that she'd rather die, she couldn't take it, enough is enough, she doesn't want to see the day. The Lord can't punish her like that. She's done enough in her life, she's suffered enough.

I mustn't be her murderer like these miserable goyim, her neighbors on the fifth. Here on the fifth, they're all born killers, each and every one of them.

I understood deep down that she was casting a spell, and also her negative prophecy and my projected expulsion, and I didn't forget it, except I had nowhere to store it linguistically, because I didn't understand a single word with respect to its true subject. I wondered what she was trying to protect me from, or from whom, or what she was trying to keep me from doing. What she was trying to keep me from with her spells. How could I have understood what Elemér had done that brought the wrath of the family down on him. Still, a person's senses pick things up and whisper to one way ahead of his intellect. He sees a structure, and supplies the missing pieces only afterward. Structural comprehension is prior to objective knowledge, and it develops earlier, too. Without the structure, there'd be no place to store objective knowledge, nor could it be enhanced. Be that as it may, I explained to myself what I'd heard from my grandmother by concluding that a person must be careful, and he must be especially careful with one's first cousin, but perhaps he can be less careful with his second cousin, that's why Grandmother and my idiotic mother keep emphasizing this first.

On Pozsonyi Street, meaning in the geographical center of the universe, in the earth's magma, no one threatened me, meaning that they didn't threaten me with superstitious linguistic exaggerations, and they didn't threaten me with emotional exaggerations or exaggerated temperaments, not even with occasional outbursts of temperament. At most, with jokes. And also, parables to drive home a point. Once, my father related the story of the mountain shepherd who cried people, people, the wolf is coming, the wolf is coming, from the top of the big mountain, when there was no danger, no wolf. There was no danger of any kind threatening the flock. But the people of the village rushed to his aid wielding axes and pitchforks. But when he cried for the third time that the wolf is coming, because the wolf was really coming, no one rushed to his aid and the wolf gobbled him up along with his flock. He didn't have to relate the parable more than once. If I fell into exaggeration or used exaggerated expressions, they just had to warn me that I'd suffer the same fate as the mountain shepherd and his flock. They mocked everything that smacked of exaggeration. In line with liberal thinking, they didn't place the individual things that had been ritually named under indictment, they placed emotional and verbal exaggeration under indictment. Which meant that they replaced the object of tribal ritual, or else offered up mental rituals in place of magical rituals. The mental rituals were hardly more permissive than the tribal, the magical.

Which is not a complaint after the fact, I merely wish to point out that this freethinking period in history replaced the object with abstraction, thus turning the earlier objects of ritual conceptual.

Look at him, all got up like a dog's dinner. Which was to be understood as an annihilating judgment. Dressed to kill to impress us. Just the other day his ass was hanging out of his pants, and now look at the show he's putting on. Shitty-pants Steve on Jesus's name day. I can't believe it.

I didn't understand this either, for a very long time I didn't understand the differences in degree hidden inside words and why I was not allowed to say any of the words that were all right for my outspoken mother to say. Why my father's brothers and sister laugh when my mother says the forbidden words, *ass*, *shit*, and *horse's prick*, words that they'd never say themselves, and which they strictly forbid me from saying. I can't even call anyone a moron. Rózsi Németh was no different from my mother. She had a loose tongue too, and when she was up in arms, she said things that were otherwise forbidden. On the other hand, no one ever stopped me from doing something just because of my clothes or shoes. They didn't stop me from playing even when I had a white shirt and white socks on. If I got dirt on them, then I got dirt on them, they put it in the light wash. They washed the bed linen, the towels, and the tablecloths in the big wash. They did the big wash in the laundry room and not the apartment, and the laundry woman came once or twice a month. But Rózsi Németh and I went to the laundry room the afternoon before they did the big wash to check if the neighbors had left everything in order. And if we found everything in order, we brought the clothes with us to soak, the colored separately, and the white separately. The laundry woman arrived at dawn, by the time I got up the fire was blazing in the kettle and she was already doing the wash. When they brought me home from kindergarten, or later when I came home from school, the laundry woman was still doing the wash. She finished in the late afternoon, sometimes in the evening, and then she went up to the attic to hang the wash up to dry, even in winter, even in the dark. Needless to say, the laundry woman only had a first name, or else just her surname, with the obligatory definite article. The Hadasné, the Zsófárné, these two I remember.

If my knees got dirty, Rózsi wiped them clean with washcloth mittens, or if we were in Szent István Park or on the promenade in front of Parliament, she rubbed them with a wet handkerchief. But no one ever said to me that I got them dirty or that I got grime on them. In my family, such expressions were used figuratively, they gained their meaning by extension.

After my grandmother, armed with a wet comb, or what was even more unpleasant, a wet brush, won her struggle with the recalcitrant curls hanging down my forehead, which I didn't always have the patience to suffer without objection, my grandfather and I could start off on our Sunday walk. When Grandmother wetted it, the brush smelled foul. A horrid hair smell, head smell, it had a pronouncedly bad hair oil smell. I inherited the recalcitrant curls falling over my forehead from Grandfather. My mother called this to my attention once when she was brushing my freshly washed hair. I remembered it because she had wrapped her quiet hope in her comment, to wit, that in my temperament and mentality I would take after her father, rather than her mother. She was in love with her father all her life. For his part, my grandfather paid more attention to the course of her life than his two other daughters', this despite the fact that my mother's Communist radicalism horrified him and prompted him into mute opposition that at times lasted for years. All the same, he couldn't help but let her have her way, just as, for the sake of peace, he did not bristle against my grandmother's bullying either. When she cackled about Grandfather's incompetence, Grandmother may have been referring to this inner disposition for yielding.

Once a surely decisive argument ensued between father and daughter, whereas they didn't even raise their voices. They closeted their anger behind the bulwarks of the most complete self-control. Argument followed argument, rebuttal followed assertion, they pushed on, it would have never occurred to them to stop until one of them had convinced the other. They were continuing an earlier, possibly a very old argument, one that had always driven a wedge between the social-democratic workers' movement and the Communist workers' movement and made left-wing unity impossible, even in the most crucial situations. The Communists wanted to save the world from egoism, to save it in the face of man's animalistic anthropological givens, if need be; hand in hand with the small vanguard of organized proletarians they strove for anti-egoist autocracy, thereby endangering democracy in the most classical manner imaginable, and they didn't even make a secret of it. Clear enough, they could not eliminate the primacy of egoistic private property in one fell swoop except by resorting to tyranny. To dictatorship. According to their intentions, with the dictatorship of the proletariat, but in fact, in line with the spirit of the Yalta Conference, with the outrageous dictatorship of a small group of Muscovites. On the other hand, the social democrats were of the opinion that the advent of socialism is contingent on government reforms and voters' rights reforms promoted within a democratic framework and based on respect for private ownership. In the argument between them, which was sparked by some current political affair, they'd reached an impasse, neither of them would give an inch, either forward or backward. My memory retained the subject and choreography of their argument, but deleted its details. At one point my father joined in the argument from the sidelines, but my mother put him down with a supercilious hiss which meant that you will now keep your mouth shut. Her rudeness had a social content that even I understood. As much as she loved him, my father was a spoiled bourgeois. Given their estate in Gömörsid, their construction company, his stream of handpicked governesses and his uncles, who were bankers, lawyers, high-level managers, chief physicians, and parliamentary representatives, how could he possibly understand what she and her father were talking about. This was one of the sensitive points of my mother's life, one might say its most profoundly mistaken leitmotifs. She considered herself a proletarian, she alternately referred to herself as a proletarian and a proli, but how could she have been a proletarian. The truth is that the dynamic culture based on solidarity with the poverty-stricken was best suited to her temperament, the group outings and cooking, the glee clubs, the choral speaking, the cheerful self-abandonment, the pyramids formed of masses of bodies in response to barely audible commands, snapping fingers or the quick, sharp sound of a clapper, the full light arsenal of anti-egoism; I still have the clapper made of walnut that she used to lead the calisthenics of the workers' gymnast groups; they were poor, that's true, at the time of the Great Depression poorer than a church mouse, but all the same, my goldsmith grandfather was not a proletarian. True, as an employee he was smitten with a sense of social responsibility and insisted all his life that he should be an organized worker. But not a proletarian. The clapper has our father's faded words of love on it. Under the clapper's tongue he wrote in minuscule letters, guess who, guess why, and he didn't even use question marks. Which means that our mother received this clapper from him as a present. She couldn't have been a proletarian if for no other reason than because of my grandmother's mentality or worldview. How could Cecília Nussbaum have dispensed with her hopes of being rich one day. As a proletarian, she couldn't have continued admiring Queen Elisabeth's beauty and white lace evening gown adorned with pearls, nor her riding frock made of the finest kidskin, clothes that she didn't just slip into, they were sewn onto her frame by hand every time, and as for Janka Tauber's fortune, she couldn't have set her sights on it. Besides, printers, silversmiths, goldsmiths, and turners were the crème de la crème of the working class, outsiders, detached individuals, aristocrats of the working world, and by no means proletarians. My mother used this word *proletarian* as linguistic self-flattery. She empathized wholeheartedly with those who came from the bottom, the outcasts, the destitute. For two years during the time of the great unemployment crisis of the mid-thirties, when my father didn't have a stable job, she worked as a laborer herself, she was an electric welder at the Tungsram factory, she worked on a conveyor belt, in accord, as they said back then, meaning that she was paid by the piece, and this lifestyle made a profound impression on her. By all odds, her activities in the illegal Communist movement lacked proletarian experience to begin with, but later she relied on the proletarian self-awareness linked to this period of her life. During this time she also became the head of the physical training section of the Vasas Sport Club, which entailed the preparation, direction, and organization of the training, the competitions, travel, and various current events. This was still the glorious period of amateur sports. Everything strictly in their free time; they even had to come up with the money for travel, and also for their gym outfits and dance clothes, and if they didn't have the money, they chipped in and sewed them themselves, the girls sewed the boys' clothes, and sometimes even their gym shoes for the gymnastics presentations. They cut, layered, and glued the soles from old hats, they cut and sewed the upper parts from some stiffer canvas. They traveled third class, they slept in the gyms or locker rooms of their hosts, sometimes on borrowed mattresses, sometimes on straw laid on the floor. Sometimes they got back to Budapest on Monday at dawn and went straight from the railway station to their workplaces. Her co-workers recognized our mother's gift for organizing and leadership, they shared their most intimate problems with her, and when the next election came around, they made her their trade union steward. From then on, she represented the female welders before the company management. I also remember that there were two huge dogs at the Tungsram plant in Újpest, they were not what you'd call tame animals, they were kept in chains, bloodhounds of sorts, and in keeping with their reputation they growled, barked, and bared their teeth, and so the workers called one Benito, after Mussolini, and the other Adolf, after Hitler. It didn't take long before the chief engineer of the plant, whose name I've been trying to remember for weeks, also recognized our mother's gift for organizing, and after a couple of months, she was transferred to the office. Those sly bourgeois, they knew what they were doing. Not only was her Hungarian spelling faultless, but so was her German spelling, and so they dictated the company's German-language correspondence to her, not to mention the fact that this way they could keep her from representing the female workers.

Miss Klára Tauber was sixteen when she found work at Rudolf Walkó's law office on Erzsébet Boulevard, and on her father's advice, she immediately joined the Hungarian Employees Association. She found her first visit to the lawyer's office quite an adventure. In the spacious and comfortably furnished office masses of folders stood in glass cabinets, the so-called Linger shelves, but there were no clerks around. There was nothing but the silence of the objects, yet everything was in order. The open doors afforded a view of the row of empty offices. After Dr. Walkó informed the young lady about her duties, he took her through the silent offices looking out on the inner courtyard that led to the two huge rooms connected by a door that he used as his library. The lawyer lived with his family on his estate in Zemplén, God only knows how long he'd had his practice on hold, he tended to the estate, wrote expert legal opinions, worked on monographs on jurisprudence, and often needed one or another of his books or folders. He communicated his needs via telegram, and my mother had to find the pertinent folder and the pertinent books with the help of an inventory, mail them, and also file the books and papers the lawyer returned by mail in their proper place. At times, in line with the lawyer's instructions, she had to go find rare books in libraries or secondhand bookshops. Besides the library and document files, my mother was also in charge of the lawyer's abundant correspondence, she was also in charge of the petty cash, she paid the smaller bills, the bills for larger sums she took to the lawyer's bank, where she was given a voucher, proof of payment, which she then forwarded to the estate in the mountains. Where she'd never been. In the morning the offices and the library rooms had to be aired out along with the eight additional rooms furnished to impress clients, which looked out on the boulevard, and were likewise connected by wide-open doors. On the other hand, in the afternoon, before the sunlight hit the left facade of the building on the boulevard, she had to close the shutters of all the windows. Every Tuesday two cleaning ladies came, who cleaned the already immaculately clean apartment; they picked up every single object, wiped it, dusted it, they scrubbed every single floor tile, cleaned every window, and polished every piece of furniture. My mother had to oversee their labors. But they worked deliberately and in silence, there was nothing to oversee. They were sisters, big, bony women, two old maids, real proletarians, whom the Walkó family made to work mercilessly for their wages, though for some reason they also supported them; come Easter and Christmas, they gave them extra pay in the form of apples and walnuts that the family sent them from their estate in wicker baskets covered with calico, which my mother then had to send back to the family's Zemplén address. My mother thought they must be distant relatives. But if the two of them couldn't finish in a day, because once a month in the morning they had to haul the rugs down to the yard, where they had to beat the last particle of dust out of them, then before giving them a final brush, they had to wax the parquet floors with Tangó wax, then buff them with the parquet

466

brush attached to their bare feet or, as they said back then, buff them up, or when they cleaned the windows and wiped the doors clean, or cleaned the silver and the copper utensils, she had to call them back for an extra day or even an extra two days. She paid their wages. They worked by the day, but she was not allowed to help them. That was not part of the young lady's duties. When she wanted to breach the rule once, because she wanted to help the women roll up the big carpets of the two library rooms, her mere intention made them so indignant, she gave up and never tried again. They thought that she was trying to short-change them in some way. On the other hand, she had to see to everything, the cleaning supplies, the clothes and rags and brushes. She had to bring their lunch from the Erzsébet Restaurant across the street, and she was even given instructions about what the lunch should consist of and how much it should cost. They were allowed thick soup or soup with plenty of noodles and creamed vegetables thickened with lots of flour or roux, served with a topping they called *feltét*, after the German *auflage*. The word *feltét* sounded to me like *feltételes*, something incidental, you either got some on your plate, or not. Today few people know what this sort of topping was, something thrown onto the vegetables as an afterthought. They flung some low-grade meat, possibly a thin slice of meat from a soup, a thin slice of meat loaf, some shreds of stewed meat, they threw this on top of the creamed vegetables and doused it with the fatty gravy left over from roast meat that, if you were lucky, included some scraps of meat. The topping, but especially the gravy, was a constant bone of contention between the guests and the waiters, and also between the waiters and the chefs. The guests felt there was not enough gravy, they complained that it was just some fat with paprika, there's nothing in it, the waiter should return it and bring a proper portion, a man's got to fill his stomach with something, especially considering how much he paid for it, and if the waiter took it back to the kitchen, the scene between the waiter and the chef was subject to further escalation. Be that as it may, scenes like this always took their toll on me. The chef pushed back the plate, saying he ladled out more than enough, that's the proper portion, that's all they're entitled to. The greatly honored guest shouldn't want to stuff himself with gravy. Or else, cursing as he did so, he dumped another ladleful of gravy atop the creamed vegetables in the soup plate with such force, it splashed all over the place. At such times, the arguments coming from the kitchens, meant to be heard outside to begin with, sent electric sparks through the air and the guests stiffened at their tables. If the greatly honored guest can't afford anything except creamed spinach, why did he come here. What I paid for I paid for. I have a right to it. I can't believe this is happening. Can't they turn the volume down in that kitchen. You know what, nothing surprises me anymore, seeing how they lead an honest man by the nose and cheat him every chance they get. At the same time, everyone must have felt that although they're not about to raise their voices at the injustice, the poor man being deprived of his rightful gravy, they know what it's like, they'd been cheated out of it more than once themselves. Cheaters, all of them. They were reduced to fuming inside. These people cheat everyone right and left. A bad lot. At other times, a veritable epidemic broke out among the guests. After a short pause, they all grumbled, the portion is wanting, it's not nearly enough. There were other complaints. One didn't have a napkin, there's no salt on the table, he's been waiting for the girl to bring him bread, the food's gone cold, mine is too hot, this isn't freshly made, the potato smells, and so on.

When she had to oversee the spring and the fall cleaning, her duties were even more difficult, because she had to hire skilled, reliable women to do the scrubbing. Using plenty of lye water and root brushes, these nameless work machines on two feet not only scrubbed the parquet floor with circular movements, they picked up the lye water with cloths rinsed repeatedly in plenty of clean water, then went over the floor with more clean water only to pick it up yet again, this was the expression they used, they picked it up, because with the big, soft cloths they veritably coralled the foaming puddle of lye, I did it myself many times with Rózsi Németh, and also later, after my mother had died and we didn't have a maid either anymore, then they wrung them dry over the pails, they didn't say rag but cloth, this is the word they used, it seems these people don't have decent cloths, which in this case didn't mean that their clothing was not made of decent cloth. There's no way I'm going to pick up the water with these little scraps, your ladyship. Kindly give me proper cloths. And then, once the parquet had more or less dried and the lady of the house had inspected it, looking for smudges, there followed the so-called staining, they dissolved yellow powder paint of different hues in lukewarm water, depending on their preference, and applied it to the parquet. After that, there was truly no stepping on the floor anymore in the room that had been emptied of furniture. When the following day or the day after they judged it to be completely dry, there followed the waxing, they waxed it or, as they said, waxed it up with a soft cloth, it had to be flannel if at all possible, this is the expression they used, soft cloth, and when the wax had more or less dried, then came the polishing with a brush, but not without applying wax to the brush first. If they don't apply wax often enough, they shouldn't be surprised if the parquet doesn't shine.

She had to pack or move every movable object out of the way, and there were hundreds of these in the apartment. She had to commit the place and position of every object to memory. But she spent most of her working hours reading in comfort. There were no literary works in the lawyer's library, but there were books on history and sociology, the correspondence and diaries of famous people, political pamphlets and biographies, all of which she read, even works on economics that she thought were interesting, and which occasionally she even understood. She always did her reading under pressure of time, at the ready every moment. Sometimes she got a terrible headache, at other times a stomachache. The basic rule of the house was that except for the weekly cleaning days, any member of the family, or even the entire family, might come to Budapest at any moment, and they had to find everything just as they had left it months before. Sometimes only the mailman, the superintendent, the landlord, or the maid from next door rang the bell, but this was enough for her to suddenly be confused about where she was and what she should do with the book she was reading. In the afternoon the mailman might come with a parcel or the telegraph man might show up at any time. Despite the regular and frequent cleaning, everything had to be put back into its strictly appointed place, the knickknacks, the rugs, the books in the glassed-in bookshelves, and the armchairs and chairs had to stand at a precise preappointed angle. She didn't read in the two library rooms, but at the desk in her own office, always ready to stash the book in the drawer or take it back to the library room posthaste. She told me about these things while she was trimming my nails, putting my clothes on, washing my hair, cleaning our shoes on Sunday night, tying my ankle-highs on Monday morning, or during similar, less important chores. She told me that she had read about prostitutes for the first time, though for a long time, possibly until I was fifteen, I had no idea what a prostitute was, even though I'd heard the word, along with all its imaginable synonyms, in Sándor and Dembinszky streets, and even Damjanich Street, in contexts that were a mystery to me, and they spoke about these women with grave accusation in their voices, and so I wouldn't have dared ask my mother what a prostitute is, my father even less.

Our mother also lets prostitutes into our apartment and then they talk under their breath for hours.

If only I knew what they're gabbing about like that.

I am under the impression that such people do not exist on Pozsonyi Street, but in the Péterfy Sándor Street house, on the other hand, two prostitutes shared an apartment. This mysterious difference was also one of those secret phenomena that separated one corner of the city from another. I kept looking to see what was prostitute about them, but I discovered nothing. When they were at home, they gave no thought to their appearance. There was one in Dembinszky Street as well, she lived in a miserable little apartment on the ground floor that opened onto the yard. In Damjanich Street there was a so-called *edelprosti*, a noble prostitute, but she lived upstairs on the fourth, in an apartment facing the backyard. The tenants also called her a kept woman. I didn't understand this either. What was it she kept doing. Or did others keep doing something to her, for instance, they kept dangling her over the railing on the fourth floor because she mis behaved, she was disobedient, she was up to some mischief, and her maid picked her up and kept her dangling over the railing, just like Rozália Kiss had done to me, who according to surviving documents started working for us as a maid on November 18, 1946, and my parents paid 24 forints social security for her because she was their live-in domestic employee, but on December 2 of the same year, she was no longer in our employ because I'd done something terribly wicked and Rozália Kiss grabbed me and dragged me to the balcony rails screaming for all she was worth that she's going to teach me a lesson, she's going to throw me off the seventh floor, and as she hoisted me up and over the railing, she yelled that I'd better promise I'd never do anything like that again or she's going to let go of me this instant. Under me a seven-story drop. She had me dangling, suspended above that frightful precipice. The afternoon was just turning into night. Superintendent Tavaly's light on the ground floor was already on. But I was in no state to promise Rozália Kiss anything, because I'd never seen the yard from this angle, and also, the unfamiliar feeling of such depth stunned me. I didn't hear my mother coming out into the hall, from where she saw what was happening on the balcony outside. The words got stuck in her throat. But she thought that it's better like this, it's best if she doesn't say anything now. She must stop herself from screaming. She must not do anything at all. And to keep herself from doing anything, she pressed herself close to the wall and got as far as the open door just as Rozália Kiss kept dangling me over the railing because I'm a perverse child, I refuse to promise her. Whereupon, unbeknownst to me, my mother slid along the length of the door post and passed out. This must have made some noise, because Rozália Kiss hauled me back over the railing and in her helpless rage threw me down on the stone floor, where I was surprised to discover my mother lying, just like me, her head hanging over the threshold of the front door, resting on the stone floor of the balcony. At which Rozália Kiss became hysterical. I don't remember whether my father was at home or not, but there was someone else in the apartment with whom my mother may have been talking in the studio, a stranger, a visitor, I don't remember whether it was a man or a woman, I only remember the person kneeling by my mother's head, slapping her and shouting, don't just stand there, bring some water, Rozália Kiss.

But what had that certain woman on the fourth floor been up to, the prostitute who must have been kept dangling over the railing, just like me. On that particular December 1, all sorts of things happened in our home that never happened either before or after. As soon as she regained consciousness, my mother told Rozália Kiss to pack her things and go. But Rozália Kiss started crying, screaming as if they were skinning her alive, shouting, where is she supposed to go and she wants to be paid for the entire month.

When she's packed and dressed, she'll get her pay for the month. But she'd better get out right now.

I remember just this one prostitute, the kept one from the fourth with the rollers in her hair, and she wrapped her hair, weighed down with the rollers, in a kerchief. I remember her shiny purple satin robe bursting from her copious flesh, her slippers with the pom-poms, which I'd have loved to slip my feet into, and also as she smoked, leaning against the railing of the balcony, which she must have considered very classy; but in fact, she was waiting for someone to come, so she could talk to someone, anyone. It seems that my grandmother was willing to let such people inside her apartment, and even my grandfather couldn't talk her out of it. She talks with them for hours under her breath. I wish I knew, Mother, what you could possibly have to talk about with a woman like her. I know that the whole house talks behind my back. But as God is my witness, they're human beings, too. Also, they're our neighbors, and a person should be on good terms with her neighbors. They pour their hearts out. What's wrong with that.

And then decades later, on an antiquarian bookseller's list, I found the description of the book my mother had read in Rudolf Walkó's library six decades previously, when she was sixteen. *The Question of Prostitution. Presented at the 1917 Meeting of the National Association.* The spine bears gold lettering, hardback binding, in good condition. In his recommendation the antiquarian further states that Georg

Lukács, Lajos Nékám, professor of venereal diseases, the radiologist Emil Weil, and the criminologist Ferenc Pekáry were among the speakers, to name just a few of the most prominent participants. Needless to say, I wanted to buy the book right away, but unfortunately, it had been sold by then. Still, later on I was terribly impressed that, despite the general censure, my grandmother had chatted with prostitutes in her kitchen. My grandfather couldn't talk her out of it throughout a lifetime. This may have been her one characteristic, this stubborn social sensitivity of hers, that truly impressed me. And by all odds, our mother read the young Lukács and the young Emil Weil, who was still a medic back then, so she could understand why the tenants disapproved of my grandmother befriending that prostitute.

Then one morning someone rang the doorbell of the lawyer's apartment on Erzsébet Boulevard, whereupon veritable hand-to-hand combat ensued, because a young man of doubtful appearance tried to get into the apartment; my mother tried to shut the door in his face, but she failed, because the young man in question prevented it with his knee and foot, upon which my mother stepped on the man's foot with her buckled, high-heeled shoe, the man howled and pulled his leg from the gap by reflex, and she managed to force him outside the door.

Locking it, trembling, she even secured the door chain.

There they stood, the two of them, panting and trembling on two sides of the door.

And who knows why, in his anger, his outrage, the man on the other side of the door cried out amid his tears, but young lady, I'm a friend of the family, I brought an urgent letter, I beg you, young lady, for just a moment, so I can hand it over. She ran through the rooms, slipping on the rugs, until, having reached the farthest office giving onto the courtyard, she flung open the window and shouted that there's a sneak thief in the house, help, help, until by and by the tenants and the servants appeared out on the round balcony, and the superintendent down in the courtyard. The thief, he's crying, this is what they saw. But by the time they recovered and started running

along the balcony and the stairwell, there was no trace of any crying thieves. Another afternoon, the lawyer's son, who was finishing
his last year of high school, showed up with his small suitcase. He
was handsome, gentle, and timid, they stood awkwardly, face-to-face;
apart from a couple of courteous banalities, they couldn't get out one
sensible sentence. But then, they had no business with each other to
begin with. In the days that followed, they kept out of each other's
way. But while they kept out of each other's way in the big apartment, they could still feel the other's presence on their skin. They were
careful to close the doors that until then had been left wide open.
This went on until my sixteen-year-old mother, who one week read
Ernest Renan, the reputed anticleric, on the life of Jesus, another week
Lukács on prostitution, and on yet another *The Secrets of the Gallows*,
the memoirs of the famous executioner Károly Henrik Sanson, one
morning found a humble present from Gerbeaud on her desk. It was
a box of bonbons decorated with violets in a small box embellished
with a wreath of violets. She was so taken aback, she wouldn't have
touched it for anything in the world.

Besides, she wouldn't have shown interest in the timid young man
anyway, because a couple of weeks beforehand the house had another
visitor, whose name was László Bódog, a friendly young man with
wavy hair and brown eyes, about ten years older than my mother.
He'd come bearing a bundle of documents. In those days, a bundle of
documents consisted of sheets folded in half lengthwise, each separate
file tied with string, or else it consisted of individual sheets sewn together with string. The young man, who was the manager's chauffeur,
brought it from the South Railway Joint Stock Company. The following afternoon he stood by the gate waiting for my innocent young
mother, who, for her part, didn't think that it made any sense to be
coy, because it was clear that the previous day, as she opened the door,
they fell head over heels in love. On the other hand, they had to keep
what they felt for each other within the bounds of reason. They had
to keep themselves from doing something they might regret. This is
how they talked about such morally delicate matters back then. As for
me, for a long time, a very long time, I had no idea what they were

talking about. At least another thirty years had to pass before I could get a grip on the concept of morals from their point of view. She'd never felt or experienced anything like it before. Her caution had to stand up to the inner strength of a man who was a stranger to her. Once when she told me the story, because she related her stories many times, under many circumstances, and in many acts, because she'd tell me her story from one aspect, then another, rambling; anyway, a slight conceptual duel flared up between us. I couldn't understand why she called him a stranger, how could he be a stranger, when he was no longer a stranger. He most certainly was, she didn't know him, they didn't take the cows to pasture together, she didn't know him for a long time to come, love is knowing a person, I don't even know your father, whereas I've loved him for quite some time. I still don't know him, and she gave a strident laugh, as long as you're in love, you don't know the other. And when you're no longer in love, why bother. With which she managed to throw me into a frenzy. My mother can't be in love with my father, that can't be. I didn't know what to say. I raged. I was beside myself. And when something like this happened and incomprehension raged inside me, adding insult to injury, I felt ashamed as well. This always surfaced at the same time, the rage and the shame felt over the rage. My mother was the only person who could throw me into a frenzy like this, and no one else. I also felt that this was not me. I don't know who. At which she said that it's no use flying off the handle and if I persist, she's going to give me two horrendous smacks. But for the other person inside me, this was like adding fuel to the fire. She's trying to derail me. To confuse me. But I'm a match for her. I'm not putting up with her insults. Your father is not my relative, she yelled, how would I know him. It doesn't happen at the drop of a hat. A person gets to know the other by degrees. My mother understood even better than I why I was raging. Which made my jaw drop. Because it may actually be true that he's not her relative, just a stranger she once met; on the other hand, the stranger became my relative, the one she's still getting to know, which means that I should accept the fact that I have two relatives who don't know each other.

The next morning there was another box of bonbons from Gerbeaud, even bigger and more elaborately packaged than before. She didn't know what she should do about these beautiful boxes. She left this one, too, just as she had found it. She couldn't tell Bódog either, the man she didn't know, because he was out of town, chauffeuring his boss around. Whereas she'd have liked to tell him. Meanwhile, at the time, after work, twice a week, she attended eurhythmics sessions in Mrs. Madzsar, Alice Jászi's gymnastics training school on Ménesi Street. I don't know who held these late-afternoon sessions for earning women, as the expression went back then, Mrs. Madzsar, Alice Jászi, or one of her former students, possibly Ágnes Kövesházi. I'd like to remember, my effort at remembering nearly reaches the pertinent contents of my mind each time, but then I don't. She and Elemér, Aunt Szerén's son and two years her senior, went dancing every chance they got. They danced with a passion. Back then girls looked enchanting when they went dancing, they wore exquisitely yet lightly styled silk dresses with round necklines and short skirt lengths, the dress afforded them freedom of movement, and they wore buckle shoes on their silk-stockinged legs, these shoes made even their wildest steps secure thanks to their chunky heels, and they didn't have to teeter in them. At most they hung a long rope of pearls, imitation or real, around their neck, but no other ornament, nothing else. She was already deadly ill, in and out of the hospital, when she taught me the basic ballroom dancing steps, the tango, the foxtrot, the slow foxtrot, and also the waltz, the polka, and the csárdás. She had a God-given talent for dancing. She didn't dance with her feet and she didn't dance with her head; instead; she knew how to create direct contact between her hearing and her muscles, but she didn't have to teach me how to do this, because I could see on her emaciated body what was happening. She taught me both waltzes, the Viennese and the English. Her maimed body was radiant with joy. Her passion for dance flooded into me, or else I inherited it, I don't know how these things go. Later I went to dancing school, but I learned the rhythm and the basic steps of the various dances from her. For a long time there was no quick dance that I could not follow and record with my eyes, then play back with my feet. Dance is reflection, dance memory recalls what the foot had previously imagined through the rhythm. People thought that she and Elemér were a couple, a couple accustomed to each other whom people circled around in the dance salons and on dance evenings with good reason and watched with admiration. And if so many other things had not interfered, they couldn't have avoided a career in dance. If, for instance, in the midst of paying court to her, László Bódog had not taken my mother and Elemér to the Nature Walkers and Gymnasts Club at the big athletic stadium in Peterdy Street. But he did. Also, if our mother had not begun to engage in gymnastics there in earnest so she could join Bódog and Elemér on their challenging nature walks, because Bódog was an Alpinist, and there was a physical-training course at the club. Once in the Alps, when they reached a clearing, she and Elemér cast off all their clothes and danced like that for the others. Laci Bódog was supposed to have taken a photograph, my father and she chuckled, but I never saw that photograph myself.

Or if at a slightly later date she hadn't met my father at this club.

Along with many other fashions, the love of nature, excursions, freestyle dance, and body culture appeared at the end of the nineteenth century as a reaction against urbanity and the successive industrial revolutions. To this day I regret that I did not become a dancer. Perhaps my physique was not suited to it. Perhaps I'd have succeeded in suiting my body to dance. I could be an aged choreographer now, musing over my former glory. Let's face it, my grandmother saw right through me, she had good reason to fear that there was an Elemér inside me and one way or another I must be purged of him. The two of them knew the wildest American and South American dances, they could step-dance, they could do the samba, the rumba, the tango, they knew the two-quarter-rhythm one-step, the quarter-note boogie-woogie, the shimmy, and the scandalous shimmy-shake. Our mother loved Elemér even toward the end. She brightened when she remembered their shared love of dancing. The photograph showing her dancing naked in the clearing has to be around somewhere. She didn't even criticize Elemér over his death. He went bonkers, she said briefly and to the point when I wanted to check Grandmother's over-heated comments with her pertaining to Elemér. Going bonkers happens in the best families. One Sunday afternoon when I was cleaning the big apartment in the Perczel villa on Svábhegy, I turned on the radio so I wouldn't be so bored and, like Jack-in-the-Box, when she heard the familiar music she leaped out of her sickbed, and a couple of months before she died she demonstrated the shake for the sake of her two sons and her husband, meaning that she showed us how she and Elemér shook their hips obscenely in front of each other.

The third untouched fancy box was lying on the desk when, on the fourth morning after his arrival, the young man himself appeared at the door of the office in his pajamas. He asked my young mother to go with him because he wanted to show her something from the window of his room. Even three decades later, our mother would giggle and laugh at the memory as she cut my toenails. Not so my father, who took the young man's infantile offering of himself to heart when he rather tastelessly wrote down the scene for us in his unfinished manuscript. He appraised the innocent story from what you might call the aspect of the class struggle. In his memoirs he praised our mother's proletarian self-consciousness and held it up to us as an example to follow. So we should grow up to be self-conscious proletarians like her. Proletarian self-consciousness is so strong that it makes one resistant even in the face of a box of bonbons from Gerbeaud. When at the age of sixteen I found this unfinished typescript among my father's papers, I must have had plans for it, because I made rather rough marginal notes on it in ink and red pencil. The First World War, just like the Second, took its toll on every proletarian family. Check this, I wrote in the margin at the age of sixteen. Your grandfather heard the speech Mihály Károlyi gave from the steps of Parliament, from close up, standing on the side steps. Check this, I wrote above the line, because by all odds I wanted to find the speech Count Károlyi gave on November 16, 1918, in which he proclaimed the First Hungarian People's Republic. In the dictatorship that followed the Second World War, this first Hungarian republic, whose last maimed and fragmented remains and aged raconteurs I kept bumping into as a journalist, became vitally important to me. The square was jam-packed with veterans, rebellious workers, and disgruntled citizens, our father writes, and this was no exaggeration. In footage from four contemporary films of Károlyi's speech, many interesting figures can be seen standing on these steps to the side, civilians, soldiers, but I failed to identify my grandfather in any of them. There must have been two hundred thousand people on the square on that Saturday, as many, more or less, as on that memorable balmy late afternoon merging into the night on Tuesday, October 23, 1956. By eight there was shooting at the Radio. Your grandfather's presence was documented by *Érdekes Újság* magazine. I haven't yet gone searching for the picture taken that Saturday. Your grandfather is working in a small workshop in Dob Street fashioning rings. I marked this sentence, too, in awful handwriting, at the age of sixteen. The small workshop making rings looked suspicious to me, I could feel the intent to belittle it, although for a long time to come, I had no idea why he should have done so. Wealthy relative, I wrote on the margin in red pencil. The goldsmith's workshop that I was familiar with from Holló Street, though before the siege it may have in fact been in Dob Street, was neither small nor did they make rings only, they made all sorts of gorgeous jewelry as well; they also repaired jewelry, and the owner was no stranger, but the wicked Janka Tauber herself. Who by all odds was not wicked, just strict, farseeing, and circumspect. But she couldn't be circumspect enough. In line with ministerial decree no. 50.000 on commerce and public supplies, on April 21, 1944, the authorities first impounded her workshop and shop along with its stock and furnishings, then in line with prime ministerial decree no. 3.840 of November 3, 1944, pertaining to Jewish property, they appropriated it. Any and all properties owned by Jews shall constitute the property of the State as part of State holdings. Nevertheless, Janka succeeded in saving some of the jewels and scrap gold through the siege. The weeks and months following the siege saw many dramatic scenes unfold because of Jewish properties left in the care of close friends and acquaintances who were considered Aryan. My Aunt Eugenie also went in search of her jewels and other valuables, impressive both in weight and number, that she had previously consigned to the care of friends. These dramatic scenes made a lasting impression on my mind as well. Check, I wrote on the margin of the manuscript at the age of sixteen. Does friendship exist in the world, that was the question. Does anything exist apart from elemental objective interests, this, too, remained the question. There were only three possibilities. These valuables were destroyed because the apartment or house where they were safeguarded had been hit by a bomb and was burned to the ground, the person to whom they had illegally given the valuables in question for safekeeping had perished along with them, furs, paintings, furniture, carpets, jewelry, scrap gold, silver dinner sets, or the Arrow Cross had taken them, or else looting Russian soldiers had carried them off, or possibly all three. Or else the owner didn't get them back with resort to one of these excuses, whereas it was obvious that the valuables had survived intact. Janka got her scrap gold and carpets back in mint condition from a person whose name I can't recall, whereas my grandmother had repeatedly referred to this person as a true hero. Accepting Jewish property for safekeeping was a risky undertaking, and it meant that man is not a wolf to man, there is hope, there is friendship, there is love of humanity, there are excellent people, and respect for law is innate to the species. In his 1945 decree no. 200 in which he repealed the anti-Jewish laws and decrees, Prime Minister Béla Miklós declared, in the name of the provisional national government, that the laws and decrees pertaining to the confiscation of Jewish property are contrary to the constitution-mindedness of the Hungarian people, and ceremoniously reinstated the previous rule of law, in short, full equality for all citizens. At least Janka got her shop back, robbed of all its contents, and also the workshop, and with the help of the superintendents in Holló and Dob streets, some of the tools and furnishings as well. And then, when amid the general building and rebuilding fever it seemed she was back on her feet again, in the presence of the police, and on the basis of a previous inventory, all her tools and equipment, her entire stock, in fact, which included raw materials, were taken into state ownership, meaning that the state required that in line with the police inventory, she voluntarily hand over the workshop and shop, along with all their appurtenances, to the National Watch and Jewelry Industry Company.

For a couple of days she adamantly and shortsightedly refused to sign the necessary papers, whereupon she received a police summons, and then she signed them after all in Gyorskocsi Street, flanked by two silent agents of the secret police.

During the days of the Commune your mother and her sisters joined the Workers Association for Children, our father wrote in his curtailed memoirs. Which meant that they could go to Margaret Island for free, and they even got a warm lunch and an afternoon snack. The snack consisted of a slice of bread and a summer apple, which they took home to share with their parents. Check Republic of Councils, I wrote in ugly, staggering letters on the typescript. But they preferred playing on the big horse-market square, our father wrote. He related this to me in person as well, in minute detail, describing how on summer mornings they'd sneak out in a group and how the superintendents sprinkling the sidewalk chased after them. This is where the downfall of the Commune caught up with her in August, smack in the middle of a wedding scene in which she played the bride and an old lace tablecloth served as her veil. The band was drumming on the bottom of patched-up, creaking pots and pans and hummed to the wedding march with the help of combs covered with thin tissue paper. Amid this loud scene Grandfather pushed the bushes aside and told them to come home with him. But why should we. Why now. Because the dictatorship of the proletariat has failed and Romanian troops will now occupy the city.

And then, when the Great Depression came, your grandmother made up for what they lacked with unflagging industry and self-sacrifice; the small apartment filled up with a boarder and several students for whom she cooked, so she could pay for the girls' schooling. Next to the student I wrote in red, her love. Surely, I must have been thinking of some innocent love story I'd heard but which unfortunately I can't remember anymore. On the other hand, I remember that Felix Salten colored our mother's story in my mind from when she was a young girl. The world-famous author of *Bambi*, the respected president of the Austrian PEN club, who came into the world on September 6, 1869, in Budapest as Zsigmond Saltzmann, didn't just write charming tales, but under the pseudonym of Josephine Mutzenbacher, he penned a juicy pornographic novel, *The Life Story of a Viennese Whore, as Told by Herself*. As a young man I had read it in German, the book hadn't been translated into Hungarian yet, and for a while I not only considered translating it, I actually launched into it to try my hand. Against all odds, the first pages of the translation have survived among my papers. I was curious to see the effect such an unconstrained text would have on my mother tongue. Even though I knew nothing about ethics or the erotic, I'd been interested in the system of erotic and ethical hypocrisy since I was twelve. Even in my autoerotic experiences, incomprehension held sway. What a person does, that's one, what he is willing to admit to in public, that's two, and how he is expected to comport himself in public, that's three. The holy trinity of bare truth, appearance, and intention. I even remember the overcast Sunday afternoon when I decided that I would dedicate my whole adult life to this two-, or rather three-facedness. This was in the sweltering summer of 1954, when I found a till then unfamiliar illustration of Janus in a lexicon. On it he had a third face wedged in between his two faces looking in the opposite direction, the one facing the observer. And oh my God, the look in his eyes, the look in his eyes was demented. It was a visual revelation. Ah, so that's how it is. Thanks to it, I suddenly understood something I couldn't understand before. The image, someone's three faces, the three perspectives of his face, drove me out to the summer garden, and I walked around out there, deep in thought. The two small events may have occurred at different times; be that as it may, my memory had merged them into one. I would write about everything, everything that people keep from each other. Anyway, at that moment, that was my decision. I had come to a decision about something, what's more, something that would be my mission in life, about which I knew nothing. How could I. I also realized that it would not be pleasant, it was not the road to glory. As a young person, I dauntlessly went in search of linguistic models in the field of eroticism to serve me in good stead in the endeavor I chose as my life's mission, and that's when I happened upon Mutzenbacher's memoirs, except I was soon bored with the monotony of the erotic descriptions. As I was working on the translation, without realizing it, I used my grandparents' apartment in Péterfy Sándor Street as the scene of the brutal pedophile first chapter. It seemed to me that this was just the kind of address Salten had in mind, that this was the house he was describing, along with all the architectural and hygienic poverty of mature capitalism. The neoclassical and eclectic architecture of Budapest and Vienna bear identical structural elements and follow identical decorative principles, and they are subject to identical financial considerations. The same open balconies with their ornate railings, unknown in other cities, the same stucco ornamentation, the same stairwells which, floor by floor, gradually dispense with ornamentation, and where the top-floor apartments, the apartments opening from the yard or the backyard, are for the poor, who are not entitled to stuccoes. But all the apartments have the same door posts and window frames, painted in the same manner, with identical color combinations, the interiors and the size of the apartments do not differ either, neither those of the bourgeois and haut bourgeois, nor those of the poor and destitute. The same back stairs, the same awful toilets on the landings. The master builders were also often the same, the same Slovak foremen, the same Moravian carpenters, and even more often, the same architects. Without realizing it, I had substituted the innocent love story of my grandmother's meal student for the history of Salten's sexually driven boarder, the way the writer possessed the little five-year-old girl in the part of the bed renter. I remember the seduction scene from Felix Salten's novel, but not the love story of our mother and the meal student. In my mind, the identity of the two apartments linked the two stories together, the one in Salten's book and the small apartment that opened from the balcony where my grandmother had a bed renter and chatted with prostitutes in the kitchen.

Which says a great deal about the mechanism of forgetting and the motivistic work of remembering.

My mother wasn't quite sure how mature grown-ups handle such matters, but she did know that after a year and a half she wanted another job so she could get away from this silent Erzsébet Boulevard apartment as soon as possible, in fact, immediately. Attorney Walkó tried to calm Miss Tauber, have her change her mind, don't do it, you won't find a better job than this, young lady. Not that he was unaware that the young girl with her shock of blond hair wanted to be with other people and had had enough of the silent apartment. On the contrary, her resolve finally impressed him, have it your way, young lady, go; he even found her another clerical job at the campaign office of a small party founded just a year and a half before. It was István Vági's party, a so-called splinter party that had split off from the left wing of the social-democratic movement; it was called the Socialist Workers Party of Hungary, the closest precursor of the Kádárist Hungarian Socialist Workers Party, and in fact one of the cover names of the illegal Hungarian Communist Party caught between the striving for independence and Moscow's directives. Walkó may have suspected as much, but the police actually knew it. When people mentioned it among themselves, they just called it the Vági party, the splinter party that could hope for a couple of parliamentary seats at best, and which, from the moment it was founded, Dr. József Sombor-Schweinitzer's political police had kept under surveillance. Even after the siege this is how they referred to it, and only by making certain connections did I understand where the Party was situated between the social democrats and the illegal Communists. When on November 1, 1956, the Janus-faced Kádár founded his own party on the smoldering ruins of the Hungarian Workers Party, which on December 1, 1955, had 871,497 registered members and was a mass party the size of which had never before been seen in Hungarian history, he said that his would be a small party, a dwarf party, if for no other reason, may I add, than because, may I add, thanks to the murders he'd ordered, his huge party now had fewer Communist members than the Communist Party had during its years in illegality, but he would now purge the Communist movement of the sins of Stalinism, the Janus-faced Kádár said, although when he made this promise, he knew perfectly well that some of these sins were tied to his own name and that he would never have to account for them to anyone, just as he knew that he would leave Budapest in a matter of hours and would play the charade of going to Szolnok to ask the Soviet government for the Soviet army's intervention, when in fact he headed straight for Moscow to return with the Soviet troops to Budapest and jointly put down the counterrevolution, and after Rajk, this time to set a trap for Imre Nagy as well. He had probably never been to Szolnok in his entire life. Had it really been Kádár who put down the revolution with our father, which already back then they called a counterrevolution, Hungary's history would have turned out very differently. But it wasn't Kádár who put it down and it wasn't our father who put it down, but the Soviet army, and Kádár didn't call them in, rather, they hired him to call in their troops, whereas in the days just before the revolution, as a member of Imre Nagy's government, he called it a revolution and was looking into ways of removing the Soviet troops stationed in Hungary. For his new party, Kádár adopted the name of István Vági's party knowingly. While serving Moscow's striving for hegemony, he wanted to keep up the appearance of independence, an intention the two men had in common. Except, while István Vági, the squat, shrewd, and able-bodied master joiner from Nagykőrös who, according to my mother, was honest to a fault, served the cause of his party's independence in all innocence, thirty years later János Kádár, who had already murdered László Rajk, fully cognizant of what he was doing, now murdered Imre Nagy as well. He was not murdering strangers but two fellow comrades who had served their party with a commitment equal to his own.

On Sunday, the police raided the Party offices. The headquarters of Vági's cover party was located in Hernád Street, but our mother was working in the Party's election office in Óbuda, situated in the yard of an old Swabian house. One of its windows gave out on the yard of the house next door. He and some others fled through this window. Vági was arrested and sentenced to four and a half years, and his party was disbanded. Upon his release, his comrades whisked him off to Moscow, where a couple of years later he was accused of spying and was killed. Even when I was a child, the question for me was not whether I should accept any one perspective of the Janus face as the sole reality, or whether someone couldn't have even more faces. The question was how I could see them converged, as one. After Vági's party was dissolved, our mother took it easy for a couple of weeks, she went dancing with Elemér, and then, thanks once again to Walkó's efforts, she was hired as secretary to Dr. József Csécsy, retired ministerial counselor and editor-in-chief of the *Közgazdaság* journal of economics and finance. She said that she learned a great deal there, but did not specify what that great deal might have been. When the journal folded because the aristocratic ladies who had been supporting it till then grew tired of financing it, she started working for the National Handicraft Association. Regardless of the perspective from which I look at her life, I can't discover the least trace of the proletarian in her. She attended the illegal Marxist seminars given by József Madzsar, Pál Sándor, and later Endre Ságvári, that's true, but these men were not proletarians.

She was a first-class organizer, good at seeing the full picture; she saw the possible hurdles ahead of time, she was attractive, she dressed well, and she was a first-rate stenographer and a faultless typist; she had studied certified public accounting, her handwriting was beautiful and legible, which at the time was important, because they recorded the ledgers and accounts by hand, and most of all, she conversed openly and cheerfully with anyone in Hungarian as well as German; in short, she was considered a reliable partner, as they said back then, someone you could count on for results. She hated the petite bourgeoisie with all her heart, which I understand, and in retrospect approve and support this inclination of hers; she had no intention of identifying herself with them, which must have been a question of intellectual disposition with her, a sign of good taste and social empathy. She was a staunch opponent of convention and a champion of equality. I understand this, too, and despite my elitist leanings, I followed her in this throughout my life. Her false, or at least coquettish self-definition, to wit, that she was one of the proletariat, had its advantages for me. Very early on, it practically took no more than a glance, and I could tell a lumpen apart from a proletarian merely on the basis of her comments about their character. That's a decent proletarian family. No, I'm afraid he's a lumpen, he drinks to excess, just look at the lump on his nose. Look, that's a decent proli, that's what a decent proli should look like. Except my mother's coquettish self-definition had a serious drawback to it. In line with their own self-deception, when I started school, they had me pegged as being of working-class origin, and there was nothing to do about it, like a lamb, I followed in tow. I walked into a fold where, with the mannerisms I'd learned from them, I did not fit. They locked me into the political structure of appearances they nurtured, and locked me out of my own reality; it's best if I don't even know what my own reality is. Come September of each year, I had to declare in front of my classmates that I was of working-class origin and I had to announce my parents' salary. Come September of each year, my cheeks burned from shame. Their combined income was four times as much as that of the other families. If any of my classmates came to our home, one look around, and they could see that there was nothing of the proletarian about us. They must have wondered why we had lied like that. In the Pozsonyi Street apartment with its furniture and tableware from the Gömörsöd estate, we were just ordinary well-off citizens compared with the proletariat, but in the villa up on Svábhey, we were considered gentry of dubious origin who were out of their minds, because they didn't have a single piece of decent furniture. Either in their past or present, there was no interpretation of the word that could have legitimized their proletarian origin so much prized by the ruling ideology of those days. For a long time the whole thing puzzled me, I paid close attention, I watched the entire staging wide-eyed, I kept my ear to the ground, but could find no explanation for why my parents insisted on it. The young female proletarian gymnasts who came to visit their beloved coach in our apartment on Pozsonyi Street to see me, her newborn, stood agape, they couldn't figure out how Klári came to be there, but were afraid to ask.

In the course of their heated argument, Grandfather's forehead took on a bright red hue. The ever-present little smile disappeared from the corner of his lips. As for his daughter, her neck turned crimson, her lips pale. She trembled in every part of her now bulky frame. At this moment, her sense of humor, lauded by so many, had vanished, Beelzebub had taken it. As far as I can judge by the historical dates, it must have happened right before my brother was born, in June, or possibly more like July 1948, but in any case, during the increasingly happy and increasingly bright last trimester of her pregnancy, when apart from the well-being of the embryo nothing whatever could affect her deeply. Her sisters-in-law even reprimanded her that when she's pregnant, she loses all her social sensibility and turns into a maternal beast. She did the same thing before Petyonka was born. A moment ago they were still screaming with laughter that with her big belly the maternal beast can't sit down, or once she's seated, she can't get up, but at this juncture, there was dead silence in the studio. The armchairs and chairs, an inheritance from my paternal grandmother Klára Mezei's informal salon, the so-called green salon, were too low and too soft. She can't control herself, she can't stop eating, she's not eating, she's guzzling her food. I for one was not allowed to use the expression, this guzzling, but she could guzzle her food to her heart's delight. You'd be wiser remembering that animals guzzle, we humans eat or take nourishment. Sure thing, except she can do as she likes, because she's just a proli in this decent bourgeois family. She meant it as a joke, but with these jokes, with her playful but focused use of words, she drove a wedge between herself and her sisters-in-law, who were incapable of freeing themselves of their bourgeois conventions, and who did not wish to be free of said conventions in the first place, because they weren't even aware that they were conventions. In the end, someone brought a stool from the kitchen. Even if it's in a spacious studio apartment in Újlipótváros, a pregnant proletarian woman is entitled to sit on a stool. Judging by the shape and size of her belly, her sisters-in-law, her two sisters, and even her own mother were expecting the arrival of a boy. Seeing how I'm Péter, let the newcomer be Pál. They decided this well in advance, it was Rózsi Németh's idea, and they laughed every time, as if with this cultural joke they were concocting an attempt on our lives, Péter and Pál, the two Communist apostles. This little premeditated joke concerning our names was typical of Rózsi Németh's thinking. She turned it into a game, she gave the naming a humorous cast, and with the Protestant earnestness, she sneaked her own convictions into the family. But wouldn't you know, neither of us became Communist apostles.

Still, they couldn't be absolutely sure, because before I was born, and on the basis of similar signs, everyone was sure I would be a girl, something that my mother, my free-talking, playful, laughing, brutal mother, later told me time and time again, the idiot.

That they were expecting a girl. Not me. Not a boy. She wanted a girl. And I knew this to be true because boys my own age left her cold, but girls my own age got her going. With which she drove me into a quiet but all the more profound desperation. What, I wondered, should I have done to be a girl. And what, I wondered, could I do after the fact.

For a while this was how she exercised her maternal tyranny over me. But only for a very short time, because we were made of the same cloth, she and I, though to this day I don't know what makes for this being made of the same cloth. All I remember is that Grandfather suddenly spoke up in the middle of this expectant, happy family cacophony. He and Grandfather Tauber were also made of the same cloth.

With her huge breasts and majestic airs there sat my grandmother Cecília Nussbaum, radiant in a neo-Romantic aristocratic armchair, while the flock of mother's chirping women's movement friends were sitting all over the place when, without the least sign of heightened emotion, Grandfather announced that he was not about to transfer his allegiance to the Communist Party. After the siege, my mother had extorted a promise from him that he would apply for membership. He did so, except he was not admitted, because during the Commune he was an adherent of the down-to-earth social-democratic politician Ernő Garami, who, with his republican beliefs, was very far removed from the Communists. My grandfather remained within the fold of the social-democratic party and was obviously relieved that he did not have to belong to his favorite daughter's party. For her part, his favorite daughter called him a bourgeois lackey, a simpleminded Garamist who is being led by the nose. Decades later I went to the library to find out about Garami, whose name my mother used as a term of abuse in the face of Grandfather; I wanted to know who these despised Garamists were. If she had her way, she'd have liked to turn his profession against him as well and deny it in front of the world. Instead of saying her father is a goldsmith, she's quick to emphasize that he's a goldsmith's assistant, a mere assistant, and she never failed to add that her father worked as an assistant all his life. Which means that her father has every right to be called a proletarian. She belittled the goldsmith's trade and shifted it into the sphere of poverty. By all odds, this heated exchange must have taken place between them on the eve of the underhanded and coercive unification of the two leftist parties, the Hungarian Communist Party and the Hungarian Social-Democratic Party, in short, on the eve of the Communist takeover, in which case it had to take place in June rather than July 1948.

I remember their argument, I remember the subject of their argument, but word for word only this one sentence, and neither the arguments nor the justifications, nor the counterarguments that followed my grandfather's no-nonsense declaration. Nevertheless, a couple of weeks later my mother convinced her father, possibly using coercion, because he joined or transferred his membership to the unified party, now called the Hungarian Workers Party. But from then on, father and daughter were careful to avoid starting up any further arguments, they even avoided having to speak to each other. For many long years this scared me, it oppressed me, it compelled me to keep a close eye on them. Catching the smallest change in their relationship was like sensing the ups and downs of the political barometer. They were mutually courteous to their dying day, but their courtesy was precarious, it threw off sparks. They kept the number of words they exchanged to a minimum. Which by all odds meant that despite their love for each other, despite their mutual respect for each other, they insisted on sticking to their original convictions.

From then on, my mother wore a supercilious expression in my grandfather's presence, aloof and haughty, and this expression reminded me of her own mother's emotional mannerisms.

I didn't like this face of hers one bit. I watched from as close up as

I possibly could to see what a political victor is like as she loses everything and alienates everyone around her for a lifetime. The objectivity of her sentences, too, suffered as a consequence, they took on a ritual cast.

After two years, she must have realized that there was no political self-consciousness, no ideological arrogance with which she could bridge the abyss between reality and her own ideas. As for my grandfather, he looked on in eloquent silence, he was on the alert like me, he did not speak, he did not reproach her, it would have been too late. Pointless. Still, he kept to himself like a patient moneylender who, when the time comes, is nevertheless intent on collecting a rather hefty loan.

In the two years that followed, both of them must have seen by the complete pauperization of the country the triumphant results of the by now triumphant dictatorship, a dictatorship that had nothing to do with the proletariat, either before or after, nothing whatsoever. I kept an intent watch on our grandfather as he silently and intently watched our mother and father, which threw into an even sharper light their daily struggle with the political roles they had adopted for themselves.

When my grandmother called my attention to the fact that I had inherited the strands of curly hair falling over my forehead from my grandfather Arnold Tauber, they hadn't yet diagnosed him with cancer, but for my parents the political game had, for all intents and purposes, drawn to a close. Though for different reasons, both had already been stripped of the high offices they held. They had both suffered a mercy killing, except they chose to pretend otherwise. For a while they tried to keep up appearances, to hold on, but the debacle of their lives could not have been more complete. I can't rule out the possibility that the stress she felt, the thorough bankruptcy of her enthusiastic and dynamic temperament, must have contributed to my mother's untimely death, to the development of her own cancer. Though thanks to her enthusiasm she managed to convince her father, in turn, the events unfolding before them convinced her of her father's truth, in short, of the legitimacy of the suspicion he'd harbored with respect to the Communists all his life.

On the other hand, I couldn't help feeling that when Grandmother was combing and brushing the waves and curls away from my forehead so intently, she wasn't thinking of Grandfather's curls, she was waging a battle against Elemér. She used her stinking hairbrush to purge my head of the family's great shame; I mustn't have golden locks, lest by chance I become as handsome as Elemér had been with his golden locks. Except by doing so, she stood in the way of me looking like my grandfather, something that my mother, in opposition to her own mother, supported, even urged with imperatives. When a person reflects on these hidden family maneuvers and feuds, he'll see how parents and grandparents weave the tangled web of their emotional problems, the web of the ignorance, the misconceptions, the meanness, the fears, and the trembling that they'd been carrying around and nursing for centuries, into the fabric of their children's lives, a tangled web in which they themselves have become entangled, and which makes them suffer as much as they. Although I was later able to shake myself free of some of these entanglements, the ones I could recognize for what they were, to break their encrypted, interlacing codes and seals and separate the cultural from the family-specific, still, there was nothing liberating in the attempts, and it seems to me that with all his uniqueness and his unbridled freedom reflex, a person remains a physical and psychological mash-up. He rebels, but at the first opportunity falls right back into the lap of his family's traditions. His personal freedom functions only in a second dimension independent of the social dimension. Within a socially determined framework he can hope for a bit of independence only in his capacity as a mash-up, or put another way, he can extract the intellectual and emotional framework of his striving for independence only from the uniqueness of the awkward admixture that is he. But uniqueness is a far cry from independence. Along with my mother, my brother, and my cousin Márta, we inherited the emphatic shape of our pelvic bones from Cecília Nussbaum. My shoulder is possibly my father's, my arms and chest belong to my maternal grandfather, from whom I also inherited the two purple warts called strawberries, which grow larger with time, and darker, too, the smaller one adorns my chest, the larger the inner crook of my thigh; with him it's the other way around, the larger one adorned his chest, the smaller the inner crook of his thigh. I asked a surgeon once and he said that if it bothers me he'll remove it, but he can't guarantee that there won't be complications. Every morning as I pull on my socks, I see my mother again in my shins, ankles, and feet. I don't know who my thighs belong to. They're rather too rounded to be masculine, but they're not weak, they're not my father's, they're not my mother's, possibly Elemér's, but my distinct impression is that they belong to a peasant woman from Vecsés pressing cabbage with her bare feet. I saw a group of women once pressing cabbage with their bare feet, though not in Vecsés, but Nagyréde; with their skirts hiked up into their waistbands, with their blackened calves and their thighs crisscrossed with a web of bluish white veins, they went about it with such indecent abandon that I was too shocked to take a picture. Whereas they'd have liked me to. At the sight of the stamping feet and the trembling varicose-veined thighs, the strength drained out of my own inherited limbs.

At an earlier time, the characteristic features of my face had reminded me of my mother's features, but they altered with the years, because now, while I shave or brush my teeth, I catch my father's features looking back at me from the mirror, and also the features of his brothers and my own younger brother. The back of my hand, the length of the fingers, the shape and consistency of the nails, the nail bed, and my wrists are identical with the back of the hand and the wrists of my paternal grandmother, Klára Mezei, and in turn her hand is just like the hand of her own mother, Eugénia Schlesinger, who was born in Vienna, and who was my great-grandmother. Her figure has come down to us thanks to a chromotype showing her in an evening gown and carefully color-tinted by Lipót Strelisky in 1866; it was even exhibited at the Paris World's Fair, though by now it is almost completely faded; there is also a life-size portrait of her from 1886 painted by Vilma Parlaghy, the infamous Court painter of the age. Eugénia passed away of postpartum fever in 1887, the year of the World's Fair, just a couple of days after the birth of her fifth child, in the apartment in Nagykorona Street. The family fell into such deep mourning that it can be felt to this day. Princess Parlaghy's painting was made on the basis of the colored chromotype nearly twenty years after Eugénia's death. Her oldest daughter, Klára Mezei, passed Eugénia's hand down to her own daughters, Eugénia, who was named after her, and Magda, and it is my impression that my Aunt Özsi passed these full and finely articulated forms on to Vera, who would not hear of it, she insisted that she had inherited Grandmother Rendl's hand, and Magda passed the special shape of the *ur*-hand to her granddaughter Yvette, but not her son, who had inherited the gallant physique of his grandfather Adolf Nádas, but the small hands of his father, Pál Aranyossi. On the other hand, his feet were anything but small. Of course, these are just contingent details, the contingently named links of the human patchwork, and then we haven't even touched upon the components of a person's soul or mental makeup. Who is to say what strategic design or blueprint serves to assemble us from these various alien physical and psychological components or whether Creation, at the moment of conception, has a worked-out strategic design for the family and individual to begin with which then has no choice but to be integrated into the greater social design, after which the individual can wonder all he wants whether, considering the limbs he has and not some other limbs, people will accept him.

We walked to City Park, we walked so that on his Sunday morning walk we could join my grandfather's friend who was a watchmaker and wore his magnificent musical gold watch hanging from the pocket of his vest over his big belly, and about whom my grandmother Cecília Nussbaum said, belittling him, whether his pocket watch plays music or not, he's not what you'd call a *lumen*, he's nothing but a great big washout, an incompetent no-go. This was more than I could fathom. I understood that my grandmother was equating incompetence with being a no-go, except I couldn't understand why she'd say that, considering that Grandfather's friend would often join us on our Sunday walk. Also, I couldn't follow Grandmother's reasoning because for a very long time I thought that if someone has a watch hanging from his vest pocket over his big, firm belly that played such beautiful music, and his grandchildren are much older than I and he can't take them for a walk on Sunday morning anymore, he must be fabulously wealthy. My grandfather's gold pocket watch, the one he got from Janka for his birthday, and thus they couldn't hock it, meaning they couldn't pawn it when, due to Janka's stinginess or implacability they had nothing to eat, was a Swiss watch, meaning the Watch of All Watches, even though it didn't play music. Which meant that my grandfather's friend had to be richer even than Janka, and even richer than the family of Janka's husband. One time in City Park, Grandfather's friend even bought me cotton candy, which also meant that he was very rich. Grandfather never bought me cotton candy. Grandfather never bought anything. On the other hand, no one expected him to. But then, he never wanted anything for himself either. Throughout his life, he made objects with the greatest of care, beautiful, finely wrought objects with the use of all sorts of precision instruments, but there was perhaps no object in all the world that he would have wanted to own. As if he were filling up his life with pure reason, and not desire. Or else we'd go to Wesselényi Street on Sunday morning to visit Grandfather's sister, the formidable Aunt Janka, who didn't look wealthy at all or, put another way, for a long time I lacked the eye for the hell-bent modesty that, either as a family trait or part of their family upbringing, bound her very tightly to Grandfather. We had to be back for lunch five minutes before the noonday ringing of the church bell so we'd have time to wash our hands and sit down by the kitchen table before it rang, which I didn't mind, because it cut short our Sunday visits to Janka. The maid conducted us into her presence along a stretch of badly lit hallway. Janka sat in the spacious bay window of the corner room, which at this time of the day was drenched in light, and she barely just turned her head to acknowledge our arrival as she watched us approach her in that huge room, almost completely empty of furnishings. Nothing on the white walls except emptiness. No table, no chair in the empty space. A rolled-up carpet, Grandmother said it's a Smyrna. I had no idea what a Smyrna was, but what a miraculous sentence. She has a Smyrna. When they unrolled it on holidays, it took up the entire room. That's what a Smyrna is like, it takes it up. A couple of old armchairs stood against the wall, and in front of the window giving out on Rumbach Sebestyén Street a wing chair and an ottoman. Our steps creaked loudly in the hall, then creaked across the spacious room. The maid silently closed the door once we were inside. The big bay window had a built-in platform with two armchairs. Janka sat on one armchair, Grandfather on the other. Janka once asked me to bring the ottoman, she kept it brief, without the slightest sign of personal intent, son, bring the ottoman, you can look out the window from it. If you stepped up on the platform, you could look out in many directions at once, not that there was much to see on the street. If I then did as I was told and got up on the ottoman, I felt like I was about to crash through the glass and fall out. But frightened as I was, something caught my eye that surprised me, and I never forgot it, though I needed three decades to understand it. An optical phenomenon that the architectural quirk of the bay window must have caused in my field of vision, but by all odds it was not the result of architectural intent but the work of chance, and it must have also been pure chance that I noticed it in the first place.

I had always wanted to be a discoverer, and this time I really did discover something.

Across from us lay the empty yard of the Dohány Street Synagogue, destroyed during the siege, behind the twin Moorish arcades. We all knew that the yard was far from empty. Beneath the ground lay the mass grave of the people who had died in the ghetto, and when after the siege I kneeled or stood on the ottoman in the bay window like this, the dead were still buried there dumped on top of one another. They were so tightly packed that when I looked at the yard, not a blade of grass grew over them.

Janka combed her hair straight back with not a stray strand, curl, or wave anywhere; she was completely gray, nearly white, her mass of hair gathered in a bun over the nape, tightly packed, immaculate. She always and strictly wore nothing but gray. They were housedresses, soft, unadorned, long, with only her ankles in their cotton socks and her uncouth but immaculate house slippers showing. They turned my stomach. Even decades later I saw similar shoes, made without the least pretention to beauty, in the windows of the few surviving shoemakers on the Grand Boulevard. On these short Sunday visits, Janka never offered us anything to eat, ever. Brother and sister sat facing each other, their conversation mutually restrained. Kneeling on the ottoman and leaning against the window frames, I looked out the window, meaning that I looked out through three different windows in three different directions, and the sunlight that came streaming in from the top of the great synagogue that lit up the entire bay window area behind me shone straight in my eye. This strong effect made the eye seek refuge on the periphery, in peripheral vision, and thus sensed the two side windows of the bay window more distinctly than otherwise. They mostly kept silent behind my back, or they spoke about something that because of its incomprehensibility and staccato did not reach my consciousness. This phenomenon was even more pronounced when I stood up on the ottoman, but I was afraid Janka would say that I was getting the patterned velvet upholstery dirty with my feet. They nodded their consent, as if they knew what the other was thinking. They were frugal with their nods, no more than twice, and slowly, with a certain dignity. Sometimes one of them would say something as if in answer to the other's inner monologue. How they did it and what they were thus doing to each other boggled the mind. When once, shortly before he died, I asked Grandfather where his family came from, he said that they came from Bohemia, they first lived in Bratislava for two generations or so, but their father was born in Pest.

Which is as much as I know about the Tauber family to this day. Once I received a letter from one of my German readers, his name was Tauber, who came upon my mother's name, Tauber, in a short biographical sketch, and he asked where my mother's family was from. The Taubers are an ancient family, he wrote, which I invariably find highly amusing, let someone show me a family that is not every bit as ancient as everyone else's. Given a well-structured family tree, who couldn't go as far back as the Big Bang. They were originally from Austria. Their family name first appeared in a document dated 1533, and according to this document, Anton Tauber was the overseer of a princely estate whose name is not given. As a reward for his services, in 1588 he even received a title of nobility along with a coat of arms. Needless to say, their heraldic animal was the *taube*, or dove, as it stands all alone and unarmed in a divided black-and-gold field. By 1592, an ancestor of theirs by the name of Peter Tauber was living in Augsburg, they found his name in the record of the town's patrician families, he was a merchant, he died in 1620, and they also know that he left behind a populous family many of whom settled in Bavaria, though some of them returned to Austria, and a branch of the Austrian family then moved to Hungary, essentially, they spoke Hungarian, the German reader wrote, meaning that they kept their German mother tongue, but they lived in Pápa, spoke Hungarian, and one of their descendants, Alexander Tauber, became a prelate of Szombathely.

As for me, every time I looked, it seemed to me that Wesselényi Street with the sidewalk opposite and behind it the badly damaged row of twin arcades and the synagogue yard with its hidden mass graves was much closer than it actually is. It made my head reel. This strange optical phenomenon plays such an important role in my life that every time I'm in the neighborhood, I take a look at the building. The bay window is now gone. Sometime in the early sixties of the last century they turned the mezzanine-floor apartment into a workshop of some sort, dismantled the bay window, and replaced the window frames with industrial frames. But back then, the cars and buses came into my field of vision through the two sides of the bay window, and though thoroughly blinded by the direct light, I could nevertheless see them passing by in two opposite directions. My body went numb from the unusual sensation. I became a pair of eyes with the raw perception perched on the brain stem, but meanwhile I had to take care that in this great Sunday looking through the window I shouldn't knock my forehead against the windowpane and that I should mind my manners so that Janka won't have to reprimand me. I was terribly afraid of Janka, who was stricter even than my grandfather. When they were together, they did everything differently. Behind my back, their denials were even briefer than their approvals; you could see what sort of people the Taubers are. Their denial was mute, as mute as my grandfather's laughter. A person naturally says no twice. No, no. But they were frugal, they said it only once. They must have regarded the second no as some sort of emotional excess, and redeemed the thought with gestures. Don't say it, I don't want to hear. But as they kept their silence to themselves, they, too, were looking out the window at the dead synagogue yard hidden behind those twin arcades.

And so I was still a child, I was of preschool age, when I already sensed the immeasurable differences, rifts, crevices, and abysses of the complex, multiply delimited yet interconnected family topography of my native town that connected and divided the city's strange human stock along the lines of surviving customs and individual endowments. On the other hand, the division and the bond functioned strictly behind the verbal, basically covertly, isolated from its own conventions. I now see that it is thanks to this profound yet banal knowledge, the knowledge of the web of relationships of the human stock, that we can talk about a native town at all, and why we subsequently cannot replace our native town with any other town. As for the customs pertaining to food, my grandmother's daughters, my aunts Erzsébet and Irén Tauber, followed similarly strict rules in their households in nearby Damjanich Street and in Dembinszky Street. They also sat down to Sunday lunch in their respective homes by the ringing of the church bell, they wouldn't have dreamed of mixing up the dairy pots and pans with the utensils used for meat, unlike in our home on Pozsonyi Street, where these rules went unobserved, not that there was much sense in observing them in Dembinszky Street and in Damjanich Street either after a while, because they ate things that my grandmother considered treyf, an abomination. They ate knackwurst and Gyulai sausage, they ladled sour cream on top of the bean soup that contained pork knuckles, and so on.

They're eating garbage, may their insides rot. They're eating offal. They may not eat pork cracklings, but they devour everything else.

They ate goose cracklings as long as there was goose to be had, and although goose cracklings were available for a while, once the geese vanished, so did their liver and their fatty skins; there was nothing to make fat from anymore, there was nothing, not even bread.

Grandmother's kosher butcher still had matzoh, though. There was also potato bread baked into a brick shape, Russian bread the way the occupying army made it; when they cut it, it crumbled under the knife, so it was better to break it off, but before you raised it to your lips, you had to squeeze it to prevent it from falling apart, but then it stuck together from the squeezing because it was sticky from the potatoes. We stood on line for bread and potatoes, we stood on line for everything. They doled it out, the news got around that they're doling something out someplace or other. This is the expression they used. They're doling out fat. They're doling out sugar. They're doling out margarine today. People got on line because they were doling out yeast. They were doling out socks. On Pozsonyi Street we ate pork cracklings and were happy to do so, with sour pickles or very hot sour peppers, why shouldn't we have eaten pork cracklings when my uncle István Nádas's workers brought pork sausages and other delicacies up from Törökszentmiklós after pig slaughter. He had workers. Which is another thing I couldn't understand. They came from Törökszentmiklós every autumn and stayed until spring. They wouldn't let strangers in their midst, all six had to be one of their own from Törökszentmiklós. But how can strange men, grown men, be had. Or why do they say it. This propriatory relationship was more than I could fathom, because I would have never ever said that someone was someone else's property. I began to work out a language strategy for myself, a way of getting around or bailing out a sentence that was needed because of its place value. I didn't say like they did that I'm taking a tram, or we're grabbing a tram, because it was obvious nonsense. I would have also never said that they're doling something out somewhere. Such linguistic conventions got on my nerves. How can we grab a tram. We're not that strong. I'm taking a cab. That, too, was nonsense. I had to get around it. I'm getting a woman. Which meant that I'm calling someone in to help with the spring cleaning or the wash, to be paid by the day. By now, I was hampered not only because the marks and the visual transformation of the numbers when I was counting; I came up against the same difficulty when I spoke, because at every turn I kept coming up against sentences that I refused to say out loud, but had to get around them or find substitute sentences for them.

Except these sentences weren't always at hand.

I had to consider everything first, and only then could I construct a new sentence to replace the old.

But a bit farther from us, in the thick of town, in the homes of the Chicago area, there were families whose daily customs were even more peculiar. They turned their back on this whole Sunday rigma-role. The noonday ringing of the bell had no effect on them. You'd think they hadn't heard. On the other hand, their children were not allowed to eat anything in our home, because our food wasn't kosher, meaning that it was treyf. I found these families fascinating. They acknowledged no one except themselves, and in front of us, in front of such loathsome strangers, they were sparing even of their words and gestures. We mustn't hear, we mustn't catch on, we mustn't see. I followed, I stared after them, I'd have liked to go inside their homes. The men wore dark suits and long, dark coats and black hats. The women wore wigs, and they even wrapped them around with ker-chiefs. Which didn't make sense, maybe because it didn't have any. Though they were constantly arguing with one another, we were not allowed to hear. We were not allowed to discover anything about their lives, because in their eyes we were even more hateful than the goyim. They had their own language that people who spoke my grandmother's language understood. While the grocery shop in Dembinszky Street was closed on Saturday but open on Sunday, everywhere else in the city they were open on Saturday and closed on Sunday. This is where they did their shopping. I was often sent to their grocery on Sun-day, but by now I can't remember the grocer's name, although I've been trying to remember for months what they called the Orthodox Jewish grocer in Dembinszky Street who made marks in a notebook with an ink pencil for those who bought food from him on credit, and this is how I know about this long-gone practice of buying on credit. Four marks down and one across, that makes five. The grocer pinned his ink pencil behind his ears, behind his impressive, thick payot, and before writing with it, he wet the pencil with his tongue. In these houses the Orthodox boys wore skullcaps and payot as well, and we, who wore nothing, were in the minority, and so in their eyes we were a lot more wicked than the goyim, which is yet another thing I couldn't understand. I still remember that Uncle Nádai, Árpád Nádai, was the superintendent of the house at 37 Dembinsky Street, I even found his name on some surviving documents, which gave me a chance to check if I remembered correctly; he was among the few who acted honorably after the siege, but I can't remember the grocer's name, no matter how hard I try. I didn't like being sent down, go on down, bring this or that, because I felt like I had no business going in there and their strange aversion would make mincemeat of me. Even the character of their aversion was strange. As soon as I entered, they fell silent. In families like this grocer's, on Saturday life came to a stop. We couldn't set foot in their homes, except in the greatest secrecy. Sometimes, after lengthy negotiation, Márta could go see them for a while. She was Márta Szántó, the daughter of Irén Tauber and Imre Szántó, born Imre Schwarz, apropos of which, amid general laughter, he joked that years ago he had been the *schwarzundnigger* of the workers' movement. Once I nevertheless gave it a try. She arranged it, this Márta. But they must have known just by looking that I was a stranger many times over, and the minute I set foot in the apartment, they sent me away. You can't come in here. Not you. But yesterday you said he could come. He doesn't live in this building, that was their argument. Only those that live in this building can come in here. Which meant that since I didn't live there, they had no way of checking up on me. Nevertheless, Márta Szántó was a gifted negotiator. I can't imagine what arguments she brought up or what she was explaining with such vehemence to them, but her tongue was always very quick.

These children couldn't eat at our house, they couldn't even play with us on the stairs or in the yard. They attended a different school. They could play only among themselves, in complete isolation. They had to pass us as if we were made of air, just as their parents did, as if the slightest breeze from us might touch their arm. They didn't greet us even when we gave it a go and greeted them, how do you do, and they didn't bat an eye when we neglected to greet them on purpose. Nowhere else had I ever seen someone taking another person for air with such haughty nonchalance. Once on my way back from New York, I decided to see if the Orthodox rabbi and his wife who were sitting on the other side of the aisle and who were more or less the same age as I would allow a fleeting look in the eyes of one of them, by chance, as it were. When a person is of a certain age, he's more tolerant, at their age the rabbi, or at least his wife, must surely be more tolerant, this is what I based my battle plan on. The same thing happened that had happened half a century before. I could look in their eyes, the children's eyes and the grown-ups' eyes, but I was surprised yet again that they didn't see me, neither the rabbi nor his wife. As far as they were concerned, I did not exist. The ideological fiction of racial seclusion can work miracles that can be followed neither intellectually nor with one's senses. It was just like out on the balcony or in the yard when we were children. These people had blinds drawn over them. Their shutters were closed. The rabbi and his wife didn't pretend I don't exist, I really did not exist. As far as they were concerned, only the six rabbinical students traveling with them existed. The stewards and stewardesses did not exist either. They accepted certain things, they accepted the kosher drinks and the kosher meals, they even said thank you, unwillingly forcing the empty linguistic formula out of themselves. From time to time the students appeared from the depths of the crowded tourist-class section, quietly and with obvious trepidation muttered something to the reverend rabbi, and when they received his short, ritually grudging answer, silent and diffident, they returned to their seats. Surely, their glance had to express profound respect, even adulation, their posture real humility, some pretended humbling of the self, but the rabbi didn't even acknowledge these real or pretended visual signs of ritual feeling, which itself was also part of the ritual. Just as there is no aesthetics in orthodoxy outside of ritual, there is no emotion outside of ritual either. For instance, at dawn they asked him what direction they should face for their prayers, and when they were given the answer, what's more, the rabbi even took care to show them where the sun rises, that's where the sun rises, which they must have seen for themselves through the windows of tourist class, backing away and bowing, they thanked the rabbi for his wise guidance. There we were, slipping from the thick of night into the purple glimmer of dawn.

In these small Orthodox communities in the Dembinszky Street building or the Damjanich Street building, life was regulated to the extreme. The Orthodox families lived in close proximity to one another and communed only with one another. Even after the Holocaust, they lived there as if nothing had happened and as if they weren't living there at all. They avoided contact with the goy families, just as they avoided contact with their Neolog Jewish neighbors, unless their children got around the draconian rules behind their parents' back and we covered for them in their suicidal rebellion. In my Aunt Bözsi's, that is, Erzsébet Tauber's kitchen in Dembinszky Street, they stuffed themselves with fatty noodles that, to be sure, my Aunt Bözsi made with goose fat as long as she could, but when there was no more goose fat to be had, she made it with pork fat. Or they gobbled up the crepes filled with sweetened cottage cheese, which my aunt fried in sunflower oil, not goose fat, in treyf. But she could have fried it in anything she wanted, the cottage cheese and sour cream was treyf, disgusting treyf. Everything. Even the pots and pans that she'd defiled, even if just once. This I understood, I felt what it was like, not to mention the disgusting, apostate person who made these foods. In Budapest, from the time that the Jewish Congress was founded by my great-grandfather in 1868, both Orthodox factions, the Hasidic and the Status Quo Ante, as they called themselves, were forbidden to enter the synagogues of the Neologs, meaning the Congress Jews. They couldn't even go to each other's synagogues, a mutually agreed-on prohibition that, as far as I know, is still in force today.

Nowhere else in the world except for Budapest is it forbidden for the Orthodox and Neolog Jews to enter each other's synagogues.

But in Damjanich Street, they got around their Orthodox parents so they could try out my brand new tricycle in the small yard in the back, where no one could see them. These children were greedy, starved for anything unfamiliar, but even in their animality, they remained more distant than anyone else. It was a strange thing to experience. They could talk to me and tell me to give them my bike or my hoop, they could even hiss at me, angrily, not here, I said, not here. They felt they could order me around, a total stranger whom they would consider a total stranger the following day as well. Okay then, where. They would even snap at me. They harbored a steady, smoldering rage against unfamiliar knowledge, along with the perplexed reactions of strangers. In the backyard. Where else. As if they expected me to know all about the superiority they were nursing and nurturing against me, in isolation from me, and without my knowledge. On the other hand, I got nowhere with them when I called to them out on the balcony or down in the yard. They didn't see me, they didn't hear me. Also, they didn't always speak Hungarian. Sometimes half of it was in Yiddish. Which made it immediately clear that they thought I was an idiot compared with them, because I can't even speak their language, but the minute they stuffed themselves with the last remnants of the pancakes my aunt or my grandmother made or had a go on my brand-new bicycle, they knowingly abused our mutual lack of knowledge. And so their superiority became very real indeed. At that moment they also abused their parents' confidence, which was also part of their real superiority. This real superiority must be taken seriously, it's the sort of superiority that you can't pick a quarrel with, nor can you deprive them of it.

Okay. So it's the yard in the back.

As if they didn't see me, the two little boys the same age as I walked in front of me with the skullcaps on their heads and their wonderfully curly side-locks, and I had to keep in the rear, carrying my bicycle up the stairs and down the stairs to the ruined backyard with its burned-out wall, so they could try it out to their heart's content.

Obviously, they can't carry it themselves, because they might be caught red-handed, or else their religion prohibits them carrying anything that's treyf, that belongs to goyim. Or who knows. I knew nothing, nothing at all about them and was intrigued by all the things I didn't know. My pride couldn't get the better of my thirst for knowledge, and the affront I felt couldn't get the better of it either. It wasn't me, it was the power of enlightenment in me, which wasn't entirely missing from them either; after all, their interest in treyf continued unabated. If I now do their bidding without a word, they will realize that I'm not their enemy and they needn't be quite so harsh with me. And then it came to an end just as quickly. They left me high and dry with my tricycle, as I called after them in vain. They didn't walk away hurriedly, they didn't walk away leisurely, they'd done with me for the day, they'd reached the end of their momentary outburst of freedom, and so off they went in the little black suits they'd outgrown, as if they had no intention of sniffing the air of my alien world ever again.

Still, my cousin Márta had a little friend from among them in Damjanich Street. I don't remember her name. In the greatest secrecy, of course. Who didn't taste the food at our table because she was hungry, or because she wanted to taste the unfamiliar food but, fighting back her tears, she was intent on violating the law. It felt good watching this little girl in the act of sinning. It was a great discovery for me. To see why she does what she does. In her excitement over breaking the law, she stuffed herself with the forbidden food as if she didn't even enjoy it. She stuffed herself from sheer intellectual pleasure, the audacious pleasure of the rebel. Trying out whether she'd die of it, or if the heavens would come crashing down on her. She was perched on a stool, and after a couple of bites, she veritably grew limp from her breach of the law. I witnessed such rebellious eating later on as well, but only from girls. The boys, I think, were not ready or were not up to such rebellion. Perhaps dogma occupies a firmer place in the minds of boys. They ate only to sate their appetites, and even that much less frequently than the girls. But by the early fifties, these families were all gone from these houses down to the last man, having made Aliyah, as they called it, meaning they wanted to be free of this foreign land and emigrate to Israel.

For instance, there was the time when the great love of my adolescent life, Hédi, the wonderful Hédi Sahn with her wonderful eyes, whom I respected, among other things, because she could chat with our teacher, Dezső Gulyás, at the blackboard about higher mathematics so that our jaws dropped, we didn't even understand the conjunctions, she would chat at the blackboard like the little countess Steinmann in Karinthy; anyway, there she was, squatting in the corner of the immaculate pantry of their apartment in Dohány Street, stuffing herself with something all the same, stuffing herself for all she was worth in spite of God's laws. She had to be quick, she had to chew and swallow in haste, before her mother in the salon could grow suspicious and come out, or in her infinitely bored manner, call out into the hall after her, Hédi, Hédike, Hédi dear, what are you doing in there all this time, Hédi, Hédikém. It was Yom Kippur. On this Jewish holiday that's an hour longer than a full day, she shouldn't have eaten at all. Their home had to be cleaned beforehand of the tiniest crumb. When I asked her once how she knew so much math, she shrugged. I was hoping she'd reveal the secret of secrets to me, because I couldn't even understand the most basic operations properly. From Kati, who else. Kati was her older sister, six years her senior, a grown woman, perhaps even more beautiful than she, which caused no small amount of anguish for Hédi. Kati was in college studying mathematics. Quickly, quickly, she must stuff herself with something, she must have her revenge. But why. I don't know. For everything. It was my impression that mathematics was the only thing that did not have its antithesis in her, because everything else did, even our love. She was jealous. She was in love with several boys at once, but even when she pretended that she considered me a snot-nosed crybaby, nothing more, she was tormented by jealousy.

She loves only me and no one else.

Which wasn't true, but she kept saying it. She was hoping that she might actually end up feeling it, and then her loving so many others wouldn't torture her anymore.

Anything, just so her mother shouldn't have the last word, her mother, of whom she was more afraid than the Almighty, may the Devil take her.

As for me, I wasn't in love only with her either, but no matter how we fought against it, I was also in love with Maja and Margitka and Éva, and also Lívia.

How can you love that dim-witted Éva Juhász.

This gorgeous big girl, this born rebel had enormous almond-shaped blue eyes framed by long, thick lashes and an abundant crown of hair, dark brown but tending to black because of its deep red highlights, that cascaded down to the middle of her back, and she let me sink my fingers into this hair for hours and comb it for hours, I could hide my face in its wilderness for hours leaning so far into it that its strands didn't tickle anymore, and she was happy to do the same with me. She kissed my neck, she snorted into my neck. She trembled from fear and the even greater pleasure of transgressing the law. She was terrified of her mother, and she was terrified of her mother's mathematical genius even more, because their mother was also an exceptional mathematician, and possibly her severity was an offshoot of her mathematical skills, but from the point of view of the dictatorship of the proletariat she was a dangerous class alien, because their jewelry shop had been even bigger than Janka's, until it, too, was nationalized. She managed to land a job with a big company as a certified chief accountant, which as far as I remember had nothing whatsoever to do with jewelry. Sometimes all three women had migraines at the same time, and then they would lie down all over the place in the big apartment, groaning and whining. On the other hand, Hédi dreaded not only this fearful chief accountant, she also dreaded the will of the Almighty. As far as I could tell, she made no distinction between the two, between her mother and the Almighty.

Years later, there was also Mari, the wife of my very fickle friend several years older than I, whom he repeatedly abandoned, then repeatedly talked into taking him back. Mari was the secretary of the generally respected and no less feared eminent Jewish scholar Professor Scheiber. When Scheiber retreated into his office crammed full of books and papers, Mari pulled out the drawer of her desk and would stuff herself with things like scones with cracklings, cheese pockets, and cocoa Danish, foods that were made under suspect conditions from forbidden ingredients that she should not have even touched, at the Rabbinical Seminary, at any rate. Because if someone ate unclean food, the people around him concluded that he had turned his back on religion. She grabbed the liver paté that, needless to say, was made from pork liver, what else, she pressed a hefty portion of the paté from its tight skin casing into her mouth, then she tore off a piece of the nice white bread and stuffed that in, too, then took a bite of the fiery hot pickled peppers. As with a mixture of trepidation and enjoyment she chewed, chumped, devoured, tasted, and swallowed the treyf that we'd bought just ten minutes before at the corner butcher's on the other side of József Boulevard, because except for pork cracklings, perhaps liver paté was the cheapest spread to be had in contemporary Budapest, as the liquid from the preserved peppers she'd bit into dribbled from her hand into the open drawer, and as she huffed and puffed from the hot peppers and her teeth, lips and chubby cheeks were pure, loathsome *khazir* from all that treyf, she kept glancing at the doors, she kept her ears open, she enjoyed it, she enjoyed waiting for this wrathful scholar god to come back in for something and catch her at it.

And so he did, he came back in again and again because he was preoccupied or forgetful, but visibly also to enjoy the company of the young woman grown quite chubby from eating the forbidden food. It was a very wholesome, firm chubbiness. The gentleman scholar couldn't have cared less what the woman was eating, how she could afford it, how much she was being paid, but he cared all the more for her legs, lap, and breasts. He was a Vengeful God who cared only for philological minutiae. He harkened to the details only from the vantage point of the universal horizon. He came so he could keep under control every breath, every movement, every stirring of her breast under her blouse, to keep the woman's breathing under his control, and if he can't have his way with her even now, because this blond scapegrace is in the room, if he can't force her to the floor of her office, then at least he should thunder at her and not be the loser. This much at least he is entitled to. After all, he's the tribal chief around here. Mari wore light blouses, at times very tight turtleneck sweaters. Her manners were not refined, but her innate intelligence was ostentatious, bordering on the offensive. She lived in a hellish marriage with my photographer friend and colleague Miklós. They relied on me to act as justice of the peace, an impossible undertaking because it wasn't one or the other at fault, because without rhyme or reason, they were mutually intent on turning each other's life into a living hell. It was no use reasoning with them, and it was no use laughing at them for their mud wrestling. But mud wrestling may not be an apt analogy. It was more like they wanted to push each other underwater. They gave no indication of loving or even liking each other, nor were they attracted to each other. But they would not stand the other cheating on them, whereas they cheated on each other mutually and repeatedly. Still, for some time they were not on equal footing because, whether on purpose or not, my friend Miki always let on that he'd cheated, then sat back and watched triumphantly to see what would come of it, all the while that he himself harbored no suspicion of his wife's infidelity.

Theirs was the very early marriage of two war orphans, right away with a beautiful and charming child, and their mutual cheating had just one object, to make the other suffer, as if in the interest of their own survival, they had to kill each other, the sooner the better.

I forgot to mention it to you just now, Mari.

Will you please bring me that file, Mari.

Why must I beg you repeatedly for everything, Mari.

Scheiber spoke to Mari in an affected nasal tone, while he spoke to others with true contempt for their infinite feeblemindedness, vulgarity, and ignorance. In which he was theoretically correct; after all, in those years he was among the few erudite enough to sustain the continuity of interrelated cultures.

Call the Chevra Kaddisha, Mari.

You let the date drop from your head again, Mari.

That someone drops something from their head I heard for the first time in my life from him.

He'd leave three times and come back three times, because this slipshod young man who, to add insult to injury, was unashamedly leaning against the huge desk packed with books and papers, and who was wearing out the floor and chair of the institution in his charge where he had no right to be, this obviously sexually mature blond male who did not deserve his attention to begin with, because no one could have stood lower in the social hierarchy than he, refused to leave. An industrial student. An orphan. Someone who obviously had nothing and no one in the world and never would. In short, he lacked a nexus to help him. Back then, this is what they called social connections. And Scheiber was right. In a dictatorship, connections are what you are measured by, and I had none. In those days it must have been all too obvious just by looking at me that I'm just barely tolerated in the world, for the time being, still tolerated. The question was for how much longer. There was no knowing. Accordingly, he did not acknowledge my greeting, which I did not offer as a formality but proffered with the profound respect due to his enormous knowledge. He did not even nod. I liked the feel of his ritual indifference on my skin. It was an enjoyment akin to the sensual. I read all his short, pithy publications in the papers and journals; they belonged to the sphere of classical Hungarian literature and brought into play an enormous philological apparatus. He called attention to errors, he rectified, he amended, he disaffirmed, he put things in their proper place. And he was invariably right. I was surprised to discover that objective, disengaged knowledge could have such a quality, I'd never experienced anything like it before.

No two ways about it, this eminent scholar was jealous the moment he laid eyes on me. He looked ritually right through me as through a pane of glass. He did not want to see a fly like me in his institution, a civilian like me; he didn't want the young friend of the despised husband on his premises. The husband hadn't made anything of himself either, he was just a rabbinical student who'd left the fold to become a salesman at a photography shop in the Inner City, and by all odds, Scheiber considered him a *niemand*, a zero, a nobody. But because of Mari, he accepted his ritual flattery. Miki was the grand master of flattery, an artist at beguiling, though with his exaggerations he invariably placed his flattery in quotation marks. There was an air of liveliness and mischief about him, something inherently kind. In no time at all, he swept everyone off their feet. Everyone except his wife, that is. On the longest wall of the secretariat of the Rabbinical Seminary, ascetically furnished to the extreme, between the upper ledge of the filing cabinets and the ceiling, there hung twelve perfectly aligned portraits. They were medium-size paintings set in frames of the same size, but the work of very different artists. The first time I set foot in this place, Scheiber was standing by the open filing cabinets, poring over some document. With his glasses pushed up over his forehead, he was intent on studying it, leaning in very close, he almost had to touch the document with his nose to see. Besides the glasses pushed up over his forehead he needed another pair that he generally left in his study or else could never find.

When I entered, he looked up from the document but did not see me. He did not return my greeting. As for me introducing myself or for Mari to introduce me, that was clearly out of the question.

Mari, must I petition you for everything.

About six months later, I nevertheless chanced an introduction, which surprised him so much that he accepted it; also, the moment I entered, I saw that everything was in the best possible order between the two of them. I was familiar with this form of Jewish asceticism devoid of any and all aesthetic principles from earlier; Hédi Sahn's apartment in Dohány Street was like this, and Janka Tauber's, too, in Wesselényi Street.

My great-grandfather Mór Mezei's likeness hung among the portraits of eminent men.

I didn't say to Mari that that there is my great-grandfather, it would've been useless, we had no historical background in common. Whereas I even knew who had commissioned the portrait and for what occasion. This knowledge came from a bygone world with which neither of us had anything in common anymore. Mari worked for Scheiber out of necessity and not conviction. She didn't have anything or anyone either, she hadn't learned a trade, at most she had a high school diploma. She'd have preferred to work somewhere, at least, this is how she fantasized, where she wouldn't have had to keep her aggressive godlessness, which however was by no means atheism, under wraps. As for me, I had nothing whatever to do with the situation, at least that's what I thought, that I have nothing whatsoever to do with what is going on here, a place where by all odds they'd forgotten my great-grandfather just as they'd forgotten everyone else; why shouldn't they have forgotten, considering how, as a consequence of the mass extermination, they themselves had barely survived, and everything but everything that belonged to the conservative liberal anteworld with its sham ceremoniousness and rancid elegance had disappeared in the depths of time.

Still, the memory of his person might not be displeasing to those who with their bare survival were moving about in this place fallen through the net of space and time. This is how I comforted myself.

She never slept with Scheiber, I never asked, but she never missed a chance to tell me why she never ever slept with him.

This never ever didn't sound convincing to me.

She insisted that really, not her, she swears, what an idea, and I should stop laughing, she dragged out the words, she slowed them down and modulated them into a veritable falsetto, the way Jewish women of breeding used to stretch out their nasals in Pest back then.

She respects him, she veritably idolizes him, she really shouldn't, but she's never met anyone with such formidable knowledge in all her life. Besides, he's too old for her. And also, she can't abide men as ill-groomed as he. Miki is sloppy, slovenly, she hates him with all her heart, but at least he takes a shower, he goes to the pool, and if she persists, he'll even wash his hair. An insufferable human being, surely I agree. Never. Not with him. Ever. I should believe her when she says that she'd find him repulsive as a man.

When Mari spoke about anything, she did so as if she were fighting off her world-weariness, but more than anything, was tired unto death of her fellow men. She especially finds the male of the species boring. Handsome, hideous, old, young, brainy, dim-witted, to her it's all the same. Scheiber, too, me too, her husband, too. Her little girl may have been the one exception. Had she had a son, she might have found him boring as well. A stream of monotonous prayers snatched from a never-ending melody issued from between her lovely lips, but with her acute presence, she kept your gaze captive all the time.

She had no one; soon after the siege, her parents simply died from what had happened, and Mari, a young girl of high school age, found herself alone in the big apartment in Damjanich Street. An aunt who lived in the countryside may have survived the concentration camps, at least, that's what I seem to recall.

This slovenly dressed eminent scholar was forever in a huff over this orphaned young woman, not that Mari was the only woman who exercised such a visibly pronounced effect on him. His jackets, worn at the elbows, hung from him, as did his slacks and his ties shining with grease, his always rumpled shirts, which at times were missing a button. In his wounded pride he was forever unsatisfied with Mari, he had it in for her, and obviously, not because of the various documents and missed phone calls.

It costs me money, Mari, your negligence, it costs me a lot of money, it costs me dear. As if he had reason to call Mari to account. Or if he doesn't, Mari makes sure every minute to furnish him with one.

I'm going to fire you, Mari.

You won't fire me, Professor.

And he didn't.

If he came out or wasn't there at the moment, or went to give a class or to the library, or he went off to give a lecture in his ungainly hat, you could look into his study from the secretary's office, it was a spacious corner room that was filled with nothing but books, manuscripts, and documents and the musty smell of old books and papers. It was a yellow smell, the smell of yellowed paper. The smell of the slow progress of acid and cellulose toward a shared destiny, and it held me in thrall. All those books and manuscripts stood piled sky-high, they buried every piece of furniture under them or barred the way to them, and there were not a few Latin and Hebrew incunabula among them. When he was not there, the door to his study had to remain open so Mari could make sure there was no one sneaking around inside among the antique documents and incunabula. There was a war being waged which, because of the wicked rabbinical students and the even more wicked city antiquarians, was a losing battle. Manuscripts and books kept disappearing in the Seminary, and the two of them were always ready to pounce or were busy searching for things. Something was always missing or was missing yet again. It lay hidden beneath the piles of paper and was later found, or had in fact been stolen. Because of the suspicions and accusations that never let up, a light insanity vibrated in the air between them.

I also knew that the impressive block of buildings where the Rabbinical Seminary of Pest opened its doors in 1877 along with the Jewish teachers' school was built neither from public funds nor public donations, but from the reparations that His Highness the emperor and King Franz Joseph had exacted from the Jews after the defeat of the 1848–49 revolution and freedom fights because they dared bear arms against him, then decided to pay back from the generosity of his heart. Thanks to Great-grandfather Mezei's gift as a tactician, coupled with his political clear-sightedness, His Majesty returned the money expressly for the establishment of the Rabbinical Seminary and Teachers' Training School. The wise Mezei, because this adjective invariably graced his name, had invited his king to make this gesture, one he could hardly refuse. At least, this is how political public opinion had it at the time.

Taking into consideration that the newspapers and those who laud someone may exaggerate on special occasions, wrote the anonymous correspondent of the conservative liberal *Magyar Hírlap* on January 16, 1916, the fact remains that his friends and those who respect him had showed him every sign of love and affection already one day before his eightieth birthday.

Already at the time of the morning visit, an exceptional number of people looked him up at his apartment in Nagykorona Street, or sent him letters and telegrams from all levels of society, the reporter wrote. Deputations from the countryside came to pay homage. Among them were the Israelite village district presidents, the purpose of their visit being to surprise the president of their national office with the resolution of their extraordinary general assembly, which accepted, amid general approval, the proposal that his portrait be painted and given temporarily to the Hungarian Jewish Museum until such time when their self-government shall possess a place worthy of displaying it, and they now handed him the elegant leather-bound copy of the extract with due ceremony. Prime Minister Count István Tisza, with whose father, the former prime minister Count Kálmán Tisza, he enjoyed playing *tarok* so much in the Liberal Club, as he did with Jókai, congratulated him in a letter, wrote the anonymous correspondent.

Mikszáth had called him Tisza's mamluk, as if Tisza had acquired him from slave merchants at some exotic oriental market, while Jókai called him Tisza's kibitz, who does not participate in the game, just sits on the side, watches, and at times makes some unwarranted comment, which couldn't have seemed too complimentary in the eyes of a young man who was an avid and discerning reader with regard to his ancestor. The novelists Kálmán Mikszáth and Mór Jókai bore greater respect in my eye than my ultraconservative great-grandfather. Mikszáth was not a kibitz and he was not a mamluk, and in his reports on the activities of the National Assembly, he jovially lampooned subjects that my great-grandfather and his political friends took so much to heart. On the other hand, today I'd say that because of my professional interest, Mikszáth was the greater authority in my eyes, but Jókai I adored, and for a long time I nursed the ambition of reading everything he ever wrote, yet my great-grandfather, the kibitz, the mamluk, dwelling at a mystifying distance affected me more than they, a fact that I not only ignored for decades, I didn't even realize that that was the case.

My intellectual orientation contained a hidden current that by all odds I should have noticed so that sooner or later I could acknowledge it as my own.

My dear friend Móric, allow me to join the ranks of those who approach you on your birthday. With the feeling of the utmost respect and friendship, may I wish you the best of health in body and soul so that you may see the turn of the century and find inner satisfaction in the success you have achieved in public life.

With hearty greetings, your most devoted István Tisza.

Sándor Wekerle from Dresden, Count Béla Serényi, Baron Kuffner, Baron Kohner, Béla Weith, Endre György, and Gusztáv Gratz greeted the celebrant. I have no idea why from Dresden. Perhaps they had gone there as a delegation to see the king of Saxony. It is interesting in the protocol list published in the paper that Baron Kuffner and

Baron Kohner are mentioned only by their surnames, as if the anonymous correspondent of *Magyar Hírlap* wished to call attention to their Jewish origin, this despite the great European current of conservative liberalism and the principle of equality. So now, one hundred years later, I wish to append their first names in print. Baron Kuffner's first name was Károly, Baron Kohner's was Adolf. Our great-grandfather was also well acquainted with Baron Adolf Kohner's father, Zsigmond, who for half a century was the legal advisor to the Commercial Bank of Hungary in Pest, while Baron Zsigmond Kohner, after he'd been ennobled, became vice president and later owner of the bank. As far as I know, Great-grandfather had decided to deflect the confidential Court propositions to endow him with a title of nobility, membership in the Upper House, and a baronetcy precisely because of the fine little precedents and distinctions that stood in sharp contrast to the principle of equality. But his makeup may also have played a part in the decision. A bit earlier on, with his fastidious political taste, he even rejected the title of court counselor. I can understand this stance of his because, throughout a lifetime, I have also done all I could to give formal honors a wide berth, or better yet, to make sure in good time that such a thing shouldn't even come up in the first place. Which of course was neither sensible nor the proper thing to do. An attempt of this magnitude to ignore innate human vanity and the love of flaunting one's feathers is a sign of inordinate vanity or overscrupulousness, which can stir a strong sense of antipathy in others, and so a sensible person should try to steer clear of it. Seen from another perspective, it is a sign of excessive vanity and excessive narrow-mindedness when a man tries to avoid his mistakes.

When with due respect and the greatest discretion they offered him a rank or title, ready for any eventuality, the Court waited patiently for the delinquent's response. According to protocol, the answer had to consist of two parts, the sublimest degree of gratitude and thanks presented in the most elaborate and formal manner possible, yet without the least sign of familiarity, to be accompanied by a substantial donation of money. The candidate had to offer the donation for the construction of public buildings and charities as if by way of an afterthought, and with all due modesty. The Jewish candidate for a title of nobility, a baronetcy, or membership in the Upper House had to know the number of zeroes expected of him. If the number of zeroes was not commensurate with the significance of the occasion, the Court made no further efforts on his behalf, as if the confidential proposition had never been offered, which in turn was part of the highest Court etiquette.

Mezei's daughters and sons considered their father's negative answer colossal nonsense and they were outraged. He hadn't even bothered to consult them. It might look for all the world as if he had acted out of avarice, they said, as if he didn't want to spend the money. Especially Záza, Erzsébet Mezei, was furious with her accusation, but Klára, Anna, Pál, and Béla also grumbled.

What makes their father think he can interfere in their fate in such a brutal manner.

Great-grandfather had a good laugh at the not completely unfounded conjecture that his tightfistedness played a part in his rejection of the title. Mór Mezei rarely laughed. He may not have been tightfisted, but he considered carefully where he put his money and where he did not. But even with his full-hearted laugh he couldn't assuage the anger of his children.

He'd just turned down the king, Záza, who was the most beautiful and most careful with her words, said, even if, in line with the rules of Court etiquette, by all odds, the king hadn't even been informed.

You can't turn down a king, even if he never finds out. It's pure nonsense. Nonsense was the expression they used back then when they wished to characterize such lack of social sensibility.

All the same, he said, cutting his laughter short, he'd like to ask his sons and daughters, and especially Záza, or Elisa, these being the pet names for Erzsébet, who, since the death of their mother and in opposition to their grandmother, their aunts, the housekeepers, chambermaids, and nannies, acted as the chief representative of her half-orphaned siblings, a role she fulfilled throughout her lifetime and remained an old maid, she remained by her father's side and kept house for him, in short, he'd like to ask his children to give due consideration to a case that calls for due consideration.

Accepting it would have been the real nonsense.

Meaning, devoid of sense. Non-sense. *Avec un trait d'union. Absurdité.*

He'd been discoursing, debating and teasing his aristocratic friends at the Liberal Club as their equal, and so would rather not become a parvenue now. He can't expose his aristocratic friends to such an awkward situation, and especially himself.

It was a persuasive argument. At least, they had to acknowledge to themselves that a Mezei cannot commit a *faux pas* of this magnitude. Even Záza fell silent, and exactly thirty years passed without any of them mentioning this uncouth rejection of the Court's offer again.

Until this certain birthday celebration, that is.

In the evening he was celebrated by the Hungarian freemasons, of which he was an honorary grand master.

I read a number of works and manuscripts about the freemasons written with insider's knowledge, I studied their constitution, if for no other reason than to gain insight into my great-grandfather's activities, but for lack of personal experience, I managed to understand their radical freethinking and the web of their secret relationships, but nothing more. Why deny it. The thought that the secret of freemasonry cannot be revealed even if the freemasons themselves were to wish it is an intriguing proposition, not to mention the secret signs on the basis of which they recognized and surely continue to recognize one another even now, but of which we, the outsiders, know nothing and consequently cannot find ourselves in a situation where we could identify them. The Jesuit monk Töhötöm Nagy, who left the Church, wrote a book entitled *Jesuits and Freemasons*, and it was this book, which he wrote in Spanish but was later translated into German and Hungarian, that affected me the most, because its subject is secrecy as such, the system of secret networks, confidentiality and conspiracy. Had he written the major work of his life as he had planned, the one based on his own secret service activities for the Communists, and had he situated the principles of Communist secrecy within the grand secret web of Christianity, of which freemasonry and communism are two intriguing branches, the effect of his insights would have been even greater.

In the course of his long, industrious, beneficent career, the conservative-liberal paper survived, Mezei brought up several generations in the spirit of the genuine love of mankind. The ceremony was organized by the Könyves Kálmán lodge, of which he was grand master for life, but the distinguished representatives of other Budapest lodges were also in attendance, the full leadership, meaning the body of main officers of the Hungarian Symbolic Lodge, as well as the members of the Council of the Hungarian Freemasons' Association. Those present filled the hall to capacity, jostling one another for space. Surely, the celebrating crowds were jostling one another in the Podmaniczky Street headquarters of the Grand Lodge, which in the language of Freemansonry was called a workshop, I now realize. The ceremony was not only grand in effect, but was exceptionally heartfelt and intimate, writes the paper. Every time a speaker finished, the tumultuous and hearty cheering lasted for minutes on end.

Needless to say, the paper writes all this according to the style of the time, and I make minor changes in word order, spelling, and punctuation for the sake of easier reading, but have kept the language intact.

On the same day, the bourgeois radical *Világ* payed homage to the eighty-year-old celebrant with a political portrait of sorts written by Jób Bede. Bede's name and works have sunk into oblivion, but luckily, old lexicons have retained traces of his activities. He was a respected journalist of his day, he hailed from Transylvania, where he had studied law and philosophy at the University of Kolozsvár, and was already a well-known writer and translator in Pest when, succeeding Kálmán Mikszáth, he became parliamentary reporter for the liberal *Pesti Hírlap*. It was a great honor, following in Mikszáth's footsteps. A journalist could hardly have hoped for a more illustrious career at the time,

When I left the House of Representatives this afternoon, Bede wrote, and walked across Lipótváros, I pondered what I should write about Mór Mezei, the typically strong-willed eminence of Lipótváros, but first I had to cross Nagykorona Street, then Fürdő Street, and proceed up Andrássy Boulevard. The editorial offices of *Világ* were located in the building at 47 Andrássy Boulevard, in an apartment facing the Oktogon, to where just two years later, on August 4, 1918, in Turnau in Bohemia, Klára Mezei would be addressing a letter to her son-in-law, His Excellency Pál Aranyossy, who at the time was also working for *Világ*, and was thus a colleague of the elderly Bede.

The letter was really for her daughter Magda. It was the last year of war, and they did not go to Gömörsid for the summer.

Eugie, the oldest of the Nádas children, thought it best to separate their mother, who was unable to recover from her mourning and shock, for the summer months at least, from their father, who was becoming more irascible than ever, and she would not even allow her to be alone with Miss Júlia in Gömörsid, who probably left for America during the fall of that same year, or with the youngest of the children, Miklós and Laci, meaning our father. From April of the previous year, no one in the family could forget Gyuri's suicidal howling. She and László Mándoki had been happily married for just six months, and Eugie would also have liked to share this experience with her mother, if only a bit. Sometimes a person is first and foremost happy, and sometimes a person is happy in spite of everything. Mándoki was serving as chief physician in a military hospital in Turnau, Eugenie followed him to this enchanting little Renaissance town, then invited her mother to visit them, and it was from here that she sent her letters to Magda.

Magda had just recently been married to Pál Aranyossi. The newlyweds were planning to move house in the city, and Klára felt that she would be best advised to address the letter meant for her daughter to her son-in-law at *Világ*.

My dear Magda, Klára Mezei wrote to her daughter, I have already received two letters from Papa, and I also received letters from Záza and Pista, but you, it seems, are waiting for the price of the stamp promised you, and doggedly refuse to write until you have received it.

So you may not have an excuse, I am herewith sending it. But now I expect you to honor our agreement and write to me every day, even if these letters will contain nothing more than our daily telephone conversations did back home.

Surely you know by now that we are satisfied with the apartment. Naturally, you must not imagine the comforts of a lordly mansion or an elegant hotel. The apartment is furnished, but they were expecting people from Prague to use it, who needless to say would bring all sorts of furnishings and household items along with them, just as we had done at one time when we spent the summer in the house in Pesthidegkút, and accordingly there are no dishes in the apartment, so we eat from plates borrowed from here and there, we don't bother with whether they're flat or soup plates, white or flower-patterned. We use the compartments of the food carrier for bowls. No lunch or dinner passes when we don't recall how, if she were to set eyes on our table, Záza would clap her hands together in surprise. And when yesterday an ensign suffering from malaria came to visit us from Laci Mándoki's hospital, who in his happy civilian days was a designer in Budapest, and thus a colleague of your sister Eugie from one of the upper classes, we showed him the stub of a candle glued to a matchbox so he should find inspiration in it for one of his interior-decorating ventures. By the way, just today we noticed that the apartment bears an uncanny resemblance to our summer place in Pesthidegkút, at least in this regard, that there is a constant draft running through it. We discover the disadvantages step by step, and each time we discover such disadvantages, poor Doctor Mándoki bows his head just a little more. Regardless of how much our fine gentleman is in love with Eugie, he will heave a sigh of relief when he waves good-bye to us from the window of the departing train. All the problems of our household weigh on his shoulders, because with his prestige as a doctor and soldier, he can get his hands on things for us, while if I go, a stranger who can't even speak Czech, they'd make short shrift of me.

Our main concern is that despite their initial promise, they didn't give us flour tickets and they didn't give us bread tickets. But we do the best we can, and when the time comes, the children will return home having gained weight.

I won't write more today, so there'll be something left over for the next letter.

One hug, two hugs, ten hugs from your loving mother, Klára.

My dear Magda, she writes a week later. I swear by the Almighty that I have not been such an industrious letter writer as I am now. It is not my fault that I don't write to each of you on a regular basis. I had to excuse myself beforehand, because this time you had to wait for my long-promised letter so long not only because the post office is so slow. I received two letters from you this week. In the last one you acknowledge receipt of the money for stamps. Miklóska has also received your postcard. But even if I did not write a letter, I gave news of the outstanding events of the week on my postcards. Last Sunday's outing was very nice, except when tired and hungry we reached our destination, we got nothing to eat. We found only the owners living in the hotel. They didn't even open it this year. But as far as you're concerned, our journey to Reich Enberg on Friday is much more important. We left the villa at one o'clock in the afternoon, but on foot and by train the trip there as well as back took up so much time that not much was left for our stay. And so I don't really know whether the shortage of linen goods is as dire as they say, or perhaps I wandered into the wrong shops. I couldn't buy anything for Eugie. But I bought you enough fabric for a dress. Eugie and I thought that for this winter your velvet coat will still do, so it makes more sense to buy fabric for a dress rather than a suit. There's enough time for a suit in spring, when the choice of color won't be restricted. I hope the fabric will win your approval, but I might as well tell you that it is also a birthday present, along with the tailoring cost, of course.

I hope that your colleague has returned from vacation by now, and you will have days off while your aunt Záza is in Pest. Be sure to look her up. I can't say for sure yet when we will be returning. Papa writes that we should stay till September. Though I may not do this. I may prolong our stay a bit longer. It depends partly on our flour supply. They have already harvested nearly everything here, and we were inordinately surprised to see that there's no weekday and no Sunday here when it comes to the harvest. But they're wise to take advantage of the good weather. What they don't gather in the morning is sure to be soaked in the afternoon. I don't know what the weather is like back home, but we haven't had much warm weather here, on the other hand, we've had plenty of rain and wind. One day this week on an uncertain cloudy afternoon I went somewhere with Miklós and Lacika, and we got so rained on that every bit of clothing we wore got soaked through and through. There wasn't a house anywhere where we could have asked for shelter. Lacika was so frightenend, he even forgot about his constant whining. Miklóska is not behaving much better here than he does in Pest, on the other hand, he eats with the appetite of a wolf. And here, because of the scarcity of supplies, you can't be choosy about what you eat. They're in much better condition, I'm very sorry that I didn't have them weighed when we came. But there's not much hope of them learning German here. They refuse. I don't know why they're so obstinate. I think I have now written to you about everything and there is nothing left but to bid farewell to you with love and hugs.

Put war bond stamps on your letter, and put these away. This is the boys' message.

Your loving mother, Klára.

Give Pál my greetings.

She writes her next letter in August.

My dear Magda, I have received the socks for darning, and thank you for what you sent in your name. Every time I hold it in my hand and see that there are no holes in it, I shall think of the good-hearted benefactor with gratitude. Not to mention how grateful I will be for the new socks once the darning thread runs out for good. We're close to it. I still have black, but the white thread that I brought along is gone. And I can't buy any other color to replace it. It seems that Laci and Miklós will be running about in white socks with holes, because there is a shortage of around yarn. For this reason, the embroidery I brought with me will also get back home unfinished, but Eugie has finished her cross-stitch pillow at last and is embroidering her third handkerchief. I received a postcard from you dated the second of the month, in which you complain about the heat. I hope that the heat has let up since then there, too. If this letter will get there somewhat faster, you will be warned in good time that your father's birthday is the 14th. Remind Pista, too. Even if you should have remembered without being told, he is bound to forget.

For the time being I can't say when we will be leaving for home. Your father may be able to give you information about it.

Hugs from your loving mother, Klára.

Then a couple of days later.

My dear Magda, Bandi writes that you were ill. Let me know without delay what the problem was. Also write and tell me the size of your waist, measure it tight over your clothes. I bought myself a body corset here for 44 crowns, which is very cheap, considering that I had paid 78 for yours. I would now like to get one for you as well. Don't delay, their stock is limited.

Another lovely day today, in the afternoon, it being Sunday, we're going on an excursion.

Hugs from your loving mother, Klára.

And along with you, Pál.

Dear Magda, she writes in the last letter she posted from Turnau, your letters of August 3 reached here only yesterday, the 14th; I was happy to get the one meant for me because I couldn't possibly imagine the reason for your stubborn silence. The truth is I still don't understand why you had to wait with your answer until you received several of my letters, but let's forget it and turn to the contents of your letter. First, accept my thanks for your good wishes. As grateful as I am for them, Lacika was just as happy with his birthday present. After he opened it, he didn't even notice that the congratulations were missing. The reason he doesn't write to you is that he is lazy. I don't know whether I'm a degree more permissive with the children, or the children are even lazier than you, be that as it may, this year I can't get either Miklós or Laci to do anything. But as far as that goes, much of what I brought with me to sew I'm taking back in the same state. But at least I have an excuse. Keeping house has been more difficult and tiring than last year. Sometimes we even have to do the cooking, even if it's not the midday meal. And what can I say, we don't have more pots and pans for it than you do, so that before I cook, I have to wash the dishes. But when it comes to table linen, you're way ahead of the game when I let on that you will find your table linen on the bottom shelf of the linen closet. There are also two tablecloths with unfinished hems with 12 serviettes; please leave them there for the time being, because I prefer to do the hem myself. I trust that until I'm done, the rest will do for you. After all, by the time you get this letter, I should be back, more or less. But if this letter should reach you faster than I expect, let me remind you to write to me, and do so immediately, and don't forget your waist measurement taken over your clothes, tightly measured, if indeed you should still be wanting a corset. If you won't like it, we can surely sell it to someone for the purchase price.

It is a holiday, beautiful weather, I'm going to join the others in the garden. So be satisfied with this much.

Hugs from your loving mother, Klára.

My greetings to Pál.

When I reach the editorial offices of *Világ*, I will write about Mezei, this is what Jób Bede was thinking two years previously on his way there, I knew him back in the old House, where he represented the Liberal Party of Lipótváros and stood by the liberal principles he believed in.

Let us quickly add that the old House of Representatives building was in Sándor Street, in close proximity to the National Museum. It is still there. It is a beautiful neoclassical edifice, for years it has been the home of the Italian Cultural Institute, and the former assembly hall has been preserved in its original state.

A badly faded photograph of the Council Chamber has survived among the family documents, a photographic rarity, for it was taken on the spot, which at the time was still a very difficult maneuver and a curiosity; it was then enlarged on so-called salted paper, the passage of time made the paper yellow, and veritable little explosions are visible on the badly fixed emulsion, a result of the disintegration of the salt crystals. It is a fairly early snapshot, the exposure must have taken minutes. Great-grandfather Mezei is sitting in a tall bench of the Council Chamber, but the other persons seen by his side are slightly blurred because of their small movements. Already back then, as a conscientious National Assembly reporter who was bound to gain the most accurate information possible about the most influential politicians, I wanted to find out, Bede writes, how he attained such an excellent position in politics, and I also wanted to find out about his early career. Possibly I need not add that back then we couldn't have walked with anything like ease along Lipótváros from the present-day Parliament building the way we can today.

The huge buildings and streets were built later. It took the tireless wake-up calls of Mór Mezei and the others for the speedy building boom to materialize in the nation's capital.

My first memory of him is that we were jammed together in the huge crowd in front of the Lloyd Palace.

The Lloyd Palace, József Hild's admirable building, was the first headquarters and club of the Liberals, but alas, it is not standing today, I quickly add by way of an aside. It suffered grave damage during the siege, though according to trustworthy architects, the damage was not irreversible. The building could have been repaired, but instead they built two unsightly buildings unworthy of it on the spot, and further demolitions and construction are sure to follow. Europe has two cities of note where respect for architecture is a thing unknown. In Berlin and Budapest architects will sacrifice anything and everything on the altar of current demands, and so the architectural quality of these two cities is the result not of their love of construction but their love of destruction. For a couple of years after the siege, the ruins of the Lloyd Palace stood behind a plank fence. They demolished its burned-out arcades and the dignified columns that had once graced its main hall the year I started school. Since they were rebuilding the Chain Bridge, they might as well get rid of the ruins of the building where the people of Budapest had once gathered in support of Sándor Wekerle's efforts on behalf of compulsory civil marriage, and when the leaders of the Liberal Party appeared in the lighted windows and the crowd began to cheer Wekerle, suddenly hundreds of voices broke free of the general laudation and flew up to the balcony: Long live Mór Mezei! This was the building that they demolished. This was the voice of nearby Lipótváros greeting its tribal chief. But at the same time it was celebrating Mór Mezei, the adamant champion of principles, whose struggles reached back to a more distant time.

Before we reach back to distant times ourselves, I must stop Bede in his tracks once again, because it seems to me that his interpretation of the cheering was not altogether correct. Prime Minister Wekerle was undoubtedly a proponent of compulsory civil marriage, but like so many other laws, this, too, was elaborated by Mezei working unobtrusively in the background, and surely this is why the crowd was cheering him. After all, he'd fought for the emancipation of the Jews back in 1861, under absolutism, before the birth of the empire. Administrator Pálffy had him detained on remand in the Károly Barracks, and he had the late, lamented Queen Elisabeth to thank for his freedom because, after her recovery from the early stages of tuberculosis and her return from Madeira, the king showed his gratitude to Providence by calling for a general amnesty.

At the time, the New Building, the Neugebäude, was still standing in Lipótváros. It was located between Hold and Nádor streets, and with its enormous bulk and enormous courtyard it took up the area we now call Liberty Square, though possibly an even larger area. It was a colossal square-shaped edifice. Attached to its four corners stood another four square-shaped blocks, also with enclosed yards. It was the largest barracks of the Monarchy, the most grandiloquent of any strict neoclassical buildings, and the hated symbol of the loyalist Labanc supporters and the veritable annexation of the Hungarian Kingdom recently liberated from the Turks. In accordance with the wishes of Emperor Joseph, the barracks was built after the design of Isidorus Marcellus Canevale, the Viennese architect of Italian origin, and the construction was overseen by János Hild, whose son, József Hild, the preeminent master of Pest's neoclassical architecture, first worked as an architect on this structure. He later designed the much more humble but no less grand Maria Theresa Barracks on Üllői Street.

I may not be the only one who regrets that the Neugebäude was pulled down, but I am probably the last who still regrets it. With its huge inner courtyard it would be the eighth wonder of the world today. Eleven windows in the apartment of my paternal grandfather, Adolf Arnold Neumayer, looked out on the New Building, and on major holidays his two eldest children, Eugenie and György, watched wide-eyed from there as, amid the rolling of the drums and to the accompaniment of music, the soldiers marched out of the southern gate of the building, by then destined for demolition. My father couldn't see their ceremonious and slightly threatening appearance with his own eyes, but he told me about it the way his older siblings had told him. As if he saw it after all. Their grandfather, meaning my great-grandfather, lived on the second floor of the so-called Baumgarten House in Nagykorona Street, that is 13 Drei Kronengasse, where only nine windows looked out on the street, but in the yard resplendent with the leafy boughs of trees, the water came trickling from two red marble wall fountains day and night, as his grandchildren later related. The wall fountains have survived. I was later a frequent visitor to the second-story apartment where my great-grandfather had lived, because about sixty years later the Herczegs, my cousin Vera's in-laws, lived there. It had been maimed beyond recognition.

Still, back then people referred to the size of an apartment by mentioning the number of windows and not the rooms. They counted the windows giving out on the street; the stretch facing the courtyard didn't matter, the tract along the facade, the spaces used for representation were the gauge. When, accompanied by their governesses, the grandchildren approached their grandfather's apartment over the back stairs, because their instructions specified entry from here and not through the main door of the apartment, they first had to walk past the long row of empty offices packed with documents, because their grandfather's law offices were located in the same building, in premises facing the yard. For their Sunday visit, the girls were dressed in white from head to toe. And so I shouldn't forget the romantic turn of events, I must also mention that there was a young man among the clerks in one of the offices, his name was Sándor Rendl, and he followed with rapt attention every step of the oldest girl, Eugénia, who was a vision in her white lace dress and was as slender as a reed, and so he would play a major role in the less turbulent history of the family. When work piled up, Great-grandfather had him come in even on Sunday. I might as well also let on that after her divorce, Eugenie will marry him, and Vera will be her daughter. At last the children with their governesses reached a big soundproof door, behind which their feared and venerated grandfather sat at his desk piled high with papers.

But we're not there yet, because in one of the remote parts of the floor lived their great-grandfather with his nurse, our great-great-grandfather, the barkeeper from Újhely, meaning Sátoraljaújhely, almost completely blind by then, whom all his great-grandchildren also looked up and greeted on Sunday. He recognized them by touch, which made the children very happy, because sometimes they would attempt to mislead him with all sorts of ribbons and laces. By way of an aside, this blind innkeeper great-great-grandfather smoked a pipe, played music, and read even on Saturday, as if the Lord had never consecrated the Shabbat. He had his books ordered from Pest, Vienna, and Paris. He was a fine violinist. He thumbed his nose at the God of the Jews. Not so his wife, Ida Friedlieber, who, faithful to her family name, was a peace-loving and pious woman. She was of such slight physique that her children and even her great-grandchildren affectionately called her Bitsimama. She kept the Shabbat, meaning that she did not reject the Jewish faith and she brought up her five boys in Sátoraljaújhely accordingly, and refused to engage in arguments over customs or the observation of customs or the rejection of customs or the nature of the Almighty; in short, she kept knowledge and opinion strictly separate. There are things that are not a matter of opinion. But most of all, she refused to argue with her husband. In order to curb his rambling thoughts, my atheist great-great-grandfather read mostly philosophical works, because he was looking for an answer to the question of why the heck we, human beings, need gods in the first place. You might say that his curiosity prompted him to sneak a look into the dustiest corners. We also know that in Újhely, where else, a man-child from Monok lived as a boarder next door to them, a high school student who was gifted on the flute. At their house concerts they accompanied my great-grandfather's little wife with the beautiful voice. They called the man-child, who was later to study law in Sárospatak, Lajos Kossuth. He not only enjoyed playing the flute, he also enjoyed exchanging views and debating politics with Great-great-grandfather. Which later exercised a great effect on the career of the philosophizing and music-making innkeeper's son Ernő. In the family, these musical afternoons budded into a long and wide-ranging political story. For a long time, this Ernő remained a bachelor, and until he unexpectedly got married, he also lived here in this big Nagykorona Street apartment, and thanks to Kossuth's recommendation, he became a representative of the Independence Party for several election cycles, but remained an eccentric character all the same.

In line with family custom, come Sunday, they took my father, too, along with all the children of their grandfather's sons and daughters, meaning their cousins, to the apartment in Nagykorona Street. The youngest ones were also dressed in white for the occasion. There was invariably a lot of white lace, a lot of white open-work design, and a lot of frill on their white clothes. At most the wide silk belts wrapped several times around the waists of the little ones were colorful. Berlin blue or sulfur yellow. I saw these silks with my own eyes, I felt them; my fingers remember the feel and my eyes recall the bright colors. There were almost more children than you could count. Our father and his older siblings, seven all told, came from nearby Báthory Street, because when the demolition of the Neugebäude began, it seemed advisable that they should move out of Hold Street. And there came Anna Mezei's children, the Krishaber children, Frank and Eugenie, because in memory of their grandmother Eugenie Schlesinger, who died of childbed fever, there was a Eugénia in this family as well; they later magyarized their family name to Kövér, they came from Duna Street; and there came Pál Mezei's children, Tamás and Endre, they came from farther away, from an apartment building on Sugár Boulevard, meaning Andrássy Boulevard, eleven children in all. My grandparents later moved with their seven children from Báthory Street to a building on the corner of Lipót Boulevard and Pannónia Street, which marked the beginning of the family's Újlipótváros history.

But just like on any other day, on that day, too, their grandfather was working behind the padded door. May God forgive his liberal thinking, he worked even on Saturday. As well as on Sunday. I don't know why, but I also work every day. I'm not a work addict, I don't even ask myself what else I could be doing. Poor Planck, Great-grandfather's manservant who hailed from one of the small German villages nestled in the Buda hills, and who was barely ten years younger than his master, also worked every day of his long life, as if indeed the Lord had consecrated the holidays with work. When Great-grandfather passed away and he had no one to serve anymore, his last will and testament left Planck an appreciable sum, which in the time left to him he supplemented with a bit of extra income, to which only he had a right in the family. Like a ghost from the past, he looked up the members of the family twice a year. In the spring and the fall, he invariably showed up on the morning of the same day, and polished the silver. He came and he worked diligently. In any one place, polishing the silver could take two or three days. I have also polished silver. It is an exacting chore. He was past ninety when, one after the other, members of the family in Pannónia Street, Duna Street, Benczúr Street, Andrássy Boulevard, and Dobsinai Street realized that he had stopped coming. He left this world as unobtrusively as he had lived. His full name was József Planck.

Being the eldest of the children, Eugenie enjoyed the privilege of knocking on their grandfather's padded door. When they entered the study facing Nagykorona Street, they greeted their grandfather one by one, and each time, he rang for Planck, whom everyone called by his surname, and gave him the same order. Planck, go to Schück's and bring a *stanicli* of chocolate pralines for the children. While Planck was bringing the *stanicli* of chocolate pralines from Schück's, and later from Kugler's, their grandfather questioned all eleven and then, with Béla's children, all fourteen of his grandchildren. This word, *stanicli*, which entered the language of Pest from the German and the German from the Italian, I no longer used, we called it a bag, but in the seventies of the last century, you could still hear *stanicli* from the people of Pest.

It must have been a very curious hour in the lives of the children. Neither their parents nor their governesses could be present at their grandfather's examination, as he called it. The governesses waited outside, because when the examination was over, they had to see the children home. As they grew older and knew things and were familiar with the rules of conduct, the older ones didn't have to go home anymore, they could stay with their grandfather until he stood up and took his leave so that with Planck's assistance he could change into tails before their parents showed up in their evening clothes for the big family dinner, and until they were called to the table, they could chat with their aunts and uncles and cousins in the formal salon. It happened like this every blessed Sunday.

Having succeeded Wahrmann, Mór Mezei was an even more combative representative, Bede continues, than Wahrmann had been. Which was a very big deal in those days, possibly a flamboyant exaggeration to suit the occasion, I now add, because Wahrmann himself was not a shy man, even though the two of them were fashioned of very different fabric.

Mór Wahrmann was one of the driving forces behind the capitalization and industrialization of Hungary, which materialized about two hundred years late. He was stocky, with a paunch even in his younger years, he had a strikingly round face and was pathologically shortsighted, what you'd call a man of unprepossessing qualities. He was a captain of industry, the owner of vast estates, a publisher and banker rolled into one, an amazingly generous patron with admirable intelligence, the founder and publisher of the German-language daily *Pester Lloyd*, a preeminent *virilis* of the city, meaning one of its top taxpayers. Everything in one and everything at the same time. Ferenc Deák spotted his talent very early on. In his writings and speeches, Wahrmann represented the view that Hungarian industry, finance, and commerce, in short, the Hungarian economy, must of necessity become independent of Austria. It is strong enough to do so, it is

ready for independence. In the interest of liberating Hungarian finance, he founded a bank in Pest. Deák, the wise man of the nation,
approved. Wahrmann was a proponent of Jewish emancipation, and
to this end he worked hand-in-hand with my great-grandfather. Herewith I would like to point out that in their minds emancipation did
not mean assimilation, but equality. On Deák's recommendation, he
became parliamentary representative for Lipótváros, at the time considered the bastion of the Jewish haute bourgeoisie. In this capacity, he
achieved a record, he kept his position for eight consecutive electoral
terms, when smack in the middle of one of these terms, he handed
his office over to my great-grandfather. Our great-grandfather was
elected representative of the fifth district of the capital city and royal
town of Budapest on Monday, January 9, 1893, and on Thursday of
that same week the presenter of the permanent certifying committee,
Lajos Ragályi, examined the voting record, and since it satisfied the
lawful requirements, confirmed him. The 132nd National Assembly,
presided over by Baron Dezső Bánffy, approved Ragályi's findings
and conferred a Class Four ranking on him, which meant that he
would be in a special committee, namely, the Finance Committee, a
position he retained during the following cycle, when he also became
a member of the Public Education Committee.

Wahrmann was among the first who dared venture into foreign
stock markets with his brokers and he did not shrink from duels.
Which raised the hearsay of his daring to legendary heights in Pest.

In June 1882 he had a row in Parliament with Győző Istóczy, the
Hungarian leader of the anti-Semitic movement that countered the
European success of the liberal movement with regression.

Istóczy's movement did not count as a rarity in the Monarchy,
nor indeed in the world at large, even if, according to the parliamentary records, the other representatives jovially and noisily laughed off
his analyses, statistics, and prophecies. He copied and followed the
Christian Socialist movement of the Berlin Court preacher, Adolf
Stoecker, whereas he was an open-minded, independent thinker with
a far greater intellectual capacity than his German master. Stoecker's
ideology was a hodgepodge of anticapitalist, antisocialist, and antilib-

eral elements and, as was caustically remarked, the sole natural binding element of his ideology was anti-Semitism. Stoecker envisioned a Christian state freed of foreign elements, a feudal state, a state that obliterates the entire history of liberal thinking and equality before the law, as well as secularization.

Istóczy's own ideas were somewhat different. He would have liked to graft the shoot of racism onto the body of liberalism, thereby squaring the circle for his nation, one might say. Not that he was a fool. He wanted to preserve a liberal state; like Wahrmann and later on our great-grandfather, he sat among the liberals in the House of Representatives, but his intelligence was manic, he insisted on his obessions and delusions. In Europe he was among the first who wanted to resettle the Jews in Palestine en bloc. He preceded the idea of Theodore Herzl's Zionist movement by a decade. In the weakness of the Ottoman Empire and the territorial expansionism of Russian diplomacy, Istóczy saw an eminent foreign-policy opportunity for the European governments to be rid of their Jewish population within the bounds of liberal ideas, meaning lawfully. The burdensome exceptionality of the Jews migrating from the eastern half of the continent to its western half gave currency to his ideas. They were fleeing the government-supported pogroms in Russia, Poland, and Ukraine in droves, and they were in fact very different. Needless to say, Istóczy's idea was preceded by British and French models, nor was his proposal the last of its kind that liberal thinking and the liberal governments of Europe rejected.

At the 118th National Assembly, held on June 7, 1882, Géza Ónody also championed the en bloc expulsion of the Jews.

I can unequivocally declare that neither a cordon nor any other cautionary measures are sufficient to stop the Russian Jewish influx, because if a Jew can't enter the country in one spot, he will enter it in another; it is my conviction that it is best for us to provide them with a territory where they can be transported. And Palestine is the only place for this; they have been wanting to go there anyway. Let the golden hour of their dreams be fulfilled.

For a long time, this dream remained in a state of suspension, or else continued to survive in the deepest layers of European thought.

The clarification of this question gained urgency for me when I was working on my novel *Parallel Stories*, and I was preoccupied with how long it took for such anti-Semitic speculation to bear fruit. How much time it takes to go from the idea to murder, or rather, in the interest of keeping the idea alive, how often must we resort to mass murder. The anti-Judaism of the Christian churches led me back to the most distant past, to the proto-orthodox Christian communities in which commensality, the breaking of bread together, became a contentious issue and, in fact, was one of the principal reasons why those of gentile origins and those of Jewish origins eventually split apart, and as certain religious historians contend, subsequently furnished the grounds for the principle of racial segregation. I was also surprised to learn of the role that the idea of en bloc expulsion played in the lives of Hungarian secret societies that were grouped strictly around blood relations, secret societies that were both anti-German and anti-Jewish, and the extent of the involvement of these profoundly antiliberal and pagan societies when the Hungarian government later elaborated its program for the disenfranchisement of the Jews, the despoliation and redistribution of their goods, which they went about in several stages and with the utmost professional circumspection, and why their appetite for pillage and murder could not be satisfied.

Among the documents of the National Assembly that convened on August 28, 1875, there is a proposal by Istóczy, filed as document no. 890, in which he calls upon the House that should it come to pass that in one of the phases of the solution to the eastern question, and here by eastern question he is referring to the disintegrating Ottoman Empire, should the leaders of European Jewry or the government of some European state propose the idea that along with the freedom strivings of the eastern Christian peoples, and in line with European interests, the Jewish people who had been ousted from their homeland eighteen hundred years ago should also be dispensed justice at long last by the reestablishment of Palestine, its beloved original home, properly enlarged, possibly even as an autonomous province under the sovereignty of the Sublime Porte, or as a sovereign Jewish state, whereby, in its present state of expansion that is thwarting the advancement of European nations and endangering Christian civilization, the Jewish people, returned to itself, besides the boon of its own national government and national institutions, in the midst of related Semitic tribes, in the backward East, declined in power, serving as a strong, mighty new element, that said Jewish people may become the potent force of civilization, the wish of the House, the Hungarian government must do everything in its power so that the Foreign Affairs Office of the monarch should not oppose a possible proposal to this effect, but on the contrary, in the interest of European interest as well as the interest of the monarchy, and most especially of Hungary, that it should support it.

However, twelve years had passed, and Istóczy's ill success made him even more radical, distancing him more and more from the liberals, or put another way, he was not to remain among their ranks for long. And then, in the heat of a parliamentary debate, he slapped Wahrmann and the following year founded the National Anti-Semite Party.

The news that Wahrmann had challenged Istóczy to a duel spread through the city like wildfire. The seconds had already agreed on the time and the conditions. It was also rumored that Wahrmann was taking lessons from a famous master shooter, because he'd never held a gun in his hand in all his life. But just as the seconds measured out the distance, and turning to face each other, each let off his first shot, and let us mention here right away that neither of them hit his target, not only did two tardy secret policemen come charging out of the bushes to catch them in the act and prevent the bloodshed with the force of the law, but panting heavily, the city's rabble, thirsty for blood and lynching, also showed up on the clearing at the break of day.

Their second early morning encounter, on a site farther off this time, came to an even more amusing end. It was quiet on the meadow, calm, birdsong, a cloudless sky, a bit of mist. No one came charging out of the thicket, but every single shot they fired fell short of its target.

On the other hand, their duel drew legal consequences in its wake. The royal prosecutor addressed an indictment to the House of Representatives, asking for a waiver of immunity for deputies Győző Istóczy and Mór Wahrmann, as well as their seconds, Prince Gyula Odescal-chi, Géza Ónody, Lajos Hentaller, and László Visontai Kovách, for qualified dueling and qualified seconding. The Immunity Committee held a session on November 17, 1882. But no such embarrassment and no National Anti-Semite Party could cool Wahrmann's spirit. When some years later, by then almost completely blind, he exchanged heated words in Parliament with Ottó Hermann, who was by no means an anti-Semite, on the other hand, he was as deaf as a doornail, he challenged him to a duel as well.

They took up their positions in a tranquil forest clearing. For a while nothing happened. And then Wahrmann, who was almost completely blind, quietly asked his seconds where the goy was standing. They positioned his arm toward his target. And when both of them were past their first erroneous shot, Ottó Hermann, who for his part was as deaf as a doornail, asked his seconds whether the Jew had shot off his gun yet.

It happened a long time ago, it happened before the two great wars, in the heyday of devil-may-care anecdotal times, and so, needless to say, it may not have been true. But it could just as easily have been.

It is incontrovertible that Mezei expended no small effort in order to fortify the liberal camp, Bede continues his own story. Equality and fraternity, the acceptance of equal responsibility, the demand of strictly equal rights always lived on as a renewed source of spiritual turmoil in the camp of liberals. Mezei supported the liberal governments, but demanded much more than they. At the time when his party wouldn't have so much as dared to mention it, he had included universal suffrage in his program. He also continued to champion universal suffrage. And today, Prime Minister István Tisza, the fierce opponent of universal suffrage, celebrates him with a telegram. And likewise Minister of Justice Balogh, who in his greeting lauds Mór Mezei's outstanding efforts in the field of law and jurisprudence. His is a life of labor, struggles and successes, and how gratifying it must be for him now, at the age of eighty, to take stock of the past.

The miracle rabbi did in fact belong to the distant history of the family, he was called Izsák, and if my calculations are correct, he must

have been my great-grandfather's great-grandfather. But what miracles he was known for I have no idea. He was the son of a learned
man, Marcus, my great-great-grandfather, who later, after Emperor
Joseph II issued his Patent of Tolerance of 1781, became professor
of the Israelite school of Sátoraljaújhely, but could bask in the glory of
his position only briefly, because on February 20, 1790, the emperor
passed on to a better world. The emperor to succeed him, Leopold II,
disbanded the parochial schools and abolished professorships. He
found work as an accountant with a wine merchant from Mád called
Teitelbaum, and had to move to the Tokaj region about fifty kilometers from his native town. At this point it is worth following the
story of my family with the help of Béla Kempelen's *Jewish Families of
Hungary.* For it transpired, Kempelen writes, that in line with the new
emperor's order, Zemplén County received a new lord lieutenant. The
Jews of Zemplén wanted to be represented at the welcoming of the new
lord lieutenant. So far, so good, but there was no one among the Jews
of Sátoraljaújhely who spoke Latin, and at the time, the lord lieutenant
could be greeted in no other language, just the language of scholars.
Then someone remembered that there was a Jew in the county who
could speak Latin, Marcus Grinfeld. They went to Mád to fetch him
and requested that he greet the lord lieutenant in their name.

Though Marcus Grinfeld tried to excuse himself, saying that he
was not worthy of such an honor, the delegation finally convinced him
and he went with them to Sátoraljaújhely, where, with the Torah in
his hand, he delivered an oration in immaculate Latin in front of the
lord lieutenant. Soon afterward, in 1805, he was sworn in as an interpreter and charged with delivering the faithful translation of "Jewish
documents according to the current formulae." After him the office
of translator was handed down to a distant cousin, Sámuel Grünfeld,
with the proviso that "when the ordinary courts are in session, at all
times, whereas at extraordinary court sessions upon occasion, furthermore, pursuant upon the chief court official's order for said Jewish
marriage officiant to be present at the synagogue or to provide other
services, on each occasion he is to be allotted 12 silver royal payments
per day from petty cash."

The Jews called Sámuel Grünfeld Hézsi. He died in the late 1850s. By then, his son Péter was already living in Pest.

Mór and Ernő's maternal grandfather, Izsák Friedlieber, was also a Sátoraljaújhely taxpayer. He died in 1828. His wife, Ziszel Schön, passed away in 1864. They had six children, Albert Friedlieber and Pinkász Friedlieber, whose son, Ignác, was a Honvéd brigade physician during the 1848–49 freedom fights, and Mayer Friedlieber, who became a Honvéd lieutenant, but they had another brother, Samu Friedlieber, as well as two sisters, Ida Friedlieber and Klára Friedlieber.

This Ida Friedlieber became Mór Mezei's and Ernő Mezei's mother, Bitsimama because she was so small.

Mezei had always been first eminent, Bede continues, after I gave him what for for his atrocious sentences, he was eminent in all subjects. The Piarist high school of Sátoraljaújhely has now paid him a tribute, they found the old class albums, this afternoon a deputation arrived from there as well to greet the school's preeminent student, Mór Mezei, of whom they invariably think with pride. When speaking about Mór Mezei, his contemporaries remember that from the beginning of his career in public law, when he was twenty-four, he was already championing the emancipation of the Jews, and the entire country followed his efforts with expectation. In 1861 Mezei founded the Israelite Hungarian Association in Pest, and as its secretary he oversaw the work of the association. He founded a paper called *Hungarian Israelite*, the first denominational newspaper to appear in Hungarian. His efforts were aimed at the magyarization of the Jews and the attainment of Jewish equality. However, as soon as, in the name of the Schmerling type of provisorium, Vienna sent us Count Pálffy as administrator, and because of an article, the administrator had Mezei detained under remand without delay and prohibited him from editing a newspaper. As we have already mentioned, he was released from his detention thanks to clemency. When he could no longer continue his publishing endeavor, he decided to embark on a career as a lawyer.

This is not quite what happened; it happened the other way around. Mezei was among the first Jews who, with special dispensation from the emperor, could practice law, but in his capacity as the owner of a newspaper as well as in his capacity as a lawyer, he soon found himself in opposition to the administrator. It was not remotely by chance, and not remotely without consideration. And not remotely in opposition to Schmerling or the emperor, but expressly in opposition to Count Pálffy. The previous year the emperor appointed Ritter von Schmerling minister of state with the express order that he should work out a moderately liberal constitution that would be acceptable to all the peoples of the Monarchy. When as a lawyer my great-grandfather drafted the demands for equality of one of the people living in the Monarchy, he was counting on this more permissive imperial intention, which however met with opposition from the hard-liner Count Pálffy. Pálffy was by no means Schmerling's man in Buda. On the contrary. What's more, my great-grandfather was not only remanded in custody, he was sentenced to imprisonment in the infamous fortress prison at Kufstein, when he and the other prisoners were released on general amnesty on the occasion of the birthday of Elisabeth, the beloved queen of the Hungarians. Whereupon, as Bede writes, he continued to agitate on behalf of emancipation not only in his weekly paper, but in other papers as well. Similar demands by the Protestants provided him with a hearty tailwind, for it would be unworthy of us to ignore the fact that around this time, the Protestants, just like the Jews, were not equals either though their numbers and social influence far outweighed that of the Jews.

If we are to assess my great-grandfather's efforts realistically, we must consider that at least four types of political aspiration were present in the empire simultaneously, working either side by side, or else against one another, and he had to find a place for his emancipation demands among them. The Croatians, the Italians, and the Hungarians rejected the emperor's patent calling for them to attend sessions of the central parliament, but they also wanted Knight Schmerling's overthrow because he was a traitor, a common traitor, they hated him in Pest and they hated him in Vienna, he was generally hated throughout the Monarchy, an 1848 revolutionary from Vienna who had sided with the emperor, they couldn't stand him, they disavowed him. This is why my liberal great-grandfather had to strike the iron on behalf of Schmerling's views. Schmerling had betrayed the revolution, to be sure, but he remained a moderate liberal, and this is why the emperor needed him, because of the way he was, a moderately emperor-friendly moderate liberal. It was not difficult for my great-grandfather to be moderate because, unlike his radical anti-Hapsburg brother, Ernő, he was moderate by nature. The article he wrote for his own paper was the last straw in the eyes of the profoundly traditionalist Count Pálffy; after all, it supported the moderately liberal views of Schmerling and the emperor. With his traditionalism, Pálffy actually went against the emperor, he wanted neither equality nor liberal public administration. He was right. Changes must be nipped in the bud. When he was shown the article my great-grandfather had written arguing in favor of Schmerling's views, according to the contemporary newspapers, he leaped up from his desk and, beside himself with rage, he shouted, *Der mach mir ja die Juden rebellisch, wie sie es schon in der Revolutionszeit waren! Die Lumperkerle!* In short, that he, my great-grandfather, makes the Jews rebellious, just as they were in the revolutionary period, *Die Lumperkerle!* Accordingly, my young great-grandfather's arrest, sentencing, and conveyance to the fortress of Kufstein became one of the major episodes of the European liberal movement and, in its wake, of the fight for emancipation to such a degree that he had to pass beyond his momentary heroism as quickly as possible. To our great good luck, there was a sufficient reserve of sanity in his makeup and sufficient humility toward the cause of emancipation.

As soon as the Hungarian ministry was appointed, Bede writes in his next sentence, Mezei launched a greater offensive than before in the interest of emancipation. He continued agitating where he had left off not only in his own weekly paper, but in other major dailies as well. When Minister of Culture József Eötvös convened his first council to focus on emancipation, Mezei became his advisor and confidant. At the minister's behest, he drafted the blueprint for emancipation, which the minister than introduced in its original state. He also became secretary of the Jewish Congress.

So we may better understand what Bede is saying, it should be remarked that the Jewish religion is not based on hierarchy, and in their own congregations the rabbis act independently; at most, should the occasion arise, they appoint one of their number to represent them before the emperor and king. The situation is similar to the Presbyterian Church within Protestantism, where it is not the bishop who makes decisions in local matters, not even the pastors, but three presbyters. But my great-grandfather saw clearly that their rabbinical tradition left them without support, because they had no legal status. The Jewish Congress was meant to supply this legal status, to bring about an institution that, independent of the various religious trends and aims, in secular matters would constitute a united front when dealing with state administration.

The effort was thwarted, Bede writes, because the Orthodox Jews would not accept the goals of the Jewish Congress, which resulted in a parting of ways. When Ágoston Trefort was minister of public education and religious affairs, the National Assembly approved their separation, and the congressional organization that unified most of the Jews became a separate Neolog organization, of which Mezei had been president since Schweiger's death.

As a reward for his efforts in the interest of emancipation, Lipót-város had already wanted to make him their representative back in 1868. But the view that a merchant should be elected instead won the day, and Mór Mezei stepped down in favor of Mór Wahrmann. However, after Wahrmann's death, the citizens of Lipótváros nevertheless elected Mezei, who meanwhile did not wish to accept a mandate in any other district, for two consecutive terms. His efforts as lawmaker were especially beneficial in the creation of various liberal institutions, and he also took an active part in drawing up laws pertaining to commerce. Those who were not familiar with him thought his manner unfriendly, but those who came to know him could see for themselves that he was an exceptionally prepossessing, kind, and wise human being.

He remained faithful to the Liberal Party all his life. When his party became the Labor Party, he did not abandon it. Though perhaps he goes there now out of habit. He finds the usual card party of four, including Podmaniczky, there. With the passage of the years his partners changed, but Mezei always had the best. In its hall increasingly serious problems are proposed and rejected. Needless to say, they are not new to Mezei. He has always represented the vanguard of championing ideologies that would benefit the nation. Mezei watches quietly, but he knows that the time for realizing these ideas is not far off. Earlier, on the initiative of Prime Minister Tisza, there was talk of recommending Mór Mezei for membership in the Upper House in consideration of his political achievements. Except he was president of the Jewish Congress, and the Orthodox Jews got wind of the fact and came forward demanding that in that case, one of their own must also be appointed to the Upper House. Except, as far as I know, it was decided that in that case, Mezei shouldn't be considered for the honor either. So much the better, Mór Mezei must be thinking, because he'd rather be called Your Honor. He could have been Your Grace, because he had been offered a post as court counselor, but he did not like it and did not accept it, and now, as a member of the Upper House, he could have been Your Grace yet again, but things took a different turn. He did not lay claim to the title of Your Lordship either, he didn't like it even when he was a representative. Your Honor, yes, Your Honor reminds him of the days when a person of his religion could embark on a profession in law only with special dispensation from the king, and with what difficulty they had transformed the country from those days to what it is today, they, the working men, the champions of human rights, culture, and enlightenment.

Then the following day, in the morning resplendent with sunlight, there stood a long line of automobiles and elegant carriages in front of the house in Nagykorona Street, bringing the various delegations, one after the other, writes the liberal Jewish paper *Equality* on January 23. With their beautiful presents of flowers, the great bevy of friends and officeholders turned the bright genteel home upstairs into a resplendent garden. In one corner, the mass of telegrams and letters piled high on a table. The fêted person greeted the delegations in the best of health and in the best of spirits, and listened to all of them standing up. When he spoke, his former combative temperament had not faded, he could make those who had come to fete him forget that they had come to celebrate the birthday of a public notable.

Equality devotes six pages to the list of the delegations who had come to pay their respects, the texts of their orations in Hungarian or German, and my great-grandfather's formal acknowledgment, delivered in Hungarian. There are among them in Nagykorona Street the members of the board of the Rabbinical Seminary, Baron Vilmos Guttmann, member of the Upper House, Manfréd Weiss of Csepel, Dr. József Bánóczi, member of the Academy, Dr. Izsó Rósa of Várhely, national representative, and the rabbis Dr. Simon Hevesi and Dr. Lajos Venetiáner. Of the teaching staff, Dr. Mihály Guttmann, Dr. Henrik Bloch, Dr. Ármin Balogh, Dr. Mór Dercsényi, and Dr. Miksa Klein. The salutatory oration below was delivered by Mr. Ferenc Mezey, who was president of the board of directors, but was not related to my great-grandfather, who would have never thought of writing his name with a *y* denoting nobility, I add by way of an aside.

Worshipful President! My beloved Friend! In the name of the members of the board and the teaching staff of the National Rabbinical Seminary as well as our National Israelite Teachers' Training School, we have appeared before you so we may partake of the profound joy that today fills the hearts of culturally progressive Hungarian Jewry, when it celebrates the eightieth anniversary of the birth of its leader. The words of the psalm fill our souls, *Yeh hazom asah Adonai, nagilah y'nismecha vo.* This is the day that God has made, let us celebrate and rejoice in it. When we greet you with sincere love, I do not wish to praise your prized efforts in a great period for Hungarian Jewry, for this shall be the task of the history of the Hungarian Jews, which it is my conviction will mention you as among the immortal champions of Israel. Nor do I wish to bear witness to your faithfulness to the Jewish Cause, which radiates from your bright intellect into the present and your so oft-manifest faithfulness to the Jewish Cause, because as your humble colleague unworthily chosen to speak before you here, they might think me biased, fallen under the spell of your brilliant mind. First and foremost, I wish to express the gratitude we feel toward you for your efforts on behalf of the foundation and establishment of our Rabbinical Institute. You were already an enthusiastic champion of the future institute when the mere thought of the Seminary seemed audacious, when any such thought was seen as a break with the ancient faith, and so you remained when from the ruins of so many hopes it was nevertheless possible to build this bastion of Hungarian Jewry, and when new ramparts were called for to protect it. Few are aware today that our congressional rules and resolutions are in most part the product of your great intellect. Half a century has exacted its toll on the enactment of law, and because Jewish communal life could not be nourished by its fertile soil, hostile tempests have snapped off more than one of its branches.

What today may be construed as a vague reproach was, back then, an unequivocal reference to the consistent, and in this one thing unified opposition of the split Orthodox communities in response to the striving for unity, and the third party's, and Neolog Jews' no less consistent, one might say traditional political passivity and profound opportunism, I now hasten to add.

But the resolution on behalf of the foundation of the Rabbinical Seminary, which you prepared with the common will of your congenial fellows, came to life after the Congress, and may the Almighty be praised, it is now in bloom, and with its abundant yield of fruit brings joy to our religious community.

Honored Sirs, my great-grandfather began in response to the greeting, you are celebrating me here today for having first proposed the idea of the Rabbinical Seminary at the 1868 Congress and fighting to make it a reality. The fact is that I fought for it together with my illustrious friend Izsó Rósa. I hereby avail myself of the opportunity to emphasize this yet again. But regardless of the direction the affairs of progressive Jewry may take, the Seminary is the one true value that has survived from the Congress, and must not become a subject of negotiation or concession. We will not let anyone touch the Seminary, we will keep the Seminary in our hands, we will hold on to it. The Institute is the pride of the Jews of Hungary, the educator of the body of progressive Hungarian rabbis. I cannot accept praise for the Seminary and the Teachers' Training School, I did no more than what was expected of me.

Which, coming in the wake of so much ceremonious praise of the highest degree, so much exaggeration and enthusiasm, does not sound very appreciative, to be sure. At most it will do to set the record straight.

This sort of objectivity is familiar to me. I could not consider a rectification of this sort out of place either, though at times I try very hard to hold myself back from being as blunt as I would otherwise like to be. That I shouldn't think that everyone takes the basic rules of equality and objectivity as seriously as I. Though there were obvious boundaries on my father's side of the family, in the spirit of liberal thinking, these were always permeable and the hierarchies barely visible or in fact invisible.

We sat down to lunch or dinner when it was ready, and this had nothing whatsoever to do with the noonday ringing of the church bell, meaning the established customs of the Monarchy. I don't recall anyone objecting to the soup not being hot enough. But I knew, because they told me, either with intent to cheer me up or to frighten me, that for his part, my paternal grandfather, whose name, according to his birth certificate, was Adolf Arnold Neumayer, but who did not use his first name, Adolf, until he magyarized his name to Nádas, at which point he left off Adolf altogether, and it didn't appear in the birth certificates made out to him later either, though his children used it against him as a form of mischievous revenge when they brought up the scenes he made at the family table. He chose the Nádas name, the family witticized, so that the elegant monogram on the family silverware Great-grandmother Neumayer had given them as a wedding present shouldn't have to be engraved again. It might even be true. I heard the story from my Aunt Magda, who enjoyed saying derogatory things about her father. Once when they were small, she and her brother Gyuri, who was one year older than she, agreed what bad luck it was that their father should be so infinitely stupid. Actually, as far as I can reconstruct it, he was more narrow-minded than stupid, because he had brains enough to get by, but in the eyes of his Mezei relatives, he was a country bumpkin, or at best, his upbringing was profoundly rural. He was the way a landowner of moderate means, what they called a proper lard peasant, should be like. A boor. A *monsieur le baron de Thunder-ten-tronckh*, open and simple-minded. On the other hand, he was not a miser, he enjoyed spending his money, and he would do good in the world above and beyond his means on a whim, though he did it for himself, too, because his heart would stir at his own goodness every time. He was unpredictable, at times sentimental, at other times brutal. Which is not an attractive mix of emotions, but it is by no means rare among men. He was terrified all his life that one day he'd be poor, a fate that during the time of the great financial crises, when the construction booms came to an end, caught up with him and the family, and later, too, it repeatedly floored them. My grandmother Klára had more than once petitioned her brother Béla, the distinguished physician, and Pál, the legal counselor, for assistance, or in graver instances her father, because they had gone through his fortune, given to them as a wedding present, yet again. She had received her dowry three times. Meanwhile, over the years, my grandfather had threatened his children that they'd pay dearly for their prodigality. When the seven lean years will come, when they will have nothing to eat but dry bread crust, when they will have to sleep under a bridge, maybe then they'll remember how choosy they'd been. And so, everyone had to eat everything on their plate. There was no room for excuses or squeamishness. If any of the children made faces or shoved their food around on their plate, they had to stand up from the table and leave the dining room, which they did amid tears, accompanied by paternal curses and frightful prophecies, whereas crying, too, was strictly forbidden.

They said that this grandfather of mine would have never flung the soup tureen out the window of his Pannónia Street apartment, because there it would have fallen from the fourth floor straight down to the street, and in this regard he kept his unbridled nature under control, but if they didn't serve it hot enough, or something was again missing from the table, he'd fling it out the window of their summer villa in Pesthidegkút or the dining room of their manor house in Gömörsid, even when the window was closed. I can't begin to imagine how he managed it. The hot soup trickled down the tablecloth, the wall, the windowpane, his arm, the dining room rug. Also, the soup tureen at Pesthidegkút or Gömörsid had to be copious in size. The soup tureen was oval, it had two big ears, I saw two of them myself in the ornately carved, neo-Romantic and incredibly ugly ebony buffet that they called the castle. The room maid took the soup tureens by their ears and placed them on the table that matched the buffet and seated eighteen but could be extended to accommodate twenty-four. It couldn't have been easy for him to fling the tureen out the window if for no other reason than because of its weight. Apart from the parents, the seven children, the tutor Mr. Tieder, and the governesses also had to sit at the table, whether in Pest, the summer villa, or Gömörsid, meaning that it was either Jolán, the German Fraulein with the Hungarian name in attendance, or one of the French mam'selles, who replaced one another at such a dizzying pace that none of their names survived in the family's memory, or both of them at the same time, and also Júlia, the nursemaid, who had to watch the children at the table. And the children were well advised to obey her, because then their father wouldn't thunder his horrible prophecies at them from the head of the table, the dry bread, the water soup, because when they were bad, wicked, a bad lot, ill-behaved, insolent, shameless, they in fact had to eat water soup, meaning that the parlor maid put a plate of hot water in front of them and they had to spoon it out to the last drop. Magda, Pista, and Bandi often threw up because of it. And they'll end up as beggars sleeping under a bridge in the freezing cold, or they'll die in some roadside ditch, and now they'd better stand up and leave the table right away, and will get nothing to eat until noon tomorrow. No bread. Not even water. But Miss Jolán or Miss Júlia would sneak them some delicious morsels even so.

On the basis of hearsay and written descriptions, their household can be reconstructed with relative certainty. We even know that there were only eight apartments in the huge building situated on the corner of Lipót Boulevard and Pannónia Street, though I can't begin to imagine the size of these apartments. On the other hand, leaning out of the time frame of post-siege days, even I could glimpse something of their style of life. On Pozsonyi Street, in the dining room of Emil Vidor's art nouveau building inspired by Finnish models, there stood the sprawling dining table and the excruciatingly ugly buffet embellished with marquetry and pillars, carved gods, fauns, mermaids and satyrs, cornucopias, flower wreaths, fruit bowls, and acanthus leaves that held the dishes and other indispensable items for serving the food, and in its drawers the everyday silverware and the silverware and other appurtenances reserved for formal dining, and on its lower shelves sets of damask tablecloths and matching, carefully starched and ironed napkins for twenty-four, twelve, and six diners that had not been used for decades, the formal tablecloths, the everyday tablecloths, and so on, the tablecloths for the breakfast table with their matching napkins, the tablecloths for afternoon tea with their matching napkins, and needless to say, the story fragments that went with them.

The cook and the undermaid were the first to face the day. They had to rise at four a.m., the undermaid had to first start the fire in the kitchen stove, then clean the vegetables right after, so that every blessed dawn the cook, whom the family lore remembers as Dumpling Mari, could put up a kilo and a half or two kilos of beef with the vegetables in a big pot to cook. They first cooked the broth needed for the various other dishes and sauces, and it had to be ready exactly on time. At the same hour, on certain appointed days, the laundry woman would show up so that she could light a fire under the cauldron in one of the laundry rooms on the ground floor; the cauldron stood in a so-called cauldron house, in short, to boil water and get started on the light wash. Eclectic and art nouveau architecture would move the laundry rooms to the top floor just under the attic only decades later. There were two cauldron houses in the laundry rooms, in one they boiled water from dawn to late afternoon, in the other they boiled or, as they said, cooked the wash. When a big washday came, they bought a woman to assist the laundress, that's how they said it, I need to buy a woman, I'm buying a woman, we'll have to buy three women next week because we're cleaning the whole house, but during the big wash, the undermaid and even the parlor maid also had to be in attendance to help with the rinsing, the blue rinsing, the wringing, the starching, and then help hang the sheets and tablecloths up to dry, because they did the wash in several washtubs, but rinsed it in just one. At such times the afternoon would slip into night, and they would still be busy washing the smaller colored items in the much-used washing soda solution by lamplight, and also the socks, we'll just swoosh these around a bit, the laundry women said when the others were already up in the attic hanging out the wash. The wet clothes were carried up to the attic in huge wicker baskets kept exclusively for this purpose, this was done by the minor help, usually two of them. The servants could not use the elevator, servants couldn't even leave the balcony and use the main staircase. Also, the elevators serving the gentlefolk resembled small jewelry boxes polished to a gleam and adorned with mirrors, where the ladies could rest themselves on small velvet seats between floors. The servants had to move about and carry things up the servants' stairs. Not only did the people of Pest call it the servants' stairs, the signs affixed to these stairs did as well. When their *baka* came, the maids would keep their secret assignations on the servants' stairs as well. In the language of Pest, this *baka* was a double-barreled, highly equivocal, loaded word. Its meaning shifted precariously among a young man, a buck, and a beau, as well as the foot soldier it designated in the first place, but it had a cruder meaning as well and was used to refer to a city dandy and skirt chaser, especially a young one who felt an itch to do what a roebuck does to a roe. I see your *baka* is coming, Rozi, take care so he doesn't buck you. These generally meek-looking men stopped on the stairs between floors so they could sneak a peak from behind a pillar or banister. Meanwhile, their sweethearts snuck a peak from the kitchen, because they couldn't leave until the lady of the house let them. Their *baka* also called them their rose.

Sometimes, his rose would sneak away for a word or a kiss.

Pregnant, pregnant, no wonder she's pregnant, her *baka* played the buck again.

That precious you-know-who sneaked food out to her *baka* again.

Some snow-white lily, I must say.

No wonder she sneaked it out to him when these unfortunate young men, humiliated in their yearning for love, sometimes stood waiting for hours, even in the cold of winter, quietly pining after their rose. I witnessed plenty such heartbreaking scenes on Pozsonyi Street myself. When I looked down from the seventh-floor balcony, I could see all the hidden pockets of the servants' stairs of the huge house.

But the undermaid and the parlor maid also had to assist with the light wash and the big wash, so they could keep an eye on the hired help, lest the expensive stuff disappear at their hands. It disappeared at her hand. This was the synonym for stealing. It changed hands and disappeared. Everything was expensive. Everything was irreplaceable. It's my dowry, and once this was said, nothing but nothing could be missing. The dowry was sacred. If a damask napkin was missing from the twelve or the twenty-four, or a tablecloth for holiday dinners got ripped because of some disgraceful negligence, the entire set was useless. How am I supposed to lay the table now. I can't lay the table properly, ever again. They put such incomplete or faulty table linen to everyday use, but if the lady of the house had to lay the table for a specified number of guests, the deficit thus created caused a real problem. The man of the house invited guests, as often as not without a thought to their number and quite unexpectedly, but did not concern himself with incidentals such as what they could serve the unexpected guests, or what they would use to set the table. The tablecloths in the dowry were compiled with an eye to various occasions, snow-white for banquets, off-white or ivory-white for feasts, cream or salmon-colored for festive breakfasts, yellow, pink, possibly off-white for high tea, heavy Chinese silk with profuse shiny patterns, and so on, but even the bright white-on-white patterns of the damask tablecloths and napkins bore significant differences to suit the occasion. There were baroque-patterned tablecloths and tablecloths with simpler patterns for everyday use, but the napkins that belonged to a certain set could not be used as part of another, the difference in the patterns made it impossible. *Unmödlich.* Impossible. Once a tablecloth was ruined, the napkins that went with it could no longer be used either.

The lady of the house had to keep a sharp eye out to ensure that the social rules should not be violated, and these included every small detail pertaining to the table linen.

Two pillowcases are missing again.

For the most part everything was found, but they were constantly looking, because something was always missing. Nothing from the sacred dowry could be missing, every single piece was meant to last a lifetime. But even the most trustworthy laundresses stole things. No two ways about it, even the great Attila József's mother stole things, so Attila should have his buttered crescent roll or colored pencil, so he could have a blue one and a red one at least. The laundry women couldn't be left alone for a single moment, though the truth is that the undermaid stole things as well to give to her *baka*. It later came to light that the cook was also regularly stealing things. There was a tremendous to-do. A cook such as Zsófi at Great-grandfather Mezei's or a cook such as Dumpling Mari, and later, during the war years, Irma at Grandfather's home, or a cook like Gizi, Gizella Mrázik, who was at my Aunt Özsi's in Dobsinai Street, was as rare as a blue moon. Gizella Mrázik cooked for them for nearly twenty years. To be sure, she was not easy to get along with. I enjoyed her cooking more than once myself, I retain vivid memories of the tastes and smells of the dishes that came from under her hands, dishes that only she could make. The stuffed brisket of veal served with asparagus in cream sauce. The artistic way she presented her dishes. The gentlewomen wanted cooks just like her, and from time to time were able to lure them away, offering shrewd alternatives, in which case they could count on the friendship between the two families coming to an abrupt end. The parlor maids stole things. Possibly only the governesses did not steal, but without a doubt, the valets did. Planck was the sole exception. And the lady of the house stole, too, because she wouldn't have had a proper outfit for their summer vacations in Karlsbad or Abbazia. On occasion, she had to dip into the household money. For his part, the profoundly respected lord of the house stole from his own greatly honored clients, he had to fleece them repeatedly and thoroughly, so that apart from domestic expenses, he'd have enough to cover his clandestine adventures, his second life with his mistress and his illegitimate children.

Once the huge pot of soup was on the stove in the kitchen, they started preparing breakfast and lunch. The chambermaids got up at four thirty, the governesses at five or five thirty, and with so many children, the lady of the house also had to get up with them. On washdays earlier, which goes without saying, so they and the undermaid could give the wash to the laundress. The undermaid also had to put wood or coal on the fire, this was strictly her job. She had to haul it up from the basement. She also had to start up the fire in all the rooms, feed and tend to the tile stoves. This is why in the larger or more distinguished households they needed housekeepers to hand out the dirty clothes to be washed; they were also charged with overseeing the day's chores and the time-consuming shopping rounds. Which is what led Gizella Mrázik to join my Aunt Eugenie's household on the other side of Dobsinai Street, where she'd been housekeeper in Baron Bornemissza's home. I don't know how the two families reacted to the transfer, but there were no hard feelings, this I know. Gizi was not a cheerful woman, she was as lacking in smiles as my aunt, she must have carried some nagging disappointment on her shoulders all her life, but she was honor incarnate, and so I am nearly completely certain that she left the other household without conflict. She'd had enough of conflict, this is why she settled for a lesser station, this is why she abandoned her post as housekeeper; she had simply grown tired of too many people and too much to-do.

Given its strict schedule, which had to accommodate fickle changes in program, household work was akin to sprints. I witnessed the early morning operation of handing out the wash only in the most humble form possible, my mother gave out the wash to the laundry woman with Rózsi Németh, or else Rózsi Németh handed it out herself, but even so, the handing out of the wash retained a precisely elaborated, classical plan of action, and not just any old plan of action either, but a ritual plan of action laden with psychological motifs. Even for a light wash, the dirty clothes and linen had to be separated the previous afternoon. Not only were the whites and coloreds separated, because if something got colored in the wash, it was nothing short of a tragedy of major proportions, there were also pieces of a more delicate nature, these had to be carefully identified and carefully separated. For instance, there were pieces that needed to be starched not in their entirety but only in part, because the master of the house liked his cuffs to be hard and crisp, but the inner lining of his collar mustn't rub his deeply honored neck, the handkerchiefs had to be ever so lightly starched, but the pocket squares needed to be crisply starched, and so on, a veritable slew of customs, special wishes, personal monomanias a laundress had to learn and had to do justice to the best of her ability.

God forbid she should blue-rinse whites.

They emptied out the packed laundry basket the previous afternoon, sorted the wash, compiled lists, set to soak whatever needed to be soaked, or else gave it out the following morning dry, or because of the indispensible lack of trust, did so in smaller portions timed to the pace and order in which the laundress worked. They also made sure to discuss the soaked pieces with the laundress. Furthermore, the laundress had to be sparing of the lye, the soft soap, the hot water, and so the laundry operations followed a strict order in line with the various sorted groups of wash. The unsparing discussion was not only in the interest of the lady of the house, it was as much in the interest of the laundress, who had good reason to fear unfounded accusations and excessive suspicions. They washed the laundry in wooden tubs using root brushes. They had to wash various types of clothing in the same lye water. They kept a close watch on the economy involved. Boiling water was expensive, the lye didn't come cheap either, the laundress couldn't change the laundry water on a whim. This is how they said it, on a whim. The whites were first soaked, then washed, then boiled, meaning that they boiled them for at least forty minutes in hot water with lye. They then used this water to launder the colored wash. For the light wash they boiled the laundry in a big pot, for the big wash in a cauldron, partly for reasons of hygiene. To avoid possible infection, the woman who did the ironing, who was only rarely the same as the laundress, always had to do the ironing with the hottest iron possible, though with an eye to the requirements of the material. They kept checking the temperature of the iron. They heated the irons with charcoal, and because of the noxious carbon monoxide fumes they had to do the ironing with the window open; it was sweltering hot and cold in the laundry room all at the same time, and in the summer, the heat was truly unbearable. The charcoal in the iron had to be kept from flaring up, and it had to be kept from dying down.

In more humble households, they worked with irons heated over the stove.

Regardless of how careful a laundress or ironing woman may have been, such procedures were bound to eat into the fine linen, they ate into the table linen, and they ate into the bed linen. That's the expression they used. On the other hand, no stains could remain. Or wrinkles. There was also a trick to folding the bed linen and table linen without leaving wrinkles. Every stain and wrinkle became the subject of some major domestic drama. At times the house veritably shook from women's yelling and screaming, crying and wailing because of some stain. The relentlessness of the bourgeois scheme of things was cheerfully readying the way for the triumph of the dictatorship of the proletariat. Since the bed linen and the table linen had to last a lifetime, because that's how life was planned out, the lady of the house made terrible scenes if something nevertheless thinned out, got split, got torn, got a hole in it, or retained a stubborn stain, or else got a new stain on it and so on. Which is understandable. This was where the strict limits of the love of one's fellow men, the obligatory liberal trust, the striving for equality, had its most closely guarded frontier. The hapless laundress had to gauge the condition of the pieces she was given to wash with a single expert glance. She held the materials up to the light for inspection, to check if they were not too thinned out in certain places. The quality of the presoaked bed linen and table linen was invariably the subject of lively debate.

Kindly bring yourself over here, madam, and she pulled a sheet from under the root brush. The lye water ran down it as she held it up to the light, and she pointed out that here, no doubt about it, the threads are bare, and it's not her fault if it won't hold up under the brush.

Just scrub it.

Sure. And then your ladyhood will make a nice racket.

In Pest, laundresses belittled the lady of the house with hair-raising sentences. In Buda, the laundresses were more circumspect with their disparagement. But one way or another, a laundress always belittled, it was in her interest, it was her revenge. Scenes of a delicate nature were de rigueur between the laundresses and the ladies of the house; after all, the underwear, the bed linen, and the table linen were invariably adorned with the telling signs of the life that transpired in the big genteel home during the previous week. And the laundresses were adept at reading the inglorious signs. For decades it was their job to identify and get rid of such shameful traces. The laundress was the vanishing genie of a genteel home. There stood the intrepid laundress on the border of appearance and reality like the Hound from Hell. The laundress couldn't help but notice that, as she put it, your lady-ship saw fit to menstruate into your snow-white or pink panties again. The privy councillor threw up on the bed linen twice this week. Judging by the stink, he washed down his pálinka with beer and ate his roast beef drenched in red-wine sauce. There's no way I can make this clean. Make this clean, this was the term the laundresses of Pest used as, exasperated, they banged their brushes against the side of the tub. In Buda, the laundresses were more refined in their observations. The privy councillor's broadcloth underdrawers got shit on them, I am sorry to say. His Excellency has neglected to wipe his ass properly again. He was too lazy to use the bidet after he shit. Or they didn't even have a bidet, which meant that theirs was not a genteel home. They're no better than parvenus. Jesus, Mary, and the Host, what am I supposed to do with this, the laundress said at such times, displaying the very depth of her professional concerns. There it was, no doubt about it, the sleepy pool of sperm, the last sign of a languid copulation, on her ladyship's white batiste nightgown abundantly adorned with Brussels lace, the sperm had dried on the fabric. Or there stood before her eyes the stain of an attempt to prevent pregnancy, or the sprayed spots of premature ejaculation, evidence of their married lives during the past month. There's no way I can get this out without leaving a mark, the laundress announced with due indignation. Until detergents containing biological whiteners were invented, sperm stains generally remained on the bed linen, which was tantamount to a catastrophe. In Krisztínaváros and Lipótváros, or the middle-bourgeois Grand Boulevard, it was a catastrophe on par with the Ottoman hordes vanquishing the Magyar armies at Mohács. The men's broadcloth underdrawers were another case in point, because they hadn't bothered to shake the last drops from their privates, not that it can be done, and though the laundresses washed these underpants, generally biased to the left with care, after a time a big yellow stain would appear, a hideous monstrosity, on the leg. Because of the repeatedly absorbed stains of excrement mixed with urine, sperm, and sweat, the underwear was no longer immaculate, and it was no use for the mistress of the house to get her dander up. Not to mention the fact that the master of the house pleased to jerk himself into his finest white poplin handkerchief yet again. When dry, there was no mistaking it for snot. The laundresses had plenty of problems with phlegm, too. They got it out of one handkerchief with the root brush, but if they didn't slam it out of the tub fast enough, the snot would stick to the other handkerchiefs. Sometimes they didn't spot the problem until it came to ironing. *Mein Gott, mon Dieu*, you ironed it into the fabric again. They'd have never said, not for all the world, what it was that the laundress had ironed into the fabric, but it sufficed to say that she ironed it in. Even though every laundress had her own fail-safe recipe for it, red-wine stains didn't always come out of the damask tablecloths either. When nothing helped, the cheeky laundress would only say to the lady of the house, scissors. Which either made both of them laugh, or this was the last word the laundress would utter in the house, and it was the same from Königsberg to Lisbon, and from Oslo to Milan.

If it was neither a light wash day nor a big wash day, then twice a week, as soon as the parlor maid had cleared the breakfast dishes off the table, the cook would go with her to the market, even though the butcher, the greengrocer, the grocer, and the colonial produce merchant delivered their standing orders every day. When a major holiday was approaching or they were expecting guests, the menu would be more elaborate, the many ingredients finer and more discerningly chosen, and the lady of the house would go with them to give them their orders on the spot. To make sure that lunch would be ready on time, they had to be back in the kitchen no later than nine thirty. The bone broth or the consommé was ready by then, too; they were used to make the soup and to serve as the base for various sauces; they also served to lighten the roux for the cream vegetables and to make roasts. The heavier produce, the potatoes, the cabbage, the fruits for preserves, or the big baskets laden with tomatoes were brought along and carried up through the back stairs by a porter. Kitchens had doors giving out to the back stairs. Even in the immediate post-siege years, porters wearing numbered red caps with black trim could still be seen waiting in the street by the markets with their two-wheeled carts. Some elderly porters were even in evidence at Budapest's railway stations into the early seventies. But after that, the age of porters came to an end. The things bought at the grocer's, the colonial merchant's, or the druggist's were carried upstairs by an assistant or an apprentice. Carrying home the big bloody meats and bones in the big basket was the job of the undermaid. There was also a small basket, this was carried home by the cook on her arm. But at my Aunt Eugenie's, Gizella Mrázik didn't have to go shopping, this being one of her strict conditions, a sign of the times, as they said back then. The exception, the special case, achieves the great historical changes only in very small steps. They put the fragile, delicate things in the small basket, the cheeses, the cold cuts, the butter, the eggs, the cottage cheese, the heavy cream, the sour cream, everything that mustn't be broken or crushed or spilled. At least twice a week, they carried enormous amounts of food home. No wonder, considering the number of people in the household that had to be fed five times a day. They made sure that everything should be filling and go a long way, as they said back then. There was breakfast, there was the *tízórai*, or mid-morning snack, there was lunch, there was the *uzsonna*, or afternoon tea, and there was dinner. Once a week, when the cook had the afternoon off, the last of these was cold. The servants ate just three times a day, at aristocratic households generally just twice, because the greater the number of servants, the more mouths there were, and the logistics of keeping house became accordingly more complex. There's more to the universe than the spacial expansion between the stars. The leftovers were destined for the beggar, but because he wasn't even allowed to come up the back stairs, the undermaid took the leftovers down to him in the yard wrapped in newspaper.

In the manuscript version of her memoirs, my Aunt Magda described a day from the point of view of the nursemaid, Miss Júlia. There's the case of Miss Juliska, she writes. Poor Pista, the eternal scapegoat, came to the dinner table once with a shiny nose, whereupon our father shouted gruffly at Juliska. Apparently, you can't even be trusted to keep the children in line anymore.

Juliska, oh, Juliska, who sponged us down to the waist every single morning, then saw to our breakfast, and while our father's carriage took Gyuri and Pista, she took me and Özsi to the school in Szemere Street on foot then rushed back home, aired out and made our beds, helped the parlor maid clean our rooms, then dusted off all the objects herself, picking up and turning around every single object every single day, then she gave the little ones their mid-morning snack, then joined our mother at the window to darn socks and mend underwear, and this is what she had to hear. At noon she went back to the school, to pick us up. In the afternoon she probably helped our mother count the clothes for the light wash. What a big heap of dirty laundry a big household was able to produce. Then she took us for a walk. After dinner she washed each one of us head to toe, then once we were in bed, she made sure we all said our prayers. She had a bit of a fight with Özsi every time, because she insisted that she'd already said her prayers silently, to herself.

I gave myself over to my prayers with all my heart. I believed, I honestly believed that a lapsed or insincere prayer would kill me.

My Aunt Magda's friends and colleagues at the Institute of Party History and her editors at Kossuth Publishers deleted these lovely, innocent sentences about evening prayers, and my aunt agreed to the amputation. Ágnes Szabó was one of her amputating editors. The process of amputating the manuscript took a long time, ten years, if memory serves me right. Various bodies at the institute put their heads together in the interest of saving the manuscript, meaning that they had parts of it deleted, others rewritten, so as not to leave room for attack. Or else they attacked it themselves, argued with its assertions and suggested suitable omissions or ammendations. The institute also appointed certain people, Tibor Erényi, Ágnes Ságvári, and Tibor Hajdú, who were conversant with Party history, to get the manuscript ready for the press. Their job was to judge certain aspects of the work as Party historians. My Aunt Magda left out certain chapters and re-wrote others, she grumbled, and at times raged and cursed, sunk between her pillows. In a joint effort, they reshaped and retailored the story of her life. Her editor was no longer there to protect her but, in line with her professional or personal interests, she had deserted her, betrayed her, had insidiously stabbed her in the back; concurrently and along the lines of the latest arguments and counterarguments, the group was repeatedly reorganized. But as horrible or difficult as it may be to understand, my aunt suffered because she couldn't not agree with the intentions of her colleagues to mutilate and amend her manuscript.

From the start, the dramaturgy of self-mutilation in the name of asceticism was part and parcel of the Communist movement. Theo-retically, there was no limit set on the surrender of the self. In fact, they took masochistic pleasure in surrendering their own thoughts. Meanwhile, I stood by, curious to see what they were doing with each other's lives. Her colleagues cut her manuscript, rewrote it, or had her rewrite it so that it should contain as few elements of a personal nature as possible. The great imperative of the times dictated that her views should be what they were pleased to call objective, and her manuscript should be a reflection of the age. They got rid of the per-sonal, which they considered bourgeois nonsense or worse. The less that remained of the young girl she once was, the young girl who had turned her back on her own class because she insisted on the indepen-dent judgment of that young girl, the better. She had to hide the fact, and she hid it of her own free will. Communist asceticism, based on voluntary participation, denied the individual's God-given independence, it nipped people's striving for independence mercilessly in the bud, or else had the person himself nip it in the bud.

Given his innate opportunism, a person can satisfy an epoch's demands, but surely he can't help but see in his own memories that it's just not him. It is not his life. Or hers. But they wouldn't let her keep the following sentence either, which ran, I also loved poetry. They crossed it out. Comrade Aranyossi has no business loving poetry. That is why I found the torture of being sponged down with cold water every night so pleasant. But strangely enough, they left this sadomasochistic sentence in. While she sponged me down, Juliska recited poems to me. János Arany, Petőfi, József Kiss. And one by one, I learned to recite these poems, too, thanks to her. Perhaps this was fate's way of compensating me for being born tone-deaf. Juliska's labors for the day were by no means over when she got us to bed. It surprises me that this sloppy, rural expression could stay. She and my mother went to the big blue table of the children's room and checked every piece of clothing we had on during the day. They then applied their needles to every loose button, torn underclothing, and holey sock. But they wouldn't let her use holey sock, so it was changed to socks with holes. Let all traces of the way her rural elders spoke be eradicated, oh, there's another, let's be rid of it, and this born lady agreed, she gave the purificators the green light. After all, she wanted to be part of the proletariat all her life. An ascetic and a purificator. Apart from these chores, there were the weekly chores as well, bathing the children in hot water, and on Saturday night, washing their hair; on Tuesday, arranging our toy shelves, cleaning up and putting our closets in order, mending our broken toys and also mending and cleaning our stuffed animals made of cloth and velvet.

No wonder that Júlia was stung by our father's casual remark. She talked back. My father shouted, Missy ran from the dining room and started packing. My mother sat for a couple of minutes longer, then she got up, went after Missy, and talked to her as calm as can be. Don't take this incident to heart, Júlia. Juliska cried and said she couldn't take it anymore. Then my mother spoke again, in an even softer voice. You know how quickly my husband loses his patience, but he's a good man. Besides, where will you go. It is late at night. What would a girl from the countryside do in Pest this late at night.

She was going to her sister Lujza, Juliska sobbed. Lujza was governess in an equally large family. But will they let her stay with Lujza.

Missy eventually calmed down and even went back to the table, and my father finished his dinner without saying another word.

But in the summer villa or the manor house that the locals called the castle, he'd raise his voice at the slightest irregularity and fling the soup tureen out the window so that the porcelain and the window-pane would make a loud crashing sound.

He even shouted as he flung the tureen through the glass pane.

Adolf Arnold was a strong, loud, slender man, yet with an imposing physique. Behind his back, his two big daughters, Özsi and Magda, called him a breeding animal. One evening, when they were already in bed, in the dark they promised each other that they would marry only small, fine, intelligent, and ugly men. They even promised that they wouldn't let each other fall in love with a breeding animal like their father and would make sure that the other kept her promise. For a century and a half, flinging the soup tureen out the window may have been the gauge of manly behavior, a compulsory display of strength for the benefit of women, and at their expense.

Decades passed, crises and wars came and went, but the scenes remained. In the house in Rákoskeresztúr where my wife, Magda, was born, the scene was repeated even in the early forties. Her father was not Jewish, he was not a landowner, he was called László Ponižil, even if they often left the haček accent off his name; he was Moravian, he was a mason, he was a contractor, he was Catholic, but he also flung the soup tureen out the window. When his half-German, half-Slovak Protestant wife, Zsuzsanna Csajka, didn't serve his meal on time or at the proper temperature, or she forgot the ladle, didn't place the tureen on the table at an angle to his liking, or didn't turn the ladle to suit him, what Magda's father in his masonic pride called a *fandli*, or trowel, you didn't position the *fandli* properly again, he yelled, or when there was no bread on the table for the soup, there's no bread for the soup again, he yelled, he would fling the tureen out the window of the beautiful house he'd built with his own two hands so that, with a horrendous crack, the glass pane went flying all over the place. Not once. Not twice. This was the compulsory family scene; the other was his drunken return from the pub, where he got soused to the gills. And this was the case even though in the quarter of the village where they lived, inhabited by Slovaks and Moravians, now annexed to Budapest, they, the two girls and their fine-mannered and self-sacrificing mother, had to sit at the table afraid of what would come not punctually at noon, but punctually at twelve thirty, though we know that in the German quarter of the village, Magdolna Ponižil's maternal grandparents sat down to lunch when the church bell rang out at noon.

In our family, half a century earlier, in Nagykorona, Hold, Báthory, Duna, and Pannónia streets, as well as in Dalszínház Street, Andrássy Boulevard, and later Pozsonyi Street, Benczúr and Dobsinai streets, it would have been equally inconceivable to place the ladle in the soup ahead of time, meaning, bringing in the tureen with the ladle in the soup. I have no idea why. I think that even my father would have been hard put for an answer. It would have constituted the sort of serving anomaly that wouldn't have even occurred to anyone. To this day I am aghast when Magda puts the ladle in the soup tureen before she starts serving it, though I keep my masculine self-respect discreetly under wraps. I don't fling the tureen out the window in either of our two residences, in Buda or Gombosszeg, just as I had never flung anything out the window of my homes in the two workingman's districts, one on Brickyard Square in Pesterzsébet, the other on Andor Street in Kelenföld. In my family, they placed the serving utensils next to where the serving dishes would go. The grown-ups served themselves, or the lady of the house served everyone, or else the oldest woman at the table. When there were guests, the older female relatives assisted with the serving, or possibly the servants, in which case the serving utensils wouldn't be placed on the table at all, but were handed to the guests. They very rarely took me along to dinner paries or receptions, children had no place being there. Perhaps wedding lunches or family gatherings after a funeral, which we never called a wake, were the sole exceptions.

This is why my native town, which of all the places in the world I know best and am also most familiar with as the scene of my recollections, does not have a separate Jewish and non-Jewish history, nor can the history of its table manners be comfortably divided up. Urbanity will not allow us to dissect the city with recourse to either religious or ethnic concepts. Hand in hand with its German history, its Hungarian history, its Turkish history, its Slovak history, its Serbian history, even its Greek history, it has several kinds of Christian and several kinds of Jewish histories as well. It further has a Catholic history, a Reformed history, an Evangelical history, a Greek Orthodox history, and it has a Buda history, an Óbuda history, and a Pest history, which differ significantly from one another, and it also has an Ashkenazi history and a Sephardic history, an Orthodox history and a Neolog history, a Hasidic history and a more recent Lubavitch family history, it has an assimilated Jewish history and an emancipated Jewish history, and also a Zionist history, what's more, it has an appreciable militantly atheist history, an apostate history, a nonreligious history, and within all of these genres it has a history of the poor and a history of the rich, it has a history of subjugation and a history of upward mobility, it has a history of the underground and a history of industry, and so on, and these histories overlap; at times they are at odds and are in conflict, at others they exist peacefully side by side or else exist in spite of one another. It couldn't be otherwise. After all, at the beginning of the nineteenth century, only 42 percent of the eight million inhabitants of the Kingdom of Hungary spoke Hungarian. Their separate stories are inscribed as one in the stones and the streets, a city could not survive any other way, and I, too, am thoroughly at one with the various lines of descent and their individual histories or, as a consequence of my own hapless actions and in opposition to these, with all sorts of other things of which my ancestors could not have known, and possibly would have preferred not knowing.